PARLIAMENTARY HISTORY: TEXTS & STUDIES

8

The Correspondence of John Campbell MP, with His Family, Henry Fox, Sir Robert Walpole and the Duke of Newcastle, 1734–71

Parliamentary History: Texts & Studies

The Correspondence of John Campbell MP, with His Family, Henry Fox, Sir Robert Walpole and the Duke of Newcastle, 1734–71

Edited by

J.E. Davies

Wiley Blackwell

for

The Parliamentary History Yearbook Trust

© 2013 The Parliamentary History Yearbook Trust

WILEY Blackwell is now part of John Wiley & Sons

Registered Office
John Wiley & Sons Ltd, The Atrium, Southern Gate, Chichester, West Sussex, PO19 8SQ, United Kingdom

Editorial Offices
350 Main Street, Malden, MA 02148-5020, USA
9600 Garsington Road, Oxford, OX4 2DQ, UK
The Atrium, Southern Gate, Chichester, West Sussex, PO19 8SQ, UK

For details of our global editorial offices, for customer services, and for information about how to apply for permission to reuse the copyright material in this book please see our website at www.wiley.com/wiley-blackwell.

The right of J.E. Davies to be identified as the author of the editorial material in this work has been asserted in accordance with the Copyright, Designs and Patents Act 1988.

All rights reserved. No part of this publication may be reproduced, stored in a retrieval system, or transmitted, in any form or by any means, electronic, mechanical, photocopying, recording or otherwise, except as permitted by the UK Copyright, Designs and Patents Act 1988, without the prior permission of the publisher.

Wiley also publishes its books in a variety of electronic formats. Some content that appears in print may not be available in electronic books.

Library of Congress Cataloging-in-Publication Data
Davies, J. E. (John Edward), 1954
    The correspondence of John Campbell MP, with his family, Henry Fox, Sir Robert Walpole and the Duke of Newcastle, 1734-71 / edited by J. E. Davies.
      pages cm
    Includes bibliographical references and index.
  ISBN 978-1-118-71062-3 (alk. paper)
  1. Campbell, John, of Cawdor, 1695-1777–Correspondence. 2. Holland, Henry Fox, Baron, 1705-1774–Correspondence. 3. Walpole, Robert, Earl of Orford, 1676-1745–Correspondence. 4. Newcastle, Thomas Pelham-Holles, Duke of, 1693-1768–Correspondence. 5. Great Britain–Politics and government–18th century–Sources. I. Parliamentary History Yearbook Trust. II. Title.
  DA501.C36A4 2013
  324.2092'2–dc23

2013026741

A catalogue record for this title is available from the British Library
Set in 10/12pt Bembo
by Toppan Best-set Premedia Limited
Printed and bound in Singapore
by Markono Print Media Pte Ltd

1   2014

CONTENTS

Table of Figures   vi

Acknowledgments   vii

Abbreviations   viii

Primary Sources Consulted   ix

Introduction. The Welsh Campbell   1

Chapter 1. 1734–40   43
Chapter 2. 1741–2   63
Chapter 3. 1743   121
Chapter 4. 1744–51   153
Chapter 5. 1755–6   203
Chapter 6. 1757–8   227
Chapter 7. 1760–4   246
Chapter 8. 1765–6   269
Chapter 9. 1767–71   306

Appendices: Campbell's Political Essays and Other Political Writings

   1. Account of the Pembrokeshire Election (1727)   319
   2. Copy of a Letter to a Nonjuring Gentleman in Scotland Writ
      in the year 1727   321
   3. Essay on the Act of Settlement c.1758   330
   4. Comments on the Preface to Spelman's Sixth Book of Polybius,
      and upon P. Francis' *Orations of Demosthenes* (c.1759)   338
   5. The Substance of a Letter, to a Friend in Scotland upon the
      Militia Scheme, August 1762   349
   6. Statement upon the Removal of Army Officers from the House
      of Commons, 1765   357
   7. Observations (c.1770)   358
   8. Some Account of the Great Demagogue, 1765   362

Index   369

TABLE OF FIGURES

2.1: John Campbell to Mary Campbell, 5 December 1741: a hand   71
      which changed very little through his long life.
2.2: A rough plan of Lord Hay's new library as drawn by Campbell.   103
6.1: John Campbell to Mary Campbell, 7 April 1757.   231

ACKNOWLEDGMENTS

I would like to thank the following establishments: the staff of the British Library manuscripts room, the staff of Carmarthenshire Archive Service and the Cambridge University Archives reprographics department. I would also like to thank the following: Emeritus Professor David Howell for reading and commenting upon the Introduction, Dr Hannes Kleineke, senior research fellow at the History of Parliament Trust, for translating the Latin quotations, Stephen Farrell for the French translation, Melanie Unwin, deputy curator, Houses of Parliament Art Department for the cover photograph and the editor of *Parliamentary History*, Clyve Jones, for his help and his humour.

I would also like to thank the Dowager Countess Cawdor for her permission to allow these letters to be published.

I am very grateful to the Scouloudi Foundation for financial assistance.

ABBREVIATIONS

b.	born
BIHR	*Bulletin of the Institute of Historical Research*
BL	British Library, London
bt	baronet
CA	*Carmarthenshire Antiquary*
CJ	*Commons Journal* (http://parlipapers.chadwyck.co.uk/home.do)
CRO	Carmarthenshire Record Office
CUL	Cambridge University Library
d.	died
EHR	*English Historical Review*
f., ff.	folio, folios
HMC	Historical Manuscripts Commission
HPC	*History of Parliament, The House of Commons* (http://www.historyofparliamentonline.org/research)
IHR	Institute of Historical Research
LJ	*Lords Journal* (http://parlipapers.chadwyck.co.uk/home.do)
'Memoir'	Henry Fox, 'Memoir of the Events Attending the Death of George the Second', in *The Life and Letters of Lady Sarah Lennox*, ed. countess of Ilchester and Lord Stavordale (1901)
MS, MSS	manuscript, manuscripts
NLW	National Library of Wales
ODNB	*Oxford Dictionary of National Biography* (http://www.oxforddnb.com)
OED	*Oxford English Dictionary* (http://www.oed.com)
PH	William Cobbett, *Cobbett's Parliamentary History* (36 vols, 1806–20)
Sainty and Dewar	*Divisions in the House of Lords: An Analytical List, 1685 to 1857*, compiled by J.C. Sainty and D. Dewar (1976)
THSC	*Transactions of the Honourable Society of Cymmrodorian*
WHR	*Welsh History Review*

PRIMARY SOURCES CONSULTED

BL, Add. MS 32723, f. 262: John Campbell to duke of Newcastle, 12 November 1750.

BL, Add. MS 32720, f. 131: John Campbell to duke of Newcastle, 9 Mar. 1750.

BL, Add. MS 32859, f. 41920: John Campbell to duke of Newcastle, 7 Oct. 1755.

BL, Add. MS 32860: duke of Newcastle to Lord Hardwicke, 12 Oct. 1755.

BL, Add. MS 32896, correspondence of duke of Newcastle, secretary of state, etc., 1727–60.

BL, Add. MS 32970, f. 103: John Campbell to duke of Newcastle, 29 Sept. 1765.

BL, Add. MS 35599, ff. 165–9: Lord Hardwick to archbishop of Canterbury, 11 Mar. 1754.

BL, Add. MS 51406, ff. 1–181: correspondence between Henry Fox and John Campbell, 1755–71.

BL, Add. MS 51417, ff. 1–248: correspondence between Stephen and Henry Fox, 1729–46.

BL, Add. MS 51418, ff. 1–120: correspondence between Stephen and Henry Fox, 1746–7.

BL, Add. MS 51419, ff. 1–230: correspondence between Henry Fox, his wife Caroline and Lord and Lady Ilchester, 1744–55.

BL, Add. MS 51430, ff. 1–160: correspondence between Lord Holland and Lady Holland, 1756–7.

CRO, Cawdor/Campbell box 128: letters of John Campbell to Mary and Pryse Campbell, and other family members 1733–77.

CRO, Cawdor/Campbell box 128: document detailing the estate income and expenditure.

CRO, Cawdor/Campbell box 252: essays and other writings of John Campbell, 1727–c.1770.

CRO, Cawdor/Campbell box 2/285: an account of smuggling near Stackpole Court, 1798.

CRO, Cawdor/Campbell box 5/99: agreement to assign messuages in Grosvenor Square on payment of £2,496, 2 Aug. 1728.

CRO, Cawdor/Campbell box 16/192: will of John Campbell of Calder in the Shire of Nairn and Stackpole Court, Pembrokeshire, 17 Apr. 1777.

CRO, Cawdor/Campbell box 20/281: Gwynn v. Hooke, legal papers, 1738–43.

CRO, Cawdor/Lort box 5/240: copy will of Sir Gilbert Lort of Stackpool Court, 9 Aug. 1698.

CRO, FJ/13: Cawdor pedigree, c.1970.

CUL, Cholmondeley (Houghton), 2219: John Campbell to Sir Robert Walpole, 18 June 1734.

CUL, Cholmondeley (Houghton), 2687: John Campbell to Sir Robert Walpole, 15 May 1737.

NLW, MS 1352b: Stackpole letter book, 1889.

NLW, MS 6106: diary of Erasmus Philipps of Picton Castle.

NLW, MS 23274: note book of Erasmus Philipps of Picton Castle.

Introduction. The Welsh Campbell

1. *The Campbells of Cawdor*

As with many gentry families in Britain the Campbells of Cawdor created an increasingly powerful political interest by acquiring land, either by grant or by purchase, and by marrying heiresses. Their wealth enabled them to pursue political careers, first in the 17th-century Scottish parliament and, by the 1720s, in the British parliament. The growth in the Campbells' political interest coincided with a shift away from Scottish clan politics and from Scotland itself as they settled in south-west Wales. By the second decade of the 18th century the family had become one of the most powerful in Wales – and remained so until the 20th century – and firmly identified themselves with the whigs, especially as defined by that particular brand of whiggery espoused by Sir Robert Walpole.

Some of the earliest surviving records show a Cawdor Campbell being given grants of land for services to Robert the Bruce. However, it was Gill-Easbuig Campbell, who died in the late 14th century, who acquired great swathes of land in a 'dramatic expansion'[1] of the Campbell lordship, so much so that his son Colin (*d*. c.1412) could style himself 'lord of Argyll', a title long established and 'which had connotations of provincial overlordship'. His grandson, also Colin (*d*. c.1493), became the 1st earl of Argyll, and he used 'all available measures – patronage, diplomacy, litigation, and force – to advance Campbell power in western Scotland'.[2] The 2nd earl, Archibald (*d*. c.1513), continued to advance the Campbell cause, becoming master of James IV's household in 1495. Although Archibald never gained the political power wielded by his father, he nevertheless received royal grants of land, in Dunbartonshire and Inverness-shire as well as a confirmation of the free barony of Argyll. Archibald married Elizabeth, the eldest daughter of John Stuart, Lord Darnley and 10th earl of Lennox, and their third son was John, later Sir John Campbell.

Sir John Campbell married Muriel, the 9th thane of Cawdor (or Calder, an earlier name), so establishing the Cawdor Campbell clan.[3] Cawdor Castle in Nairnshire was a substantial physical remove for Campbell, situated as it is on the north-eastern coast of Scotland, the other side of the country to the Argyll lordship. As a branch of the Argyll clan, John Campbell's family was inextricably involved with Scottish Highland politics and all its endemic internecine strife, and continued to be so until the head of the family moved to south-west Wales at the end of the 17th century.

Sir John Campbell sought 'incessantly to increase his possessions and extend his influence' and acquired great power in the north of Scotland, so much so that the

---

[1] *ODNB*.

[2] *ODNB*.

[3] Muriel was born c.1494; the Cawdor ancestry can be traced back on the maternal side to Donald, 1st thane of Calder who was alive in the 1290s.

Campbells of Cawdor almost came to rival their clan chiefs, the Argyll Campbells.[4] However, Sir John died in 1546, leaving his extensive possessions under the control of the very able Muriel, who maintained her leadership of the Cawdor Campbells until 1573 when, two years before her death, she passed the thanedom to her grandson, John Campbell, her eldest son Archibald having died in c.1551. John Campbell, like his grandfather before him, acquired large tracts of northern Scotland, and large debts – two traits that recur in the history of the Cawdors. He married Mary Keith, sister to Agnes, countess of Moray and, from 1573, countess of Argyll upon her marriage to the 6th earl.[5] Campbell became the tutor and one of the principal counsellors to the eight-year-old Archibald Campbell, 7th earl of Argyll. Archibald's minority created a power struggle within the clan Campbell which 'led to rivalry, internal dissension, and a bitter feud that threatened to split the Campbells apart'.[6] After Agnes Keith's death in 1588, John Campbell effectively became the head of the clan when he kidnapped the young earl and assumed control of the Argyll household. However, Campbell's rule lasted barely four years. In one of the more violent episodes of this internecine power struggle, Campbell of Cawdor was murdered in February 1592, in a conspiracy led by Archibald Campbell of Lochell and George Gordon, 6th earl of Huntly, the former hoping to become the leader of the clan.[7]

The murdered John Campbell's son, also John, and later knighted, became the head of the Cawdor Campbell family, as the 12th thane. Continuing the family tradition, he also added greatly to the family possessions when he acquired in 1614, with the help of the English crown, the isles of Islay and Jura. Both isles were Macdonald strongholds but, undeterred, Campbell subdued resistant tenants with both economic and military might. However, both places were a constant drain on the family's resources, though they grimly held on to both islands for nearly a century, with 'large bribes, assuredly exacted by courtiers, others possibly paid to the king, for the gift'.[8] Sir John died in 1642, albeit 20 years earlier he had resigned the estate over to his son John, 'the fiar' Campbell, upon the latter's marriage. 'The fiar' lived until 1654, though in 1639 he had been declared a lunatic and relinquished control of his estates to his son Colin, who died in c.1647 whilst still a student at Glasgow University. The Cawdor estates then devolved upon John the fiar's uncle Sir Hugh Campbell (c.1639–1716), son of Colin Campbell of Ardersier and his wife, Elizabeth, daughter of David Brodie of Brodie, Morayshire. The Brodie connection would later be of use to John Campbell (the subject of this volume) in his electioneering efforts in Inverness.

Sir Hugh carried out extensive building works at Cawdor although, ironically as it transpired, he was the last of the Cawdor Campbells to reside at the castle until the 20th century. He was 'a gentleman of learning and knowledge and of great benevolence'.[9] In

---

[4] C. Innes, *The Book of the Thanes of Cawdor*, xxii (Edinburgh, 1859).

[5] Colin Campbell (c.1542–84), 6th earl of Argyll.

[6] *ODNB* entry for Archibald Campbell (1575/6–1638), 7th earl of Argyll.

[7] His murder was part of the same conspiracy that resulted in the more infamous murder, in the same year, of James Stuart (1565–92), 2nd earl of Moray.

[8] Innes, *Book of the Thanes of Cawdor*, xxviii.

[9] 'A Succinct Account of the Family of Cawdor', in *Highland Papers, Vol. I*, ed. J.R.N. Macphail (Scottish History Society, 1914), 141–91. Macphail's account is based on the work of the Rev. Lauchlan Shaw (c.1685/90–1777).

1661 he became MP (in the Scottish parliament) for Nairnshire, a seat he held until 1693. He married Lady Henrietta Stuart, the daughter of James, 4th earl of Moray. Sir Hugh supported the Glorious Revolution of 1688, and was appointed privy councillor a year later. However, by the second session of the Scottish parliament for 1690 he had been fined for non-attendance and had become a member of the opposition club. Two years later he was not reappointed as a privy councillor, and was excepted from pardon by James II. Campbell's move away from support for the administration was further emphasised when, first, his second son Archibald married the daughter of Duncan Macpherson of Cluny, a prominent jacobite, and second, in 1707, when he opposed the Union between Scotland and England. He enjoined his followers to support the 1715 jacobite rising and the fortuitous Cawdor estates were only saved from forfeiture by Sir Hugh's death in March 1716.

2. *Moving to Wales*

Hugh's eldest son and heir to the estate was Alexander, who matriculated to King's College, Aberdeen in 1677, though there is no evidence that a degree was conferred upon him.[10] In 1693 he followed his father as Scottish MP for Nairnshire, but only sat for two years. In 1688 he was contracted to marry Elizabeth, daughter – and co-heiress with her brother Gilbert – of Sir John Lort of Stackpole Court, Pembrokeshire and Lady Susannah Holles, the daughter of the 2nd earl of Clare.[11] The marriage, which took place in the following year, was the first that the Campbells of Cawdor had undertaken outside Scotland and it marks a shift for the family away from the bloody strife associated with Highland politics. Moreover, in physically moving from Scotland, Campbell was following a late 17th-century trend among the Scottish nobility, as they were increasingly 'attracted by London and the royal court'.[12] It also tended to distance Alexander Campbell from the taint of jacobitism which had begun to blight the family under Sir Hugh's lairdship. The marriage, which was cut short by Alexander's death in 1697, produced four children: Gilbert, who died an infant, John, the subject of the present study, Susanna, who married her first cousin, Sir James Campbell, 5th baronet of Auchinbrek in 1717, and Anne, who married Edmund Morris of Loddington, Leicestershire.[13]

The manor of Stackpole, originally established in the early 12th century when Archbishop Baldwin granted land to Elidyr de Stackpool, was, by the 14th century, owned by the absentee Vernon family of Hadden Hall, Derbyshire. The Vernons kept

---

[10] *Roll of Alumni in Arts of the University and King's College of Aberdeen, 1596–1860* (Aberdeen, 1900).

[11] Sir John Lort (c.1638–72), 2nd bt; Susanna Holles (1642–1710); John Holles (1595–1666), 2nd earl of Clare.

[12] B.P. Lenman, 'From the Union of 1707 to the Rise of the Franchise Reform of 1832', in *The New Penguin History of Scotland from the Earliest Times to the Present Day*, ed. R.A. Houston and W.W.J. Knox (2001), 277. Lenman continues: 'After 1707 this trend became much more marked, and the leading nobles and grander lairds tended to focus their careers and ambitions on the crown in its Westminster parliament'. John Campbell exemplifies this trend.

[13] Edmund Morris (?1686–1759), tory MP for Leicestershire 1722–7. He was listed in 1721 as a possible supporter of the Pretender. *The History of Parliament: The House of Commons, 1715–1754*, ed. Romney Sedgwick (2 vols, 1970), ii, 279.

the manor until the death of George Vernon in 1565, when it was purchased by the resident steward at Stackpole, George Lort. The latter's descendant Sir John Lort, 2nd baronet, died in 1672, leaving his wife Lady Susanna Lort and two children, Gilbert and Elizabeth, co-heirs to the estate.[14] Gilbert died unmarried in 1698, and in theory the estate should have devolved to his sister, by then Elizabeth Campbell. However, under the terms of Gilbert's will the Stackpole estate was put into a trust, the trustees being Lort's kinsman, John Holles, 1st duke of Newcastle, one Thomas Owen of Gray's Inn and Edward Harley of the Middle Temple.[15] On hearing that the tory Harley was one of the trustees, John Meyrick of Bush, Pembrokeshire, MP for Cardigan boroughs, suggested that the 'long dormant interest of Stackpole Court' could be woken in the tory interest to become a rival house to the whig Owen family of Orielton and the then whig Philipps family of Picton Castle.[16] However, any political awakening would have to wait until John Campbell came of age.

The Stackpole Court estate would have been seen as a good investment for the Campbells – one of several they made in Wales over the next 200 years. It was the second biggest estate in Pembrokeshire, after that of the Picton Castle estate, and contained some of the best farming land in Wales. Accordingly, it afforded stark contrast to the rather barren land surrounding Cawdor Castle at this time. But Alexander's early death almost deprived the family of the opportunity to reap any reward, for John, his heir, was just two years old when his father died. However, and fortunately for the Campbell family, the trustees accepted the terms of Gilbert Lort's will, and the estate was still intact on John Campbell's coming of age in 1716, two years after Elizabeth's death.[17] Reinforcing the family's separation from Scotland, the latter, in a statement of July 1708, which she reiterated in her will, dispossessed herself of all her Scottish estates, favouring the purchase of two Pembrokeshire copyholds, Carew and Wenn. And anti-Scottish sentiment is further in evidence two years later when Lady Susanna Lort, perhaps wary of the clan Campbell's volatile inter-familial past, included in her will that her estate was only to be settled on family members who did not marry 'north Britons'. It was an instruction that was followed, whether consciously or not, since thereafter the Campbells' principal seat became Stackpole Court and heiresses were sought from either England or Wales.[18]

3. *John Campbell*

John Campbell was born in London in 1695 and was raised in England and Wales. He entered Lincoln's Inn in April 1708, and matriculated to Clare Hall, Cambridge in May

[14] Elizabeth Lort (1665–1714).

[15] CRO, Cawdor/Campbell box 5/240: Will of Gilbert Lort of Stackpole Court, proved 3 Dec. 1698; John Holles (1662–1711), duke of Newcastle; lord privy seal 1705–11; probably Edward Harley (1664–1735), MP for Droitwich 1695–8 and Leominster 1698–1722. Harley became auditor of the imprest in 1702, an office he kept until his death, earning him the sobriquet Auditor Harley.

[16] John Meyrick (c.1673–1735) of Bush, Pembrokeshire; tory MP for Pembroke boroughs 1702–8 and Cardigan boroughs 1710–12. P.D.G. Thomas, 'Orielton versus Picton Castle', *Journal of the Pembrokeshire Historical Society*, vi (1994–5), 35–46.

[17] She died on 14 Sept. 1714 and was buried in Westminster Abbey.

[18] TNA, PROB/11/542/188, Will of Lady Elizabeth Campbell, 9 Oct. 1714; PROB/11/515/160, Will of Rt Hon. Lady Susanna Lort, widow of Chiswick, 26 May 1710.

1711.[19] Campbell entered a college that was heavily under the influence of Richard Laughton who, as tutor there, espoused the new natural philosophy of Isaac Newton and John Locke, the latter in particular being the doyen of the whig cause. This 'vigorously Whig atmosphere' coloured Campbell's political outlook for the rest of his life.[20]

Upon attaining his majority in 1716 he became head of the family. There is no evidence that he visited his Scottish estate and, indeed, his actions regarding Cawdor point to his increasing alienation from the Highland patrimony, though at elections he often used his politically secure ancestral home at Nairn as a safety net to fall back on should his more volatile seat in Wales become threatened by rivals. The Scottish estate that he inherited was greatly burdened by the debts left by his ancestors, particularly his grandfather, Archibald Campbell. As an indication of the scale of these debts, the agent for the isles of Islay and Jura, James Anderson, was personally owed over £2,000.[21] John Campbell attempted to unburden himself from debt; however, as was the case with many other landowners, he largely failed. In 1723 he mortgaged the isles of Islay and Jura – which had been a constant source of political and economic strife for the family since their acquisition in 1614 – to his cousin, Daniel Campbell of Shawfield, raising over £12,000 in the deal.[22] This act also emphasised Campbell's remove from his ancestral home. In fact Campbell's 'actions in the personal, commercial, and political spheres reveal just how far he had moved beyond the traditional concerns and agendas of a highland laird'.[23] And in another shift away from Highland politics, in 1726 he married Mary Pryse, daughter of Lewis Pryse of Gogerddan, Cardiganshire. He informed his uncle Archibald, laird of the Scottish estate, thus: 'I was this morning [8 Apr. 1726] married to Mrs Pryse, a young lady of North Wales, who possesses in the highest degree every virtue and agreeable accomplishment that can make a person beloved and respected. Her fortune is a small estate among the Welsh hills'.[24]

Despite the fact that Lewis Pryse was a well-known Welsh jacobite – he was returned as MP for Cardiganshire in 1715, but was expelled from the Commons for refusing to take the oaths – the taint of jacobitism does not seem to have hindered Campbell in his political ambitions, though political enemies occasionally raised that spectre as they did

---

[19] *The Records of the Honourable Society of Lincoln's Inn: I, Admissions 1420–1799* (1896).

[20] R. Browning, *The Duke of Newcastle* (1975), 7.

[21] 'Succinct Account of the Family of Cawdor', ed. Macphail, 136.

[22] Daniel Campbell (1672–1753), of Shawfield, Lanark; MP for Glasgow burghs 1716–34. Campbell's house, Shawfield, was destroyed by the Glasgow mob in 1725 after they believed he supported the malt tax of that year. The house of commons granted Campbell £6,080 compensation, which together with a called-in loan of £4,000 from Glasgow city, enabled him to purchase Islay and Jura from John Campbell. *HPC, 1715–54*, i, 520; A. Murdoch, *'The People Above': Politics and Administration in Mid-Eighteenth Century Scotland* (Edinburgh, 1980), 31.

[23] *ODNB*. In his 'Substance of a Letter, to a Friend upon the Militia Scheme', written in 1762, Campbell does declare of rejoicing in the 'Country of my fathers, to which I have so strong, and natural a tye'. However, his actions throughout his life indicate that this was merely the statement of a man whose attachment was more romantic than real.

[24] Innes, *Book of the Thanes of Cawdor*, xlv, fn., wherein he states that Campbell's letter to his uncle is a 'model of succinct and business like correspondence'.

hints of Roman catholicism.[25] However, Mary had an estate – Aberllefenni – of just over 2,000 acres in her own right, which was most likely the attraction for Campbell and which overrode any political considerations,[26] for the Aberllefenni estate had the singular benefit of being in possession of one of the oldest, biggest and most productive slate quarries in Wales, an undoubted advantage for a gentleman intent on raising his income.[27]

By sales of lands in Scotland and by a prudent marriage in Wales, Campbell's prospects for increased income began to look promising, though his attempt to rid himself of debt was always to prove a futile exercise. By the mid 18th century the Welsh agricultural estates, despite yielding an income of around £4,885, had regular outgoings of £22,000.[28] However, not to be deterred, in 1717 Campbell purchased the Ystradffin estate in the north-eastern corner of Carmarthenshire. This estate, which the Lorts had held on lease since the 1680s, was poor farming country, but it contained, at Rhandirmwyn, under-exploited lead mines, a situation that Campbell intended to change, albeit slowly.[29] By the 1780s the family was benefiting from the mines to the sum of around £6,000 a year.

With income from land sales in Scotland, good agricultural land at Stackpole and developing mineral extractive ventures in Carmarthenshire and Merioneth, the early 1730s seemed to promise a more comfortable financial future for Campbell than had the early part of the previous decade, though his spending was always in excess of his income. Many gentry families in the 18th century, especially those with ambitions to become political leaders of their home counties, began building projects – enlarging or rebuilding their family seats – and John Campbell was no exception.[30] As he saw a more stable financial future for his family, and as his political ambitions seemed to be in the ascendancy, Campbell began a grand project to rebuild Stackpole Court, which was not really completed until the mid 19th century. The Stackpole Court that Campbell inherited was a fairly large medieval manor house, probably dating from the 14th century, although the original owner of Stackpole, Elidyr de Stackpool, held land that was probably gifted to him by Archbishop Baldwin around 1100.[31] In 1670 Stackpole Court was taxed at 12 chimneys, making it the second biggest house in Pembrokeshire, though by the late 17th century it was looking run down.[32] John Campbell's ambitious rebuilding turned the house into a Palladian mansion of grand proportions, creating one

---

[25] *HPC, 1715–54,* ii, 371.

[26] Aberllefenni, Montgomeryshire.

[27] Aberllefenni slate quarry was really three quarries: Foel Grochan, Hen Chwarel and Ceunant Ddu. All three quarries had been mined since the 14th century until their closure in 2003.

[28] CRO, Cawdor/Campbell box 128, document detailing the estate income and expenditure.

[29] The mines at Rhandirmwyn had been worked since Roman times, and had been the property of the monks of Strada Florida monastery, Cardiganshire, until the Reformation. By the end of the 18th century the mines were among the biggest being worked in Wales, with around 400 miners employed. See J.E. Davies, 'The Cawdor Estates in Wales in the Nineteenth Century', Swansea University PhD, 2008, ch. 4.

[30] See D.W. Howell, *Patriarchs and Parasites: The Gentry in South-West Wales in the Eighteenth-Century* (Cardiff, 1985), for estate indebtedness in south-west Wales at this time.

[31] E.V. Stackpole, *History and Genealogy of the Stackpole Family* (Lewiston, ME, 1920), 10–11.

[32] Pembrokeshire hearth tax, 1670; rival houses Orielton and Picton Castle were recorded as having 20 and ten chimneys, respectively.

of the largest houses in Wales.[33] It was a rebuilding which reflected the whig aspirations of its owner, and indicated to local political rivals that the Campbells, relative strangers in the county, had become a major interest in the area. Stackpole Court was no longer politically dormant, to some extent thus fulfilling Mr Meyrick's desire, but it had awoken decidedly in the whig rather than the tory interest.

4. *A Whig for Life: John Campbell's Political Career*

Campbell's political awakening had actually begun several years before the rebuilding of the mansion had commenced. After the general election of September 1727, called by Sir Robert Walpole after the death of George I, Campbell became MP for Pembrokeshire, a seat he retained for 20 years. Campbell may have been fortunate in winning the county seat in this his first election, his success being largely due to the intense rivalry between the two leading whig families in Pembrokeshire, the Philippses of Picton Castle and the Owens of Orielton. Sir John Philipps of Picton Castle gave his vote to Campbell as a way of preventing his rival whig, Sir Arthur Owen from winning at the poll.[34] Sir John's eldest son, Erasmus, wrote that 'everybody owned that it was the Picton family that carried the election for Mr Campbell', in which a contested election was fought against the sitting member, Sir Arthur Owen.[35]

There had been antagonisms, both personal and political, between the houses of Picton and Orielton for a number of years. In 1715 Sir John Philipps had been passed over for the place of lord lieutenancy of the county by Sir Arthur Owen, a snub to the family that was long remembered.[36] Twelve years later, in the election of 1727, Phillips' son, also Sir John, gave his support to Campbell largely because of personal antipathy towards Owen. Sir Arthur had passed to Sir John, 4th baronet, some personal correspondence of the latter's son's, an act the young man described as 'bad and rascally', and which almost ended in a duel.[37] Some of the antagonisms between the families may have been born of political frustration on behalf of the Philippses. The Owens had held the county seat since 1689 except for five years from 1710 when John Barlow of Lawrenny

---

[33] The architect of Stackpole Court is unknown. The great Palladian architect, Coln or Colin Campbell (1676–1729), of Boghole, Scotland, and author of *Vitruvius Britannicus*, was a first cousin of John Campbell, but had died a few years prior to the building work at Stackpole. And it seems that the Coln Campbell archive has no major gaps, though the house bore more than a passing resemblance to the Campbell-designed Stourhead. Stackpole was further added to in the late 18th century, and a dammed river created a four-acre lake in the small valley at the back of the house. More building work was undertaken in the first half of the 19th century, and at its largest Stackpole contained over 150 rooms. The 5th earl destroyed the house in 1963, when he failed to receive government grants to make good the damage to the house caused by the army which had commandeered it during the 1939–45 war. The earliest letters of John Campbell to Pryse were written from Stackpole, and describe the rebuilding in a fair amount of detail, Pryse having been sent from the house for his own safety.

[34] Sir John Philipps (1666–1737), 4th bt, of Picton Castle, Pembrokeshire; MP for Pembroke boroughs 1695–1702 and Haverfordwest 1718–22; Sir Arthur Owen (c.1674–1753), 3rd bt, of Orielton, Pembrokeshire; MP for Pembrokeshire 1695–1705 and 1715–27, and for Pembroke boroughs 1708–12.

[35] NLW, MS 23274: notebook of Erasmus Philipps, son of Sir John.

[36] P.D.G. Thomas, *Politics in Eighteenth-Century Wales* (Cardiff, 1998), 96.

[37] Thomas, *Politics in Eighteenth-Century Wales*, 180.

(cousin, but political foe, of Sir Arthur Owen)[38] had held the seat. For the rest of the 18th and nearly half of the 19th century only Sir John Philipps, for three years from 1761, and John Campbell were successful in breaching the Owen family stranglehold on the county seat.[39] By contrast the Philippses had mainly to make do with the less prestigious borough seat of Haverfordwest, and the turbulent borough constituency of Carmarthen, where Sir John Philipps was returned in 1741.[40]

Even with the support of the Philipps vote Campbell was not entirely sure of his victory in 1727. He wrote a detailed account of how he won, stating that the opposition *London Evening Post* of 16 September reported that he had lost the poll. However, that and several other newspapers all reported his victory, not defeat.[41] In Campbell's account, which was probably written as his defence after Owen petitioned the Commons, he states that initially he lost the poll to Sir Arthur Owen by 374 to 229 votes, but that many of his votes had been discarded by the returning officer, until the illegality of this was pointed out since those discarded votes were from legal freeholders. On a recount Campbell became the county MP by 551 to Owen's 374 votes.[42] In return Owen pleaded foul play and petitioned the Commons; the hearing was twice postponed before lapsing.[43] Erasmus Philipps commented that the high sheriff of the county, Sir Richard Walter, the deputy sheriff, and Mr John Vaughan of Trecoon, Pembrokeshire, who sat for a while at the poll, 'were in Mr Campbell's interest', though adding that they all 'acted, I think, Impartially'. Philipps continued: 'Twas well Mr Campbell had good friends to support him for he was a stranger pretty much to the country'.[44] Strangers, though some may have resided in the locality for centuries, were often regarded with suspicion and as political outsiders in rural Wales. However, though a stranger, Campbell had powerful political connections. Sir John Philipps was related by marriage to Sir Robert Walpole, then at the height of his power, and Campbell could include among his family connections and political friends both the duke of Newcastle and the duke of Argyll.

Campbell had to contest four more elections during his 20-year stint as Pembrokeshire's member of parliament. Two of these were the mere formality of seeking re-election after being placed in government office, in 1736 and in 1746. However, at the general election of 1734, Campbell's friends again lent a helping hand, though this time it was the Owen family that enabled him to remain at Westminster. William Owen, of Landshipping, Pembrokeshire, eldest son of Sir Arthur, and whig MP for Pembroke boroughs, agreed a compromise with Sir Robert Walpole – the latter

---

[38] John Barlow (*d.* 1718) of Lawrenny, Pembrokeshire; MP for Haverfordwest 1715–18.

[39] In 1841 the Owens' hegemony over Pembrokeshire county politics was ended when Lord Emlyn, John Campbell's descendant, won the election, a seat he held until 1860, when he was raised to the peerage as the 2nd Earl Cawdor.

[40] On the debate regarding the petition against Philipps at that election Campbell commented: 'all Kilgetty [Philipps] has done to deprive the Inhabitants of Carmarthen of the Right to chose their own Member', a reference to the tory stranglehold over the town at this time. Letter 33: John Campbell to Mary Campbell, 24 Dec. 1741 (see Chapter 2).

[41] See *London Evening Post* and, for instance, the *London Gazette*, both 16 Sept. 1727.

[42] See the account of this election written by Campbell in Appendix 1.

[43] R. Thorne, 'The Political Scene, 1660–1815', in *Pembrokeshire County History: Early Modern Pembrokeshire, 1536–1815*, ed. B. Howells (Haverfordwest, 1987), 345.

[44] NLW, MS 6106: diary of Erasmus Philipps of Picton Castle.

intervening to prevent another contest between two whig families – whereby Owen agreed to support Campbell in return for a Cornish seat for John Owen, Sir Arthur's younger son.[45] William Owen, Sir Arthur's heir, believed that it was his acceptance of Walpole's compromise which allowed Campbell to succeed at the 1734 poll, writing to Walpole: 'Had I acted otherwise he [John Owen] should have been chose in Pembrokeshire'.[46] However, after Walpole's fall the agreement was no longer deemed binding and in the 1747 election John Owen formed an alliance with Sir John Philipps, by this time one of the leading tories in the Commons, and defeated Campbell, who 'retreated to the Nairnshire seat controlled by his family'.[47]

In December 1741 Campbell fought a contested election against John Symmons of Llanstinan, Pembrokeshire. He won by 556 to 529, a slender margin of 29 votes.[48] Again, in Sheriff Matthew Bowen of Camrose, Campbell had a favourable returning officer. Symmons petitioned, claiming that whereas his voters had been checked for land tax payments none of the Campbells had been scrutinised in this way.[49] Symmons' petition was due to be heard in March 1742, along with others relating to Carmarthen, Haverfordwest and Pembroke boroughs. However, the hearing of these petitions was repeatedly postponed until January 1743, when Velters Cornwall proposed to Lord Bath that they should all be withdrawn. This was agreed in early February 1743, by all parties except, initially, Symmons.[50] However, as Campbell explained, Kilgetty [Sir John Philipps], one of the others being petitioned against – for Carmarthen boroughs – 'went out to Mr Symmons & after a little bustle all was right again'.[51] That Campbell was relieved by this conclusion was conveyed in a letter to his son Pryse: 'if you remember how I was used for a long time after Mr. Symmons declared and what an expence that usage occasion'd, you will not think I can desire to undergo farther trouble & expence for the sake of that Family [Symmons] which occasion'd all the trouble I have allready had'.[52]

When Campbell felt his seat in the Commons under threat from his Welsh opponents, he also on occasion sat for his family seat at Nairnshire, which was as near to a safe political seat as the Cawdor Campbells could hope for. However, neither the Welsh nor the Scottish seat were easy picking, and Campbell resorted in the remote northern constituency to more unconventional methods than he would perhaps have dared in Wales. The Campbells were hereditary sheriffs in Nairnshire, which helped at election times – the sheriff also being the returning officer – and the office had been used on several occasions as insurance in case of failure in other

---

[45] John Owen (1698–1775), of Bath; whig MP for West Looe 1735–41.

[46] *HPC, 1715–54*, ii, 316, citing CUL, Cholmondeley (Houghton), MS 2193: Owen to Walpole, 8 June 1734.

[47] *HPC, 1715–54*, i, 379. Owen was the whig MP for Pembroke boroughs 1722–47 and 1761–74, and Pembrokeshire county 1761–74. He voted with the administration on every recorded division. He succeeded his father as the 4th bt in 1753; Thomas, *Politics in Eighteenth-Century Wales*, 125.

[48] *HPC, 1715–54*, i, 379.

[49] *CJ*, xxiv, 28, 340.

[50] *CJ*, xxiv, 403–4.

[51] Letter 78: John Campbell to Pryse Campbell, 3 Feb. 1743 (see Chapter 3).

[52] Letter 71: John Campbell to Pryse Campbell, 12 Jan. 1743 (see Chapter 3).

constituencies.[53] However, at Nairn, Campbell found a rival in the politically ambitious Alexander Brodie (1697–1754) of Brodie who, ever since his appointment in 1727 by the earl of Ilay – Walpole's election manager in Scotland – to the office of Lord Lyon of Scotland, regarded himself as the government voice in Nairnshire and was intent on controlling politics in the county.[54] Campbell had been returned for Nairnshire in 1734, but chose, as we have seen, the Pembrokeshire seat where he had also been elected (he was the only candidate to be elected for both a Scottish and Welsh constituency). At the ensuing Nairnshire by-election, Campbell supported his cousin, Alexander Brodie of Lethen, Nairnshire who took the seat, even though this meant he would antagonise his clan chief, Alexander Brodie of Brodie.[55] In this election both Campbell and Brodie of Brodie used force in an attempt to keep opposition voters away from the polls. Twelve years later, in the election of 1747, Alexander Brodie again threatened to use force but was pacified by a promise of being returned unopposed for Inverness burghs if he withdrew from the Nairnshire election, which he did. Campbell remained MP for Nairnshire until 1754, after which he represented Inverness burghs, in an election that again was fraught.[56] His opponent, Sir Alexander Grant, was snubbed by the duke of Newcastle, who had been given the nomination of the burgh by Hugh Rose of Kilravock, then the leading political power at Nairn, in favour of his relative. Grant responded and on the last day of April 1754 the Inverness town clerk reported that a mob had 'seized the court house and tollbooth' (the places chosen as polling booths) and refused access to all. Eventually it was agreed to hold the poll in Hugh Rose's house, where Campbell was returned unanimously.[57]

Campbell remained MP for Inverness burghs until 1761, when he made way for his opponent of seven years earlier, Sir Alexander Grant who, in return, gave his interest to Campbell's son Pryse, who in his second election was hoping to be re-elected for Inverness-shire. However, John Campbell, who by this time may have been hoping for political retirement – he had been a member of parliament continuously since 1727 – was then put forward by Henry Fox as the second candidate for the pocket borough of Corfe Castle.[58] Fox wanted good friends in the Commons, as he had been given what was perceived to be the politically uncomfortable task of persuading the Commons to accept the terms of what became the Treaty of Paris which ended the Seven Years

[53] The heritable sheriffs of Scotland were created by the medieval Scottish monarchy. In the aftermath of the 1745 jacobite rebellion, Lord Hardwicke saw an opportunity to abolish these and other heritable jurisdictions, as anomalies of a separate Scottish jurisdiction, with no place in a United Kingdom. However, at the debate for the second reading many Scottish whigs voted against Hardwicke's bill. John Campbell both spoke and voted against the bill, which was passed by 233 to 201 (*CJ*, xxv, 359), and went on to become the Heritable Jurisdictions (Scotland) Act of 1747 (20 Geo. ii, c.43). By his actions Campbell would not have won himself any favours with either Hardwicke or the duke of Newcastle. BL, Add. MS 35363, ff. 156–8: Philip Yorke, 2nd earl of Hardwick to Charles Yorke, 20 Apr. 1747. See B. Lenman, *The Jacobite Risings in Britain 1689–1746* (1980), 278–81.

[54] Alexander Brodie (1697–1754), of Brodie, Elgin; MP for Elginshire 1720–41, Caithness 1741–7 and Invernesss burghs 1747–54; Lord Lyon, king of arms 1727–54.

[55] Alexander Brodie (*d.* 1770), of Lethen, Nairnshire; MP for Nairnshire 1735–41.

[56] Brodie kept the seat until his death in 1754.

[57] G. Bain, *History of Nairnshire* (Nairn, 1893), 383–4.

[58] *The History of Parliament: The House of Commons, 1754–90*, ed. L.B. Namier and John Brooke (3 vols, 1964), ii, 187, 188.

War.[59] Campbell remained as member for Corfe Castle until his retirement from politics in 1768, though his last Commons appearance may have been as early as 1765.

Campbell was brought into the administration twice. In May 1736 he was given a place in Sir Robert Walpole's administration as one of the commissioners of the admiralty, which made up the board of admiralty, under the first lord, Admiral Sir Charles Wager.[60] The admiralty board was a junior branch of the administration and was often used as a stepping stone to greater office, such as a place on the treasury board. Campbell received the commission as a reward for his unstinting support of the Walpole administration since he had entered parliament. Pryse Campbell's godfather, John, Lord Hervey, lent his support in obtaining the office for Campbell, writing to Walpole that Campbell and Henry Fox had both supported the administration for several years without reward but with 'that unpopularity which always attends serving power without the profit that should be annexed to it'.[61] According to Hervey, Walpole knew the worth of both Campbell and Henry Fox, but feared that if Campbell was brought into the administration, either Thomas Clutterbuck or Thomas Winnington, both also on the admiralty board, would have to be removed.[62] It was resolved that Winnington should be promoted to the treasury to make room for Campbell. Interestingly, Fox had to wait until after Walpole's fall before he was given office in the administration, as one of the lords of the treasury in Pelham's first administration.[63]

Campbell's commission was renewed in 1738 and again in 1741, but he was removed from office in March 1742 in the aftermath of Walpole's fall from power. Campbell wrote to Pryse on 13 March 1742 that he should send all future letters to the Campbells' house in Grosvenor Square since, 'though I had the honor yesterday to sign the New Admirals Commissions, I expect to be superseded myself by the time this comes to your hands', though according to the London press he had been removed from office on 4 March.[64]

As one of the lords of the admiralty Campbell was involved with the war with Spain which began in 1739 and with the increasing tensions and affrays between France and Britain, which only formally became war in April 1744. However, it was not the admiralty board's responsibility at this time to formulate naval policy – that was undertaken by the king and his cabinet council. Rather it was the board's job to ensure that policy was carried out by making certain that the navy was in a 'state of prepared-ness . . . for detailing the ships and squadrons necessary' to undertake orders that were issued by the secretary of state – more an administrative than executive role.[65] However,

---

[59] The Treaty of Paris was ratified on 10 Apr. 1763. The Commons voted for its terms 319 to 65 on 9 Dec. 1762; *CJ*, xxix, 394.

[60] There were usually seven commissioners, including the first lord. Campbell shared his first commission with Wager, Sir Thomas Lyttelton, Lord Archibald Hamilton, Sir Thomas Frankland, Thomas Clutterbuck and Lord Harry Powlett.

[61] Lord Hervey, *Memoirs of the Reign of George the Second*, ed. J.W. Croker (3 vols, 1848), i, 403.

[62] Hervey, *Memoirs of the Reign of George the Second*, i, 403.

[63] Although he was the king's surveyor-general of works from 1737, which was probably a more lucrative office than a relatively minor government office, income always being an important consideration with Fox.

[64] Letter 45: John Campbell to Pryse Campbell, 13 Mar. 1742 (see Chapter 2); *Daily Gazeteer* (London), 5 Mar. 1742.

[65] 'The actual administration of the navy [was] divided between separate departments with very little inter-communication.' B. Williams, *The Whig Supremacy 1714–60* (2nd edn, Oxford, 1960), 223.

Campbell's letters are imbued with a sense of deep involvement at the admiralty, as they are filled with news of skirmishes, victories and defeats against the Spanish and the fear of invasion by the French.

After he was removed from the admiralty Campbell was not considered for office again until the second administration of Henry Pelham in June 1746. It is not surprising that he was not included in the short-lived Wilmington administration which replaced the Walpole government, since it was dominated by Lord Carteret, an implacable opponent of Walpole and his supporters. However, since Campbell was a relative of Henry Pelham, and had been a long-time supporter of the administration, including Pelham's first administration, it is surprising that he does not seem to have been considered for office. Pelham's first administration was filled with old corps whigs, those who remained loyal to Walpole and were 'the backbone of his party that was to prove unbreakable until its leaders grew too old to face a new king and a new generation in 1760'.[66] Campbell's whig credentials were perfect for this account and he would have been totally at home politically in the first Pelham administration. His exclusion rankled, especially as he believed less loyal men and lesser men – he was thinking of William Pitt in the first instance and Edmund Waller in the latter – were given places: 'Must it not be very grating', he wrote to Pryse, 'to me & some others to see ourselves quite neglected & such put into the most honorable and profitable Posts'.[67]

However Campbell was given a place as a lords commissioner of the treasury or lord of the treasury in June 1746, a promotion from the more junior admiralty office.[68] He remained a treasury lord until Pelham's unexpected death in March 1754. However, in another snub to Campbell, he lost his place when Newcastle established a new administration after his brother's death.

With his removal from the treasury, it seemed that any hope of other office disappeared, though when Newcastle was establishing his administration he fleetingly considered Campbell for chancellor of the exchequer: 'What think you of Campbel of Pembrokeshire', he wrote to his friend and trusted political adviser Lord Hardwicke, and, answering himself, stated: 'He is an Old Corps man, But He is a Scotch Man & a Campbel – The King will be uneasy'.[69] However, Newcastle himself had a predisposition to disliking or at least distrusting Scots, and as a novice himself in his new role at the head of the treasury Newcastle needed men of experience he could trust entirely.[70] Thus Campbell was ruled out, though perhaps regardless of the king's unease. Two years later, Campbell could remark to Fox, in a sour observation, that 'I have from a very little after Mr Pelham's death, to this time [1756], except some months last Winter been in great fear that the Duke of Newcastle's causeless jealousy's and his denying in fact all confidence, though promised it, to those who were disposed to be his friends', which, although referring to Newcastle's reluctance to accept Fox in his administration, may also be a comment upon the duke's continued denial of any office for Campbell

[66] J.H. Plumb, *Sir Robert Walpole: The King's Minister* (2 vols, 1960), ii, 280.

[67] Letter 118: John Campbell to Pryse Campbell, 18 Dec. 1744 (see Chapter 4).

[68] The treasury board was usually five in number. In this first commission Campbell shared the board with Pelham, as first lord, Charles Sackville the earl of Middlesex, George Lyttelton and Henry Bilson Legge.

[69] BL, Add. MS 32860, f. 332: Newcastle to Hardwicke, 12 Oct. 1755.

[70] Browning, *Duke of Newcastle*, 85.

himself.[71] Such a remark provides an indication that Campbell at this time was still politically ambitious for office. It was to be a vain ambition.

As a sop to his political desires Newcastle offered Campbell control of a minor Scottish office. On Campbell's removal from the treasury, Horace Walpole commented: 'The same day [4 Apr. 1755], the Duke of Newcastle obtained his full list of preferments from King. Lord Barnard, Legge, Lord Dupplin in Treasury with Nugent, in room of Campbell who had the place of Lord Lyon for two sons' lives'.[72] Campbell filled the office with his second son John [Jack]. Acceptance of the office meant that Campbell was establishing a place for a younger son without the lavish spending that either gaining a seat in the Commons or a commission in the forces would have entailed. John Campbell, who became John Hooke Campbell in 1757, when he was bequeathed the Bangeston estate, Pembrokeshire, in the will of John Hooke, remained Lord Lyon until his death in 1795. It was (and still is) the most junior of the Scottish offices of state, and therefore one of relatively little political interest, dealing principally with matters relating to heraldry. However, the office holder had a right of veto on who should or should not be granted a coat of arms, and since a grant of arms bestowed a certain amount of patronage, including the patronage of votes, on the recipient, it may have been that Campbell saw the office as a way of controlling political enemies in Scotland. By potentially limiting votes in the Scottish constituency, Campbell may have been considering his son Pryse's budding political career – he became MP of Inverness-shire in the same year that John Hooke Campbell became Lord Lyon.[73]

Campbell's chances of further office seem to have ended with his removal from the treasury, and his acceptance of the office of Lord Lyon for his younger son in addition to Pryse becoming a member of parliament tempered the father's own political ambitions. He never refers to his desiring office in any letter after 1756 and, unlike his friend Henry Fox who was voraciously ambitious for a peerage, only to be disappointed when he received merely a barony, there is nothing in Campbell's correspondence to suggest that he was likewise desirous of a place in the Lords. At the end of 1734 there is a brief report in the press that Campbell was to be created a peer.[74] However, this was erroneous and in Campbell's surviving correspondence for that year there is no mention of any such elevation.[75] Campbell seems to have become content to see two of his sons advanced in the world after he had built a modest base from which they could further their political ambitions. In Henry Fox, Campbell had had a politically well-connected, ambitious friend. However, there is no indication in the correspondence between them of Campbell having asked Fox to propose him for office. And in Fox's lists of potential administrations, which he created during the mid 1750s crisis and later, Campbell is never included. On the other side, Campbell, in his most effusive extant letter to Newcastle, does recommend Fox as a man of integrity who could greatly improve the

[71] Letter 151, BL, Add. MS 51406, ff. 19–20: John Campbell to Henry Fox, 5 Nov. 1756 (see Chapter 5).

[72] *The Yale Edition of Horace Walpole's Correspondence*, ed. W.S. Lewis *et al.* (48 vols, New Haven, CT, 1937–83), ii, 10, fn. 5.

[73] Campbell's kinsman, Thomas Brodie of Lethen, was chosen as Hooke Campbell's deputy in 1754.

[74] *Daily Courant*, 25 Nov. 1734.

[75] CRO, Cawdor/Campbell box 128.

administration: 'I am extremely glad of the good Agreement between your Grace and Mr Fox, and I heartily wish, and hope, such Measures may be taken, as all who act upon right, and public, principles may concur in'.[76] However, Campbell perhaps knew the true state of affairs between the two men, or rather three men, since Newcastle always had Hardwicke, an inveterate foe of Fox, to back him. It was a recommendation that would have done nothing for any ambitions harboured by Campbell.

Although he was a political ally of Walpole, Campbell's support for the administration in the Commons was not uncritical, and in a frank admission to Newcastle he claimed to have always voted in accordance with his conscience, which led him on occasion to vote with the opposition: 'I did, in some Instance's Vote contrary to the inclinations of Sir Robert Walpole, when he was Minister, of your Grace, and of your beloved Brother [Henry Pelham], at the same time that I was firmly, and warmly attach'd to those Administrations'.[77] Thus he voted for the bill to prevent occasional conformity in 1733 and in the following year he voted in favour of the peerage bill. He also voted against the administration's bill for granting £115,000 to make good arrears of the Civil List.[78] However, on all crucial administration bills, such as the excise and septennial bills, and on the various bills for subsidies to foreign troops, Campbell gave his support in the Commons to the whig administrations under which he served.

At the end of April 1735 Campbell was voted by a ballot of members on to the committee to inquire into the frauds of the Customs, which had been established after an opposition proposal in the wake of the defeat of the excise bill.[79] The committee, which was composed of politicians of all hues, was a veiled attack on Walpole's administration as the opposition began to realise that Sir Robert's end was in sight. Campbell would have been there to defend his mentor.

Campbell spoke on several occasions in the Commons, though over a 40-year stint as MP it cannot be said that he was a regular speaker. He certainly spoke more often at the beginning of his parliamentary career and up to the fall of Walpole than later on. Nevertheless there is a ten-year lacuna in the letters from 1745 when he could have spoken, though other contemporary sources do not refer to him during this period. It cannot be said that he left any sort of mark in the Commons as a speech maker – had he done so then others would have reported his speeches; they rarely did and then only briefly. In the extant letters he modestly mentions when he had spoken, but does not go into detail. Reports from others of the content of Campbell's speeches are only extant in one or two instances. Lord Egmont refers to a speech made by Campbell in February 1730, supporting the continued payment of Hessian troops. This is the earliest recorded speech by Campbell, though Egmont does not give any detail of the speech, merely stating that 'Mr Cammel of Wales spoke for the Court'. And in January 1732

---

[76] BL Add. MS 32859, ff. 419–20, Letter 137: John Campbell to the duke of Newcastle, 7 Oct. 1755 (see Chapter 5).

[77] BL, Add. MS 32970, f. 103, Letter 208: John Campbell to the duke of Newcastle, 29 Sept. 1765 (see Chapter 8).

[78] Chandler refers to two John Campbells voting for this bill and John Campbell of Pembrokeshire voting against. R. Chandler, *History and Proceedings of the House of Commons* (14 vols, 1732–4), viii.

[79] William Cobbett, *Cobbett's Parliamentary History* (36 vols, 1806–20), ix, 10–11.

Charles Howard states that Mr Campbell moved the address.[80] A month later he was one of the speakers listed, when he spoke in support of the salt duty, in a debate 'which lasted seven or eight hours, occasioned by whether they should revive the duty on Salt, which was taken off last year, or to have two shillings in the pound Land Tax'.[81] For all the years he was an MP, Cobbett's *Parliamentary History* only refers to Campbell giving a speech on one occasion – when he moved the address to the king's speech in January 1734.[82] However, both the king's speech and the Commons address of thanks – a response to the speech – were set pieces authored by the leaders of the administration, rather than the speaker, though the latter would have added content. The precedent for the address was that it was expected to cover all the main points of the king's speech, omitting none and adding none. However, Campbell's address in 1734 did cause a minor stir, the opposition patriots demanding to know 'why he had put in words to the Address which were not contained in the heads agreed to'.[83] The offending words implied that the British would support any measure 'on every occasion' the king thought necessary – by which the opposition believed parliament was being asked to give unequivocal support to the king's European interest, namely the Hanover Electorate. Campbell defended his position, stating that as far as he was concerned there was nothing in the address for 'room for imagining, they [the criticized words] were ever meant to comprehend his Majesty's German dominions; every man must see they relate only to the foreign rights and possessions belonging to the crown of Great Britain'.[84] Both Henry Pelham and Sir Robert Walpole spoke defending Campbell, but Walpole, according to Egmont, 'gave way that the words objected to should not stand part of the Address'. After the offending words were removed, the Address was passed.[85] This relatively minor episode, ruffling the feathers of the opposition, is the most extensively reported speech Campbell made.

These are early references to Campbell speaking at the beginning of his parliamentary career and are all before the dates of the extant letters. In the letters Campbell only refers to speaking on a handful of occasions and then usually in regard to minor matters. Thus at the end of January 1742 he spoke 'unasked [that is, it had not been a premeditated speech] and I believe unexpected but I was moved in spirit and could not refrain', over the debate regarding whether or not Speaker Onslow's speech regarding the Westminster election should be published. Campbell, along with Horace Walpole, was the only MP to speak against publication, Campbell maintaining that though a good speech it 'wants facts to support it'.[86]

More importantly, in March 1742 he did speak against establishing a committee of secrecy concerning the Walpole administration. He states to Pryse that 'I bore my testimony against it & express'd in the strongest terms my contempt for that popularity

---

[80] HMC, *Diary of the First Earl of Egmont, Viscount Percival* (1879–1923), i, 31; HMC, *15th Report, Manuscripts of the Earl of Carlisle* (1897), 80: Col. Hon. Charles Howard to Lord Carlisle, 21 Jan. 1731.

[81] HMC, *Carlisle*, 89: Col. Hon. Charles Howard to Lord Carlisle, 21 Feb. 1732.

[82] He was seconded by Stephen Fox, Henry's elder brother.

[83] HMC, *Egmont's Diary*, ii, 9, 18 Jan. 1734.

[84] *PH*, ix, 190.

[85] HMC, *Egmont's Diary*, ii, 9, 18 Jan. 1734.

[86] Letter 36: John Campbell to Mary Campbell, 26 Jan. 1742 (see Chapter 2).

which ruins us, makeing some act contrary I verily believe both to their Judgement & inclination'.[87] This is as detailed as Campbell ever becomes with regard to his own utterances in the Commons.

Campbell next mentions speaking in November 1742, defending his Pembrokeshire seat, in a debate on the election after a petition had been brought in by his opponent John Symmons of Llanstinan in June of that year.[88] Campbell had won the election by a mere 29 votes, and Symmons claimed that the sheriff had not acted impartially; however Campbell defeated the petition.

As mentioned, there is a lacuna in the letters of ten years from 1745, so the next time we have evidence of Campbell speaking is in December 1755 when he joined the debate on the Hessian and Russian subsidy treaties – speaking for the treaties, and thereby supporting his friend Fox, then secretary of state for the southern department. However, all we know of his speech is that he 'spoke a few words that I might declare my assent more explicitly than by mere voting'. In a letter to his wife, Mary, three weeks before his speech he outlines for her what subsidies were and the exact sums that were being voted upon.[89] The letter reads like a lecture, and may be the gist of what he said to his fellow members. In this important debate Campbell was lucky to have been given the chance to speak at all; those great orators, Attorney-General William Murray, and William Pitt, both spoke at length, Murray for and Pitt against the treaties. The great commoner, according to Campbell, spoke excellently, but 'outdid his usual outdoings'.[90]

So throughout a parliamentary career of 40 years, the evidence for utterances by Campbell is sparse. Not many commentators mention him, he himself refers to speeches he made only infrequently and it must be assumed that he spoke relatively few times and mainly briefly. For most of his speeches it is probably the case that commentators were silent, because they believed he added nothing substantial to debates in a house of commons that was bulging with exceptional orators. The extant evidence of his speeches tells us that they may just have been extemporised responses to the utterances of others in debate, rather than prepared statements. And in fact, most of his speeches, where acknowledged in the letters, concern local politics, particularly in defence of his own seat at such times as post-election petitions.

Campbell, who is still known in the family as 'joyless John', gives ample proof of his seriousness as an MP. When Thomas Brereton, MP for Liverpool and a fellow unstinting supporter of Walpole, spoke regarding the Pembrokeshire petition of 1742 and frivolously commented about a break in precedent regarding such petitions, making the opposition 'set up a loud laugh', Campbell was not amused: 'it is our busyness . . . to unite the Whigs of the old & new Ministry as much as possible for the Common cause, there could be nothing more imprudent . . . as he . . . more impertinent than to say a thing that raise a laugh & carry a reflection upon our new friends'.[91] But would he have been more amused if the joke had been at the expense of the opposition, rather than of the Pembroke petition?

[87] Letter 47: John Campbell to Pryse Campbell, 23 Mar. 1742 (see Chapter 2).
[88] Letter 55: John Campbell to Pryse Campbell, 25 Nov. 1742 (see Chapter 2).
[89] Letter 142: John Campbell to Mary Campbell, 20 Nov. 1755 (see Chapter 5).
[90] Letter 145: John Campbell to Mary Campbell, 16 Dec. 1755 (see Chapter 5).
[91] Letter 55: John Campbell to Pryse Campbell, 25 Nov. 1742 (see Chapter 2).

5. *A Minor Political Writer*

Although Campbell cannot be regarded as a regular, and most certainly not a major, speaker in the Commons, he did, over the course of his political career, write several essays and extended letters on political, military and religious subjects. Six of his writings are included in the present volume, those excluded being not directly political in subject matter.[92] Most of the surviving works were written in the late 1750s and early 1760s when the politically experienced author could demand some sort of respect from his fellow MPs as a commentator on parliamentary affairs. However, it is not clear why Campbell wrote any of the essays. None seems to have been published, and they may just have been for self-clarification. On the other hand, one is addressed to the reader, so it may have been his intention to publish.

All of his essays are imbued with the philosophy of John Locke, 'the evangelist of whig doctrine'.[93] Campbell maintained that since the Glorious Revolution of 1688 and the Acts of Settlement and Bill of Rights, the nation had been happy 'under a king truely great and good', though a king controlled by parliament. Behind such a belief was Locke's interpretation of the settlement of 1688 which was taken up wholeheartedly by the whigs and which justified in their eyes such acts as the Septennial Act of 1715; by extending the life of parliament for up to seven years this was instrumental in keeping the whigs in power for over half a century.[94] Campbell absorbed this philosophy whole-heartedly and his protestant, whig and Hanoverian credentials furnished a bastion against all opposition who were by their very definition, according to Campbell's outlook, defective in their beliefs, whether they were tories or opposition whigs, the latter in particular being looked upon with much disdain by Campbell.

The essays and other writings are responses to current political and other contemporary issues. The earliest extant, a long letter rather than an essay entitled 'Copy of a Letter to a Nonjuring Gentleman in Scotland', was written in 1727. The title seems to imply that this letter was published, though where remains unknown.[95] It is also unclear who the gentleman in the title is, though Campbell was a kinsman of the bishop of Aberdeen who led the later nonjurors of Scotland, and in the essay he does attack the high clergy, of which the bishop was a leading light.[96] Campbell's main argument, repeated in several of his essays, is that government was given to mankind by the will of God, and that the end and design of government was the 'good of the governed'. This argument was the orthodox whig one, and was the opposite of the nonjuror and tory philosophy that monarchy was of divine origin. To back up his argument Campbell states that a reading of Sir Robert Filmer's *Patriachia*, a defence of the divine right of kings, would convince anyone of 'the Inconsistence, and vane Nonsense of that Doctrine'.[97]

---

[92] For those included see the Table of Contents. Those not included are: 'Dr Chandler's Review of the History of the Man after God's Own Heart' (1762), 'Thoughts on Religion', 'The Athanasian Creed' and 'Some Short Remarks upon the Book of Common Prayer' (all undated but written c.1762).

[93] Williams, *Whig Supremacy*, 3.

[94] 1 Geo I, s.2, c.38.

[95] There is no indication from the British Library's early newspapers online that it was published. And it is too early for publication in either the *Gentleman's* or *London* magazines.

[96] Archibald Campbell (*d.* 1744), bishop of Aberdeen 1727–44.

[97] 'Copy of a Letter to a Nonjuring Gentleman in Scotland Writ in the Year 1727'. See Appendix 2.

In several cases the essays were written in response to published works. Such is the case with his critique of Edward Spelman's preface to his translation of the sixth book of the Greek historian Polybius' *Histories*. Polybius is most famous for the theory of the separation of the powers of government into a judiciary, an executive and a legislature. Spelman, in his preface, grafts Polybius' ideas on to mid 18th-century British government. In the process he attacks the whig-engineered Septennial Act, which he refers to as 'the severest Stab the liberties of the People of England ever received'.[98] Campbell, as an old corps whig, obviously bore no truck with Spelman's argument, and contends that self-interest was in part a motivating force for gentlemen to become MPs and that annual parliaments, as proposed by Spelman, would give no gentleman an incentive to become an MP.

Allied to the essay upon Spelman's preface is one of Campbell's more interesting writings. Although fairly short, his commentary upon *Orations of Demosthenes*, i (1757) and the *Orations of Demosthenes and Æchines*, ii (1758), as translated by the Rev. Phillip Francis (1708–73), further expounds Campbell's views of politics. Francis was an Irish-born teacher – one of his pupils was Edward Gibbon – and writer who was employed, from about 1755, by Henry Fox as a family chaplain and as a tutor to his son Charles James. On hearing that Francis was so employed Charles Churchill quipped that Francis the atheist had become the chaplain to the atheist Fox. Francis was soon found to be a useful political ally. It was rumoured that Francis was the author of the *Test*, the anti-Pitt paper first published in November 1756.[99] And in 1761, when Pitt resigned as secretary of state, Francis wrote a libel against him called *Mr Pitt's Letter Versified* and then *A Letter from the Anonymous Author of Mr Pitt's Letter Versified*. Francis also attacked with great venom both Pitt and John Wilkes in the tract *Political Theatre* (1764), in which he lent his support to the tory, Lord Bute, at a time when Fox, by then Lord Holland, was being courted by the royal favourite. Francis was helped by Holland on numerous occasions, either with minor livings or putting his name forward to political friends. It was thanks to Holland that Francis was made chaplain at Chelsea Hospital. However, around the time *Political Theatre* was published, Francis accused Holland of promoting all his friends except him when the latter failed to get him appointed to an Irish bishopric.[100]

Campbell was one of the subscribers to Francis' translation of Demosthenes' *Oration*, which includes an essay by Francis on the political state of Greece by way of introduction to the Greek writer. Campbell's comments throw light on his political views which show him to be – in his own eyes at least – steadfast in his opinion of opposition politics. Francis stated that the Greeks, at their richest and most powerful, had lost sight of poverty and probity, and love of country rested with the opposition, whose ridicule 'was reserved for another people' (that is, the opposition of the mid 18th century). Campbell retorts: 'I could never see reason to believe, that Love of Country and Probity, were the spring, & rule of Action to the Opposition in my time', and that such words coming from the mouth of the opposition were gross hypocrisy, and deserve to be ridiculed.

---

[98] 1 Geo I, s.2, c.38.

[99] Earl of Ilchester, *Henry Fox, First Lord Holland, His Family and Relations* (2 vols, 1920), ii, 34.

[100] *ODNB*.

His next comment is reserved for a footnote by Francis in which the latter refers to Chares, admiral of the Greek fleet accused of cowardice and treason. Francis' note reads: 'how near to Ruin must be that maritime state, whose Admiral dares to be a Coward or a Traytor, yet is protected from the vengeance of his Country, by the Administration, and the Ministers: for such were the Orators of Athens'. This is obviously pointed at Admiral Byng, whose failure to stop the French from capturing Minorca in 1756 resulted in his execution. Campbell believes Francis to be too harsh in his condemnation of Byng, who was let down by orators and ministers, Pitt in particular – contrary to today's belief – whilst Campbell's friend Fox resigned when he saw the storm over Byng heading his way. At the end of his comment Campbell adds: 'In truth they [popular orators] have been too often able, to destroy the best Ministers, and raise to Power Men of very different Characters', an obvious reference to Pitt's and Carteret's part in the downfall of Campbell's beloved Walpole.

Related to this criticism of Pitt is Campbell's comment about the 'licentiousness of the People taking advantage of the Ambition of the Gentry, & Rich, to extort extravagant Price's for their Votes', whereas Francis had commented that the people had been corrupted by the rich in pursuit of their votes. Here again Campbell's prejudice against the popular, as identified with Pitt in particular, is prevalent.

In other places Campbell comments directly on Demosthenes' writings. Campbell's view of the houses of parliament as sacrosanct, and that populist politics (as courted by Pitt for instance) was a danger to that sanctity are well delineated by the Greek, when he states in terms Campbell describes as 'just wise and honorable' that all concerned in the 'Administration should by custom render you gentle and humane in your Assemblies', though those who 'in your assemblies formed to Pleasure only by the most luxurious Delicacy, the most artful Adulation, you really bring the Republic, in all Affairs of Moment, into extremist Danger'.[101] Yet again there is a reference to Pitt, or Pittite populism. Campbell disliked the way politics was heading, a dislike that probably discouraged him from seriously pursuing office after the mid 1750s.

Other essays were written in response to unpublished utterances in the Commons. His 'The Substance of a Letter, to a Friend in Scotland upon the Militia Scheme, August 1762' is one such essay. It is not known to whom Campbell was writing, though Sir Gilbert Elliot of Minto had campaigned ceaselessly for a Scottish militia and the letter may have been intended for him.[102] Another possibility for the recipient is Campbell's son Pryse, who had been on the committee to draft the English militia bill of 1759, and may have used his experience gained then to assist in the Scottish militia campaign of three years later.[103] However, the most likely addressee is George Dempster MP, who had delivered a speech in the Commons concerning a Scottish militia in November 1761. Campbell's letter is a detailed analysis of the militia question and the reasons why he believed a militia for Scotland was not in the best interests of national security. It is a response to the debate regarding the protection of Scotland by a militia upon the same

---

[101] *Orations of Demosthenes*, trans. Phillip Francis (2 vols, 1757), i, 225–6.
[102] Sir Gilbert Elliot of Minto (1722–77), 3rd bt.
[103] http://www.historyofparliamentonline.org/volume/1754-1790/member/campbell-pryse-1727-68, 1 Jan 2013.

principles as the one established under the 1759 Act for England and Wales. William Pitt was behind that Act. He had introduced a bill in the Commons to establish a militia in the dark days of 1755, with the war going from bad to worse and England being threatened with invasion from France. Pitt had proposed a militia as a better – more patriotic, but also cheaper – measure than employing Hessian or Hanoverian troops to defend England. Pitt's bill failed – it was thrown out in the Lords – but in 1759 a militia bill was enacted, though only for England and Wales. Scotland was excluded, partly in fear of armed uprising, with memories of the 1745 rising still vivid in the minds of men. In response, the following year saw a campaign of agitation by Scottish members with the backing of Pitt for an extension of the militia north of Hadrian's Wall. Two years later, in 1762, Scottish MPs considered bringing in a militia bill for Scotland, but support was poor.[104]

Campbell's arguments against a militia – not just for Scotland for he hopes the militia in England and Wales will be abolished on the completion of peace – are based not on the spectre of jacobitism, but on four key points: the dangers, if any, to the nation from a standing army; the expense of keeping such an army in peacetime; the militia being paid to defend property; and the justice of putting arms in the hands of a free people to defend their country. On all four counts Campbell believes a standing army to be superior in defending liberty and property. Such an army, with its leaders drawn from the landowning class, would cost about the same as a part-time, amateur, ill-prepared militia. Fears that a standing army could become a danger to the liberty of the nation were groundless, thought Campbell. Parliaments that sat regularly would prevent an army from becoming the tool of a despotic monarch as had happened under Charles I – a dig at the house of Stuart, and by extension the jacobites. Since the Glorious Revolution of 1688, 'The Power of the Crown, the Privileges, and Rights of the Parliament, and People, are more known, ascertained, fix'd, and secured'.[105] Campbell's arguments are fully in accord with the whig doctrine of the ascendancy of parliament over crown.

Aside from allaying the fears of the nation regarding the loss of national liberty and property from a standing army, Campbell proceeds to argue that a militia, composed as it was of part-time soldiers, was wholly to the moral detriment of the nation. He chooses to illustrate this by criticising some of his enemies, namely merchants, traders and war, in so doing exposing his Walpolian roots. J.H. Plumb observed how Walpole 'hated merchants, hated them all with the intensity of a debt-loaded squire'.[106] Campbell was of the same opinion. And he saw in excessive military operations a waste of resources. He believed Britain had a split personality thanks largely to the greed of merchants: trade wanted 'to be a mercantile, and at the same time a Military People. And both these desires have been carried to extravagance'. To his mind, Campbell believed such thinking was not only incompatible with a free nation but morally degrading. Those who are taken from their families and neighbourhoods to train with the militia – for a total of 28 days a year for three years – mostly return to their homes 'debauch'd, corrupted in

---

[104] J.R. Western, *The English Militia in the Eighteenth-Century: The Story of a Political Issue 1660–1802* (1965), 174.

[105] 'The Substance of a Letter, to a Friend in Scotland upon the Militia Scheme, August 1762'. See Appendix 5.

[106] Plumb continued that Walpole 'detested the obstreperous Common-Councilmen of London; loathed their constant clamorous and wearisome petitions'. Plumb, *Walpole*, ii, 247.

their Morals, and render'd both Idle, and dissolute', becoming 'rather troublesome, and burthensome to the Neighbourhood, slothfull, vicious, and insolent'.[107]

If Campbell raises moral questions regarding the militia, in his essay 'Thoughts on Religion', he attacks church-taught religion as espoused by high church tory divines as morally debased and deliberately obscurantist. Instead he advocates a religion 'that God has reveal'd himself to us in his Works and given us reason for our Guide'.[108] This belief in the power of reason in religious matters together with Campbell's latitudinarianism are both traits of whiggery and a point of view instilled in him when a student at Clare Hall, Cambridge. At that period, Richard Laughton, the tutor at Clare until 1713, placed 'considerable emphasis on natural rather than revealed religion'.[109] Campbell is at pains to refute high church and catholic doctrine, the former usually supported by tories, the latter by jacobites. At one point he asks: 'As to the Holy Catholic Church, I would desire first, to know, what it is, and next, what is meant by believing in it'. His non-doctrinaire attitude towards religion is glimpsed when he refers to the writings of the radical baptist preacher James Forster, all ten volumes of his sermons being housed in his library at Stackpole.[110] Nevertheless, rumours persisted of his attachment to catholicism. Commenting in his diary on the 1727 election in Pembrokeshire, Erasmus Philipps recorded how, in political circles, 'Names idle and foolish going about on this occasion, Mr Campbell being called a papist at heart'.[111] In this essay Campbell again and again dismisses any hint that he had papist leanings, or even that he was overtly religious.

As a response to a sermon by the dissenting minister Samuel Chandler upon the death of George II in which he compared the deceased monarch's reign with that of King David, the author John Noorthouck wrote a satire called the 'History of the Man after God's own Heart'. Chandler responded with a review of the Noorthouck satire, which was viewed as a veiled attack upon George II's reign. Campbell, however, although acknowledging Noorthouck's writing to be full of inaccuracies, reserves most of his criticism for Chandler. The library at Stackpole had an edition of the complete sermons of Chandler, whom Campbell referred to as a 'Man of Learning, great ability and [who] has appeared as a friend both to civil and religious Liberty'; however, he believed Chandler's criticism of Noorthouck's satire was written in anger and consequently not very good.[112] What Campbell's short essay mostly reveals is his extensive knowledge of the Old Testament, though for all his erudition the purpose of this and his other essays on religion, apart from self-enlightenment, is not clear.

Apart from the longer writings there are two texts: one a short, untitled paragraph; the other called 'Observations'. The former, dated 1765, though responding to a *cause célèbre* that occurred in mid 1764 is Campbell's comment on the removal from the house of commons of a member of the army, Lieutenant-General Henry Seymour Conway,

---

[107] 'Substance of a Letter, to a Friend in Scotland'. See Appendix 5.

[108] CRO, Cawdor/Campbell box 252, 'Thoughts on Religion', 1.

[109] *ODNB*.

[110] Letter 119: John Campbell to Pryse Campbell, 20 Dec. 1744 (see Chapter 4).

[111] NLW, MS 6106: diary of Erasmus Philipps of Picton Castle.

[112] CRO, Cawdor/Campbell box 252, 'Dr Chandler's "Review of the History of the Man after God's own Heart"'.

who was also dismissed from his military post for speaking and then voting with the opposition on general warrants.[113] The opposition argued that Conway's military post had nothing to do with his position as an MP. Horace Walpole, Conway's cousin and mentor, said at an opposition after-dinner speech that the government intended to purge the Commons of army men. William Guthrie, the historian and propagandist, wrote a pamphlet on behalf of the administration supporting the king's action. There followed a flurry of pamphlets between Guthrie and Horace Walpole, the latter supporting the opposition view.[114] Why Campbell wrote this paragraph is not clear, but it may have been a short Commons speech, defending the removal of Conway.[115] If this is the case it may be the last utterance of Campbell in the Commons, as there is no evidence that he attended any later debate.

The other, much longer text, 'Observations', was written in 1770, two years after Campbell had retired from the Commons, but it presents a still politically eager mind. He was 75 years old and 'Observations' is his response to the Parliamentary Election Act of 1770 known as George Grenville's Act, which was designed to reduce corruption at times of election, by entrusting the resolution of any contraverted election to a small judicial committee.[116] Campbell is critical of the Act and believed the creation of a small committee of the judiciary to deal with contraverted or contested elections to be a step in the wrong direction, since it removed the responsibility from the house of commons as a whole. For Campbell, the lifelong parliamentarian, this was an erosion of the importance of the House he had sat in for 40 years. However, as Brooke has observed, the Act made it 'almost impossible for a government to determine a controverted election along party lines',[117] so perhaps Campbell was fearful that the Act eroded party power in the Commons rather than parliamentary power as such.

Although Campbell's essays were written from the very beginning of his career as an MP and examples survive past his time in the Commons, it cannot be said that he was a regular essayist, or a controversial one. Of course the essays that have survived may only be a small number of many more now not extant. However, there are no references in his letters to his essays and other writings. Unlike, for instance, his friend Lord Hervey, who was scathingly brilliant as a whig essayist, the most that can be said of Campbell's works is that they are interesting examples which throw light on Campbell himself rather than attempts to support the whigs or ridicule the tories.

6. *Campbell: Loyal Old Corps Whig*

John Campbell adhered to a Walpolian political philosophy for his entire life, as did his correspondent Henry Fox, though to a lesser extent. Campbell's uncompromising belief

---

[113] Conway spoke on 6 Feb. 1764 and then 18 Feb. 1764.

[114] As was frequent with 18th-century pamphlets, they deteriorated into personal abuse – Guthrie accusing Walpole of sexual frustration, since he could not consummate his passion for Conway. *ODNB*.

[115] Conway's dismissal is the last recorded instance of an MP being removed from his military post for voting contrary to an administration.

[116] 10 Geo. III, c.16.

[117] *HPC, 1754–90*, iv, 179–80.

in Walpolian whiggery tended to make him increasingly isolated in his later years as an MP, since the whig outlook, especially from the mid 1750s, 'fragmented from within', changing as political circumstances changed.[118] Campbell's whiggery must have appeared even more static after the accession of George III in 1760. The king was intent upon replacing whigs with tories at the centre of power, and any old corp whigs still politically active and wanting executive power would have to realign their thinking to fit the new circumstances. This happened with Fox, as he moved ever closer to the Bute camp. The correspondence between Campbell and Fox becomes sparse – only nine letters survive from 1760 to 1763 – a muted criticism? As Fox moved towards the centre of power, Campbell remained politically static, watching from the political sidelines as younger men, such as Fox's son Charles James, remoulded the whigs into a party that could grapple with the huge changes occurring in late 18th-century British society.

Campbell's Walpolian whiggery led him to harbour long-lasting grudges against those whom he thought were responsible for the downfall of his political mentor, and even in the late 1750s Horace Walpole could comment that Campbell 'had never forgiven Mr Pitt and the Grenvilles the share they had in overturning Sir Robert Walpole'. Campbell as a 'diehard' old corps whig could easily have come into conflict with Fox in the early months of the 1760s, when the latter had moved into the tory Bute camp. However, after Sir Robert's demise Campbell, in an inevitable compromise, 'had steadily adhered to Mr Pelham and Fox, as successors of that minister'.[119]

Campbell's continuing attachment to old corps beliefs manifested itself in his contempt for William Pitt in particular and not just because of the great commoner's political opposition to Walpole. Campbell saw in Pitt's politics an appeal to the populace and popularity, to the mob and to the London merchants, all of which seemed to Campbell a debasement of the noble art of politics, particularly Walpolian politics, since contempt for popularity, the mob and London merchants also informed Sir Robert's political outlook.[120] Not that Campbell can completely dismiss Pitt's talents as an orator, though even here he is much more guarded than some of his contemporaries. In the debate on a motion to inquire into the war, Campbell states that Pitt made 'a handsome speech but went far from the Question'.[121] Only once does he praise Pitt without qualification, namely when Pitt was (fleetingly) supporting the measures that Campbell, too, advocated. Even Fox, who likewise disliked Pitt, could admire his talent as an orator. Pitt 'made the finest speech I ever heard', he commented to his brother in April 1746.[122] Simply, Campbell saw no redeeming features and, though he may have had to accept that Pitt was a great orator at times, as is shown, his loathing for Pitt's appeal to populist politics and above all his part in

[118] J.C.D. Clark, *The Dynamics of Change: The Crisis of the 1750s and the English Party Systems* (Cambridge, 1982), 26.

[119] *Horace Walpole's Correspondence*, ed. Lewis et al., ii, 218.

[120] Plumb, *Walpole*, ii, 247.

[121] Letter 79: John Campbell to Pryse Campbell, 5 Feb. 1743 (see Chapter 3).

[122] BL, Add. MS 51417, f. 241: Lord Ilchester to Henry Fox, 15 Apr. 1746.

the removal of Walpole fog all of Campbell's thoughts on the great commoner. However, and ironically, the nicknames Campbell uses to refer to him reflect a view of someone who was haughty rather than otherwise: on numerous occasions Campbell calls Pitt 'His Serene Excellency', 'Lord Protector', 'His Highness' or 'His Sublime Protectoral Highness'.

Campbell is not only vehemently anti-Pitt. It is very clear from the letters that anyone who was in opposition to Walpole received the most critical treatment regardless of their standing with other MPs, or the public. In this camp was William Pulteney, from 1742, earl of Bath. When Pulteney spoke in the debate on whether there should be a secret committee to examine the affairs of Walpole's administration, Campbell notes that he said he was a whig, but queries what sort of whig voted with the tories. He continues his letter: 'You see into what difficultys, & contradictions a man is brought by his Passions, & Ambition; and affecting Popularity, that is in other words, prefering the false flattery & giddy Noisy applause of Knaves & fools, to the sober & sincere approbation of Men of sense, and Virtue, and of his own Conscience'.[123] Popularity, passions, ambition – three favourite dislikes of Campbell – had devoured Pulteney, who in becoming earl of Bath through ambition, it is generally agreed, lost most of his political credence and power.

Campbell's criticism was also visited upon his local rival, Sir John Philipps of Picton Castle, Pembrokeshire. The latter was the younger son of Sir John Philipps, 4th baronet, and until his elder brother Erasmus died in 1743, Philipps resided at Kilgetty, a small house on the Picton estate. That residence, and Philipps' income of around £300 per annum, would have been socially derisory in Campbell's view, and he rarely referred to his rival as anything but 'Kilgetty'. However, in his record as a parliamentary speaker Philipps contrasts greatly with that of his rival from Stackpole. As we have seen, Philipps was initially a whig, but after winning the 1741 election to Carmarthen borough as a tory, he soon became one of their leading speakers in the Commons.[124] However, Campbell thought Philipps was a poor speaker, frequently pontificating without authority or accuracy, a point Campbell frequently made to Pryse. When Philipps moved that the House should debate the state of the nation, without the backing of the tories, Campbell comments that Philipps, referred to in an earlier letter as a 'solemn superficial coxcomb', 'Shews want of Judgement, a meddleing busy temper and hurts his Character by doing such Things without the knowledge or approbation of his Friends'.[125]

The letters are imbued with incidental information relating to the house of commons and its members. MPs arriving early for debates in their slippers in order to have a seat in the cramped House, jokes being played by members upon each other, wigs falling off and other general merriment, give the Commons a life that adds flavour to the ratherserious business carried out in the chamber. In one extraordinary incident, Campbell reports that 'On Monday some Gentlewomen in our gallery, not

---

[123] Letter 48: John Campbell to Pryse Campbell, 24 Mar. 1742 (see Chapter 2).

[124] See Thomas, *Politics in Eighteenth-Century Wales*, ch. 8, which outlines Philipps' political career.

[125] Letter 33: John Campbell to Mary Campbell, 19 Dec. 1741; Letter 53: John Campbell to Pryse Campbell, 18 Nov. 1742 (see Chapter 2).

being able to hold their water, let it run on Mr. Dodington & a Scots member who sat under the first had a white duffel frock spoil'd, the latter allmost blinded'.[126] The day was 24 January and it was devoted to local election petitions and other purely local matters, together with the first reading of a bill presented by Lord Strange, MP for Lancashire, to ban the use of gold and silver lace thread and wire in wearing apparel.[127] Is it too fanciful to think this display to be a protest against the bill? Even in a period when public urination was relatively common, Campbell refers to *women* needing to relieve themselves.

7. *Campbell's Family and Later Years*

Campbell's political life was free from scandal and his private life was similarly untarnished. However, towards the end of his stint as an MP his daughter Anne (Nanny) was involved in some public gossip when in 1766 she found herself in trouble with her husband, Matthew, 2nd Baron Fortescue, whom she had married in 1752. In the letters Campbell refers on two or three occasions to Anne's misfortunes, without specifying what he meant: 'she is a Woman of an innocent, and amiable disposition. She is now with us here, deserves all the kindness I can shew her, and wants all the Comfort that can give her'.[128] However, Henry Fox's sister-in-law, Lady Sarah Bunbury, comments in a letter of January 1766 that she had heard 'Seventeen people are to be parted [i.e. separated or divorcing]', including Lady Fortescue – Lord Fortescue, being 'stark staring mad', had tried to kill his wife and their children.[129] Nothing seems to have come of this; they were not divorced and Lady Fortescue went back to her husband. She lived until 1812, long surviving his lordship who died in 1785.

A larger, more damaging scandal to the family concerned their second son, John (Jack) Campbell, who was born c.1733 and died at Bath in September 1795. He married Elizabeth Eustacia, daughter of John Francis Bassett[130] of Heanton Court, Devon in August 1762. Jack added Hooke to his name in 1757 as a condition to his inheriting the Bangeston estate, Pembrokeshire, upon the owner John Hooke's death in that year. John Hooke-Campbell caused his father a great deal of anguish during the latter's final few weeks alive, when he decided to divorce his wife Elizabeth for adultery with the master of ceremonies at Bath, William Wade.[131] Campbell senior was at the spa town attempting to regain his health when the scandal became public. Wade lost his place as master of ceremonies and moved back to his native Brighton. In Campbell's eyes all was the fault of Elizabeth. He wrote to his grandson John regarding Elizabeth:

---

[126] Letter 75: John Campbell to Pryse Campbell, 27 Jan. 1743 (see Chapter 3).

[127] *CJ*, xxiv, 387–8.

[128] Letter 219, BL, Add. MS 51406, ff. 126–7: John Campbell to Lord Holland, 28 Jan. 1766 (see Chapter 8).

[129] *The Life and Letters of Lady Sarah Lennox, 1745–1826*, ed. countess of Ilchester and Lord Stavordale (1901), 182: Lady Sarah Bunbury to Lady Susan O'Brien, 9 Jan. 1766.

[130] Elizabeth Eustacia Bassett (*b.* c.1737); John Francis Bassett (1714–57), MP for Barnstaple 1740–1.

[131] Captain William Wade (1733/4–1809), master of ceremonies 1769–77. His portrait, painted by Gainsborough in 1771, hangs in the Victoria Art Gallery, Bath.

I confess to you I think she deserves no regard; for she has shewn None for him [her husband], for her Children, or her own Family, which she has done all in her power to disgrace. Her infamous behavior is Common talk, not only of the Gentry, but the servants, Chairmen, and Laborers about this Place. I don't doubt but you might hear it from the Haymakers, and People who are mending the Roads.[132]

Hooke-Campbell divorced Elizabeth at the end of 1777, a few months after his father's death. However, Elizabeth's relationship with William Wade was a lot more than just a brief encounter. Ten years after the divorce and after the death of Wade's first wife, Katherine, he and Elizabeth married.[133]

Alexander or 'Ally', the Campbells' third son, was a career army man who rose to be a lieutenant colonel in the Scots guards. On 3 September 1768, he married Frances Meadows (*d.* 1770), the only daughter of Sir Phillip Meadows of Chattisham, Suffolk. 'Ally' never stood for parliament and died in 1785. The Campbells also had two daughters, of which very little is known: Elizabeth (Bessy) (1729–1816), who married, much against her father's will, Joseph Adams of Holyland, Pembrokeshire, a man of inferior social standing, and Mary (Molly) (n.d.), who remained unmarried.[134] However, the main focus of John Campbell's ambition for his family rested with his eldest son and heir, Pryse.

Pryse Campbell was born in St James's parish, Westminster on 26 November 1727. He was educated at Stackpole by a private tutor, the Reverend Henry Rowe, before matriculating to Clare Hall, Cambridge in November 1745. He married Sarah, daughter of Sir Edmund Bacon MP, of Garbolisham, Norfolk, premier baronet of England, on 24 September 1752.[135] They had seven children – three girls and four boys: Mary (*b.* 1753), Sarah (*b.* 1758), who married Thomas Wodehouse of Norfolk on 12 September 1782, Henrietta (*b.* 16 November 1761), Charles (*b.* 28 September 1763), George (*b.* 14 August 1759), Alexander (*b.* 14 September 1756) and Pryse's heir, John (*b.* c.1755).

Pryse's second youngest son, George Campbell, joined the navy in 1772 at the age of 13, and rose to become an admiral and commander-in-chief of Portsmouth by 1818. He became MP for Carmarthen borough 1806–13, much to his dislike and largely at the insistence of his elder brother, by then 1st Baron Cawdor. In 1821, while still in command at Portsmouth, he took his own life.

Alexander, Pryse's second son, was part of a rebellion at Eton in 1768. Many of the boys, referred to as 'Rebells', walked away from the school as a protest after a fellow scholar had been flogged too severely. However, Alexander briefly returned to the school, before being moved by Pryse to Harrow. Like his father and grandfather he then moved on to Clare Hall, Cambridge, matriculating in 1774. Alexander did not complete his

---

[132] CRO, Cawdor/Campbell box 128: Campbell to John [Jack] Campbell, 25 June 1777.

[133] For details of the depositions concerning the divorce, see *Trials for Adultery: Or, the History of Divorces* (1780), iv.

[134] The Adams family had lived at Holyland since the 16th century. The family and estate archive is held at Pembrokeshire Record Office, Ref: GB0213 D/Adams.

[135] Sir Edmund Bacon (c.1680–1755), tory MP for Thetford 1710–13 and Norfolk 1713–15 and 1728–41. He withdrew from the motion against Walpole in Feb. 1741.

degree, leaving after a year to join the 55th regiment of foot as an ensign. At the beginning of 1778 he had become a lieutenant in the same regiment. However, in late 1778 he joined, as captain, the 75th regiment of foot (the prince of Wales' regiment) which had been established in that year by his older brother and heir to the Stackpole estate, John, later 1st Baron Cawdor, and Thomas Johnes of Hafod, Cardiganshire.[136] In that regiment he served in the American War of Independence, and was wounded and then held captive in 1778. After the regiment was disbanded at the end of the war, he became MP for Nairnshire, but died in November 1785, after just a few months as a member.

Pryse had always been of a delicate constitution – his father's earliest extant letters to him are full of concerns for his health – and by November 1768 he was resident at Bath, attempting to regain his health.[137] In the early part of the month Pryse could write:

> I am now getting strength every day [and] I have got rid of the Bile but have still some Obstructions which give me uneasy feelings & have prevented by [*sic*] sleeping in the beginning of the Night but as they lesson [*sic*] I hope soon by the assistance of Dr Gasthart & the Bath Waters to get soon quite free from them.[138]

However two weeks later his father was writing: 'his stomach very weak and nerves much affected'.[139] Pryse never left Bath. He died on 14 December 1768, with a promising political career cut short. He was 39. His wife Sarah had died in May the previous year and the seven children, ranging in age from four to 12, were left to be raised by the septuagenarian John Campbell at Stackpole Court.

Campbell's main concern was for the education of the heir to the estate, John (Jack) Campbell and Campbell senior may have relished the idea of raising his 12-year-old grandson as a model whig, attempting to mould him in his political career, as he had tried to do with Pryse. Jack (also known as Jolly Jack), did become a whig and remained so, though he, like his father, supported a Pitt, this time Pitt the Younger, for which he received, in 1796, a peerage as Baron Cawdor of Castlemartin, Pembrokeshire. Campbell the elder wrote regularly to his grandson giving him moral advice in a number of areas of life as Jack grew to manhood. He was particularly concerned that the future baron should be aware of the effects of overspending and the burden of debt. When Jack was unanimously elected as MP for Nairn in 1777, just a few weeks before the old man's death, it must have cheered his heart.[140] He immediately wrote to his grandson:

> It is now your Part to make your self an able, as I am satisfied you will be an honest Member, and if you are able, I think you ought to be usefull. You will be much to blame if you do not make a better figure in the World than I have done; you come

---

[136] J.W. Fortescue refers to this as Picton's regiment, named after Sir Thomas Picton (1758–1815), but Picton was only a captain in this regiment, and joined on its creation. *A History of the British Army* (1911), iii, 248.

[137] Dating from 1733 – when Pryse was a mere seven years old. CRO, Cawdor/Campbell box 128.

[138] CRO, Cawdor/Campbell box 128: Pryse Campbell to his son John, 9 Nov. 1768.

[139] CRO, Cawdor/Campbell box 128: John Campbell to his grandson also John, 20 Nov. 1768.

[140] He remained MP for Nairnshire until 1780 when he became MP for Cardigan boroughs, a seat he kept until he was raised to the peerage.

much younger into Parliament, and with greater advantage, you are much better known than I was, you will have opportunity at London of improving your self in the best Company. I had no Friend, or near Relation to direct, or advise me when I was a young Man; and by my Mothers death, when I was nineteen, I became entirely Master of my self, and my fortune; I was very idle, and foolish, but, I thank God, I allways preserved my integrity, and sobriety.[141]

It is a letter of self-criticism, the last clause a telling self-judgement.

In one of John Campbell's last letters, to his grandson Jack, dated 1 July 1777, just two months before he died, his hand is firm and is very little changed from the hand of the letters of four decades earlier. Writing from Bath, he comments that his memory was failing him, perhaps not surprising given that he was 83 years old. Writing of estate business he refers to the marriage of his daughter Elizabeth of which he did not approve, but which 'I could not prevent without acting in a manner I was not accustom'd or inclined to'. That line precisely sums up Campbell's long political career, one of acting according to his whig principles, which were firmly implanted in him by the time he entered parliament and were honed by long practice as an MP. In his own estimation, the opportunistic Pitt and the hypocritical Pulteney were beyond the pale, however talented they were. Campbell remained true to a standard, and he was attracted towards others who stood by a similar standard, at least from his point of view, among whom was Henry Fox.

Campbell lived a long life with seemingly little in the way of physical ailments. However, he was prevented from travelling to London in the latter years of his parliamentary career by what may have been prostate problems. Writing from Stackpole in October 1765 he states: 'Wee are within what I used to think an easy walk, and should yet, with a little resting by the way, if it were not for the bloody water'.[142] He was in the capital in August 1767, but that is the last time there is any evidence that he was away from Stackpole apart from his final few months alive when he was living in Bath. He died there on 6 September 1777.

8. *Pryse Campbell: A Political Disappointment*

John Campbell's political ambitions for his family rested with his eldest son and heir Pryse. Except for those families wealthy enough to enter more than one son into a political career, this was usual practice in the 18th and 19th centuries. In 1754 Pryse entered parliament, when he became the member for Inverness-shire, though he had been 'Intended from youth for a parliamentary career [and] was mentioned as a possible candidate for Inverness-shire as early as 1746', two years before he reached his majority.[143] He was expected to follow his father as a whig, but from the beginning of his parliamentary career Pryse showed much less hostility towards the tories than John Campbell liked.

---

[141] CRO, Cawdor/Campbell box 128: John to Jack Campbell, 1 May 1777.
[142] Letter 209, BL, Add. MS 51406, ff. 102–3: John Campbell to Lord Holland, 18 Oct. 1765 (see Chapter 8).
[143] *HPC, 1754–90*, ii, 190.

Less than a year after Pryse had become an MP his father wrote to Mary his wife, expressing his concerns with regard to which way their son was going to vote on 13 November 1755, on the address of thanks for the subsidy treaties with Russia and Hesse: 'That with the uncertane [*sic*] of what my Son will do, and the fear that he may take a course quite contrary to my judgement & wishes, has kept my mind in continual agitation'.[144] A year later, Campbell was still perturbed: 'My sons political Conduct for a year past has been one of the greatest troubles I ever met with'.[145] Pryse's political independence from his father continued throughout his short life. In 1757 he voted with Campbell's hated Pitt on the Minorca inquiry, and in the same year Newcastle believed Pryse to be a supporter of Pitt.[146] Pryse also voted in opposition to his father on the motion to expel John Wilkes from the Commons – according to Newcastle, the young Campbell was one of those who were 'violently against' the motion.[147] And in 1759 Pryse was one of those who sat on the committee to draft Pitt's militia bill.

In March the same year Pryse voted for the free importation of Irish cattle into Britain, a vote that was to have negative repercussions for him in 1761 when he was seeking re-election for Inverness-shire. The county was the centre of black cattle stock farming, so Pryse's action did nothing to endear him to voters, with whom 'he had little rapport' anyway.[148] His ill-considered vote was to the annoyance of his father, Argyll and most of the Scots members, who were overwhelmingly administration supporters, and therefore opposed the cattle vote. Pryse wrote to Newcastle, commenting: 'A young Man is not allow'd to think for himself & your Grace may have been told that I am attach'd to a Faction & will blindly follow wherever that leads & tho' I have a better opinion of my own sense & honesty, it is from my Actions your Grace should form yours', a comment that seems to have been aimed, at least in part, at his father.[149]

As a consequence of his rebellious behaviour in 1759, when seeking re-election for Inverness-shire two years later, Argyll refused to support him, and Pryse lost his seat to Simon Fraser, son of the jacobite Lord Lovat. Pryse Campbell was then put forward for Nairnshire, Campbell senior giving up his seat at Inverness burghs in order to gain support for his son, who was returned unopposed. He was re-elected for the same seat at the beginning of December 1766 after being appointed to office as one of the lords of the treasury in Chatham's administration. It was a good office for Pryse to have been offered though it must have rankled with his father given the latter's opinion of Chatham.[150] Unfortunately Campbell's letters to Pryse had long since stopped, or at least none has survived; it would be interesting to have read his comments on his son's ascent into the government of the despised Chatham. Politically Pryse must have been a disappointment to his father, who had groomed him to follow in his footsteps, only to find that he surrounded himself with friends who were tory or at least not old corps whigs.

[144] Letter 141: John Campbell to Mary Campbell, 13 Nov. 1755 (see Chapter 5).

[145] Letter 153, BL, Add. MS 51406, ff. 23–4: John Campbell to Henry Fox, 12 Nov. 1756 (see Chapter 5).

[146] *HPC, 1754–90*, i, 190–1.

[147] Cited in J. Brooke, *The Chatham Administration* (1956), 359.

[148] Murdoch, *The People Above*, 98.

[149] BL, Add. MS 32,892, f. 207: Pryse Campbell at Ham to the duke of Newcastle, 24 June 1759.

[150] His fellow treasury lords were the duke of Grafton, Charles Townshend (chancellor of the exchequer), Thomas Townshend (later Lord Sydney) and George Onslow.

In 1768 Pryse became a Welsh MP. In that year Nairnshire was not to be represented at the election and he considered trying for Inverness-shire again. However, in the meantime, Cardigan boroughs was offered to Pryse when his kinsman John Hugh Pryse of Gogerddan, Cardiganshire suddenly withdrew his candidature, on being offered the seat for the county of Merioneth, while his opponent Sir Herbert Lloyd of Peterwell withdrew his opposition at Cardigan on the day of the election, in March 1768, ensuring that Pryse was returned unopposed. However, Pryse's stint as Cardigan boroughs MP was cut very short when, as we have seen, he died in December of the same year.

9. *Henry Fox: Two Stephens*

It is not known when Campbell and Henry Fox became friends.[151] In a letter of May 1746, Lord Ilchester, Fox's brother wrote that he was glad that 'My Friend Campbell is likely to succeed [to a place on the treasury board]'.[152] So it seems Campbell was a friend of Lord Ilchester's before he became so with Henry. Ilchester's reference to Campbell is the only one in the several volumes of Holland House papers between Henry and various members of the Fox family. Nor are there any references to Campbell in letters Fox wrote to various political allies – not even to Newcastle recommending an office for Campbell, at a time when Fox had political sway over the duke, Campbell's 'noble cousin'.[153] However, in the extant letters, which date from 1755, it is clear that the two men had been friends for a number of years and that there was a close affection for each other as well as a trust with regard to political matters. Campbell wrote in 1765: 'I clame the Title of your Friend as having a sincere esteem and Affection for you, from my knowledge of your great, and amiable qualities and my full persuasion of the Integrity of your heart'.[154]

In contrast to John Campbell's modest and relatively obscure political career, Henry Fox, from 1763 1st Baron Holland, had a career which was, for a few years in the 1750s at any rate, unrelentingly near the top of the political tree. Also in contrast to Campbell's was Fox's ancestry, which was relatively humble and perhaps a cause of some of the animosity with which Fox was plagued: among many, the dislike of Fox by George III stands out, the monarch writing in March 1763 to his favourite Lord Bute that Fox was a 'man I would rather see perish than at the head of Ministry'.[155] However, though of a more illustrious ancestry, Campbell was a Scot, at a time when many of the ruling English distrusted or disliked anyone from north of the border. As we have seen, it may have been a determining factor in preventing Campbell from becoming chancellor of the exchequer. So in their individual ways both men's ancestry worked against them in an era when pedigree counted for much and ability less.

---

[151] The Melbury House game books which are cited extensively by Ilchester, *Henry Fox*, were not available to the author. They list numerous visitors to Melbury House from the mid 1720s, and may say if or when Campbell visited.

[152] BL, Add. MS 51418, f. 1: Lord Ilchester to Henry Fox, 3 May 1746.

[153] BL, Add. MSS 51416, 51417, 51418.

[154] Letter 212, BL, Add. MS 51406, f. 112: John Campbell to Holland, 8 Nov. 1765 (see Chapter 8).

[155] *Letters from George III to Lord Bute, 1756–66*, ed. R. Sedgwick (1939), 199–200: George III to Lord Bute, 11 Mar. 1763.

Henry Fox's father, Stephen, began his working life at the age of 13 when, in 1640, he joined his brother John, who was closet keeper and organist in the household of Charles, prince of Wales. Two years later Stephen is found working as a page boy for a variety of aristocrats and one, Henry, Lord Percy, who was master of the prince's horse at the time, was a particular help to the young Stephen. Under Percy, Stephen became gentleman of the horse to the prince. He travelled to the continent with the exiled court after the execution of Charles I in January 1649. In 1651, back in England, he married Elizabeth Whittle (1627–96), a marriage that was to survive until her death. In 1654 Fox again left for the continent, to work in the exiled royal household and this time remained until Charles II returned to England in 1660. As a man who was trusted by the exiled king, Fox was given the responsibility of looking after the king's meagre finances. In 1661, Fox was appointed paymaster of the royal guards – a new post. It was a measure of the trust that the king had in Fox. The paymaster's responsibilities expanded over the next few years, until he was controlling most of the monies to pay the army. However, Fox made a fortune not from his position as paymaster but by acting as a risk-taking financier. He raised loans to pay the army on his own account and charged the treasury 5% poundage – a charge that was passed on to the army.[156] That he also dispensed the money he raised (as paymaster) was a coincidence.[157] However, poundage continued to be paid to the paymaster even into the 18th century and it was how Stephen's son Henry made his fortune – especially since he was paymaster during the Seven Years War, when monies granted to the army became exceedingly large.[158] Neither Henry Pelham, when he was paymaster, nor Pitt, who was paymaster immediately before Fox, accepted poundage money, making Henry Fox's willingness to do so appear to many to be particularly rapacious. Pitt emphasised his non-acceptance of poundage money by making it known publicly that on his removal from the paymastership, he had to borrow £1,000 from his brother-in-law, Lord Temple, to tide him over.

Stephen Fox was knighted in 1665 and continued to work for the king. In 1676 he was dismissed from the office of paymaster in a political intrigue by the lord treasurer, Danby, who believed that Fox had become too powerful. However, he was briefly reappointed to the paymastership in 1679, before resigning at the end of the same year on becoming a treasury commissioner; in 1696–7 he briefly became first lord of the treasury. Fox continued to work for the crown until his retirement in 1702.

Stephen Fox was also an MP for 53 years from 1661, though there is little evidence to evaluate his career in the House.[159] It seems he rarely spoke, and when he did so it was usually on non-controversial matters. However, although he was of the court party, he was never merely a yes man. On two occasions he was to vote against the wishes of the crown: first, over the impeachment of the earl of Clarendon in 1667, to whom Fox owed his initial appointment into the household, and from which time they had become

---

[156] The Restoration treasury was often desperately short of money and was often several months behind in making payments. The crown feared an army that was not paid on time.

[157] How Stephen Fox made his fortune is dealt with in great detail – and lucidity – by Christopher Clay, *Public Finance and Private Wealth: The Career of Sir Stephen Fox, 1627–1716* (Oxford, 1978).

[158] For instance in 1755 the Commons voted to grant £1.2 million for the army.

[159] For Salisbury 1661–79, 1685–9 and 1714–15; for Westminster 1679, 1691–8; for Cricklade 1699–1702.

close friends; and second, over the impeachment of Danby, the lord treasurer in 1678, when Fox voted with the Commons as an act of revenge for Danby's move to remove him from office in 1676.

Lady Fox died in 1696 and eight years later Stephen married, at the age of 77, Christian Hope, the 27-year-old daughter of the Reverend Charles Hope, rector of Haceby and then Aswarby, Lincolnshire. By this second marriage Fox had four children: Stephen (1704–76), Henry, Christian (1705–7), who fell from a window to her death, and Charlotte.[160] The latter married Edward Digby, eldest surviving son of William, 5th Baron Digby of Geashill, County Offaly, Ireland, in 1729.[161] One of their many children, Edward Digby, became Henry Fox's favourite nephew, and he was devastated when Digby died in 1757 at the age of 27.

Sir Stephen died in 1716 and Christian two years later, leaving their surviving children to be guided into adulthood by trustees. In January 1715 both Henry and Stephen went to Eton, followed by Christ Church, Oxford, where Henry matriculated in February 1721.[162] Neither Henry nor Stephen completed their degrees. Stephen had left university by the middle of 1723 to travel on the continent and, although Henry was still at Christ Church at the end of 1724, there is no record of him having completed his degree. The brothers had a very close affection for each other and 'their correspondence testifies to the reliance which each was wont to place upon the judgement of the other'.[163]

Stephen entered parliament in 1726 as MP for Shaftesbury, a seat he kept until 1741, though with a short break in 1734–5 when he represented Hindon, Wiltshire. In his biography of Henry Fox, the earl of Ilchester states that Stephen began his parliamentary career as a whig, but in *HPC* he is described as a tory, and he did vote with the opposition regarding subsidies for Hessian troops in 1730.[164] He resigned his Commons seat in 1741 on being raised to the peerage as Lord Ilchester, baron of Woodford Strangways.[165] Six years later he became baron of Redlynch, and in 1756 1st earl of Ilchester. However, Stephen was never an ambitious politician and he only attained two minor offices throughout his career: as joint secretary to the treasury, 1739–41, an office reluctantly given by Sir Robert Walpole and which was resigned when Fox was raised to the peerage, and joint comptroller of army accounts, 1747–76.[166] Stephen, as the elder brother, became an MP before Henry, though he was never really interested in politics; in the correspondence between the brothers it is Henry who is the enthusiastic politician: 'I hear of nothing but Petitions, journals, Treatys, Alliances &c', complained Lord Hervey to Stephen Fox in 1728 after being with Henry. After Henry become an MP he frequently wrote to his brother, often ensconced at Redlynch, the family seat, of debates, though Stephen's replies show a great deal more concern for estate management

[160] Ilchester, *Henry Fox*, i, 15.

[161] William Digby (1661–1752).

[162] Ilchester, *Henry Fox*, i, 17.

[163] Ilchester, *Henry Fox*, i, 16.

[164] Ilchester, *Henry Fox*, i, 28; *HPC, 1715–54*, ii, 49.

[165] J.C. Sainty, *Peerage Creations: Chronological Lists of Creations in the Peerages of England and Great Britain 1649–1800 and of Ireland 1603–1898, Parliamentary History: Texts & Studies*, vi (2008), 37.

[166] *HPC, 1715–54*, ii, 50.

than politics. On several occasions Henry wrote pleadingly to Stephen to attend important debates in the Lords, lest the king assumed him to be in opposition. Before the opening of parliament in 1742, Fox wrote to Stephen, newly raised to the peerage as Lord Ilchester, concerning the urgency of the latter attending the Lords, when Walpole was desperate for support: 'why will You contrive to shew what the K[ing] will think Ingratitude & Discontent, ev'n before there is any necessary Test brought your way? For your Non Attendance at first will be interpreted Opposition, & yet if you are there You may probably not be call'd upon to declare either Way'.[167]

Stephen Fox's marriage, like his brother's, though less notoriously so, was a clandestine affair, which took place in 1736. His wife was Elizabeth, the wealthy 13-year-old daughter of Thomas Strangways and Susanna Strangways-Horner, with whom Henry Fox was embroiled in a love affair at the time. The marriage probably ended what is the most widely known aspect of Stephen's life – his ten-year love affair with John, Lord Hervey, though the latter remained close friends of not only Stephen but of his wife Catherine and Henry Fox.[168]

10. *Henry Fox's Political Career*

Stephen's younger brother, Henry Fox, entered the house of commons in 1735 as whig MP for Hindon, Wiltshire, though he had first attempted to win a seat in 1727, the same year that Campbell entered parliament. In that year he stood as a tory at Hindon, 'a notoriously venal borough'.[169] In the following year he again failed to win a seat when he unsuccessfully stood for the rotten borough of Old Sarum, Wiltshire, a seat entirely controlled by the Pitt family. In 1728 the number of voters at Old Sarum was three, and the Pitts controlled two of those. Fox eventually entered the Commons, though by now as a whig supporter of the administration, as member for Hindon, when he replaced his brother in 1735. From 1741, for 20 years, he was returned for New Windsor, Berkshire, a borough owned by the Beauclerk family, firm supporters of the administration.[170] Fox found this constituency an expensive place in which to maintain an interest, even though he was returned unopposed on four occasions. He complained that at the 1746 unopposed election he spent nearly £400.[171] His final stint as an MP was for two years from 1761 as member for Dunwich, Suffolk, a pocket borough controlled by Sir Jacob Downing.

Fox was given his first, minor office in 1737, when he was made surveyor-general of the works. Six years later he was appointed one of the treasury commissioners in Henry Pelham's first administration. And in 1746, in the second Pelham administration, Fox was made secretary at war, an office he kept until 1755.

---

[167] BL, Add. MS 51417, f. 90: Fox to Ilchester, 28 Oct. 1742, regarding attending the Lords at the opening of parliament.

[168] For their relationship see Lucy Moore, *Amphibious Thing: The Life of Lord Hervey* (2000), and R. Halsband, *Lord Hervey, Eighteenth-Century Courtier* (Oxford, 1973).

[169] *HPC, 1715–54*, i, 347.

[170] *HPC, 1715–54*, i, 193.

[171] Ilchester, *Henry Fox*, i, 133.

On becoming secretary at war, he wrote to a friend that he could assure him: 'I shall never after even in private regret the loss of ease and leisure which is the worse for me for my having all my lifetime indulg'd myself too much in both'.[172] Without doubt, his workload did increase greatly, and he never again had time for grand self-indulgence – gambling, drinking and travelling being particular favourites – his voluminous correspondence testifying to his diligence. However, the secretaryship was an office he was initially reluctant to take up, writing to his brother Stephen: 'There are, as yet, some, but rather slender Hopes of my avoiding the Secretaryship', and hoping he could become, instead, a treasurer of the navy.[173] As secretary at war, Fox became linked inevitably to the duke of Cumberland, a younger son of George II, who was at this time commander-in-chief of the forces. Their official relationship 'soon ripened into a close and concerted friendship destined to exert a domineering influence on the politics of the time'.[174] His closeness to Cumberland made him many political enemies, but also gave him a certain amount of protection.

Fox's friendship with the duke was politically advantageous – it brought him closer to the king and all the protection that afforded – but shows in Fox a lack of concern about public or fellow MPs' opinions, since Cumberland was never a popular politician. Fox comments to his brother that 'they know me only ready to obey (not the Adviser tho' highly approving, of the measure) & yet I assure you I am reckon'd the Devil of a Secretary at War' by the house of commons.[175] It was a trait that Fox seemed to relish, and it was recognised by fellow politicians. Fox remained on good terms with Cumberland until the duke became increasingly offended by Fox's political closeness to Lord Bute. In 1762, as Fox undertook to purge the 'Pelhamite innocents' on behalf of Bute, Cumberland, who had a deep mistrust of George III's favourite, had also come to befriend Newcastle, a move set to alienate Fox. Under these circumstances it was inevitable that Cumberland and Fox's friendship would suffer. Campbell wrote to his wife:

> Since my last Mr Fox has been here & sat two hours with me. The Sluices of Abuse will be again let out upon him stronger I suppose than ever. And he will be abused for leaving the Duke of Cumberland that is for not following him where it is amazing he should desire to lead. Who some years ago could have thought of a league between him & my Cousin of Newcastle. But People at my age should wonder at nothing.[176]

The rupture became irreconcilable and up to the duke's sudden death in 1765 their friendship remained in breach. Fox had attempted several reconciliations, writing to Campbell on one occasion: 'my heart & my Judgement, avow the friendship & wish to be restor'd to it'.[177] But his efforts were all ignored by the duke. Campbell, if not an enemy of the duke, was warmly critical of the man. On Fox's efforts to restore his

---

[172] Fox to Fawkener, 11 June 1746, cited in Evan Charteris, *William Augustus, Duke of Cumberland: His Early Life and Times (1721–48)* (1913), 287.

[173] BL, Add. MS 51418, f. 3: Fox to Ilchester, 3 May 1746.

[174] Charteris, *William Augustus, Duke of Cumberland*, 287.

[175] BL, Add. MS 51418, f. 88: Fox to Ilchester, 4 Dec. 1746.

[176] Letter 184: John Campbell to Mary Campbell, 14 Oct. 1762 (see Chapter 7).

[177] Letter 210, BL, Add. MS 51406, ff. 104–7: Lord Holland to John Campbell, 22 Oct. 1765 (see Chapter 8).

friendship with the duke, Campbell remarks: 'As to the Great Person who [you] wish to be Friends with, I will not say a word more, because I fear I could say nothing agreable to you upon the subject'.[178]

Until 1753 Fox never put a political foot wrong. But in that year he vehemently opposed Lord Hardwicke's marriage bill in the Commons. The bill was meant to bring an end to clandestine marriages, which Fox had undertaken when he married Caroline as, too, had Stephen when he married the 13-year-old Susanna Horner in 1736. During the debates Fox vented his spleen upon Lord Hardwicke, the creator of the bill, and political alter ego to the duke of Newcastle. Turning the argument towards the personal, he created an unbridgeable rift between himself and Hardwicke and Newcastle. However the real reason behind Fox's outburst may have been what he believed was 'the desertion of Sir Robert Walpole, whom Fox had idolized', by the duke and his cohort.[179] Fox survived the fallout from his attack, but was never really trusted again by Newcastle. Although the latter promoted Fox to the office of secretary of state in 1754, which was declined, and then again in the following year, when it was accepted, it was done so from mistrust and a desire to curb Fox's perceived power and political influence in the Commons rather than from any real inclination to include him in the administration. In March 1754 Hardwicke expressed his fears of Fox to the archbishop of Canterbury:

> If he should succeed to the plenitude of power which Mr Pelham had, there is an end of this Administration, and of all that you & I wish well to in that respect. He would also, by his Connection [to Cumberland] in a certain place, have another Power added to it, which Mr Pelham had not for several years, the Army. So here would be the *Treasury*, the *House of Commons* & *the sword* joined together'.[180]

Fox was offered the office of secretary of state for the southern department, the senior of the two secretaryships, in April 1754. Much of the work of the office involved dealing with foreign affairs, of which Fox had no practical experience. However, what Fox wanted along with the secretaryship was the leadership of the Commons, a place of real political control, but Newcastle, whose administration it was, ensured that this would not occur, vainly hoping to control the Commons himself from the Lords. So, after much consultation with friends, Fox, feeling that he would be politically emasculated by the deal Newcastle offered, declined the office, which was a political blunder from which he never really recovered since Newcastle's administration was, at this point in time, in a relatively strong position.[181] He did accept the same office in November 1755, after also accepting a cabinet council place, on condition that he relinquish his uneasy political alliance with Pitt. Browning has pointed out that this, too, was a disaster for Fox, since he accepted an office in a Newcastle administration that was

[178] Letter 211, BL, Add. MS 51406, ff. 110–11: John Campbell to Lord Holland, 3 Nov. 1765 (see Chapter 8).

[179] T.W. Riker, *Henry Fox, First Lord Holland* (Oxford, 1913), 134–5. See also Clyve Jones, 'Henry Fox's Drafts of Lord Hardwicke's Speech in the Lords Debate on the Bill on Clandestine Marriages, 6 June 1753: A Striving for Accuracy', *British Library Journal* (2005), regarding the efforts by Fox to report the debate accurately.

[180] BL, Add. MS 35599, ff. 165–9: Lord Hardwicke to the archbishop of Canterbury, 11 Mar. 1754.

[181] Clark, *Dynamics of Change*, 58–63.

floundering.[182] He wrote to Campbell seemingly knowing this himself. The king, Fox informed him, 'yesterday declar'd His Intention of making me Secretary of State, & giving me the Conduct of the House of Commons', but added wryly: 'I don't know that I ought to tell you this with much pleasure'.[183] His stint as secretary and leader of the Commons lasted for a mere 12 months, again with Newcastle at the head of the administration. However, Newcastle's administration was entering the furore over the loss of Minorca and the intending court martial of Admiral Byng. This political maelstrom gave Fox an excuse to abandon Newcastle, and he resigned the secretaryship at the end of October 1756.[184] This was the first time Fox had been out of office since his first appointment as surveyor of works in 1737. It was the highest office attained by Fox, and he held it for just about a year.

Nine months later Fox was installed in the newly formed Devonshire–Pitt administration, this time as paymaster-general of the forces, a lucrative office he had coveted for some time. He remained paymaster until reluctantly resigning in 1765. It was an office that made Fox's fortune just as it had his father's, as we have seen. The paymaster's office was 'sole domestic banker of the Army'.[185] All the money voted for the army by the Commons was passed to the paymaster, who then paid out sums as and when they were needed, with interest accruing in Fox's favour. His enemies increasingly resented his stint as paymaster, especially after he became Lord Holland in 1763 when it was mistakenly assumed by the king and Bute that he would resign the office. His refusal to remove himself created new enemies from former friends such as John Calcraft, Richard Rigby and William Shelburne, the latter being blamed by Holland for not reporting accurately to the king his intention not to resign. Rigby was particularly incandescent, turning against Holland, a man who had done nothing but encourage his political aspirations. Rigby, as others did, believed that Holland was at fault for continuing in an office he had agreed to resign, but he snubbed Holland entirely, a political reaction to a man he knew was about to lose any real power by 'retiring' to the Lords. As paymaster Fox may have – legally – accumulated around £500,000 during the period 1757–74, so it was hardly surprising that he was reluctant to relinquish such a lucrative office.[186]

In 1762 Fox was made 'cabinet councillor and his majesty's minister in the House of Commons', a place that gave him real power in the Commons, which he used, not only to get the Treaty of Paris accepted – in the end not too difficult a task – but to wreak havoc upon his political foes. Although it was undertaken on behalf of Bute, it was an act of revenge by Fox, whose ruthlessness shocked fellow politicians. Pitt was prevented from gaining office and Newcastle lost patronage. The latter was stripped of the three lord lieutenancies he controlled, and most of his friends were likewise removed from places of political influence in this 'massacre of the Pelhamite innocents'.[187]

---

[182] Browning, *Duke of Newcastle*, 215.

[183] Letter 135, BL, Add. MS 51406, ff. 1–2: Fox to John Campbell, 27 Sept. 1755 (see Chapter 5).

[184] Newcastle resigned in mid Nov. 1756. See Clark, *Dynamics of Change*, ch. 5; Browning, *Duke of Newcastle*, 244–5.

[185] L.S. Sutherland and J. Binney, 'Henry Fox as Paymaster General of the Forces', *EHR*, lxx (1955), 230.

[186] Sutherland and Binney, 'Henry Fox as Paymaster General of the Forces', 239.

[187] Ilchester, *Henry Fox*, ii, 214–20; Browning, *Duke of Newcastle*, 292. See J. Black, 'The Making of the British Atlantic', *History Today*, lxiii (2013), 22–6, on the importance of the Treaties of Utrecht and Paris to today's world.

When Bute resigned as prime minister in 1763, he recommended to the king that Fox be allowed to form a ministry, but neither George, who could not abide Fox, nor Fox himself, who was not really intent on becoming first lord of the treasury, wanted this. Fox's chance of becoming head of the administration vanished, as did much of his remaining political ambition. Several times among the Campbell correspondence of the 1760s Fox states that he has no interest in further office, his only ambition being with regard to the advancement of his immediate family. He did so by ingratiating himself with Lord Bute, in the hope of receiving a peerage. The latter came as a baronetcy, though for Caroline, who was made Lady Holland, baroness of Holland, Lincolnshire and Foxley, Wiltshire, in May 1762. Fox had to wait until the following year for a baronetcy, becoming Baron Holland of Foxley.[188] The baronetcy was a disappointment, since he was hoping for a viscountcy at the very least, and he pestered Bute among others in the vain hope that he would be further honoured.

Despite his activities in the early 1760s any real political ambition that Fox had seems to have faded. The elderly Lord Granville, who by the late 1750s had become a political patron to Fox, found him an unadventurous politician and wrote:

> Fox, I don't love to have you say things that will not be believed. If you was of my age, very well. I have put on my nightcap; there is no more daylight for me; but you *should* be ambitious. I want to instil a noble ambition into you, to make you knock the heads of the kings of Europe together, and jumble something out of it that may be of service to this country.[189]

And Luff comments that Fox 'had never displayed much enthusiasm for administration or policy making, but his role as a debater in the lower House did matter very much to him'.[190] Fox wanted power, but only the power that came with the leadership of the Commons. In the mid 1750s he could have grasped the nettle and formed an administration, but seemed more content to propose various others to the king as potential first ministers. Moreover, he flatly refused to form a ministry in 1763, even though Bute was handing over the office on easy terms.

Holland lived until 1774. He resigned the paymastership in 1765, two years after receiving his peerage which was in effect his political retirement. John Campbell, who never indicated in his surviving letters that he was interested in a peerage for himself, continued to be an MP, though not a very active one, until 1768, when he was 73 years old. Holland and Campbell continued to correspond, but their views were increasingly those of outsiders as they were superseded by a younger generation, which included Charles James Fox and Pitt the Younger; the sparring of these two formidable politicians curiously reflected the similar battles that Henry Fox and Pitt the Elder had fought. Meanwhile, Campbell's ambitions for his son were cut short by Pryse's death in 1768, the same year Campbell retired from the Commons, and the family had to wait until 1777, the year John Campbell died, to see another member of parliament from Stackpole Court in Pryse's son John. The latter's abilities and burning political ambition

---

[188] On 16 Apr. 1763. Sainty, *Peerage Creations*, 46.

[189] William Coxe, *Memoirs of Horatio, Lord Walpole* (2 vols, 1808), ii, 178.

[190] P.A. Luff, 'Henry Fox and the "Lead" in the House of Commons, 1754–55', *Parliamentary History*, vi (1987), 33.

would set the family on a course that would see its members rise to become earls Cawdor by the 1820s.

11. *The Campbell Correspondence*

The John Campbell letters held by Carmarthenshire Archive Service were deposited by the late 5th Earl Cawdor in 1963. They form part of the extensive Cawdor archive. In 1889 these letters were partially transcribed into a single volume by one Hugh Owen. This manuscript is known as the Stackpole letter book and is held by the National Library of Wales (ref: NLW, MS 1532b). It has been the main route to Campbell's letters for historians and although the transcripts are of a high standard there are occasional errors, and Owen omitted that which was not strictly of a political nature as defined by the late 19th century. The other main source of Campbell's letters is the Holland House papers held by the British Library (ref: BL, Add. MS 51406). These form the correspondence between Campbell and Henry Fox, later the 1st Lord Holland.

There are one or two other places of deposit that hold a small number of Campbell letters. There are four letters, written in the mid 1730s, in the Cholmondeley (Houghton) papers held in Cambridge University Archives, from Campbell to Sir Robert Walpole. Two of those are included in the present volume as they are of a political nature; those not printed pertain only to Pembrokeshire patronage matters. Perhaps surprisingly, considering they were related, there are very few letters between Campbell and the duke of Newcastle or between Hardwicke and Campbell. A mere half dozen or so letters survive between the three men. Those between Hardwicke and Campbell are concerned exclusively with west Wales matters – of Campbell asking to excuse individuals from the financially onerous task of serving as high sheriff for the counties of Pembroke or Cardigan. Of course, Campbell was making or keeping political friends by doing so, which may have been useful to him at election times, but as they are repetitive requests they are not included in the present volume.

Among his letters to Newcastle, in one instance Campbell lends his weight, however insignificant, to promoting Fox to office. And on another occasion he uses his familial connection to Newcastle to scupper the chances of his local political rival, Hugh Owen of Orielton, being given a promotion to the head of the Pembrokeshire militia.[191] However, most of Campbell's handful of extant letters to 'his noble cousin', as he refers to Newcastle, again concern local patronage matters, and are not included in the present volume.

There are no political letters either to or from Campbell in the National Archive of Scotland (where there is a large Cawdor archive pertaining to the Scottish estate). The Bute archive contains one or two letters but is currently a closed collection.[192] Apart from those, there are no known Campbell letters not included in the present volume.

All in all, the political letters of John Campbell of Stackpole Court, Pembrokeshire, are extant from 1734. However, the main body of those letters do not commence until

---

[191] Letter 208, BL, Add. MS 32970, f. 103: John Campbell to Newcastle, 29 Sept. 1765 (see Chapter 8).

[192] The Bute papers are held at Mount Stuart, Isle of Bute.

February 1739, when he begins a series of missives to his 12-year-old son Pryse, then resident at Stackpole Court. These are interspersed with letters to Campbell's wife Mary. In 1755 the extant correspondence commences between Campbell and Henry Fox, later Lord Holland. Four main areas of political history are referred to in some detail: Walpole's fall from power and the rise of the Pelhams; the crisis of government of the mid 1750s – the period covered by Clark who used the letters in his *Dynamics of Change* – when Fox was at his zenith politically; the Stamp Act crisis; and finally the parliamentary turmoil caused by John Wilkes in 1769–70.

The most densely concentrated group of letters – the earliest extant Campbell letters dealing with political matters – concern the fall from power of Walpole and his administration and its supersession by the Pelhams. Most of these letters are written to Pryse Campbell, with eight written to Mary Campbell. This group of letters is unique in that they are the only substantial source available written from the point of view of a staunch supporter of Walpole. John Owen's comment, although written over half a century ago, that 'The sole authorities for the period [of Walpole's fall] are the Opposition and its scribes – Pulteney, Egmont, Secker, Newton, Pearce and Glover', is still pertinent, as no major sources supporting the Walpole administration have subsequently seen the light of day, excepting the letters of John Campbell.[193] There is, for instance, only one extant letter pertinent to Walpole's fall, as viewed from an ally's point of reference, among the Fox correspondence in the Holland House papers.[194] After the detailed letters to Pryse and Mary relating this momentous event in British political history, the letters become less and less frequent, and by the eve of the jacobite rebellion of 1745 they are no longer extant.[195]

From February 1745 until September 1755 there is a ten-year gap in the letters. During this lacuna, correspondence between father and son stops or, more likely, has become lost, with a single exception which may be dated 1751. The latter is the last known letter to Pryse. Letters to Mary are not extant after February 1742 until November 1755. They then continue until 1763, though only intermittently. During the whole period of Campbell's political letter writing, only 26 letters are extant between Campbell and his wife, and considering that on occasion he wrote three or four times a week it can be assumed that many letters have become lost.

After the ten-year lacuna, there begins, from September 1755, a relatively lengthy correspondence between Campbell and Henry Fox. The two men had been friends from around 1746, so again it can be assumed that there were earlier letters no longer extant. The John Campbell–Henry Fox correspondence is extant for the period when the latter was at the height of his political power and was vying with the duke of Newcastle and William Pitt the Elder for leadership of government and more particularly and crucially for control of the house of commons. There are five main periods for which the correspondence between the two men is more plenteous than at other times: the end of September 1755 until the end of September 1758; November 1760–January 1763; March–May 1763; November 1764–February 1765; and September 1765–April

---

[193] J.B. Owen, *The Rise of the Pelhams* (1957), 88 and fn.

[194] BL, Add. MS 51417, ff. 79–82: Fox to Stephen Fox, 19 Dec. 1741.

[195] Henry Fox's correspondence with his brother Stephen is extant and replete with news of the rebels' advances into England. See BL, Add. MSS 51417, 51418.

1766. Between these dates and from 1766 until 1771 there are periods of relative silence, the correspondence dwindling to one or two letters a year. However, even at more intense periods the letter writing cannot be said to be other than irregular. For instance, in 1760–1 only four letters are extant, all from Fox to Campbell, and two of those addressed to 'Dear Sir', though the internal evidence indicates they are to Campbell. After the middle of October 1762 they become more numerous, covering the administration of George Grenville and then the Stamp Act crisis of 1765–6. Of the latter period, P.D.G. Thomas has written of the paucity and unreliable nature of the sources, so the letters between the two men are a welcome addition to the primary evidence for the debate.[196] In 1766 there are 14 letters between the two men, which cover all the major debates regarding the American colonies, the repeal of the Stamp Act and the passing of the Indemnity Act. The last years of correspondence between Campbell and Holland, sparser in number again, deal with the parliamentary crisis that occurred with the rejection of John Wilkes from the house of commons in 1769. By this period Campbell was ensconced at Stackpole Court, in poor health and no longer an MP, and Fox, by this time Lord Holland, was politically *persona non grata*, and spent much of his time either travelling on the continent – as a remedy for his or his family's health – or creating follies on his estate at Kingsgate, Kent. Thus, both men were outsiders, viewing politics with an old man's perspective, cynical and nostalgic for their heyday. It is the correspondence of two isolated men, and in the case of Holland at least, one occasionally wishing for his physical end. However, he was blessed with seeing the rising political star of his son Charles James, and commented to Campbell: 'I am told, that few in Parliament, ever spoke better, than Charles did on Friday. Off hand with rapidity, with spirit, & such knowledge of what he was talking of, as surprize'd every body, in so young a Man. If you think this Vanity, I am sure you will forgive it'.[197] As is well known, the younger Fox was to have an even more illustrious (and notorious) parliamentary career than his doting father.

There are no extant letters between Fox and Campbell after 2 April 1771. Fox did not die until July 1774 and Campbell until September 1777. Both men continued to write to other correspondents, Campbell up to a month or so before his death. However, given the warmth of the letters between the two men, it is probable that the fate of time has intervened to deprive readers of later letters, rather than a cessation of writing between them as the two men headed towards death. However, Holland was having trouble writing in his own hand from about 1767, and Mr Fannen, his amanuensis, wrote increasing numbers of letters from that time, which Holland, often in a very shaky hand, signed. This may explain why there are no letters from Holland after 1771, although no such excuse can be made on Campbell's behalf as his hand remained clear and remarkably unchanged up to his death.

The period of Campbell's letters more or less coincides with the embargo parliament placed on the reporting of debates, which dates from April 1738. The embargo was not lifted until Wilkes' efforts to establish free reporting of debates in 1768–70. Journalists

---

[196] P.D.G. Thomas, 'Introduction', in *Parliamentary Diaries of Nathaniel Ryder, 1764–7*, ed. P.D.G. Thomas (Camden Society, 4th ser., xxiii, 1969), xxiii, 230.

[197] *CJ*, xxxii, 385, 14 Apr. 1769. The debate on the Middlesex election, in which Fox spoke in support of Luttrell. Letter 236, BL, Add. MS 51406, ff. 161–2: Lord Holland to John Campbell, 18 Apr. 1769 (see Chapter 9).

found ways around this ban by using pseudonyms, though this may have been at the cost of accuracy. Thus debates were reported in the *Gentleman's Magazine* as 'Debates in the Senate of Lilliput', while the rival *London Magazine* reported debates from the 'Political Club'.[198] So Campbell's and from 1755 Fox's surviving political letters, reporting details of Commons debates from the beginning of 1739, are an invaluable source, giving increasingly extended reports from debates in the Commons, including division figures, from the very beginning of the reporting embargo. They also have an advantage over the published reports in immediacy, as Campbell frequently wrote his letters within hours of coming from the House. The nearness in time to the debates of Campbell's correspondence may lend more accuracy to his reports to Pryse and Mary than other, printed reports, for instance those written by Samuel Johnson for the *Gentleman's Magazine*, which were often the altered accounts of debates that William Guthrie took from the rival *London Magazine*.[199] Boswell comments that Johnson stated, just before his death, with regard to his Commons reports that he regretted 'having been the author of fictions, which had passed for realities'.[200] And on the quality of memory, Jane Austen was later to reflect: 'our powers of recollecting and of forgetting, do seem peculiarly past finding out'.[201] Indeed, on one occasion Campbell does admit: 'Yesterday Wee sat till allmost night, and I am so stupid I can't recollect what it was about'.[202] However, that instance apart, Campbell is very assured in his reporting. Fox, it seems, was not as assiduous in his writing, at least to Campbell, and often wrote several days after a debate. On one occasion, when writing to Campbell, he repeats information he had already sent to Stackpole nearly six weeks earlier.[203]

Campbell's extant letters are voluminous enough to indicate that he was a regular and fairly substantial letter writer. From internal references in the surviving letters it is clear that he wrote a lot more than those that have survived. However, it is fortuitous for researchers that his surviving letters concerning the demise of Walpole's administration and the rise of the Pelhams provide probably the most detailed account extant, from the point of view of a Walpolian whig. Furthermore, his correspondence with Holland, pertaining to the repeal of the Stamp Act, is also a valuable addition to the primary evidence. The Campbell–Holland correspondence written during the mid 1750s political crisis, used by Clark, is presented here for the first time in its entirety, and their comments about the Wilkes affair reflect the conservative whiggery of two elderly politicians.

As mentioned above, J.C.D. Clark used the letters when writing *The Dynamics of Change*. J. Black has also used them in his work, principally *Pitt the Elder* and *Walpole in Power*. Professor Black was the first historian to point out the importance of the letters, especially for the 1740s.[204] Other historians who have used the Campbell letters, though

---

[198] M. Ransome, 'The Reliability of Contemporary Reporting of Debates of the House of Commons, 1727–41', *BIHR*, xix (1942–3), 76.

[199] D. Nokes, *Samuel Johnson, a Life* (2009), 69.

[200] J. Boswell, *The Life of Samuel Johnson* (1791), 87.

[201] J. Austen, *Mansfield Park* (1814), 222.

[202] Letter 81: John Campbell to Pryse Campbell, 10 Feb. 1743 (see Chapter 3).

[203] Letter 217, BL, Add. MS 51406, ff. 122–3: Holland to John Campbell, 2 Jan. 1766; Letter 222, BL, Add. MS 51406, ff. 132–3: Holland to John Campbell, 25 Feb. 1766 (see Chapter 8).

[204] J. Black, 'Archival Sources for the Parliamentary History of Britain in the 1740s', *Archives*, xix (1991), 404–22.

usually from the late 19th-century partial transcriptions found at NLW, MS 1532b, include D.W. Howell, particularly in his *Patriarchs and Parasites* and more extensively P.D.G Thomas, in his extensive writings on 18th-century politics.

12. *Editorial Method*

The letters have been fully transcribed, the only omissions being Campbell's usual closing sentence which most frequently begins 'Pray God bless . . .' followed by an exhortation to good health, and the valediction. All spelling has been kept as in the original, as has Campbell's usage of capital letters, or non-use, as with his frequent use of lower case for the initial letter of days of the week. Very occasionally I have added a full stop where confusion might otherwise have ensued; otherwise all punctuation is as Campbell used it, including his frequent use of the semi-colon to indicate the end of a sentence.

Chapter 1. 1734–40

Unless otherwise stated all letters in this chapter are from CRO, Cawdor/Campbell box 128.

1. CUL, Cholmondeley (Houghton), 2219
John Campbell, Stackpole Court to Sir Robert Walpole, 18 June 1734
I have received an account of my being unanimously chosen for the shire of Nairne in Scotland, but as it is expected I should make my Election for this County, I believe they are allready thinking of another Candidate for Nairne, the Person I would desire to recommend is a very near Relation of mine Mr Brodie[1] of Lethen, I have writ to my Lord Ilay[2] in very pressing terms to favour him, I will not trouble you now with a long story, only in general beg leave to say, that I think my Interest, honor & Credit so much concern'd in this Affair, that if I am so happy to have any share in your Friendship I promise my self your assistance for my Friends. I hope the Returns to Parliament are such as will answer the warmest wish's of the kings Faithfull servants, and your Friends, in both which Characters none can be more zealous or sincere.

2. CUL, Cholmondeley (Houghton), 2687
John Campbell, Wimbledon[3] to Sir Robert Walpole, 15 May 1737
I am inform'd by a letter from the Country, that the Place of one Lloyd a Tidewaiter at the Hubberston in the Port of Milford, is or will very soon be vacant. I beg it may be given to Stephen Evans, recommended to me by a Gent[leman][4] of Great Fortune in Pembrokeshire, to whom I was very much obliged for the Quiet of my last Election. I am your most obedient and obliged humble servant . . .

[1] Alexander Brodie (d. 1770), of Lethen, Nairnshire. See Introduction.

[2] Archibald Campbell (1682–1761), known as Lord Archibald Campbell (1703–6); earl of Ilay (1706–43) and 3rd duke of Argyll (1743–61). He helped rein in his brother's (John Campbell, 2nd duke of Argyll) 'intractable perversity' and when the latter opposed Walpole, Archibald remained in Walpole's confidence. Archibald was sent to Edinburgh to put down the Porteous riots in 1736. *ODNB*.

[3] The Campbells had a house in Wimbledon. John Campbell was robbed of a gold watch and 12 guineas on Wimbledon Common by a highwayman in the summer of 1737. This may have something to do with his apprehension regarding Pryse's journey to London in the following year. *London Evening Post*, 16 June 1737.

[4] Sir John Philipps (1700–64), of Kilgetty and later Picton Castle, Pembrokeshire; MP for Carmarthen 1741–7, Petersfield 1754–61 and Pembrokeshire 1761–4. Philipps was related to the Walpole family; however, by the early 1740s he was supporting the opposition and became one of the leading tory MPs, speaking regularly in the Commons. He was a prominent member of the Society of Sea Serjeants of south Wales, a tory club with jacobite leanings, and was elected its last president in 1762 though even as early as the 1750s Philipps was 'anxious to rebut charges that it was a Jacobite group'. See J.P. Jenkins, 'Jacobites and Freemasons in Eighteenth-Century Wales', *WHR*, ix (1979), 395; P.D.G. Thomas, *Politics in Eighteenth-Century Wales* (Cardiff, 1998), esp. ch. 8; for the Sea Serjeants see F. Jones, 'The Society of Sea Serjeants', *THSC*, i (1967), 57–91, and F. Jones, 'Disaffection and Dissent in Pembrokeshire', *THSC, 1946–7* (1948), 221, where he states that 'the Society seems to have confined its activities to assemblies, dinners, cards and snuff-taking'.

3.

John Campbell to Pryse Campbell,[5] Wimbledon, 13 February 1739
My Dearest Boy
I pray God this may find you in perfect health. Wee are all well here. Yesterday I received in the Lobby a Copy of the Convention[6] &c. As soon as they are published I will send you one, or else bring you this when I come to you. Dodsley[7] the Poet & Bookseller was yesterday order'd into custody by the House of Lords for printing the Poem called Manners[8] (which I will bring to you). The author Whitehead[9] absconds.

Your Mama's Love & Blessing & your Brother & Sisters[10] Love attend you. I pray God to bless you many Years in Virtue, Health and Peace. I am always with the most tender affection My Dearest Pupsy Your most loveing Pa' and most Faithfull Friend.

My service to Mr Cargill.

I beg of you my dearest to continue a proper application, to your Learning, and by all means to avoid & resolve against wrangling at Play &c. And I intreat my Dearest to be carefull of himself, and to mind where & how you run &c.

4.

John Campbell to Pryse Campbell, Wimbledon, 5 March 1739
I am very glad to here you had a good ride to day, I hope your Cold is quite gone. I was surprised when I went to the House to day to find them calling over the Names.[11] Wee could not safe [sic] Mr Rolle[12] this time. Wee divided upon the Question to excuse him and lost it, so he is order'd into Custody.

[5] Pryse Campbell (1727–68), John Campbell's son and heir; the main recipient of the letters. See Introduction.

[6] The Convention of Pardo or Treaty of Pardo, signed 14 Jan. 1739, between Spain and Britain, was an attempt to put to an end various grievances between Spanish and British merchants.

[7] Robert Dodsley (1703–64), bookseller and writer.

[8] Lord Delaware commented that the poem was 'one of the most flagrant instances of abuse and virulence that this age had seen'. LJ, xxv, 290.

[9] Paul Whitehead (1710–74), satirist. The poem Manners (published 3 Feb. 1739) was a satirical attack on parliament. It was voted 'scandalous' in the Lords and a question of privilege was raised. Dodsley and Whitehead were summoned to the Bar: the former appeared, but Whitehead, a friend of Bubb Dodington, absconded.

[10] Pryse had five siblings. See Introduction.

[11] The Call of the House was a roll call of members undertaken near the beginning of the session. After being given four to six weeks' notice, members were expected to attend for the Call. It was frequently delayed, especially in Walpole's ministry, as a way of keeping MPs at Westminster, since once the Call had been taken members could go home. In the particular instance referred to by Campbell several MPs failed to appear at the Call, all being excused due to illness or 'extraordinary Avocations or on the road' except Rolle. He failed to give an excuse. The vote was 145 to 171 in the negative. CJ, xxiii, 269. The last member taken into custody for not attending the Call was in 1781. See P.D.G. Thomas, The House of Commons in the Eighteenth Century (Oxford, 1971), 105–10.

[12] Henry Rolle (1708–50), MP for Devon 1730–41 and Barnstaple 1741–8.

I was obliged to be at Sir R[obert] Walpole's[13] this Evening by seven, & staid there till after nine, and I must go by nine to morrow morning to secure a Place in the House.[14] The speaker says there are 518 members in Town.

My Dearest I beg of you when your eyes are well to give good attention to your learning. You know I do not desire to confine you. I only beg that the time you are at your Book may be well employ'd, that you will apply in earnest and avoid trifleing. But my Dearest I would not upon any account have you run the hazard of straining or hurting your eyes by reading when they are out of Order or in any Book that the Print is not quite easy & agreeable to you.

I pray God . . .[15]

Give the enclosed with my kind remembrance to your Dear Faithfull Gil Blas.[16] I send you three Apricot Cakes; eat but one in a Day. My Service to Mr Cargil. Let Johnny send me word by the Post what is the number of the last Vote you had, that I may bring the rest.

5.

John Campbell to Pryse Campbell, Wimbledon, 9 March 1739

I was very glad to hear from Johnny that you continued very well and were down so early yesterday. I thank God I am perfectly well after the long attendance yesterday. The Debate began before twelve at noon, Mr H[oratio] Walpole[17] moved for an Address much the same with that from the House of Lords.[18] He was seconded by your Pa.[19]

---

[13] Sir Robert Walpole (1676–1745), of Houghton Hall, Norfolk; MP for Castle Rising 1701–2 and King's Lynn 1702–42. Secretary at war 1708–10; treasurer of the navy 1710–11; paymaster of the forces 1714–15; first lord of the treasury and chancellor of the exchequer 1715–17; paymaster of the forces 1720–1; first lord of the treasury, chancellor of the exchequer and leader of the house of commons 1721–45. He was created earl of Orford in 1742. Both John Campbell and Henry Fox remained loyal to Walpole long after he had lost power and, indeed, long after his death.

[14] The house of commons 'chamber measured only 57 feet 6 inches by 32 feet 10 inches [and] the lobby through which it was entered being 28 feet by 30 feet'. After the Union with Scotland in 1707 there were 558 members, and although Wren had enlarged the galleries the Commons was still far too small for the number of members. Thomas, *House of Commons in the Eighteenth Century*, 1; *HPC, 1715–54*, i, 1.

[15] This is Campbell's valediction.

[16] Gil Blas was the nickname of John Wright, an agent at Stackpole Court. The original Gil Blas was the hero of the picaresque novel of the same name by the French author Alain-René Lesage (1668–1747).

[17] Horatio Walpole (1678–1757), MP for Lostwithiel 1710, Castle Rising 1710–15, Bere Alston 1715–17, East Looe 1718–22, Great Yarmouth 1722–34 and Norwich 1734–56. Ambassador to France 1724–30 and to the United Provinces 1734–9; secretary to the treasury 1715–17 and 1721–30; chief secretary to Ireland 1720–1; cofferer of the household 1730–41; teller to the exchequer 1741–57. Second son of Sir Robert Walpole, and was commonly known as Horace. He was created Baron Walpole of Wolterton, Norfolk, in 1756. The Address referred to is of thanks for the Convention of Pardo. Walpole spoke for two hours and the debate, held on 8 Mar., took up all the business of the day. William Cobbett, *Cobbett's Parliamentary History* (36 vols, 1806–20), x, 1246.

[18] On 1 Mar. the Address of Thanks followed a debate in the Lords which was voted: contents 71, non-contents 58, with proxy votes of 24 contents and 16 non-contents, giving total votes of 95 contents and 16 non-contents. *Divisions in the House of Lords: An Analytical List, 1685 to 1857*, compiled by J.C. Sainty and D. Dewar (1976), hereafter Sainty and Dewar.

[19] *PH*, x, 1258–9, gives Campbell's speech. John Selwyn writing to Thomas Townshend stated that Campbell 'did as well as Mr Walpole left him room to do'. William Coxe, *Memoirs of the Life and Administration of Sir Robert Walpole, Earl of Orford* (3 vols, 1798), iii, 519.

Wee divided Ay's 260, No's 232,[20] and the House adjourn'd a little after twelve at night.[21] This day it is to be reported to the House, for yesterday it was in a Committee of the whole House. If the Address is presented on Saturday it will hinder me comeing to you till after dinner.

Last night poor Gammer[22] was some way thrown of the box just as the House rose, and much hurt. Jo' drove me home, and I must get some one to drive me to Wimbledon.

Jack stands by me and sends his love to you & his compliments to John Wright. Give my service to Mr Cargil, and remember me most kindly to our dear Faithful Gil Blas.

Pray my Dearest be very careful not to hurt your eye by any means. I pray God . . .

6.

John Campbell to Pryse Campbell, 30 October 1739

I was greatly rejoyced to see your hand writeing yesterday, I thank God that your eyes are so well and pray they may long continue so. Your Mama sends her Love to you & Many thanks, She has not time to write to you to night being obliged to make several Visits, & intending to see the Ball at Court. There was a good deal of Company there in the Morn. I was not extravagant for I had a plain Cloth Coat with a gold button & a green silk Wastcoat with an open gold triming.

While I was at the Admiralty[23] yesterday, Wee received a letter from Admiral Haddock[24] with account that he had taken in sight of Cadiz a Spanish Ship from the Caracca's call'd the St Joseph laden with Tobacco & Cocoa with 15 Chests said to contain 50000 Dollars, & besides the Chests there were 20421 dollars 2087 Pistoles and some Jewells & Plate of no great Value. He send [*sic*] her guarded by the Chester Man of War for Portsmouth, and to day they say they are arrived at Spithead, The Tobacco & Cocoa are supposed to be of considerable value. You may be sure Wee are very much pleased with this News.[25]

I send the inclosed to make you laugh. When Frank was in Town I went with him to see the Duke of Argyll's,[26] and when I came out a man desired to speak

---

[20] This was one of the largest attendances in the Commons to that date. See Thomas, *House of Commons in the Eighteenth Century*, 123–6, concerning attendance in the Commons. Campbell's figures accord with those recorded in *PH*, x, 1247.

[21] *PH*, x, 1246–7, gives 9 p.m.

[22] Campbell is probably referring to his horseman, although it could mean grandmother or could refer to any elderly woman. *OED*.

[23] The admiralty building, officially the Ripley building, was completed in 1726 and lies in Whitehall.

[24] Nicolas Haddock (1686–1747), MP for Rochester 1734–46. Commander-in-chief in the Mediterranean, 1738–42. He was made a vice admiral in 1743 and admiral a year later.

[25] Haddock allowed the Spanish squadron at Cadiz to escape in Oct. 1740, which caused an outcry in England. *HPC, 1715–54*, ii, 94.

[26] John Campbell (1678–1743), 2nd duke of Argyll; chief of the clan Campbell, and a relative of John Campbell. Argyll supported the Act of Union, fought in the War of Spanish Succession under the duke of Marlborough and became commander-in-chief of the British army in 1742. In 1705 he recommended for Scotland a protestant succession and union with England. In 1740 he blamed the ministry for the failure of the harvest and the widespread disturbances that followed, with such venom that he was immediately relieved of all his offices. From this time he attacked Walpole's ministry at every opportunity. However, 'he played in politics a part not only comparatively subordinate, but glaringly mean and contemptible'. He regained many of his offices after Walpole's fall, but then resigned them, believing he was not rewarded sufficiently for the role he had played. *ODNB*.

to me & his busyness was to offer himself for a Tutor to my son, Frank thought it had been to offer himself for a footman, and wonder'd at his assurance to offer for that in such a Dirty shabby Pickle, You will see it is the same Person who writes this Fine letter.

Give my Blessing & Love to Dear Trub and my kind service to Mr. Rowe.[27] I pray God . . .

Remember me to all your Friends and Favorites. I pray God grant us a happy meeting. I continually long for it.

7.

John Campbell to Pryse Campbell, Wimbledon, 1 November 1739

I give you many thanks for your letter which gave me very great Pleasure to hear you had Spent your time so pleasantly and to see you write so well after being so long prevented useing your Pen. You make me long to dine with Mr Leach. Yesterday when I was at the Admiralty there was a Master of a Merchant man call'd in, to inform the Board, that he came directly from Gibraltar, & before he came away saw a Spanish Prize brought into that Port, which they said at first was worth £40,000 but soon after he heard it was richer than the St. Joseph which Wee reckon to be worth above £100,000. It is true as you see in the news that Captain Ambrose[28] took some Spanish Goods out of a Genoise Ship, but I fear they magnifie the Value for the Letters to the Admiralty mention very little money, and do not describe the Goods as of much Consequence.

My Dearest let me repete my earnest desire that you will be very carefull of yourself; the accounts I receive of you from Mr Rowe and from Johnny are so Good that I find no occasion to give you more Advice, haveing so much reason to believe you are very Good and behave yourself as I wish you to do; I pray God ever to Bless and direct you, and to preserve you many years in Virtue, Health and Peace. Give my Blessing and Love to dear Trub. I thank God I am in very good health, as is your Mama, Bessy and Ally [Alexander]. The schole Dabs were so when Wee heard from them. Your Mama sends her love to You and Trub so does Bessy, but Ally minds only munching bread and Butter. Give my Kind service to Mr Rowe. A happy meeting at Stackpole is the constant Prayer of My Dearest Boy Your most Loveing Pa' and ever Faithfull Friend.

J. Campbell alias Pudge[29]

---

[27] Henry Rowe was Pryse Campbell's tutor and the vicar of Stackpole Elidor 1724–65, rector of Hogeston 1724–8, of St Petrox 1728–9, of Stackpole Elidor 1749–79 and Burton 1765–79, and canon of St David's 1752–79, all in Pembrokeshire. He went to St John's College, Cambridge, matriculating in Oct. 1717. Campbell wrote to the duke of Newcastle asking for the duke's influence to get Rowe the living of Narberth, Pembrokeshire, which was in the gift of the crown: 'Mr Henry Rowe a very worthy Clergyman who was Tutor to my son'. BL, Add. MS 32720, f. 131: Campbell to duke of Newcastle, 9 Mar. 1749/50. Campbell wrote again the following November (see Chapter 4, Letter 133, 12 Nov. 1750), but Narberth eluded Rowe.

[28] John Ambrose (d. 1771), appointed captain of the *Greyhound* frigate in 1734. See J. Charnock, *Biographia Navalis* (1799), iv, 252–61, for his naval career.

[29] It is not known why Campbell is referred to as Pudge.

Remember me kindly to R[oger] & F[rancis] Evans[30] your Friend Adam, your Gentleman Val,[31] Johnny my Jewell,[32] Johnny Bowen[33] etc not forgetting your honest Huntsman who I hope continues to deserve everybodys good opinion.

8.

John Campbell to Pryse Campbell, 13 November 1739

I am just now come from Sir Robert Walpole's where Wee heard the Speech[34] that is to be made on Thursday, there is nothing new in it, nor indeed could it be expected there should. The King informs us that the Injustice Breach of Faith &c of the Spaniards had made it necessary to declare War against that Crown. He depends upon the Support of the Parliament and hopes that a Union of all who wish the true interest of their Country will disappoint our Enemies both at home & abroad who have been chiefly encouraged by our domestic divisions & animosities &c.

Sir Robert [Walpole] at the same time inform'd us that the King has given his Servants leave to declare his Intention to distribute the Prizes allready taken from the Spaniards between the Captors, and the Merchants who were Sufferers by the Spaniards Depredations, but the Several Proportions cannot be Settled till the Value of the Prizes is known.

I am sorry for poor Tenby's indisposition and that you are not yet provided with another Horse, but if you have at present the same weather Wee have here I think you can't ride, Wee have had two or three days hard frost & excessive Cold. Pray my Dearest be carefull of your Self.

I am willing you may dine some day with Mr Phillipps of Bosherston[35] if it be agreable and convenient for you, and the days are not too short. I would have you do nothing that may be in the least inconvenient.

I was glad to hear you presented Mr. Cuningham[36] with a hunted Hare. Give my Love & Blessing to Dear Trub & kind service to Mr. Rowe. Our Dear Faithfull Gil Blas is allways sure of my best wishes & sincere Love.

My Dearest Boy, I pray . . . God Grant us a happy meeting at Stackpole and preserve us to one another . . .

I wish much joy to Johnny my Jewel.

[30] Roger Evans was the Stackpole estate steward who died c.1770. F. Evans is Frank or Francis Evans, brother of Roger. Francis was clerk of works for the rebuilding of Stackpole Court, which Campbell was undertaking in the 1730s.

[31] Val was Pryse Campbell's valet, constant companion and confidante, even into Pryse's early 20s. CRO, Cawdor/Campbell box 128: letters from Pryse to Val, 1749–56.

[32] Johnny my Jewel is probably John (Jack) Campbell.

[33] John Bowen was a servant at Stackpole Court. He was still working there at the time of Campbell's death and received an annuity from the latter's will. He did not die until 1793. CRO, Cawdor/Campbell box 16/192 for Campbell's will and CRO, Cawdor/Campbell box 3/49 for Bowen's certificate of burial.

[34] Walpole, as was usual practice, gathered his most important supporters to read the king's speech and the Address two days before they were heard in parliament. That Campbell was included in this inner circle is an indication of his position within the whigs. The king's speech can be found at *CJ*, xxiii, 382–3.

[35] Pembrokeshire.

[36] This could be Dr Cuningham, or a relation.

9.

John Campbell to Pryse Campbell, Stackpole Court, 15 November 1739

Wee had a fuller House to day than I expected. The motion for the Address[37] was made by Mr Harry Archer[38] one of the members for Warwick, & seconded by Mr Mordaunt[39] who is, I think, for Nottinghamshire, then Mr Pulteney[40] made a pretty loud speech in which though he declared a dislike of past Measures, yet he spoke warmly for the present Establishment & Royal family & for vigorously & unanimously supporting the King in the War, and letting every thing give way to the Common Nation & the support of this Government. He concluded with saying I third the Motion so when the Question was put Sir J[ohn] H[ynde] Cotton[41] gave the only Negative. I hear they had a Debate & Division in the House of Lords about the mentioning [*sic*] Animosities at Home.[42] The Question there was carried 68 Against 41.[43] Lord Scarborough[44] the Duke of Argyll & Lord Halifax[45] both Voted & Spoke on the side of the minority.

I took Particular Notice that Mr Pulteney said it would not have it thought he was makeing advances to some Gentlemen (meaning the Ministry) he scorn'd it, and he also despised any unjust mean suspicions from any other Quarter (meaning his own Party or rather perhaps the Torys). I was very glad to hear him speak in that manner and declare so warmly & honestly for his King and Country, I hope he will continue to act suitably in great and necessary Points. In the middle of Mr. Pulteney's speech rubbing his forehead & giveing a little motion with his head, his Wig fell quite off upon the seat behind him, which made both himself and others laugh.

My Dearest Pupsy you will easily know how great joy I have in receiving so good account of your health & eyes. I pray God continue it. I hope this Cold weather will agree with you. Pray my Dearest be carefull for slips and falls are very bad in hard frost and it needs Care to avoid them.

---

[37] *PH*, xi, 83. This was the usual response of the Commons (and the Lords) to the king's speech.

[38] Henry Archer (1700–68), one of the MPs for Warwick, the other being his brother Thomas. The Archers, government supporters, gained their seat when on petition the returned candidates, Sir William Keyt and William Bromley, were ousted.

[39] John Mordaunt (?1709–67), MP for Nottinghamshire 1739–47, Winchelsea 1747–54 and Christchurch 1754–61.

[40] William Pulteney (1684–1764), MP for Middlesex 1734–42. One of the leaders of the patriots, in opposition to Walpole. He was created 1st earl of Bath on 14 July 1742.

[41] Sir John Hynde Cotton (c.1688–1752), tory MP for Cambridge 1708–22 and 1727–41, Cambridgeshire 1722–7 and Marlborough 1741–52. Lord of trade 1713–14; treasurer of the chamber 1744–6. Cotton was one of the leading English jacobites. After Watkin Williams-Wynn's (see Note 58 below) death in 1749, Cotton assumed the role of tory leader in the Commons, and his death 'virtually silenc[ed] the Tories' as a party. J.C.D. Clark, *The Dynamics of Change: The Crisis of the 1750s and English Party Systems* (Cambridge, 1982), 36.

[42] The king's address referred to 'The Heats and Animosities, which … have been fomented throughout the Kingdom', which he said was one of the chief causes of war against Spain. *CJ*, xxiii, 383. These animosities may refer to the supporters of Charles Stuart.

[43] These figures agree with those in Sainty and Dewar.

[44] Richard Lumley (1686–1740), 2nd earl of Scarbrough. This was his last speech in the Lords – he committed suicide in Jan. 1741. *PH*, xi, 54.

[45] George Montagu-Dunk (1716–71), 2nd earl of Halifax. First lord of trade 1748–61; lord lieutenant of Ireland, 1761; first lord of the admiralty 1762; secretary of state for the northern department 1762–3 and 1771, and for the southern department 1763–5. He succeeded to the earldom in 1739.

Give my Love & Blessing to Dear Trub your Mama's to yourself and him. I pray God . . .

God grant me a happy meeting with you at Stackpole and may Wee live to shew our gratitude to your Dear Gil Blas, and may he assist you in the Care of your Sons. I am . . .

10.

John Campbell to Pryse Campbell, 17 November 1739

Inclosed is one of your Gloves & the Lords Address by which you will see how little Occasion there was for a Debate. I told you in my Last that Lord Scarborough was with the Minority, it seems about a week or more before he desired to have his name Struck out of the Cabinet Councill,[46] what is the Occasion of his disgust I can't tell, but I am apt to think the Division was made cheifly to shew him on that side.

Our friend Mr. Hill[47] & another Commissioner of the Customs were sent to Portsmouth to secure the Ladeing of the St. Joseph & to bring up some Chests suppose to contain Silver they return'd in a Coach attend'd by two Waggons laden with the said Chests, & a party of the Grenadier Guards. The People in all the Towns & Villages crowded to see them go by, and fancying that the Spanish fryar[48] was brought up, were very curious to see him, the Weather being extreme Cold, it seems Mr Hill had got a red great Coat with a Cape & hood that cover'd his head, so those Wags the Grenadiers told all the Country People that the man in the Coach with the red hood upon his head was the Fryar. The Commissioners who knew nothing of the matter, wonder'd what made the People crowd so much about and stare into the Coach.

This day Wee went with our Address,[49] which was agreed to Yesterday without the least debate, but Wee had a Debate that day upon a Motion for a Bill to encourage the Seamen,[50] not that any body was against such a Bill but as they who moved it explain'd what they intended to put in the Bill, it was thought to be moved for so early that the King might not have the thanks due to him for giveing the Prizes as I told you he would, however after sometime the Court not being able to prevail with the other side to defer it for a few days, that the favor might come originally from the Crown, rather than divide the yeilded & let the Bill be order'd; Mr Pulteney, Mr Sandys[51] and Lord

---

[46] The cabinet council was the equivalent of today's cabinet but it advised the king – its origins were in the privy council.

[47] John Hill (c.1690–1753), of Thornton Hill, Malton, Yorkshire. Commissioner of customs 1723–47; MP for Higham Ferrars 1747–53.

[48] John Hill dressed to resemble a Spanish friar. *The Spanish Fryar*, a tragi-comedy by John Dryden written in 1680, was being performed regularly at both Covent Garden and Drury Lane playhouses throughout c.1738–44. The popularity of this play may have been the cause of the crowd's interest.

[49] *CJ*, xxiii, 283: address of thanks to George II expressing the Commons' satisfaction with the king's declaration of war with Spain.

[50] Motion brought in by William Pulteney. The ensuing bill was read for the first time on 26 Nov. and after debate in both Houses was given royal assent. *CJ*, xxiii, 385.

[51] Samuel Sandys (1695–1770), MP for Worcester 1718–43. Chancellor of the exchequer 1742–3. Second to Pulteney in the whig opposition to Walpole's ministry, Sandys brought in the motion to remove Walpole on 13 Feb. 1742. He was created Lord Sandys on 20 Dec. 1743.

Baltimore[52] to prepare & bring it in; Lord Carteret[53] Spoke in the House of Lords in the same way that Mr Pulteney spoke in our House & was not for divideing, but the Question on which they divided, was moved by Lord Chesterfield[54] & seconded by Lord Scarborough. Lord Talbot[55] made a speech an hour long most of which he read out a large Paper like a Lawyers Brief, he went over all the Treatys that have been made, & all the Forces & Tax's that have been raised for near twenty years, he Voted with the Minority but his speech might have serve many other Occasions as well as that.

Your Mama sends her Love & Blessing to you & Trub. Pray give mine to him. My Dearest Boy I Pray God to Bless & preserve you . . . and to grant me a joyfull happy meeting with you and all the Friends I left at Stackpole. I am always . . .

The other Glove is inclosed to Mr. Rowe.

11.

John Campbell to Pryse Campbell, Stackpole Court, 22 November 1739

I thank you kindly for your letter & am very well pleased with the Account you inclosed of your Lessons; I hope in a few Years to see you a much better scholar than your Pa. I Bless God for the good Account I hear of you in every respect.

I believe the account you heard of poor Mr. Philipps is too true, it is a Melancholy thing that a Gent should destroy himself by such a mean irrational practice, I hope my Dearest you will allways have the greatest abhorrence of such beastly intemperance.

Give my love to Dear Trub. I am very glad to hear he is so good, it is a great pleasure and satisfaction to me that you and he are good & loveing Friends to each other. Give my kind service to Mr Rowe, and remember me kindly to all your Friends & favorites about Stackpole.

I heard to day at the House that the Spanish Ambassador to the Court of France, had left Paris in disgust, People seem'd to believe the Fact, but I could not learn the reason, I suppose Wee shall soon hear it.

The late seceders[56] seem much divided among themselves, I believe the Tories are heartily angry with Mr. Pulteney for expressing so warmly his zeal for the present Establishment, I hope he despises their Anger as much as he dislikes their Principles.

---

[52] Charles Calvert (1699–1751), 5th Baron Baltimore (Irish peerage), proprietor governor of Baltimore, MD, North America. *CJ*, xxiii, 385, also refers to Sir John Barnard, Mr Hooper and Mr Gybbon to prepare the bill.

[53] John, Lord Carteret (1690–1763), whig opposition leader to Walpole in the house of lords. Carteret became 2nd Earl Granville, on the death of his mother, in Oct. 1744. He was fluent in German, so was one of the few English statesmen able to communicate directly with George II.

[54] Philip Dormer Stanhope (1694–1773), MP for St Germans 1715–22 and Lostwithiel 1722–3. He was known as Lord Stanhope until he succeeded to the peerage as 4th earl of Chesterfield in 1726. Gentleman of the bedchamber to the prince of Wales 1715–27; lord of the bedchamber 1727–30; ambassador to The Hague 1728–32; lord steward of the household 1730–3; secretary of state for the northern department 1746–8. He opposed the excise bill for which he was dismissed from his position of lord steward. Thereafter Chesterfield worked strenuously in the Lords for Walpole's downfall.

[55] William Talbot (1710–82), 1st Earl Talbot, of Hensol, Glamorgan; whig MP for Glamorgan 1734–7, though by 1735 he was voting with the tories. He became lord steward of the household and lord high steward of England on George III's coronation. He was made Baron Dynevor of Dynevor Castle, Carmarthenshire, in 1780.

[56] Those whigs who, in 1725, had combined with some of the tories to form the patriotic opposition to the Walpole ministry.

I believe to morrow or next day both Houses will wait on the King with an Address[57] to desire he will conclude no Treaty will [*sic*] Spain till they acknowledge our Right of Navigation to and from our Colonies in America, without being search'd, vilified, or stop'd, on any pretence. It was first moved in our House by Sir William W–[58] perhaps they hoped the Ministry would oppose or try to put it off, but they came heartily into it, and it pass'd Nemine Contradicente.[59]

I thank God . . .

12.

John Campbell to Pryse Campbell, Stackpole Court, 8 December 1739

I thank you very much for your letter and the Latin inclosed in it, any instance of your improvement gives me great Pleasure, and the Good Account I receive from Mr. Rowe and Johnny both of your health, & behaviour, is the greatest happyness I can have at this distance from you, I pray God to continue it, and to grant us a happy meeting.

Give my Love & Blessing to your Apprentice, I am glad his Complaint was soon over, I hope it will not return; I heard yesterday that Alester, & Bessy were very well. The other Dabs came here from Schole the same day, all alive. Mouse carried them to Wimbledon this morning where they are to stay till after the Holydays, Mouse returns to morrow, I stay'd being engaged to dine with Lord Hervey[60] who came to Town just before the Parliament in very good health from Bath, while he was there it was confidently reported here that he was out of favor at St. James,[61] but I have the pleasure to be well assured of the contrary.

I am very glad your Frock gave you an agreable surprise, I am very much pleased with the accounts of your being so well diverted at Pembroke & on your Birthday. It shall allways be my greatest & endeavor, as far as I am able, to make you happy, and I hope both you, and I, shall ever remember that you can't be truely so, without Virtue, and a competant degree of Knowledge; and as nothing of this world can be enjoy'd without health, I beg of you my Dearest to be carefull of your self. I pray God . . . may you be long the delight & Comfort of your Friends & Dependents as you are of my Dearest Boy.

I can't express how much I rejoyce when I hear of your Good health, Good humor, high spirits, and innocent Mirth and that your Dear Eyes have so long continued well & clear.

My Dearest I observe in your Translation you have neglected makeing full stops at the end of sentences, & beginning a New sentence with a great letter, the want of

---

[57] 23 Nov. 1739. *LJ*, xxv, 433, with the king's answer at *LJ*, xxv, 435.

[58] Sir Watkin Williams-Wynn (1692–1749), 3rd bt, of Wynnstay, Denbighshire. A leading opponent of Walpole and openly jacobite, Williams-Wynn headed the Welsh jacobite club The Cycle of the White Rose, based in north Wales.

[59] Without dissent.

[60] John, Lord Hervey (1696–1743), eldest son of John Hervey, 1st earl of Bristol. Vice-chamberlain 1730–40; privy councillor 1730; lord privy seal 1740–2. He was a staunch supporter of Robert Walpole. For several years from c.1730 Hervey was the lover of Henry Fox's brother Stephen. Hervey's sexuality was frequently in doubt, and when, in 1731, William Pulteney referred to Hervey in a pamphlet as Miss Fainlove, a duel resulted. See R. Halsband, *Lord Hervey: Eighteenth-Century Courtier* (Oxford, 1973); L. Moore, *Amphibious Thing: The Life of Lord Hervey* (2000), 113–22.

[61] That is, at court.

which makes one apt to mistake and confound the sense in reading; the Latin would have guided you in that, and you should endeavor to write correctly in those respects, I often mistake in such things myself but should rejoyce to see myself out done in that, or in any desireable accomplishment, by you.[62]

13.

John Campbell to Pryse Campbell, Wimbledon, 10 January 1740

I bless God that you & your Dear Brother have continued so well in the excessive Cold, and that your spirits are so high, I hope they will not be the lower for my letting you know that your Tickett[63] is come up a Blank.

I thank you for the Lines of Latin – inclosed in Mr. Rowes letter, indeed I did not expect so much writeing from you while the hard weather continues, and Wee see here no sign of its going off. The snow still lyes & it Freezes hard, but is not quite so cold, as yesterday when all the Trees were candy'd white, but that is gone off to day either melted by a fog or blown off in the night, I don't know which.

The Parliament adjourn'd to Monday so Wee continue here this Week. Allys Cold is better, the two youngest Dabs have Colds & your Mama a little but Bessy & I continue quite Free. I go very seldom out of Doors, it being very cold, often misty & the ground cover'd with snow. If I was with you, I believe I should stir a little more. God grant me a happy meeting with my Dearest & all my Friends at Stackpole. Your Mama sends her Love to you and Trub, so does Bessy. My Love to your little Apprentice. My kind service to Mr. Rowe, for I fear I shall not have time to write to him or Johnny because here I receive my Letters & send the Answers in a short time the same day. Tell our Dear Faithfull Gil Blas, that I remember him with sincere affection and thank God for the recovery of his health.

My Dearest Pupsy I long impatiently to come to you, I pray God . . .

Remember me to Val, Adam, Johnny my Jewel &c.

Pray my Dearest be very carefull of yourself that you don't get falls, and be very carefull when you handle a Gun.

I suppose the hard Weather will have kill'd your poor Woodcocks in the Garden. I should have been mightily pleased to see them there. My Dear did the Wind that drove you out of the Dineing room make you wish your self here, and think Stackpole not quite so good a Place as you had thought it in bad weather.

14.

John Campbell to Pryse Campbell, 10 o'clock, 21 February 1740

I am just come from the House and have only time to tell you that I am very well and Bless God for the happy accounts I receive of you. Give my Love to your little Apprentice. My kind service to Mr. Rowe and remember me most kindly to our Dear Faithful Gil Blas.

I pray God . . .

---

[62] This final paragraph appears as a note inserted into the letter.

[63] Lottery ticket. The state lottery, which was begun in 1694, raised money for both the navy and the army. It was abolished in 1826.

Our Debate was on a Motion to Address for all the Negotiations relateing to the Convention in order to their being examined by a Secret Committee profess'dly in imitation of that the beginning of the late Kings reign, which form'd the impeachments against Queen Annes last Ministry.[64] The Motion was made by Mr. Pulteney, seconded by Sir William Wyndham,[65] pass'd in the negative Ay's 196 No's 247.[66]

15.

John Campbell to Pryse Campbell, 26 February 1740

I was in such a hurry when I writ to you last, that I had not time to tell you that I thank you kindly for yours of the 12th,[67] and I don't know when I shall be at leisure. Yesterday Wee sat till between six & seven upon the Navy, and after all the Papers call'd for & the rout made, it vanish'd in smoak, without any Question. To day Lord Polwarth[68] made a Motion about some of those Matters, which it would take up too much time to explain, and it is not worth while, for after five o'Clock he withdrew his Motion, and our Debate ended in Nothing.

I was glad to here by Johnnys last letter that you were going on horseback, let me beg of you my Dearest to be carefull. I hope you will not fatigue your self too much at first, after being so long without rideing. I thank you for the Lines of Latin Mr. Rowe inclosed to me, I please myself with the hopes that in a few Years you will be much before me both in Greek and Latin; and that reading books in those Languages will be one of your favorite Pleasures, I hope reading will not make you neglect Exercise, nor Sports in the Field, take off your thoughts from Books, but that useing both those pleasures in a proper degree & giveing a due proportion of your time to each, you will enjoy both with a higher relish. May you long enjoy those innocent usefull and healthfull Amusements; and may you never want that greatest truest Pleasure which attends a Conscience void of Offence towards God & Man. Nil Conscire sibi, nulla pallesceri Culpa.[69]

The Poem you desire, Hobbinol,[70] is too big for the Post, but when opportunity serves, you shall have it but you will find it no way equal to the Chace. When there is a ship, I will send some Arrack,[71] but now the Cold weather is gone I suppose you don't much want it.

---

[64] The ministry headed by Robert Harley (1661–1724), 1st earl of Oxford and Earl Mortimer. Harley was imprisoned for two years at the beginning of George I's reign, for treason – for his part in the Treaty of Utrecht (1713) with France.

[65] Sir William Wyndham (?1688–1740), 3rd bt; MP for Somerset 1710–40. A leading jacobite and faithful follower of Bolingbroke. However, he was 'the one statesman who had enjoyed the trust of both opposition whigs and many tories', and his death led to schism between these factions, most noticeable in the voting debacle over Sandys' motion to remove Walpole. C. Gerrard, *The Patriot Opposition to Walpole: Politics, Poetry, and National Myth, 1725–42* (Oxford, 1994), 43.

[66] *CJ*, xxx, 474–5; *PH*, xi, 315, states that this motion was passed after several hours' debate.

[67] Not extant.

[68] Hugh Hume Campbell (1708–94), Lord Polwarth, opposition MP for Berwick-on-Tweed 1734–40, until his accession to the peerage on the death of his father, Lord Marchmont. However, Lord Ilay who controlled the election of the representation of Scottish peers excluded him from the upper House. *HPC, 1715–54*, ii, 160.

[69] Horace, *Epistles*, i, 61: 'To be conscious of no fault, to turn pale at no accusation'.

[70] *Hobbinol or the Rural Games, a Burlesque Poem* by William Somerville (1740).

[71] A spirituous liquor, of south and east Asian origin, distilled from the fermented sap of the coco palm. *OED*.

The inclosed Petition [not extant] from the Thames is I think a good piece of humor, but I dislike the latter end, for by the Supreme Court of Judicature the Author must mean Heaven which ought never to be mention'd in a ludicrous way, but allways with Awe and Reverence.

I had a letter last Post from your Uncle Morris[72] who mentions you very kindly. I should have your Mama's Love to send you but she is gone out & don't know of my writeing. Give my Love & Blessing to your Dear little Apprentice and my kind service to Mr. Rowe.

My Dearest I pray God . . .

I am glad to hear your Gentleman Val is recover'd. Remember me to him & to your Friend Adam, Johnny my Jewel &c.

The Laird[73] is here and sends his Compliments to you. He has some thoughts of makeing you a Visit before he goes to Scotland.

16.

John Campbell to Pryse Campbell, 11 March 1740

It is a great pleasure to me to hear that you & your dear little Apprentice are so well; by a letter I had from Dr. Cuninghame last Post, I have the Comfort to find that he thinks the little appearance upon the Corner of your right eye, of no Consequence, and hopes your eyes will soon be so strong as not to be liable to such things, Wee cannot expect a weakness in any part to go off at once, some time must be allow'd, I bless God it is so well, and earnestly pray for your continuance in perfect health in every respect.

I dined abroad & did not come home till after nine so have very little time to write. A master of a ship from Jamaica has brought News of Admiral Vernon[74] have taken Porto Bello & twelve ships (I suppose empty) in the Harbour but this wants confirmation. I really believe it is at present no more than a ghess. I send you inclosed a Paper which I think is very well writ, there is only one paragraph of Party abuse in it, which I have mark'd at the beginning and end, it seems only cram'd in because it must be a party Paper.

Your Mama joyns in Love & Blessing to you & Trub. Wee are very glad to hear he is become so gallant a Horseman as to ride alone.

Give my kind service to Mr. Rowe

Remember me most kindly to our Dear Faithfull Gil Blas. Remember me kindly to R[oger] & F[rancis] Evans and give the inclosed to the Latter. I received it to day at the Admiralty.

My Dearest, I pray God . . .

---

[72] Edmund Morris, tory MP for Leicestershire 1722–7, who married Anne, Campbell's sister, in 1720.

[73] Probably Sir Archibald Campbell, brother of Alexander, John Campbell's father. CRO, FJ/13: Cawdor pedigree.

[74] Edward Vernon (1684–1757), opposition MP for Portsmouth 1741 and Ipswich 1741–57. As Admiral Vernon he captured Porto Bello, Panama, from the Spanish during the War of Jenkins' Ear (1739–42), which made him a national hero. Lord Egmont said Vernon was 'a remarkable brave man, sober well experienced, and zealous for the honour and interest of his country', cited in *HPC, 1715–54*, ii, 498. The Spanish offered no defence and continued to use the port after the British had left, so the victory 'was nugatory'. R. Browning, *The War of the Austrian Succession* (Stroud, 1994), 29. He was disliked by Campbell, partly because of the cult of Vernon which established itself after Porto Bello. See K. Wilson, *The Sense of the People: Politics, Culture and Imperialism in England, 1715–1785* (Cambridge, 1998), ch. 3.

17.

John Campbell to Pryse Campbell, 13 March 1740

This Evening a letter came from Admiral Vernon, with account of his haveing Taken Porto bello, & three Spanish men of War in that Harbour, he has destroy'd all the Fortifications of that Place, render'd useless above 80 Iron Cannon, and brought away 50 brass Cannon, 4 brass Mortars, 18 brass Paterero's and all their shot & Ammunition, the Admiral says he made the terror of our Cannon be felt at Panama & by that means engaged the President there to send him all the South Sea Company's Factors & Servants who had been imprison'd there, and are now on board Mr. Vernons Ships. The Admirals letter which is now before me is dated on board the Burford at Sea 18 of December 1739 & he says he sent it by one of the Spanish Prizes. The first attack was on the Castle call'd the Iron Castle which surrender'd at discretion after some resistance in which Wee had only 7 seamen & 3 soldiers killed & 10 sailors wounded. This was on the 21 of November the next day he was prepareing to attack the Castle called Gloria Castle but was happily prevented by their hanging out a white flag & that afternoon they surrender'd upon Capitulation.

The last Bell rings I have only time to add my Love to dear Trub and my earnest prayers to God for your health & happyness . . .

18.

John Campbell to Pryse Campbell, 18 March 1740

I was greatly rejoyced to see your hand, by which I knew that your dear eyes were well, I bless God for it, and pray for the continuance, and that I may soon have the happyness to see you at Stackpole, perfectly well in every respect. I am very glad Dear Trub is so well & so good but am affraid he should rather disturb your studies, than profit much by his own, while he is so very Young.

Inclosed is the Copy of a Paper Dick Lloyd[75] shew'd me to day, which he said he had from the Customhouse, it appears by that, the St. Joseph is a richer Prize than Wee thought she was. Some of the Patriots[76] lately put into the London Evening Post[77] a very florid Funeral Oration upon the late Earl of Marchmont,[78] it was chiefly intended to Compliment his son the present Earl, whom I lately mention'd by the name of Lord Polwarth. It apply's to the Old Earl and his two sons the following lines out of Virgil Aeniad 9

Di patri, quorum semper sub Numine Troja est,
Non tamen omnino Tecros delere paratis,
Cum tales animos jurenum, & tam certa tulistis Pectora.

[75] Richard Lloyd (c.1703–57), of Mabws, Cardiganshire; MP for Cardigan boroughs 1730–47.

[76] The patriots were a group of whigs headed by William Pulteney who, in 1725, formed an opposition to Walpole, believing he had too much power. In 1726 Pulteney, together with Lord Bolingbroke, established a patriots' journal, the *Craftsman*, which was used to attack Walpole and his supporters outside parliament.

[77] 6 Mar. 1740.

[78] Alexander Hume-Campbell (1657–1740), 2nd earl of Marchmont. His son, the 3rd earl, was Hugh Hume-Campbell (1708–94), Lord Polwarth.

Sic memorans, humeros dextrasque tenebat
Amborum, & vultum lacrymis atque ora rigabat[79]

Mr. Pitt[80] is by some said to be author of that Oration, and the Common sense[81] I sent you is given to Lord Chesterfield. This day both Houses waited on the King with an Address to congratulate him on the success at Porto Bello.

Your Mama joyns in Love & Blessing to You & Trubshaw. My Dearest I pray God . . . My kind service to Mr. Rowe. Remember me kindly to all Friends.

I don't know why you call me C. Calpurnius Piso[82] but any name my Dearest gives me, pleases me. Your Brother & Sisters were well yesterday.

19.

John Campbell to Pryse Campbell [undated]

I was very glad to here your eyes were so well as to be going a hunting, though the hearing that, gives me some anxiety, after all this wet weather; however I will trouble you no farther with my fears, than to repete my most earnest entreaty that you will be carefull of your self, and not be heedless.

My Dearest forgive me that I cannot help wishing that you, your Brother, Mr. Rowe and Johnny were at Wimbledon; when you were there, I could hear from you every day, and pleased myself all the Week, with the hope of spending Saturday and Sunday with you.

I and your Mama went to Court at Kensington to day, there was not much Company, very few Ladys, all the news I learn'd there is, that the King & all his Family look'd very well, Sir Robert [Walpole] & the Duke of Newcastle[83] are both well again and were there. A Councill was held to order a Proclamation for the Parliament to sit

---

[79] Lines 247–51. Translated and published in 1740 by Christopher Pitt as:

Ev'n yet, ye guardian gods, your pow'rs divine
Will spare the relics of the Trojan line,
Since you the bosoms of our youths inspire
With such high courage, such determin'd fire.
Then in his arms the boys by turns he took
With tears of joy;

[80] William Pitt the Elder (1708–78), of Hayes, Kent; MP for Old Sarum 1735–47, Seaford 1747–54, Aldborough 1754–6, Buckingham 1756, Oakhampton 1756–7 and Bath 1757–66. Groom of the bedchamber to the prince of Wales 1737–45; joint vice-treasurer 1746; paymaster-general 1746–55; secretary of state, southern department 1756–7 and 1757–61; lord privy seal 1766–8. One of Cobham's cubs, an antagonistic speaker who never ascended to the position of first minister, though he gave his name as earl of Chatham (created 1766) to the 1766–8 ministry and was, effectively, its leader. Pitt was disliked intensely by Campbell.

[81] *Commonsense or the Englishman's Journal* was an opposition journal first published 1 Feb. 1737. It was a successor to the earlier *Craftsman*. The key authors of *Commonsense* were Lord Chesterfield and William Lyttelton. Gerrard, *Patriot Opposition to Walpole*, 42.

[82] *London Magazine* appendix, 14 Nov. 1739, contained several speeches including that of 'Calpurnius Piso' (that is, Campbell) upon the question of whether an address should be presented to his majesty for the late convention with Spain. The historical Calpurnius Piso was a Roman senator in the 1st century AD. He was the focal figure in the Pisonian conspiracy of 65 AD, the most famous and wide-ranging plot against the throne of Emperor Nero.

[83] Thomas Pelham-Holles (1693–1768), 1st duke of Newcastle-upon-Tyne (3rd creation). A protégé of Walpole, who served as secretary of state of the southern department 1724–48, secretary of state for the northern department 1748–54 and first lord of the treasury 1754–62, on the death of his brother, Henry Pelham (see Chapter 2, Note 12). Newcastle and Pelham were dominant whig forces in the two Houses, though they often argued about policy.

the 15th of November. I saw the french Ambassador[84] there, he has been made Knight of the Holy Ghost[85] while he was in France, it is a blue water'd Ribbon paler than our own Garter,[86] & wore upon the right Shoulder, as our Bath Ribbons are; I did not see the King speak to him.

Your Mama gives her Love to you and Jack. She is very glad your eye is so well, & will be glad to hear from you when it suits your convenience. My Love to Trubshaw. Remember me most kindly to our Dear Faithfull Johnny. Remember me to R[oger] Evans and to Wil Thomas, Val, Adam, Johnny my Jewel &c.

My Dearest Boy I pray God . . .

Di charum servate Caput.[87]

20.

John Campbell to Pryse Campbell, 27 March 1740

I send you herewith inclosed a Plan of the Harbor &c of Porto Bello which was publish'd this day, I will have one framed but I was resolved to send this by the quickest conveyance, because I thought it would be a pleasure to you to see it soon.

I Bless God for your Good health & most earnestly pray it may continue, and that Wee may soon have the pleasure of a happy meeting at Stackpole, and that I may have the joy to see you perfectly well and your eyes clear & strong. I yet hope I may see you the latter end of April. My Love & Blessing to Dear Trub and my kind service to Mr. Rowe. I Pray God . . .

21.

John Campbell to Pryse Campbell, 29 March 1740

This is cheifly to tell you that Jacks Godfather[88] will in a short time be declared Lord privy Seal, which I am very glad of for I have known him and had a Friendship for him above twenty years. He has great abilitys, and great knowledge and I believe him a very honest Man. I don't yet know who succedes him in his present Employment.

My Dearest I long very much to see you, I hope I shall before may day. God grant us a happy meeting. Give my kind service to Mr. Rowe and my Love to Dear Trub. I pray God . . .

22.

John Campbell to Pryse Campbell, 3 April 1740

I thank you kindly for your letter and the Latin inclosed with it. I am allways rejoyced when I see your hand upon a letter, because then I know your dear eyes are well; but I don't mean to trouble you to write often because your Book and writing your Latin Exercise takes up your time, and when those employments are over, I would not confine you from your diversions so a letter now and then contents me very well.

---

[84] Jacques François, Count de Cambis or his successor.

[85] The order of the holy spirit which was established in 1578. The order's symbol is a Maltese cross hung from a blue ribbon, the knights of the order becoming known as 'les cordon bleus'.

[86] The most noble order of the garter, the highest order of knighthood in England, was founded in 1348.

[87] 'Oh Gods, preserve the esteemed head.'

[88] John Hervey, 2nd Lord Hervey. He was made lord privy seal in Apr. 1740 and dismissed in July 1742.

Upon your telling me I had the name of C. Calpurnius Piso from the Appendix to the London Magazine[89] I bought that Pamphlet, & there I found a speech under that name, but indeed my Dear they have mended it so much, that I can by no means call it mine, I can only acknowledge one sentence viz: nothing can be honorable that is not just, and no War can be just that is not necessary.[90] This they have transposed, and introduced it in a very different manner from what I did, for I was not so sanguine in my expectations of the Spaniards doing us justice as C. Calpurnius Piso seems to be.

I fear the account I sent you of the Cargo of the St. Joseph was too high, though Dick Lloyd said it was given him as authentic at the Custom house, but I have since heard a much lower account. Wee now hear that the story of five Coasters being taken by a Spanish Privateer in the Channel was a lye formed by some pressed sailors that escaped in a Boat from a Tender. I wish it may prove so, but however I believe at worst the five will prove but two.

Sir Charles Wager[91] has had a Cold, & not come out of his own lodgings for a week, but has not been dangerously ill as said in the Papers. Wee see him & indeed he sees every body else for several days past.

Wee have expected every day to hear of the King of Prussia's death,[92] which would put our Court in deep mourning,[93] but they would lay it aside for some days to be fine at the Princess Mary's Wedding[94] which is to be very soon after the Parliament rises, Mouse has bought a gay Gown for it but I shall escape.

I am obliged to your Uncle & Aunt Philipps[95] for their visit to you, but I hope you did not think of rideing after your Uncles Fox hounds. I am glad to hear Johnnys spod is a jolly Boy. I wish he may be like his Father & live to enjoy your Friendship. I Bless God that you & your Brother have so good health. Give my Love to dear Trub.

I pray God preserve you many Years in Virtue, health and Peace, that you may be a Blessing to all your Relation's and dependants, and God grant you may be happy in

---

[89] *London Magazine*, appendix, 14 Nov. 1739.

[90] Inaccurate reporting of debates and speeches from parliament was one of the reasons – another being attempts to keep debates a secret – why a standing order to prohibit reporting was issued each session. P.D.G. Thomas, 'The Beginnings of Parliamentary Reporting in Newspapers', *EHR*, lxxiv (1959), 623–36; J. Black, 'Archive Sources of the Parliamentary History of Britain in the 1740s', *Archives*, xix (1991), 404–22.

[91] Sir Charles Wager (c.1666–1743), MP for Westminster 1734–41 and West Looe 1741–3. Lord of the admiralty 1718–33 and first lord of the admiralty 1733–42, though he had been de facto first lord during Lord Torrington's spell in that office (1727–33). Wager was a career naval officer and was appointed an admiral in 1731 and vice admiral of Great Britain in 1742.

[92] Frederick William I of Prussia (1687–1740) died on 31 May.

[93] Frederick was married to Sophia Dorothea of Hanover (1687–1757), George II's younger sister, hence the reason for the court to go into mourning.

[94] The Princess Mary (1723–72), daughter of George II, was married to Prince Frederick Hesse-Kassel (1720–85), first by proxy in London (8 May 1740), and then in person in Kassel (28 June 1740).

[95] James Philipps (c.1709–94), of Pentyparc, Pembrokeshire. He married Jane, the daughter and co-heiress of the jacobite Lewis Pryse of Gogerddan, Cardiganshire, and was thus the brother-in law of John Campbell. High sheriff of Pembrokeshire 1734 and 1787. In the early 1740s Philipps actively promoted Sir John Philipps' (see Chapter 2, Note 79) tory interests in Carmarthen boroughs, which led to a tory stranglehold of that borough which lasted for the rest of the century. He was an avid fox hunter, hence Campbell's comments.

them, and see your Children and their Children such as may give true Comfort & satisfaction to a Wise & Good Man. I am, My Dearest Boy spes & solatia Nostra.[96]

My kind service to Mr. Rowe & many thanks for his letters, which are very agreable to me. Wee have a very dry East wind, but not at all windy weather & the sunshines all day yet the air has not the softness to be pleasant & 'tis dusty.

23.
John Campbell to Pryse Campbell, 12 April 1740
I thank you very kindly for the great desire you express to meet me at Stepaside,[97] but my Dearest my time will be very uncertain, and I should be very sorry to disappoint you, and though I could be sure of the day, Wee can't be so sure of the hour, and if you should come there before me, it is not a good Place for you to wait in especially if the Weather is not better than as yet Wee have reason to expect. I assure you my Dearest I long to see you as much as I can long for anything, but I prefer your safety to everything in this World, so I would have you consider of it and consult with your Friend Johnny.

I hear the Parliament will be up on tuesday sevenight and I do not intend to stay here two days after, but as I have not been on horseback since I came to Town in september I shall be but a poor Traveller & probably be soon tired and not able to make long stages, but the hopes of seeing you in perfect health will make my journey pleasant.

> Incolumen Pallanta mihi, si Fata reservant;
> Si visurus eum vivo, et venturus in unam:
> Patior quemvis durare laborem.[98]

I sent to the Carrier this morning a Box in which was the last Edition of Severinus[99] your Almanach from the Admiralty, a Box of Rhubarb & a bottle of the same in Powder, a small Horace[100] printed at Dublin, and Knee & Garter Buckles for Trub. Your Garter Buckles I could not get time enough, and a Bottle of Hartshorn drops. Give my Love & Blessing to your dear little Apprentice. Remember me most kindly to our dear Faithfull Gil Blas, tell him for the future to write to your Mama but directed to me, till I come home, I may perhaps stay here long enough to receive an Answer to letters I write to Night but I am not sure, for I long to begin my journey to my Dearest. I pray God . . .

[96] Virgil, *Aeneid*, viii, 514: 'our hope and consolation'.

[97] In south Pembrokeshire.

[98] Virgil, *Aeneid*, viii, 575–7. Translated by Christopher Pitt (1740) as:
    With due regard, a king's and father's pray'r!
    My dear, dear Pallas, if the fates ordain
    Safe to return, and bless these eyes again.

[99] Probably Anicius Manlius Severinus Boethius (480–524 AD), Roman philosopher. He wrote treaties on music and mathematics and *De Consolatione Philosophiae/The Consolation of Philosophy*, a dialogue in prose.

[100] This could be *The Third Ode of the Third Book of Horace, Imitated: On Occasion of the French Fortifying Dunkirk*, which was printed in Dublin in 1740.

I am glad your Friend Adam is like to find Benefit by Dr. Cuninghames Prescriptions. I believe the Embargo[101] will be taken off on Monday, a General Councill being to be call'd that day on purpose to determine it.

24.

John Campbell to Pryse Campbell, 26 April 1740

I was very glad to hear by Johnnys letter to your Mama that you & your dear little Apprentice were in good health, I was sorry poor Johnny had a little sore throat. I hope he took Care of himself & got soon rid of it. This morning I drew my Tooth it was very large with vast spreading Fangs, I should have drawn it yesterday, but was obliged to go to the Admiralty at eleven in the forenoon, and staid there till three, in order to get Lieutenant Holcombe[102] made a Captain which at last I effected. I must take care to keep from Cold, till it is quite heald. Wee have yet Winter weather excessive cold, Northerly Winds, & this morning Wee had rain hail and snow.

About noon I had a letter from the Admiralty with account that the Lenox, Kent, and Orford have taken a Spanish Man of War of 68 Guns and 700 men after an Engagement of seven hours, which was very gallant in the Spaniard, for ours are 70 Gun ships all three. The Ships are expected every hour at Spithead. This account was brought by the Seahorse who fell in Company with them after they had taken the Prize.

I forgot whether I sent you word that I have made Mr. Vaughan of Trecoons[103] Brother[104] a Lieutenant. I doubt whether Captain Bishop knows that he could not be made a Lieutenant without passing an Examination at the Navy Office.[105]

Your Mama sends her Love & Blessing to you. Bessy came here to day very well and left Ally so, your Uncle & Aunt Morris are just gone, they desire me to give their Love to you. I hope next Post to give you account of my journey. Remember me most kindly to our Dear Faithfull Gil Blas. Give my Love & Blessing to Dear Trub. I pray God . . .

25.

John Campbell to Pryse Campbell, 1 May 1740

I was troubled to hear that you & your Brother had Colds, but Johnnys letter to your Mama says you were both well, I pray God I may find you in perfect health. I am vex'd at being so long in Town, several things have hinder'd me, but indeed if nothing else had, I could not have ventured to travel in such Cold weather till my mouth was pretty well heal'd after drawing that great Tooth, I hope nothing will hinder me leaveing this Town on Saturday, but I can't name a day for being with you, that I must write from the road.

---

[101] An embargo on all shipping except coasters had been in place since 1 Feb. 1740, by order of the lords of the admiralty. A petition from merchants, shipowners and others concerned in trade asking for increased protection from the navy had been rejected in the Commons by 166 to 95. The embargo was lifted on 14 Apr. after merchants agreed to furnish one in four of their crews for navy service. *PH*, xi, 579–82.

[102] Essex Holcombe (*d.* 1770) was appointed captain of the *Winchester* frigate in Oct. 1740. He retired in 1755 at the rank of rear admiral. Charnock, *Biographia Navalis*, v, 42–3.

[103] Erasmus Vaughan of Trecwn, Pembrokeshire.

[104] Possibly John Vaughan who was made a lieutenant on 17 Apr. 1740. *Court Kalendar* (1744), 139.

[105] Samuel Pepys had introduced an examination for prospective lieutenants in 1677.

Your Uncle & Aunt Morris are gone to day to the Wedding of Lord Noel
Somerset & Miss Berkley.[106] Last Night the Duke of Argyll was dismiss'd from all his
Employments. It is said there are to be three Camps this summer, the Command of the
greatest was offer'd to his Grace but he declined it unless he had the chief Command
of the whole Army.[107] The Princess is to be contracted on Wednesday next, very soon
after, the King goes abroad,[108] I suppose she will go with him; His Majesty's journey
surprises us, for it was not spoke of but within these very few days.

Remember me most kindly to our dear Faithfull Johnny & tell him I have sent the
Protection to Owen Davis. Mr. Early has received his salary and paid it me, according
to the inclos'd Note.[109] Give my Love and Blessing to Dear Trub. I pray God . . . My
Dearest Angel I long to see you, God grant us all a happy meeting . . .

My kind service to Mr. Rowe & remember me to all Friends.

There is a great deal of Ship News in the Papers that I fear has little foundation.

[106] Lord Charles Noel Somerset (1709–56), tory MP for Monmouthshire 1731–4 and Monmouth 1734–45.
He was made the 4th duke of Beaufort in 1745. He married Elisabeth Berkley, daughter of John Sims Berkley
of Stoke Gifford, Gloucestershire.

[107] However Argyll became commander-in-chief of the British army in 1742, only to die a year later.

[108] George II left Britain for Hanover, for several months, in most years of his reign.

[109] Not extant.

Chapter 2. 1741–2

All the letters in this chapter are from CRO, Cawdor/Campbell box 128.

26.

John Campbell to Pryse Campbell, 8 January 1741

Blank News uses to fly fast, but I forgot last Post to send you the inclosed. I wish I may never send you worse news, I dare say this will not grieve you, though no doubt a good Prize would have given you some joy. I was very glad to hear you spent New Years day so pleasantly. I hope you will not be the worse for the bitter Cold weather Wee have had these three days.

Give my kind service to Mr. Rowe, and thank him for his letter with your Exercise inclosed, which pleased me very well, and the writeing was better than the last. Remember me most kindly to Johnny and give him the Protection.

My Love to Dear Trub and Ally. I made my Compliments to Dab in your Mama's letter. Your Joyner Tools will be sent next week to Bristol to go from thence by sea to you. I entreat you dearest to be extremely carefull not to cut or hurt yourself with anything of that sort.

27.

John Campbell to Pryse Campbell, 12 February 1741

I Bless God that you continue in so good health & spirits and I earnestly pray you may continue so many years.

You must desire your Mama to read to you the News in her letter, and then you will understand what follows viz: Sir Robert Walpole ended his short answer to Mr. Sandys with this Verse.

Nil conscire tibi, nulla pallescere culpa.[1]

but instead of nulla he said nulli. As soon as he sat down, Mr. Pulteney, who sat near him told him his mistake, but Sir Robert would have it that nulli was right, & laid a guinea upon it, which I saw him pay to Mr. Pulteney, for he was convinced he had lost.

Give my Love to Dear Trub & Ally. I am very glad they are so well, My Dearest I have not leisure to add more but pray God to preserve you to a good old age . . .

28.

John Campbell to Mary Campbell, 13 February 1741

The House of Commons being very full Mr Sandys at one a Clock rose up to speak & concluded with the following Motion, which was seconded by Lord Limerick[2] That an

---

[1] Horace, *Epistles*, i, l. 61: 'To be conscious of no guilt, to turn pale at no blame'.

[2] James Hamilton (c.1691–1758), 1st Viscount Limerick (Irish peerage); opposition MP for Wendover 1727–34 and 1735–41, Tavistock 1742–7 and Morpeth 1747–54. Horace Walpole described him as 'a pale ill-looking fellow with a bent brow, a whoreson voice and a dead eye of saffron hue . . . belonging to Lord Bath', cited in *HPC, 1715–54*, ii, 101.

humble Address be presented to desire His Majestie will be graciously pleased to remove the Right Honorable Sir Robert Walpole Knight of the most noble Order of the Garter, first Commissioner for exercising the Office of Treasurer of the Exchequer Chancellor & under the Treasurer of the Exchequer and one of his Majesties most honorable Privy Councill, from his Majesties Councill & Presence for ever.

Mr Sandys in his speech complain'd of the great Load of Tax's & Debts, the Nation being in War with Spain, near a War with France & no Ally appearing to help us, this state of Affairs was said to owing to the Treaty of Hanover[3] & several subsequent Treatys, the Debts being so great owing to the Sinking Fund being applied to the service of the year, and he complain'd the War was not carried on with Vigor Supplys being sent too Slowly to Admiral Vernon, & Sir John Norris[4] not having Sail'd at all, and all these grievances were to be charged on Sir R[obert] W[alpole] who had been Prime Minister or as many call'd it sole Minister for 20 Years. Mr Wortley Montague[5] on Mr Doddington[6] who was ill & but just come into the House rising to speak stop'd him to move that Sir R[obert] might withdraw immediately which he said was necessary, and that by Order none could speak till he was withdrawn, he was Seconded by Mr Gybbon[7] who call'd for Journals & read Several Precedents, but unluckily those two Gentlemen could not find a third in the House who thought their Precedents in point to the present Case & it was agreed on all hands that the Charge & Evidence being to arise from the speeches of the Members who supported the Question, it was just and necessary for Sir R[obert] to hear the whole debate, so they gave up their Motion & the Debate went on, but Mr Dodington was too ill to stay while this journal Learning was display'd & withdrew in the mean time. Upon the whole I can safely & impartially say, I never saw a Question of importance so ill maintain'd, it was certainly the weakest the most extravagant, & unjust, motion I ever heard, toward the latter end of the Debate Lord Cornbury[8] got up & said he did not rise to debate only in a few words, to justifie the Vote he was to give, he said he thought Affairs in a very bad State, he disliked the Measures had been taken perhaps he strongly suspected that Gentleman was to blame,

[3] Of 1725 between Britain and France. It was a response to the Treaty of Vienna, between Austria and Spain, also of 1725.

[4] Sir John Norris (c.1670–1749), MP for Rye 1708–22 and 1734–49 and Portsmouth 1722–34. He joined the navy at the age of ten, and was made an admiral in 1709. He was one of the lords of the admiralty 1718–30 and admiral of the fleet and commander-in-chief 1734–49. In 1741 he offered to fight Pulteney in the Commons when the latter said the fleet had done nothing in the war.

[5] Edward Wortley Montagu (1678–1761), of Wortley, Yorkshire; opposition MP for Huntingdon 1705–13 and 1722–34, Westminster 1715–22 and Peterborough 1734–61. He was the son of the writer, aristocrat and eccentric, Lady Mary Wortley Montagu. They were painted together by the Flemish-French artist Jean Baptiste van Mour (1671–1737).

[6] George Bubb Dodington (1691–1762), MP for Winchelsea 1715–22, Bridgwater 1722–54 and Weymouth and Melcombe Regis 1754–61. Initially he supported Walpole, who had made him a lord of the treasury in 1724, but by 1727 he had become one of Walpole's enemies. In 1760 he commented that during Walpole's administration 'the interest of the House of Walpole, not of England, was the centre of action'. J. Carswell and L.A. Dralle, *The Political Journal of George Bubb Dodington* (Oxford, 1965), 390.

[7] Phillips Gybbon (1678–1762), of Hole Park, Kent; whig MP for Rye 1707–62. He was a commissioner of revenue 1714–26; chairman of committee of privileges and elections 1722–7; surveyor-general 1726–30; lord of the treasury 1742–4. He was a supporter of Walpole's administration.

[8] Henry Hyde (1710–53), Viscount Cornbury; MP for Oxford University 1732–51. Until 1735 he supported the jacobites, but in that year severed his connections with the Pretender. He died of a fall from his horse whilst in Paris.

he should be willing to go into any proper enquiry, and should at the end of it be ready to censure any who should appear to deserve it, but his Conscience would not permit him to pass such a Censure upon any Man without Evidence & therefore he must give his Negative. Mr Southwell, Mr Bowes & Mr Ed[ward] Harley[9] spoke much to the same effect, only Mr Harley said he would not Vote, & Mr Bowes did not express his dislike of the Measures &c so strongly. Mr Pulteney was the last that spoke & was unwilling either to rise or to declare he would not speak but being strongly urged either to say he would not speak or to speak before Sir R[obert] who by Mr P[ulteney]'s own confession, in the beginning of the Debate, ought to hear the whole of his charge, Mr P[ulteney] at last got up vex'd & confused, spoke some time said some hard things & threw out some new and odious but unsupported charges, and indeed did not Speak with anything of his usual spirit & force. Sir R[obert] . . . rose & spoke a little more than an hour . . . after such an attendance he could not be . . . & I think did not speak so well as . . .[10] would if he had not been so fatigued, for when he ended, it wanted but a quarter of three in the morning, so the Debate had lasted very near fourteen hours.[11] Mr Pelham[12] Spoke the best against the Question he had indeed such a strength & clearness of reason such a Dignity such appearance of Integrity as cannot easily be described, he expressed his Friendship for Sir Robert [Walpole] in such a Manner as did honor to them both, he spoke with warmth, but such a warmth as added to the grace & dignity of his manner and expression, Friendship, Justice, & Courage seem'd to appear in their noblest & most amiable Forms. The Attorney General[13] Spoke indeed very handsomely & very sensibly, Henry Fox[14] charmingly.

When Sir R[obert] had done Speaking he went behind the Chair & throw [*sic*] the speakers private room to his son Lord Walpole's[15] House & the Question was immediately put a very Faint Ay & a loud No. I think the loudest I ever heard. Mr Lyttelton[16]

---

[9] Edward Southwall (1705–54), of King's Weston, Bristol; MP for Bristol 1739–54; George Bowes (1701–60), of Stretham Castle, County Durham; whig MP for Co. Durham 1727–60; Edward Harley (?1699–1755), of Eywood, Herefordshire; MP for Herefordshire 1727–41.

[10] Part of the letter is missing.

[11] William Cobbett, *Cobbett's Parliamentary History* (36 vols, 1806–20), xi, 1388, states that the debate began on 13 February at 11 a.m. and continued until 4.30 the following morning.

[12] Henry Pelham (1695–1754), brother to the duke of Newcastle; MP for Seaford 1717–22 and Lewes 1722–54; treasurer of the chamber 1720–2; lord of the treasury 1721–4; secretary at war 1724–30; privy councillor 1725; paymaster-general 1730–43; first lord of the treasury 1743–54; chancellor of the exchequer 1743–54. Pelham created the so-called broad-bottomed administration after Walpole's fall, though it contained a majority of old and new whigs.

[13] Dudley Ryder (1691–1756), of Tooting, Surrey; MP for St Germans 1733–4 and Tiverton 1734–54; attorney-general 1737–54. Robert Walpole thought highly of him as did Horace Walpole who said he was a man 'of singular goodness and integrity'; cited in *HPC, 1715–54*, ii, 398.

[14] Henry Fox (1705–74). See Introduction.

[15] Robert Walpole (1701–51), eldest son of Sir Robert Walpole who, in 1723, eschewed a peerage for himself in favour of his son who became known as Lord Walpole, until 1745 when he succeeded his father as 2nd earl of Orford. He was auditor of the exchequer 1739–51.

[16] George Lyttelton (1709–73), MP for Oakhampton 1735–56. One of Lord Cobham's cubs, Lyttelton was appointed the prince of Wales' secretary 1737–44; lord of the treasury 1744–54; chancellor of the exchequer 1755–6. Created 1st Baron Lyttelton in 1756. He was a writer and poet as well as a promoter of both Alexander Pope and of Fielding's *Tom Jones*. Lyttelton was satirised in Smollett's *Peregrine Pickle* as Sir Gosling Scragg, a character with little in the way of intelligence and 'the best milch-cow that any author ever stroaked', Oxford World Classics edition (1751), 659. He was also ridiculed by Lord Hervey and Horace Walpole because of his ungainly appearance and general awkwardness.

divided the House, & the Noes being affraid the Ay's should yeild without telling creid out strongly withdraw, withdraw so they went out & the House was told Yea's 106 Tellers Lord Limerick, Sir John Bernard[17] No's 290 Tellers Mr Pelham, Mr How.[18]

List (I believe not complete)[19] of such Gentlemen who used to be constant in the Opposition & staid to the end of the Debate, or very Near it, & did not vote for the Question.

Voted against it
Lord Cornbury
S[i]r H[enry] Pakington
Mr Mansell
Mr Rolle
Alderman Perry
Alderman Marshall
Mr Mackworth
Mr Prade
Dr Cotes
Mr Rutherford
Mr Bowes
Mr Southwell
Mr Ch[arles] Gore
Mr T[homas] Gore
Mr Packer
Mr Banks
S[i]r William Heathcote
Mr William Moore
Mr Cartwright
Mr Whichcot
Mr Viner
Mr J[ames] Noel
Mr H [*sic*] Noel[20]

---

[17] Sir John Barnard (c.1685–1764), MP for London 1722–61. Opposed Walpole's excise bill, and generally voted against the government. After Walpole's demise Barnard allied himself more with the government, though he remained independent.

[18] John Howe (c.1690–1742), of Stowell, Gloucestershire and Great Wishford, Wiltshire; MP for Gloucester 1727 and Wiltshire 1729–41. Initially a tory, by 1735 he had become a warm supporter of Walpole.

[19] *British Parliamentary Lists 1660–1800*, ed. G.M. Ditchfield, D. Hayton and C. Jones (1995), 51; *PH*, xi, 1226, citing W. Coxe, *Memoirs of Horatio, Lord Walpole* (2 vols, 1808), does not include Praed, Cotes or Packer, listed by Campbell but does include Coningsby Sibthorp, Lord William Manners, George Compton, Sir G. Oxenden and P. and H. Mackworth, none of whom are listed by Campbell.

[20] Sir Henry Perrott Pakington (c.1701–48), 5th bt, of Westwood, Droitwich; MP for Worcestershire 1727–41; Bussy Mansell (?1701–50), of Briton Ferry, Glamorgan; MP for Cardiff boroughs 1727–34 and Glamorgan 1737–44; Micajah Perry (d. 1753), of St Mary Axe, London and Epsom, Surrey; MP for London 1727–41; Henry Marshall (1688–1754), of St Mary at Hill, London, and Theddlethorp, Lincolnshire; MP for Amersham 1734–54; Herbert Mackworth (1687–1765), of Gnoll, Glamorgan; MP for Cardiff boroughs 1739–65; William Mackworth Praed (1694–1752), of Trevethoe, Cornwall; MP for St Ives 1734–41; Charles Cotes (?1703–48), of Lichfield, Staffordshire; MP for Tamworth 1735–41 and 1742–7; physician for Westminster Hospital 1733–9; John Rutherford (1712–58), of Edgerston, Roxburgh; MP for Roxburghshire 1734–42; Charles Gore (?1711–68), of Tring, Hertfordshire; MP for Cricklade 1739–41, Hertfordshire

Withdrew to avoid voteing
Mr Shippen
Lord Guernsey
Mr Digby
Mr E[dward] Harley
Mr R[obert] Harley
Mr Lechmere
Mr Taylor
S[i]r Edmund Bacon
S[i]r Harry Northcote
S[i]r William Courtney
Mr Hilton
Mr George Vernon
S[i]r Charles Mordaunt
S[i]r James Dashwood
Mr Noel
Mr Brown   } Counsellors at Law
Mr Fenwick
Lord Gage
S[i]r William Irby
Mr Charles Stanhope
Lord Carnarvon
S[i]r Nathaniel Curzon
Mr Curzon
Lord Baltimore
Mr Prowse
Mr Charles Pelham of Lincolnshire
Mr Evelyn
Sir Hugh Smithson
Lord Arch[ibald] Hamilton[21]

[20] (*continued*) 1741–61 and Tiverton 1762–8; Thomas Gore (?1694–1777), of the Inner Temple, London and Dunstan Park, Berkshire; MP for Cricklade 1722–7 and 1754–68, Amersham 1735–46, Portsmouth 1746–7 and Bedford 1747–54; Wichcombe Howard Packer (1702–46), of Donnington and Shellingford, Berkshire; MP for Berkshire 1731–46; John Bankes (c.1691–1772), of Kingston Lacy, Dorset; MP for Corfe Castle 1722–41; Sir William Heathcote (1693–1751), of Hursley, Hampshire; MP for Buckingham 1722–7 and Southampton 1729–41; William Moore (1699–1746), of Polesden Lacey, Surrey; MP for Banbury 1740–6; Thomas Cartwright (1671–1748), of Aynho, Northamptonshire; MP for Northamptonshire 1695–8 and 1710–48; Thomas Whichcot (?1700–76), of Harpswell, Lincolnshire; MP for Lincolnshire 1740–4; Robert Vyner (c.1685–1777), of Gautby, Lincolnshire; MP for Great Grimsby 1710–13 and Lincolnshire 1724–61; James Noel (1711–52), of Exton, Rutland; MP for Rutland 1734–52; Thomas Noel (c.1704–88), of Exton, Rutland and Walcot, Northamptonshire; MP for Rutland 1728–41 and 1753–88.

[21] William Shippen (1673–1743), MP for Newton 1715–43. He was an ardent jacobite, refused to acknowledge the accession of George II and in 1729 was almost incarcerated in the Tower for an attack on the government which was published in the *Craftsman*. Heneage Finch (1715–77), Lord Guernsey; MP for Leicestershire 1739–41 and Maidstone 1741–7 and 1754–7. Succeeded his father in 1757 to become 3rd earl of Aylesford. Edward Digby (c.1693–1746), of Wandsworth, Surrey; MP for Warwickshire 1726–46; Robert Harley (?1706–74), MP for Leominster 1734–41 and 1742–7 and Droitwich 1754–74; Edmund Lechmere (1710–1805), of Hanley Castle, Worcestershire; MP for Worcestershire 1734–47; Joseph (?1693–1746) or William (c.1697–1741) Taylor (*HPC, 1715–54*, ii, 464, lists both as withdrawing). Joseph was MP for

I heard Mr Shippen call this Question a Mare's Nest[22] on Thursday in talk after the House rose.

29.

John Campbell to Pryse Campbell, 28 March 1741

I send you inclosed a Print[23] which came out yesterday, the fancy of the old Duchess of Marlborough[24] being cheif mourner pleased me, there were several Prints came out as it were in answer to the Motion.[25] If they had either Wit, or Humor in them, I should have sent them to you, but they were extremely dull. I believe my Dearest does not think me so partial not to see Wit on the other side if it is to be seen; however if you have a mind I will send or bring you those Prints.

---

[21] (*continued*) Ashburton 1739–41 and William MP for Evesham 1734–41. Sir Edmund Bacon (c.1680–1755), 6th bt, of Garboldisham, Norfolk; MP for Thetford 1710–13 and Norfolk 1713–15 and 1728–41. Pryse Campbell married Sir Edmund's third daughter and co-heiress, Sarah, in September 1752. Sir Henry Northcote (1710–43), 5th bt, of Haynes and the Pynes, Exeter, Devon; MP for Exeter 1735–43; Sir William Courtenay (1710–62), of Powderham Castle, Devon; MP for Honiton 1734–41 and Devon 1741–62; John Hylton (1699–1746), of Hylton Castle, Co. Durham; MP for Carlisle 1727–41 and 1742–6; George Venables Vernon (1710–80), of Sudbury, Derbyshire and Kinderton, Cheshire; MP for Lichfield 1731–47 and Derby 1754–62; Sir Charles Mordaunt (?1697–1778), 6th bt, of Walton D'Eiville, Warwickshire and Little Massingham, Norfolk; MP for Warwickshire 1734–74; Sir James Dashwood (1715–79), 2nd bt, of Kirtlington Park, Oxon; MP for Oxfordshire 1740–68; William Noel (1695–1762), of Bloomsbury Square, London; MP for Stamford 1722–47 and 1747–57; John Browne (1696–1750), of Forston, Charminster, Dorset and Lincoln's Inn, London; MP for Dorchester 1727–50; Robert Fenwick (1688–1750), of Burrow Hall, Lancashire; MP for Lancaster 1734–47; Thomas Gage (c.1695–1754), 1st Viscount Gage, of High Meadow, Gloucestershire; MP for Tewkesbury 1721–54; governor of Barbados 1738–9; Sir William Irby (1707–75), 2nd bt, of Whaplode, Lincolnshire; MP for Launceston 1735–47 and Bodmin 1747–61; Charles Stanhope (1673–1760), of Elvaston, Derbyshire; MP for Milbourne Port 1717–22, Aldborough 1722–34 and Harwich 1734–41; Henry Brydges (1708–71), marquess of Carnarvon; MP for Hereford 1727–34, Steyning 1734–41 and Bishop's Castle 1741–4; succeeded his elder brother as Lord Carnarvon in 1727; Sir Nathaniel Curzon (?1676–1758), of Kedleston, Derbyshire; MP for Derby 1713–15, Clitheroe 1722–7 and Derbyshire 1727–54; William Curzon (?1681–1747), of the Inner Temple; MP for Clitheroe 1734–47; Thomas Prowse (c.1707–67), of Compton Bishop, Somerset; moderate tory MP for Somerset 1740–67; Charles Pelham (c.1679–1763), of Brocklesby, Lincolnshire; MP for Great Grimsby 1722–7 and Beverley 1727–34 and 1738–54; John Evelyn (1706–67), of Wotton, Surrey; MP for Helston 1727–41 and 1747–67 and Penryn 1741–7; Sir Hugh Smithson (1715–86), 4th bt, of Stanwick, Yorkshire and Tottenham, Middlesex; MP for Middlesex 1740–50; trustee of the British Museum 1753–86; lord of the bedchamber 1753–63; vice admiral of Northumberland 1755; lord chamberlain to the queen 1762–8; vice admiral North America 1764; master of the horse 1778–80. In 1740 Smithson married Lady Elizabeth Seymour, daughter of the 7th duke of Somerset, whom he succeeded as Baron Warkworth and earl of Northumberland in 1750, taking the name Percy in lieu of Smithson. Lord Archibald Hamilton (1673–1754), of Riccarton, Linlithgow and Motherwell, Lanark; MP for Lanarkshire 1708–10 and 1718–34, Queenborough 1735–41 and Dartmouth 1742–7. Coxe, *Memoirs of Walpole*, lists both Joseph and William Taylor, Lord Quarendon, George Wrighte, Edward Smith, James Wigley, Lord John Chetwynd, Harry Waller, George Chaffin, Thomas Carew, John Proby, William Levinz, Lord Andover [William Howard], Jacob Houblon, Bejamin Bathurst of Gloucester, [William Pitt] of Sarum and Eliot Montagu. Campbell lists Digby and Lechmere, not recorded by Coxe. *PH*, xi, 1226.

[22] A complex or confused situation. *OED*.

[23] *The Funeral of Faction* (1741), BMC 4287. A political print attacking the opposition to Walpole.

[24] Sarah Churchill (1660–1744), duchess of Marlborough, 'politician and courtier', the youngest daughter of Richard Jenyns, MP for St Albans. Groom of the bedchamber, then groom of the stole and then keeper of the privy purse to Queen Anne. She was a favourite of Anne's and enormously powerful, though they had a very stormy relationship. In 1677 she married John Churchill, later 1st duke of Marlborough (1650–1722). *ODNB*.

[25] *The Motion* (1741), BMC 2479, depicting leading opposition members 'proceeding along Whitehall to Westminster in a precipitate quest of office'. H.M. Atherton, *Political Prints in the Age of Hogarth* (Oxford, 1974), 121.

I am vastly pleased to hear that you don't incline to foxhunting,[26] the very name of a foxhunter gives me disagreable Idea's. I am apt to think of a man[27] who gives his whole time & thought to sport, which is below a rational Creature; of one who glory's in foolhardiness calling it bravery, and who is a zealous Tory, as it were to shew that he lives talks and acts (one can scarce say he thinks) in contempt & defiance of reason. To spend a whole life in sports is below a Man; & to think of liveing without any recreation, is attempting to rise above human Nature, & you know when a man attempts anything above his strength, he is sure to come off very poorly. Do you my Dearest avoid both extremes, and may God direct & assist you, to divide your time, between Virtuous, prudent, & beneficent actions usefull & elegant studys, and innocent healthfull recreations; and I earnestly pray that your life maybe long & comfortable to your self, usefull & dear to all who are, or may be, concern'd in you.

Give my Love & blessing to Dear Trub, & Ally. I made my Compliments to Dab in your Mama's letter. Remember me most kindly to Gil Blas with my best wishes to Spud,[28] but as for his New Wench you may tell him I don't care if she was in Mr. Whitfields Nursery in Georgia.[29]

I pray God . . .

Remember me kindly to R[oger] & Francis] Evans your Gent &c. I don't write to R[oger] Evans till I hear he is got home which I expect next Post. The Lairds Compliments.

30.
John Campbell to Pryse Campbell, 1 December 1741
I heartily thank you for your kind, I would not trouble you too often, but your letters will allways give me great Pleasure. Wee had to day a full appearance in the House of Commons,[30] and Mr. Onslow[31] was chose speaker unanimously. Nobody spoke but Mr. H[enry] Pelham & Mr.Clutterbuck[32] who moved & seconded; Mr. Onslow's speach's were very short, & decent; I think he judged very right, not to act such an affected Farce, & to refute or make long speech's to excuse himself & pretend inability, this being the third time he is to be presented on fryday, after which all the House must take the Oaths, so that I think Wee can't enter upon busyness before Monday, or

---

[26] In his will Campbell inserted a clause which attempted to stop his grandson, also John Campbell (later 1st Baron Cawdor), from pursuing fox hunting, as it was expensive and the sport of idle fellows. CRO, Cawdor/Campbell box 16/192.

[27] James Philipps of Pentyparc. See Chapter 1, letter 22.

[28] Not indentified: 'a short or stumpy person'. *OED.*

[29] George Whitefield (1714–70), co-founder of methodism, established an orphanage in Savannah, Georgia in 1740.

[30] *CJ*, xxiv, 7–8.

[31] Sir Arthur Onslow (1691–1768), of Imber Court, Surrey; MP for Guildford 1720–7 and Surrey 1727–61. Unanimously voted Speaker of the house of commons on 23 Jan. 1728, he was likewise voted on four other occasions and on his retirement in 1761 he was given an annuity of £3,000. His tenure as Speaker was defined by his generally incorruptible stance, and he realised the 'Speaker must himself be no respecter of persons'. P.D.G. Thomas, *The House of Commons in the Eighteenth Century* (Oxford, 1971), 351.

[32] Thomas Clutterbuck (1697–1742), MP for Liskeard 1722–34 and Plympton 1734–42. Initially he supported Carteret, but from 1730 attached himself to Walpole. He became one of the lords of the admiralty in 1732. He was one of Campbell's sources of political gossip.

perhaps this day sevenight. There are a great many strange faces[33] in the House of Commons, I don't know when I shall come to know them all.

Wee have frosty weather but with a West wind. The morning & evenings are foggy, but I believe the days are pleasant out of Town. My Dearest I can't help repeteing my earnest desire to you to be carefull of yourself, particularly I beg of you to be very cautious of rideing when it is slippery. The more smooth and even the ground is the more dangerous in that Case, and if then Horses are smooth shod, they will be very apt to loose their feet, and when a horses feet slip from under him he can't recover himself, nor can you save your self from a dangerous fall. I was talking yesterday with a Member who got a terrible fall which has lamed him, rideing on a slippery green turf, at a Horse race. He assures me he was going but a foot pace, when his horses feet slipping he came down at once.

My Dear when I came to look over your Paper of directions, I found a laced Hat & a pair of spurs, neither of which Wee can buy by guess. Wee must have the diameter of the Hat, and for the spurs I should be glad to have a piece of paper or Parchment cut to as to shew not only the size but the shape. Bailey says that Johnny has a pair of spurs of a very convenient Form. You have also put down Pencills but I don't whether you mean black lead or brush's for coloring. James[34] says he thinks you have enough both of the one & the other, but if you want any, Wee can send them I believe in a Frank.[35]

Give my Love to your Mama. I was sorry to hear by Johnny that she had a return of her headach. My Love & Blessing to Trub & Ally and tell them I hope they will both be good Boys. My Love & Blessing to Bessy. My service to your Uncle & Aunt &c. My Compliments to little Molly.

My Dearest Boy I pray God . . .

31.
John Campbell to Mary Campbell, 5 December 1741[36]
Your letters can never be insipid while they bring me account of your own & my Children's good health, I can't promise mine will have much other entertainment.

The Lords sat yesterday till between eight & nine. The King's speech[37] you will see sufficiently modest & respectfull to his Parliament, & I am told the Motion made by Lord Malton[38] was in so general terms that it was not easy to find fault with it, but they opposed addressing at all, for the present, which is more than has been done I think since the Revolution,[39] however when they came to divide there were 88 for the address & 43 or

---

[33] As a result of the general election, held between Apr. and June 1741.

[34] James Haycock was John Campbell's manservant. He was bequeathed two annuities, one of £60 and one of £70 and Campbell's wearing apparel, buckles and buttons in his master's will. CRO, Cawdor/Campbell box 16/192.

[35] The free franking of letters by MPs which continued until the penny post was introduced in 1840.

[36] See Figure 2.1.

[37] *LJ*, xxvi, 7.

[38] Thomas Watson-Wentworth (1693–1750), whig MP for Malton 1715–27 and Yorkshire 1727–8, though he frequently voted against the government. Created Baron Malton in 1728, earl of Malton in 1734; marquess of Rockingham 1746; earl of Malton (Irish peerage) 1746–50; Earl Malton 1750; lord of the bedchamber 1760–2; first lord of the treasury 1765–6 and 1782; leader of the house of lords 1765–6 and 1782. Malton's address is in *LJ*, xxvi, 9–10.

[39] The Glorious Revolution of 1688.

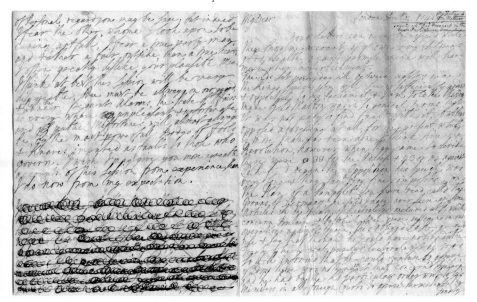

Figure 2.1: John Campbell to Mary Campbell, 5 December 1741: a hand which changed very little through his long life.

44 against.[40] Lord Chesterfield began the Opposition his speech was very long & they say a very fine composition on the Plan of a Pamphlet you have read call'd the Groans of Germany,[41] he said I dare aver there are some Articles in the Treaty of Neutrality[42] concluded at Hanover which concern Britain, & by which Wee were restrain'd in our operations against Spain, this obliged Lord H[arrin]g[to]n[43] to rise & say that though he could have no hand in the Treaty which was purely Electoral yet he was so well inform'd that he could venture to assure your Lordships there was nothing in it that concern'd Britain and he had by the King's particular order writ to his Ministers in all foreign Courts to assure them that the Treaty was entirely Electoral[44] & that H[is] M[ajesty] was as K[ing] of G[reat] B[ritain] at full liberty to act with his allies &c if Men at the head of Parties had not thrown off all shame they would blush at such impudent & wicked falsehoods. The Duke of Argyll made a long speech in much the same style I don't know whether quite so strong, Lord Chesterfield was unswerv'd by Lord Cholmondeley[45] & the Duke of Argyll

[40] Not recorded in the *LJ*. The figures agree with those in Sainty and Dewar.

[41] *Groans of Germany: Or the Enquiry of a Protestant into the Original Causes of the Present Distraction of the Empire . . . Translated from the Original lately Published at The Hague* (1741).

[42] Treaty of Hanover between Britain, France and Spain, 1725.

[43] William Stanhope (c.1683–1756), created Baron Harrington in 1730 and 1st earl of Harrington in 1742; whig MP for Derby 1715–22 and 1727–30 and for Steyning 1727. Ambassador to Spain 1721–7 and 1729–30; vice-chamberlain to the household 1727–30; secretary of state for the northern department 1730–42 and 1744–6; lord president of the council 1742–5; lord lieutenant (Ireland) 1746–51.

[44] That is, concerned entirely with Hanover.

[45] George Cholmondeley (1703–70), styled Viscount Malpas 1725–33 and 3rd earl of Cholmondeley 1733–70; whig MP for East Looe 1724–7 and New Windsor 1727–33. Cholmondeley married Robert Walpole's daughter Lady Mary Walpole in 1723. He held several important offices, including master of the robes 1726–7, lord of the admiralty 1727–8, lord of the treasury 1735–6 and chancellor of the duchy of Lancaster 1736–43.

by Lord Hardwicke[46] Lord Carteret spoke but like one who was not desperate at C[our]t I think that is some Comfort to the Friends of the Administration for I fancy if his Lordship thought them falling he would not be the last to give them a kick. I think those who have another King[47] act very consistently when they abuse our King, but what can they mean who say they have no other I cannot tell you know what Wee thought of the Groans of Germany. This is all I have yet heard from the House of Lords. I was last night at Sir R[obert] W[alpole] to hear the Motion[48] which is to be made in our House next Tuesday by little Herbert,[49] Seconded by Trevor[50] Mr Rices son[51] who married Sir Thomas Frankland's Daughter.[52] Our Motion is drawn as carefully to avoid Debate as could be, but that you know will not do, if the other side are resolved to Debate, as I fancy they are; but in what manner, whether like the other House, or no is uncertain. So far is no secret.

I promised to tell you my thoughts of this new Parliament to say truth they are but indifferent, I think 'tis past all doubt. The Court have a majority, but I fear 'tis not a large one. There are a great many Boys,[53] one knows not what whims may get under their toupees, nor how far they may be led by their Companions in whoreing and drinking if our friends should not attend well, the Consequence may be bad; and the Party out of Power I believe generally attend best. If a few Elections should be determined the wrong way, it may make an ugly hole in a small Majority; They talk of setting up Dr Lee[54] for Chairman of the Committee of Elections, & against Earle,[55] he is a Whig a Dr of Civil Law, a Sensible pleasible man and of Character, speaks well & with great volubility is Brother to my Lord Chief Justice,[56] & of their elder son: is a Bar[one]t of good Family & fortune; all this to set against G[iles] E[arle] many fear Wee shall loose it and if Wee do,

[46] Philip Yorke (1690–1764), MP for Lewes 1719–22 and Seaford 1722–33. He was solicitor-general 1720–4; attorney-general 1724–33; chief justice of the king's bench 1733–7; privy councillor 1733. Raised to the peerage in 1733 as Baron Hardwicke and as earl of Hardwicke in 1754. He was appointed lord chancellor in 1737, a position he kept until his resignation on 19 Nov. 1756, the same day as his lifelong friend and mentor, the duke of Newcastle, resigned as prime minister. Yorke kept a parliamentary journal during the years 1743–5.

[47] That is, the jacobite supporters of Charles, the Pretender.

[48] *CJ*, xxiv, 11–12.

[49] Henry Arthur Herbert (c.1703–72), of Oakley Park, Montgomeryshire; MP for Bletchingley 1724–7 and Ludlow 1727–43. He was created Baron Herbert of Chirbury 1743 and in 1748 he became Baron Powis of Powis Castle, Viscount Ludlow and earl of Powis.

[50] John Trevor (?1717–43), of Glynde, Sussex; MP for Lewes 1738–43. Owed his place to the Pelhams to whom he was related.

[51] Trevor was the son of John Morley Trevor (1681–1719), not 'Mr Rice's son'.

[52] Elizabeth, daughter of Sir Thomas Frankland (c.1683–1747), MP for Harwich 1708–13 and Thirsk 1713–47.

[53] The boy patriots or Cobham's cubs.

[54] George Lee (?1700–58), MP for Brackley 1733–42, Devizes 1742–7, Liskeard 1747–54 and Launceston 1754–8. Brother to Sir William Lee (see Note 56. Although he entered parliament as a whig he frequently acted with the opposition. He was elected chairman of the election committee in December, defeating the government candidate by four votes, a defeat which signalled the end of Walpole's administration.

[55] Giles Earle (c.1678–1758), MP for Chippenham 1715–22 and Malmesbury 1722–47. A wealthy Bristol merchant. Hervey said he was a man of 'a sordid avaricious temper, a very bad character, and as profligate in his discourse as his conduct', while Horace Walpole reported him as saying 'Lord God! what fine things oysters would be if one could make one's servants live on the shells'. *HPC, 1715–54*, ii, 1.

[56] Sir William Lee (1688–1754), lord chief justice from 8 June 1737, being nominated by and replacing his close friend and colleague Lord Hardwicke, who became lord chancellor. In the year of his death he was made, as a temporary measure, chancellor of the exchequer on the death of Henry Pelham. *ODNB*.

I think it will be of very bad consequence; for I am of opinion Lee will serve The Party who chose him more strongly than a less plausible Man could do; besides it will be stumbling at the threshold, looking an important question at the begining of the Session, I am most heartily for Earl[e], not out of Personal regard you may be sure; but indeed I fear the other, whome I look upon to be cuning, artfull, I fear a true party Man, and rather a fair outside, than a true heart; I often greatly dislike your plausible Men. I think at best this Session will be very disagreeable, Wee must be allways on our guard & shall be under frequent Alarms, the state of affairs is every where unpleasant & unfortunate, and public Misfortunes will allmost allways be, by the most powerfull Bodys of Fools & Knaves, imputed as faults to those who govern. I wish I may give you more agreable accounts of this Session from experience, than I do now from my expectation.[57]

32.
John Campbell to Mary Campbell, 17 December 1741
It was past nine when I got home to night. Wee were upon the Westminster Election[58] & are to go upon it again to morrow. Yesterday all our Friends were desired to dine, at the Crown in Kingstreet that Wee might go from that to the Committee of Elections to choose a Chairman, Sir R[obert] W[alpole] dined among us & went to the Committee, where I never saw him before; not withstanding all this Wee lost it, for when the Question was put for G[iles] Earle to take the Chair Wee divided Ay's 238 No's 242[59] upon which the majority made a great noise laughing, shouting and even claping their hands. The tellers were Winnington,[60] & Sandys so there were in all 482 members present: Thomas Hervey[61] was against us, but poor man he is by what I heard from Brudenell[62] quite out of his senses. If things continue to go in this way Wee shall see strange alterations I suppose, but really it is a melancholy thing to have such a Convulsion at home, when Affairs have so sad a face Abroad, & I don't know what Wee may soon hear from the Mediterranean if the French & Spanish Squadrons are united and act together . . .[63]

---

[57] The last nine lines have been obliterated.

[58] The Westminster election of May 1741, which returned government opponent Sir Charles Wager, was declared void on 22 Dec. In the ensuing election John, Viscount Perceval, was returned unopposed for the opposition. The presence of armed soldiers near to the polling area, before the poll had closed, was deemed 'a high infringement of the Freedom of Elections, and an open defiance of the laws and constitution of this Kingdom'. *PH*, xii, 326–8.

[59] Not recorded in *CJ*, since it was a committee vote

[60] Thomas Winnington (1696–1746), MP for Droitwich 1726–41 and Worcester 1741–6. Although brought up a tory, from 1729 he became one of Walpole's chief supporters. Horace Walpole stated that Winnington had 'infinitely more wit than any man I ever knew', cited in *HPC, 1715–54*, ii, 550. He became secretary at war 1741–6, a lord of the treasury 1736–42 and paymaster-general of the forces 1743–6. He died as a result of excessive purging and bleeding as a treatment for rheumatic fever. His doctor Thomas Thomson and several other medical men wrote pamphlets regarding the case. *ODNB*.

[61] Thomas Hervey (1699–1775), of Bond St, London; MP for Bury St Edmunds 1733–47. The brother of John, Lord Hervey, he voted with the government, except on the vote referred to by Campbell – the division on the chairman of the elections committee. He said he did not know why he had voted with the opposition on this occasion, saying 'Jesus knows my thoughts, one day I blaspheme and pray the next'. Hervey had spent some time in an asylum. *HPC, 1715–54*, ii, 135.

[62] James Brudenell (c.1687–1746), MP for Chichester 1713–15, Andover 1715–34 and Chichester 1734–46. Voted consistently with the government of the day.

[63] The rest of this letter has been cut out.

33.

John Campbell to Mary Campbell, 19 December 1741

I am glad I can send you a little better news from the House of Commons (where I sat till eleven last night) than I did the last time; Wee carried a public question by ten a Second by a somewhat greater Majority. I don't remember the last numbers but the first division was 237 against 227.[64] After ten o'Clock wee were forced to divide to put of [*sic*] the farther hearing of the West[minster] Election till Monday to which day Wee adjourned & got a day of rest, which you will think not unreasonable when I tell you Wee had sat upon Westminster Election on Thursday till about 8 at night. When I send yesterdays Vote[65] I will if I can get time explane what Wee divided upon. I may venture to affirm the heads of the Opposition knew Wee were in the night. The News you will see in the nights Papers from Russia[66] is very bad, that Revolution was plotted between the French the Swedes and the Devil, I believe our Court got some intelligence of it & immediately sent notice to the Duchess[67] Reg[imen]t but she believed it a device to bring her forces into Germany to the assistance of our friends, so she did not credit our information by which I fear she has lost her life[68] for it is said she is murder'd, her husband[69] infant son[70] and the Counts Osterman[71] & Munich[72] sent to Prison 'tis said Keith[73] had a great hand in it. There seems now to be no hope left for the Queen of Hungary[74] or the Liberty of Europe, I fear all the Maritime Powers[75] can do is to defend themselves as long as they are able, how unfortunate that at this juncture Wee have thrown away so much blood and Treasure in America.[76]

[64] *CJ*, xxiv, 33.

[65] *Votes*, a weekly publication of the house of commons giving brief proceedings of the House, first published in 1685.

[66] Elizabeth Petrovna (1709–61) became empress of Russia in a bloodless coup on 25 Nov. 1741. She brought Russia into the war.

[67] Anna Leopoldovna (1718–46), also known as Anna Karlovna, grand duchess, and from Nov. 1740 to Dec. 1741, regent of Russia.

[68] Anna, her family and her chief ministers, were first imprisoned and then exiled rather than executed.

[69] Anthony Ulrich (1714–74), duke of Brunswick-Lüneburg.

[70] Ivan VI, Antonovich of Russia (1740–64), emperor of Russia 1740.

[71] Count Andrey Ivanovich Osterman (1686–1747), German-born Russian statesman.

[72] Count Christoph von Münnich (1683–1767), Danish-born German soldier who became a field marshal and politician in the Russian state.

[73] James Francis Edward Keith (1696–1758), known as Marshall Keith, an army officer in the Russian and Prussian service. *ODNB*.

[74] Maria Theresa of Austria (1717–80), queen of Hungary 1740–80, queen of Bohemia 1740–1 and 1743–80, archduchess of Austria 1740–80 and holy Roman empress 1745–65. Maria Theresa's father Emperor Charles VI had, by the Pragmatic Sanction of 1713, ensured that Maria would become sovereign upon his death, contrary to Salic Law, which prohibited female succession. However, several signatories to the Pragmatic Sanction – Saxony, Prussia, Bavaria and France – rejected the agreement after Charles' death. Prussia invaded Austrian Silesia at the end of 1740, thereby commencing the War of the Austrian Succession. In Britain, she was referred to as the queen of Hungary.

[75] The Netherlands and Great Britain were known as the Maritime Powers.

[76] A reference to the War of Jenkins' Ear (1739–42), 'essentially a commercial conflict', which escalated into the War of the Austrian Succession. R. Browning, *The War of the Austrian Succession* (Stroud, 1994), 23.

The House is every day entertain'd by[77] empty hoddle & the solemn stupidity of the Lord M[a]y[o]rs[78] round face, I think our friends see Kilgetty[79] is a solemn superficial Coxcomb but the opposition seem still to like him, and don't doubt the hard heads in the Tory Corners will continue to admire him as long as they think him of their side.

I was this morning at Chelsea where I found the little Wench's very well & carry'd them some French Books . . .[80]

'Tis certain there was a Treaty late signed between our Court & the late regent of Russia.[81]

24 December 1741[82]

When you hear what hard service Wee have had in the House of Commons, I am sure you will not blame me for not answering your letters, for which I give you many thanks. I am sorry you are troubled with Chilblains; wear warm gloves let your hands & arms be well rub'd with the flesh brush, endeavor to keep your hands warm by rubing them one against the other, or let somebody else chafe them with warm hands, but don't put cold hands in your bosom for fear of hurting your breast to warm your hands. I have given your Mama an account of the House[83] I must tell you of the Committee of Elections last night, the other Party were a great Majority for a great number of them dined togather an [sic] a Tavern just by, but our Friends were gone all the Town over, and many did not come down. Mr. Symmons's Petition is order'd for the 19th of March but every body thinks it can't possibly come on this Session, indeed Kilgetty himself told me that day in the House, that he thought it co[u]ld not be heard this Session. The Petition for Carmarthen is order'd the 22[n]d of March & pray tell your Uncle that our Friends in that Town are in the wrong if they wish'd it to come on soon, for should it be heard is such . . .[84] or such a House as Wee had lately . . . ld certainly explane the last Resolution in such a manner as to confirm all Kilgetty has done to deprive the Inhabitants of Carmarthen of the Right to chose their own Member, but indeed whatever might be our desire, the Committee was so form'd that Wee durst not have divided upon any question and if Kilgetty had thought it necessary for him to put off the hearing that Petition till June Wee could not have help'd it; nor can Wee promise ourselves a Majority in a future Committee though Wee must hope for the best.

Sir Robert Walpole is in very good health notwithstanding these fatigues & keeps up good Spirits notwithstanding these disappointments. Some I believe have deceived him very basely, I am sorry to say there are two or three Scots Members in that number. Give my Love & Blessing to dear Trub & Ally, my affectionate service to your Uncle.

---

[77] The next word has been obliterated.

[78] Sir Robert Godschall (c.1692–1742), of College Hill, London, and Weston, in Albury, Surrey; MP for London 1741–2; alderman of London 1732, sheriff 1735–6 and lord mayor 1741–2.

[79] Sir John Philipps (1700–64), 6th bt; MP for Carmarthen borough 1741–7, Petersfield 1754–61 and Pembrokeshire 1761–4. See Introduction. Kilgetty (Cilgeti in Welsh) House is near Picton Castle, and Philipps, as a younger son, only began to reside at the castle on the death of his elder brother Erasmus in 1743. Campbell uses the sobriquet 'Kilgetty' for Philipps as a way of referring to his relatively lowly status as a younger son.

[80] The next four lines have been obliterated.

[81] The treaty was signed on 3 Apr. 1741, the regency being that of the infant Ivan VI (1740–64).

[82] This unnumbered letter is attached to letter 33 of 19 Dec. 1741.

[83] Also dated 24 Dec. 1741.

[84] Part of the letter is missing, hence this and the following blanks.

When you see Dr. Cuninghame pray present my best Service to him. Pray my Dearest . . .

34.
John Campbell to Mary Campbell, 24 December 1741
One of the inclosed [not extant] will shew you why I could write no letters last Post; and what Wee did that day[85] and what I have writ on the Vote, will shew you, how exactly conformable to truth our resolves were; as the question was at first worded, the Church yard was expressly said to be the Place where the Poll was taken,[86] though the Poll was taken in the Portico which is before the East end of the Church and the church yard is on the West & comes up a little on the North & South Sides, but not so far as the Portico; yet that Question was not drawn in a hurry but brought written to the House, I suppose it was hoped it might pass in a hurry, and then it would have gone all over the Kingdom by authority of the House that soldiers, surrounded the Place of Polling during the takeing the Poll.[87] A Motion was made after three o'Clock but was after some debate withdrawn, to Vote Mr Blackerby[88] guilty of high Crimes & misdemeanors, for writeing to the soldiers, though the only knowledge the House had of his writeing, was from his own evidence being call'd as a witness for the sitting members, and in his evidence he declared the Poll to have been finally closed an hour before the letter was writ, & the occasion of writeing was he and the two other justice's being inform'd that the Mob declared they would have the blood of Lord Sandon[89] & the High Bailiff[90] & that if they did not come out they would pull down the Church and Vestry, so Wee were to believe Mr Blackerby so far as tended to accuse himself but not, in anything that tended to justifie or excuse him. If a man should refuse to come before the House as an Evidence, I suppose it would be a breach of privilege; if he came to the bar & would not answer questions asked, that I suppose that would be the same, and when he does answer wee are by pricking out a part of his Evidence to Vote him guilty of high Crimes & misdemeanors can anything be more like the Inquisition, more unjust, more cruel, or more absurd; yet this was for some time warmly insisted on, but at length they yeilded to name a day for the Justices to appear, and I believe they scarce know themselves what then to say to them, or prove about them, consistent with common justice, or Common sense. I think Wee have gone far to put all Elections in the hands of the Mob, for if an Election is not ended till there is public declaration made

[85] 22 Dec. 1741, when the house debated and voted on the Westminster election. *CJ*, xxiv, 36–7.

[86] St Paul's Church, Covent Garden, the standard venue for the Middlesex constituency.

[87] *PH*, xiii, 63, states that 'the Presence of a regular Body of armed soldiers at an Election of Members to serve in Parliament is an high infringement of the Freedom of election's, and an Open Defiance of the Laws and Constitution of this Kingdom'.

[88] On 22 Jan. Nathaniel Blackerby, George Howard and Thomas Lediard were ordered to attend the house of commons to be reprimanded for their part in ordering the army to close the election. *PH*, xii, 323.

[89] William Clayton (1671–1752), of Sundon, Bedfordshire; MP for Woodstock 1716–22, St Albans 1722–7, Westminster 1727–41, Plympton 1742–7 and St Mawes 1747–52. He was created Baron Sundon (Irish peerage) in June 1735.

[90] John Lever, high bailiff, City of Westminster, 'acted at the said elections in an illegal and arbitrary manner'. It had been resolved on 22 Dec. by 217 to 215 votes to take him into custody. *CJ*, xxiv, 37. Lever, 'a simple, perplext creature', was a brewer by trade, had six children and was discharged on 26 Jan. *PH*, xii, 324.

(which no law requires) and no military assistance can be had till that is over, if the Mob of a Town where an Election is held are of a different Party from the Electors for that Town, or County, for which the election is; they may by Riot leave the returning Officer the Melancholy choice, of either being torn to pieces, or making a return contrary to Law, & his Oath; this it seems is Liberty and Patriot Justice. I must also tell you that their debate ran against the civil Magistrate calling the Military Force to his aid in any exigence whatever, which is subjecting all our Lives and fortunes, and giveing up the civil Power bound hand & foot as I may say to the most arbitrary & merciless of all Tyrants an enraged Mob. This day Wee adjourned to Monday the 18th of January. God grant Wee may do better things when Wee meet again, I think to go to Lodington[91] the beginning of next week & return a few days before the House meets again. I thank God I am very well but you will easily believe I have had no time to do or to thing [sic] of anything else but what I am writing account of. Wee had Sat till Seven I think on Monday night yesterday I lay in bed till eleven, went to the House at two & to the Committee between six & seven where I staid till nine at night. The Year forty one is wretched stuff, and I have not lately had time to read or enquire about the new things advertised. My Love & Blessing to all . . .

You need keep none of this Secret our case Can't be conceal'd I would fain hope it will mend or is not really so bad as it seems, if our Friends will be brought to attend, the rejoiceing were not so great as the news says, I saw several Bonfires, but no great noise or Crowd about them, and no illuminations between this & the House in my way to the Committee, but in Hanover Square the Duke of Roxburgh[92] Lords Westmoreland[93] & Cobham[94] & others had illuminations some House's had Candles in the Windows some only flambeaux's stuck on the Iron rails some I believe both for I did not see them but Bailey was there & told me, I think it was very humble doings for men of their quality, but they do right, for when the Mob is declared sovereign, it is right to make one self a part of the Sovereign Power.

I forgot to tell you that the Mob being pretty quiet soon after the Soldiers came to common Garden, Lord Sandon was advised to go home without a guard he went from the Church to his Coach through the church yard through a Lane of soldiers quietly but as soon as the Mob Saw the Coach drive off without a Guard they began to pelt it with stones dirt & brick bats, immediately broke both the glass's to pieces, & persued it quite home & no doubt had kill'd him if his Coachman had not drove so hard that they could not lay hold on the Coach, this was proved by Sir Thomas Cross,[95] who was in the

---

[91] Loddington, Leicestershire, the home of Edmund and Anne Morris (John Campbell's sister).

[92] Robert Ker (c.1709–55), 2nd duke of Roxburghe.

[93] John Fane (1686–1762), of Mereworth, Kent. Initially a whig MP for Hyde 1708–11, Kent 1715–22 and Buckingham 1727–34, he became an enemy to Walpole, supporting the mob in burning his effigy in 1742. He succeeded to the peerage as 7th earl of Westmorland on the death of his brother on 4 July 1736.

[94] Richard Temple (1675–1749), 1st Viscount Cobham; MP for Buckinghamshire 1697–1702, 1704–8 and for Buckingham 1708–13; created Baron Cobham in 1714 and Viscount Cobham in 1718. Cobham initially supported Walpole, but opposed the excise bill, from which his opposition faction, known as Cobham's cubs, grew. The cubs included William Pitt, the Grenville brothers, George and Richard, and George Lyttelton.

[95] Campbell is here mistaken: Sir Thomas Crosse died in 1738 leaving an only son, John Crosse (1700–62), MP for Wootton Bassett 1727–34, Lostwithiel 1735–47 and Westminster 1754–61. Crosse voted with the government at every recorded division.

Coach & thought his life in the greatest danger, & Sir Robert Rich[96] who saw the Coach go by a Coffeehouse. But our Patriots think it a pretty joke they could not prove the least affront offer'd to any of the Voters for Vernon & Edwin, but it was fully proved that the Voters for Sandon & Wager were outrageously insulted by the Mob & some beaten to the hazard of their lives & confined to their Beds for weeks by the wounds & bruises, of these were some of the Guards who went to Vote not in their Regimentals and without so much as Sticks or Canes in their hands.

I thought myself fully justified from the Evidence in Voteing Lord Sandon & Wager duely Elected and thought it very unjust to confuse the High Bailiff who yet had certainly been sent to Newgate if Mr Pulteney had not shewn more humanity than many of his Party.

35.

John Campbell to Mary Campbell, 23 January 1742

I could not write to any body by the last Post, an unexpected debate[97] of the highest consequence haveing lasted till between 11 & 12 at night & the House sat I think ½ a hour after 12. Mr Pulteney moved to refer some Papers to a Committee which he declared he should if that question was carry'd move to consist of 21 chose by Ballot & to be a Committee of Secresy, and that many other Papers should afterward be refer'd to them such a Committee would have been a Sovereign Councill, & an Inquisition. This you will say was a struggle for the whole & wee carried it only 253 against 250.[98] I believe no man alive remembers so great a number present at any Debate yet three of our side were at the Yorkshire Election (note 3 of the other side came up from it on private notice) and three were absent on account of their Mother the Duchess of St Albans[99] death a point of decency in my mind very unnecessary, she had been dead a Week but was not buried. I would not have come out at such a time to encrease a certain majority, or to carry a point of ordinary Consequence, but on so great an occasion I would have come though my affliction had it extremely painfull to me to appear; In their Case it could not I think have been so for the good old Lady had been dead to the World for some time & Scarce come out of her Chamber, & two of them came publicly to the House next morning. On the other side Sir William Gordon,[100] though allmost a dying himself & one of his Sons drown'd that day sevenight, came to the House out of mourning, he has the longest, the blackest, & the most emaciated face you ever saw, and he enter'd the House after night, with a dirty flannel hood under a black old Wig, and with a very long red Cloak, your imagination cannot paint I believe

---

[96] Sir Robert Rich (1685–1768), 4th bt, of Roos Hall, Suffolk; MP for Dunwich 1715–22, Bere Alston 1724–7 and St Ives 1727–41. A career army officer who had risen to the rank of field marshal by 1757. Groom to the bedchamber to George II both as prince of Wales and king, 1718–59.

[97] Motion for referring to a select committee the several papers laid before them relating to the conduct of the war. *CJ*, xxiv, 53. For the debate, in which Pulteney refers to a committee of secrecy, see *PH*, xii, 332–73.

[98] *CJ*, xxiv, 53.

[99] Lady Diana de Vere (1679–1742) married the 1st duke of St Albans, the illegitimate son of Charles II and Nell Gwyn, in 1694. The three absent sons were Lord Henry Beauclerk (1701–61), MP for Plymouth 1740–1 and Thetford 1741–61; Lord Sidney Beauclerk (1703–44), MP for New Windsor 1733–44; and Lord Vere Beauclerk (see Chapter 4, letter 118).

[100] Sir William Gordon (*d.* 1742), 1st bt, of Invergordon, Cromarty, and Dalpholly, Sutherland; MP for Sutherland 1708–13 and 1714–27 and for Cromartyshire 1741–2.

anything equal to his figure, one could not but expect a prophetic All Hail, indeed one could easily believe that the Prince of the Air who greeted Mackbeth by his Ambassadors,[101] was come in Person to declare the approaching Power of some greater favorite, and chose the long swarthy visage in honor to a certain Family.[102]

As to the Merchants Petition[103] I don't doubt its being push'd as far as possible to help to ruin the Ministry, but I believe nobody wants to hurt us farther than the loss of our Places, & with or without that Petition I scarce expect to keep mine longer, than the end of this session, for I confess I cannot think this Ministry can stand with so small & uncertain a Majority. Who or what will succede I cannot ghess, I can see no prospect that pleases me. Mr Pitt declared on thursday in the strongest terms that he would not be a Minister, . . .[104] I am going to sit all day at an Election.[105] If Wee can carry no Elections Wee must soon loose every thing. His Enemys own Sir R[obert] W[alpole] behave greatly; he looks easy, preserves great temper, & presence of mind, & reasons strongly. He seems as if he would shew Mr D[odington] a Fall like what he so finely describes in his Epistle.[106] I confess my dislike to many of the Patriots rises to perfect detestation. I have not time to give you account of our last Debate but do assure you I think it was not possible to be more Strongly in the right than Wee were.

Love & service to Dal &c.

Wee are only to reprimand the Westminster Justices for what they did **Not**[107] do. This is oweing to Mr P[ulteney] who has a favor for one of them, otherwise the Rage of lesser Patriots might have gone much farther; I can scarce help saying, Cursed be their Rage for it is cruel.

36.
John Campbell to Mary Campbell, 26 January 1742
[108] . . . think it will be agreed not to hear either Pembroke or Haverford[109] Petitions this session Sir W[atkins] W[illiams] W[ynn] & Mr Sandys encline it should be so but you need not mention it as yet. Inclosed is the Speakers [Arthur Onslow] Speech to the West[minste]r I suppose he speaks the sense of that Majority which order'd the High Bayliff into custody &c It is a very good Speech & only wants Facts to support it. I made a short speech against printing it which you will think was a disagreeable subject to speak on, but I could not consent to print I [*sic*] reprimand which I had not thought

---

[101] *Macbeth*, Act I, Scene iii.

[102] The Campbell family: for long Cawdor Castle has been associated with Macbeth, though the present castle was not built until the 14th century, long after the historic King Macbeth who died in 1057.

[103] The Merchants' Petition 'sets forth the Hardships they have sustained in their Trade and Commerce by the capture of their ships, by those contemptible Vessels the Spanish privateers'. The petition 'meets with universal Approbation and is already sign'd by above 400 Gentlemen of the greatest concerns in Merchandize in the whole Kingdom'. *Daily Post*, 8 Jan. 1742. It was presented to the house of commons along with other petitions from other parts of England on 20 Jan. 1742. *CJ*, xxiv, 49.

[104] Four lines obliterated.

[105] That is, Campbell was hearing petitions as a member of the committee of privileges and elections.

[106] George Bubb Dodington published his poem *Epistle to Sir Robert Walpole* in Dec. 1725.

[107] Written large.

[108] Letter incomplete.

[109] Haverfordwest, Pembrokeshire.

they deserved, there were several negatives but no division & no body spoke against it but Horace[110] and I what I did [*sic*] was unasked and I believe unexpected but I was moved in spirit and could not refrain.

To morrow Wee are to hear the Merchants Petition[111] & Leonidas[112] is to harangue instead of Councill,[113] I suppose it will last several days.[114] Lord Perceivell [*sic*] is a lamentable Speaker & I believe thought so by his own side, when all his Friends agreed to discharge the high Bayliff yesterday he alone Spoke for a severer punishment when all allow he in common decency should have been the last man in the House to have spoke on that side, if capable of feeling he would have been severely mortified by four of the Opposition Speaking after & against him.

37.
John Campbell to Pryse Campbell, 30 January 1742
I thank you very kindly for your letter. The writeing is most of it good, and though there are some little inaccuracy's in your style, I have the pleasure to observe it is in the main easy & manly. The greatest Pleasure this World can afford me is to see you answering my fond hopes & wishes, and to find so much reason to hope, that not only I, but all that are concern'd in you will have Cause to bless God for you. My Dearest it has pleased God to give you a good capacity and it is both your Duty & your Interest to cultivate & improve it. Let it be the great Maxim of your Life, on all occasions and in spight of all temptations to preserve your Truth & integrity inviolable, in order to which you must resolve to be temperate, for a Man may as well think to ride a high Mettled Horse without a bridle as to govern his Passions without Temperance which imply's not only moderation in eating & drinking, but in all other pleasures, & enjoyments; for if a man gives himself up to any pleasure, he becomes the slave of it, and cannot be sure that his Integrity may not some time fall a Victim to it. But I no more mean by this to forbid you the moderate use of innocent Pleasures, than I should intend to forbid you ever to ride if I desire you not to throw the bridle on your Horses neck & let him carry you how & where he pleased. No my Dear I am persuaded that a reasonable use of innocent diversions is beneficial both to your Body and mind, and as I would indulge you in nothing hurtfull, so I would restrain you from no pleasure you

---

[110] Horace Walpole.

[111] That is, they heard Godschall's report on the committee established after the petition had been read on the 20th. *CJ*, xxiv, 62.

[112] Richard Glover (1712–85), of Exchange Alley, London; writer, politician and merchant; MP for Weymouth and Melcombe Regis 1761–8. He was known by the sobriquet of Leonidas after the publication of his anti-Walpole poem of that name in 1737. Glover allied himself with the whig patriots and continued to support the merchants even after Walpole's fall. The merchants' petition was written by Glover, and presented to the Commons by Sir Robert Godschall, mayor of London. Glover also wrote a speech which he presented, as the merchants' representative, at the Bar of the House which outlined the complaints of the merchant community and its fears regarding the lack of military protection against the Spanish.

[113] 'Whether their case was before a Committee or at the Bar of the House, petitioners could be heard either by themselves or by counsel, but not by both methods.' Thomas, *House of Commons in the Eighteenth Century*, 19.

[114] The *Gentleman's Magazine*, xii, 150, states that there were several days of examinations before Glover summed up the evidence.

can safely enjoy. My Dearest will I am sure understand that I mean the safety both of your body & mind, it is my earnest endeavor to educate you in such a manner as to lay a sure foundation for your true and lasting happyness.

I can send you no good News from Westminster. On thursday Wee sat till 12 at night & divided upon a question relateing to the right of Election at Chipenham,[115] to my apprehension our Friends were most clearly in the right yet Wee lost it, 236 against 235. Yesterday Wee heard the Merchants again but every body being weary adjourn'd at six, to Monday, this is luckily a day of rest & Jehew's Rhubarb for a pain & swelling in my upper gums on one side, and it is now easy. I think the Merchants have as yet produced no great matters. You will see in the Votes the Petition from the City of London which is indeed a most insolent Libel upon the Government. The Merchants Petition[116] is entirely managed, & all the Witness's call'd & examined by Leonidas a most impudent affected Coxcomb.

I was diverted with the most ridiculous reports you tell me are going at Pembroke. Sir Robert Walpole is far from hideing himself, & indeed never appear'd so great to me as in his present behavior. He looks cheerfull & composed, & speaks with spirit, ease, & modest dignity. Yet I think he must know that he cannot carry on the public busyness against so strong a tyde, and I confess I see no probability of its turning more in his favor; I know not what will happen. I pray God that the Liberty & constitution of Britain may be preserved.

Give my Love to your Mama & Blessing to your Brother and sister. I pray God . . .

Your Uncle sends his compliments to all.

errat: in your last for T & I gives there duty Write give their duty.

38.

John Campbell to Mary Campbell, 4 February 1742

You will now see I had reason to bid you expect great news by this Post. The Adjournment of the Parliament is droping the Curtain[117] while a new Scene is prepared. How it will appear at the drawing up the Curtain this day fortnight, I cannot tell; I fancy most of the changes will be kept till the end of the Session because of re elections. All

---

[115] Chippenham election of 1741: the opposition candidates, Edward Baynton Blunt and Sir Edmund Thomas, were made freemen of the town, enabling them to take control of the corporation and nominate the bailiff who acted as the returning officer. A key government supporter, the sheriff, was arrested on a trumped up charge, with bail set at £10,000, until after the poll, at which the opposition were narrowly returned. At the ensuing petition in the Commons, the administration defeat by one vote referred to by Campbell was the immediate cause of Walpole's resignation. A second vote on 16 Feb. finally determined the outcome with a defeat for the administration of 16 votes. *HPC, 1715–54,* i, 344; *PH,* xii, 402–4. William Coxe, *Memoirs of the Life and Administration of Sir Robert Walpole, Earl of Orford* (3 vols, 1798), iii, 244, commented: 'At length, on the 28th, the opposition finally triumphed. A question on the Chippenham Election was carried against the Minister, by a majority of one . . . and the party gained so considerable an accession, by the desertion or absence of several members of the court party, that the final decision of the Chippenham Election was carried against the minister, by a majority of 16; 241 against 225'. Cited in *PH,* xii, 402.

[116] The merchants' petition of 20 Jan. 1742. The *Daily Post,* 21 Jan. 1742, stated that the merchants of the City of London 'in as decently grand a train as perhaps ever seen on such an occasion attended at Westminster with their Petition to Parliament, setting forth the great losses they have sustain'd in the capture of their ships by Spanish Privateers'.

[117] Parliament was adjourned by the king 3–18 Feb. *CJ,* xxiv, 84.

I know certain is, that Lord Wilmington[118] will be at the head of the Treasury, Sir R[obert] W[alpole] went to court to resign yesterday before the King went to the House; but he is not actually out of the Treasury till the new commission supersedes the old which may be to morrow or next day; He had a great Levee to day, I was there, he took me by the hand to the Window, desired me & all friends to attend the House for else, say'd he, they will break the Army & ruin the Government. I thought his looks shew'd great Concern, and I confess I felt a good deal of concern my self. I pray God this fortnight may be so well employ'd as to bring the Whigs to agree so far as to support the Government & disappoint the Tories, indeed many of them look'd yesterday as if it was a matter in which they had no concern; I wish it may be so; Sir J[ohn] H[ynde] C[otton] look'd pleased, is he less a Tory, or only less honest than Shippen who did not look at all pleased. Wee cannot expect a real Settlement in this fortnight only hope they may be patch'd up so as to carry on the public busyness this Session, but if the Patriots should persue the same Measures they did before this resignation, why then it has only hasten'd our ruin but sure the Cheifs of them cannot be so mad. Sir R[obert]'s words Surprized me, I hope he only judged from the obstinacy & inveteracy they shew'd towards him; I hear the King was to the last most firm & affectionate to him from the answer to the Message one looks upon the P[rince']s return to C[ourt] as the necessary consequence of this Change. I however think it odd that that is all I can yet say of that matter. There was a report to day I know not how, that the Duke of Richmond[119] had resign'd. Its said a Peer can't be Chancellor of the Exchequer, I don't know why, some name Doddington some Sandys for that Office, they also talk of the Duke of Newcastle going to Ireland & Lords Chesterfield & Carteret being Secretarys, but it seems to be all conjecture. Lord Gage[120] has taken upon him all this Session beyond what one can endure with Patience.

Kilgetty has several times shewn himself a formal Coxcomb. Gogerthan[121] never Spoke but once except about his own Election, & now and then asking a Question,

[118] Spencer Compton (?1674–1743), MP for Eye 1698–1710, East Grinstead 1713–15 and Sussex 1715–28. On the accession of George II, in 1727, Compton was briefly considered, although 'almost totally devoid of political ability', for the head of the treasury until Walpole was asked to continue. J.H. Plumb, *Sir Robert Walpole: The King's Minister* (2 vols, 1960), ii, 165. Until then Compton had supported Walpole (though he regarded him as 'an old woman'). Compton was placated with a peerage, becoming Baron Wilmington in 1728, and earl of Wilmington in 1730. Upon Walpole's resignation Wilmington was briefly made first lord of the treasury, though he was a mere cipher in that position. *HPC, 1715–54*, i, 568–9; *ODNB*. Hanbury-Williams (see Chapter 6, Note 86) in his 'New Ode to a Great Number of Great Men Newly Made', stated:
> See yon old, dull, important lord,
> Who at the long'd-for money-board
> Sits first, but does not lead;
> His younger brethren all things make;
> So that the Treasury's like a snake,
> And the tail moves the head.

[119] Charles Lennox (1701–50), 2nd duke of Richmond, of Goodwood, Sussex; created earl of March at birth. MP for Chichester 1722–3. A staunch whig supporter of both Walpole and the Pelhams. Lord of the bedchamber to the king 1726–35; lord high constable 1727; master of the horse 1735–50; privy councillor 1735; ambassador to France 1748–9. The father of Lady Caroline Fox. *ODNB*.

[120] William Hall Gage (1718–91), of Firle, Sussex and High Meadow, Gloucestershire; MP for Seaford 1744–7 and 1754–80. Succeeded his father as 2nd viscount in 1754, and was created Baron Gage of Firle in 1780 and Baron Gage of High Meadow in 1790. Voted with the government until 1747 when he followed the prince of Wales into opposition.

[121] Thomas Pryse (?1716–45), of Gogerddan, Cardiganshire; tory MP for Cardigan boroughs 1741–5.

what he said was so little it was I am sure not worth repeteing of remembering; but it is easy to become the Admiration of Fools.

What times we live in; Sir R[obert] W[alpole] must resign to make way for Sandys's bright Parts, Dodingtons prudence, Chesterfield's & Carteret's integrity and Argyll's humility & moderation. Who would have believed two years ago that Sir R[obert] W[alpole]'s or indeed any Ministry should be overturn'd by the Members from Scotland & Cornwall yet so it is; from what quarter Cornwall was influenced you may easily ghess,[122] and in Scotland the Duke of Argyll managed against the C[ourt] his brother for it, but in some instances the latter was either grossly deceived or did deceive, but whether remembering how he was attaqued in the Ed.r Bill[123] he sought to make himself independent on the Ministry and was himself deceived in chooseing for that end such as would not be guided by himself, or whether . . .[124]

Pray do what you judge best & like best as to Aberllefeny House.[125] I suppose nothing can be done till pretty far in the Spring on account of the Weather.

39.
John Campbell to Pryse Campbell, 6 February 1742
I received you short letter of the 31 of January and though when you have leisure and inclination to write a long letter, I shall allways take great pleasure in reading it; yet when you write enough to let me know that you are in good health and spirits, that is enough to make me happy; and I would not put any constraint upon you in that respect; but my Dearest when your letter was so short, you should have taken more care to have it well writ. Not that you need make any ceremony how you write to me, only to give your self a habit of writeing clear & correct.

I was this morning with Lord Privyseal,[126] who is better in health than when I saw him last. I believe he may keep his station if he pleases, but as yet no body knows what either the Men, or the Measures will be; so no honest Man can say whether he will joyn with, or oppose, the future Ministry; for at present all is Confusion, the Victorious Party are not come to any Agreement with the Conquer'd; nor are they I believe agree'd among themselves. It is easier to throw down, than to build up, to confound things, than to put them in order. I saw Mr. Hervey[127] who is a gentile youngman & still preserves that sweetness and Modesty he had when but a Boy. Lord Bristol[128] has given up his House in St. James Square to Lord Hervey who has altered & improved it, that it is a very good & a large House, with many fine Pictures, some of which Lord Hervey

---

[122] The prince of Wales, who in 1741 had 27 of the county's 44 MPs representing his interest. S. Ayling, *The Elder Pitt* (1976), 67.

[123] Edinburgh bill – referring to the Act of Sederunt issued by the court of session in Edinburgh during the malt tax riots of 1725 which made it illegal for Edinburgh brewers to refuse to work.

[124] This part of the letter is missing.

[125] Aberllefenni estate, in the parish of Talyllyn, Meirionydd, was the property of Mary Campbell. At its greatest extent this mid Wales property was over 2,000 acres in several parishes. Most was sold off to help clear debts in the period 1799–1802. See Introduction.

[126] John, Lord Hervey.

[127] Probably one of John, Lord Hervey's four sons who were born to Mary Lapell, Lady Hervey: George William, (1721–75), later 2nd earl of Bristol; Augustus John (1724–79), later 3rd earl of Bristol; Frederick Augustus (1730–1803), later 4th earl of Bristol and bishop of Derry; William (1732–1815).

[128] John Hervey (1665–1751), 1st Lord Bristol, father of the 2nd Baron Hervey.

bought, & many of them were Lord Bristols; who is now in Town, & has an Apartment in the House, & lives with his son. Lord Hervey told me to day, that he is as much Master of his Fathers Estate now, as if his Father was dead; I think my Lord Bristol acts like a Wiseman, and I am persuaded he will never have Cause to repent it. How happy it is when a Father & son have a mutual affection for & confidence in each other; and God be praised I think I have no occasion to envy any Father; I pray God direct me to do every thing that is best for you; and may his Goodness ever bless, preserve and guide you.

Give my Love to your Mama & the two inclosed letters. My Love & Blessing to Ally and Dab. I am very glad my pretty little fellow is quite well again. I intend to visit your sister on monday. I did intend to have gone to day but was runing from one shop to another till it was too late. I am glad you have had your will of the Old Hut, I suppose I shall find the scite of it finely improved.

Give me leave my Dearest to repete my earnest entreaty that you will be carefull of yourself. I am allways O dulce Decas meum.[129]

Remember me most kindly to Gil Blas. I am heartily glad he is well again. Remember me to Val & tell him I mended the direction of the letter to Griffith, Frank'd it & left it at the Admiralty for the Post.

I am as yet wholely uncertain whether I shall be allow'd to keep my Place[130] if I will, or whether I will keep it, if I may. But I am sure my Dearest believes I look upon that as a Trifle. Indeed the Confusion and uncertainty of the Public Affairs give me Concern.

40.
John Campbell to Mary Campbell, 9 February 1742
Not having a letter from you last Post makes me fear you had a fit of your ugly headach. Public Affairs (and nobody thinks or talks of anything else) are in a very uncertain state & wear a gloomy Aspect. Sir Robert Walpole kiss'd the Kings hand yesterday as Earl of Orford; when he first resign'd & the Parliament was adjourn'd, most People took it for granted, there was a sort of agreement that he should retire in Peace, & that there would be a mixt Administration; but I find it is no such thing; he has not the least assurance of Security, and they talk now of a thorough sweep; the Victorious are to have a great meeting at the fountain[131] in the Strand next Fryday, and if no Treaty can be made with some of their Leaders before that time, God knows what a League may be then made; They talk of a Petition from the City for Justice, and of violent proceedings against the late Minister and his Family, to ask what is he guilty of is an idle question; a powerfull Faction can easily find, or make guilt, if they want to satisfie their Vengence. I heard to day that it was doubtful whether the Admiralty Commission

---

[129] Horace, *Odes*, i, l. 1: 'The glory of my life'.

[130] As one of the lords of the admiralty.

[131] The Fountain Tavern, London: after Walpole's resignation the opposition held a meeting at the Fountain Tavern, headed by the duke of Argyll and attended by 'not less than three hundred members of both houses of parliament'. The meeting was a reaction to the news that the opposition would not be forming a ministry. Lord Perceval referred to this meeting as a schism which was 'the death of the late opposition'. *PH*, xii, 411–12; J.B. Owen, *The Rise of the Pelhams* (1957), 97–8, gives an account of the gathering.

would be charged this week or after the Parliament meets again, Lord limerick & Sir John Barnard talk'd of for two new Commissioners, not known who would be at the head, Wee were ghessing possibly Lord Winchelsea, it is lucky I did not remove. Sir Robert has had his daughter made a Lady to take place as an Earls Daughter, which I think a weakness but no crime. The King would have given him a Pension of £4,000 per annum but he wisely declined it,[132] however they clamor much at his procureing a reversionary Grant of some Patent Sine Cure for Keene[133] & Legge,[134] a good natured thing that no humane Man would be angry at. Legges Case is hard, to have so fair a prospect nipt in the bud. I don't believe Mr P[elham][135] is inclin'd to acts of Violence, but how far his Party & the fear of loosing his popularity may carry him, God knows, and if there is no hope of moderate measures from him, I know no other quarter one can look for it from.

I was two days ago with Lady P[elham][136] she is so mercifull she would not hurt a hair of his head, but except that, she sets no bounds to her railing . . .[137]

On Sunday night it came to hard frost with high North wind, it has been excessive cold ever since, but the wind is now East & pretty calm.

You may continue to direct to the Admiralty till farther notice, my Gammer will bring my letters though I should be out of the Commission; I hope she will not loose her place, she is, I think too low to feel the storm. I can't yet learn what share the Tories are to have in the spoil, surely they must have some; for if the new managers are resolved; as is said, to give no quarter to the friends of the old Ministry, they will want the assistance of the Tories, who I think can't All be such Idiots as to fight under them for nothing. I heard W[atkins] W[illiams] W[ynn] asks only the management of Wales

---

[132] *PH*, xii, 404, citing the Secker MSS: 'He was persuaded to refuse a grant of £4,000 a year during the King's life and his own, but could not be dissuaded from accepting a letter of honour from the King, to grant his natural daughter, Maria, precedence as an earl's daughter'.

[133] Benjamin Keene (c.1697–1757), whig MP for Maldon 1740–1 and West Looe 1741–7. Highly regarded by Walpole who ensured that he and Henry Legge had equal shares in a reversion of a place in the customs referred to here by Campbell, worth £1,200 to each man. Keene left Britain to become British minister in Lisbon in 1746 and never returned to his homeland.

[134] Henry Bilson Legge (1706–64), of Mapledurham, Hampshire; MP for East Looe 1740–1, Orford 1741–59 and Hampshire 1759–64. Legge became secretary to Robert Walpole in c.1735; a lord of the admiralty 1745–6, of the treasury 1746–9 and treasurer of the navy 1749–54. He was made chancellor of the exchequer on three occasions: 1754–5, 1756–7 and 1757–61. On becoming chancellor for the first time he was referred to by Newcastle as 'that creature of ours' and was dismissed when he gave a speech against subsidies which Horace Walpole said was 'humble, artful, affecting moderation, gliding to revenge'. Cited in *HPC, 1715–54*, iii, 30. He was driven into the political arms of Pitt by Newcastle's later harsh treatment. Legge was an erstwhile friend of Campbell's but came under criticism from both Campbell and Fox in their correspondence for his alignment with Pitt. Fox quotes the duke of Newcastle as saying: 'you despise him [Legge], and the D. of Bedford hates and despises Legge, & the D. of Devonshire, and Mr Pitt hates or despises Legge, and I don't care a farthing for Legge'. Henry Fox, 'Memoir of the Events Attending the Death of George the Second', in *The Life and Letters of Lady Sarah Lennox*, ed. countess of Ilchester and Lord Stavordale (1901), 39.

[135] Henry Pelham – as head of the whigs in the Commons, and a year later first lord of the treasury.

[136] Lady Katherine Pelham (1700–80), daughter of John Manners, 2nd duke of Rutland and Catherine Russell, his wife. Described as a political wife: 'A formidable woman who seldom minced words and did not suffer fools gladly, she used the patronage system astutely and successfully'. *ODNB*.

[137] Six lines obliterated.

which, as a trifle, is granted to him; I shall be afraid to go to North Wales[138] lest I should be set in the stocks for drinking K[ing] G[eorge]'s health[139] or some such misdemeanour . . .[140]

41.
John Campbell to Pryse Campbell, 9 February 1742
Inclosed are some seeds that James brought from Lord Burlingtons.[141] You may find an account of them & the method of raiseing them in Millers Gardiners Dictionary.[142]

My Love & Blessing to Dear Trub & Ally. Your Uncle Morris sends his Compliments to your Mama your self &c. Remember me most kindly to Gil Blas, tell him I have taken care of Mr. Rice's letter. I was to day at Lord Orford's[143] but was told he was very busy & desired to be excused. I believe more than a hundred had the same answer, I believe he avoided haveing so great a Levee on the occasion, which might inflame the envy, & malice of his wicked, & cruel Enemy's.

42.
John Campbell to Pryse Campbell, 16 February 1742
I thank you for your letters of the 3rd & 10th instant. I am very glad you liked the things I sent you. I was glad to hear your Chilblanes were better, though you told it me in a Pembrokeshire phrase, for you said My Chilblanes are gone better. You should have said, They are grown better or else only They are better. I am pleased that you like Greek because I have a great likeing to it myself though, I am ashamed to say it, I know very little, next to nothing of it.

Wee had an account to day at the Admiralty of the Otter sloop being lost near Alborough. The Captain, all the Officers & I think 37 men drowned, a few of the men I think about 17 were saved. The Captain, Sir William Gordons son, was a very moderate hand. Sir Charles Wager tells me the Prize taken by the Superbe will be worth to the Captor £40,000. This is all the News I have yet heard. Only that some time ago a Message was sent to H[is] R[oyal] H[ighness][144] by the Bishop of O[xford][145] to offer

[138] That is, Sir Watkin Williams-Wynn's stronghold.

[139] In a strongly jacobite area, though perhaps Campbell is being facetious.

[140] The rest of the letter is cut out.

[141] Richard Boyle (1694–1753), 3rd earl of Burlington, known as the 'Apollo of the arts' and as 'the architect earl'. He was instrumental in establishing Palladian architecture in Britain. Among his collaborators were William Kent, the landscape gardener, and Coln Campbell the architect cousin of John Campbell.

[142] Phillip Miller (1691–1771), botanist and gardener at Chelsea Physic Garden from 1722 until just before his death. His *Gardiner's Dictionary* was first published in 1731, and had gone through eight editions by 1768.

[143] Walpole was presented at court as Lord Orford on 8 Feb. *PH*, xii, 404.

[144] Frederick Louis, prince of Wales (1707–51). With familial rifts of monumental size, and a personality that seemed to antagonise many, Frederick, under the counsellorship of George Bubb Dodington, established an alternative court to his father's, George II, first at Norfolk House, St James's Square, and then Leicester House, where he used his influence to undermine Walpole's ministry. Bolingbroke, Chesterfield, Carteret, Wyndham and Cobham were among his special friends. He applied to parliament to raise the £50,000 offered from the civil list by his father but was voted down in both houses. *ODNB*.

[145] Thomas Secker (1693–1768). He was appointed rector of Houghton-le-Spring, County Durham in 1724 and prebend of Ryton, in the same county, in 1727. Secker became rector of St James's, Piccadilly in 1733, bishop of Bristol in 1735 and bishop of Oxford two years later. In 1758 he was translated to the archbishopric of Canterbury where he remained until his death.

him £100,000 per annum & to be made easy as to his debts, to come to Court upon a proper submission to the King without being obliged to part with any of his servants or being restrain'd from seeing any he now see's. Unhappily for the public this offer was not accepted. This I believe is very true & maybe told to Friends but should not be talk'd of publicly, you will tell it to your Mama in the first place.

My Dearest I beg of you to be very carefull of your self at all times & in every respect, for the sake of your poor Pa' who can't help frequent & great anxiety's for the dear Treasure of his Heart. I pray ever . . .

43.

John Campbell to Pryse Campbell, 16 February 1742

It was a great pleasure to me to hear from your own dear hand that your cough was departed & your sty going away. I hope in God you are now in perfect health and I most earnestly pray you may continue so many years.

This day the new Commissioners of the Treasury viz Lord Wilmington, Mr. Sandys Chancellor of the Exchequer, Sir John Rushout,[146] Mr. Gybbon, and Major Compton[147] Brother to Lord Northampton,[148] kiss'd the Kings hand, and I saw the Marquis of Tweeddale[149] at Court, as I was told, to receive the seals as third Secretary of State,[150] an office erected at the Union & held first by the late Duke of Queensbury,[151] and afterwards by the late Duke of Roxburgh,[152] upon whose dismission about eighteen years ago, that office was dropt, and the busyness of it added to the Duke of Newcastle's Office, in form but the care of Scots Affairs was left to Lord Ilay, but not the third Secretary is revived all will be done by him. Lord Ilay I hear is to continue keeper of the Scots Great seal a Place of honor & £3,000 per annum salary. It is said that our Commission is reprieved for some time to avoid makeing so many vacancys in the House of Commons at once; and it seems uncertain whether they will sweep our Board so clean as the Treasury. For my own part as I did not ask the late Ministry to put me

[146] Sir John Rushout (1685–1775), 4th bt; MP for Malmesbury 1713–22 and Evesham 1722–68. Together with Sandys and Gybbon he was a key supporter of Pulteney in the treasury.

[147] George Compton (1692–1758), MP for Tamworth 1727 and Northampton 1727–54. Cornet, royal horse guards 1707; guidon and major 2nd life guards 1713; lord of the treasury 1742–4.

[148] James Compton (1687–1754), 5th earl of Northampton, known as Lord Compton to 1727; MP for Warwickshire 1710–11. He was created Baron Compton in 1711.

[149] John Hay (1695–1762), 4th marquess of Tweeddale. Chosen as one of the representative peers of Scotland in 1722 and 1727. He then attached himself to Lord Carteret, and was not elected in either 1734 or 1742. After Walpole's ministry Tweeddale was again elected and continued to be until 1761. He was made principal secretary of state for Scotland in 1742, until that office was abolished in 1746. He married Lady Frances, Carteret's daughter.

[150] Secretary of state for Scotland, which was created in 1707 and abolished in 1746.

[151] James Douglas (1662–1711), 2nd duke of Queensbury. Created marquess of Queensbury (Scottish peerage) in 1695 and duke of Dover in 1708. Keeper of the privy seal for Scotland 1695–1702 and 1705–9; secretary of state for Scotland 1702–4 and 1709–11.

[152] John Ker (c.1680–1741), 1st duke of Roxburghe. He was made a secretary of state for Scotland in 1704 and helped bring about union with England, for which he was created duke in 1707. A representative peer for Scotland in four parliaments and secretary of state for Scotland 1716–25. He helped put down the jacobite rising in 1715, but in 1725 opposed the malt tax for Scotland for which Walpole eventually removed him from office. He was a zealous supporter of Carteret and Cadogan in their opposition to Walpole and Townsend. *ODNB.*

in Office I certainly shall not ask the present to continue me, but if I see they serve the King and the Public honestly, & prudently, I shall be satisfied whatever they do with me. As long as the King & Constitution stand our Estate will be secure to me & you, but if the Enemys of the present Establishment should prevail, then indeed Wee can call nothing our own. However I hope that many whose Passions carried them unjustifiable lengths in opposition to the late Minister have still too much sense & Honesty to let in the Common Enemy; though some I fear, would hazard all to gratifie their own Pride, Malice & Revenge.

Give my love & Blessing to Dear Trub & Ally. Remember me most kindly to Gil Blas. I pray God . . .

44.
John Campbell to Pryse Campbell, 27 February 1742
I thank you for your letter of the 11th which I observed with pleasure was well & correctly writ, only the ink very pale. I am glad you approve my Conduct in respect to the Admiralty, I think it very right for you to begin to exercise your Judgement in things of Consequence, and I hope that a frequent agreement in our opinions will add to the Pleasure of our Friendship. I had heard of the Comet here, but I believe it is not possible to see it out of this House.

The Merchants have not yet finish'd their Evidence.[153] I believe they will on tuesday next if no other busyness prevents. I think the only fault they can prove against the Admiralty, is not being severe enough in punishing those who did not obey their Orders, which in truth was oweing to Sir Charles Wager the board haveing been often uneasy at his too great lenity, but this is only for your self, for it would be very ungenerous at this time, to throw the fault upon the good old Gentleman. All agree that my Lord Mayor [Godschall][154] makes a wretch'd figure in the Chair of the Committee, and Leonidas (who is Orator and Manager for the Merchants) a very poor one at the Bar. Several of the Witness's have been very insolent and impertinent.

The Sheriff of Denbighshire[155] had managed so ill, that no one could speak in his behalf, yet one may say that the house did not in their Justice, think much of Mercy. There is a very angry spirit in some parts of the House, which I fear will produce Mischief. I am sure when Wee were the Majority, Wee used the then Minority with much more decency and good Manners than Wee now receive from them.

---

[153] The resolutions of the grand committee on the merchants' petitions was heard on 4 Mar. 1742, the main resolution being that due and necessary care had not been taken to protect merchant shipping from the enemy. After hearing the resolutions it was ordered that a bill for the security of trade and navigation in time of war be prepared. The bill was rejected in the Lords on 20 May 1742: contents 25, non-contents 59. *PH*, xii, 446–7 and xii, 788.

[154] Sir Robert Godschall (c.1692–1742), lord mayor of London from Sept. 1741 until his death in June 1742. Some commentators referred to his talent as a speaker, but Horace Walpole had a different opinion: 'This gold-chain came into Parliament cried up for his parts, but proves so dull one would think he chewed opium'. Cited in *HPC, 1715–54*, ii, 67.

[155] William Myddelton, high sheriff of Denbighshire in 1741. In the county election for Denbighshire Myddelton had declared his kinsman John Myddelton of Chirk Castle the successful candidate, discounting over 600 votes of his rival Sir Watkin Williams-Wynn. On petition the Commons overturned the decision and sent William Myddelton to Newgate for seven weeks for acting 'partially, arbitrarily and illegally'. *CJ*, xxiv, 92.

Inclosed is an account of things sent in a box this morning to the Carrier. Give my Love to your Mama. I am sorry she was troubled with her headach. My Love & Blessing to Trub, Ally & Dab. I am very glad Ally was so much better. I liked Trubs letter mighty well.

I pray God . . .

45.

John Campbell to Pryse Campbell, 13 March 1742

You are very good & kind in being so much pleased with my approbation and I assure you My Dearest it is the greatest Pleasure I can have to see you deserve it. I pray God continue your health in this very cold dry northwest wind. It is here hard frost and extreme cold & the streets as dusty as in the middle of summer. Your Latin Proverb is of great use at this time, when I neither see nor hear anything that pleases me. I would have you direct your letters for the future to Grosvenor Square, for though I had the honor yesterday to sign the New Admirals Commissions, I expect to be superseded myself by the time this comes to your hands. Sir Charles Wager is not yet made Vice Admiral of England though it is all in the Newspapers. I don't know whether Sir John Norris would be understood to have resign'd, I believe he repents and would explane it off. Some talk of Sir Charles Wager going to sea, but so many things are said & contradicted again that one knows not what to believe.

I have not yet had leisure, to get a Salust[156] & compare your translation; indeed I am too much a Politician I cannot help haveing my thoughts taken up with public Affairs, when I think the Peace & safety of the Nation so much endanger'd by the Ambition of foreign and domestic Enemies, for otherwise who are in or out of the Ministry would signifie little to me.

My Love & Blessing to Dear Trub & Ally, and kind service to Mr. Rowe. I pray God . . . The account I received lately from Mr. Rowe of your learning, gave me great satisfaction.

46.

John Campbell to Pryse Campbell, 20 March 1742

When I read your kind & agreable letter I can't forbear saying to my self O felix Nati pietate.[157] When I gave you account of our carrying that Question, I was in great hopes of somewhat like a settlement upon a Whig bottom, but things do not look so promising now.

Excutimur cursu, et caecis erramus in undis[158]
Incerti quo fata ferant.[159]

I shall be very glad to see Cato's speech all your own.

What you say upon the loss of my Place pleases me very much. Had all who pretend to be Patriots had the same brave, honest, & generous sentiments, Wee had not now

---

[156] Gaius Sallustius Crispus, known as Sallust (86–34 BC), Roman historian.

[157] Virgil, *Aeneid*, iii, l. 480: 'Blest in a son' (John Dryden's translation).

[158] Virgil, *Aeneid*, iii, l. 200: 'Cast from our course we wonder in the dark' (Dryden's translation).

[159] Virgil, *Aeneid*, iii, l. 7: '. . . uncertain yet to find' (Dryden's translation).

been in the dangerous & uncertain condition Wee are brought to, by Ambition, covertousness and revenge, under the Masks of Public spirit, Virtue and justice.

Wee have very cold & dry weather which I fear will have a sad effect in the Country. I pray God keep you in good health. I hope my Dearest you are carefull of your self. Your sisters enquired after you kindly to day & send their Love to you. Nanny [Anne] talks to me but Molly, who is mightily improved in her looks, only smiles & laughs & holds up her hand curiously. My Love & Blessing to Dear Trub & Ally. Give my kind service to Mr. Rowe and remember me most kindly to Gil Blas. I pray God . . .

My Dearest in your last you writ sucsess instead of success.

47.

John Campbell to Pryse Campbell, 23 March 1742

It has happen'd as I fear'd it would. They have carried the Question to appoint a Secret Committee to enquire into the Conduct of Robert Earl of Orford for the last ten years of his being at the head of the Treasury 252 against 275.[160] The Committee to be 21, chose by Ballot next fryday. They had as I told your Mama several new members since last time, and by the alteration in some Peoples Conduct several who did not vote then voted against us now. About four of our Friends, like fools, were shut out. I bore my testimony against it & express'd in the strongest terms my contempt for that popularity which ruins us, makeing some act contrary I verily believe both to their Judgement & inclination. I pray God . . .

48.

John Campbell to Pryse Campbell, 24 March 1742

When I was in the Country I told you my intention to bring you to Town next Autumn. I have often thought of it since, as I must often think of whatever concerns you. Omnis in Ascanio cari stat cura Parentis[161] and indeed I am not willing to let you be much longer without seeing this Place, at the same time I consider that you will not have finish'd your schole learning so soon, that it may not be convenient for Mr. Row[e] to come up and stay, here with you all next winter & spring, and that it may be neither agreable nor profitable to you to change your Instructor before you go to the University; I have therefore thought to propose to you to come up with Johnny & spend a few weeks with me here this Spring, & then return & spend another Winter at Stackpole; If you like this my Dearest propose it to your Mama, you must lend Val for that time to Trub, and I dare say Mr. Rowe will take a little more than ordinary trouble with your Brother, while you and Johnny are away. I suppose as the Parliament were so long before they began public busyness and have now order'd this cursed Committee they will not be up before the latter end of may, so if your Mama has no objection, you may take what time you think proper for your journey and if Mr. Rowe will let me know what books he would have you read while you are here, I will provide them, and give you any assistance I am able. I thank God I don't doubt

---

[160] Debate on Lord Limerick's motion for a committee of inquiry into the conduct of affairs at home and abroad during the last 20 years. *PH*, xii, 588–90. The names of the MPs voted on to the secret committee are given in the same place, col. 588.

[161] Virgil, *Aeneid*, i, l. 646: 'All his fond parental care was centred on Ascanius'.

your being able for the journey, but if you undertake it, I must beg of you to travel very moderately, & be extreme [*sic*] carefull of your self. As you will bring Johnny & either your Huntsman or Johnny Bowen with you, I will send Bailey to wait on your Mama for Wee shall not want him here, I brought him up to help me in removeing to the Admiralty, it is well Wee did not take that trouble. I say all this upon supposition of your journey which however I leave your Mama & you to determine. I was this day to pay my duty to H[is] R[oyal] H[ighness] where I was received at least as well as I expected, for he spoke to me, & asked if your Mama was in Town. There was a vast crowd it being the first time H[is] R[oyal] H[ighness] saw company since he had the Measles, and the second time since he went to Court. I write to night because Fryday being appointed for the ballot possibly my good Lord Mayor may move to repeal the Septennial Act[162] to morrow. I don't know whether he will do it in so pathetic a manner as he introduced the Merchants Petition which was literally, Multa gemens, largoque humectat flumina Vultum.[163] The first who spoke against the motion yesterday was Lord Orford's youngest son Mr. Horace Walpole.[164] He spoke very prettyly, and even Mr. William Pitt took notice that his filial piety made him appear in the most amiable light. Mr. Pulteney in his speech declared that for his own part he could have wish'd that the Person being removed from power, might be allow'd to retire in Peace, but said the enquiry was necessary to satisfie the People; that is, he must Sacrifice his Principles, his inclinations & his good faith to Popular Clamor, a Devil of his own raising; He talk'd much of restraining the committee within the bounds of justice, reason, & moderation; but would a Wise man rouse and let loose a lyon, hopeing to lead him tame about to destroy vermine, but by no means to hurt any innocent Creature. He strongly profess'd himself a Whig, and desired to unite us all, in the Cause of Liberty, & support of the present royal Family; but surely it is a new way of uniteing the Friends of Liberty, for some of them, to joyn with the Tory's, in calling the rest, and majority part, Mercenary rascals; for if Lord Orford's Administration was iniquitous, what must Wee be who supported and approved it. You see into what difficultys, & contradictions a man is brought by his Passions, & Ambition; and affecting Popularity, that is in other words, prefering the false flattery & giddy Noisy applause of Knaves & fools, to the sober & sincere approbation of Men of sense, and Virtue, and of his own Conscience. After They had voted the ballot &c. last night, Mr. Pulteney moved an address to give strong assurances of our zeal & fidelity to his majesty, and our resolution to support him, which he said he hoped would pass nemine

---

[162] An Act for Enlarging the Time of Continuance of Parliaments (1 Geo I, c.38), known as the Septennial Act, allowed parliament to sit for up to seven years, and ushered in a period of political stability. The Septennial Act repealed the Act for the Frequent Meeting and Calling of Parliaments (6 & 7 Wm & Mary, c.2) or the Triennial Act of 1694 which allowed three-year parliaments.

[163] Virgil, *Aeneid*, i, l. 465: 'Sic ait, atque animum pictura pascit inani, multa gemens, largoque umectat flumine voltum'. In Dryden's translation:
He said (his tears a ready passage find),
Devouring what he saw so well design'd,
And with an empty picture fed his mind.

[164] Horatio Walpole (1717–97), youngest son of Sir Robert, of Strawberry Hill, Middlesex. He was the whig MP for Callington 1741–7, Castle Rising 1754–7 and King's Lynn 1757–68. This was Walpole's maiden speech. His *Memoirs*, begun in 1751, are a major source for political historians, though they have to be used with caution.

contradicente and it did so, but I was told, for being talking to some near me, I can't say I observed it myself, that Sir Watkins Williams Wynn beckon'd & carry'd out a number of his choice Friends that they might not be present at the Vote. In truth this address is but a poor amends to the King for dividing & distressing his Friends & throwing Things into the present Confusion.

Give my Love to your Mama & tell I received the Bloodstone & hope to send the blue box by Mr. Holcombe. The Bloodstone fits the silver very well. My Love & Blessing to Trub, Ally and Dab. I pray God . . .

49.

John Campbell to Pryse Campbell, 1 April 1742

I received yours with your translation of Cato's speech inclosed for which I kindly thank you. I have bought a Sallust to day that I may compare it as soon as I have leisure. I think allready that the language reads as well as I could expect from your Age and the opportunitys you have had, but I will let you know my opinion of it fully & Freely 'ere long; I observed an abbreviation in your writing, 'em once or twice for them, which I would not have you use your self so it is allways best to express your self fully & plainly that minceing of Words spoils the language.

Yesterday my Lord Mayor made his Motion to repeal the Septennial Act, which was rejected by 204 against 184.[165] Mr. Pulteney, the New Treasury, and several other Patriots voted with us; you see the House was not very full, for the ballot haveing prevented it the day it was design'd for his Lordship did not think fit to give us any other notice; he was pleased on this Occasion to be facetious, whatever Character he assumes, he has the good luck to be equally ridiculous. A Gentleman said very rightly of him, that he is abusive without being angry, laughs without being pleased, and cry's without being sorry; acts every part, and feels none; and this you must understand is not from the perfection of his Art, but the stupidity of his Nature. Mr. Pulteney spoke and strongly shew'd that Septennial Parliaments were better than Triennial, he said indeed that he prefer'd annual, to either, but he did not favor us with his reasons for that preference, confessing that it was not proper to reduce it to annual in the present conjuncture of Affairs; and truely I am apt to believe he will never find a time when he will think it proper; but I suppose he had a mind to say something to sooth the Populace, and I think he voted for the repeal of this Act a few years ago, so Wee must suppose he then would have made it annual; but could not venture to do so, in the present dangerous, & uncertain state; and that way wee must reconcile the two Votes, and make this great Man consistent with himself. But it is not as plane as the light at noon, that those Patriots who voted against it now, were for it a few Years ago, only to raise a popular Cry against the then Prime Minister. My Lord Mayor was a little roasted about the Surrey Election, it seems he was very busy in procureing subscriptions for to carry on the Opposition against Lord Baltimore;[166] and either gave, or sold a good deal of Wine on that occasion. There was an outrageous Mob who knock'd down many, and threaten'd and insulted all who came to Vote for Lord Baltimore, this to

---

[165] *CJ*, xxiv, 160, 31 Mar. 1742.
[166] Nevertheless Baltimore won the election.

preserve the Freedom of Elections, as the Money Subscription was to prevent Bribery and the Duke of B[edfor]d[167] & Earl of Ay[les]f[or]d appearing publicly and makeing harangues against Lord Baltimore, was to preserve the Privileges of the Commons, from being infringed by the Peers. So do Tories protect Liberty, and such is the fashionable Virtue, and Patriotism.

To day the Chancellor of the Exchequer [Samuel Sandys] deliver'd a Message from the King desireing an Aid to assist the Queen of Hungary, it was, Nemine contradicente, refer'd to the Committee of Supply which I suppose will sit upon it to morrow, I think they talk of £500,000.[168]

Your sisters at Chelsea send their Love to you but Nanney complanes you have owed her a letter a long time. Give my Love & Blessing to Dear Trub & Ally, and my kind service to Mr. Rowe. I am sorry to hear of Mr. Ricksons illness, I hope he will do well again; I have a sincere kindness for our Friend Mr. F Meare, and should be very glad to do a thing agreable to you, but my Dearest I have no Interest, scarce any acquaintance with the New Treasury, and you may be sure it is not very pleasant to ask favors of those who have, as I may say, just now kicked me down stairs.

If you think of comeing up upon what I said in my last, I intreat you my Dearest to be very carefull of your self & not to fatigue yourself. If you come, I hope the Wind will change first for I should be uneasy to have you take a long journey with such a terrible wind full in your face. I pray God . . .

50.
John Campbell to Pryse Campbell, 3 April 1742
I have compared your translation of Cato's speech with the original, and think in the main it is very well, when I have the pleasure to see you, I shall tell what corrections I would make in it, but I can't pretend to be a good judge, haveing, to my sorrow, very much neglected my learning.

Give my Love to your Mama. I am sorry her headach has been so troublesome lately, if it was occasion'd by change of weather, I believe it would make her bear it more easily, it has look'd very like rain this Evening & dropt a little once, but as the wind is N.E. I fear it will blow over. Pray give the inclosed to your Uncle Philipps with my Compliments. I suppose by his last he may be at Stackpole when you receive this.

I have no News. Lord Orford came to Chelsea yesterday. I sent James there with a howdee ye this morning and he sent word he should be very glad to see me, so I intend to go to morrow, or next day, being very willing to shew all civility, and respect, to a Man who appears to me to be unjustly persecuted, and to have been drove from his place, by false & Malicious storys, and most unjust arts, by which his Ambitious & revengefull Enemies have influenced the minds of ignorant unthinking fools.

---

[167] John Russell (1710–71), 4th duke of Bedford. He was hostile to Walpole. On the fall of Carteret in Nov. 1744 he was appointed first lord of the admiralty (1744–8); secretary of state for the southern department 1748–51; lord privy seal 1761–3; lord president of the council 1763–5; British ambassador to France 1762–3.

[168] *CJ*, xxiv, 161.

I drank your health & all your Friends at Stackpole with your Uncle Owen & Mr. Edwardes[169] who dined with me to day. Give my Love and Blessing to your Brothers and Sisters. I was glad to hear by Johnny you had taken a doze of Rhubarb this spring, I would wish if it please God to prevent the return of weakness or redness upon your dear eyes dearer to me, if I know my heart, than my own. If you come to Town bring with you Dr. Cuninghams prescription for the powders and Tea you used to take; pray present my best respects to the Dr. and his Lady. If you come to Town I think to get a danceing Master to teach you to make a bow &c gentiely, and I will endeavor to make your short stay here, as usefull & agreeable to you as I can; for it is my great desire to serve and please you; I am sure you will understand I mean to please you in such a manner, as is consistent with your good, & with the utmost care to make you a Virtuous, knowing and valuable Man; and I am persuaded you do not desire I should indulge your Pleasure in any way inconsistent with that care, and undoubtedly that man will enjoy the most Pleasure, who keeps his Pleasures within the bounds of honesty, prudence & moderation. I pray God . . .

51.

John Campbell to Pryse Campbell, 3 November 1742

I am very glad to hear by Johnny that your Cold is gone I pray God continue your health. I am sure my Dearest will be sorry to hear that I have lost the best Friend I had in this part of the World, poor Mr. Clutterbuck; he died this morning, was Free from feaver, or pain on Sunday, continued well yesterday, rested well all last night, eat his breakfast heartily and seem'd very well this morning, and sometime before noon was suddainly taken with fainting, and died in half a quarter of an hour; he was an able & usefull man of busyness, a valueable and agreable Friend. If all this was occasion'd, as is thought, by the prick of a thorn going through a hedge, what reason there is to be carefull. Let me entreat you my Dearest to be carefull of yourself both when you ride & when go a sporting on foot.

Yesterday Mr. Philipps presented the Petitions[170] from Wiston[171] & From Mr. R[awleigh] Mansel[172] against Mr. Owen[173] and moved they might be heard at the Bar

---

[169] William Edwardes (c.1712–1801), of Johnston, south Pembrokeshire; MP for Haverfordwest 1747–84 and 1786–1801. He sat in the Commons for 52 years and no speech by him has ever been recorded. After 1760 he voted with the government in every division. Edwardes leased Holland House, Kensington to Henry Fox in 1745 until 1768 when Fox purchased it. *HPC, 1754–90*, ii, 382. He was created Baron Kensington (Irish peerage) in 1776. For Edwardes' role in Pembrokeshire politics see P.D.G. Thomas, *Politics in Eighteenth-Century Wales* (Cardiff, 1998).

[170] *CJ*, xxiv, 340. Thomas Phillips, former mayor of Pembroke, presented several election petitions from burgesses of the borough of Wiston, Pembrokeshire; and Rawleigh Mansell of the county borough of Carmarthen, and also a burgess of Wiston, presented an election petition stating that his voters 'were obstructed and prevented from going into the said Hall [to vote] by a great number of persons, who were placed on the stairs . . . armed with pitchforks, and other offensive weapons'. Cited in Thomas, *Politics in Eighteenth-Century Wales*, 109.

[171] Wiston: a parish and tiny borough in Pembrokeshire. Since the Acts of Union (1536 and 1542) Wiston burgesses had had a right to vote in elections for the borough of Pembroke. However, the latter place frequently objected to Wiston burgesses voting and often petitioned parliament in protest.

[172] Rawleigh Mansel (1705–49), of Limestone Hill, Carmarthenshire. He was high sheriff of Carmarthenshire 1730 and was a member of the tory Society of Sea Serjeants.

[173] William Owen (c.1697–1781), of Orielton, Pembrokeshire; MP for Pembroke boroughs 1722–47 and 1761–74 and Pembrokeshire 1747–61. He voted with the administration in every recorded division.

as was order'd last year, the House divided and wee carried it against him by 160 against 82.[174] He had given the Petition against me to Lord Strange[175] who (after acquainting me) presented it & moved to refer it to the Committee without saying anything more about it. The Committee will meet next Monday. I have not heard that Mr. Symmons is come to Town.

Give My Love to your Brothers. I pray God Bless you all. My kind service to Mr. Rowe. God grant you . . .

52.

John Campbell, Llandovery [Carmarthenshire] to Pryse Campbell, 7 November 1742

The Post so long comeing in that I believe I shall not receive the letter I hope for from you, till I come to Brecknock [Brecon] this Evening. It was lucky I staid here yesterday for it proved a sad day: rain, hail, Lightening & Thunder. I believe Sir Erasmus Philipps[176] was very wet between this and New Inne. I fancy he went no further for I find by Mr. Price he was not much pleased with the thoughts of being at Carmarthen which he said was very noisy. Compliments pass'd between him & me but wee did not come together, I wonder'd to see him going to Picton[177] just before the Parliament meets when there is a Petition against him. My dearest I beg of you to be carefull of yourself & not venture any danger you can avoid, for my sake, remember you are the dear treasure of my heart, the Comfort & Joy of my Life. Give my Love to your Brothers, my kind service to Mr. Row[e], most kind remembrance to Johnny and make my Compliments to all Friends. I pray God . . .

James desires me to give his duty to you.

53.

John Campbell to Pryse Campbell, 18 November 1742

I thank you for your very kind letter what a comfort & joy it is for a Father & son with equal arder & sincerity to pray for each others long life, health & happyness. I was sorry to hear you had a cold, I hope you would take care to get it off as soon as possibly, such things should be taken care of when they are slight at the very first, then they are easily removed, but may grow very troublesome if neglected at first. You will be carefull of sitting near the Window in your dressing room when the wind is North, one is never so liable to cold as when sitting or standing still.

I was in great hurry when I writ last, but I intend when I have leisure to send you all the news I can and shall probably in writing to my Dearest speak with greater

---

[173] (continued) Succeeded his father Sir Arthur Owen (see below, letter 63) as 4th bt in 1753. With the help of Sir John Philipps, Owen defeated Campbell in the 1747 election, the latter retreating to his family borough of Nairn, Scotland. Owen was only concerned with local matters, particularly in strengthening his family's political hold on Pembrokeshire. He attended the Commons rarely. Thomas, *Politics in Eighteenth-Century Wales*, 125. See Introduction.

[174] *CJ*, xxiv, 340.

[175] James Murray (1690–1764), of Garth, Perth; Baron Strange 1736–64; MP for Perthshire 1715–24. Although classed as a tory he voted with the government on all recorded divisions.

[176] Sir Erasmus Philipps (1699–1743), of Picton Castle, Pembrokeshire; MP for Haverfordwest 1726–43. Returned as a whig he voted consistently against the administration. He was the elder brother of Sir John Philipps, 6th bt. He drowned in the river Avon near Bath when his horse was frightened by some pigs.

[177] Picton Castle, Pembrokeshire.

Freedom both of Men & things than I would to another, therefore when you have a mind to communicate the News to your Friends, and neighbors, it may be proper only to tell them the Facts, without shewing, or reading my letters to them. I believe your Mama gave you account of our meeting at the Cockpit[178] only she mistook in saying Lord John[179] instead of Lord George Sackville.[180] Our young Lords perform'd extremely well, you may be sure it was great pleasure to me to see my Favorite shew he has a head worthy of his heart. Mr. Walter[181] began the Opposition, to lay aside this Motion & for an Address of thanks for the speech[182] & assurances of Duty & affection in general Words, without comeing to any particulars. This they call reverting to the ancient method of Parliament, and to say truth our New Ministers have often contended for it, against the late Minister, and allways received the same Answers. They now gave to the broad Bottom,[183] all they could say to avoid the charge of inconsistency was, that the present conjuncture of Affairs was much more extraordinary than any of those in which they were for general Address's; but you will think Wee made a better figure who our Enemies must allow act consistently. The part of the Address most objected to, was that which mentions the 6000 Hanover Troops march'd into Flanders which are design'd to be in British pay, and indeed they talk'd of Hanover in a way one would not expect from Gentlemen who profess being Friends to the present Government. Some of the Wrongheads were for amending the Motion by leaveing out such words as they thought might imply an intention to pay the Hanover Troops, and they were above an hour puzzleing themselves, & both teizing, & diverting the House about it, but that being not the Measure of the Party, when a Question was put upon it, the negative was given without any trouble. Shippen spoke but seem'd to do it only to distinguish himself from those who have, or would have, left him; and to express his contempt for patriotism. Sir J[ohn] Cotton seems to set himself at the head of the Torys; but Mr. William Pitt I believe does not intend to be under any one, and he has to be sure a very good way of speaking, & parts very fit to make a figure in Parliament. Mr. Dodington would I believe make the first figure, but I fear it will be only in his own opinion, for though he has good parts, and accomplishments, yet the Coxcomb prevales over the Man of Sense; he spoke long in his affected familiar style, with several prettyness's but not in a way that will ever make great impression, or raise a Mans Character high in the House; they all agreed in calling this a stronger address than the late Ministry ever did, or would

---

[178] In a letter dated 16 Nov. 1742, CRO, Cawdor/Campbell box 128. The Cockpit was a government building in Whitehall, originally a cockpit. It was used by ministerial supporters to prepare for debates in the Commons and was also the location of the offices of the secretaries of state. Thomas, *Politics in Eighteenth-Century Wales*, 40–1.

[179] Lord John Philip Sackville (1713–65), MP for Tamworth 1734–47; lord of the bedchamber to Frederick prince of Wales 1745–9. Sackville died in a private lunatic asylum in Lausanne.

[180] Lord George Sackville (1716–85), known as George Germain from 1770; MP for Dover 1741–61, Hythe 1761–8 and East Grinstead 1768–72. Chief secretary (Ireland) 1751–5; joint vice-treasurer (Ireland) 1765–6; first lord of trade 1775–9; secretary of state of the American department 1775–82. In the power struggle between Fox and Pitt, Sackville leaned towards the former until Feb. 1757, when he supported Pitt's motion for a subsidy for Hanoverian troops.

[181] Peter Walter (1715–53), MP for Shaftesbury, Dorset, 1741–7.

[182] *CJ*, xxiv, 336–7. The debate on the address divided 259 to 150 in the affirmative.

[183] The new ministry combined old and new whigs as well as a small number of opposition members and became known as the broad-bottom administration.

have attempted; Sir J[ohn Hynde] Cotton took notice of the speech being artfully & Ministerially worded, he said he remember'd a very Ministerial Letter (meaning that from the late King to the King of Spain[184] about Gibraltar) and he knew who was the Author of that letter. He believed he could ghess who was the Author of the speech (meaning Lord Carteret) and gave several hints of that Lord going greater lengths than ever Sir Robert did or would have done, and makeing his court to the King by Hanover & Pitt, L[yttelto]n & some others all hinted that the Ministers flatter'd the King by Takeing his Hanover Troops, in order to secure their Places, and infer'd that they would never venture to dismiss them, for fear of being turn'd out. On our side Winnington spoke very well & with great spirit, Mr. Sandys did very well as a private Gentleman[185] but Mr. Pelham made the speech that ought to have come from a Chancellor of the Exchequer.[186] He spoke long with great knowledge and judgement, force of reason, & expression, and both with Modesty and Dignity. Sir John Barnard spoke well strongly, explicitely & resolutely, highly approved all the Measures have been taken abroad, said in supporting the Queen of Hungary Wee did not fight others Battles but our own, as Wee would exert ourselves to the utmost to extinguish a fire in our Neighbors House to prevent our own being burnt next, he said he thought the March of the Hanover Troops had done great service, it was not now the Question whether Wee would pay them, but if that came before us, and it should appear that the Electorate was not able to maintain so great a body of Troops out of their own Country, at the same time they had so many in the Electorate; he should think it right for us to pay them; saw no reason Wee should not take them as well as any other foreign Troops, into our Pay, and had no fear of their being continued longer than necessary, his Speech had a very good effect, and Struck a damp upon the Opposers, Lyttelton spoke next & grieved most ruefully at his differing from Sir J[ohn] B[arnard].

I forgot to tell you that at the Cockpit, the Chancellor of the Exchequer [Samuel Sandys] came to me ask'd about the Petition against me, and affected to talk with me in the most Friendly & intimate manner. Wee lean'd on the back of the same Chair, with our heads togather, and he held my hand in his, allmost all the time Wee talk'd; Wee never were so great before, or anything like, or near it. I saw Lord Orford on tuesday in a little sort of Levee, he took me by the hand aside from the Company and with great kindness said if he could serve me in anything I might command him as freely as his own son.

Yesterday after the Address was agreed to Mr. Philipps of Kilgetty Stood up & moved[187] for the House to go into a Committee on the state of the Nation the 17th of January. Carew[188] Seconded but nobody else on that side said a Word, So the

---

[184] Philip V (1683–1746), Bourbon king of Spain 1700–24 and 1724–46. In 1724 he abdicated in favour of his son Louis I (1707–24), but returned to the throne after Louis' death a few months later.

[185] That is, he was not speaking as chancellor of the exchequer.

[186] Henry Pelham became chancellor of the exchequer on 12 Dec. 1743, replacing Sandys.

[187] *CJ*, xxiv, 339.

[188] Thomas Carew (1702–66), of Crowcombe, Minehead, Somerset; MP for Minehead 1739–47. He was descended from the Carews of Carew Castle, Pembrokeshire. *PH*, xiii, 1056–63, for Carew's speech. Horace Walpole wrote that he was 'a crazy zealot, who believed himself possessed by the devil, till he was cured by his apothecary's assuring him that he had met the devil upon the stairs coming from him'. Cited in *HPC, 1715–54*, i, 528.

Chancellor of the Exchequer [Samuel Sandys] got up made a pretty brisk Answer, & moved to Adjourn, upon which without any Debate, Wee divided and carried it for adjourning by 169 against 121.[189] This was between 2 & 3 o'Clock. This Motion was I suppose merely his own, for had it been concerted the Party would doubtless have spoke to Support it; a man Shews want of Judgement, a meddleing busy temper and hurts his Character by doing such Things without the knowledge or approbation of his Friends, for no Party can do anything to purpose, but when they act in concert. Kilgetty was for Granting no Supplys till the State of the Nation was known, & yet would put off that enquiry for two Months; how absurd unless he would confess he would destroy the Government by putting such a full stop to all Measures, but perhaps he only wanted to make this Session as long as the last. This day I expected him to present the Petition against me,[190] & I believe he intended it but was stopt by Winnington presenting the Petition against him & moveing to refer it to the Committee.[191] Kilgetty spoke brag'd of the Goodness of his Cause and desired to have the Petition heard at the Bar as soon as possible. Winnington would not agree to the Bar, but said if the Gent pleased he would be for hearing it the very first in the Committee, the Question being put to refer it to the Committee. Kilgettys Friends divided the thin House, and Wee carried it for the refering 90 against 37. This dampt the Party so much they would present no Petitions to day. H[enry] Fox presented that against Sir Erasmus which was referr'd to the Committee, and then after appointing monday for the Committee of Supply Wee adjoun'd to that day, & went to Court with our Address. Probably Mr. Philipps[192] will present Mr. Symmons[193] Petition[194] on Monday [22 November] or watch some time when our Friends are absent, but I hope Wee shall not let them catch us. I can't believe he so much desired the trouble and expense of a hearing, but may be he thought that if his went to the Bar Wee could not easily hinder that against me to go there too & perhaps thought he might make a bargain, he look'd very much disconcerted. I spoke with Lord Wilmington to day at Court. He was very obligeing and talks as if he gave the Collectors Place to me, but who will have the Credit of it in the Country I can't tell.

I forgot to tell you that Sir J[ohn] Rushout got up to Speak the first day, but was put out and he said the Speaker trying to make the House quiet put him out worse than anybody and he scolded the speaker, as they speak aside in a Play, but so that I heard him planely & could have laugh'd very heartily. My Compliments to the Laird. Love to your Brothers, kind remembrance to Mr. Rowe, Johnny &c Pray my Dearest be very Carefull of yourself in every respect. I pray God . . .

[189] *CJ*, xxiv, 339.

[190] This was presented on 22 Nov. by John Symmons (see Note 193). *CJ*, xxiv, 340.

[191] A committee of privileges and elections was appointed on 17 Nov. 1742 to examine election petitions. *CJ*, xxiv, 337.

[192] Sir John Philipps of Kilgetty, Pembrokeshire.

[193] John Symmons (1701–64), of Llanstinan; tory MP for Cardigan boroughs, 1746–61 and a member of the Society of Sea Serjeants.

[194] *CJ*, xxiv, 340: 'Presented to the House, this petition and that of Rawleigh Mansell, complaining of undue elections in both Pembroke Borough and the County were voted 82–160 in the negative'.

54.

John Campbell to Pryse Campbell, 20 November 1742

I hope you have got rid of your Cold & that you will be carefull of your health (I don't by that mean to make you tender) and read to follow the Drs. advice when there is occasion. I take Allys to be the Chicken pox which is a very slight thing, I hope it may help to carry off his Cough. I was yesterday at Leicester House,[195] it being the Princess's Birthday.[196] H[is] R[oyal] H[ighness] spoke to me graciously enough. There was one of the greatest Crowds of Company that I ever saw. Poor Mr. Clutterbuck cannot yet recover his health, I saw him so well on Monday that he talk'd of comeing to the House next day but had on tuesday some return of feaver. I saw him on wednesday better, but on thursday he was much out of order, some what better since but far from well I fear. Your Mama sends her Love to you & your Brothers, my Love to them & affectionate service to the Laird. Wee had terrible cold raw ugly weather ever since I came to Town till this day which was mild. I think a south west wind, a damp air, but I had a long walk this morning in most nasty streets. I was enquiring for Gloves but fear there are none here quite so good as those your Mama sent you from Woodstock, there has also been enquirys about Horses but I think without success. Remember me very kindly to Johnny, and make my Compliments wherever you think proper. I hope my Dearest you apply with Care & diligence to your studies, you will be amply paid by the Pleasure you will hereafter reap from them. I don't intend by what I say to confine you any more than usual only desire a good application, which I don't doubt you will give. I pray God . . .

I send you the Worcester Instructions[197] which are so remarkable insolent.

Going through Leicester Fields to day I observed all the rails round the Square Garden entirely taken away, and was inform'd that the Mob pull'd them down and made a Bonfire of them last night.[198] They were somewhat old and decay'd yet I think the independent Inhabitants of Westminster took a liberty not very pleasant to peaceable People who have any property to care for.

55.

John Campbell to Pryse Campbell, 25 November 1742

The inclosed will give you a little diversion, you must compare it with the London Instruction[199] & remember those from Edinburgh calling London their sister City. The

---

[195] The prince of Wales had established his (opposition) court at Leicester House, The Strand, by this date.

[196] Princess Augusta of Saxe-Gotha (1719–72), princess of Wales 1736–51 and thereafter dowager princess of Wales. Mother of George III. She was born on 30 Nov.

[197] Just prior to the opening of parliament the mayor, aldermen and citizens of Worcester sent instructions to their MPs, Winnington and Sandys, on how they expected them to vote in forthcoming debates. Neither MP complied. *HPC, 1715–54*, i, 356. After the fall of Walpole there were two 'waves of instructions' to various opposition MPs from frustrated constituents, a campaign begun as a response to failure of the opposition to form an administration. Many of the instructions were published in opposition newspapers. R. Harris, *A Patriot Press: National Politics and the London Press in the 1740s* (Oxford, 1993), 26–7.

[198] *Westminster Journal*, 27 Nov. 1742, reported that while a ball was in progress at Leicester House to celebrate the birthday of the princess of Wales, 'the Mob pull'd down the Wooden Rails that inclose'd the Gardens in the Middle of the Square, and burnt them, declaring, while they were doing it, that it was scandalous his Royal Highness should live in a Place that had so mean Appearance, and that it would be a means of Making the Place beautiful – Which is probably the case'.

[199] Instructions from the common council of London were issued to its two MPs telling them how they were expected to vote on a variety of subjects, such as the war with Spain. The London Instructions were published on 16 Nov. 1742 in an advertisement appearing in the *London Evening Post* of that date.

Names are Paul Whitehead & Edward Carey, the first a sawcy poet (I think a Taylors son) who is under a Censure of the House of Lords for abusing some of the Peers in an Impudent Satyr call'd Manners a few years ago, the second is a Chirargion. They with Guthry[200] who I think should not have been forgot, were Managers of the Westminster Mob, alias independent Electors, and they two were the managers of the Scald miserable Procession.[201] I forgot to tell you that when the Pembroke (Wiston) Petition and R[awleigh] Mansels were present[202] [sic] & moved for the Bar, after Mr. Owen & I had spoke the great Mr. Brereton[203] thought he must say something so he said it was the fashion last year for Petitions to go to the Bar, but now he hoped the fashion was alter [sic], upon which the Broad bottoms set up a loud laugh. You know my Dear it is our busyness at present to unite the Whigs of the old & new Ministry as much as possible for the common Cause, there nothing could be more imprudent, and in such a supply as he more impertinent than to say a thing that raise a laugh & carried a reflection upon our new Friends, everybody of sense was much vex'd at his impudent folly. Wee expect some attack upon Lord O[rford] next week. They will try by that to disunite us, and if that fails double their abuse upon the New Ministers, who I hope will not be such Fools as to fall into their Trap, or value their Censures.

The King has promised Sir Charles Wager Poor Clutterbucks Place. I am truely grieved for the loss of my Friend but since the Place is vacant I am glad Sir Charles will have it. He is not to kiss the Kings hand till after next week. Murray[204] the famous Orator is to be chose by the Duke of Newcastles interest for Boroughbridge so I suppose Wee may depend on his assistance in the House. My love to your Brothers I hope they are very well & good Boys Trubs letter is long comeing. My Dearest Boy remember all my advice & my earnest entreatys. I pray God . . .

My Compliments to the Laird, Kind service to Mr. Row[e] and remembrance to Johnny.

You must also look in the Westminster Instructions.[205] The City of Bristols letter to Mr. Southwell[206] in the Gentlemans Evening Post[207] is very handsome & decent.

---

[200] William Guthrie (c.1708–70), historian and political journalist. From 1743 to 1746 he wrote under the pseudonym of Jeffrey Broadbottom producing scurrilous works such as *Old England: Or, the Constitutional Journal*, and the scatological *Serious and Cleanly Meditations upon an House-of-Office (a Boghouse)*. In 1744 Henry Pelham awarded him an annual government pension of £200.

[201] The 'Scald Miserable Procession' was organised by the poet Paul Whitehead and Esquire Carey, surgeon to the prince of Wales, as a parody of freemasonry. Carey was grand steward of the masons in 1741. He was dismissed by the prince for his involvement in the procession.

[202] On 22 Nov. *CJ*, xxiv, 340.

[203] Thomas Brereton (*d*. 1756), of Shotwick Park, Chester; MP for Liverpool 1724–9 and 1734–56. He was an unstinting supporter of Walpole. Campbell and Brereton were the tellers for the noes in the vote on the Pembroke petition. *CJ*, xxiv, 340.

[204] William Murray (1705–93), of Ken Wood, Middlesex; MP for Boroughbridge 1742–56. He became an MP in order to be appointed solicitor-general on the resignation of Sir John Strange in Dec. 1742. A talented lawyer and an excellent orator who remained loyal to the administration, being placed in the Commons by the duke of Newcastle. He is regarded as the founder of English commercial law. Created 1st earl of Mansfield 1776.

[205] Drawn up by the Westminster Society of Independent Electors, 'a collection of the more extreme and malcontent elements of the metropolitan opposition'. Charles Pratt believed these instructions were the product of a 'brutal fierceness of misrule and anarchy'. Cited in Harris, *A Patriot Press*, 116.

[206] Edward Southwell.

[207] The letter, stating the city of Bristol's support for the war with France and Spain, was actually published in the *Gentleman's Magazine*, xii (1742), 595–6.

Last Sunday our Aunt of Mabws dined here. Mr. Owen Carried her home in his Coach. She took notice to him that I drank very little, and very gravely & wisely said she thought it was better to drink too much than too little.

56.

John Campbell to Pryse Campbell, 27 November 1742

I heartily wish you joy of completeing your 15th year. I pray God grant you may see many years in health and Peace. He has given you good sense and a virtuous dispo-sition, I hope you will be carefull to improve the one and preserve the other invio-lable. Wee were in some mistake about your Birthday, I thought this was the day, but upon farther enquiry find it was yesterday. I was very sorry to hear my Dear Ally was so ill, but by the Drs. letter I hope the worst was over, I pray God it may, for he is a sweet Boy.

Wee certainly expect an attack upon Lord Orford next week but are in [sic] yet sure what day or in what manner it will be made. They have talk'd of going upon some part of the Report of the Secret Committee which they say may be call'd for as a part of the journals, but now it is rather thought they will go upon the Convention, but how they can either make it a Crime or fix it on Lord Orford is above my understanding. Wee have no doubt of a Majority against it, but don't exactly know how it will be managed, whether by a flat negative, or some less direct way of throwing it off, you may be sure Wee should wish for the first. Mr. Worcester[208] would join us in that, but perhaps some wiser folks (alias greater fools) may be more mealy mouth'd. Lord Weathercocks[209] word was, depend upon it Sir Wee will battle it, a word not very distinct, beside what he says is not so much to be regarded unless he is got above the eddy Winds that whirl'd him about so last Spring; I am not sure neither who will be the mover, Fazakerley[210] says he is too old to undertake so laborious a part, Bubb some say declines it some say is not approved for it: the Noble person who presented the petition against mee has been named & may probably be the man, if so Fazakerley will really undertake the Thing though he pretends to decline it; he is no doubt the great director of it. The broad bottom have certainly sent very pressing letters to call up their Friends, these particulars I had in a private conversation therefore you may keep them to yourself. Lord Hay[211] yesterday assured me that the Duke of Argyll is quite against makeing anymore attacks upon Lord Orford, that he was vex'd at his Nephew Mackenzie[212] for not being in the

---

[208] This could be George Lyttelton who was MP for Worcester at this time.

[209] William Pulteney – he is referred to as such in a ballad reputedly written by John, Lord Hervey in Oct. 1742:

> All that weathercock Pulteney shall ask we must grant
> For to make him a great noble nothing I want;
> And to cheat such a man demands all my arts,
> For though he's a fool, he's a fool with great parts.

Cited in Thomas Wright, *A Caricature History of the Georges* (1868), 145.

[210] Nicholas Fazakerley (?1685–1767), of Preston, Lancashire; MP for Preston 1732–67. A tory lawyer.

[211] Lord Charles Hay (c.1700–60), of Linplum, East Lothian; MP for Haddingtonshire 1741–7.

[212] James Stuart Mackenzie (?1719–1800), of Rosehaugh, Ross and Belmont, Angus; MP for Argyllshire 1742–7, Buteshire 1747–54, Ayr Burghs 1754–61 and Ross-shire 1761–80. Brother of James Stuart, 3rd earl of Bute and nephew of the 2nd and 3rd dukes of Argyll, under whose guardianship he was raised. He failed to be present in the Commons on a number of occasions, when expected by Argyll. In 1743–4 he was absent

House to Vote for the Address the first day. Lord Hay seem'd to desire what he told me should be known.

This day Judge Parker[213] kiss'd the Kings hand for being Cheif Baron of the Exchequer and Mr. Murray for being Solicitor General, Sir John Strange[214] resigning who has a Sign Manual from the King to take place between the Attorney and Solicitor General. High Bred Harry F[urnese][215] will certainly be out of his Place they talk of Jeffreys[216] of Brecknock to succede him, I was told that Weathercock gives up High bred & says he deceived him this I heard privately. I believe K[ilgett]y[217] may be in some danger of looseing his seat in the House. I don't know whether that will be for my private advantage, I fancy he sees his danger and might be glad of a bargain to make me quite easy in order to secure himself, but if he is turn'd out I may expect he will revenge himself by giveing me as much trouble as he can; and if I should keep it off this Session they may bring it on next.

Lord Hay is building a fine new Library 90 foot long 22 broad & 21 high.[218] Towards each end a bow window where the greatest bread [*sic*] will be 27. The form of the room is like this . . .[219] I was this morning with Lord Orford in Arlington Street.[220] His House I believe is a good one by candlelight, but the back rooms are very dark in the day time, worse than where he lived in St. James Square. Give my Love & Blessing to your Brothers. I hope Trubs cold is well before this. Let Dear Ally Know his Mama & I were very sorry for his illness. Your Sisters are all very well. My compliments to the good Laird & kind service to Mr. Row[e]. I pray God . . .

---

[212] (*continued*) from the Commons, pursuing Barberina Campanini (1721–99), an opera dancer in Venice. The 3rd earl of Argyll arranged for Stuart to be deported from Prussia when he followed the celebrated dancer there. *HPC, 1715–54*, ii, 454.

[213] Sir Thomas Parker (1695–1784), of a Staffordshire family. He received the patronage of Lord Hardwicke throughout his life. He remained chief baron until he retired in 1772.

[214] Sir John Strange (1694–1754), of Leyton Grange, Essex; MP for West Looe 1737–41 and Totnes 1742–54. Solicitor-general 1737–42 and recorder of the City of London 1739–42, both of which he resigned in 1742, for reasons commented upon in the satire by Porcupinus Pelagius (pseudonym of Macnamara Morgan), *Causidicade, a Panegyri-Satiri-Serio-Comic-Dramatical Poem on the Strange Resignation and Stranger Promotion* (1743).

[215] Henry Furnese (c.1688–1756), of Gunnersbury House, Middlesex; MP for Dover 1720–34, Morpeth 1738–41 and New Romney 1741–56. From 1739 Furnese attached himself to Pulteney for which he was rewarded after Walpole's fall with joint secretaryship of the treasury with Henry Legge though at least one satirist, Hanbury-Williams, believed Furnese had to pay 'Bath's doxy' (Lady Bath) half his salary. *HPC, 1715–54*, ii, 56. The line 'High bred Harry Furnese' appeared in 'A New Ode' by Hanbury-Williams and refers to Furnese's lowly origins as an apprentice to a London merchant.

[216] John Jeffreys (1706–66), of the Priory, Brecon and Sheen, Surrey; MP for Breconshire 1734–47 and Dartmouth 1747–66. Pulteney rewarded his support by making Jeffreys – a remarkably incapable – joint secretary to the treasury after Walpole's fall. He kept the office until 1746. From 1752 to 1754 he was secretary to the chancellor of the exchequer. *HPC, 1715–54*, ii, 173.

[217] Kilgetty, that is John Philipps. He had been returned as the MP for Carmarthen by the tory borough in 1741, a seat he kept until 1747. However, Campbell is referring to petitions against Philipps, which were eventually dropped in a trade-off with a petition against Campbell. See Thomas, *Politics in Eighteenth-Century Wales*, 117–18. See Introduction.

[218] Probably at the family seat of Linplum House, Lothian.

[219] See Figure 2.2.

[220] The Walpole residence in London was in Arlington Street, near St James's Street. Horace Walpole was born there and Sir Robert Walpole died there.

Figure 2.2: A rough plan of Lord Hay's new library as drawn by Campbell.

57.

John Campbell to Pryse Campbell, at night, 30 November 1742

I writ in the morning in a great hurry being obliged to go out & not being sure of returning early enough in the evening and now I have been forced to answer a hatfull of letters I had upon Monocles death.[221] The first application I had was from Mr Bowen of Camrose[222] and I have ask'd it for his son,[223] but don't yet know my success.

I would have told you that last night at the Committee Mr Pelham in speaking for the long day for the Petition against me, profess'd his regard for me in the most obligeing manner, and I thought did me great honor for tho' I despise what is commonly call'd popularity, yet few things give one greater satisfaction, than the regard & Friendship of Men of sense, knowledge, honor, & Virtue, and such indeed I am convinced Mr. Pelham is.

[221] This is most probably the Rev. George Phillips who died in Nov. 1742. He was rector of St Thomas's church, Haverfordwest, the living of which was with the crown. 'Monocle' is probably his nickname – 'one eye'. OED.

[222] The Bowen family of Camrose, Pembrokeshire. Campbell is referring to Charles Bowen (b. 1683); he owed the Bowen family a favour – Matthew Bowen was the high sheriff of the county, and thus the returning officer, in Campbell's election of Dec. 1741. See F. Green, 'Bowen of Roblinston and Camrose', West Wales Historical Records, xi (1926), 37–62.

[223] Hugh Bowen, who became the rector of St Thomas's church, Haverfordwest, in 1743.

This day Lord Hillsborough[224] presented the Petition against Mr. Wynne[225] for the Town of Denbigh[226] & moved for it to be heard at the Bar, there was, a short but sharp debate, the Tories reflected, both irregularly, & indecently, upon the proceedings of the Committee last night, and the youngest Greenville[227] so much upon the New Ministers, that the speaker stopt him; their anger was very great, which I was glad of, being sensible it proceded from their despare; yet I could not but admire their modesty, in complaneing of hardships in regard to Elections after such things as I have seen them do; Wee divided & carried it against hearing at the Bar 235 against 190.[228] Then it was refer'd to the Committee, with an Instruction to hear it next after Pembrokeshire. I presented one from Dick Lloyd which is to be heard next after that.[229]

I ought to have acknowledged that Sir Watkins Williams Wynn though he complaned loudly in the Committee of putting off Mr. Symmons Petition to so long a day that it could not be heard, yet was very civil to me personally, saying he knew nothing of the merits of the Election, and did not speak at all in regard to or against the Gentleman concern'd, only for doing justice by letting the Petition be heard; not that I believe they desired it should be heard, but if it could have been got to an early day, they hoped I fancy to make a bargain for Kilgetty. Today Before the Petitions were presented Mr Waller[230] moved for the defensive Alliance[231] (concluded as he call'd it) between the King and Russia, & Prussia should be laid before the House but it happen'd, unluckily for him, that the King in his speech only says those Alliances were agreed upon, for a Treaty cannot be said to be concluded till the Ratifications by the respective Princes are exchanged, which is not yet done. I don't know whether that with Russia is as yet sign'd by the Plenipotentiarys, that with Prussia was sign'd here lately, as you saw in the News, so Mr. Waller changed the Word concluded for the word agreed so his Motion which before contain'd a false fact, was now only absurd, & without precedent, for as there is no example, so in truth it is contrary to Common Sense, for the House to call for a Treaty before it is concluded; he would not withdraw his Motion, so there was a very faint ay, a loud no, and no division: The call of the

[224] Wills Hill (1718–93), of North Aston, Oxon; opposition whig MP for Warwick 1741–56. Known as Viscount Hillsborough (Irish peerage) 1742–51 and earl of Hillsborough 1751–89. Secretary of state for the colonies 1768–72.

[225] Sir John Wynn (1701–73), 2nd bt, of Glynllifon and Bodfel, Caernarvonshire and Melai, Denbighshire; whig MP for Caernarvonshire 1740–1 and 1754–61, Denbigh boroughs 1741–7 and Caernarvon boroughs 1761–8. Deputy cofferer of the household 1743; deputy treasurer of Chelsea Hospital, 1744–54; surveyor-general of the mines in north Wales. Wynn was employed by Lord Bute in 1762 to establish a ministerial majority. For the election contests between the Wynns of Glynllifon and the tory Wynns of Wynnstay, see Thomas, *Politics in Eighteenth-Century Wales*.

[226] *CJ*, xxiv, 347.

[227] James Grenville (1715–83), MP for Old Sarum 1742–7, Bridport 1747–54, Buckingham 1754–68 and Horsham 1768–70. Third son of Richard Grenville (1678–1727) of Wotton and brother of George, Richard and Thomas Grenville.

[228] *CJ*, xxiv, 347.

[229] *CJ*, xxiv, 348. After his defeat in the 1741 election Richard Lloyd repeatedly petitioned the Commons until his petition was rejected in 1746.

[230] Edmund Waller (c.1699–1771), of Barn Hall, Beaconsfield, Buckinghamshire; opposition whig MP for Great Marlow 1722–41 and Chipping Wycombe 1741–54. Cofferer of the household 1744–6.

[231] Treaty of alliance between Britian and Russia concluded 11 Dec. 1742 and ratified by Russia 10 Feb. 1743.

House is adjourned to this day fortnight,[232] I don't know what day Wee are to expect the Motion upon Lord Orford. Winnington said a very good thing yesterday to Sir John Hynde Cotton on the reading the Land Tax Bill[233] to me complan'd, as usual, of Officers haveing their Tax's repaid them, it was answer'd that many of their salarys were so small that they could not live if their Tax's were not repaid. Sir Broadbottom[234] said there were some considerable Officers who had their Tax's repaid if he was well inform'd as the Commissioners of the Navy & Admiralty, Winnington reply'd that the Navy Salarys were but small, for the Duty they do, and if the Honorable Gentleman had ever been in the Admiralty he would have known their Tax's were not repaid, this raised aloud laugh allmost all over the House & Sir John really knew not how to look. The accounts of Preferments in the News papers are very wrong, I think I told you all that was true. Mr Murray kiss'd hands as Solicitor before his Election, he is not yet return'd I don't but it may come to morrow. I fancy the latter part of My letter last Post would let you know in what private Conversation I heard what I told you; and you would ghess whose Closet Weathercock was in, when he said depend upon it Sir Wee will battle it. The Broadbottom Gentlemen loose no opportunity of being severe upon the Chancellor of the Exchequer who does not value it a pin, and I hope will act as true Whig in spite and contempt of them, and our Friend ought to support him. This my Dearest is all the News I can think of at present. I have not time to write in regular order, but put things down as they come in my head, my desire is both to divert and improve you by the best informations I can give you of men & things. Pray my Dearest be carefull of your self. I pray God . . .

58.
John Campbell to Pryse Campbell, 2 December 1742
The accounts I received last Post from Mr Brodie & Mr Rowe of your good health good behavior and improvement brought tears of Joy into my eyes, I pray God continue such happyness to me, and make me truely thankfull for it.

I send you this Post a Pamphlet[235] which I am sorry is publish'd, because I think the best thing Wee can do in our present Circumstances is to support the present Administration, therefore I would not have Truths told publicly to their disadvantage, for though falshoods are to be spoke at no time yet there are many Truths not to be spoke at all times, for which reason I would not have you put it in many hands, and I desire you not to tell any body who you believe the Author, though I think myself as sure it was writ by one you & I visited one morning just, I think the very day, before you left London, as if I had seen it under his hand, it is writ with so much Life, & Wit that I am sure it will entertain you very much. I don't doubt your finding out who are meant

[232] The call was not made until 18 Jan. 1743. *CJ*, xxiv, 383.

[233] The land tax was initially established in 1693 and 'was always a sore point between government and . . . opposition'. W.R. Ward, *The English Land Tax in the Eighteenth Century* (Oxford, 1953), 1.

[234] Sir Francis Fane (c.1698–1757) of Brympton, Somersetshire; MP for Taunton 1727–41, Peterfield 1741–7, Ilchester 1747–54 and Lyme Regis 1754–7. Fane was chairman of the committees of supply and ways and means 1739–51, and as such he took the chair in the Commons in the place of the Speaker who left the chamber, when these subjects were debated, as he did for all committees of the whole House.

[235] This could be Lord Hervey's *Miscellaneous Thoughts* which was published in the autumn of 1742.

by the Triumvirate,[236] if you do not ghess them immediately, read over the Ballad call'd the Patriots are come,[237] and that will explane the Characters. I divide it in three for the franks the first part I direct to Mr Brodie, the second to Mr Row[e], the third to J[ohn] Wright. I would not put any of it with this because of what I tell you of the Author Triumvirate and one is not sure but Pacquets with Prints inclosed may be open'd.

Yesterday Mr Lyttelton moved for a Secret Committee upon Lord Orford exactly in the same words that it was resolved last Session. The Debate began about two and lasted till sometime after six in the Evening When Wee divided ay's 186 No's 253.[238] Lord Limerick, Sir J[ohn] Barnard, Lord Percival, Mr. Hume Campbell, Mr. Hooper, Sir Edmund Thomas, voted for the Motion.[239] Sir W[atkins] W[illiams] W[ynn] seconded. While he was speaking he was obliged to sit down for some time to see the new Solicitor general [William Murray] introduced by Mr Pelham, & the Attorney general [Dudley Ryder]. The speakers that I can recollect for the Motion were Mr Lyttelton, Sir W[atkins] W[illiams] W[ynn], Sir J[ohn] Barnard, Lord Strange, Mr Waller Mr William Pitt, Mr Dodington the eldest,[240] Mr Greenville, Lord Hillsborough, Mr Powney, Mr Carew, Sir Cordell Firebrass, Sir Edward Turnor, Mr Viner Nugent.[241] Against the Motion Mr Edward Walpole, Lord Donneraile, Mr H[enry] Legge, Colonel

---

[236] The Triumvirate were Carteret, Sandys and Pulteney. The opposition *London Evening Post*, 31 Dec. 1743, published the following on their rise and subsequent consequences:

John, Sam and Will
combin'd of late
To form a new Triumvirate;
To share Authority and Money,
Like Caesar, Lepidus and Tony.
But mark what follow'd from this Union:-
Will left his Countrymen's Communion,
And tho' in Office he appear'd,
Was neither honour'd, lov'd or fear'd.
Sam in the Sunshine buzz'd a little;
Then sank in Pow'r, and rose in Title;
So Will and Sam obscure remain'd.
And John with gen'ral Odium reign'd.

See also Wright, *Caricature History of the Georges*, 50, and the *ODNB* for William Pulteney.

[237] *The Patriots are Come or, a New Doctrine for a Crazy Constitution*, was published on 22 Oct. 1742. *Daily Advertiser*, 22 Oct. 1742.

[238] *CJ*, xxiv, 348.

[239] John, Viscount Perceval (1711–70), MP for Westminster 1741–7, Weobley 1747–54 and Bridgewater 1754–62; Irish MP for Dingle 1731–49. He succeeded his father as 2nd earl of Egmont (Irish peerage) in 1748; lord of the bedchamber to the prince of Wales 1748–51; first lord of the admiralty 1763–6; Alexander Hume Campbell (1708–60), opposition whig MP for Berwickshire 1734–41 and 1742–60; Edward Hooper (?1701–95), MP for Christchurch 1734–48. A supporter of Pulteney, Hooper sat on the committee to inquire into the last ten years of Walpole's administration; Sir Edmund Thomas (1712–67), 3rd baron, of Wenvoe Castle, Glamorganshire; MP for Chippenham 1741–54 and Glamorgan 1761–7.

[240] Was Campbell mistaken here? George Dodington (c.1681–1757), of Horsington, Somerset, MP for Weymouth and Melcombe Regis, died in 1741 according to *HPC, 1715–54*, ii, 615.

[241] Peniston Powney (?1699–1757), of Ives Place, Maidenhead; tory MP for Berkshire 1739–57; Sir Cordell Firebrace (1712–59), of Long Melford, Suffolk; tory MP for Suffolk 1735–59; Sir Edward Turnor (1719–66), of Ambrosden, Oxon; tory MP for Great Bedwyn 1741–7, Oxfordshire 1755–61 and Penryn 1761–6; Robert Nugent (1709–88), of Gosfield, Essex; MP for St Mawes 1741–54 and 1774–84, and Bristol 1754–74. Horace Walpole commented of Nugent that 'This modest Irish converted Catholic stallion does talk a prodigious deal of nonsense in behalf of English liberty'. Cited in *HPC, 1715–54*, ii, 302.

Bladen, Chancellor of the Exchequer [Samuel Sandys], Dr Lee, Mr Fox, Mr Pelham, Colonel Cholmondley.[242]

The new Ministers were charged with self contradiction with self interested few [sic] and with manageing Affairs worse than Lord Orford in the bitterest and most provokeing language that could be invented, which the Chancellor of the Exchequer [Samuel Sandys] received with intredpidity & contempt. Mr Carew had got a Magazine[243] in which Mr. Sandys speech upon the Motion for removeing Sir Robert Walpole from H[is] M[ajesty]'s Person & Councills was printed. He held it in his hand and read most of it[244] very distinctly as part of his own speech it was an odd thought, not a bad one, but required good assurance to put in execution. As soon as he sat down Colonel Cholmondeley rose & said as he not [sic] a printed speech in his Pockett to read in answer to the Gentleman he should only repete two lines he happen'd to remember out of Martial.[245] I have no Martial by me & can't remember them exactly but the end with these words: male dum recitas incipit esse tuum.[246] I really think this little sort of turn was the only thing that could be done upon the occasion. You may be sure that as the New Ministers were charged with changeing for their Place's, they did not fail to retort speaking with Anger and resentment for their disappointment, upon those who would have come in & did not. The Dear joy Poet Laureat[247] happen'd to say that discontent was occasion'd by disappointment raised a great laugh from our side of the House. H[enry] Fox rejoyced & triumph'd on the Union of the Whigs and insulted the Tories for not being able to prevent or break it charmingly. Mr Pelham used all the proper arguments against the Motion & gave a noble testimony to Lord Orford saying that he firmly believed that dureing the whole course of his long administration, his view was the public good and his sincere endeavor to serve his King & Country faithfull I gave you the meaning not perhaps the exact words. He farther said my belief is founded on knowledge I know that it was so. Mr. Dodington spoke much better than ever he has done since he was in opposition but from him it was shamfull, he was put in mind of his joining so long with Sir Robert Walpole to which he only answer'd that he join'd as long as he thought it right & left them when he could no longer honestly join. This was a poor come off for he did not resign but was turn'd out & never gave a Vote in

---

[242] Edward Walpole (1706–84), of Frogsmore, Berkshire; MP for Lostwithiel 1730–4 and Great Yarmouth 1734–68; Sir Robert's son. Martin Bladen (?1680–1746), of Aldborough Hatch, Essex; MP for Stockbridge 1715–34, Maldon 1734–41 and Portsmouth 1741–6; supporter of Walpole. James Cholmondeley (1708–75), whig MP for Bossney 1731–4, Camelford 1734–41 and Montgomery 1741–7. A consistent supporter of Walpole. He was given a colonelcy in 1741 and distinguished himself at the battle of Falkirk on 17 Jan. 1746 against the jacobites, preventing an English rout by standing firm against the enemy.

[243] Sandys' speech was reported in the *Gentleman's Magazine*, xi, May–July 1741. A different version of the speech was reported in the *London Magazine*. See M. Ransome, 'The Reliability of Contemporary Reporting of Debates in the House of Commons, 1727–41', *BIHR*, xix (1942–3), 76–7.

[244] According to *PH*, xii, 906, Carew read Sandys' printed speech in the debate on the Place Bill, 3 Dec. 1742.

[245] Marcus Valerius Martialis (c.38–104 AD), Latin poet best known for his *Book of Epigrams*, of which he wrote over 1,500.

[246] Martial, *Epigram* 1.38. The full quote is: 'Quem recitas meus est, o Fidentine, libellus; sed male cum recitas, incipit esse tuus'. Translated: 'Oh Fidentinus, the book which you recite is mine; but when you recite badly, it will begin to be yours'.

[247] Campbell is referring to an MP, perhaps Charles Hanbury-Williams (see Chapter 8, Note 110) or George Lyttelton rather than *the* poet laureate, Colly Cibber, who was not an MP.

opposition till after he was turn'd out, he join'd Sir Robert Walpole about 18 Sessions & opposed him about one & ½ were Measures right so long, & only wrong the two last years, or did it require 18 years for Mr Dodingtons fine parts to discover Sir Robert Walpole Iniquity though he sat & acted with him in the Treasury allmost daily, and heard all the Debates in Parliament yet could never be convinced till he was removed from the Treasure, how shameless how profligate is such behavior. Dr. Lee said that he had long opposed Sir Robert Walpole's Measures because he thought them wrong, but even while he opposed the Minister he did, if he might be allowed so familiar an expression love the Man for his many great & amiable qualities, and never desire'd more than to remove him from his Power, but even if he thought him guilty & deserveing Punishment there were many reasons from the state of our Affairs both at home and abroad, why he could not think it expedient for the public Wellfare to renew the Enquiry.

Wee expect another Motion in relation to Lord Orford to morrow whether for an Impeachment or what else I know not, but the Tory Squires & brought up, and must have some sport for their Money before Christmas for I believe many of them will not be persuaded to be here after. It is talk'd that after they have try'd all their great Questions they will make another secession. I should think they would hardly try that Measure a second time, it had so little effect and was so little approved without Doors, besides I think some Gentlemen like to display their Oratory in public too well to deprive themselves of the Opportunity of doing it. Mr. William Pitt is indeed an Orator & has great Talents to rob a People of their Liberty under the pretence of giveing them more. Mr. Mckenzie,[248] Lord Bute's[249] brother voted for the Motion to my surprise, his uncle I[la]y express'd great concern at it & assured me it was directly contrary to the plane advice of Duke of Argyll who I find recovers so slowly that he does not talk much upon a subject, and it was even supposed People might persuade Mr. Mckenzie not to regard his advice as being out of his senses.

Give my Love to your Brothers. I have not time to write to Trub tonight but will do it the first leisure. I pray God . . .

59.
John Campbell to Pryse Campbell, 4 December 1742
I thank you for your kind & agreable letter, as I allway hear of your health from some other hand; I would never have you put your self under any constraint, to write to me But when you have leisure, and it is agreable to your self to write, you may be sure that nothing can be more acceptable to me, than a letter from you. I thank God both your own letters & those of Mr. Brodie & Mr. Row[e] in what they say of you give me the

---

[248] James Stuart Mackenzie.

[249] John Stuart (1713–94), 3rd earl of Bute; a Scottish representative peer 1737–41 and 1760–80. A favourite of the prince of Wales. After the prince's death in 1751 Bute became tutor to his son, the future George III, creating a close friendship. In 1761, Bute became secretary of state to the northern department and a year later the first lord of the treasury (1762–3). His premiership saw the ending of the Seven Years War, with the signing of the Treaty of Paris on 10 Feb. 1763. Popular opposition to the peace brought death threats, riots and hundreds of satirical prints and verse to Bute, and in April he resigned. Contemporaries widely believed Bute to have been the secret influence over George III's policies and administration, until his friendship with the king fell apart upon the monarch's alliance with Pitt in 1766. Wright, *Caricature History of the Georges*, 283–5; *ODNB*.

greatest satisfaction, in furnishing me with fresh reasons for my judgement to approve, the strongest & warmest inclination of my heart, to love you above anything on Earth.

As to public News the Times I hope are happily alter'd, for now allmost every letter brings you account of some Victory. Yesterday instead of an Impeachment Lord Barrington[250] moved for a Place Bill[251] Seconded by Sir W[atkins] W[illiams] W[ynn]. Lord Barrington has a pretty manner of speaking, but his reflections on the New Ministers were bitter & plane & beyond anything said before if possible. Sir William Yonge[252] retorted upon the Broad bottom & then Lord Barrington got up again when the speaker found it high time to interpose, & put an end to that way of debateing nothing being so contrary to order as personal reflections, this most just & necessary interposition cut the Debate very short, only Velters Cornwall[253] contrived in his odd way but with a good deal of true humor, to make an Ironical speech in which he abused them very sufficiently without being disorderly. He stood very near the Chair and, I am told, said softly to the speaker, Sir if you take me down, I shall get up again & speak for an hour. Wee divided before it was quite 4 o'clock Ay's 196 No's 221.[254] You need not wonder our Majority was smaller on this Question than the others, for Wee used allways to be weakest upon this Bill, many of our Friends either haveing particular ways of thinking about it, or imagineing it an occasion of doing a popular thing, without danger of doing hurt, because they were sure the Lords would not pass it. However they were abused, it is certain, the New Ministers had firm ground to stand on in this Question, for last year Mr. Sandys brought in a Bill the same Lord Barrington now moved for, it went through the House of Commons, & was rejected by the House of Lords,[255] which put then Mr. Pulteney in a rage, for he thought that in regard to him, & compliance with his dictates, they would only have amended it; to appease that, then most powerfull, Man a Negotiation was set on foot & it was agreed by the leading Men in both Houses that a Place Bill, of less extent, and with a somewhat different Title, should be brought into the House of Commons, and being sent up in the Manner agreed upon, should be pass'd by the House of Lords, to avoid quarrelling with the Commons about the other Bill, which the Lords had several times

---

[250] William Wildman Shute Barrington (1717–93), 2nd Viscount Barrington (Irish peerage) of Beckett, Berkshire. Opposition whig MP for Berwick-upon-Tweed 1740–54 and Plymouth 1754–78. In c.1744 he went over to the government side under the influence of the Cobham group. Secretary at war 1755–61; chancellor of the exchequer 1761–2; treasurer of the navy 1762–5; secretary at war 1765–78; postmaster general 1782. Described by Fox, 'Memoir', 40, as a 'frivolous, little minded man . . . but is devoted to the duke of Newcastle'.

[251] Place bills or the ensuing acts were passed to exclude people holding office under the crown from sitting in the Commons. For the debate, which according to *PH*, xii, 873, was moved by Velters Cornwall (see below, Note 254), see *PH*, xii, 873–905.

[252] William Yonge (c.1693–1755), of Colyton, Devon; whig MP for Honiton 1715–54 and Tiverton 1754–5. He supported Walpole's administration to the end of its term. John, Lord Hervey stated that 'his name was proverbially used to express everything pitiful, corrupt, and contemptible'. Cited in *HPC*, *1715–54*, ii, 567.

[253] Velters Cornwall (?1697–1768), of Moccas Court, Herefordshire; tory MP for Hereford 1722–68. He voted consistently against the administration. Cornwall sat up for 22 hours during the scrutiny of the lists of members of the secret committee on Walpole's administration.

[254] *CJ*, xxiv, 351; *PH*, xii, 873–905, for the debate.

[255] The votes were contents 44, non-contents 63. Sainty and Dewar.

rejected and were determined to reject, if offer'd them again; this Agreement was intimated in the House of Commons, as planely as in a parlimentary way it could be, and our Friends, to promote Peace & Union, among the Friends of the Government, and to humor the Man, who could then either heal our breach's, it was thought, or connfound all things, as he pleased, agreed not to oppose, though they could not approve, the Bill so brought in. Those who had a mind to prevent all agreement among the Whigs, attempted to make additions to that Bill, not in hopes to gain more, but because they knew no more would pass the Lords than was agreed to, and if they could get more into the Bill, the Lords would reject it; and the agreement being broke, our Breach's would be wider than ever; but upon several divisions Wee carried it to keep the Bill as first proposed; and the reason for doing so, was avow'd by the New Ministers & their Friends; so the Bill pass'd into a Law, which takes effect the next general Election. The Case being thus, you will see that though Mr. Sandys should be as much in Love with the Bill, which he brought in the beginning of last session, & Lord Barrington moved now, as ever he seem'd to be, yet he could not at this time agree to send it to the Lords, without being guilty of a scandalous breach of Faith.

I was diverted the other day with hearing that Lord B[ath],[256] the very first time he open'd in the House of Lords fell into his old custom of rambling from the Question. It was upon a Writ of Error from the Kings Bench about the Corporation of Weymouth, and his Lordship continued to talk of the Army, the War, & the reduction of the Army when a Successful War shall have produced a good peace. It was Mr. Dodingtons Cause, on whose side his Lordship spoke, against an unanimous Judgement of the Court of Kings Bench; which notwithstanding his Lordships Eloquence, was affirm'd by the House of Lords.[257] Indeed the great E[arl] of B[ath] after displaying his Oratory, modestly withdrew and did not Vote.

I must tell you a good thing Lord Chesterfield said to Lord Orford meeting him at Court just when the Parliament met. Lord Orford said he was come to Town to be an ay & no Man in the House of Peers, my Lord said Chesterfield you must now say Content, which you know is the form of voteing in that House, but wittily alluded to the good state he thought Lord Orfords Affairs were now in. I must add a good saying of Mr. Shippen who the first time he saw Sir Thomas Wynne[258] in the House wish'd him joy & said I think Sir you are the only Man that has reaped any Lawrels from this Campaign. You know Sir Thomas was made a Bar[one]t on the prospect of his attending the King to Flanders. The Opposition have agreed not to interrupt the Money days next Week, so Monday Wee shall have the British Army, Wednesday the Malt Bill,[259] and Fryday the Hanover Troops which I fancy will be the greatest debate this Session. I pray God . . .

---

[256] William Pulteney, created earl of Bath 14 July 1742. *LJ*, xxvi, 158.

[257] *LJ*, xxvi, 174.

[258] Sir Thomas Wynn (1677–1749), of Glynllifon, Caernarvonshire; MP for Caernarvon borough 1713–49. A loyal supporter of Walpole, he was rewarded with a baronetcy in 1742. He bragged that he had cost Sir Watkin Williams-Wynn above £20,000 in election expenses in three contests in 1740, 1741 and 1747. Thomas, *Politics in Eighteenth-Century Wales*, 175–6.

[259] Malt tax was first introduced in 1697. 9 Wm 3, c.22.

60.

John Campbell to Pryse Campbell, 7 December 1742

I was very glad to hear by Johnny that you and your Brothers were well. I pray God continue it, and I hope my Dearest you will be mindfull of my earnest & frequent entreatys to be carefull of yourself, both in rideing & every other respect.

Yesterday Wee were in the Committee of Supply and voted the British Forces the same that were last Year. The first question was on continueing the 16000 men in Flanders on which there was a debate that lasted till about eight at night when Wee divided Ay's 280 Noe's 160.[260] The New solicitor general [William Murray] spoke very well for the question. The chief speakers against it were Mr Dodington, Mr Pitt, Mr Lyttelton, Mr Waller, Mr Fazakerly, Mr Philipps would have begun the Debate but was prevented by the Chairman pointing to two or three other Gentlemen before him, however he spoke but begun his speech with declareing his aversion to standing Armies, which happening not to be directly to the question, perhaps was the occasion of the House not being so attentive to him as decency & the regard due to his merit, & abilitys required. the Speaker spoke I thought not so well as he used to do, he was for the question yet blamed the Ministry for haveing undertaken the Measures that occasion'd it without, as he thought, the advice of Parliament. I thought he blamed them more than they deserved, and more than was proper for one who voted for the Question. Mr. Pelham on these occasions, takes the Part which, from what Wee have formerly seen, one should naturally think belonged to the Chancellor of the Exchequer [Samuel Sandys], but Mr. Pelham is equal to it, and the Chancellor has not yet been long used to act the Minister. I should have told you that Sir William Yonge open'd the Question very clearly and handsomely, Mr. Winnington was a speaker for it, he is allways a good one. When that question was over Sir J[ohn] H[ynde] C[otton] moved to adjourn & some of them, I know not why, divided the Committee upon that Question which Wee carried by a very great majority in the negative. Then the rest of the questions for the different parts of the Forces on the British Establishment pass'd without any one word said about them. This day these resolutions were reported to the House & agreed to, Mr. Philipps had made some little remarks on the Estimates which he desired to have explaned which was soon and easily done; to the satisfaction of every body, by the Secretary at War [Thomas Winnington]. When the question came upon the number for Guards & Garrisons at home, Mr. Bramston[261] made a speech not very long, nor extremely fine, against it, but being neither answer'd nor seconded by anybody, the question was immediately put, however he divided the House Ay's to agree with the Committee 199 Noes 133.[262] The House was not full no debate being expected. To morrow Wee are to Vote the Malt tax,[263] as that will not take up time, perhaps Wee May have some other Question. To be sure Wee shall soon have a Motion for repeleing the Septennial Act for the Tories I think must be able to tell their Country Friends and

---

[260] *PH*, xii, 940.

[261] Thomas Bramston (c.1690–1765), of Skreens, Essex; tory lawyer; MP for Maldon 1712–34 and Essex 1734–47.

[262] *CJ*, xxix, 354, gives figures of ayes 199 and noes 113.

[263] No vote was recorded as the House was in committee. *CJ*, xxiv, 355.

Christmas, that they have complied with the great Articles of their Instructions; and it will doubtless cost a great quantity of liquor to wash down the bitter sorrow these disappointments will occasion.

The Pamphlet[264] I sent you last is much talk'd of, I believe all admire the wit of it, and most are pleased with some Truths in it, but it lash's so many, that few are not angry at some part or other of it. I have little concern for Octavius [Carteret] the Dr for a crazy Constitution, or Antonius Weathercock [Bath] but I am sorry Lentulus[265] so nearly related to a Gent I so much honor, & in truth related to me, should be so roughly handled. Indeed there are many truth's in it. I would not have publish'd at this time, especially by one who speaks so much in favor of, or rather in Justice to Lord Orford. You will easily see that the Author of that, and of the Ballad, The Patriots are come,[266] is the same, he is confidently named for the Author by everybody, but there are good reasons why it should not come from me which you will remember, for if you should name the Author, every body would know it came from me. The Pamphlet I send to night is not new, or anything extraordinary, but it will serve to make up your Collection of Political scandal.

Give my Love & Blessing to your Dear Brothers. Your Mama sends hers to you. All here are well. Mr. Owen went this morning for North Wales but is to return soon. I pray God . . .

61.
John Campbell to Pryse Campbell, 9 December 1742
Yesterday and today were idle days in the House of Commons, but I expect tomorrow will be the greatest debate of the session, upon the Hanover Troops, if one may ghess by some expressions that have already been dropt in the House, and from some Pamphlets that have appear'd. I am well informed, that the Government know, the Pretenders Instructions are to run down Hanover as much as possible, and say nothing of him, which is no doubt the wisest councill that ever was taken by his Court, for if the Present Settlement[267] was overturn'd, he must come in; and it is a much easier task by false assertions, and suggestions, to set the People against the Government they live under; than to raise a zeal for him, in any but old Women (whether in petticoats or breech's) upon the old absurd Notions of indefeaseable hereditary Right, and absolute passive obedience to lawless tyranny; I will not say these Pamphlets are Writ in obedience, but I must say they are writ in perfect conformity, to those Instructions; I keep them by me, but do not care to send them into the Country.

I told you in my last that your Uncle Owen was gone to North Wales but yesterday while Wee sat at dinner he surprised us with an unexpected return, he went as far as Nettlebed,[268] and then finding it very bad travelling, by reason of Frost & Snow, he very prudently return'd. He knows how scarce great & valuable Men are so takes the just and

---

[264] *Miscellaneous Thoughts.*

[265] In *Miscellaneous Thoughts*, the third of the triumvirate is Lepidus – Samuel Sandys – why Campbell refers to Lentulus is a puzzle, except as a slip of memory? Lentulus is referred to in the *Gentleman's Magazine*, Sept. 1742.

[266] John, Lord Hervey, *The Patriots are Come, or a Doctor for a Crazy Constitution* (1742).

[267] The Act of Settlement of 1701, 12 & 13 Wm III, c.2, which settled the succession of the English throne on Electress Sophia of Hanover (1630–1714), mother of George I, and her protestant heirs.

[268] In Oxfordshire.

proper care of his person; and he could not I think be in must [*sic*] hast, to fetch any Papers or Intelligence necessary to finish the busyness that brought him to Town; for you may remember when he first came, the beginning of July he allow'd himself a whole fortnight at least, to complete the Affair he came about. I have taken several Journeys in severe Frost & Snow it is true, I proceeded slowly, but I never turn'd back; but he says it is a shocking road to Oxford, whether you go by Henley,[269] or the Wickhams.

You will see by the News that my poor old Friend Tom Willoughby[270] is dead. He was a truely good natured, honest Man; but his Father being a hard drinker, he had the Misfortune to learn it very young. While He & I lived much togather, my advice & persuasion kept him pretty well from it, & he did not often excede; but since he married & lived mostly in Yorkshire, I have but seldom seen, or corresponded with, and he gave himself up to drinking, ruin'd his Constitution, became gouty several years ago and has at length kill'd himself by it, before 50. I lament it, for I think he might have been a very valuable Man.

To day Nancy & Molly came home in great joy for the holydays. Wee are all very well and remember you with the affection you deserve. Give my Love and Blessing to you Brothers, my Kind service to Mr Row[e], remember me very kindly to R[oger] Evan[s]. I have intended to write to Brett about the Garden ever since I came to Town, but could never find leisure; as he is one of the Political Club,[271] he will not wonder that public Affairs take up all my time, and that I am more concern'd to preserve the Queen of Hungarys Dominions, than to improve my own.

Remember me to Val. I hope he will be a sober, carefull, Faithfull, and affectionate servant to you and then he may be sure I shall allways be his Friend. I am very sorry to hear his Father hearken'd so much to the Methodists. I hope he will come to his senses again, and not fancy it is Religion to be Mad, melancholy, or useless.

I pray God . . .

You see I Love writeing to you so well that I can make a long letter when I have no News.

62.
John Campbell to Pryse Campbell, 11 December 1742
I was very glad to hear that you & your Brothers were well, and am very much pleased that my letters are so agreable to you; your letter was extremely so to me except that it was ill & incorrectly writ, blotted some words omitted, and one or two writ twice, Now my Dear I am affraid that writeing so hastily while you are young should spoil your hand, & lead you into a bad Custom, for otherwise I should not mind how carelessly you writ to me but be rather the better pleased.

[269] Henley-on-Thames, Oxfordshire.

[270] Thomas Willoughby (1694–1742), of Birdsall, Yorkshire; tory MP for Cambridge University 1710–27 and Tamworth 1727–34. Recorded as voting only once, against the excise bill. His father, also Thomas Willoughby, was 1st Baron Middleton. Willoughby and Campbell probably became friends whilst at university – Willoughby went up to Jesus College in Nov. 1711, Campbell to Clare in May 1711.

[271] Campbell may be referring to the Pembroke Society, a reading club established c.1741 for clergy and gentlemen. See G. Walters, 'The Eighteenth-Century "Pembroke Society"', *WHR*, iii (1963), 291–8.

Yesterday Wee voted the 16000 Hanover Forces in the Committee of Supply Wee divided about 9 at night 260 against 193.[272] A greater Majority that [*sic*] I expected upon that question so much pains haveing been taken to make it unpopular. The Secretary at War [Thomas Winnington] open'd it very well, Lord Perceval was one of the first that spoke for it, Mr. Waller I think the one of the first that spoke against it, which he did with bitterness, Sir John St Aubin[273] spoke as he allways does, a good set speech but severe against the Ministry, strong about Hanover & very plane though guarded charges of corruption upon the late and present Parliaments. It was fit he should have been answer'd with spirit, Colonel Bladen happen'd to be pointed to & seemed very desireous of speaking, which he did for half an hour but so coldly that he was the most improper of all that offer'd (for several had got up) to answer Sir John, unless I may except Lord B[altimore][274] one of my successors, who I fear had done worse; Mr. Pitt spoke in his oratorical way but I thought had not much argument he complaned of a former speech of his haveing been grossly misrepresented as I thought to H[is] R[oyal] H[ighness] he gave the Misrepresenter the epithets he deserved if it was true, and said I know not who he is, but let him take that, and tell me; or words to that effect, several of them used the strongest words they could think of against the Minister meaning Octavius [Carteret]. Sir J[ohn] H[ynde] C[otton] abused the Chancellor of the Exchequer [Samuel Sandys], but I think with little success for he misrepresented or rather falsify'd Mr. Sandy's speech so grossly, that everybody must see the injustice of it. Harry Fox spoke extremely well on our side, Sir Barnard was not in the House, nor did I see Lord Cornbury; Lord Limerick voted with us so did Sir Edmund Thomas. Kilgetty was up to speak once or twice but prevented by others so kept his speech, perhaps for monday. Lord Quarendon[275] who is reckon'd a might pretty sort of young Man spoke, I thought, very moderately, he is, I think, quite a Tory. Sir Watkin was silent, & Mr. Shippen sat all day in the Gallery, Horace alias Lord Sheffield[276] spoke I thought well & not very long, which was his wonted fault. I send you a Westminster journal[277] intended for an Answer, or at least a return to the seal'd Miserable Instructions, but you will see he comes poorly off, he attempts to ridicule Lord Percevals Answer, but I think he had better have left it alone.

Wee have had frost for some time, to day it is very hard, yesterday & part of to day were clear & pleasant, but wee had very dark weather for somedays. Tuesday I think, I could neither write nor read easily in my study any time of the day and Wee had

---

[272] See *PH*, xii, 940–1058, for two versions of the debate and a list of those voting for and against the motion.

[273] Sir John St Aubyn (?1702–44), of Clowance and St Michael's Mount, Cornwall; tory MP for Cornwall 1722–44.

[274] Lord Baltimore succeeded Campbell at the admiralty in 1742.

[275] George Henry Lee (1718–72), Viscount Quarendon, a courtesy title of the eldest son of the earl of Lichfield. As such he was able to sit as an MP, of Quarendon, Buckinghamshire, and Ditchley Park and Spelsbury, Oxon; tory MP for Oxfordshire 1740–3. He abstained from voting on the motion to dismiss Walpole though he sat on the committee to inquire into the latter's administration.

[276] Horatio Walpole (1678–1757), but why alias Lord Sheffield? An indication of his worthiness but lack of any real talent – Sheffield plate was copper coated with silver.

[277] The *Westminster Journal or New Weekly Miscellany* (11 Dec. 1742), by Thomas Touchit.

Candles when Wee sat down to dinner, though it was but just past three. Yesterday I got to the House about ½ hour after 8 in the morning and had good luck to get a Place I liked then, Kilgetty was there in his slippers, I am told he has taken a Lodgeing close by. I am apt enough to believe the Tories will bring him in for some Borough, if he looses Carmarthen.

Lord Essex[278] is return'd home & I am told quite out of his senses which is a melancholy thing. I [*sic*] my Chief[279] is not quite Master of his, I see his Nephew[280] constantly with the Tories.

Give my kind service to Mr. Row[e] my affectionate Compliments to the Laird and Remembrance to Johnny. I sent his Warrant to him last Post. Give my Love and Blessing to your Brothers. I pray God . . .

63.
John Campbell to Pryse Campbell, 14 December 1742
I was sorry to hear that you had a little hoarseness, I hope you will be carefull to get it soon off again; but I was glad you did not go to Orielton[281] this day sevenight, the days are too short, & the Weather too cold to go any where that you cannot perfectly command your time to be home before night. Sir A[rthur] O[wen][282] is so used to ride in the night that he thinks nothing of it. I reckon soon after the House meets after Christmas, I shall be able to give a tolerable ghess at the length of the Session; you may be sure I shall be glad to go to Wales as soon as I can; and will send for you in good time before the end of the Session that you may then be ready to go with me home. I shall be extremely glad if the Laird will see you safe here, it will save me some difficulty and uneasiness. You may depend upon it I shall be very glad to serve the Cab[283] for the Lairds sake but have no great expectations from the War Office.

Yesterday the Resolution for the Hanover Troops was reported from the Committee of Supply, and Wee had a Debate; after some time, Mr Waller moved for an amendment to leave out the levy money and Wee divided upon that, & carried it against the amendment 230 against 177.[284] The opposition it is thought would have done more wisely if they had spoke less upon the main question, & stuck more to the amendment, which was our weak side, for I believe most of us wish'd the levy money had not been ask'd. When Wee had carried it against the amendment, they did not divide upon the

---

[278] William Capel (1697 1743), 3rd earl of Essex.

[279] Cobham.

[280] Pitt.

[281] Orielton, Pembrokeshire, the seat of the whig Owen family.

[282] Sir Arthur Owen (?1674–1753), 3rd bt, of Orielton, Pembrokeshire; whig MP for Pembrokeshire 1695–1705, Pembroke boroughs 1708–23 and Pembrokeshire 1715–27. Owen lost the county seat (541 votes to 374 votes) to John Campbell in 1727, largely because of Owen's local unpopularity, though Campbell had powerful friends in the dukes of Argyll and Newcastle. Owen's almost total control of local patronage had also alienated the tory Philipps family of Picton Castle, Pembrokeshire, who threw their considerable political weight behind Campbell at this election. Thomas, *Politics in Eighteenth-Century Wales*, 96. See Appendix 1, 'Account of the Pembrokeshire Election' (1727). See Introduction.

[283] Cabinet.

[284] *CJ*, xxiv, 362.

main question; Lord Conways[285] Brother[286] spoke on our side, he had never spoke before; he did it very handsomely but with a very weak voice, Mr Berkeley[287] the late Lady Herefords[288] son spoke for the first time on the other side, but did not do so well as I expected from the Character I have heard of him; Lord Guernzey spoke on that side better than I expected. This day the call of the House was adjourned to the 18 of January which makes us think Wee shall have no more great questions before Christmas, but that they keep somewhat back, and put off the call, to have the House fall about the time Kilgettys Election comes on.

Give my Love & Blessing to your Brothers, my Compliments to the Laird & kind service to Mr. Row[e]. Wee have very hard frost, much Ice I hear in the Thames, if it is so with you pray speak to Brett to take care of the Rosemary lest it suffer as it did two years ago. Pray my Dearest be carefull of your self both as to takeing cold & falling which is very dangerous in frosty weather. I heard they were scateing either in the Park or Kensington Gardens I don't know which.

I pray God . . .

Mr. Hooke[289] was here on Sunday & asked very kindly for you. He has been laid up with the Gout but says it was not violent. My compliments to the Dr when you see him.

64.

John Campbell to Pryse Campbell, 16 December 1742

I thank you kindly for your letter which was very well writ. I am very sorry you are so trouble'd with the toothach, & Johnny told me your face was somewhat swell'd with it. I hope you will be carefull to keep your face from cold when it is so; when you come to Town I fear Wee must have that tooth drawn, but you can't venture in the Country, they are not enough used to it, to be expert. Indeed I believe there are but very few good tooth Drawers here.

This day the House adjourn'd till tuesday, Wee shall have no busyness till after Christmas. Wee had a ridiculous diversion to day, Lord Perceval presented a Petition

---

[285] Francis Seymour Conway (1718–94), 2nd Baron Conway and 1st marquess of Hertford.

[286] Henry Seymour Conway (1719–95), of Park Place, Berkshire; whig MP for Higham Ferrers 1741–7, Penryn 1747–54, St Mawes 1754–61, Thetford 1761–74 and Bury St Edmunds 1775–84. Groom of the bedchamber 1757–64, secretary of state of the southern department 1765–6 and of the northern department 1766–8, and on Cumberland's choice, leader of the house of commons. He was also returned to the Irish parliament as MP for Antrim 1755–61. He was a cousin of Horace Wapole (1717–97). Conway was a career militarist and had become a lieutenant in the 5th dragoons by 1737. He was made aide-de-camp to commander-in-chief, General Wade, in the Netherlands in 1744 and in the following year fought at Culloden against the jacobites. In 1757 he was appointed second in command to raid the French fort of Rochefort, which he had doubts about. In 1764 Conway was dismissed from the bedchamber and his colonelcy for voting against the government regarding John Wilkes (see Chapter 7, Note 137). However, by 1782 he had risen to become commander-in-chief of the army and was made field marshal in 1793.

[287] Norborne Berkeley (?1717–70), tory MP for Gloucestershire 1741–63. Groom of the bedchamber 1760–4; lord of the bedchamber 1767–70.

[288] Elizabeth Norborne (*d.* 1742), Dowager Viscountess Hereford, wife of Edward Devereux, 8th Viscount Hereford who died in 1700. Elizabeth then married John Symes Berkeley, of Stoke Gifford, Gloucestershire.

[289] John Hooke (c.1699–1757), of Bangeston, Angle, Pembrokeshire. Hooke left the Bangeston estate to Pryse Campbell's brother, John (Jack) Campbell, on condition he took the name Hooke, which he did in 1757. See Introduction.

from the Dean & Chapter of Westminster praying for some money toward repaireing
& beautifying the Abby, & moved to refer it to the Committee of Supply. Lord Strange
opposed it & divided the House. Wee carried it to refer by 44 against 11.[290] You will
wonder at the small numbers but Wee only met to day for the form of reading the Malt
Bill the 3[r]d time and sending it to the Lords. Sir Charles Wagers Writ[291] was moved
for so he will be reelected before Wee meet after the Holydays.

Give my Love & Blessing to your Brothers and Compliments to the Laird, tell
Johnny I will be sure to speak as he desires on behalf of Jack Morris. Wee have here
very hard frost, the Thames is so full of Ice that I believe no Boats can go upon it.
I pray God . . .

65.

John Campbell to Pryse Campbell, 18 December 1742

I was heartily glad to hear by Johnny last Post that your Cheek was well again. I hope
you will be carefull of your Dear Person.

The Parliament not sitting I have no news, only it is said that Lord Perceval has
writ his own life[292] but speaks in the third person, one Chapter haveing given
account of his Patriotism either in Ireland or Westminster, ends with words to this
purpose viz: and here Wee leave the Noble Youth[293] struggling for the Liberties of
his Country. Speaking of the Westminster Election he says he was invited to stand by
the earnest solicitations of many 1,000s of Independent Electors, and after says, that
at length he was join'd by one Edwin;[294] which gives great offence to that Gentleman. I heartily wish it was printed; though Wee should not laugh at the Noble
Youth now he both Votes & speaks on our side. He has some parts, much Industry,
& infinite Vanity. Some time ago he came early to the House & left a paper with
his name writ on it to keep his Place & then went away, Jack Pitt[295] (Brother to Mr.
Burton)[296] took his Paper carry'd it cross the House & pin'd it to the Place where
Mr. Sandys usually sits, and then they whisper'd about that there was a new
Chancellor of the Exchequer.

[290] *CJ*, xxiv, 365.

[291] *CJ*, xxiv, 364. Wager had resigned as first lord of the admiralty after Walpole's resignation. However, after being refused permission to step down from public life by the king, he took on the office of treasurer to the navy, in December (grant dated 20 Dec. 1742: http://www.history.ac.uk/resources/office/navy), so a writ, issued on 27 Dec., was needed to re-elect him. *HPC, 1715–54*, i, 214.

[292] Lord Perceval contributed to the third volume of a fanciful account of his family history which had been begun by his father, John Perceval, 1st earl of Egmont (1683–1748). The first edition was entitled *Genealogical History of the House of Yvery in its Different Branches of Yvery, Luvel, Perceval, and Gournay* (1742). *ODNB*.

[293] Perceval.

[294] Charles Edwin (c.1699–1756), of Plas Llanmihangel, Glamorgan; tory MP for Westminster 1741–7 and Glamorgan 1747–56. Edwin was, it seems, chosen accidentally as the candidate for the Westminster election, the first of which was declared void by parliament. He was re-elected in Dec. 1742 along with Perceval. Horace Walpole referred to Perceval as 'Lord Perceive all' and Edwin as 'Mr Perceive-nothing'. *HPC, 1715–54*, i, 286 and ii, 6.

[295] George Pitt (1721–1803), of Strathfieldsaye, Hampshire; tory MP for Shaftesbury 1742–7 and Dorset 1747–74.

[296] William Burton (?1695–1781), of Ashwell and North Leffenham, Rutland; MP for Rutland 1730–4. In 1737 Walpole gave him a place on the excise board which he kept until 1776. He married Pitt's daughter Elisabeth in 1738.

Give my Love & Blessing to your Brothers & Compliments to all Friends. I pray God . . .

The lairds & your letters are Frank'd & forwarded.

Pray my Dearest direct R[oger] Evans to give half a guinea to John Reynols for bleeding the poor People. It has thaw'd all day. I hope the Frost is gone.

66.

John Campbell to Pryse Campbell, 21 December 1742

I have no news but that the Parliament is adjourned to Monday the 10th of January. The King made a short speech expressing his thanks for what Wee have done and his confidence that Wee will go on support [*sic*] the Queen of Hungary & restore the Balance of Power.[297] I hear Wee are to take 10,000 of the Duke of Wolfembutte's[298] Troops into our pay. If Wee can find money to support, it I shall like our exerting ourselves to the utmost to curb the Power of France & prevent, if possible, their enflareing all Europe.

Wee have had two or three warm days, they say there was a little frost last night, but this was the finest day I've seen since I came to Town. Just now the Kings speech is brought me. I was affraid it would have been too late.

My Love to your Brothers & Compliments to all Friends. I hope my Dearest you are carefull in your shooting. I pray God . . .

I have by Good Authority corrected one word in the Pamphlet your Mama sends the Laird viz: Litany for Creed. Our Kensington Friend was with me this Evening.

67.

John Campbell to Pryse Campbell, Christmas day 1742

I thank you for your latin Epistle, it is very true your first attempt should not be criticised, and I must confess I am a very poor Judge of such performances, but I have no fear of your doing well if you apply. I intend to send a Box with the things you desire this day sevenight. I believe the Verses I spoke of were left in one of the upper drawers of my Library Table the Keys are in one of the drawers of the small Table. I lately met your Friend Old Mr. Campbell that had been in Ireland, at Court he ask'd kindly for you & spoke very handsomely of you to another Gentleman that was by us.

I dined yesterday at Lord Herveys he is greatly recover'd since you saw him, looks plump & fresh, his eyes clear & says he is mighty well, he attributes it in great measure to lowering his diet, in quantity, for it was scarce possible to do it in quality. He did not come into the room till the meat was taken away & the Desert set on then he came to Table & his dinner was brought him viz: a pint of milk & a pint of water gruel which he mixt in a China Bowl & then pour'd into a small Bowl or large Cup which he supt out of, eating a half penny rowl. His breakfast is Green Tea & Milk & a Sea Biscuit and he eats no supper he has an appetite to eat hearty and does not want digestion, but if he excedes his ordinary diet he is sure to be feaverish & restless all night. It is an odd

---

[297] *CJ*, xxiv, 367.

[298] Karl Eugen (1728–93), duke of Wurtemburg.

Case, and requires great command of ones self never to satisfie ones appetite, for he is all most allways hungry, and is it not surprising that he should look well, & be lively, & strong upon such a Diet.

Your Mama & I drank your health to day at Governor Morris's[299] where Wee dined upon a very fine Wild Turkey. Every body that has a Country Place within reach are out of Town, so 'tis a very dead time that I can hear nothing. I was with Lord Hay on thursday; he says his Brother is very low spirited, and uses few words but is for the present Measures he fancy's that he repented his resigning, that the steps he made at that time, and the attempt to draw him into a Jacobite Plot by the papers Lord Barrymore[300] brought him, affected his spirits & vex'd him very much. I suppose the proceedings of the Jacobites shew'd him the Mistake of his own Conduct. But this he does not declare only Lord J[301] thinks he has reason to ghess it is so.

Your Mama joins me in the good wishes of the season to your self & your Brothers. She says she will write when she can hear any News to send you. My kind service to Mr. Rowe & remembrance to Johnny & his spud with many good Years. I pray God . . .

James is very thankfull & much pleased you are so kind to think of him. Remember me to Val. I am much concern'd for poor Will Thomas.

68.

John Campbell to Pryse Campbell, 28 December 1742

I think this will come just in time to wish you a happy new year, and I am sure you believe there is nothing in this World I wish so ardently as that you may enjoy very many years in the truest happyness the World can afford.

I hear a little news at this time, it is said there is more hopes of the Dutch comeing to act in concert with us,[302] only two Towns hold out, viz: Dort and Bril, the latter they make little doubt will come in. It seems to enter into any New engagements there must be the unanimous consent of all the little Republic's the Dutch State is composed of; but a Measure begun, may be carried on by the Majority, and if Dort can no way be brought to consent, they say it has been talk'd, that the States General[303] may declare that joining with the english now is only in consequence of the Treaty's and Alliance's by which their State is allready bound, and that it is no new Engagement or undertakeing; it is they say the Right of the States General to judge that matter, and a Right they make [*sic*] safely exercise in this Case, a great Majority of all ranks of the People in all the Province being inclined to act with us in the present conjuncture; if the Dutch come in, I hope it will have a happy effect abroad, & confound, if nothing can silence, our Gainsayers at home.

---

[299] Lewis Morris (1671–1746), chief justice of New York and governor of New Jersey.

[300] James Barrymore (1667–1747), 4th earl of Barrymore (Irish peerage); MP for Stockbridge 1710–13, 1714–15 and Wigan 1715–27 and 1734–47.

[301] This could be I, but from the context Campbell means Lord Hay.

[302] The Dutch, after much prevaricating, joined the British and allied forces in the spring of 1743 in what became known as the Pragmatic Army. R. Browning, *The War of the Austrian Succession* (Stroud, 1994), 113, 134.

[303] The states general of the Netherlands: the Dutch parliament.

I had the luck not to find our new Bishop[304] after takeing a journey beyond Westminster Abby to wait on him, but my Lord of Llandaffe[305] promises to bring us togather.

I hear Lord Essex is like to dye[306] which is rather to be wish'd by his Friends than that he should continue in the unhappy condition he now is.

Give my Love & Blessing to your Brothers. I wish them many happy New Years. Make the Compliment of the day from me to the Laird, Johnny, and all their Friends. I pray God . . .

Pray make my Compliments to Dr. Cuninghame when you see him.

Wee have had several foggy days, & this day small rain.

---

[304] Edward Willes became bishop of St David's in 1743 in the place of Nicholas Clagett (1685/6–1746) before being translated a year later to Bath and Wells. His place at St David's was taken by Rev. Richard Trevor, bishop 1744–52.

[305] John Gilbert (1693–1761), bishop of Llandaff 1740–8 and archbishop of York 1749–61. Neither a scholar nor theologian, Horace Walpole stated that Gilbert was 'composed of that common mixture of ignorance, meanness and arrogance'. Horace Walpole, *Memoirs of the Reign of George the Second* (2 vols, 1822), ii, 245.

[306] He died on 8 Jan. 1742.

Chapter 3. 1743

All letters in this chapter are from CRO, Cawdor/Campbell box 128.

69.

John Campbell to Pryse Campbell, 1 January 1743

I thank you for your kind letter and was extremely glad to hear you & your Brothers keep so good health; 'tis true the want of Fresh air & a Little exercise makes the time hang heavy here, but I wish more for the Parliament riseing than for their meeting after the Holydays.

The cessation of arms between the King of Sardinia[1] and the Spaniards is not very agreable News, it being fear'd he may make a seperate Peace. I should in my last have told you that the Town's of Dort & Bril are two out of 19 Towns in the Province of Holland, and it is the consent of that Province which would be completed by their agreeing to assist the Queen of Hungary. You know there are six more Provinces that form the Dutch Republic, but I think the Province of Holland makes a third part of the whole, & commonly leads the rest to expostulate with those Towns, a thing only done upon extraordinary occasions. I learn'd this from H[orace] Walpole who made me a visit yesterday.

Lord Wilmington is in so declineing a state of health that it is thought he cannot live long.[2] I hear Dr. Mead[3] says the Bath is the only thing that can continue his life but I don't know whether he has resolved to go. His death would occasion some events of importance, one great Man, but I don't know who, would get his Place, and one other, at least, would be disappointed & displeased for want of it. I should be very sorry to see Antonius [Bath] in that Place for I think a Man of such passions, & inconstancy, to say no worse, would guide the Helm very ill, & if he was at the head of the Treasury he would think he had a right to be our Pilot, I had rather have Octavius [Carteret] though I have a very moderate Opinion of his Integrity, but were I to choose a head of the Treasury, it should be Mr. Pelham, for I have a good opinion both of his head, and heart.

I am very sorry to hear so bad an account of my friend Muff. I suppose you made a proper complaint to Mr. Philipps of his Turnspit; and I hope Muff may be reclam'd, but it will, I believe be necessary for you to confine him at home.[4]

I have this day sent a Box to the Carrier of which the Contents are inclosed, all the curiosity's are presents from Johnny Morris, the Nuts like kidneys have a kernell good to eat, but require great caution for there is an oyl between the shell & the kernell which will burn & blister the Mouth, or the hands if it lies some time upon them, the mouth immediately. The way is to take the kernell out of the shell & wash it well in

[1] Charles Emmanuel III (1701–73), king 1730–73.
[2] He died on 2 July 1743 and was succeeded by Henry Pelham as first lord of the treasury.
[3] Dr Richard Mead (1673–1754), physician and collector of books and art.
[4] Pryse's dog Muff had been attacked by Philipps' turnspit dog!

warm water till the oyl is clean off, if you tast any of them, pray let somebody clean them well for you first. There is a skin like that of a Chestnut under the shell to be peel'd off before the kernell is eaten.

You will find the Observations on Miscellaneous thoughts[5] a very wretched performance, the little Pamphlet call'd the new Ministry contains all the Verses I left at Stackpole & some more; I heard that a Messenger was at the Printers to seize them, if so, they will be scarce.

The weather is not at all cold. Wee had a good deal of rain all the middle of this day. Mrs Porter[6] dined with us she complaned you disappointed her of the visit you promised her last Summer, I said I hoped you would make amends this Spring. Your Mama's Love & Blessing attends you.

My Dearest I hope you are very carefull of your health, & of your self when you ride hunting &c. You cannot blame me for haveing some anxiety about the dear Treasure of my Heart in whome I place all my hopes & all my joy in this World. I pray God . . .

Captain Rickson[7] dined here yesterday & sends his Compliments. He sets out for the Country next week, haveing leave to come over to settle his Affairs upon his Fathers death.

Pray remember me kindly to poor Will Thomas. I am very sorry for his illness.

Remember me to R[oger] Evans.

The small seeds in the little parcell are Indigo, the five Pea's are great curiosity's to try what the seeds, Pea's, Nuts &c will produce you must give them to the Gardiner to sow in a hotbed, for I believe they are all from Jamaica which is a very hot Climat.

Don't cut the kidney like nuts your self lest you cut your fingers, as I did the other day two fingers & a thumb at one stroke trying to cut a hard skin'd Pomegranate.

70.

John Campbell to Pryse Campbell, 8 January 1743

I thank you for your letter of the 2[n]d I was very glad to hear you were all well, and had a pleasant hunting on News years day; I had a letter from your Uncle Philipps dated that day & he said it was a terrible stormy rainy day; I was glad you did not go with the Crowd to Orielton. You cannot conveniently dine at this time of year, in any place where you cannot be sure of your time, & take your own way, for I would by no means hope you ride after night.

Lord Wilmington is better but I believe in a weak state I wish he may hold it for some time, though I hope the Person I wish for would succede him. I don't doubt Lord Bath would desire to be there, but I think the King would not be at all willing to put him there, and I know many of our Friends could not bear the thoughts of acting under such a Man. Lord Carteret would be much better than he, yet not quite to my satisfaction. I have a great opinion of the Man named in my last,[8] I hope I shall not find reason to alter it.

---

[5] *Observations upon a Late Pamphlet, Entitled Miscellaneous Thoughts &c in a Letter to the Noble Author* (1742), was a response to Lord Hervey's *Miscellaneous Thoughts* (1742).

[6] Mary Porter (*d.* 1765), tragedienne actress, active 1698–1743.

[7] Probably Captain William Rickson, correspondent with General Wolfe.

[8] Henry Pelham – see letter 69.

Lord Essex died this day, his Friends could not wish for his life in the melancholy way he was.

Your Friend Jeffrey French & his Lady[9] have been about parting, but I hear to day that they have on farther consideration & the advice of Friends resolved to continue togather. I don't yet know whether Vernon is come, I heard, but I can't say with what authority, that he will not be admitted to the Kings presence, Wentworth[10] and he haveing highly accused each other I believe it difficult for either to clear himself, but Vernon is much worse spoke of than the other, if half that is said of him be true he deserves to be hanged as a Monster of inhumanity, Pride, & Insolence.[11]

I send you a sawcy journal that abuses the Chancellor of the Exchequer [Samuel Sandys], & turns Cibbers[12] Birthday Ode upon Lord B[ath]. It is commonly a sawcy jacobite Paper. The Inclosed Bills shew what is sent from Mr. Pyes by Captain Warton if he comes safe to you, but the storm some days ago made us in great fear for him. There is with the Grocery 6th of Chocolate from this.

I thought you might want Sperma ceti Candles[13] to read by, or to avoid a bad smell in your Bedchamber, let them not be wasted, for money is scarce & Wee must be frugal even to Candles ends. My Love & Blessing to your Dear Brothers, I am very glad my pretty Ally continues in good health, compliments to the Laird, Mr. Rowe, Johnny &c. Pray my Dearest be allways carefull to preserve your health, & Limbs in safety, & to improve your mind. I pray God . . .

I have writ Frank Meare a full and true Account of the sheriff Affair.

71.
John Campbell to Pryse Campbell, 12 January 1743
I was very glad to hear by our Friend Allys letter to your Mama that you were all well. I pray God continue it long.

I have lately had several letters from the Laird in which he speaks of you greatly to your advantage, in short says every thing of you that can answer my fondest wishes, and as I believe he is too honest & sincere and too much my Friend to say more than he thinks. No words can express the joy that overflows my heart when I read the Character he gives you; many People might think me indiscrete for telling you this, thinking it might make you vane & conceited, but I promise my self it will have a very different effect, that it will make you diligent & carefull to deserve and act up to the Character given to you, and make you constantly upon your guard not to do anything unworthy of, or inconsistent

---

[9] Jeffrey French (c.1701–54), MP for Milborne Port 1741–7 and Tavistock 1754. His wife, Catherine, daughter of Richard Lloyd of Croghan, County Roscommon., held elegant assemblies in London and was accused of being unfaithful. They were reconciled, as Campbell states, but in 1751 they separated again.

[10] General Thomas Wentworth (?1693–1747), of Sunninghill, Berkshire. He was returned as a government supporter for the vacant Whitchurch seat 1743–7. Major general 1741, lieutenant general and colonel of the 5th dragoon guards 1745; second-in-command and then commander-in-chief of the land forces at Cartegena 1740.

[11] Vernon and Wentworth were joint commanders of the failed navy and army attack on Cartagena in what is now Columbia, in Mar.–June 1741. It was the major battle of the War of Jenkins' Ear. R. Browning, *The War of the Austrian Succession* (Stroud, 1994), 58–60.

[12] Colley Cibber (1671–1757), actor, playwright and poet. He was appointed poet laureate in 1730, a reward for his unstinting support of Walpole. His *Birthday Odes to George II* were particularly poor verse, ferociously attacked by Pope in *The Dunciad*.

[13] Candles made from spermaceti, the wax found in the head of the sperm whale.

with such a Character. My Dearest God has given you sense, lively spirits, and a pleasant temper, you must think your self bound in duty & gratitude to use those Gifts in the manner most pleasing to the Allwise & Good Giver, and that you will easily know must be to make your self usefull & innocently agreable to your fellow Creatures, especially those with whome you are by his Providence more immediately related or concern'd. I bless God you have hitherto done so as far as could be expected from one of your Years, it is my earnest prayer that your Virtue may increase & strengthen with your age.

The House sat yesterday but only received Petitions was not full & rose early.[14] I expect little busyness before tuesday, I am told the broad bottom will be up, but what to do I can't tell. I met, & made my Compliments to, Mr Symons yesterday in the Court of requests.[15] To day Velters Cornwall came to me in the House & told me that they had proposed to Lord Bath to have the Carmarthen, Haverford[west], Pembroke Town, & County Petitions[16] all withdrawn that his Lordship approved it, & he intended to speak of it to the Chancellor of the Exchequer [Samuel Sandys] and desired I would stay till the House was up & join with them in it; I told him he might be sure if other Gentlemen were satisfied, I could have no objection to a thing that would make me easy, and secure me from trouble, and expence; but it was a Case I could not speak in, because it would be call'd desireing to sacrifice other Gentlemen to my own Interest. I staid, in Case they had a mind to speak to me, but I thought proper not to go among them unless I was call'd; when the House adjourn'd I saw Mr Cornwall, Sir Erasmus & his Brother,[17] & Mr Carew go & talk to the Chancellor of the Exchequer. I stood at some distance near Mr Pryse of Gogerthan & Mr Powell of Nanteos,[18] who were both very much for Mr Cornwalls Project.[19] I repeted to them what I had said to Mr. Cornwall, what pass'd in the Conference I can't tell; as I came through the Court of Requests I saw the above named welch Gentlemen giveing an account, I suppose of their Conference to Mr. Symmons, I fancy'd by Kilgetty's face he had met with but little encouragement, Indeed I do not expect anything from this negotiation, though between you & I it would not displease me if it took effect. And if you remember how I was used for a long time after Mr. Symmons declared and what an expence that usage occasion'd, you will not think I can desire to undergo farther trouble & expence for the sake of that Family which occasion'd all the trouble I have allready had. I think my Lord Baths name will make our Friends the more averse to this Treaty though I know at the begining of the Session, both Mr Pelham & Mr. Sandys would have been glad to have

[14] *CJ*, xxiv, 372–6.

[15] The court of requests was within the palace of Westminster, situated between the Lords and the Commons and open to the public, and was used as a meeting place by, among others, lobbyists. See introduction to *The London Diaries of Bishop William Nicolson, Bishop of Carlisle, 1702–18*, ed. C. Jones and G. Holmes (Oxford, 1985). Mr Symons is probably John Symmons of Llanstinan, Pembrokeshire.

[16] Sir John Philipps of Kilgetty, Pembrokeshire, as MP for Carmarthen borough (1741–7), was opposed by Griffith Philipps (see below, Note 58) of Cwmgwili, Carmarthenshire. At Haverfordwest Philipps of Picton Castle was petitioned against Hugh Barlow (see below, Note 32) of Slebech, Pembrokeshire.

[17] Sir Erasmus Philipps and Sir John Philipps, both of Picton Castle, Pembrokeshire.

[18] Thomas Powell (c.1701–52), of Nanteos, Cardiganshire; tory MP for Cardigan boroughs 1725–7 and Cardiganshire 1742–7; lord lieutenant of Cardiganshire. A jacobite from a jacobite family – his father was William Powell and he and Lewis Pryse (?1683–1720) of Gogerddan, Cardiganshire, were 'the greatest incendiaries and most disaffected persons in the principality of Wales'. Cited in *HPC, 1715–54*, ii, 371.

[19] The project to have the various Welsh petitions withdrawn.

all Petitions dropt, & Winnington would have under taken it soon after the Committee settled the days of hearing, if Sir W[atkin] W[illiam]s Wynn would have given up the Denbigh Petition; but it is very late to talk of it now, & I think it will come to nothing. I will only say that if our Friends reject this Offer they should make sure of turning out both the Philipps's or else Wee shall make a very ridiculous figure.

Your Friend who walks as if he rid on a stick, told me to day that he had a letter from a Man of rank in Jamaica who told him that in the tryal of Sir C[harles] Ogle for assaulting the Governor which you saw mention'd in a letter to me, Vernon was an evidence & prevaricated most dirtily & shamefully.[20]

If you have not allready, you may, lend Miscellaneous Thoughts to Dr. Cuninghame, but desire him not to shew it his Neighbors, for if he did, little Bowen[21] & twenty Fools would want it, though none of them could be at all capable of tasting, or understanding it.

My Love & Blessing to your Brothers & Compliments to all Friends. I pray Preserve you . . .

Your Uncle Owen was on Sunday at Henley's Oratory,[22] by his account it was a most impudent, dull incoherent Rhapsody of Blasphemy, Treason and Scandal, too bad I think it will be suffer'd but one thing was ridiculous he spoke against scandalising People, and treating them with contempt (though by the way he did so by everyone from the highest to the lowest) at last he said Wee ought not to ridicule any body not even the little Monsieur Bussy[23] the French envoy.

72.
John Campbell to Pryse Campbell, 15 January 1743
I received yours of the 9th (though dated the 10th) with great pleasure. I cannot as yet give you any account of Vernon, he came to Town thursday night, I believe did not go out anywhere yesterday, and I have been nowhere to day to hear. It is said the mutual complaints between him & Wentworth will be hush'd up if possible there being no want of anything to perplex the Court or inflame the People. I was told that to this end Lord Bath met Vernon at Brentford, but all this is report of which I have no certainty, possibly I may be able to say more next Post. Lord Hervey came here this evening he told me that it is said Mr. Sandys will be made a Peer to make way for some changes, but his Lordship is not now in a scituation to know such things but by hearsay. If Mr. Pelham is to be Head of the Treasury & Chancellor of the Exchequer I shall be extremely satisfied with the change; not that I expect any advantage to my self but it is the best thing I can think of for the Public. Make my compliments to the Laird & tell him I had rather he made a visit to Pentyparch & return'd to Stackpole, for I think my Dearest you had better begin your journey from home, & defer your visit to Pentyparch till Summer. I hear Mr. Phillipps has had a fall with his horse & hurt himself, I beg of

---

[20] Sir Charles Ogle was a member of the supreme council ruling Jamaica during the early years of the War of Jenkins' Ear. Other members were Admiral Vernon, Generals Wentworth and Bulkney and the governor of the island, General Edward Trelawney.

[21] Probably one of the Bowen family of Camrose, Pembrokeshire, who were distantly related to the Campbell family.

[22] John Henley (1692–1759). Orator Henley used to stand on a tub in the neighbourhood of Lincoln's Inn Field and hold forth. For some years he edited a weekly paper, *Hyp Doctor*, in opposition to the *Craftsman*.

[23] François de Bussy (1699–1780), French chargé d'affaires in London 1740–3.

you my Dearest to be very carefull of yourself when you ride. I think very soon to mention a time for your comeing to London.

Yesterday Lord Strange moved for a Bill to prevent for the future wearing any Gold or Silver in Cloths,[24] he had on a rich french Wastcoat, he was elaborately Seconded by Mr. Gybbon of the Treasury,[25] the finest performance Wee have had from him since he so worthyly fill'd that Place. Mr. Sydenham[26] thired in a rapture of joy hopeing that such frugality would enable us to pull down France & preserve the Liberty of Europe; and this wise Triumvirate are to bring in this Bill, which I suppose will never pass and if it did I fear would ruin some Tradesmen without preventing the ruin of any others, extravagance would find some other way and I believe 'tis as vane to expect to cure a Nation abandon'd to all manner of luxury and extravagance by such a Bill, as it would be think of cureing a very Scorbutic Constitution of body by putting a bit of plaster on a Pimple.

The same day the Chancellor of the Exchequer [Samuel Sandys] moved for some alterations in the Gin Act and hinted that it might possibly prove a fund on which all the Supplies of the Year might be raised, upon which, as on every other occasion, they abused the new Ministers & Pitt, Lyttleton, & Sir J[ohn] H[ynde] C[otton] spoke some handsome things of Lord Orford as a contrast to the present Chancellor of the Exchequer. I should be very sorry to alter the Gin Act[27] if I thought it answer'd the intention, but I fear that Mischief is too big to be remedied, and People too ungovernable to submit to any such Law; I believe nothing can keep them from Gin unless one could persuade them that they insulted the Government every time they drank small liquor.

Give my Love & Blessing to your Brothers, his Mama & I are very glad to hear Ally grows stout & plump. Remember me most kindly to Johnny. My Dearest I pray God . . .

My Dear when I was in the Country I observed that the little Fool Punch had painted my study so that all the knots in the Wainscote appear'd & looked yellow. Pray don't let him paint or finish anymore till I send some directions which I intend very soon.

James desires to send his duty & many thanks.

73.

John Campbell to Pryse Campbell, 18 January 1743

This day the House was call'd[28] over, and Sir John Astley, Mr Speke, & Mr Wyndham Ashe[29] were order'd into custody for not attending, Wee divided the House

---

[24] *CJ*, xxiv, 379.

[25] Phillips Gybbon. After Walpole's fall he was placed on the treasury board by Pulteney, along with Sandys and Rushout in order to combine their votes against the nominal first lord, Wilmington. *HPC, 1715–54*, ii, 93.

[26] Humphrey Sydenham (1694–1757), of Coombe, Dulverton, Somerset and Nutcombe, Devon; tory MP for Exeter 1741–54. He moved to introduce a bill for annual parliaments in Jan. 1745, seconded by Gybbon (see Chapter 4, letter 126).

[27] See *PH*, xii, 1191–440, for the debates in the Lords (though not the Commons) on the sprituous liquors bill, held between 15 and 25 Feb.

[28] The call of the House.

[29] Sir John Astley (1687–1771), of Patshull, Staffordshire and Everley, Wiltshire; tory MP for Shrewsbury 1727–34 and Shropshire 1734–71; George Speke (*d.* 1753), of White Lackington, and Dillington, Somerset; whig supporter of the administration. MP for Milbourne Port 1722–7, Taunton 1727–34 and Wells 1735–47; Joseph Windham Ashe (1683–1746), of Twickenham, Middlesex; whig MP for Downton 1734–41 and 1742–6. They were committed to the custody of the serjeant at arms for defaulting.

to save them, but so many were gone off after their names were call'd that Wee were beat every division.[30] This attendance has made my head incline to ach so I can't write much. Lord Wilmington is gone to the Bath, Wee are very anxious for his life, for I fear it would not be easy to settle matters as Wee wish in case of his death, in the mean time his absense from the Treasury though necessary is an inconvenience. The Sensible People of our Party are in some pain about the Carmarthen Election,[31] but say nothing of that. Mr Barlow[32] &c are come to Town, Master Owen was at Court on Sunday, I thought he look'd awkward, though in Scarlet & gold.

Your Mama has her headach to day, the Dabs are all well My Love & Blessing to your Brothers, Compliments to the Laird &c. Be carefull of the dear Treasure of my heart I pray God . . .

I had half an hours Conversation to day morning with Mr. Pelham Spes fidisima Teucrum.[33]

74.
John Campbell to Pryse Campbell, 22 January 1743
It would be very difficult to express the Joy and Satisfaction I had in reading your letter of the 16th. It has been the great object of my desires & cares ever since you were born to see you a Man of Sense & Virtue, and affectionate to me; and Young as you are, I think that letter shews me already in possession of all my wish's. I pray God grant a long continuance of so great happyness. The very inaccuracy's of the language gave me pleasure as they were so many proofs that all said was your natural thoughts without study, or art: Your Friendship is the greatest pleasure I can have in this world, and if it pleases God to continue us to one another, in a competent state of health, and prosperity, you will give a Pleasure to my Age, beyond anything my Youth enjoy'd. I will endeavor to behave so, if possible, that my Age may not prevent my being an agreable Companion, as well a zealous Faithfull Friend to you, I hope in such a Manner that you may never be unwilling to tell even your Faults to me, for Wee can none of us be perfect, and when you do fall into any Mistakes, I hope you will never have reason to fear the reproofs of an angry Father; but will be desireous to receive the advice of a true and kind Friend, that will give you the best advice he is able not only to prevent your falling into the like error for the future, but to set the past as far right as may be possible.

Your thoughts upon Pride & covetousness please me very much. I am sure it was never possible to suspect you of either. I wish my Dearest I was better able to instruct you, for it would be the greatest delight & satisfaction to be usefull to one I love so much, and thanks to God, my Judgement justifies all the fondness of my heart. Pardon me my Dear if I often repete my earnest desire that you will allways be very carefull of

---

[30] *CJ*, xxiv, 383: 110 to 129 against Astley, 111 to 23 against Speke and 102 to 21 against Ashe.

[31] The 1741 Carmarthen election was notorious as a trigger for mob violence in the town which continued at regular intervals until a new charter was issued in 1764. The election was between Sir John Philipps of Picton Castle, Pembrokeshire and Griffith Philipps of Cwmgwili, Carmarthenshire. The former won but Griffith Philipps petitioned, though this was withdrawn in Feb. 1743.

[32] Hugh Barlow (*d.* 1763), of Lawrenny, Pembrokeshire; MP for Pembroke boroughs 1747–61. A supporter of the Pelhams. See P.D.G. Thomas, *Politics in Eighteenth-Century Wales* (Cardiff, 1998), 118–19.

[33] Virgil, *Aeneid*, ii, 281: 'O most faithful hope of the Trojans'.

your health and your Person in all respects. If you are every day shewing your self more valuable and consequently makeing your self more dear to me you must expect my anxiety for you [*sic*] safety and wellfare will increase.

I hope the little swelling that was on one of your under eyelids after a sty, is quite gone, if there is any remanes of it you should not neglect it, but use the white oyntment the Dr gave you. I have taken it for granted your eyes were well because nobody has mention'd them to me; I hope I was not mistaken.

Last Post I writ pretty planely to the Laird about the visit you desired my direction whether you should make or no. Ask the Laird to shew you the letter if he has not allready for I did not mean to keep my thoughts from my Dearest Boy.

On Wednesday [19 January] Wee went into the Committee of Supply in order to Vote a Grant of £500,000 for supporting the Queen of Hungary & restore the balance of Power in Europe. The same sum was voted in the same words last year & was disposed of £300,000 to the Queen of Hungary & £200,000 to the King of Sardinia to enable those Princes to keep up their Forces. The Opposers knew that Sir J[ohn] Barnard would vote for the question & if he spoke declare for all the present warlike measure [*sic*] so they endeavor'd to put the busyness of [*sic*] till fryday knowing Sir J[ohn] Barnard would then be absent for he scarce ever come to the House on a Fryday or monday. So Wee divided whether the Speaker should leave the Chair Ays 212 no's 159.[34] When Wee were in the Committee they did not directly oppose nor approve the question but found fault rail'd at all the Measures & abused the Ministers. Our Treasury did not make much of it, but Mr. Pelham made a long speech & with great strength, spirit, and dignity even exceeded himself. Sir J[ohn] Barnard spoke for the question, approved the present Measures, and was not a bit affraid of the French. I wish I could say as much. The Committee did not divide But yesterday upon the report to the House there was another short debate in which the Solicitor General [William Murray] spoke excellently for the Question. Mr. Pitt took occasion to express his aversion to the Hanover Troops in terms that were Surpriseing from one who is in the Service, and one should think desires to be thought in the Interest of the present Royal Family. Sir J[ohn] H[ynde] C[otton]. also spoke very strongly against the Hanoverians and Mr. Pit[t], I think in a 2[n]d speech[35] said he should allways agree with that Gentleman when he spoke in that manner of those Troops, and he believed should allmost allways agree with him in every thing or words to that effect, his was also very surpriseing. Mr. Pelham said somewhat that gave the Speaker a handsome opportunity to give Pit a sort of rebuke for his irregularity for speaking in such terms of takeing the Hanover Troops into our Pay after it has been Voted by the House.

I think the Heads of the opposition had no inclination to divide, but when the Question was put to agree with the Committee & the Speaker gave it for the Ay's Carew divided the House, and Wee were not willing to let them yeild so Wee divided

---

[34] *CJ*, xxiv, 385.

[35] Speakers were only allowed to speak once in any debate, hence Campbell's comment. Very few instances of this rule being broken have been recorded, especially under the Speakership of Onslow, who kept tight control of the Commons. P.D.G. Thomas, *The House of Commons in the Eighteenth Century* (Oxford, 1971), 193–4.

Ays 245 No's 156.[36] I think the Merionethshire Instructions produced some good for Mr. Vaughan[37] voted with us in this Question, though Sir W[atkin] W[illiams] W[wyn]. was one of the Teller, [*sic*] Vaughan faced him with his hat on.

Give my Love & Blessing to your Brothers. Compliments to the Laird & kind remembrance to Johnny. I pray God . . .

75.

John Campbell to Pryse Campbell, 27 January 1743

Last night the Committee of Elections sat again up [*sic*] the Carmarthen affair, after much wrangling Wee divided upon a question whether Mr. Richard Dalton[38] should be admitted as a Witness to prove that several Persons were not resident in the Borough before their being admitted Burgess's, he being a Burgess who was resident in the Borough before his admission. The objection against him was frivolous & absurd, I believe the like was scarce ever made before, Yet Wee were beaten by a Majority of 49. What then may Wee expect on other Questions in this Election which probably may not be so plane in our favor. I look upon Kilgetty as quite sure of his seat, and probably Sir Erasmus too our Friend would not let their Leader compromise these Elections & yet they will not attend, for Wee divided but 116 and our own Friends could have made much more than that, the New Minister ought to have dealt more planely and by selling what the [*sic*] would, or fancy'd themselves engaged to, do have shewn our Friends the necessity of makeing up an Affair they could not carry, I mean our New Ministers in the House of Commons, for I believe Lord Tweedale[39] wish'd us well Wee had some of his Friends Lord Winchilsea[40] the same I believe Octavius [Carteret] would have done well if he could but he has few dependents in our House. Antonius [Bath] I hear acted perfectly up to his most admired & virtuous Character, first saying Kilgetty ought by all means to be turn'd out, then promiseing him his assistance, and at last acting a neuter part makeing as many as he could, keep away. On Monday some Gentlewomen in our gallery, not being able to hold their water, let it run on Mr. Dodington & a Scots member who sat under the first had a white duffel frock spoil'd, the latter allmost blinded.

My Love & blessing to your Brothers. I am sorry to hear of dear little Ally haveing a cough. My Compliments to the Laird and kind service to Mr. Rowe. My Ancle is a good deal better but I have not been out of Doors except in a Chair to the Committee last night. I saw great flash of lightening through the Windows there about 12 at night, and while I was there the Wind blew down a Chimney in Hanover Square. I pray God . . .

---

[36] *CJ*, xxiv, 387.

[37] William Vaughan (?1707–75), of Gorsygedol, Merioneth; tory MP for Merioneth 1734–68, though he supported the whigs in the 1740 Caernarvonshire election against Sir Watkin Williams-Wynn.

[38] Described in a variety of documents as gentleman of Carmarthen town. CRO, names indexes.

[39] George Hay (1700–87), 6th marquess of Tweeddale.

[40] Daniel Finch (1689–1769), 8th earl of Winchilsea and 3rd earl of Nottingham; styled Lord Finch until 1730. MP for Rutland 1710–30; first lord of the admiralty 1742–4 and 1757; lord president of the council 1765–6.

76.

John Campbell to Pryse Campbell, 29 January 1743
I receaved yours last night with great Pleasure. I am very thankfull for the kind
concern you express for my health. I thank God I am very well & my foot much
better, though I staid at the Committee till near three this morning. Wee had no
division for indeed Wee saw our selves too weak to divide,[41] the Cause is not ended
but there can be no doubt of our looseing it, were it a much stronger Case than it
is. I wish Mr Barlow[42] may have better fortune I think him an honest good natured
Man and believe he has a Strong Case, but that will signifie little if there is a strong
Party against him.

I think my Dearest you make a very good & proper use of Dr. Middletons Tullys
Epistles.[43] I think it is rather too early for Ally to begin latin but if he desires it one
would not cross him. I was very glad to hear that Trub and he were so well & his
Cough but slight thank Trub for his letter to me, & tell him I will write to him soon.

The account you will see in the News of the Fire[44] which begun they say by airing
sheets or somewhat like that in a careless way at a House taken for the Duchess of
Beaufort makes me think it proper for you to speak to Frank to give a strick charge
to & keep a carefull eye upon all the workmen in that respect, and see that the
Chimneys where they work are safely brick'd, and let R[oger] Evan[s], & the
Housekeeper give strickt charge to all the servants, your sleepy Man Dick Dawkins
should never be trusted with a Candle up stairs, your own Man Val is apt to be sleepy
you will make him be carefull. As to your journey, I would have you, if you please,
come here the beginning of March but don't tye yourself to a day either for setting
out or comeing here, but do as the Weather & roads make proper. I beg of you not
to expose your health or Limbs to danger by rideing in bad weather, makeing long
stages to hazard being out after night, or rideing fast in bad way indulge a little my
fears if you have none of your own.

My Compliments to the Laird, kind service to Mr. Rowe &c. My Love & Blessing
to your Brothers. Your Mama has a cold but is gone to the Opera. I pray God . . .
James desires his duty with many thanks.

Lucerce says that the flower roots with the following Names should have a little Dung
strew'd over the Mold they are Planted in Faisen I suppose he means Pheasant
Queen of Great Britain
Albino
Riceto
Sultana
Mogol
I think these are all Hyacinths.

[41] Referring to the petition against Sir John Philipps of Kilgetty as MP for Carmarthen borough.

[42] George Barlow (1717–56), of Slebech, Pembrokeshire; tory MP for Haverfordwest 1743–7. He was
petitioning against the return of Sir Erasmus Philipps of Picton Castle as MP for Haverfordwest.

[43] 'The Epistles of M.T. Cicero to M. Brutus and of Brutus to Cicero', the Latin with English Translation, and a
Prefatory Dissertation in Defence of the Authenticity of the Epistles (1743).

[44] In Southampton Row. Two houses were completely destroyed and a third badly damaged. The duke of
Bedford was on hand to direct the working of the seven fire engines. Daily Post, 28 Jan. 1743.

77.

John Campbell to Pryse Campbell, 1 February 1743

I send you inclosed a Print, which I believe cheifly alludes to a voluminous account of his family which the noble youths Father is said to have sent into the Heralds Office, I suppose what is under the Print in Italic's is an extract from that Pedigree, and by what is in the blast[45] above I imagine they have derived the Name from the latin Words, Per se Valet, or Valens, Let him Vote how he will now, I can't forget the Westminster Election nor consequently be sorry to see him hunted & worried by his own hounds. I send A vote that was Mislaid and a Pamphlet of an extraordinary Case of a man liveing upon allmost nothing in Argyllshire but that Pamphlet is too big to be under Your cover so I shall put it in two, directed to the Laird & John Wright. As I keep mostly at home to favor my foot which mends, I hear no News. There is a great Debate to day in the House of Lords, I think upon the Hanover Troops,[46] if I can get any particulars by next Post you shall have them. I am very desireous if it please God to have my foot well by the time you come to Town, that I may sometimes have the Pleasure to walk with You without being very troublesome to you. My Love & Blessing to your Brothers. I pray God . . .

The Life of the Noble Youth[47] I gave you account of some time ago makes part of the Genealogy, which I believe ends with an account of the Christening of his son viz this young Nobleman had for his Godfather & Godmother the Right Honorable the Earl & Countess of Egmonts[48] his Grandfather & Grandmother. I forgot the other Gossip but believe it was some Right Honorable Earl.

78.

John Campbell to Pryse Campbell, 3 February 1743

I sent this morning to my Neighbor the good Lord of Llandaffe for an account of the Questions in the House of Lords on Tuesday [1 February],[49] I inclose his answer.[50] I wish I could have sent the Question at large I heard E[arl] Stanhope[51] had his Speech writ down[52] & was often forced to look on his Paper, & as he is not very happy in his Person, & his action not the best he alltogather made rather a merry figure, he was Seconded by the Earl of Sandwich[53] who took occasion to tell a story of a King of France hireing Troops of a Duke of Hanover, which I am not sure is to be found in the

---

[45] The balloon-shaped scroll proceeding from the mouths of speakers in caricatures.

[46] *LJ*, xxvi, 195–7.

[47] Perceval, 1st Earl Egmont.

[48] John Perceval, 2nd Earl Egmont.

[49] The debate on taking the Hanoverian troops into British pay. See *PH*, xii, 1058–189, for the debate.

[50] See note at the end of the letter.

[51] Philip Stanhope (1714–86), 2nd Earl Stanhope.

[52] *PH*, xii, 1058–9, citing Secker: that Stanhope 'spoke a pre-composed speech which he held in his hand with great tremblings and agitations, and hesitated frequently in the midst of great vehemence: but his matter was not contemptible'.

[53] John Montagu (1718–92), 4th earl of Sandwich; first lord of the admiralty 1748–51, 1763 and 1771–82; secretary of state for the northern department 1763–5 and 1770–1. Became known as Jemmy Twitcher, the betrayer of Macheath in Gay's *Beggar's Opera*, since his political behaviour was deemed very similar. He was dismissed by Newcastle, and later Bute, as being untrustworthy. However, as first lord, especially in his final stint, he reformed the gross mismanagement of the navy dockyards.

french History, he said the Duke charged that King with such a jam for the maintenance or Pay of his Troops & another large jam for levy Money which the king refused saying the Troops were raised before & not on purpose for his service. The Duke of Hanover replied that he hoped H[is] M[ajesty] would consider he was a very poor Prince & wanted money very much the King of France told him if he raised more Troops on purpose for his service, he would pay him half what he demanded, for levy money, but he would not be his bybble.[54] N.B. The Prince of Wales & Duke of Cumberland[55] were both in the House when this story was told. Lord Hervey spoke long & handsomely against the Measures of Forming an Army in our Pay in Flanders but said nothing of the Hanover Troops in particular, Lord Lonsdale[56] Spoke & Voted for Lord Stanhopes Question & Lord Gower[57] L[ord] P[rivy] S[eal] spoke for it. The Earl of Bath spoke against it. Lord Orford was not in the House haveing been some time indisposed with a feaverish disorder he is now pretty well but I believe has not yet been out of his House I saw him Yesterday. The Lords sat till near eleven at night, several makeing very long speechs.

This day by agreement the Petitions of Mr Griffith Philipps,[58] Mr [Hugh] Barlow, Mr R[awleigh] Mansel & Mr Symmons were all withdrawn[59] and considering how matters went it was certainly a good bargain on our side (I have heard no one but Brereton[60] doubt it) for Lord Bath was more for Sir Erasmus than for his brother so if the Petitions had gone on Mr G[riffith] Philipps & Mr. Barlow would have been put to farther expence & lost their Causes, and next Session the petitions against Mr. Owen & me might have been renew'd, when Wee had none to set against them; had there appear'd any hope of carrying Mr. Barlows Cause the Case had been very different.

My Dearest I beg of you to be carefull of your self both to avoid getting cold & to get well when you have any Cold, especially upon changes of weather. Mr. Maynard[61] was here this evening & enquired kindly of you & your Brothers. Wee have had mighty fine weather but to night it is high wind & hard rain.

I had forgot to tell you that this agreement for withdrawing the Petitions was made yesterday, but this morning Kilgetty said Mr Symmons would not consent to withdraw

---

[54] Bubble, a word used with regard to delusive or fraudulent commercial or financial schemes, after the South Sea Bubble of 1720. *OED.*

[55] Prince William (1721–65), duke of Cumberland, younger son of George II. He fought at Dettingen in June 1743, where he was wounded, made a lieutenant general and a British hero. He was later responsible for destroying the Young Pretender and his forces at Culloden and ruthlessly destroying the jacobite forces, earning him the title 'butcher Cumberland' by his enemies. Henry Fox was the leader of the Cumberland faction in the Commons in the 1750s. They fell out over Fox's (or Holland as he had by that time become) increasingly close political friendship with Lord Bute, the hated favourite of George III.

[56] Henry Lowther (1694–1751), 3rd Viscount Lonsdale; lord privy seal 1733–5.

[57] John Leveson-Gower (1694–1754), 1st Earl Gower. Leader of the tories in the Lords, he became the only tory to take high office, as lord privy seal, after the fall of Walpole. Lord privy seal 1742–3 and 1744–54. *ODNB.*

[58] Griffith Philipps (c.1715–81), of Cwmgwili, Carmarthenshire; whig MP for Carmarthen 1751–61 and 1768–74.

[59] *CJ,* xxiv, 403–4. Philipps for Carmarthen borough, Barlow for Haverfordwest, Mansell for the boroughs of Pembroke and Wiston and Symmons for Pembrokeshire.

[60] Thomas Brereton.

[61] Probably Charles Maynard (c.1699–1775), known as Lord Maynard 1745–66. Created 1st Baron and Viscount Maynard in 1766.

his Petition. I am told his desire was to have the Petition for Carmarthen voted frivolous, & vexatious, but Sir W[atkin] W[illiams] W[ynn] who was witness to the agreement yesterday upon Mr. Winningtons complaneing to him said the agreement should be kept, so he spoke to Kilgetty & I believe went out to Mr Symmons & after a little bustle all was right again. The new Ministers and their Friends would have stood by Mr. Owen & me and I believe would greatly have resented Kilgetty's going back for the agreement if he had persisted in it.

Give my Love & Blessing to your Brothers kind service to Mr. Rowe & remembrance to Johnny. I pray God . . .

James's Duty, he hopes ere Long to wait on you to the Monument. Remember me to Val.

[62]I have not the Words of either Question: both were very long: the First to Address the King against the Measure &c of sending Troops to Flanders.

For this Address: 35. against it: 90.[63]

The next was a Vote of Approbation mov'd by Lord Scarborough.[64]

For it: 78. against it 35[65]

The first Question was mov'd by Lord Stanhope.

79.

John Campbell to Pryse Campbell, 5 February 1743

I am very thankful for the kind concern you express for my hurting my Ancle, your affection is the best Comfort I can have in any Misfortune. One must not expect so weak a Limb as mine to recover fast, but it is a great deal better allready. I hope I may be able to take a Walk with you when you come to Town. My Dearest you shall be allways wellcome to tell me of my faults, & I will take any caution from you very kindly, but I assure I was not to blame this time. I wish I could prevent any of my Friends haveing Marble Pavements for they are both dangerous and disagreable.

I am Sorry to hear our Country[66] was so hard hearted to the poor Men upon Gresholm.[67] I heartily wish they may be saved, & shall be glad if they owe their preservation to you.

I am very sorry I could not give you a better account of Haverford[west] & Carmarthen but as things went every body thinks Wee did the best Wee could. Yesterday Wee had a Motion to address the King to lay before the House all Letter Memorials &c that have pass'd between his Majesty's Ministers & the Ministers of the Queen of Hungary for more than a Year past,[68] much in the same terms that such a Question pass'd last year our New Ministers supported it then and opposed it now. Sir

[62] This is in a different hand – I assume it to be the note referred to by Campbell in the body of the letter, written by Lord Llandaff. See *LJ*, xxvi, 196–7.

[63] The figures agree with those in Sainty and Dewar.

[64] Thomas Lumley-Sunderson, Lord Scarbrough (1691–1752).

[65] The figures agree with those in Sainty and Dewar.

[66] That is, Pembrokeshire.

[67] Gresholm (Grassholm today) is a small, uninhabited island six miles north of the entrance to Milford Haven, Pembrokeshire.

[68] *CJ*, xxiv, 406.

J[ohn] Rushlight[69] attempted to prove himself consistent, but he had better have fairly said he would act a wiser & honester part now than he did then. The Chancellor of the Exchequer [Samuel Sandys] spoke not quite so rashly as Sir John but he made no great figure, Mr Pelham, Mr Winnington Sir William Yonge & H[enry] Fox spoke well against the Question and might with a good grace for they opposed it last year. Pitt made a handsome speech but went far from the Question, it was moved by Mr Waller & supported by Pitt, Lyttelton, Dodington, Lord Barington & Lord Strange who made no great figure in it. Wee divided Ay's 154 No's 212.[70] I send you inclosed the Lords Protest,[71] you will consider that in such a thing they are at liberty to affirm & argue as they please there being no Answer to be made and one might be most grossly imposed upon if one judged of any Question by a Protest against it. I hear the great Earl of B[ath] made but a moderate figure in the Debate. I saw Lord Orford to day he grows better but I can't say that he looks quite well.

Vernon has not yet come to the House which I[72] nor declared what Place he will serve for which I think is most insolent & impertinent.

Pray my Dear direct R[oger] Evan[s] to send a Man to the Sheriff Mr. Paynter.[73]

I hope you are quite rid of your Cold & will be very carefull of your health. My Love & Blessing to your Dear Brothers, Compliments to the Laird. I pray God . . .

80.

John Campbell to Pryse Campbell, 8 February 1743

I can write but little to night haveing sat in the House till after six when I left them talking about a Petition from some Master of Colliers,[74] which it seem'd agreed should lye upon the Table,[75] and I was quite tired with so much prateing to no purpose, for they talk about some parts of the Gin Bill,[76] till four o'Clock, without attempting to divide or haveing anything like a Question. I hear General Wentworth is to come into the House in the room of Mr. Charles Clark[77] who you will see by the News is made a Baron of the Exchequer.

My Love & Blessing to your Brothers, Compliments to the Laird, Mr. Rowe, Johnny &c. My Dearest I pray God . . .

---

[69] Sir John Rushout. Campbell refers to him at times as Rushlight, which could be a comment on Rushout's character or size, a rushlight being steeped in fat or grease!

[70] *CJ*, xxiv, 406.

[71] *LJ*, xxvi, 195–7. The debate on a motion of Lord Stanhope's to reject taking Hanoverian troops into British pay took place on 1 Feb. (see letter 78 above) with a vote in the negative 90 to 35. For that debate and the 'Protest against Rejecting Lord Stanhope's Motion', referred to by Campbell, see *PH*, xii, 1058–189, protest reported at cols 1180–9. *LJ*, xxvi, 196–7.

[72] A letter or part of word scribbled out here.

[73] David Paynter of Dale, Pembrokeshire.

[74] *CJ*, xxiv, 412.

[75] If it was agreed to place a paper on the table of the House, it effectively allowed any member to peruse its contents, except where a paper was placed on the table unread in which case it was not allowed to be taken up. This was an effective method of extinguishing unwanted petitions. However, the colliers' petition was read. Thomas, *House of Commons in the Eighteenth Century*, 24–7.

[76] *CJ*, xxiv, 410.

[77] Charles Clarke (c.1702–50), of Godmanchester; whig MP for Huntingdonshire 1739–41 and Whitchurch 1743.

81.

John Campbell to Pryse Campbell, 10 February 1743

I thank God for the good account I receaved of you & your Brothers healths last Post by Johnny.

On tuesday [8 February] after I left the House they Put off the call, & Lord Strange's Lace Bill for two months which I was glad of.[78] Yesterday Wee sat till allmost night, and I am so stupid I can't recollect what it was about. To day Wee were puzzleing till three upon a Bill about County Elections, then Wee took a night to consider of it and are to go with maturer deliberation upon it to morrow.[79] When that was put off Mr. Waller moved to address the King for all Letters Memorials or verbal negotiations between our Court & that of Berlin; or Berlin and the State General which had been communicated to our Court concerning the Marching of Foreign Troops into Germany after a Debate in which there was but few Speakers viz Mr Waller, Mr. Pitt, Mr. Lyttelton, Sir J[ohn] H[ynde] C[otton] and Lord Strange for it, and Lord Baltimore, Mr Pelham, the Solicitor General [William Murray], and as I may say Mr. Vyner against it Wee divided ay's 130. noes 164.[80] Then Mr. Waller moved for all letters & Memorials between our Court & the King of Swedes, Landgrave of Hesse[81] concerning the Hessian Troops in our pay acting in Germany on that Wee divided ays 134 Noes 148.[82] Some Wiseheads that were with us in the former question being against us in this. You will observe the House was but thin I suppose many thought busyness over because the call was put to a long day, but the other side attended better than ours probably many of them had notice of the motions being intended.

I send inclosed a new ballad that has some things pretty well. I must conclude the Bell ringing for the Letters.[83] I pray God . . .

82.

John Campbell to Pryse Campbell, 15 February 1743

Johnny tells me you think to set out about the 23[r]d. I pray God direct & preserve you & grant us a happy meeting. It is a great satisfaction to me that you promise you order your journey according to the condition of the Weather &c. Johnny desired me to send down some of the Oyl'd Silk to line the Sleeves of your Great Coat. I have several times ask'd Mr. Clive, he could not tell where it was had but allways promised to enquire & let me know & as often forgot. I hope you will take all the care to secure yourself against bad weather that you can, and expose yourself to it as little as may be. I would advise you to have such a hood as Will White made for James. I think it much more convenient than those that are fast to the Coat. Your Man may Carry it in his Pocket when you don't wear it, & then your Great Coat need not have two Capes. I think a loose Joseph Coat keeps one from the Wet better than the Closebodied great Coats.

[78] *CJ*, xxiv, 412. The House divided on delaying the call for a fortnight or two months, and voted for the latter 130 to 103. It was the second reading of Lord Strange's bill.

[79] *CJ*, xxiv, 415.

[80] *CJ*, xxiv, 415, gives ayes of 30.

[81] Frederick I (1676–1751), king of Sweden and landgrave of Hesse.

[82] *CJ*, xxiv, 416.

[83] Postmen rang bells in the streets of London to announce time for the collection of letters to be posted.

I thank you my Dearest for your Translations but can't give my judgement upon them for I have no Tully here, but I think they seem to read well.

Admiral Vernon spoke in the House to day and I find him exactly the same than as when he was last in the House. There had been a Bill brought in for the importation of Spanish Oyl. This day it was by consent put to a long day to be dropt for this session at least, but the Admiral took that occasion to scold like a fishwoman at the Spaniards till he set the whole house a laughing. He said this Kingdom was more burthen'd with Debts and tax's than any Country on this side Hell.[84]

My Love & Blessing to your Dear Brothers, Compliments to the Laird, Mr. Rowe &c. Most kind remembrance to Johnny. I am sorry Dr. Crowther talks of returning the Saddle, but I think they did ill to persuade the poor Beast to drink so much Brandy.

I pray God . . .

James Duty to you. He says he found the hood very convenient either for rain or Cold. The wind does not get under it as it does under the Cape of a Coat.

I was last night at the Play to see Mrs. Porter[85] act for the last time & for her own benefit she had a full House & good Company.

83.

John Campbell, Huntley[86] to Pryse Campbell, 10 November [?1743]

I fancy you will smile at the date of this, but Wee could not win[87] Glocester, & I assure you Wee are very well entertain'd here, I eat a fine Partridge for Supper, & have very tolerable Portwine, better than most Innes; & a good comfortable house, the White Heart. I intend for Frogmill or if I can Norlech to morrow.[88] I thank God am perfectly well may this find you & all with you the same. My Love to your Brothers, best service to the Laird, kind remembrance to Mr. Rowe, Johnny &c. I pray God . . .

Wee could have reached Glocester if the Maid at Hereford had call'd as she was order'd. Her excuse was, she had sat up two nights till three o'Clock to let in a learned divine, who doubtless was persueing his studies in the College Library till that hour.

My Landlady when she was makeing the Partridge sawce to night very civilly asked James if I had any sort of diversion to an Onion.

84.

John Campbell to Pryse Campbell, 19 November 1743

You will find by my letter to your Mama that I ended my journey very gallantly, I thank you for your letter which I found here, you may be sure I am ill pleased to find myself in Pandæmonium[89] a fortnight sooner than need. I believe by the date, that

---

[84] No reference is given concerning this bill in either *CJ* or *PH*. However *CJ*, xxiv, 423–4, refers to several petitions being presented to the House regarding the prohibition on the importation of Spanish olive oil.

[85] Mary Porter acted by command and for the last time in her own benefit at Covent Garden in John Banks' *The Albion Queens*, on 14 Feb. 1743.

[86] Seven miles west of Gloucester, at the northern end of the Forest of Dean.

[87] That is, they could not reach Gloucester.

[88] Frogmill Inn, Andoversford, near Cheltenham. Norlech, today Northleach, is to the north-east of Gloucester.

[89] London.

Pelhams letter to stop me came to Stackpole the very day I left it. Mr Pelham fancy'd it was Mr Barlow of Lawrenny[90] that stood for Haverford [west] and says in his letter to me that he heartily wishes him success. I congratulate Trub upon his heroic atchievement. I am pleased to hear of you being well diverted in the field, if I am well assured, you are carefull of your self and run no hazards I beg you often to think how anxious your poor Father is for you safety, and then I am sure your good nature will make you carefull. I think you did very right to excuse your self from going to Bush as Mr Meyrick[91] has not for several years been to Stackpole. My compliments to Mr Rowe and all Friends. I pray God . . .

85.

John Campbell, London to Pryse Campbell, 26 November 1743

I hope in God you are now in perfect health and good spirits with your Friends keeping your Birthday, and I earnestly pray that you may see many of them in Virtue health Peace & honor. Mr Edwards dined with me today in his way to Wimbledon to drink your health. I give you many thanks for letter of the 20th for I know that must be the day it was writ, though you forgot to date it. Nothing can be more welcome or agreable to me than a kind letter from you, though I would never have you confine yourself to write to me but when you have leisure and convenience I shall allways rejoice to hear from you.

I see I might have stay'd longer at Stackpole and yet have had good travelling weather, and what is worst of all I was told today by Sir R[oger] Bradshaigh[92] whom I met in my walks, that the Parliament will not do busyness till after the Holydays. It is said the Cabinet Councill cannot yet agree what to say to us. I believe both affairs and Persons are in great uncertainty and confusion, Several changes and promotions have been talk'd of, but I know nothing for certain, it is said that hints have been given Mr Pitman,[93] but that he refuses every thing & will starve for the Cause he is engaged in what that Cause is or means I can't tell, I wish he knows. I shall send you two or three wicked Papers by Jack the Carter,[94] but I would wish you only to shew them to your Mama and Mr Rowe, not to let them go about, for I think the Clamor had but faintly reach'd the Country when I left it & one would be cautious of giveing any help to its spreading, but it is grown to a terrible height here, & the Jacobite Libels I think are more impudent and more openly dispersed than ever I remember, I fear a certain Person did show more partial countenance to his Native Countrymen than Wee could wish, a very natural failing, and I believe it made them foolishly sawcy and impertinent; but the pride of our own Officers has made many much more of it than needed, or than was just, as I believe, and the malignity of People at home

---

[90] It was George Barlow of Slebech, Pembrokeshire (the Barlows of Lawrenny, Pembrokeshire, were a minor branch of the family). He became MP for Haverfordwest on the tory interest 1743–7. However rumour had it that the townspeople wanted to elect Hugh Barlow of Lawrenny, even though he had canvassed for his namesake. Thomas, *Politics in Eighteenth-Century Wales*, 119.

[91] John Francis Meyrick of Bush, Pembrokeshire.

[92] Sir Roger Bradshaigh (c.1675–1747), 3rd bt, of Haigh Hall, Wigan, Lancashire; MP for Wigan 1695–1747. He was father of the House of Commons 1738–47.

[93] Pitt?

[94] The carrier of the papers rather than the author of them.

has taken advantage of the Cockade Gentlemans[95] discontents such an odium & clamor as really frights all honest and well meaning men. Lord Bath went out of Town just before the Birthday[96] and return'd a day or two after it, by the Birthday I mean last tuesday [22 November]. He pretends not to be displeas'd about the T[reat]y,[97] but if he is satisfied with his usage at Court, he cannot deny being displeased with the usage he meets from every other quarter. So he talks of being quiet joining in what he thinks right, but not concerning himself further with busyness. However he never knew his own mind yet, or could keep long in any temper. I expect Wee shall have a hot uneasy Session, every thing & person seems out of tune, but perhaps they may come better than I expect. I kiss'd the Kings hand[98] on wednesday, some time after I was retired to a distance in the Circle, he turn'd to me and ask'd me with a pleasant Countenance if I had been all this summer in Wales, this was shewing he knew me, & distinguish'd me from many other Gentlemen who kiss'd his hand that morning. Lord S[tai]r[99] I hear behaves with great decency & modesty has been several times at Court & had a fine military Coat on the Birthday, I wish I could say he had been taken notice of. I fear he has most reason to complane and yet says least of any of the offended Officers, but I can't help fancying he was too sanguine in his schemes for humbleing France and going to the Gates of Paris, but Errors in judgement if they were so, seems not to deserve what I fear he has met with, but it is hard to know the Truth.

I can't yet tell who will be B[isho]p of St David's I hear that if the A[rch]b[isho]p of Cant[100] lives he will have it for his son in law Dr Sayer,[101] but if the A[rch]b[isho]p dies his sons interest dies with him, and they are willing to delay the matter till it appears whether his Grace is likely to recover, which many think he is not. I have been much inclined to be vain lately for Lord Carteret took me by the hand and was mighty glad to see me, and the Chancellor of the Exchequer [Samuel Sandys] came cross [*sic*] the room to make his Compliments to me, he had a fine french wastcoat and his Coat unbutton'd. Several have ask'd kindly for you particularly the B[isho]p of Llandaff who sat above an hour with me in my study yesterday night. Harry Fox tells me he staid but one night in Cardiganshire at Mr Jones's.[102]

---

[95] White cockades were worn by supporters of the jacobites, referred to here. Black cockades were worn by supporters of the Hanoverians.

[96] 2 Nov. had been appointed as the day to celebrate the king's birthday at St James's Palace. *Country Journal or the Craftsman*, 19 Nov. 1743.

[97] The Treaty of Worms, signed 13 Sept. 1743.

[98] To become a lord of the treasury.

[99] John Dalrymple (1673–1747), 2nd earl of Stair (Scottish peerage), of Castle Kennedy, Wigtownshire; general, diplomatist and foremost agriculturalist of his day. Initially a whig, he came to oppose Walpole's administration. He fought at Dettingen alongside the king. Scottish representative peer 1707–8, 1727–34, 1744–7.

[100] John Potter (1674–1747), archbishop of Canterbury from 1737. A high-church whig, he entered into a long and tedious theological controversy – known as the Bangorian controversy – with the bishop of Bangor, Benjamin Hoadly, in 1716–21, which may account for Campbell shortening his title.

[101] Rev. Dr George Sayer (1696–1761), archdeacon of Durham 1730–61. He married Martha, daughter of John Potter, archbishop of Canterbury, in 1739.

[102] Probably Thomas Jones (1721–80), of Llanfair Clydogau, Cardiganshire.

I fancy Captain Hammond makes good sport with the Haverford[west] People. When I see Mr Corbett[103] I will speak about J. Morris. Give my Love to your Mama & my Love & Blessing to your Brothers & Sisters, I am every day doing somewhat about your & your Mama's Commissions, J[ohn] Wright writ to me for a pair of spurs for Trub but I know not what size to buy them, I think it scarce worth while to pay a great deal for the fashion of silver spurs that probably will be too little in a twelve month. My Compliments to all Friends I won't use to trouble you with nameing particulars. I beg of you my dearest to be very carefull of your self, to give good application to your studys, in the day & to read somewhat in the study in the evenings, but pray my Dearest be carefull of your eyes, keep the Candles from them with the brass reading Candlestick sit upright & both read & write upon a Desk. Pray My Dearest keep a watch upon yourself not to pick your nose bit your fingers, or sit with your mouth open, these things seem trifles but are really of Consequence, for they make a man look odd & disagreable and may raise prejudices in strangers who can only judge by appearances, and some times prejudices raised by trifles are not easily got over, you may now easily prevent any little trick of that sort getting the better of you, and growing into a habit, but you can scarce imagine how very difficult you would find it in a few years hence to overcome any habit you may contract now. My Dearest it is the busyness of a fond and Faithfull Friend to be watchfull for your good in all things from the greatest to the least and to be allways ready to advise you for the best & warn you against every thing that is wrong. I will endeavor to do it in the best & most agreable manner I can, and hope I shall be able to serve you Faithfully without makeing either my advice or my seld disagreable or uneasy to you, and I beg you my Dearest Allways to use me with the most Free & unreserved Freindship, never be afraid to let your failings or mistakes be known to me, but rather desire I should know them, that my advice and assistance may be had when most wanted. I pray God . . .

86.

John Campbell to Pryse Campbell, 29 November 1743

The information I had from Sir R[oger] Bradshaigh proves a mistake though it was generally believed for a day or two, all the World haveing got a Notion that the Cabinet Councill could not agree among themselves what to say to us; I believe it true that they differ'd about a Treaty[104] made by Octavius [Carteret] but not yet ratify'd, I think it is for a subsidy to the King of Sardinia, such agreements used to be for a year or some certain term not very long, this is said to be for an indefinite time which was not thought proper, or at all fit, to be laid before the Parliament who would certainly take offence at such an agreement, made without the knowledge of them who must furnish the money; it is said they debated it for several hours, and then divided Octavius [Carteret] had with him only Bolton,[105] Tweedale & Winchilsea on the other side were Canc Presdt,[106]

---

[103] Most probably Thomas Corbett (c.1687–1751), of Nash, Pembrokeshire; MP for Saltash 1734–51. Clerk in the admiralty 1715–23, chief clerk 1723–8, deputy secretary 1728–41, joint secretary 1741–2 and secretary 1742–51.

[104] A treaty contemporaneous with the Treaty of Worms but never formally ratified, between Britain, Maria Theresa and Charles Emmanuel, king of Sardinia, guaranteeing £300,000 p.a. to Maria Theresa for as long as she was deemed in need of this sum.

[105] Charles Powlett (1685–1754), 3rd duke of Bolton.

[106] Council president: lord president of the council, the earl of Harrington.

Grafton[107] Richmond, Montagu, Dorset,[108] Newcastle & H[enry] Pelham. Argyll thought it might be ratified with an explanation which I believe was a soft word for an alteration to bring it to what the others would have it, & I believe that will be done. I hear the Kings Speech & Address upon it will be for supporting the Queen of Hungary vigorously but in very general terms. I believe what is to be done with the Hungarian Forces is not yet settled, some think the animosity between them and the British has rose so high that they cannot serve togather again, yet if Wee continue the War it is certain wee cannot dismiss such a number of the Troops in our pay without takeing others in their room, and I don't know where Wee shall have them besides if Wee change these for others, all the World must see the reason, & draw strange consequences from it. It will be look'd upon as a Confession of what I can't express, but you may easily ghess, from the printed scandal and the Clamor I have told you has been so strongly raised. On the other hand if Wee should take the Hungarian troops for another Year, besides what Wee must expect to hear upon that occasion at Westminster, what would it be if they and the British should quarrel in the Field. I can scarce tell which of these evils is the greatest. It is said of Octavius [Carteret] in one of the Libels, that when abroad he Talk'd like a G[e]r[ma]n, dress'd like a G[e]r[ma]n, drank like a G[e]r[ma]n and they call'd him the G[e]r[ma]n Hero. You remember what is said in the Miscellanious thoughts of the way he took to promote his Interest in the Closet, and indeed I fear he rather studys to serve himself by flattery that [sic] to serve his Master by good advice. It is said he is every evening fluster'd with wine, and when he is so his insolence & vanity are beyond imagination, think what a task his fellow servants have to bear with him, yet if they broke with him, he and the few he could draw after him might in these uncertain dangerous times do great Mischief, otherwise he would surely be treated as he deserves, the Man however has parts and Genius, but vain, insolent, hot, extravagant, in his schemes, and I believe entirely free from sincerity & moral honesty.

The Duke of Marlborough[109] has resign'd not only his Military employment but that of Lord of the Bedchamber. I am very sorry for it. Many changes & promotions have been talk'd of, but none as yet made that I know of, indeed I know very little, though what I have told you I believe is true, you will see it is not fit to be spoke of only to your Mama who will let you go no farther.

My Dearest you will see in this nights News the Duke of Portland[110] has broke his arm a hunting for Gods sake let such things give you warning not to risk your Life, health, or Limbs in so foolish a way. Give my Love to your Mama. Tell her I saw Molly very well yesterday. She sends her Compliments. My Love & Blessing to your Brothers & Sisters, kind service to Mr. Rowe &c. I pray God . . .

---

[107] Charles Fitzroy (1683–1757), 2nd duke of Grafton; privy councillor 1715; lord lieutenant of Ireland 1720–4; lord chamberlain 1724–57. Fitzroy became duke in 1690 and was made earl of Arlington in 1723. He was 'closely associated with the generation of ageing old corps whigs led by the duke of Newcastle, and there were key moments when his mollifying interventions on their behalf were vital in smoothing dissensions between king and ministers'. ODNB.

[108] Lionel Cranfield Sackville (1688–1765), duke of Dorset.

[109] Charles Spencer (1706–58), 3rd duke of Marlborough. In 1734 he became a member of the Liberty Club formed by opponents of Walpole. He was a major supporter of the prince of Wales. However, in 1738 he went over to the court and became a lord of the king's bedchamber in August. He fought at Dettingen (27 June 1743) but he and Lord Stair resigned afterwards, as a protest regarding the Hanoverian troops.

[110] William Bentinck (1709–62), 2nd duke of Portland.

87.

John Campbell, London to Pryse Campbell, 6 December 1743

I give you many thanks for your letter as to its being blotted, I would wish you to use your self to write fair for other People, otherwise it is no matter how you write to me. I am very glad that you and all at Stackpole were well, I hope you would be carefull not to get cold standing looking at the wreck. I was surprised to hear of such a thing, for Wee have had no wind here, but a good deal of Fog, not very thick till to day, and I expect to hear of many wrecks in the streets this night, for when I came from the House between two & three o'Clock, the Coachs were ready to run foul of one another at Charing Cross, it was not quite so bad hereabout, many People have not [sic] colds, I think all my little Family except myself upon the change of the weather from very warm to very cold.

I hear Mr Pelham is to be declared Chancellor of Exchequer on Saturday,[111] his Election[112] in Sussex is to be the 15th when that is over I suppose other Writs will soon be issued. I believe Mr Winnington will be Paymaster Mr Sandys Cofferer, & Sir John Rushout Treasurer of the Navy which makes two vacancys in the Treasury. I think all agree Harry Fox is to fill one seat, & I have heard Lord William Manners[113] & Mr Arundel[114] named for the other but I am not inform'd who will have it, Sir Charles Hardy[115] & Mr Philipson,[116] which some of the Papers have blunder'd into Sir J[ohn] Philipps, are to come into the Admiralty. Sir Charles haveing the rank of Admiral makes him equal to the thing, but I believe he is not very high in Character. Mr Philipsons Father was master of the Pacquet Boats at Harwich he was bred a clerk in the Navy Office & at the end of last Parliament or sooner I can't exactly remember, he was made a Commissioner of the Navy, I believe he dos not want sense, is a Man of busyness in that way and in good circumstances (as a South Sea Director I think) but I should never have thought he was of a rank to be a Lord of the Admiralty[117] but I heard Lord W[inchil]sea insist on it & for ought I know Sir C[harles] Hardy is made the same way. I suppose his Lordship likes to have People at the Board that can have no pretence to take much upon them. This is all the News I hear, I have not such good intelligence now as when poor Clutterbuck was alive.

I saw Legge lately he enquired kindly after you. Give my Love to your Mama & tell her I have sent her letter to Mr Edwards but have not seen him since fryday. I hope you will like the Gloves I sent they were all the sorts I could think of, the worsted are very

---

[111] 10 Dec. However, Pelham took his place as chancellor on Monday, 12 Dec.

[112] His re-election after being appointed to office.

[113] William Manners (1697–1772), of Croxton Park, Lincolnshire; MP for Leicestershire 1719–24 and Newark 1738–54. He sometimes voted with the administration, sometimes against. Lord of the bedchamber to the king 1727–38. Portrayed in the gambling scene in Hogarth's *The Rake's Progress*, Manners reputedly made a fortune as a professional gamester. He died of a fall from his horse.

[114] Richard Arundell (c.1696–1758), of Allerton Mauleverer, Yorkshire; MP for Knaresborough 1720–58. Master of the mint 1737–44; lord of the treasury 1744–6; treasurer of the chamber 1746–55; clerk of the pipe 1748–58. An intimate friend of the Pelhams, Arundell was made a treasury lord in Pelham's broad-bottom administration.

[115] Sir Charles Hardy (c.1680–1744), MP for Portsmouth 1743–4.

[116] John Phillipson (1698–1756), of Park Hall, Harwich, Essex; MP for New Shoreham 1734–41 and Harwich 1741–56.

[117] Phillipson, despite Campbell's doubts, became a lord of the admiralty 1743–4.

good to wear under wash leather in cold weather. I shall send the box to the Carriers this week. My Love & Blessing to your Brothers & Sisters.

By what he has writ to Mr Edwards I find Mr J Phillips[118] thinks of comeing to Town in the Spring I really believe to come with you is his only reason which does not please me, but I don't know how to help it, however I wish you would if he ask you what time you up [*sic*], speak of it as uncertain how soon or how late. I can't help telling you a trifleing incident when I was at Carmarthen because it shews a little the humor of the Man. He & I & Mr Jenkins the Exciseman were sitting together & one of us happening to mention the late Queen Caroline.[119] Mr P[hilipps] spoke mighty well of her for her gracious behavior and told us that when he was presented to her soon after he married, she ask [*sic*] him so many questions & talk'd so much to him, that he was greatly out of Countenance, and he believed he would have continued the conversation longer, if she had not seen the confusion he was in and so relieved him, he said if she had lived a little longer he was a coming to Town, as if he meant Wee should believe he would have come purely to wait upon H[er] M[ajesty]. Now you must know I was close by when he was presented & and I do assure you the Queen only wish'd him joy (her words were a happy Marriage, probably the Form for wishing Joy abroad and she did not say one word more to him. I remember very well that he asked me one of the questions that he told us she ask'd him. One knows not when to believe a man that either has so little regard to truth in his common Conversation, or else liable to such odd mistakes.

My Dearest I pray God . . .

88.
John Campbell to Pryse Campbell, 8 December 1743
Yesterday Mr. Waller moved for an Address[120] to desire His Majesty forwith to issue for the Hanover Troops not be continued in the british [*sic*] longer than the 25 inst[ant] his speech seem [*sic*] to be confused and was deliver'd in such a manner that I could not hear or understand the greatest part of it, he was seconded by Lord Barington who spoke, as I think he general does, very well. The speakers for the question were Mr Pit[t], Mr. Lyttelton, Sir Francis Dashwood,[121] Admiral Vernon, Mr Noel,[122] Kings Councill, Lord Hilsborough, Mr Dodington, the eldest Greenville[123] & his Brother George,[124] Sir J[ohn]

---

[118] James Philipps of Pentyparc, Cardiganshire, Campbell's brother-in-law.

[119] Caroline of Brandenburg-Ansbach (1683–1737), queen consort of George II and supporter of Walpole.

[120] *CJ*, xxiv, 487; *PH*, xiii, 232–74, for the debate.

[121] Sir Francis Dashwood (1707–81), of West Wycombe, Buckinghamshire; opposition whig MP for New Romney 1741–61 and Weymouth and Melcombe Regis 1761–3. 15th Baron le Despencer 1708–81. Chancellor of the exchequer 1762–3. He was a founder member of the Hell Fire Club.

[122] Either William (1695–1762) or Thomas (c.1704–88).

[123] Richard Grenville (1711–79), of Wotton, Buckinghamshire; MP for Buckingham 1734–41 and 1747–52 and Buckinghamshire 1741–7. First lord of the admiralty 1756–7; lord privy seal 1757–61.

[124] George Grenville (1712–70), second son of Richard Grenville of Wotton; MP for Buckingham 1741–70. Lord of the admiralty 1744–7; lord of the treasury 1747–51; treasurer of the navy 1754–5, 1756–7, 1757–62; first lord of the admiralty 1762–3; first lord of the treasury 1763–5; leader of the Commons 1761–2 and 1763–5. The hallmark of Grenville's ministry was efficiency and economy; however he lost his place as first lord because George III disliked him intensely, finding him insolent, tedious and verbose. His verbosity was commented upon by many others. He is perhaps best known as the man who introduced the Stamp Act to America, thereby precipitating the War of American Independence. *ODNB*. See Chapter 8, letters 220–3, regarding the debate on the Stamp Act and its repeal.

H[ynde] Cotton, Mr Banks a Lawyer,[125] Mr Forster,[126] Captain Strickland,[127] Honorable Captain Charles Ross,[128] Mr Nugent, against the question Mr Winnington, Mr Chancellor of the Exchequer [Samuel Sandys], Mr Murray, Solicitor General [William Murray], Mr Edward Finch,[129] Mr H[enry] Fox, Lord Baltimore, Dr. Lee, Brigadier General J[ohn] Campbell,[130] Lord Charles Hay, Colonel Cholmondley, Mr Ellis,[131] Mr Calthrop,[132] General Oglethorp,[133] Mr. Horace Walpole Senior,[134] Lord Cornbury. I may perhaps have forgot some speakers on each side.

The Matter of the [King']s partiality to the Hanoverians was handled more tenderly than I expected and by most as decently as one would expect if it was mention'd at all, but they strongly insisted that there were such jealousys & animosities between the English & Hanoverians that it was impossible for them to serve togather another Campaign, some said if they did there would be much more likelyhood of a Battle between the E[nglish] & H[anoverian] than between the Allied Army & the French. Mr. Pitt I think professing his loyalty to the Royal Family said that the Family of King [*sic*] was the greatest Blessing but the Electorate[135] would probably prove the greatest Curse to this Nation I am not quite sure whether it was he or another of that set I mean the Cobham Nephews,[136] I believe it was he. The eldest Greenville spoke strongly of Hanover being incompatible with England and said that was an opinion he was ready to seal with his blood, or that effect are not these monstrous expressions, when one considers that Wee have no right or pretense to require the King to resign his Electorate that it is highly improbable anything could persuade him to do it, and indeed that he cannot transfer it to a younger son without the consent of the Emperor & Empire if then they are not to be seperated does not all that is said against the Electorate hold strongly against the Person of [the King]. I think it is a melancholy time when such things can be said openly in the House with Impunity.

The Solicitor General Murray made a very fine speech.[137] Mr. Edward Finch said some things that seem'd to me to beat very hard upon the Earl of S[tair] it haveing been

---

[125] Henry Bankes (1700–76), of Broad Chalk, Salisbury, Wiltshire; tory MP for Corfe Castle 1741–62.

[126] Brooke Forster (1717–71), of Willey Park, Salop; whig MP for Wenlock 1739–68.

[127] William Strickland (1714–88), of Beverley, Yorkshire; tory MP for Beverley 1741–7.

[128] Charles Ross (1721–45), of Balnagowan, Ross; MP for Ross-shire 1741–5. He died in action at the battle of Fontenoy, 30 Apr. 1745.

[129] Edward Finch (?1697–1771), of Kirkby Hall, Rockingham, Northamptonshire; MP for Cambridge University 1727–68. Diplomat patronised by Carteret.

[130] John Campbell (c.1693–1770), of Mamore, Dunbarton, and Coombe Bank, Kent; MP for Buteshire 1713–15, Elgin burghs 1715–22 and 1725–7 and Dunbartonshire 1727–61.

[131] Welbore Ellis (1713–1802), of Tylney Hall, Hampshire; MP for Cricklade 1741–7, Weymouth and Melcombe Regis 1747–61 and 1774–90, Aylesbury 1761–8, Petersfield 1768–74 and 1791–4. A lord of the admiralty 1747–54; joint vice-treasurer of Ireland 1755–62 and 1770–7; secretary at war 1762–5; treasurer of the navy 1777–82; secretary of state for America 1782. Henry Fox's chief manager at the Minorca inquiry, 1757. He was a close friend of Fox to whom he owed many of his appointments.

[132] Henry Calthorpe (c.1717–88), of Elvetham, Hampshire; MP for Hindon 1741–7. Supported the administration in all recorded divisions.

[133] James Edward Oglethorpe (1696–1785), of Westbrook, Haslemere, Surrey.

[134] Horatio Walpole, Sir Robert Walpole's brother.

[135] Of Hanover.

[136] Lord Cobham's nephews were the Grenville brothers James, George, Richard and Thomas.

[137] For Murray's speech, see *PH*, xiii, 246–56.

said on the other side that the Hanoverians were well provided with every thing while the British were allmost starved, he that the Person who had contracted to furnish the British Troops was turn'd off, he knew not why, and another contracted with who was a bankrupt & neither did nor could provide a sufficiently [sic] that the Hanoverians took the Contractor Wee had turn'd off and were by him well supplied, he spoke of two march's made before the King came to the Army which being consider'd at two Councills of War to which no Hanoverian or Austrian Generals were call'd, and all the British Generals gave their opinions against the March's yet they were made. All these things must have been the sole acts of the Earl of S[tair] and I must observe Mr. Finch was not contradicted by any one, and he was upon the spot. Mr Thomas Pitt[138] elder Brother to the famous William Pitt said that he should be against the Motion if it was practicable for the British & Hanoverians to serve togather another Campaign, but if they could not then he should be for it, and he wish to hear the opinions of Officers that were there, this, some time after, call'd up Captain Ross (not quite 21 when this Parliament met) and Captain Strickland Nephew to the late Sir William was it not a modest undertakeing for two such young Captains to take upon them to judge whether the British & Hanoverian Troops could serve together, they both were of opinion they could not, Captain Ross told of a quarrel between some Hanover soldiers & a Groom belonging to an english officer who I think is a Dukes son, and the Hanover Officer, he said try'd & acquitted their own Men without giveing notice to those who were to have brough [sic] evidence and carried on the prosecution against them. He also said that he himself haveing made one Hanoverian soldier, togather with several english, Prisoner for some disorder they had committed in a Village, a Hanover General sent to desire the Hanoverian might be sent to him Captain Ross accordingly deliver'd him to the Person sent who he says set him at liberty after he carried him a very little way. Lord Charles Hay said such little quarrels & partialitys would happen in all Armys that he was assured there were much greater in the French & in Princes Charles's Armies though each were composed only of the subjects of their respective sovereigns; he said he remember'd to have every body agree that the Groom was a drunken quarrelsome fellow. Captain Strickland founded his opinion solely upon the Hanoverian Soldiers takeing away straw that was laid for the english soldiers to put in their Tents, but he did not say there had ever been any complaint made about it. Some body afterward said that possibly the straw originally belonged to the Hanoverians, the english soldiers might have seised it & so the Hanoverians only took back their own. Captain Strickland did not think fit to rise again to clear this important Point, were not these storys fitter for Schole Boys than Senators & Officers. Mr. Dodington said that at Dettingen[139] the Hanoverians were only spectators as if the British were Gladiators to fight for their diversion, Brigadier Campbell said[140] that some of the Hanoverians were engaged & he saw them behave well. I scarce ever saw a Man under so much concern at speaking in the House which he never did before he spoke warmly & like a brave Man shewing that the greatest courage & the greatest modesty are very consistent, he express [sic] a warm affectionate

---

[138] Thomas Pitt (c.1705–61), of Boconnoc, Cornwall; MP for Oakhampton 1727–54 and Old Sarum 1754–5 and 1761.

[139] Battle of Dettingen, 27 June 1743.

[140] PH, xiii, 141.

zeal for his royal Master & indignation at his being so treated for one could not but consider the Motion it self & many things insinuated in the Debate as the highest reflections upon [the king]. Mr. Thomas Pitt spoken again to say he had heard nothing to satisfie him that the British & Hanoverian Troops might not serve togather again therefore he should Vote against the Question.

Mr. Horace Walpole spoke very indiscreetely saying several things very distastfull to our old Antonius's [Bath] but now Allies, the New Ministers, of all People that Family should forbear such things at this time, Mr. Edward Walpole express'd his concern for it to me very strongly after the House was up. Wee divided I think between eight and nine Ay's 181. No's 231.[141] Several who voted with us the first day of the Session were against us in this, but our number I believe would have been greater if our People had expected the Debate.

My Love & Blessing to your Brothers & Sisters. I pray God . . .

89.

John Campbell to Pryse Campbell, 10 December 1743

I thank you for your letter of the 4th I believe though you forgot to date it. I am glad every body think [sic] the Captain innocent of the loss of the ship Three Friends, pray order R[oger] Evans not to use or dispose of any part of the Wreck till he is sure the Owners or Insurers will not desire it, for though it is reasonable I should not be out of Pockett by saveing it, yet I never desire to be a Gainer by the Misfortunes of other People. I was sorry to hear Harry White dislocated his knee about the Wreck, I wish he had staid at home to mind his proper busyness, and not gone about what he was not find [sic] for.

You are much in the right to desire I would distinguish my public & private News. I will put all my public togather in a Postscript, or if you had rather I will upon notice from you put the private News in the Postscript.

Me Dearest I don't doubt you could ride such a journey without any body but your own Man & a groom but I think I had rather you had some body else in Case of any accident, and perhaps your Mama will not be quite easy if you have only your Man and a Groom, and you know I would if I could, take from Mr P[hilipp]s[142] any pretence of your wanting his Company or care; I had lately an extraordinary letter from him, desireing me to ask Mr Pelham for a Place for him. I intend to send it to you, when I have answered it. If Mr Rowes goes with you to Gl[ouceste]r he can be absent but one sunday, and I think he will not find it difficult to have his Churches served for one day. My Dearest you are very kind in saying you will readily and Cheerfully do what ever I think right, and I desire you will most freely tell me what you think upon it, between this and the time you left the Country last year which I believe will be early enough for you to come this Year.

My Dearest I beg of you not to write in so much hurry, for you frequently omit words & thereby leave the sense imperfect, you should read your letters over after you have writ them to correct any Mistakes in the stile, Grammar or Spelling, what I mean is for you to learn to write correctly otherwise it would be no matter how you writ to

---

[141] *CJ*, xxiv, 487; for the debate, see *PH*, xiii, 232–74.

[142] James Philipps, of Pentyparc, Cardiganshire.

me, who can allways find out your meaning & I thank God allways see sense at the
bottom though the expression may be faulty through hast of negligence.

Lord Carteret in the last debate spoke against founding an Address on common
Fame which was so uncertain and might be absolutely false, upon which Lord Halifax
and Lord Chesterfield, both very well reminded him of his Motion to remove Sir
R[obert] W[alpole] upon common Fame. I send you inclosed the most impudent
Jacobite journal that I have yet seen. Give my love to your Mama I am very sorry
she had the headache, I intend to send her next Post an account of the things sent
in the Box by the Carrier to day. My Love and Blessing to your Brothers & Sisters,
tell Trub I hope he will be very good and apply diligently to his learning. I can't
forbear repeting my entreaty's that you will be very carefull of your self in every
respect, and never let your eagerness at sport make you forget a just and prudent &
proper caution. I pray God . . .

P.S.

I was assured to day that Captain Stricklands story of the straw[143] was as suggested in
the House the english took away the straw provided for the Hanoverians by their own
Commissary, and the Hanoverians only retook their own. I dare say there were
Craftsmen in the Camp who endeavor'd to foment jealousies there to be made use of
at home. On Thursday Lord Gower & Lord Cobham resign'd as is said in the Papers.
The Privy seal is given to Lord Cholmondeley. Yesterday Mr Sandys resign'd the Seal
of the Exchequer and the same day Mr Pelham kiss'd the kings hand for it, he goes out
of Town on tuesday to be reelected in Sussex.[144] Mr Winnington is to be Paymaster, Mr
Sandys Cofferer and a peer (I think Lord Sandys) Baron of Evesham[145] Sir John Rushout
the Treasurer of the Navy, Mr H[enry] Fox a Lord of the Treasury. Mr Ord[146] who was
Secretary to Chancellor Sandys, is to be deputy Cofferer. Jack Wynne[147] to have some
what else, I know not what. All this is certain but who is to be the other Lord of the
Treasury or how the Places of the Chancellor of the Duchy of Lancaster, Surveyor of
the Works & I think a Commissioner of Trade, are to be filled I know not.

Yesterday the Lords had the same Question[148] that was in our House on wednesday,
leaving out the word 'forthwith' & adding at the end these words 'Thereby to remove
the discontents of his Majesties subjects here at home', or to that effect.[149] It was
moved by Lord Sandwich seconded by Lord Talbot, the [sic] divided Content 36 not
Contents 71.[150] Proxy's not called for. The speakers I heard for the Question besides

---

[143] Strickland had recited this story in the Commons and appeared 'very frivolous' to that House. HMC,
Egmont Diary, iii, 278.

[144] When an MP was appointed to an office he could not sit in the Commons until he had been re-elected.

[145] Sandys was created Lord Sandys, baron of Ombersley on 20 Dec. 1743. He became cofferer of the
household at the same time. *ODNB*.

[146] Robert Ord was deputy cofferer until Dec. 1744. J.C. Sainty, *Officials of the Royal Household 1660–1837*
(2 vols, 1997), ii, 135.

[147] Sir John Wynn. He became deputy treasurer of Chelsea Hospital in 1744, which the Place Act of 1741
had declared incompatible with a seat in the Commons. *HPC, 1715–54*, ii, 564.

[148] The question was regarding the ending of British payment of the king's 16,000 Hanover troops.

[149] *LJ*, xxvi, 276. Here the words are more poetic: 'to put a stop to the Jealousies and Heart-burnings
among His Majesties faithful subjects at Home and His British Forces Abroad'.

[150] *LJ*, xxvi, 276, only records a negative vote but does not give the figures. Sainty gives the same figures
as Campbell.

the two above, were Lord Chesterfield, Lord Halifax, Lord Westmoreland, Lord Lonsdale, Lord Lichfield, Lord Haversham[151] against it Lord Chancellor, Lord Carteret, Lord Cholmondeley, Lord Bathurst,[152] Lord Winchelsea, Lord Raymond,[153] Earl of Moreton.[154]

Duke of Marlborough voted for the Question but did not speak Duke of Newcastle kept away by the Gout, Dukes of Richmond & Grafton & Lord Delawar[155] out of Town. The Proxys if call'd for would have been 4 Contents 20 not Contents.

90.
John Campbell to Pryse Campbell, 17 December 1743
I am extremely thankfull for your kind letters which give me double pleasure, as they shew me that you are highly deserveing of my love, and at the same time truely affectionate to me, there is nothing in the World I value so much as your Love and it is my great desire and endeavor to make my Friendship usefull to you.

I have been strangely puzzled with the news from Haverford[west]. The Post before last Mr Prust[156] writ me word that he believed the People of the Town would Choose Mr H[ugh] Barlow in opposition to himself, but that it was what neither Mr Geo[rge] Barlow nor Mr H[ugh] Barlow expected. Last post brought word to Sir John Philipps, as I have writ to your Mama, that Mr H[ugh] Barlow is a declared candidate against his namesake. I shall be very sorry if Mr H[ugh] B[arlow] is drawn to do any thing not easily to be reconciled to his honor, and I confess it must be somewhat very extraordinary, that can in my opinion justifie his being a Candidate, after gives [*sic*] his Interest to Mr B[arlow] of Slebech and going about to ask Votes for him but I must suspend my judgement till I hear the whole story. I told Sir J[ohn] P[hilipps] that Mr Barlow had never writ to me for my Vote, he said it was very odd, and that he told him when he went to ask Mr Tucker's[157] Vote, that he ought not to expect it till he had asked me. I have not seen Mr Owen these two or three days I don't know but he may be gone out of Town for he told me he was to spend the Holydays a [*sic*] Chester and then bring his Lady to Town, perhaps he could have given me some light into the Haverford[west] affair. I believe Wee shall have no more busyness of moment before Christmas, I expect Mr Pelham will be introduced next monday, and all the preferments I have mention'd, will be declared time enough for the Writs to be moved for before the Adjournment.

The B[isho]p of Llandaff is a very friendly neighbor to me, and invites me to his Table in a Family way. I wish he had come to St David's for the time he has been, & will stay at Llandaff, I believe he will get a good remove as soon as such a vacancy happens. I pray God . . .

---

[151] Maurice Thompson (1675–1745), 2nd Baron Haversham.

[152] Allen Bathurst (1684–1775), Lord Bathurst and from 1772 1st Earl Bathurst.

[153] Robert Raymond (c.1717–56), 2nd Baron Raymond, of Abbots Langley, Herefordshire.

[154] James Douglas (1702–68), 14th earl of Morton. A patron of science, particularly astronomy, Morton became the president of the Royal Society from 1764 until his death.

[155] John West (1693–1766), 1st Earl De La Warr.

[156] John Prust, deputy sheriff.

[157] Josiah Tucker, 'a leading Whig election manager'. Thomas, *Politics in Eighteenth-Century Wales*, 188.

   I am inform'd (I fear too well) that the Duke of Marlborough, will certainly speak if the Hanover Troops come again before the House, whatever he says will make a very different impression to what was made by the story's of two such Lads as Ross & Strickland, but I can't think H[is] G[race] has done himself any credit by signing a Protest[158] which condems his Votes last Session in things that can not be alter'd by whatever happen'd in regard to the Hanover Troop's, if the Forces kept at home were necessary last year, nothing the Hanoverians have done can have made them useless (as they are call'd in the Protest) now.

91.

John Campbell to Pryse Campbell, 15 December 1743

This day Mr. George Greenville moved for an address to desire His Majesty in consideration of the reduced and impoverish'd condition of this Nation & the unequal burthens Wee have hitherto born, not to engage us any farther by acting as Wee have done or entering into any farther engagements without first concludeing a treaty with the States General to assist in a certain proportion as was done in the last War.[159] He was seconded by Mr. Lyttelton and this odd perplex'd question[160] was debated for some time. Mr Pitt in answering Mr. Sandys who I think had found fault with the Preamble giveing such a dismal account of our condition, said that he did not regard the preamble he only spoke for the matter of the Address, he suppose a Gentleman would not much mind the preamble of it His Patent to create him a Peer the Peerage he would think a substantial good & not trouble him self whether the preamble were true, or false, he concluded with saying that the little finger of the hand Wee had felt for about 20 months past (meaning Lord Carteret) was heavier than the loins of a former 20 years Administration. At length several of their own Friends not seeming quite pleased with the preamble & wording of the question, they alter'd it to a desire that His Majesty would act no farther in support of the Queen of Hungary unless the Dutch enter'd into a treaty to furnish a proper proportion of the Force & expence as was done in the last War. Upon this Wee divided between 5 & 6 I believe near six Ay's 132 Noes 209.[161] Lord Petersham[162] & Mr Poulett brother to the Earl[163] were in the Minority. I hear there some arrears of a Pension due to the late Earl

---

[158] *LJ*, xxvi, 276–7: Protest against rejecting the motion for an address to the king against the continuing use of Hanoverian troops in British pay.

[159] *CJ*, xxiv, 492–3.

[160] *PH*, xiii, 385–6, citing Philip Yorke's *Parliamentary Journal*: 'The improper, loose and inaccurate manner of wording this question was exposed with great spirit and force by the solicitor general'.

[161] *CJ*, xxiv, 493.

[162] William Stanhope (1719–79), of Elvaston, Derbyshire; MP for Aylesbury 1741–7 and Bury St Edmunds 1747–56. First son of William Stanhope, 1st earl of Harrington. Styled Lord Petersham from 1742. Nicknamed Peter Shambles because of his peculiar gait. Walpole referred to 'his nose and legs twisted to every point of crossness'. Cited in *HPC, 1715–54*, ii, 438; *PH*, xiii, 387, citing Philip Yorke: Lord Petersham, 'to the surprise of everybody, voted with the minority'.

[163] Vere Poulett (1710–88), of Hinton St George, Somerset; MP for Bridgwater 1741–7. 3rd Earl Poulett 1743–64. Walpole strongly supported Poulett, who supported the administration until 1744. His brother was John Poulett (1708–64), who became 2nd Earl Poulett in 1743.

Poulett[164] unpaid, which would come to the younger Brothers. As to Lord Petersham I know nothing. I pray God . . .

I think it will be best for the future to put private News in the Postscript. Inclosed is the letter I told you of which you may open & read in private. Haycocks duty to you he will be mighty glad of a letter from you. Last Sunday I was walking in the Park a Blackamore Groom gallop very fast upon plane ground. His horse fell with him & roll'd upon him, he was a good while quite senseless & did not bleed when a vein was open'd; they carried him to the Hospital. I don't know whether he recover'd for Gods sake be carefull my Dearest.

92.

John Campbell to Pryse Campbell, 22 December 1743

Your Mama would tell you for what reasons I was glad you did not go to Haverford[west] and that she excused it in the manner she did, indeed I never heard anything more absurd than the management of our Friends about the Haverford[west] Election seems to have been, I am really very sorry for it. This day the House adjourned to the 9th of January. I will writ [*sic*] a list of the Late Promotions on the other side several you know before but I will put them all togather. I met Mr Paulett[165] Lord Harry's[166] son at Gov[erno]r Morris's yesterday he asked very kindly for you I think he seems a good sort of young Man.

I send you an Ode just come out which I think is not bad. Pray bid Val begin a register of the weather again the first of January & I will endeavor to keep one here to compare with it.[167]

The loss of Horses is very bad News because it calls for was [*sic*] is not, nor is like to be, plenty with me viz: money. Pray my Dearest be very carefull of your self, let me know particularly how your dear eyes are; if they are well I hope you read somewhat in the evenings at my Desk in the great study; you will remember I recommended to you *The Religion of Nature Delineated*.[168] Pray my Dear be carefull to spell right. I am sorry when I see a false spelling in one of your letters. My love & Blessing to your Brothers & Sisters. I pray God . . .

List of Ministers:

Mr Pelham first Lord of the Treasury & Chancellor of the Exchequer
Mr West his Secretary

---

[164] John Poulett (c.1668–1743), 4th baron and created 1st Earl Poulett in 1706. First lord of the treasury 1710–11 and lord steward of the household 1711–14.

[165] Harry Powlett (1720–94), MP for Christchurch 1751–4, Lymington 1755–61 and Winchester 1761–5. A career navy man, Powlett became a rear admiral in 1756, vice admiral three years later and admiral in 1770.

[166] Lord Harry Powlett (1691–1759), of Edington, Wiltshire; whig MP for St Ives 1715–22 and Hampshire 1722–54. Succeeded his brother as the 4th duke of Bolton in 1754. Lord of the admiralty 1733–42.

[167] Unfortunately neither of these weather journals has survived.

[168] By William Wollaston (1659–1724), moral philosopher. The basic premise of the book was that religion was the pursuit of happiness by the practice of truth and reason. His lack of orthodoxy led him to resign as a clergyman. See Introduction for John Campbell's religious and moral views.

Mr Winnington Paymaster of the Forces
Lord Sandys Cofferer & Baron of Evesham
Henry Arthur Herber [*sic*] Lord Herbert of Cherbury
Lord Middlesex & Mr Harry Fox Lords of the Treasury[169]
Sir John Rushout Treasurer of the Navy
Sir Charles Hardy & Mr Philipson Lords of the Admiralty
Mr Harry Finch Surveyor of Works
Sir Charles Gilmour a Commissioner of Trade
Mr Denzil Onslow Treasurer of the Board of Works
Mr Hamilton brother to Lord Abercorn receiver of the kings rents in Minorca, in the
    room of H[enry] Finch
Mr Ord deputy Cofferer[170]

General Wade the Lord Cheif Justices Lee, and Willes and Mr Anthony Duncomb[171] were talk'd of for Peers, it is not done, whether intended or no I can't say.

93.
John Campbell to Pryse Campbell, 31 December 1743
I must begin my letters as you did yours by makeing the Compliments of the season not only to your self but to all the family for I really forgot to do it in your Mama's letter

---

[169] Herbert never became a lord of the treasury.

[170] James West (1703–72), of Alscott Park, Gloucestershire; whig MP for St Albans 1741–68 and Boroughbridge 1768–72. He was secretary to the chancellor of the exchequer 1743–52, loyally serving Henry Pelham, and on his death transferring that loyalty to the duke of Newcastle, as joint secretary to the treasury 1746–56 and 1756–62; Charles Sackville (1711–69), earl of Middlesex; MP for East Grinstead 1734–42 and 1761–5, Sussex 1742–7 and Old Sarum 1747–54. He was lord of the treasury 1743–7, and master of the horse to the prince of Wales 1747–51; Henry Finch (?1694–1761), MP for Malton 1724–61. Receiver general of revenues of Minorca 1729–43; surveyor general of works 1743–60. Unlike his brothers, Edward and Heneage, he voted consistently with the government; Sir Charles Gilmour (*d.* 1750), 2nd bt of Craigmillar, Edinburgh; opposition whig MP for Edinburghshire 1737–50. Paymaster of works 1742–3; lord of trade 1743–4. He was removed from the latter post after the fall of Carteret; Denzil Onslow (c.1698–1765), of Mickleham, Surrey; MP for Guildford 1740–7. Receiver general of the Post Office 1727–40; paymaster of the board of works 1743–55; commissioner of stamp duties 1755–7 and commissioner of the salt office 1757–65; Charles Hamilton (1704–86), of Painshill, Cobham, Surrey; brother to the 7th earl of Abercorn (Scottish peerage) (1686–1744). Hamilton was MP for Truro 1741–7; clerk to the household of the prince of Wales 1737–47, an office he owed to his sister, Lady Archibald Hamilton, the prince's mistress. He was receiver general of the Minorca revenues until 1756. On the loss of Minorca in that year Hamilton's friend Henry Fox secured him a secret service pension of £1,200 p.a. *HPC, 1715–54*, ii, 100; Robert Ord (1700–78), of Petersham, Surrey and Hunstanworth, Bingfield and Newbiggin, Northumberland; MP for Mitchell 1734–41 and Morpeth 1741–55. An intimate friend of and legal adviser to William Pulteney; secretary to the chancellor of the exchequer 1742–3; deputy cofferer to the household 1743–44; chief baron of the exchequer (Scotland) 1755–75.

[171] George Wade (1673–1748), of Abbey Courtyard, Bath; MP for Hindon 1715–22 and Bath 1722–48. A strong supporter of the administration, though he never received a peerage. However, he became commander-in-chief of the Flanders army in 1743 and briefly commander-in-chief in the north of England 1745; Sir John Willes (1685–1761), of Lincoln's Inn and Astrop, Northants; MP for Launceston 1724–6, Weymouth and Melcombe Regis 1726–7 and West Looe 1727–37. Attorney-general 1734; serjeant-at-law 1737; lord chief justice of common pleas 1737–61; commissioner for the great seal 1756–7. In 1757, Willes was offered, but refused, the great seal of the lord keeper, hoping instead for a peerage. However, the king denied him that honour because of his support of the prince of Wales. *ODNB*; Anthony Duncomb (c.1695–1763), of Barford, Wiltshire; MP for Salisbury 1721–34 and Downton 1734–47. A supporter of Walpole, he did not receive a peerage.

till after I had seal'd it, she knows indeed that I don't mind such ceremonies much, but 'tis right they should have that Compliment to make from me wherever it is proper.

I dare say my Dearest you are satisfied that no words can well express how earnestly & ardently I wish that you may enjoy very many years in Virtue, health, and Peace; and may you be as happy in your Children & Grandchildren, as I am in you, more cannot be. The greatest pleasure of my Christmas is to hear that yours is merry, otherwise mine is indeed very dull.

I need say nothing of Mr Brodie to you because I frankt a letter from him to you last Post, I heartily join in your wish. I was very dull in marking your Pockett book for Pentyparch.[172] I am sorry the battledores & shuttlecocks were not right in truth I thought the large Clackens[173] had been the best, I will send you some less the 1st opportunity I think Wee could not get larger battledores. I met Mr Dunoyer in the street t'other day, he immediately ask'd for you, I told him you would want his assistance in the Spring & he said he should be in the way to serve you. I heard to day that Mr Winnington has opposition at Worcester[174] they say he was offer'd to be chose without any if he would not support young Mr Willes,[175] the Lord Chief Justices Son but he said he had promised in Town to assist Mr Willes & could not go from his word, so then they said they must oppose him but it is thought Mr Winnington will carry it but Mr Willes may probably loose it. I have lately heard from your Uncle Morris he send [sic] his Compliments to all at Stackpole & says, in answer to an enquiry I made, that your Cousin is five feet four inch's without Wig or shoes, pray send me your Measure, and let it be taken fairly: not that I trouble myself much about your height as long as you have good health, with such a head at heart as answers I think my warmest wishes and prayers. My Love & Blessing to your Brothers & Sisters, I presume you will receive Mollys Compliments from some of them, tell Nanny I was mighty well pleased with her french letter to her sister which I could make shift to understand without assistance. My kind service to Mr Rowe & tell him I intend to write to him soon, he must excuse my being no regular Correspondent. Compliments to all Friends. I pray God . . .

I am sorry Winnington meets with any trouble at Worcester but shall not be very sorry if Willes looses it; for I hear his cheif Interest besides Winnington is Sir Richard Lane[176] the most contemptible scoundrel I ever saw. I believe it was to please Octavius [Carteret], that Winnington engaged for Willes whose Father[177] they say is quite devoted to Octavius [Carteret], I therefore am not inclined to wish for him.

---

[172] Pentyparc, near Llanon, south of Aberystwyth, Cardiganshire, the home of James Philipps.

[173] Clacken is a wooden hand-bat or racquet. *Scottish National Dictionary.*

[174] Winnington had been re-elected on 27 Dec. 1743 after being appointed paymaster general. Campbell is referring to the election of 10 Jan. 1744, when Winnington, as the town recorder, was involved in the election of the tory, Sir Henry Harpur, Sandys' nominee on the latter's elevation to the Lords. The *Univeral London Morning Advertiser*, 2 Jan. 1744, reported that Sir Watkin Williams-Wynn and others had gone to Worcester to give their interest to Harpur.

[175] John Willes (?1721–84), of Astrop, Northants; MP for Banbury 1746–54 and Aylesbury 1754–61.

[176] Sir Richard Lane (c.1667–1756), of Worcester; opposition MP for Minehead 1721–2 and Worcester 1727–34.

[177] Sir John Willes (1685–1761), see Note 171.

I sent your letter to Haycock who is gone to Yarmouth to visit Mr John Haylor, I had a letter from him to day he desires me to give his duty to you, and tell you that he intends to write to you soon, I expect him home about the time the House meets again.

I have no hopes of the Gent[leman][178] giveing over his design of comeing to London (where I believe he has no busyness but to follow you) unless the looseing all hopes of a Place may put him off it. I am sure if he does come he will give me great uneasiness, and rob me of a great deal of the Pleasure I propose in your Company, for I know he will haunt you continually, I must use him civilly for the reasons you know, yet shall be heartily tired of his Company, when you are with me, much more than if he was here when you are not, Pray my Dearest if he will come with you let him planely know that you look upon it as an accidental travelling togather, both haveing a mind to go to London at the same time, and that you will not consider it as attending upon, or takeing Care of you that being wholely needless, I shall never think my self obliged to any man for a Service he forces upon me when I neither desire nor want it. Believe me my Dearest he has a mean, interested Mind, he will I know always shew the best side to you, because it is his great desire to insinuate himself into your favor that he may pin himself upon you for life; I believe he is satisfied he can take no immediate hold of me, so he thinks to manage me through those that are nearest and dearest to me. But I think you can see through & despise Flattery.

Pray my Dearest be very carefull of your self in rideing and shooting & of your health in every respect.

---

[178] Almost certainly James Philipps of Pentyparc. He had written to John Campbell on 1 Dec. 1743: 'I wish you would be so kind to take an opportunity to ask your cos Pelham for some Place for your humble servant . . . and would accept of one could I get it . . . [for] . . . I fear I shall not clear the incumbrances on my estate without assistance'. NLW, MS 1352b.

Chapter 4. 1744–51

Unless otherwise stated all letters in this chapter are from CRO, Cawdor/Campbell box 128.

94.
John Campbell to Pryse Campbell, 12 January 1744

I thank you for your letter from Bangeston[1] and I was very glad to hear from your Mama that you were come home in good health, I wish my Dearest you would not make too many holydays for consider how much time is lost from your learning by your hunting twice a week, which, though I have allways freely allow'd it for your health's sake, is a liberty which perhaps no Youth in the Kingdom besides your self is allow'd; unless such whose education is entirely neglected; I do not say this my Dearest as in the least grudgeing the liberty I have allow'd, for your health will ever be most dear to me and next to Virtue is the most valuable thing in this world; I only put you in mind of it that you may avoid unnecessary avocations from your Studies. You remember that you were in respect to Books entirely idle when you were last here, and if you loose all your time when in Town, and too great a share of it in the Country, what will be the consequence, I hope when you come next to Town as you & I shall be alone togather, Wee shall find some hours to look in latin & greek books, though in truth I cannot pretend to give you any assistance in the latter, which I am very sorry for.

Yesterday the english Army was voted in the Committee of the whole House, there was a faint attempt to put it off on pretense of some accounts not yet laid before us, & at the end of the Debate the same reasons were given for a Motion made by Sir J[ohn] H[ynde] C[otton] to leave the Chair upon which Wee divided ays 165 noes 277. I believe the [sic] avoided divideing upon the main question it being so apparently absurd to lay down your Arms before you have made Peace. Today the resolutions of the Committee were agreed to by the House without the least opposition only a few cry'd No when the questions were put. Last night the Solicitor Gen[era]l Murray spoke extremely well, & really Percival spoke well, much better than I expected. Mr York[e][2] Lord Chancellor's son spoke short but very well. Mr Winnington made the Motions, Sir W[illia]m Yonge being not well enough to attend, he had a short fit of the Gout in his stomach but is recovering.

The best speakers I think on the other side were Mr Geo[rge] Greenville & Oswald[3] a wild looking Scot. Mr Dodington made a long speech but I think his hand was out, Fazakerly spoke sometime & would I believe have spoke a good deal longer, if he could have been heard, but the Committee were not at all complaisant to him, talking aloud & calling for the question, & some time calling order to those that stood at the bar & behind the Chair not really to make them take places, but merely to disturb Fazakerly & make him sit down. Wee divided I think a little after seven o'Clock, I do not expect

[1] An estate in Angle parish, south-west Pembrokeshire – bequeathed to John (Jack) Campbell in 1754.
[2] Philip Yorke (1720–90), of Wrest, Bedfordshire; MP for Reigate 1741–7 and Cambridgeshire 1747–64.
[3] James Oswald (1715–69), of Dunnikier, Fife; MP for Dysart burghs 1741–7 and 1754–68 and Fifeshire 1747–54.

anything of Consequence again until we meet till next wednesday when I hear the
Hanover Troops are to be moved for. I hope Wee shall carry that question, but I neither
expect, nor desire, to carry it by so great a majority. Mr Corbett has promised me to
recommend J Morris to Captain Griffin.[4] If my Friends in Pembrokeshire had heard the
civil things Lord Winchelsea said to me last night, meeting accidently after the House
was up, they would expect me to make Captains and Lieutenants by the dozen, but I
have seen enough of Courtiers to understand their language a little better. My Love &
Blessing to your Brothers & Sisters. I pray God . . .

Haycock is just come home he gives his duty to you & will write soon he defer'd it
till he came home.

My dearest I should not have been against you staying a night or two with Mr
Hooke, but had much rather your had gone by yourself, than with that Gent[leman]
you cannot indeed avoid haveing so much of his Company at home, but there was no
necessity I think for you to go with him to stay with him at another Gent[leman']s
House & longer than you stay'd when I was with you; I confess I did not expect you
would have done it so immediately after I had told you my opinion of him in very plane
terms. You might at least have gone home on Saturday, and press'd him not to come
away on your account, taking that opportunity to let him planely see you did not think
your self or desire to be thought by others, under his Care, and that you will not think
it at all necessary for you & he to come and go togather, if you had done so, it would
have been pleaseing to one who has studied to make you happy ever since you were
born, and will endeavor to do you the best service he is able as long as he lives. My
Dearest one may avoid intimacy & friendship without wanting in civility.

I thought myself very happy in your company here the two last Springs, and when
I travell'd with you to Shrewsbury, & so home, I thought it the pleasantest journey I
ever took in my life. I have hoped for much pleasure in your Company next Spring, but
if that Gent[leman] comes up with you, & follows you here, as he does in the Country;
I can have no satisfaction, or expect one pleasant day while you are here. I do not
believe he has any busyness that would bring him to Town if you did not come, I
heartily wish my giveing him no hopes of my asking a Place for him may displease him
so much as to prevent his journey; unless he is cunning enough to know that comeing
up with you is doing the most disagreable thing to me in his power.

Pray take care not to drop, or mislay this.

95.
John Campbell to Pryse Campbell, 14 January 1744
Inclosed [not extant] is a political Print which if it has not much wit, has however a serious
and certain truth in it. I have also sent you an old London evening Post for the sake of
Mr. Willes's letter to the Freemen of Worcester,[5] his saying he stands upon no particu-
lar bottom, put me in mind of a scene between Orator Henley & Punch in one of

---

[4] Probably Sir John Griffin (1719–97), of Audley End, Sussex; MP for Andover 1749–84. A supporter of
Henry Fox, he was made a captain in 1743. He ended his military career as a general in 1778.

[5] *London Evening Post*, 7 Jan. 1744. Willes' letter, published after he had lost the Worcester election,
declared that he stood 'upon no particular bottom', but was a proper person for Worcester. In reply the
Evening Post, in the guise of 'Ben Broadbottom', said that Willes, after unsuccessfully canvassing for two days,
'sneak'd off being not a proper person' for Worcester citizens.

Mr. Fieldings[6] Farce's.[7] The Orator says let every Tub stand upon his own bottom, you fool say's Punch my Tub has no bottom. I should have told you that in the scene Punch and the Orator appear as preaching against one another in two Tubs, but I fancy you have the Farce. The letter in the whole is like an advertisement I have seen in a Newspaper to this effect. Observing with great concern how mankind are daily imposed upon by Quacks, has induced a regular Physician to offer his advice to the Public, who may be heard of every day at the Green Hatch in Holborn[8] &c.

This Independent Candidate is the son of one whose Estate they say does not excede £800 per annum and has a debt upon it besides. When I heard so much talk of the Independent Electors of Westminster I used to say they were such as had nothing to depend on. I do not know any News at all. My Love to your Mama, Blessing to your Brothers & Sisters & Compliments to all Friends. I pray God . . .

My Dearest Haycock has told me what you say about Horses. I am sensible of the necessity, but don't well know how to go about a busyness I am so very ignorant of. As to Coach Horses the money frights me. I don't mean my Dear that I am unwilling to lay it out if I have it, but I believe you would not wish me to spend more than I can afford; I did it at the last cursed Election which vex's me.

96.

John Campbell to Pryse Campbell, 24 January 1744

I received last night two letters from you one dated the 13th which should have come two posts before. You may be assured I neither did nor I hope ever shall impute Your silence to want of Love or regard for me, I am allways glad when I receive your letters, but I should be sorry if you were confined or put to any inconvenience to write them. I don't doubt you will do the best you can to recover the time you lost, but though I caution you against too frequent, or too long interruptions of your studys I dare say you will allways understand, that I do not desire to confine you too long a time to your Books; I believe you will give good attention while you are at them, but to be long at any one time poreing upon books as I know it would be disagreable, so I really think it would be improper for one of your sprightly temper, and I thank God that you are so sprightly, long may you continue so. Your Mama tells me she is assured you are carefull of yourself and do not run any hazards when you are hunting which gives me the greatest satisfaction and is the strongest proof of your love to me and your care to make me easy & happy.

I will get a great Coat for you & send by the Carrier the last time I went to Chelsea I was enquireing of Mr Latouche[9] about their drawing Master upon your account, so you see my Dearest I remember'd my promise. I wish you may soon get a good Portmantle Horse. Speak to R[oger] Evan[s] about it who I dare say will allways be ready to obey your directions the best he can. Haycock is very thankfull & much pleased that you remember him so kindly, indeed I think he well deserves it & sincerely loves you.

---

[6] Henry Fielding (1707–54), novelist, dramatist, satirist, JP and, in 1749, co-founder of the Bow Street Runners.

[7] *Author's Farce and the Pleasures of the Town*, first performed at the Little Theatre, Haymarket in 1730. It was Fielding's first theatrical success.

[8] A 'Dr Russel' regularly advertised his potions in the London press as being available from the Green Hatch, Holborn. See for instance, *London Daily Post and General Advertiser*, 7 Mar. 1744.

[9] James Digges la Touche (1707–63), a poplin merchant and banker.

I believe when you come to Town if you order your huntsman to wait at Table, and bring my Man Johnny Bowen up it may do well to polish him & let him see the World a Little. I forgot to tell you before that it is not judged proper for the Parrott to travel in Winter, but she is very well & talks a few. I pray God . . .

Kind service to Mr. Rowe and remember me to all Friends. You forgot to tell me how your dear eyes have been since I left you. Inclosed is for your self.

97.
John Campbell to Pryse Campbell, 24 January 1744

> Care puer, mea sera & sola voluptas,
> Ante annos, animunque gerens curamque virilem[10]

Nothing could give me greater satisfaction than your last affectionate, sensible, & manly letter. I promise myself I Shall never be angry with you for I do believe you will never give me cause, and I hope I shall never be so unreasonable, or so far abate the most tender affection I have for you, as to be angry without. You may have little failings & inadvertency's which may give me concern, because I love you so passionately that I cannot think of you on any occasion with indifference, but I hope that concern will never have any mixture of anger. I believe no Parent had ever less occasion of dissatisfaction given them by any Child than I have hitherto had by you, and I am persuaded that the older you grow the more reason I shall have to be satisfied with your behavior, to rejoice in your Virtue, and to thank God for the good sense, and amiable temper he has blessed you with. Macte nova virtute, puer: sic itur ad astra.[11]

I was speaking to your Friend Groves about your Great Coat just as I received your letter. I hope you will get a horse to carry your Cloak bag & then I believe I shall send you sailing Orders soon after you receive your Coat and I shall be very glad if you escape that Gentleman's[12] company, for I am sure he would give us frequent uneasiness here, though I am convinc'd you do whatever I desire, and that your behavior will be alltogather in every respect answerable to my wishes. My Dearest Boy I earnestly pray to God . . .

98.
John Campbell to Pryse Campbell, 26 January 1744
Yesterday Mr. Waller made a long Motion which you will see in the Votes next Post for all Papers relateing to the Treaty of Worms.[13] I cannot recollect exactly the numbers

---

[10] First line: Virgil, *Aeneid*, viii, 581: 'dearest child, who art my last and only joy'. Second line: Virgil, *Aeneid*, ix, 311: 'bearing a mind and manly concern beyond his years'.

[11] Virgil, *Aeneid*, ix, 640–1: 'persevere in virtue my boy, thus is the way to the stars'.

[12] Almost certainly James Philipps of Pentyparc.

[13] The Treaty of Worms was signed on 13 Sept. 1743. It was a heavily criticised alliance between Great Britain, Austria and Sardinia. Pitt commented: 'I wish that treaty could be erased from our annals and our records, so as never to be mentioned hereafter: for that treaty, with its appendix, the convention that followed, is one of the most destructive, unjust, and absurd that was ever concluded. By that treaty we have taken upon ourselves a burden which I think it impossible for us to support', the burden referred to being the £200,000 yearly subsidy that Britain agreed to pay to the king of Sardinia. However, 'It was Carteret's greatest hour'. R. Browning, *The War of the Austrian Succession* (Stroud, 1994), 148.

by which it pass'd in the negative.[14] Lord C[arteret] was as usual loaded with epithets; I think two were new viz delirious Minister & High German Doctor much good do it him, nec lex est justior ulla &c.[15] To day Wee sat till after five on the Bill for divorceing the Duke of Beaufort[16] which meet with no opposition.[17] To morrow the Lords are to debate about the Hanover Troops.

It is exceeding cold disagreable black weather. I hope My Dearest is very carefull of himself.

Haycock is gone to set up tonight with poor Governor Morris who may they say live a fortnight perhaps, but the [sic] give no hopes of his recovery.

Give my Love to your Mama, blessing to your Brothers & Sisters & Compliments to all Friends. I pray God ...

I have by this Post return'd the Plan of the Grove[18] to R[oger] Evan[s]. You may look on it & give any Farther directions you like, I forgot to bid him the wit to you.

After Lord Sandwich had made a long Motion[19] against the Hanover Troops, which was seconded by Lord Harvey,[20] the Chancelor [Lord Chancellor Hardwicke] Observ'd that it was the self same with the last upon which the sense of the House had been already taken & therefore in Point of Order it could not be debated again. We[21] urangled [sic] about this til near six: at last the Motion was disposed of by a Previous Question & the Affair adjourn'd to be introduc'd by a Motion in a new shape & fully debated on tuesday next. We had no Division.[22]

99.
John Campbell to Pryse Campbell, 2 February 1744
This morn Captain Broderick[23] who had been order'd to observe the Brest Squadron[24] brought account that they were come out & entending themselves in a line from Ushent[25] to Scilly. 'Tis said they are 21 in number, and what they design is uncertain, upon this an extraordinary Councill was held at the Cockpit, & it is said that upon its riseing Sir J[ohn] Norris immediately set out for Portsmouth. This is the subject of all

[14] *CJ*, xxiv, 520. The votes were 149 to 207.

[15] The full quote is from Ovid, *Ars Amatoria*, i, 655: 'Neque enim lex est aequior ulla, Quam necis artifices arte perire sua'. Translates as: 'Nor can there be a juster law than that the artificers of death should perish by their own invention'.

[16] Henry Somerset (1707–45), 3rd duke of Beaufort. In 1729 he married Frances Scudamore, and by act of parliament took her name. He divorced her in 1743 for an adulterous affair with William, later Lord Talbot.

[17] *CJ*, xxiv, 522.

[18] At Stackpole Court.

[19] *PH*, xiii, 505–52, for the motion and the ensuing debate in the Lords.

[20] John Hervey (1665–1751), 1st earl of Bristol.

[21] The house of commons.

[22] Note attached to the letter in a different hand.

[23] Thomas Broderick (1704–69), entered the navy as a volunteer in 1722 and rose to become rear admiral of the blue by 1759. He was promoted to captain in 1741.

[24] The Brest fleet had orders to attack the British channel fleet to make way for an invasion of Britain. A great storm, which raged on 7 Mar., destroyed these plans as well as many of the French and British ships involved. Browning, *War of the Austrian Succession*, 157–8.

[25] Ushant, an island off the western tip of mainland Brittany. It marks the southern entrance to the English Channel.

Conversation & Speculation at present. I make no doubt but the Politicians in our Stewards Hall will conclude the Cardinal Tencin[26] resolveing to out do his Predecessor Fleury,[27] has projected no less than the Conquest of Pembrokeshire.

Yesterday the Opposition would have put off the Committee of Supply in order to call for Papers relateing to the Treaty of Worms, but it was carried to go into the Committee by 214 against 146.[28] In the Committee Wee voted several sums the first of which was £200,000 for His Majesty to pay to the King of Sardinia persuant to Treaty (viz of Worms). Wee had but very short debate & no division in the Committee, it being allmost six o'Clock when Wee went into it, but to day upon the report it was moved to leave out the paying to the King of Sardinia persuant to Treatys & grant the sum to his Majestie to layout in satisfieing such engagements as he has thought fit to enter into for the Common Cause. I can't pretend to give you the exact words, only the sense, what they meant was to avoid giveing any Countenance to the Treaty of Worms, they were told that giveing money in Consequence of a Treaty was not approveing it, the Crown has the sole power of makeing Treatys & when made and ratified they are valid without asking the consent of Parliament yet if the Parliament thinks a Treaty contrary to the Interest of the Nation they may call to account & punish the Minister who made & ratified that Treaty. Q[ueen] Anne's Ministers were impeach'd[29] for makeing the Treaty of Utrecht yet that Treaty allow'd to be valid, & binding. It was carried to agree with the resolution of the Committee without amendment by 167 against 125,[30] a thin House but many people imagined there would be no debate. Scarce any of the P[rince]'s family[31] were at the House except those in opposition, and I fancy a Board continued sitting at the Admiralty to give Orders upon the Account brought by Captain B[roderick]. Young Stanley[32] made a long speech yesterday without much meaning, but in a pompous and most theatrical manner one would have taken him for an Actor rehearseing a part in one of Nathanial Lee's[33] Plays.

The Motion made in the House of Lords on Tuesday [27 January] was a resolution against the Hanover Troops.[34] I don't doubt I shall soon send it you in print with a flameing Protest. It was made by Lord Sandwich seconded by the Duke of Marlborough

---

[26] Cardinal Pierre Guerin de Tencin (1679–1758). Tencin was a disciple of Fluery, and 'hard, spiteful, and vindictive by temperament, serious and prudent in his station', he believed that the true enemy of France was Britain rather than Austria. Browning, *War of the Austrian Succession*, 129.

[27] Andre-Hercule de Fleury (1653–1743), chief minister to Louis XV.

[28] *CJ*, xxiv, 539.

[29] Queen Anne dismissed Robert Harley, 1st earl of Oxford and Earl Mortimer, at the end of July 1714. On the accession of George I, Harley was impeached and imprisoned in the Tower for his part in the drafting of the Treaty of Utrecht, which George deemed hostile to Hanover.

[30] *CJ*, xxiv, 544.

[31] Followers of the prince of Wales.

[32] James Stanley, Lord Strange (1717–71), MP for Lancashire 1741–71. Horace Walpole described him as 'of a party by himself, yet voting generally with the Tories'. Cited in *HPC, 1715–54*, ii, 439.

[33] Nathaniel Lee (1653–92), dramatist. He spent five years in Bethlehem madhouse, and died in a drunken fit. His play *Alexander the Great* remained popular into the 19th century.

[34] *LJ*, xxvi, 299–300. In the debate Sandwich stated that until a final determination was reached he would raise the subject 'proteus like' at every opportunity in order for it to be debated again. For the debate, see *PH*, xiii, 505–52.

who said by little and in very general terms that by what he had observed when he was abroad he did not think the English and Hanoverians could serve togather. He did not speak with much Force or Spirit which no doubt greatly disappointed the Patriots, & Turianum Maxima[35] was so enraged that she sent him a most bitter letter either that night or next morning. I am very glad for the public good that he was prevaled upon to be so mild, but to be sure H[is] G[race] made but a poor figure saying so little and being so calm in public after haveing said a great deal & been pretty warm in private I mean out of the House for he did not desire those he talk'd to would keep it secret, but the contrary. Lord W[es]ttm[orla]nd reflected very brutally on Marshall Wade for what he said in our House, & on Lord Orford whom I suppose he brought in by head & shoulders, Octavius [Carteret] haveing spoke of the Libels that are spread abroad, Earl of Moreton condemn'd them very much, but said that if some who had for many years encouraged, such things now suffer'd by them it was a just judgement upon them, and as far as such People were concern'd he could not help being pleased to see it. He said this in a much better & stronger manner than I tell it pray drink his health for it. He spoke long & I am told said many good things, but he has somewhat an odd maner, have been allways, till he was chose one of the 16,[36] a retired studious man. Wee sat till after six this evening and I believe shall sit as long to morrow though I can't well tell what about.

I have not time to write to your Mama but give my Love to her & tell her that Haycock carried her letter to Mrs Bramstons who was in Town but not at home. My Blessing to your Brothers & Sisters. I pray God . . .

I send you the infamous & traiterous Libel[37] of last Saturday who can read such things without reflecting on the cursed wickedness of Antonious [Bath] who taught the People such destructive Licenciousness.

The Report[38] from the Committee On the Hanover Troops passed without a Duty to adjourn the Debate till Monday Noes 266 Ay's 178.[39]

London, 28 January 1744

Horace Walpole Junior was one of the first Speakers in the Debate about Hanover Troops in the Committee & spoke extremely well. The second day on the Report the Solicitor General [William Murray] spoke as well as possible & Mr. Pitt exerted Himself to the utmost to answer Him or Rather by Eloquence & at Full applying to the Passions to take off the impression He had made & inflame so far as to leave no room for the Operation of cool reason. The youngest Grenville James made a furious Speech it did not attempt to reason but was a severe invective against the People & Country of Hanover, fill'd with all the reproachful Language used by Heroes in old & Oyster Women in Modern times. Young Stanley was resolved to be outdone by nobody &

[35] Sarah, duchess of Marlborough.

[36] Scottish representative peers, those peers, 16 in all, elected from the peerage of Scotland to sit in the house of lords after the Acts of Union of 1707.

[37] Perhaps *Miscellaneous Reflections on Miscellaneous Thoughts*.

[38] This report is included with the letter. It is not written by Campbell.

[39] *PH*, xiii, 462–503, for the debate which took place on 19 Jan. 1744.

used a Sacred Name in a manner I never Heard used in the House & I scarce think anyone has heard these 110 Years. But the rash impudence of a Boy was not so surpriseing as the Rage & Noise & almost Tumult with which it was supported when call'd to order. One would have thought that all would have gone into Confusion till the Speaker [Arthur Onslow] (it being in a Committee) got up to speak & with difficulty procured attention which I Believe nobody else could have done; & then gave Stanley a Rebuke & advice in a manner fit to appease the Disorder rather than adequate to the Offence. Before the Speaker spoke I saw Him take some pains to clear the Way to the Chair which He thought He must have resumed to prevent the last degrees of Disorder & Confusion, for I believe at first He scarce hoped to be heard from his Place in the Committee. Stanley seemed neither daunted or abash'd Remark: it is a Melancholy thing to see Gentlemen trample upon all order Law & decency & ready to involve their County in all the miseries of a Civil War to gratifie their Ambitions or their resentments I pray God grant times against you come into *Public Scenes.*

100.

John Campbell to Pryse Campbell, 9 February 1744

Wee spent this day till after eight at night upon an incidental question in the Denbigh Election which I have not time to explane; upon a division Wee were 193 against 181.[40] In the Debate Mr William Pitt without any provocation used Mr. Pelham with the utmost brutality, it seems to me to be the Measure of the opposition to bear down the Freinds of the Government by rage, fury, noise & insolence. Your acquaintance Mr. Legge came home to share my hodge Podge[41] he often enquires after you. God preserve you . . .

101.

John Campbell to Pryse Campbell, 14 February 1744

I came from the House this Evening a little after seven the Denbigh Election comes on again on thursday, Wee were very dull at it to day, it [sic] truth it is a poor employment for this time. To day about noon and Express brought account that five of the French Ships of War are gone to Dunkirk where there are thirty Transports the rest of their Fleet are at Torbay, it seems the general opinion that they design an Invasion but I believe there is no certain intelligence of their design, the Cabinet Councill sat immediately upon the arrival of this express, I hear Sir J[ohn] Norris was yet at St. Helens. I heard some talk as if there were accounts from Scotland of Cabals among the Clans, but I did not hear any thing of it at the Duke of Argyll's where I was this morning. I heard an imperfect account of 3000 People calling themselves Methodists being got togather at Bermingham in such a manner as was thought to require the attention of the Government. Whatever the French Fleet design it is a very disagreable Affair, and may give us much trouble.

My Dearest I pray God . . .

---

[40] *CJ*, xxiv, 555.
[41] A type of mutton soup.

102.

John Campbell to Pryse Campbell, 16 February 1744

Yesterday between 2 & 3 Mr. Pelham brought a message[42] to the [*sic*] sign'd by His Majestie (the like was sent at the same time to the Lords) to acquaint them that he had received undoubted advice of the Pretenders[43] eldest son[44] being come into France, and that a Invasion was being intended from France, in concert with some disaffected Persons at home, to be supported by the French Squadron that has appear'd for some time in our Channel.[45] As soon as the Message was read Lord Hartington[46] moved for an Address to express our indignation, abhorence &c and to assure his Majestie that Wee would stand by him with our Lives & Fortune's in defence of his Person & Crown and of our Religion, Laws & Liberty. My favorite Lord[47] Spoke like himself, & was very handsomely seconded by Sir Charles Wyndham,[48] and who would have thought any honest Man could have spoke on that occasion but to express his zeal when all is at stake, and to shew his desire that the House might unanimously concur in the loyal & affectionate Address proposed to them; yet Mr. Doddington & Mr. Waller moved & seconded an Amendment of which I give you an exact Copy, though I could only give you the substance of the King's Message & Lord Hartington's Motion the amendment was as follows: And to assure His Majestie that this House will enter into a serious consideration of the disposition & state of the Naval Forces of this Kingdom, as also of the time of the fitting out & sailing of the French Fleet who does not see that such an addition would have taken away all the Force of the Warm & affectionate expressions that went before, reduced them to mere empty Form and shewn that in a time of the greatest danger Wee were more inclined to attack the Ministers than to defend the King, to have shewn such a Coldness in defence of the Government must have fill'd all its Friends with Fear, & Amazement, and given courage and confidence to our Enemies both at home & abroad. Soon after this debate began Wee received a Message from the Lords to desire Wee would continue sitting and in a little time another Message by two of the Judges to desire Wee would agree with the Lords in their Address which they sent to us.[49] Their Address was read, and then Wee Went on with our debate. Mr. Doddington said what assistance could Wee give the King, as for money the Nation was allready exhausted nor could Wee either increase our Land Army or our Fleet both of which he represented as to weak for our Enemies. Yet I think he had begun his speech with saying that he heard this News rather with indignation than fear, the two parts of his speech were the planest

---

[42] *PH*, xiii, 641–5.

[43] James Francis Edward Stuart (1688–1766), the Old Pretender.

[44] That is, Prince Charles Edward Louis Philip Casimar Stuart (1720–88), or Bonnie Prince Charlie or the Young Pretender. The instigator of the jacobite uprising of 1745.

[45] *CJ*, xxiv, 568. This is the Brest fleet referred to above in letter 99.

[46] William Cavendish (c.1720–64), marquess of Hartington 1729–55, and then 4th duke of Devonshire; whig MP for Derbyshire 1741–51. Master of the horse 1751–5; lord treasurer 1754–5 and 1761–3; (nominal) first lord of the treasury 1756–7; lord chamberlain 1757–62.

[47] Probably Sir Robert Walpole.

[48] Charles Wyndham (1710–63), 2nd earl of Egremont; MP for Bridgwater 1734–41, Appleby 1741–7 and Taunton 1747–50. Initially a tory, by 1741 he had gone over to the whig interest. Secretary of state for the southern department 1761–3, in which office he worked closely with his brother-in-law George Grenville to bring about a war with Spain in 1762.

[49] *CJ*, xxiv, 568.

contradiction unless his indignation against our own Government makes him not affraid of the Success of a foreign Invasion. Sir Francis Dashwood gave a long account of King James 2nds ill Government and said that was the reason his People would not defend him when he was invaded from Holland. Mr William Pitt speaking in his usual insulting & menaceing stile used some words, that made the speaker [Arthur Onslow] think it necessary to take him down, & he after riseing to defend himself, the Speaker rose again & spoke in such a manner as brought Mr. Pitt to temper and made him very modest & complaisant towards the Speaker. Many who on other occasions vote with the opposition left them on this Occasion as the Aldermen Gybbon, Marshall, Lambert,[50] & Calvert,[51] Mr Digby, Mr Velters Cornwall, G [sic] Fox & others. Lord Cornbury spoke early in the Debate in a very proper manner to persuade to unanimity & to avoid delay upon so great an occasion. Lord Strange was mighty hot for the amendment & upon Mr. Winnington saying Wee ought on such an occasion to agree without Debate to the Lords address he made a passionate childish complaint that Mr. W[innington] attempted to take away the Freedom of Debate. Sir John Philipps ingeniously said that they who refused the amendment prevented unanimity for they who offer'd it were very ready & desireous to be unanimous. Soon after seven o'Clock Wee divided for the amendment 123 against it 287.[52] Then Lord Hartington desired to withdraw his Motion & moved to agree to the Address sent us from the Lords which was the same in effect, and it was agreed to Nemine contradicente and I suppose both House's will wait upon the King with it to day. A great many Peers came into our House to hear this most extraordinary debate among the rest the Earl of Winchilsea & Nottingham. Mr William Pitt in his Speech made some quotations from Bishop Burnets History[53] regarding the late Lord Nottingham[54] and took care to direct his eyes when he spoke to the place at the bottom of the House where Lord Winchilsea sat. I must not omit that Admiral Vernon haved [sic] raved as usual & several others reflected strongly upon the Admiralty. Lord Baltimore spoke surpriseing well in their defence, shew'd they had not been negligent, & shew'd that the intelligence the Patriots seem'd to boast of was in Several instances utterly false. In truth he put them to shame & did it in a very handsome and becomeing manner, I did not think it possible for him to speak so well, indeed he need not wish to do better.

The account yesterday was that Sir J[ohn] Norris was in persute of ten sail of French men of War, which prevented his receiveing the last orders sent from here. I believe some are in pain lest he should persue them to the West and in the mean time the Ships & Transports from Dunkirk, come here. It is not certainly known where the Pretenders son is, but I believe one can scarce doubt his being at hand to embark with the French

---

[50] Alderman Daniel Lambert (1685–1750), of Savage Gardens, Tower Hill and Perrots, Banstead, Surrey; tory MP for London 1741–7.

[51] Alderman Sir William Calvert (?1703–61), of St Katherine's, Tower Hill; MP for London 1742–54 and Old Sarum 1755–61.

[52] *CJ*, xxiv, 569.

[53] Gilbert Burnet (1643–1715), historian and divine; professor of divinity at Glasgow University 1669–74; bishop of Salisbury 1689–1715. The history referred to is the *History of His Own Time* (1723).

[54] Daniel Finch (1647–1730), 2nd earl of Nottingham; tory MP for Great Bedwyn 1673–9 and for Lichfield 1679–82. First lord of the admiralty 1681–4; secretary of state for the northern department 1689–90 and 1692–3; secretary of state for the southern department 1690–3 and 1702–3; lord president of the council 1714–16.

Troops. I hear all the Forces in England have had orders immediately to draw near London, the defence of which is indeed the main chance. I write this in the morning lest busyness should keep me long at the House if I hear any news when I go out I will, if I have time writ it to your Mama at night. I believe there is little or nothing, in the Story I sent last Post from Bermingham, there was a story of an Insurrection in Yorkshire yesterday but I hope without any grounds, Wee must expect such Story's every day while this alarm lasts. J[ohn] H[ynde] C[otton] & W[atkin] W[illiams] W[ynn] were prudently silent in yesterdays debate.

I believe Sir Norris's last orders were to go to the Downs[55] & I wish he had received them, I suppose if our Fleet was there it would be difficult for the French to get by them in order to land in Kent, or on the Northside of the Thames which they probably would rather chuse, as I believe they would then have the easiest March towards London. But if it pleases God he should destroy those ten ships before the others are ready to come from Dunkirk it may have a very happy effect. Probably Wee shall soon see some very happy, or very unhappy event, God grant the former. I must now dress to go to the House. I was very sorry you sprain'd your thumb in ramping,[56] for Gods sake my Dearest be carefull & think how bad a thing a sprain is, Haycocks thumb is not recover'd yet. Tell your Mama he says he left a bottle & a piece of a bottle of Verjuice in the Wine Cellar on the Top of the Brick work on the right hand as you go in. I pray God . . .

Extract from Bishop Burnets History
Volume 2[n]d, page 94
It was believed . . . that this Victory (meaning that over the French Fleet at La Hogue)[57] might have been carried much Farther than it was; but Russel[58] was provoked by some Letters & orders the Earl of Nottingham sent him . . . which he thought the effects of Ignorance. The Seamen . . . complaned that the Earl of Nottingham was ignorant of Sea Affairs, and yet that he set on propositions relateing to them, without consulting Seamen, and sent Orders which could not be obey'd without endangereing the whole Fleet.

16 February, evening
Comeing home before this letter was gone to the Post Office I open'd the cover to tell you that now it is believed there is but one French Man of War with the Transports at Dunkirk, and 'tis said that a Considerable part of the Brest Squadron is gone to the Mediterranean, but I don't know if it be true. Wee are to go with the Address of both Houses to morrow the King haveing a cold I think prevented his receiveing it to day. I hear the City have agreed upon a handsome Address, the stanch [*sic*] broad bottom

---

[55] A roadstead or area of sea, part of the English Channel, off Dover.

[56] 'To ramp: to gesticulate with or raise the arms, to stretch; to clutch wildly at.' *OED*.

[57] The battle of la Hogue was fought at the end of May 1692, and was one of the naval battles of the Nine Years War (1688–97).

[58] Edward Russell (1653–1727), admiral and from 1697 earl of Orford; first lord of the admiralty 1694–9, 1709–10, 1714–17. He was one of the Immortal Seven, of mainly whig noblemen, who sent the invitation to William of Orange to come to England in 1688, the result of which was the Glorious Revolution, ousting the catholic James II and replacing him with the protestant William.

endeavor to ridicule the apprehensions of an Invasion, but other People think it a Serious thing. Sir John Cope[59] is gone to Scotland, & this morning General Wentworth set out to fetch 6,000 Dutch Auxiliary Troops, Lord Stair offer'd his service on this occasion, and it has been said he would have the chief at home, and then that he was to resume the cheif command abroad & M[arshall] Wade command at home, but I cannot say that either are true. I had been told to day that Lord Orford had been summon'd to Councill, but on enquiry I don't find it true, but I believe the New Ministers have been glad to have his advice and opinion in this emergency.

Yesterday the Duke of Marlborough moved for the Address in the House of Lords,[60] Lord Chesterfield moved for an amendment a good deal like that moved in our House, Lord Lonsdale spoke strongly against the amendment, and I think it was dropt without comeing to a question. I was told by one that lives over against him that there were many Chairs & some with the curtains drawn at the quondam Viscount Barrington's yesterday so probably these amendments might be concerted there.

The Duke of Marlboroughs takeing that part yesterday was I think a good thing both for the Government and for his own Character. I send you strange uncertain & contradictory accounts but I can have no better. The Dutch they say are thoroughly alarm'd and very hearty to exert themselves to the utmost against France.

I believe all stories about insurrections are entirely groundless.

I am sorry there were any in the House of Commons who could do so wrong a thing as to move such an amendment, but as it was moved & debated I am very glad they divided to shew how great a Majority were against it.[61]

I can't send you sailing orders yet. God keep & direct you my Dearest.

103.
John Campbell to Pryse Campbell, 18 February 1744
Not haveing my Notes from the House yesterday I send you those that should have gone to Mr Morris chiefly that you might see the Kings Message.[62] When you have read them you will send them to Mr Morris. I have told your Mama that I had no News. I walk'd about the rooms at Court yesterday three Hours & was never the Wiser. I saw Lord Orford sometime alone yesterday morning. He has not been summon'd to Councill and would not by any means wish to be summon'd for which he has I think very good reason. I pray God . . .

104.
John Campbell to Pryse Campbell, 21 February 1744
If Burton[63] should become vacant I believe there is no doubt of its being my turn.[64] I think with you that I could not bestow it on a more worthy Person than Mr. Row[e], and I am sure no recommendation can have so much weight with me as

---

[59] General Sir John Cope (1690–1760), MP for Queensborough 1722–7, Liskeard 1727–34 and Orford 1738–41. Defeated by jacobites at the Battle of Prestonpans, 21 Sept. 1745.

[60] *LJ*, xxvi, 312.

[61] *CJ*, xxiv, 568: a vote of 287 to 123.

[62] Of 15 Feb. concerning the threatened French invasion. *CJ*, xxiv, 568.

[63] Burton Rectory, near Milford Haven, Pembrokeshire.

[64] That is, to choose who should fill the vacancy.

yours. I will recommend Mr. Bishop to Lord Winchilsea, who has indeed press'd me to make applications to him and assured me of his inclination to oblige me in strong terms. How far I may rely on them I cannot tell, but I beg you would not mention it, for if my good Friends in the Country knew what Lord Winchilsea said to me there would be no end of their applications, nor any bounds to the extravagance of their expectations.

The King did not go to Chapel on Sunday but came into the Drawing room & I hope is now very well.

Yesterday Lord Barrington moved for an Address to the King for an account of the intelligence received by his Majesty or any of his Ministers, concerning the fitting out of Ships in any of the Ports of France since April last, his Lordship ridiculed the Notion of an invasion & spoke of it as a fear now over; he was some how supported by Mr. Dodington & Mr. Waller & nobody else, only Lord Strange Seconded the Motion for form without saying any more, Mr. Pelham spoke extremely well upon it, spoke of the Invasion as a Matter very Serious, & the danger not over. They divided on this question though they did not think fit to debate upon it. Wee rejected it by 234 against 141.[65] Then Wee received from the Committee of Ways & means the Report of their Resolution to lay an additional duty on sugars imported, and Lord Limerick proposeing instead of it to lay an additional duty on foreign Linen, moved to recommit the resolution. This debate lasted till seven at night, or past, and then it was carried for recommiting by 176 against 168.[66] This was cheifly owing to the folly of the Scots,[67] who hoped by laying a duty on foreign Linen to raise the price of their own, at least hoped to get a little dirty popularity at home by seeming to do so; a popularity which if they get at present, will be forgot long before the next Elections, in the meantime they do a real injury to the Government, makeing it appear weak, giveing strength, & encouragement to the opposition, & such an obstruction in raising the Supply may make it very difficult for the Administration to raise money at 3 per cent as they hoped to do, and will probably be very pleasing to the Power Wee are to Struggle with. There are so great objections to laying the Duty on foreign Linen that I can't think it will be done, and fear if it is, that the public will loose much more by it, than will be gain'd by the little, low, dirty, provincial Scots politic, which was the result of a meeting of Wiseheads at the British Coffee house[68] by the Court of Requests. I don't see how the public busyness can be carried on at this rate, if Mr. Pelham is so used, that a parcell of Wiseacres, without saying a word to him before hand, will join with the opposition to

---

[65] *CJ*, xxiv, 576.

[66] *CJ*, xxiv, 577.

[67] *PH*, xiii, 652: Lord Limerick's project, to replace the tax on sugar with one of 1*d*. per yard upon foreign linen, 'was extremely relished by the Scotch members, who thought the duty upon foreign linnens would promote that manufacture amongst them, so by their means, and that of the absentees, it was carried on the division to recommit'. This would also damage a trade treaty established with the queen of Hungary, Maria Theresa, which explicitly stated that no such tax should be levied on linen from countries under her jurisdiction.

[68] The British Coffee House was a recognised venue for Scots in London. The 'coffee-house provided a centre of communication for news and information. Runners were sent round to the coffee-house to report major events of the day, such as victory in battle or political upheaval, and the newsletters and gazettes of the day were distributed chiefly in the coffee-house'. J.D. Pelzer, 'The Coffee Houses of Augustan London', *History Today*, xxxii (1982), 40–7. The whigs patronised St James's and the tories the Cocoa Tree, both houses in Pall Mall.

obstruct the means of Supply. If he cannot go on, who can, I am sure none of the old Stock have near so much credit, and to set at the head of the Treasury any of the Patriots now in the House of Commons would in my opinion, be no better than setting up a pissing Post. The Solicitor General [William Murray] spoke long and exceedeing well for agreeing with the Committee, but some are so honest, & some so Wise, as never to be convinced by the strongest or planest reasoning. Wee go again into the Committee of Ways & means to morrow, & if the sugar is not moved again, I fancy, it will be an additional Duty on Spirits, which Sir J[ohn] Barnard was for when the sugar was first proposed, he was not in the House yesterday.

There was a report yesterday that Admiral Matthews[69] had sunk 8 of the Toulon fleet & the rest were retired back to that Port but I fear it had no foundation, the French haveing stopt all Post and Pacquets & forbid any body going out of that Kingdom help'd to gain credit to it, but those precautions may be only to conceal the designs against this infatuated Island.[70]

I am now to go to the Denbigh Election,[71] if I hear any news there and come home time enough I will it you in a Postscript. Pray make my Compliments in the kindest manner to Dr. Cuninghame when you see him. My Love & Blessing to your Brothers & Sisters. I have with great pleasure heard of your diligent application to your studies, and makeing up what time you had lost for which I most heartily thank you. I pray God . . .

105.

John Campbell to Pryse Campbell, 23 February 1744

I think I told you that when Wee were last in the Committee of Ways & Means, after Mr. Pelham had moved the sugar Sir J[ohn] Barnard opposed it, & proposed an additional duty on Spirituous liquors, & mention'd a surplus of the duty laid on last year, after paying the interest of the money borrow'd on it, it was carried in the Committee, as I told you, for the sugar but that Resolution being recommitted, Wee were yesterday in that Committee & had a pretty full appearance. As soon as Mr. [Francis] Fane had taken the Chair, Mr. Pelham stood up & said that though he had heard nothing to convince his private judgement that the sugar was not the best means to raise the Supply wanted, yet he submitted to the opinion of the House, & had not the least thought to resume that matter, he thought in [*sic*] necessary to raise the supply without delay & therefore to avoid as much as he could all variety of opinions as to new duty's he would at present propose none, but move to raise the sum wanted upon the surplus of the duty laid last year on Spirituous Liquors, which he computed for this Year at £70,000, and

[69] Thomas Mathews (1676–1751), of Llandaff Court, Glamorgan; MP for Glamorgan 1745–7 and Carmarthen 1747–51. Mathews entered the navy at the age of 14, and by 1703 was a captain. Commander of the navy at Chatham 1736–42; vice admiral 1742; commander-in-chief Mediterranean and minister to Sardinia and the Italian States 1742–4; admiral 1743; rear admiral Great Britain 1744–7; dismissed from the navy in 1747.

[70] Mathews was given the command of the Mediterranean fleet at the age of 66. His second in command, Richard Lestock, with whom Mathews was on bad terms, failed to capture the French and Spanish fleets at the battle of Toulon, 11 Feb. 1744. A court martial ensued which resulted in dismissal from the navy for Mathews, though it seems Lestock may have been more at fault since he refused to obey his admiral's orders. *HPC, 1715–54*, ii, 247.

[71] *CJ*, xxiv, 578–80. The Denbigh election of 1741 was petitioned by Sir Watkin Williams-Wynn against the government candidate, John Wynn. The hearing was postponed on several occasions and was only resolved, in Wynn's favour, 193 to 167 votes, on 23 Feb. 1744. *CJ*, xxiv, 584–5.

as there the distillers had a great stock in hand when that duty commenced, which lessen'd the product for this Year, it may probably amount next year to £80,000 which is about the Interest of the sum to be raised upon it. The reason Mr. Pelham proposed a New Duty in the Last Committee, was because this surplus if not disposed of by parliament goes to the Sinking Fund and he was not willing, if he could have avoided it, to take it from that; Mr Pelham was Seconded by Mr. Gybbon who gaped very wide but has unfortunately lost his voice by a hoarseness, which to the unspeakable detriment of public affairs, has been upon him all this Session; next Lord Limerick rose & proposed, as he had done before, an additional duty on foreign Linens, which been well prepared, he spoke very fully upon, and it was debated some time, but Sir John Barnard haveing spoke Strongly for Mr. Pelhams Motion and been Supported by Sir William Calvert, Mr. Hume Campbell after speaking much for the Linnen, proposed to agree without dividing, to Mr. Pelhams Motion provided he would agree afterward to go into a Committee to consider about the Linnen. Mr. Pelham assured him that he would not oppose such a Committee, but would attend it and after hearing all that could be said about it would Vote as he should think best for the Public Interest. Mr Pitt, Lord Limerick &c. agreeing to this the matter ended much better than I hoped for when I came into the House, for indeed I expected a long debate & then to have carried Mr. Pelhams Motion by a Small Majority, but I believe whe [sic] the Opposition saw the City come in so heartily the [sic] thought it prudent not to divide lest they should have lost the Credit they gain'd by carrying their Point for recommitting the Sugar. Both Mr. William Pitt & Mr. Hume Campbell exerted themselves to cut Sir J[ohn] Barnard but I think they found him invulnerable. However I hope he will not forget their kind intentions, and I do not think him of the most forgiving temper.

Many of the Opposition still treat the account of a French Invasion as a Ministerial Act which is monstrous, when it is notorious that a French fleet has been so long in the Channel; they are particularly angry at those words in the Message, that say it is in concert with disaffected Persons at home; I am convinced the Government are well assured of some at Home being concern'd I most heartily wish, they could make public such proof of it as would silence that most impudent falsehood one so often hears that there are no Jacobites in the Kingdom.

The inclosed scrap from todays Advertiser gives, I believe a true account of Sir J[ohn] Norris,[72] if he gives the French a good blow he will get great Fame & a Peerage if he trifles, he will deserve & meet with great reproach; but he may indeed do his best & fail; one would think he would exert himself to gain a Title, with honor, which is the point he has so long persued perhaps not allways by the most laudable means. I wish to God Wee may have good News from the Mediterranean, the French & Spanish Fleets are safe as long as they please to stay in Toulon, Mr. Matthews on the contrary is more exposed to accidents of the Weather, and if by that means some of his Ships should be disabled, the French & Spanish may take that advantage to come out upon him, beside it is believed that 7 or 8 French Men of War went into the Mediterranean in January. The French Fleet in the Channel has hinder'd our sending any supply either of Force or Stores to Matthews, if he should meet with a Misfortune the Consequence would be bad.

---

[72] The *Daily Advertiser*, 23 Feb. 1744, stated that Norris intended, wind permitting, to pursue ten French ships of the line reported to be passing Boulogne.

I believe your Mama has told you the reason I have not sent you sailing Orders, had you been here at first, there had no reason for my being uneasy but it was not thought proper by Mr. Grahame[73] to send for you out of fresh Country air. I believe the distemper is not so much about as it was, nor of a bad sort, but I beg of you My Dearest to have patience till it is thought proper to send for you, the disappointment is great to me as well as you for I wish very much for your Company though for a fortnight or more last past, I could have had but little of it, I was so much confined in the House of Commons. Wee were up yesterday half an hour after five, to day Wee finish the Denbigh Election; Wee sat upon it, but without any question, till after ten on tuesday night.

Give my Love to your Mama. I have not time to write to her this morning. If I come home soon enough I will tell her at night what becomes of Denbigh. My Blessing to your Brothers & Sisters. I pray God . . .

Denbigh Election J. Wynne for 193 against 167.[74]

There is a call of the House order'd on Lord Stranges Motion for tuesday sevenight which they say is for Sir Charles Gilmours Election,[75] a New Courtier. The inclosed letter [not extant] upon him was given me by Lord Moray.[76] I would not lose his Vote, but he deserves all they say, though nonsense in it self.

106.

John Campbell to Pryse Campbell, 23[77] February 1744

I send you the papers I mention'd in my last with the Address moved by Lord Orford,[78] I was well inform'd this morning that Lord was to be to day at the Prince's Court & that His Royal Highness talks much of him since he made that motion.

I went pretty early to the House to day to secure a place expecting a Debate. Mr. Pelham acquainted the House[79] (which was very full) from the King that His Majestie haveing reason to suspect the Earl of Barrymore[80] of treasonable practices had caused

---

[73] Thomas Graham, apothecary to the person – that is, the king's apothecary, was appointed in 1741. J.C. Sainty, *Office-Holders in Modern Britain, IV: Admiralty Officials 1660–1870* (1975), i, 50. Graham was from Garthmore, Perthshire. His will, in which he is described as 'his majesty's apothecary in London', is dated 2 May 1764. TNA, PROB11/898.

[74] Written in pencil squeezed between the signature and postscript. This is referring to the vote on the petition regarding the creation of 1,500 burgesses in the 1741 Denbigh borough election. The returning officer only accepted resident freeholders, the petition upholding this, and thus ensuring that Sir Watkin Williams-Wynn was kept out of the borough, the successful candidate being the nominee of Chirk Castle, John Wynn. *HPC, 1715–54*, i, 376, and P.D.G. Thomas, *Politics in Eighteenth-Century Wales* (Cardiff, 1998), 116.

[75] Gilmour's re-election after his appointment to the board of trade in Dec. 1743. The election was contested, Gilmour's cousin, Sir John Baird (1685–1745), being his opponent. Baird lost the election and petitioned the Commons, which he also lost. The hearings were held on 8 and 9 Mar. 1744. *CJ*, xxiv, 605, 607.

[76] James Stuart (1708–67), 8th earl of Moray (Scottish peerage).

[77] From the contents of the letter this must have been written after the Commons debate of 28 Feb.

[78] *LJ*, xxvi, 322, 24 Feb. 1744. Orford's address, on the debate concerning the intended invasion by the Pretender, is given in *PH*, xiii, 662–5.

[79] *CJ*, xxiv, 591–2.

[80] In his early seventies Barrymore became a prominent and leading jacobite and he, together with the duke of Beaufort, Lord Orrey, Sir Watkin Williams-Wynn, Sir John Hynde Cotton and Sir Robert Abdy had signed a letter to Monsieur Amelot, requesting French help in restoring the Stuart monarchy. After his arrest habeus corpus was suspended and Barrymore was incarcerated until the end of March when he was released on bail. See *PH*, xiii, 668–75; E. Cruickshanks, *Political Untouchables: The Tories and the '45* (1979).

him to be seized. Then Mr. Coke[81] moved for an address to thank His Majestie for informing them & to desire he would detane & secure the said Earl. There was some little altercation by Lord Strange, Sir J[ohn Hynde] Cotton, Sir W[atkin] W[illiams] W[ynn] & Sir J[ohn] Philipps, & I think Mr Pitt slightly Complaned of our not being informed yesterday, but the Address was order'd with very few negatives. Then the Attorney General [Dudley Ryder] moved for a Bill to suspend the Habeas Corpus for two months, he was seconded by the Solicitor General [William Murray], there was a little opposition by Lord Strange, Sir J[ohn] Philips and, which I wonder'd at, Mr George Grenville who spoke warmly upon it though he was not supported by any of the set he used to be with, as he is a sensible Man I did not expect he would have acted so much by himself; when the question was put there were very few negatives. The Attorney immediately went to the Bar & offer'd the Bill which was read twice to day & committed for to Morrow I suppose it may have the royal assent on thursday. There is yet no certain account from the Mediterranean, but Wee hope the best because the French conceal it. I wish the first Article of London News in the General Evening Post were true, but our ships received much damage, and it is fear'd one of them, the Kingsale, founder'd at Sea, & I think two or three more are missing as yet; Wee have not any account how the French Fleet came off in the Storm that did this damage in the night between fryday and Saturday, the wind is now high.

I hear D[uke of] Beaufort is allready discharged, Lord B[arrymore] was to be examined to day. They had been in the mean time examining his papers, but I don't know what has been discover'd.

General Wade is ill which I am very sorry for, fearing he will not be able to go abroad. Lord Stair is to command here. I pray God . . .

107.

John Campbell to Pryse Campbell, 25 February 1744

Yesterday Mr. Pelham by the Kings order laid before the House[82] some Extracts of Letters[83] from the Duke of Newcastle to Mr. Thompson[84] our Agent at Paris & that Gentlemans Answers & the Affidavit of Ridley the Master of the Pacquet Boat between dover & Calais, by the letters it appears that the Duke of Newcastle directed Mr Thompson to acquaint the French Ministry that His Majestie had received advice of the pretenders eldest Son[85] being come to France that if it was so His Majestie made no doubt but the French King would according to the Faith of the Treatys subsisting between the two Crowns order that person immediately to depart his Dominions & do every thing else that His Majestie had by the Treaty's a right to expect. Mr. Thompson

---

[81] Edward Coke (1719–53), only son of Thomas Coke, 1st earl of Leicester; whig MP for Norfolk 1741–7 and Harwich 1747–53. A loyal supporter of Walpole.

[82] CJ, xxiv, 586–7.

[83] PH, xiii, 656–60, for the letters concerning the intended invasion of Britain by the Pretender and for Ridley's affidavit.

[84] Rev. Anthony Thompson, chargé d'affaires to France 1740–4. He was ordered to leave Paris on 17 Mar. 1744, without taking leave. British Diplomatic Representatives, 1689–1789, ed. D.B. Horn (Camden Society, 3rd ser., xlvi, 1932), 20.

[85] Charles Edward Stuart, 'Bonnie Prince Charlie' (1720–88), eldest son of the Old Pretender, James Francis Edward Stuart (1688–1766).

waited on Monsieur Amelot[86] to deliver this Message & for more exactness read to him the Duke of Newcastles letter, upon which M[onsieur] Amelot said Sir, Since you speak to me by order, I cannot give you any answer but by order also, I will therefore take the first opportunity to acquaint the King with your Message that I may be able to give you His Majestie's Answer. After this it was seven days, before Mr T[hompson] had any answer from Mr A[melot] who at length told him that Treatys were no longer binding on the one side than they were observed on the other, and that when the Court of England should give satisfaction upon the many Complaints made by France for the breach of those Treaty's on the part of England, then the King of France would be ready to explane himself upon this demand of the King of Great Britain. Mr. Thompsons account of this Answer was the Pacquet which was stopt at Calais and had not been here now but for the prudence of Hammond the Messenger who gave it privately to Ridley as soon as he came to Calais, and he hid it in the Pacquet Boat, where it could not be found by the French though the Boat was search'd by an officer with a File of Musqueteers. I told you in my last that the Messenger was seized just as he was going on board upon which the Pacquet Boat sail'd without him. The Information upon Oath of the Master of the Pacquet is much the same with what I told you in my last, he saw at Calais the Count de Saxe[87] natural son of the late King of Poles,[88] who is to command this Expedition, and he saw with him a tall slender young Man about 24 who had great respect paid him, and the French said was the Chevalier, he supposed the Pretenders eldest son, there was another young Man who he heard was his Brother,[89] he could not get a distinct view of the Young Chevalier's Face. Mr. Pelham explaned to us that the Complaints made by the French mention'd by Mr. Amelot, were for our stoping & searching French ships for Spanish effects, which they have from time to time complaned of ever since Wee were at War with Spain. This I observe is a plane proof that from the very first the [sic] took care to have a pretence for joining Spain against us whenever they should think fit. Mr. Pelham told us that our burning the Spanish Vessels in a French Harbor & our blocking up Toulon, though they seem more offensive have never been complaned of; he concluded with moveing for an Address to desire His Majestie to encrease his forces by Sea & Land in such proportion as he should judge proper and assureing His Majestie that Wee will make good any expence he may be at for the defence of his Sacred Person, and so for the safety of the Kingdom. Vernon who is much fitter for Bedlam than an Assembly of Gentlemen, made a long mad rant for leaveing out land Forces, of which his addled brain could conceive no possible occasion. Mr William Pitt Spoke handsomely for the Address, Sir J[ohn] Philipps was extreme [sic] he could not agree with him for whome he had the greatest respect, but he could not agree to this Address which he call'd a Vote of Credit. He could not put such trust in Ministers, but if an addition of Force was necessary Wee might go into the Committee of Supply & grant it, Sir J[ohn] had the same misfortune with his Friend Vernon to be Seconded by nobody, on the Contrary Lord Strange said much the same

---

[86] Jean-Jacques Amelot de Chaillou (1689–1749), French minister of foreign affairs 1737–44.

[87] Maurice, comte de Saxe (1696–1750), French general and later marshal and then grand marshal of France. He was chosen to command the land forces of the planned French invasion of Britain on behalf of the Old Pretender in 1744.

[88] August II the Strong (1670–1733), king of Poland 1709–33.

[89] Henry Benedict Stuart (1725–1807), cardinal and duke of York (in the jacobite peerage).

of him that he had said of Mr Pitt, & was for the Address; said he was as jealous of Ministers as his worthy Friend but found it necessary to trust on this occasion, for the evil of refuseing but be greater than what could arise even from their abuseing the trust for which they might be punish'd by Parliament. Mr. Waller spoke to the same effect. Then poor Sydenham who is I believe very sincere but very Mad, made a long speech which was scarcely heard for declareing War against France,[90] & nobody either second-ing or answering him the Question was put on the Address to which Sir J[ohn] P[hilipps] gave his single only negative.[91] Mr. Pelham desired the House might sit to day,[92] it being possible though he thought not probable some what might happen proper to be communicated to them.

The Duke of Newcastle laid the same Paper before the Lords[93] that his Brother [Henry Pelham] laid before the Commons & when they had been read said that as both Houses had lately Address'd and given His Majestie the fullest assurances &c he would make no Motion so they were going to call in Councill upon a private Cause, then Lord Orford rose up with all the appearance of extreme concern, beg'd pardon for giveing their Lordships a trouble he did not intend, and which he had allmost resolved never to give them as long as he lived but he could not forbear telling them he thought it would not become the Peers of Great Britain to receive such information with silence, and to go upon a private Cause, he beg'd they might make an Address to shew their affection to His Majestie & zeal for their Country on this occasion, in such a manner as might raise an english Spirit in the People against France. He spoke with great earnestness & concern, allmost tears, frequently beg'd their Lordships pardon for the trouble he gave them which he said was the overflowing of his heart, which he could not refrain. Indeed I can witness that he has for some time in the most private conversation express'd the same warm affectionate concern for the present Government & for his (I almost said ungratefull) Country. As soon as he sat down Lord B[ath] rose, as my informer thinks to second him, but the Duke of Newcastle riseing at the same time B[ath] sat down. The Duke appear'd somewhat hurt as if what Lord Orford said had been reproach upon him for not makeing a Motion, he excused himself but was ready to agree to Lord Orford's Motion, so without makeing more speaking the Lord Chancellor [Hardwicke] took pen and Ink & Lord Orford going to him they soon drew up a strong Address[94] which was unanimously agreed to & I suppose you will see it in Print. The Prince and Duke[95] were both in the House, the Prince sat by the Lord Chancellor & look'd over the Address as he drew it. The Lords Sit to day, if I hear any News at the House I will add it to my Letter after I come home. Colonel Cecill[96] who gave the Treasonable Pacquet to D[uke of] Beaufort which he sent by old Lord Barrymore to the late Duke

---

[90] It was France that finally declared war against Britain on 15 Mar. 1744.

[91] *PH*, xiii, 665–6, gives an account of the debate citing Philip Yorke's journal in which he wrote that only two in the Commons dissented against Pelham's address: Philipps and Admiral Vernon.

[92] A brief Saturday sitting was undertaken. *CJ*, xxiv, 588.

[93] *LJ*, xxvi, 320–2.

[94] *LJ*, xxvi, 322.

[95] The prince of Wales and the duke of Cumberland.

[96] William Cecil (1676–1745), of Northgate Hall, Wakefield, Yorkshire; jacobite conspirator and agent. He was arrested on 24 Feb. 1744 on charges of high treason and committed to the Tower three days later, to be released in May on £4,000 bail. *ODNB*.

of Argyll;[97] was taken up yesterday, so I hear was the famous Parson Carte,[98] & I heard search was makeing for a son of Lord Weymiss[99] who took the name of Chartres & is lately come from France. I hear a Roman catholic Gentleman of £4,000 per annum in Sussex is gone to Dunkirk.

I hear nothing at the House but that the last express brought word that Sir J[ohn] Norris was within a league of the French Fleet off the Coast of Kent. What effect the high Wind might have I cannot say. My Dearest I pray God . . .

Private.

I hear that Sir J[ohn] N[orris] desired to be employ'd on this occasion but insisted on the payment of £1,600 which he clamed upon some former reckoning, if this be true I think a man who could be capable of makeing a dirty Bargain for money in the present conjuncture ought not to have been employ'd but rejected with the last contempt, and the infamous reason publicly declared; I fear he is capable of it, I believe many are uneasy at his haveing so important a command in this great conjuncture, knowing him to be mean, selfish, surly, obstinate & not to be advised, besides many think him dilatory & all are not convinced of his intrepidity. If he behaves well he will gain & deserve a Coronet, if otherwise he will deserve[100]

108.
John Campbell to Pryse Campbell, 1 March 1744
Yesterday when it was moved to go into the Committee upon the Bill to suspend the Habeas Corpus for two Months,[101] Lord Barrington who had been out of Town when the Bill was brought in made a warm Speech against it, but concluded with moveing to put off the Committee for a week, he was Seconded by Admiral Vernon who made a mad raveing Speech as usual. Sir J[ohn] Philipps spoke on the same side very little was said on the other it being thought scarce worth while to answer them. However they divided on Lord Bar[r]ingtons motion ay's 83 noes 181.[102] Mr William Pitt, Mr Lyttelton, Mr Prowse, Mr Shuttleworth[103] & one who I think is his Son in Law,[104] went out for sometime before the division to avoid voteing. Haveing carried that question Wee immediately went into the Committee,[105] & this morning the Bill was read the

---

[97] John Campbell, 2nd duke of Argyll, died in Oct. 1743.

[98] Rev. Thomas Carte (1686–1754), historian and jacobite. In 1722 he was accused of high treason and fled to France. Pardoned in 1728, thanks to the influence of Queen Caroline, he later alienated his patrons by writing in his *General History of England* that the king's evil would be cured by the Pretender. A large collection of documents collected by Carte are held in the Bodleian Library.

[99] James Wemyss (1699–1756), 5th earl of Wemyss; his son was Francis Wemyss Charteris (1723–1808), 7th earl 1787–1808.

[100] Letter ends.

[101] *CJ*, xxiv, 594.

[102] *CJ*, xxiv, 594.

[103] Richard Shuttleworth (1683–1749), tory MP for Lancashire 1705–49 and prominent jacobite, though Egmont thought he was reconciling himself to destroying the jacobites towards the end of his life. He was Father of the House 1748–9. *HPC, 1715–54*, ii, 424.

[104] John Crewe (1709–52), of Madeley, Staffordshire and Crewe Hall, Cheshire; tory MP for Cheshire 1734–52.

[105] Of the whole House.

third time & pass'd without any farther opposition when it came to the House of Lords it was immediately read three times & pass'd without the least contradiction.

The account of Admiral Matthews in the General Evening Post[106] finds credit it came yesterday morning in a letter writ in arabic from a Jew at Marseilles to another who I think is his Brother at London. The account of Sir J[ohn] Norris's fleet is better than was expected. The last account of the French Fleet that I heard, the [*sic*] were at Torbay. I was to day with Lord Orford & wish him joy of haveing been to wait on His Royal Highness who he told me was very civil to him. There is one Captain Morris[107] who affirms that in December last he say [*sic*] Count Saxe in St. James Park about 8 in the morning that he immediatly knew his face but did not on the Suddain recollect who it was but soon after meeting him in Spring Garden[108] he knew him paid his respects to him, the Count own'd himself, call'd the Captain by his name, & told him if he had any commands to Paris he should set out early the next morning. It seems odd that a Person of that rank should be here incognito & yet appear in St. James Park, but Captain Morris is extremely positive in the thing & did not seem to discover it to make a merit but to mention it accidentally upon hearing Count Saxe named to command this Invasion. A person who heard him told Lord Orford and after at his Lordships desire brought the Captain to him, and from Lord Orford I had the Story. If their Second meeting was also so early as 8 o'Clock the Count might think himself private, for few who can be supposed to know him walk there so early, but this Captain happen'd I think, to be a Prisoner at Philipsburgh[109] after the Action at Dettingen and there saw Count Saxe.

I pray God . . .

109.

John Campbell to Pryse Campbell, 3 March 1744

I sincerely assure you that your last letter made me very happy by telling me that my company is most agreeable to you. I still expect the pleasure of seeing you here this Spring, though I am unhappily prevented sending for you so soon as I intended, but I believe the Town is allready much healthy than it was, and when Mr. Grahame approves it I shall be very glad to send you Sailing Orders. I believe I must stay to have your judgement in buying me a Horse. I am very glad Mr. Hooke has seen a happy end to his Lawsuit.[110] They are expensive, vexatious, & hazardous things. I writ to congratulate him upon it. My Dearest it is a great pleasure to me to comply with a request of yours and I am satisfied from the honesty of your heart, the sweetness of your temper, and the goodsense God has bless'd you with, that your requests will allways be agreeable to me.

---

[106] *General Evening Post*, 1 Mar. 1744, referring to what became known as the battle of Toulon which, despite the news reports of victory, ended in failure for the British who, on 11 Feb., had allowed combined French and Spanish forces to escape a blockade of that port.

[107] Possibly Bezaleel Morrice (1678–1749), writer and sea captain. *ODNB*.

[108] Near the Mall, London.

[109] In Germany.

[110] Against Priscilla and Dorothea Gwynn regarding the ownership of the Bangeston estate, Pembrokeshire. CRO, Cawdor/Campbell box 20/281.

The Jews letter was in the Spanish language only writ in arabic Characters, the [sic] talk'd yesterday of Sir J[ohn] Eyles[111] haveing received a letter hid in a bale of silk confirming the Jews account & saying that thirty of the Enemies Ships were destroy'd & fourteen of ours. They say the Master of the Mahone Pacquet lately arrived heard the fireing and saw 20 Ships steering Eastward which did not Fire, they are supposed to be the Spanish Transports for Italy who took, it should seem, opportunity to slip away dureing the Battle. That I fear if true is a bad matter but all these things are uncertain, but Wee draw great hopes from the French silence, Lord Gage endeavors to destroy them by assureing us the French know no more than Wee do, that does not seem to me very probable, but his Lordships accounts are, I think allways (to be sure quite contrary to his wishes) partial to the French. I don't know if there is anything new to day, the House did not sit & I have been no where. I am my Dearest with the most Faithfull & tender affection . . .

Haycock is very thankfull for your kind remembrance & wishes much to see you here. You & he may choose Paper to hand [sic] your dressingroom when you are here.

All the Ships under Sir John Norris have at length appear'd viz the Princess Royal that was lost, the Kingsale that founder'd and the Aldborough that was taken by the French, and I hope they are not so much damaged as was at first apprehended.[112]

110.
John Campbell to Pryse Campbell, 6 March 1744
Notwithstanding what you see in the General Evening Post, there is no express from Admiral Matthews, nor can one be expected in less than eight days, as I hear, all the account Wee have is what came yesterday or this morning from Mr. Thompson. It is the account sent from Spain to France, they collect from it that the Spaniards engaged Admiral Matthews, that one of their great Ships was taken & another I think destroy'd, that the French did not support the Spaniards, I think they pretend they could not see their Signal, that both the combined Fleets fled to the Coast of Spain & the English would have the advantage in sailing being just come clean out of Port. The French I think were got to Alicant,[113] & some of the Spanish, the rest were dispersed they hoped they would not fall into the hands of the English. It is believed the French were guilty of the Like treachery to the Spaniards, that the [sic] shew'd to the English in one of King Charles the 2[n]d Dutch Wars, and to the Dutch I think in the other, and lately by land to the King of Prussia[114] when they stood by & saw him beat by the Queen of Hungary's Forces. 'Tis said that 10 or 12 of the French Transports & one of their Men of War, were drove on Shoar in the Storm, that all their Men were relanded & it was thought the design'd Invasion laid aside for the present. Yesterday, this rested on the report of the Pacquet Boat from Calais this afternoon I heard that the loss of the French Transports had been confirm'd by an account from Sir J[ohn] Norris but I am not sure of that. There is a loud cry against Sir J[ohn] N[orris] great numbers affirming that no other Officer would have let the French Fleet off

---

[111] Sir John Eyles (1683–1745), of Gidea Hall, Essex; MP for Chippenham 1713–27 and London 1727–34. He was a rich London mercer and wool stapler. He became lord mayor of London in 1726.

[112] The *Daily Advertiser*, 2 Mar. 1744, reported that ships under Norris were safely in the Downs. However, the *Kingsale* is not mentioned.

[113] Alicante, Spain.

[114] Frederick II 'the Great' (1712–86), king of Prussia 1740–86. By invading Silesia in 1740 he was responsible for embroiling Europe and the Americas in what has become known as the War of the Austrian Succession.

Dungeness escape. I would not be too hasty to condemn him, but appearance's seem to be against him; I have long thought that avarice, insolence and obstinacy were the great ingredients of his composition. How happy, how glorious would it have been for us if those 14 ships had been taken, they slipt their Anchors & went off when the wind shifted at 8 at night, it did not blow a storm till one in the morning; Sir J[ohn] [Norris] staid till he was blown from his Anchors & did not know the French were gone till 8 the next morning. They say never any Fleet lost so many Cables and Anchors; the [*sic*] suffer'd so much by endeavoring to stay there. The French by going out to sea had little damage. How justly I know not, but most people are fill'd with indignation against, & contempt for Sir J[ohn] N[orris] some of the Admiralty treat him with as little ceremony or regard as he treated them. It is said he insisted upon an independent absolute power over all the ships in the Channel, the Admiralty think much inconvenience has proceded from the Power over all the Ships being taken from them, and it seems pretty plane Wee are not much the better for its being given to Sir J[ohn] N[orris]. I must do the Admiralty the justice to say that the accusations against them were infamously false for it appears they had a Noble Fleet perfectly complete immediately. I pray God . . .

You will be cautious of speaking too freely as from me of Sir J[ohn] N[orris].

Poor Legge is in a good deal of uneasiness, the Medway which is commanded by his Brother[115] being the only ship that has not been heard of since the Storm. Last night was pretty stormy. I Hope Sir J[ohn] N[orris] did not take the opportunity to loose more Anchors Cables &c.

Mr. Keppel[116] enquired after you the other day at Court which I Took very Kindly.

In the inclosed List the Yellow voted for the Hanover Troops, the red against, the black were neuter.[117]

111.
John Campbell to Pryse Campbell, 10 March 1744
I heartily thank you for your last kind letter, your waiting with so much patience and cheerfullness, for orders to come to Town, is a proof of your good sense, good nature and affection to me. I must confess you are more reasonable than I in not being affraid. I was never affraid of the smallpox for myself before I had it, nor was I in any concern when I was taken ill of it, more than for any other disorder. But my tenderness for you will sometimes excede the bounds of reason, though I will endeavor to make it as little troublesome to you as I can; and I know your kindness will make you bear some little inconvenience for my ease.

I can tell you no News but that Legge was yesterday in great joy, the Medway being safe arrived at St Helens. Wee sat till after seven last night on Sir Charles Gilmours Election[118] & then voted him duely elected without a Division, the Petition was only for a void Election on account of some little informalities, it was not denied that he had a fair majority of good Votes, & had this Election been made void he would have been

---

[115] Edward Legge (c.1710–47) was the captain of the *Medway* from Nov. 1743 until Mar. 1744. He was elected MP for Portsmouth in Dec. 1747, but had died in September whilst on duty in the West Indies.

[116] George Keppel (1724–72), MP for Chichester 1746–54. Styled Viscount Bury until 1754, when he succeeded his father as 3rd earl of Albemarle. He captured Havana, in 1762, near the end of the Seven Years War.

[117] List not extant.

[118] *CJ*, xxiv, 607.

I suppose elected again without difficulty so it was not worth while for the opposition to be very earnest in it, and they had a very slender presence for it. Sir C[harles] Gilmour & some of his Friends wanted to have the Petition voted frivolous & vexatious, but our Friends persuaded them not to attempt it; it was not very modest for them to expect Wee should do a thing for one of our new Allies which I never knew done for one of the old Trojans,[119] while Troy stood. Had such a question been moved I and I believe, many more who attended for Sir C[harles] G[ilmour] so far as to support his Election, should have voted against it. I am told if the Duke of Argyll had not assisted with his Interest in the Country, Sir Charles could not have been chose by his Patron Secretary Tweedledum.[120] It would have been unreasonable to void the Election but it was much against the grain with many of our Friends to attend for Sir Charles, he and his Friends attended Jack Wynne [John Wynn] and therefore on Mr. Winningtons account and desire I attended, otherwise seeing Sir Charles's Friends, M[arcus] Antonius [Bath] & Tweedledum at the bottom of the House almost turn'd my Stomach.

I have as yet but very little faith in or expectation from our Mines[121] though I heartily wish they may prove good for your sake, I confess in [sic] often grieves me to think how great a Debt I fear I must leave upon your Estate, which will make you in difficult Circumstances, unless good fortune, or your own good Management makes them easy; I Wish on your account I could be as good a Manager as my Father[122] was, who dureing the short time he lived paid part of the Family Debt, with a moderate Income and a growing Family. Had it pleased God to continue his life instead of his Fathers[123] I should most probably had a free & plentifull fortune, and then I should have been much to blame if I had not left it so to you, as it is, I cannot alltogather excuse myself, but I believe you are satisfied of my good intentions towards you, and therefore will think kindly & candidly of me, and forgive my unskillfull or negligent management, more easily than I forgive myself. Give my Love to your Mama. I am very sorry she is so much trouble'd with the headach. My Love & Blessing to My Dear little Ally and your Sisters. I hope it may not be long before I shall think my self at liberty to send for you, I long very much for your Company. I pray God . . .

I thank Val for his journal. I wish I had kept one as I did intend, to compare with it but first the hurry of busyness prevented & then I forgot it.

Pray give R[oger] Evans the inclosed Voucher for £363 which I forgot to inclose in my letter to him.

112.
John Campbell to Pryse Campbell, 13 March 1744
I have very little news, though our expectations were mightily raised about the time I went to the House to day, by a Person arriveing express from Turin. What he brings is

[119] The old corps whigs.

[120] Lord Tweeddale? Tweedledum: a high-pitched musical sound or combined with other words such as tweedledee to denote an insignificant difference between two arguments. First usage in 1725. *OED*. It could refer to Tweeddale having a high-pitched voice, or to his propensity for scheming.

[121] In 1717 the Ystradffin estate, north-east Carmarthenshire, was purchased by Campbell, principally for the lead mines at Rhandirmwyn. By the 1780s the mines were making the Campbells around £6,000 p.a.

[122] Alexander Campbell who died in 1697. See Introduction.

[123] Hugh Campbell (c.1639–1716), of Cawdor. See Introduction.

the Account given by the Captain of an english Man of War that put into Nice viz that Admiral Matthews attack'd the Spanish fleet very briskly, and order'd Rowley[124] to engage the French who appeard to assist them. The French soon thought fit to retire, and the Spaniards who behaved well being left by the French were obliged to run one Spanish Ship the Poder (I think of 70 Guns) was destroy'd, Admiral Matthews slightly wounded by a Splinter, Captain Cornwall[125] & one of his Lieutenants kill'd. Our Fleet persued the French & Spaniards, but what became of them, Wee must wait some time to know, I suppose by Sea from Mr. Matthews. I wish the Queen of Spain[126] may be convinced of the French treachery & shew resentment like her self.

It is believ'd that Count Saxe being put in to Calais after the Storms went from thence to Paris, but whether he is to return & how the French design goes on I know not, neither can I tell anything of the most serene & fortunate Sir J[ohn] Norris. I heard that he cryed & stampt like a Madman when he found the French had escaped him; æstuat ingens.

Imo in corde pudor, mixtoque Insania luctu.[127]

I can't answer for the truth of the Conversation between the States [General] & the Abbe de la Ville,[128] but I believe anybody that should doubt of the French design against Britain, at the Hague would be thought Mad.

I inclose the Advertisement refer'd to in Sir Thomas Deveils[129] (he was knighted this day) long Article, as the Advertisement was repeted for a week together it is amazeing to me no better care was taken to prevent the disorder,[130] I can only suppose Octavius [Carteret] got drunk and forgot it. They might, I think most easily have prevented it, and sure all wise men would rather prevent Crimes than punish them.

Wee have a strong very cold N[orth] E[ast] Wind, I hope my Dearest you are carefull of your self. I would not have you neglect the use of the flesh brush for what opens the pores & promotes circulations must help your growth both in size & strength and conduce so your health.

My Love & blessing to your Brothers & Sisters. I pray god . . .

I send you a Pamphlet which though not so correct as I could wish it contains a good deal of honest Truth.

---

[124] William Rowley (c.1690–1768), of Tendring Hall, Suffolk; MP for Taunton 1750–54 and Portsmouth 1754–61. He joined the navy in 1704 under Captain, later Admiral Sir John Norris. Rowley became rear admiral in 1743, vice admiral in 1744 and admiral in 1747; lord of the admiralty 1751–7; admiral of the fleet 1762.

[125] James Cornewall (1698–1744), MP for Weobley 1732–4 and 1737–41. He was made a captain in the navy in 1724.

[126] Elizabeth Farnese (1692–1766), consort queen of Spain to Philip V. She had great influence on Spanish foreign policy.

[127] Virgil, *Aeneid*, xii, 666–7: 'Rage, boiling from the bottom of his breast, And sorrow mix'd with shame' (John Dryden's translation).

[128] Jean Ignace de la Ville (?1699–1774), French ecclesiast and diplomat. He occupied seat 26 of the Acadámie Française 1746–74. De la Ville wrote two memorials to the states general which together with the king's declaration were published in London in 1747.

[129] Sir Thomas De Veil (1684–1746) was a leading London magistrate whose zeal for prosecuting crime in the metropolis earned him a knighthood in 1744. His house in Bow Street was used as a court and was occupied by Henry Fielding the novelist, who established the Bow Street Runners there in 1749.

[130] The advertisement referred to is probably one for the sale of an unstamped newspaper. De Veil committed Maybella Smith and Frances Bowles to Clerkenwell Brideswell for selling this. *Penny London Morning Advertiser*, 14 Mar. 1744.

113.

John Campbell to Pryse Campbell, 17 March 1744

You very rightly judge that I neither expect nor desire a formal letter from you, that you writ the 11th inst[ant] if perfectly wellcome and agreable to me. The weather here is much the same as you describe it, only you perhaps are a little more exposed to it than Wee are in the Town. I am however at this instant so sensible of the Cold that I write, with my table close to the Fire, in my dressingroom from the East Wind makes my Study Smoaky as well as cold, & I have been driven out of it for about a week past. I am however very glad I can tell you that Mr. Thomas Grahame who has been with me this Morning tells me the Town is so healthy that he thinks it a very proper time for me to send for you, and you may be sure that I shall be exceding glad to have your Company now that I think it quite safe. I believe you can't decently begin your journey before Easter Monday, I suppose if the weather is good you will hardly defer it longer; I beg of you my dearest to be very carefull of your self, to ride carefully & not hard and not to expose your self to bad weather. Consider how dear you are to me, what concern the least accident befalling you would give me and therefore have fears for my sake that perhaps you would not have for your self. You will let me hear from you on the road when you have opportunity; you have not told me how you liked your great Coat & oil'd hood. I think the latter will be very usefull to keep your neck dry if rain comes upon you, indeed I would not have you ride in Wet more than need must, and if your Feet or any part is wet I beg of you to shift them dry, as soon as ever you come into a house. Pray order Val to take care that your room & bed are well air'd. I believe it will be the better that you have taken somewhat to cool your blood before your journey as I suppose you have by what your Mama told me of the Drs. desire.

Yesterday there came an account which I hope is authentic, that Prince Lobkowitz[131] come up to the Spanish Army in Italy, though they were said to be so strongly intrench'd they did not think fit to defend their lines, but made a hasty retreat towards the Kingdom of Naples. 500 threw down their Arms and were made Prisoners. I doubt whether the Spanish Army will be very wellcome ghests to the Neopolitans, & I fancy H[is] M[ajesty] of the Two Sicily's[132] will be in some perplexity.

Yesterday Mr. R[ichard] Greenville moved that the Account of the extraordinary charges of the Troops in British pay, which served in Flanders & Germany for the years 1742 & 1743, incurr'd, and not provided for by Parliament, might be refer'd to a select Committee. The Debate was chiefly managed on one side by Mr. R[ichard] & George Grenville, Mr Pitt & Mr Hume Campbell, & on the other by Mr Pelham, Sir William Yonge, Mr Winnington & Mr H[enry] Fox. A little after seven Wee divided on the Question, Ay's 115 No's 173.[133] Wee Sit to day to go into the Committee, to consider of the state of the linnen Manufacture and I expect to stay till 8 o'Clock at night or so.[134]

---

[131] Johann Georg Christian, Fürst von Lobkowitz (1685–1755), Austrian field marshal. He was governor of the Duchy of Milan 1743–5, and imperial commander in Italy. He lost the battle of Velletri (1744) against the Spanish-aligned kingdom of Naples.

[132] The duke of Parma (1716–88) conquered Naples and Sicily and from 1735–59 ruled as King Charles. In 1759 he became Charles III of Spain.

[133] *CJ*, xxiv, 621.

[134] *CJ*, xxiv, 622. A Saturday sitting, this was the only item discussed.

My Love & Blessing to your Brothers & Sisters. I must repete my earnest entreaties that you will be carefull of your self and I pray God . . .

You see my Dearest I leave the manner of your journey to your own discretion which I thank God I have great trust in.

114.
John Campbell to Pryse Campbell, 20 March 1744

Yesterday being the day for the Committee of Supply, to vote the Estimates which I told you they moved to refer to a Select Committee; before the order of the day was read Mr. Lyttelton made a fine tragic Speech which he ended with this Motion. That the issueing & paying £40,000 to the Duke of Arembery[135] to put the Austria Troops in Motion, was a dangerous Misapplication of public money & destructive of the privileges of this House.[136] Mr. Pelham said it was by no means a proper time either to censure or approve that payment, the regular way was to refer the Estimate to the Committee of Supply where the question might be fully discuss'd, and the money either granted or refused, and even though it was granted, if it appear'd to have been wrong to pay it, the House might censure it, he therefore moved the previous question in order to go first into the Committee. This was debated till after 7 at night, & then divideing whether Mr. Lytteltons question should be now put it was carried in the negative by 232 against 144.[137] Wee were desired to stay & go into the Committee, which otherwise the Opposition might put off the Committee from time to time by Starting questions; they exclamed much against going into the Committee so late, though when they had the upper hand they have moved questions of importance much later, so Wee divided again upon refering the Estimate to the Committee Ay's 207 No's 146.[138] Then after some debate just when the question was ready to be put on the Estimate, in the Committee the [*sic*] moved for Mr. Fane to leave the Chair[139] & divided upon it Ay's 111 No's 182.[140] Then the money on the Estimate was voted without farther debate or division, and the House rose about 5 minutes before twelve at night. The resolution is to be reported to day & I suppose will be debated again. The chief speakers were Mr. Lyttelton, Mr William Pitt, Mr R[ichard] & Mr. George Grenville, Mr. Dodington, Mr. Waller, Mr. Hume Campbell on the one side & Mr. Pelham, Sir William Yonge, Mr Winnington, Mr H[enry] Fox on the other.

My Dearest I pray God . . .

Haycock sends his duty & hopes you will pardon his not writeing as he had only to wish you a good journey. He is mighty glad you are to be here so soon. If you come up alone would you have him meet you on the road at Gloster or elsewhere.

---

[135] Leopold Philippe d'Arenberg (1690–1754), 4th duke of Arenberg, Austrian field marshal. He led the Austrian army in the Battle of Dettingen on 27 June 1743.

[136] *PH*, xiii, 677–80, for the debate.

[137] *CJ*, xxiv, 623.

[138] *CJ*, xxiv, 624.

[139] It was routine procedure for the chairman of any committee to vacate his chair before a debate pertinent to the committee ensued. Fane was the chairman of the committee of supply.

[140] *PH*, xiii, 680, states that the motion was rejected by a majority of 73, but does not give voting figures.

By good luck I came home to night before eight so can add what was done to day. Lord Hillsborough moved to Address for all letters memorials &c relateing to the £40,000 paid to the Duke of Arembery.[141] His Lordship took care to say some Spitefull things but his Motion was not opposed. Then Mr. Hume Campbell in a long Speech moved to recommitt the resolution of last night he was seconded by Lord Guernsey and Supported by Mr Pitt, Mr Lyttelton, & Mr. Waller answer'd by Sir William Yonge & Mr Pelham. Their were a few other Speechs the Division was Ay's 123 No's 196.[142] Pray tell your Mama Lord Carteret is married this Night to Lady Sophia Fermor.[143]

115.
John Campbell to Pryse Campbell, 9 December 1744

What I chose not to write by the Post was to tell you that Macheath[144] had by his arts & flattery gain'd so far upon Father & Son[145] that it was with the utmost reluctance he was parted with, & I believe he had commission to offer allmost any terms to any party that would support him, but he could find none, if he could have had any encouragement he had stood his ground & Macduff[146] been dismiss'd. I am sorry to say that the partiality to Macheath has been shewn too publicly since his demission[147] while Macduff stood by quite neglected, I hope that behavior will not last, for if it does it must have bad consequences. Macheath has spared no flattery to the Old Coachman[148] but he was not to be catch'd; his Son in Law[149] indeed was, and would wisely and honestly have help'd Macheath to catch his father in Law, I really believe his behavior did occasion some little jealousy in his Father in Law's old Friends, which the Old Gent took a little unkindly for he, in my opinion justly thought his Friends Should have known him better no doubt Macheath did his best to make it be thought the Old Coachman was inclined to his interest, but they should have known the one too well to doubt him & the other too well to give credit to him. But their not writeing

[141] *CJ*, xxiv, 628.

[142] *CJ*, xxiv, 628.

[143] Lady Sophia Fermor (1721–45), daughter of Lord Pomfret. They were actually married on 14 Apr. 1744, the marriage being delayed because Sophia was suffering from scarlet fever.

[144] Granville. Macheath is the leader of a gang of thieves in John Gay's *The Beggar's Opera* which was first performed in 1728, partly as a satire upon Walpole's administration. In the play Macheath, the leader of a gang of thieves, marries Polly the young daughter of Mr Peachum.

[145] King and prince of Wales.

[146] Henry Pelham? Macduff is one of the main players in Shakespeare's *Macbeth*. Both *The Beggar's Opera* and *Macbeth* were being staged in London during Dec. 1744.

[147] Carteret had resigned as northern secretary on 24 Nov. 1744.

[148] The Old Coachman is Sir Robert Walpole. A ballad published in 1742 by Charles Hanbury-Williams tells the tale of Lords Bath and Carteret being driven away from the duke of Newcastle's residence by a coachman who, in a drunken state, overturns the coach. Another passenger then helps the two peers, who were in a mire, to reach their destination – St James's Palace, the centre of power. The other passenger is the old coachman. The implication is that it was thanks to Walpole that Bath and Carteret came to the centre of power, and that although no longer chief minister, 'That Orford, old coachman, still governs the reins'. The overturned coach is a reference to a print called 'The Motion' (a pro-Walpole print published after the failed motion of Sandys to have the prime minister removed from office in Feb. 1741/2) which shows an out-of-control coach, driven by the duke of Argyll, with Bubb Dodington between his legs in the form of a spaniel, hurtling towards the treasury building in Whitehall with Carteret a passenger and the earl of Chesterfield riding postilion. P. Langford, *Walpole and the Robinocracy* (Cambridge, 1986).

[149] George Cholmondeley, 3rd Earl Cholmondeley, who had married Walpole's daughter Mary in 1723.

anything to the Old Coachman of what was in agitation shew'd they had doubts & was I think not kind & not right. His Master would most gladly have had his help to save Macheath, but he had the good fortune to avoid seeing him till it was over, & has not yet been with him in private. His Son in Law sent for him by his Masters order, & as soon as the Messenger was gone Macheath publish'd it to all the World, the Son in Law did not write the old Gent word what was about, which was base, however his own good sense prevented his being Caught.

116.

John Campbell to Pryse Campbell, 13 December 1744

Though I hope your foot is perfectly well before this time, yet you must give me leave on this occasion to renew my most earnest entreaties that you will at all times be carefull of your self, and remember that the happiness & comfort of your tender Father & most Faithfull Friend depend on you; and on your wellfare. Pray my dearest be allways carefull in steep places, you know of how very bad consequence Sprains sometimes are, even never to be recover'd; the Duke of Argyll some years ago Sprain'd his ancle getting hastily out of a Coach & steping in a kennel,[150] he has been lame ever since & you might observe, that leg is wasted & grown much less than the other. I don't know but you might do well when the swelling is quite gone to use the receipt[151] I recommended to Miss Lloyd & Colonel Murray[152] to me, viz a large handfull of bay salt & a pound of Castile Soap dissolved in as much hot water as in a pan, or some such thing, will cover your ancle, to put your foot into it every night hot & hold it there a Quarter of an hour or more, if the water is as hot as conveniently it may be, when you put in your foot it will retane a good degree of warmth so long, I thought it strengthened my foot after the last Sprain.

I do not know whether anything is yet Settled, only it seems past doubt that the Duke of Bedford is to be at the head of the Admiralty & Lord Sandwich one of the board, I hear his G[race] will not accept before he has seen some of his Friends taken care of, if so the Admiralty will not, as was expected, be the first thing declared; but surely all things of consequence must be declared before Christmas which draws very near. I fear MacHeath makes things go very heavily, he may do mischief, but he will surely feel his full share of it, for if he continues to obstruct, and to triumph in the strength his vile arts have procured he will certainly raise a Spirit against him in the House of Commons which he will not be able to resist, or pacify. How different is his behavior from that of the good old Coachman three years ago. One acted like an honest Friend to his K[in]g & C[ountr]y the other acts like an interested K[ing] abandon'd to all sense of honor, honesty or shame. I hear'd a bon mot of Lord Cobham which pleases me; he was talking with the Duke of Newcastle that Sir J[ohn] N[orris] must not by any means be at the head of the Admiralty. The Duke said what can Wee give him then to make him easy, Cobby [Lord Cobham] replied Give him a guinea. I believe I am truely inform'd

---

[150] The surface drain of a street. *OED*.

[151] Recipe.

[152] This could be Lord John Murray (1711–87), of Pitnacree, Perth and Banner Cross, Yorkshire; MP for Perthshire 1734–61. He was made colonel in 1743.

that Leonidas[153] writ circular letters to call a meeting of Citizens to consider of proper persons to be recommended for the Admiralty. He was somewhat vex'd to see a much thinner meeting than he expected, However he made them a fine harangue which ended with proposeing the Duke of Bedford & Lord Sandwich. He had a Friend ready prepared to applaud his Speech and Second his motion, but then another whose name I have forgot Stood up & said he thought it was a thing highly improper & impertinent for that company to talk upon them, & desired that at least his name might be minuted as protesting against it. It is said all the rest of the Company agreed with the last Speaker & so they broke up, this was doubtless the last degree of insolence & impertinence in Leonidas yet as far as it concern'd the Noble persons I think they deserved it, as the proper reward of their absurd, dirty patriotism.

As to my being in the Treasury[154] I have had not the least hint of any such thing from Mr. Pelham or the Duke of Newcastle and therefore as the time draws so near, I believe no such thing is thought of; if it were I have too good an opinion of Mr. B[arlow] of L[awrenny] to think him capable of what Mr M[aynard] charges him with. If my great Relations[155] do not design anything for me upon this occasion, it cannot indeed be said they think kindly of me; but I think it must be own'd they have a good opinion of me.

I was this morning with Mr Corbett, he told me that two Sloops (I think they were) went to bring home the Officers and men of the Northumberland, the men on board one of them rose & instead of comeing to the Port where they were order'd, run her on Shoar in some place & made their escape into the Country to avoid being press'd. The other ship is not yet come. My Dearest I pray God . . .

117.
John Campbell to Pryse Campbell, 15 December 1744
I am very glad my letters are agreeable to you, I assure you they cannot express half the kindness of my heart. The greatest happyness I desire in this World is to have your love and that both my Company & Correspondence may be agreeable to you. I was very glad to hear your foot continued mending it is very kind in you to let me have a constant account of him from your own hand. I hope you will be as much as possible on your guard against such accidents for the future. I pray God protect and preserve you.

I have not heard a word of news since my last, but Mr. Maynard told me that Lord Cobham disowns the story of the guinea, 'tis however a very good one and I don't like it the worse for his not being the Author but I wish the Duke of Newcastle may know what everybody thinks of his great Admiral.

I dined today with my good neighbor the Bishop of Llandaffe who kindly remember all my Family, he received a letter from Glamorganshire that told him Admiral Matthews was like to carry it.[156] Mr. Morgan of Ruperra[157] is a most active & indefatigable Solicitor for

---

[153] Richard Glover.

[154] Campbell did not become a lord of the treasury until the second Pelham ministry, 1746–54. See Introduction.

[155] That is, Newcastle and Pelham, who were related by marriage to Campbell. See Introduction.

[156] Admiral Thomas Mathews stood in the Jan. 1745 election for Glamorgan, which he won.

[157] Thomas Morgan (1702–69), of Ruperra, Glamorganshire; whig MP for Brecon 1723–34, Monmouthshire 1734–47 and Breconshire 1747–69.

the Whig Interest. I do not know that he has any other attachment to Mr. Matthews, who has not the happiest manner to gain upon people's affections.

To be sure it was quite a blunder in the Jury to give the whole Quay[158] to Mr. Allen,[159] Mr. Wogan[160] of Norfolks part haveing never been disputed. My Dearest I pray God . . .

Haycock desires his duty to you & thanks for your kind remembrance of him. He was very sorry for the accident of your foot. He desires me to tell you he has got a black dog for you if you like to have it. 'tis a Spaniel as high as Pompey but not so thick.

118.

John Campbell to Pryse Campbell, 18 December 1744

I can't help being a little uneasy, to hear there was yet a little swelling upon your Ancle, and that there was one place still sore when press'd by a finger. I should be much more uneasy if your Mama was not so kind to tell me the exact truth and to assure me nothing that concerns you shall ever be conceal'd from me. I hope my Dearest you are very carefull of it.

As to public matters I was much better pleased some days ago than I am now. I understood that Pitt & one or two of his Cousins were to have some considerate things, and that the Tories were to have some places of profit but of no power or great rank, but I little dream'd of what I now hear that Bubb [Dodington] is to be Treasurer of the Navy & Waller Cofferer & that Pitt accepts nothing i.e. keeps himself quite at liberty to act what part he pleases. Must it not be very grating to me & some others to see ourselves quite neglected & such put into the most honorable and profitable Posts. What can be a greater insult on the old Trojans than to let Bubb [Dodington] who so lately and basely deserted, & then impudently abused them in so high a station to look down & laugh at us honest Fools; is this what the Duke of Newcastle call'd to me standing upon the Bottom of their old Friends & only takeing some help from others, is it not rather accepting a partnership with I don't know who and standing upon what bottom they please to let you. If it is said a better bargain could not be made, I should be apt to answer how could you have made a worse, I understand all the New Courtiers that came in when Lord Orford went out are to go out again, and their places to be entirely fill'd by Patriots or Tories without McDuff[161] adding one more of his old Friends. I hoped upon his getting rid of Macheath, he was to be at the head & a number of the opposition to come in to him, but I wish he has not exchanged one Macheath for another, and indeed if Pitt does not come in Macduff seems to have paid a mighty price without getting the best part of the purchase. When I look upon their Successors, I feel a sort of respect & esteme for Lord S[tair] & Sir J[ohn] Rushlight which I never had before, or ever thought it possible I could have. I hear Sir [John] Philipps is to have a place but I know not what, but I am pretty sure it is so intended. Sir John Broadbottom,[162] I'm told is to be master

---

[158] Creswell quay, south Pembrokeshire – from which John Allen and other coal owners exported coal to London.

[159] John Allen (*d.* 1752), of Cresselly, Pembrokeshire.

[160] John Wogan (1713–75), of Gawdy Hall, Norfolk and Boulston, Pembrokeshire.

[161] Henry Pelham?

[162] William Richard Chetwynd (1684–1770), 3rd Viscount Chetwynd. Entered parliament as a whig but from 1734 was counted as opposition. MP for Stafford 1715–22 and 1734–70, and Plymouth 1722–7. A lord of the admiralty 1717–27; master of the mint 1744–69, with which lucrative appointment he became a government supporter, and undersecretary of state 1745–8.

of the Mint & Mr. Arundel[163] to go into the Treasury. I was glad when I first heard Sir John was to be no higher, not suspecting that B[ubb Dodington] & W[innington] would be set so far above him, some talk since of Mr Broadbottom haveing a staff, but really if the Treasury, the Navy & the Cofferers Place, are to be filld, I don't much care how any other place's are disposed of; I hear the lank lean long Orator[164] is to come into the Treasury, can that be pleasant to Macduff, had he not much better keep Nurse Gybbon.[165] If he is forced to comply with all this, how is his condition mended. The Admiralty List on sunday was Duke of Bedford, Earl of Sandwich, Lord Vere,[166] Lord Baltimore, H[enry] Legge, Chetwind, & Anson[167] but as it is not yet declared it may possibly be alter'd. I heard Lord Gower was to be L[ord] P[rivy] S[eal].[168] & Lord Cholmondley to have Harry Veres[169] Place,[170] a little time will shew. I wish it ends well, the present appearance is not very pleasing to me, nor to some others. I saw the old Coachman yesterday I thought he look'd better than when I saw him before. He declares he has no knowledge or participation of what is doing, and I believe would be sorry any one should think he had a hand in preferring his Cousin or Bubb [Dodington] & W[innington]. I had a short private conversation to day with Winnington; he does not like it, he indeed thinks they had better not have removed Macheath. I can't yet go so far as that, but I am apt to agree with him in thinking they had better have try'd to go on without a farther change, & trusted for a session the People who came in with Macheath, than have made such a bargain as seems to be now concluded, for Wee think that if those People had deserted, Wee might then have made as good a bargain at least, for the old corps are too numerous to be despised. No Minister can in this Parliament do without them and I doubt whether the Cobhamites could find their account in calling a new one. Winnington and I perfectly agreed in concludeing that Wee must endeavor to make the best of it, and that the best seems to be very bad. In truth till within these two days I hoped better things for the Public, though I expected nothing for myself. You may tell the News in this to who you please, but the opinions & reasoning upon it only to your Mama, for the present at least. Give my love to your Mama & Blessing to your Brothers & Sisters. I pray God . . .

---

[163] Richard Arundell.

[164] George Lyttelton.

[165] Phillips Gybbon.

[166] Lord Vere Beauclerk (1699–1781), of Hanworth, Middlesex; whig MP for New Windsor 1726–38 and 1738–41 and Plymouth 1741–50. A lord of the admiralty 1738–42 and 1744–9. Appointed admiral in 1748 and Baron Vere in 1750.

[167] George Anson (1697–1762), admiral. During his circumnavigation of the world (1740–4) he captured a ship with about £500,000 of treasure on board, for which he was promoted to rear admiral, made a lord of the admiralty and MP for Hendon (1744–7) by Pulteney. And in 1747 he captured a ship with £300,000 of specie and was rewarded with a peerage as Baron Anson. *HPC, 1715–54*, ii, 415.

[168] Gower did replace Cholmondeley as lord privy seal.

[169] Not Vere but Henry Vane (c.1705–58), of Raby Castle, County Durham; MP for Launceston 1726–7, St Mawes 1727–41, Ripon 1741–7 and Durham County 1747–53. Joint treasurer and paymaster general of Ireland 1742–4; lord of the treasury 1749–55; joint paymaster of the forces 1755–6. Succeeded his father as 3rd Baron Barnard in 1753 and was created 1st earl of Darlington a year later.

[170] As joint vice-treasurer of Ireland, an office Cholmondeley held 1744–57.

[The following undated list repeats much of what Campbell had written to Pryse in the letter of 18 December 1744, so it may have been intended for Mary Campbell.]

Lord Chesterfield Lieut[enant] of Ireland, not yet declared I think

Duke of Dorset Lord President of Ireland in the room of Lord Harrington

Duke of Devonshire Lord Steward in the room of Duke of Dorset

Lord Gower Lord Privy Seal in the room of Lord Cholmondeley

Lord Cholmondeley joint vice Treasurer of Ireland in room of Harry Vane

Lord Halifax Master of the Buckhounds in room of Mr Jennison[171] who I understand is to be provided for in some other way

Lord Hobart[172] Captain of the Gent[lemen] Pensioners in room of Lord Bathurst

Sir John Hynde Cotton Treasurer of the Chamber in room of Lord Hobart

Mr Dodington Treasurer of the Navy in the room of Sir John Rushout

Mr Waller Cofferer in room of Lord Sandys

Mr Chetwynd Master of the Mint in room of Mr Arundel

Mr Arundel
Mr Lyttelton } Lords of the Treasury in room of Mr Compton,[173] Mr Gybbon

Duke of Bedford
Earl of Sandwich
Lord Arch[ibal]d Hamilton   Lords of the Admiralty
Lord Baltimore Mr Cockburne[174]   Mr Philipson turned out
Lord Vere Beauclerck   Sir Charles Hardy dead
Mr George Greenville
Mr Anson

Sir John Philipps
Mr John Pitt[175] } Commissioners of Trade in room of Mr Keene, Sir Charles Gilmour

Mr Keene Paymaster of the Pensions in room of Mr Hooper

Mr Oswald a Commissioner of the Navy but his Warrant can't come out till the new Admiralty can countersign it.

Lord Cobham to have some what in the Army & be in the Cabinet Councill

119.

John Campbell to Pryse Campbell, 20 December 1744

A few days past it was said Wee were to adjourn this day till after Christmas, but it seems the distribution of the places could not yet be finally settled, so after the K[ing] had been

---

[171] Ralph Jenison (1696–1758), of Elswick Hall, Northumberland and Walworth Castle, County Durham; MP for Northumberland 1724–51 and Newport, Isle of Wight 1749–58. Master of the buckhounds, 1737–44 and 1746–57.

[172] Sir John Hobart (1693–1756), of Blickling, Norfolk; MP for St Ives 1715–27 and Norfolk 1727–8. Lord of trade 1721–7; treasurer of the chamber 1727–44; captain of the gentlemen pensioners 1744–56. Created Baron Hobart of Blickling in 1728 and earl of Buckingham in 1746.

[173] George Compton (1692–1758), MP for Tamworth 1727 and Northampton 1727–54. Lord of the treasury 1727–54. Became 6th earl of Northampton in 1754.

[174] John Cockburn (c.1679–1744), of Ormiston, Haddington; whig MP for Scotland 1707–8, and Haddingtonshire 1708–41. Lord of trade 1714–17; lord of admiralty 1732–3 and 1742–4.

[175] John Pitt (?1706–87), of Encombe, Dorset; tory MP for Wareham 1734–47, 1748–50 and 1761–8 and Dorchester 1751–61. He was a member of the broad-bottom administration of 1744, a lord of the board of trade 1744–55 and of the admiralty 1756.

at the House to day & given his assent to the Land tax Wee adjourn'd to saturday. I had allmost forgot that Mr Carew presented today a Petition against Mr Anson who was chose by Lord Bath at Heydon,[176] & it was agreed to be heard at the Bar on the 15 of January. Wee have a new List of Admiralty[177] every day, yesterday I heard the D[uke] of B[edford], E[arl] of S[andwich], L[or]d Vere, L[or]d Balt[imo]re, G[eorge] Greenvile [Grenville], Mr Philipson & Mr Anson, today I hear Philipson out & L[or]d Glenorchy[178] in his Place, Mr [George] Lyttleton in the Treasury, I can't learn what Sir J[ohn] P[hilipps] is to have, but I think on saturday Wee must know all, the appearance does not please me I wish it may turn out well. The D[uke] of Somerset[179] is to have a Patent[180] for Earl of Northumberland, with remainder failing Heirs Male of his body, to Sir Charles Wyndham whose Mother[181] was the Dukes daughter this was obtaned by Lord G[ranville] at his departure,[182] it was said to be stopt by a letter Lord Hertford writ to the K[ing] but 'tis supposed it will 'tis said Lord Aylesbury[183] a zealous Tory is to be a Duke but with what remainders I can't say, I believe this noble person is as wise as old Justice Colby[184] was. I was very glad when Macheath went out, but as to the alterations proposed among the Commons I have scarce heard of any but what I think are from bad to worse, and I wish Macduff has not taken in help that will be too strong for him I shall be much mistaken if the old Trojans are not a good deal uneasie with some of these preferments.

I beg you my Dearest to be very carefull of your Ancle, for it will some time be much more liable to an accident than it was before and second sprain of the same ancle might be of very bad consequence.

I think your Mama judged very right to give you the Cheltenham Waters to keep you cool when you could not take exercise and I hope you will take them more than once or take some other gentle physic for it can't be proper for you to use much exercise for some time, and a sedentary life is what you are not at all used to. I wish you would consult with Mr Rowe whether you are enough Master of the Greek & Latin to go to the University this Spring, in all events I believe I shall think of your journey to Town pretty early; hopeing to be my self at Stackpole about two months sooner than I was last summer.

Pray look in my Study how many volumes there is of Forsters Sermons[185] & let me know how they are bound and letter'd, that I may get the Volumes that came out

---

[176] Heydon, Norfolk?

[177] The final admiralty board, established on 27 Dec. 1744, consisted of the duke of Bedford (first lord), the earl of Sandwich, Lord Vere Beauclerk, Lord Archibald Hamilton, Lord Baltimore, George Anson and George Grenville.

[178] John Campbell (1696–1782), 3rd earl of Breadalbane and Holland, styled Lord Glenorchy 1716–52.

[179] Algernon Somerset (1684–1750), 7th duke of Somerset.

[180] Letters patent. A royal proclamation granting, in this case, a title.

[181] Catherine Seymour (*d.* 1731).

[182] 24 Nov. 1744, as secretary of state for the northern department.

[183] Thomas Brudenell-Bruce, 1st earl of Ailesbury?

[184] Probably Lawrence Colby of Bletherston, Pembrokeshire, who became high sheriff of the county in 1722.

[185] James Forster (1697–1753), baptist minister who published ten volumes of sermons on various subjects between 1732 and 1755. Although he was a radical, moderate protestants and catholics as well as deists were attracted to his writings.

since. My Dearest I am extremely pleased with and give you many thanks for the latter part of your letter in which you shew good sense, good nature, and true affection & esteme for me. I readily consent to your going for two days to Pentyparch, if I made any difficulty about it I should seem to doubt either your sincerity or your discretion, you have from your very Cradle made it impossible for me to doubt the first, and your behavior since you grew towards Man has been such, that I should do you great injustice if I had not a greater confidence in your discretion, than is usual to be shewn to one of your age. I only desire you will not prolong your stay, unless for bad weather, and I beg you not to expose yourself to that, on any account but otherwise you may excuse your self & me, that as your time in the Country will be but short I am not willing you should loose much of it from your studies.

Haycock defer'd writeing to you till he had sent your things he presents his duty and thanks to you, I believe he would write much oftener to you if he was not a bad scribe for I am sure he thinks often of you and I dare say loves you very much & sincerely. My Dearest I pray God . . .

I think myself very greatly obliged to Mr Hooke for comeing to see you on your confinement.

I send you inclosed a simple sort of political Print [not extant].

Undated list:
Noes:
Lord William Manners
Mr Compton
Sir George Oxenden
Withdrew:
G. Wright
Lord Chetwynd
C. Montagu
H. Waller
Mr Crew
Sir Edmund Isham
Lord Barrymore
Shuttleworth
Lord Quarendon
Mr Carew[186]

---

[186] Sir George Oxenden (1694–1775), 5th bt, of Deane Court, Kent; MP for Sandwich 1720–54. Lord of the admiralty 1725–7; lord of the treasury 1727–37; George Wright (c.1706–66), of Gayhurst, Buckinghamshire and Brooksby Hall, Leicestershire; MP for Leicester 1727–66; Charles Montagu (c.1695–1759), of Papplewick, Nottingham; MP for Westminster 1722–7, St Germans 1734–41, Camelford 1741–7 and Northampton 1754–9; Harry Waller (c.1701–72), of Lincoln's Inn and Grosvenor St, London; MP for Chipping Wycombe 1726–47; Sir Edmund Isham (1690–1772), of Lamport Hall, Northamptonshire; MP for Northamptonshire 1737–72; either Richard (1683–1749), MP for Lancashire 1705–49, or James Shuttleworth (1714–73), MP for Preston 1741–54 and Lancashire 1761–8.

120.

John Campbell to Pryse Campbell, 22 December 1744

At length the great Affair[187] is settled and the House adjourned to the 10th of January I inclose an authentic List of Preferments, Mr John Pitt is Brother to Mr Burtons Lady.[188] Mr. William Pitt has nothing says in his infirm state of health he has more money than he wants so did not desire a lucrative Employment without busyness should have liked to be Secretary at War, but could not desire or expect H[is] M[ajesty] to part with so old & usefull a servant as Sir W[illia]m Yonge, but he hoped to behave so as to deserve H[is] M[ajesty']s favor when an opportunity should offer, these are fine Words but I fear they will butter no Parsnips, 'tis said that – should say, tell them (meaning they who treated on the side of the Patriots) I will have Mr P[itt] have one of the P[rivy] C[ouncillor] places viz T[reasurer] of the N[avy] or C[o]ff[e]r[e]r, and they may leave out which of the two R[a]sc[a]ls they please, it was spoke like a Man, & I wish he had not been persuaded from it.

It is a very melancholy account you give me of the Boat that was lost in the Harbor, the poor Master was vastly to blame but he paid his Life for it, I greatly honor the bravery and humanity of the Sailor who ventured to stick on the keel and bid them to try to save the others, I lament the poor Chirurgeon very much. I am a little uneasy that there is yet some swelling about your ancle pray my Dearest be very carefull. My Love to your Brothers & Blessing I pray God . . .

121.

John Campbell to Pryse Campbell, 10 January 1745

I give you hearty thanks for your letter and was very glad to find you well come home again. I am glad the Plaister was taken off your foot & verjuice applied I hope that has quite reduced the swelling. I had a letter from Mr. Barlow of Lawrenny in favor of Mr. Smith of Jeffreston,[189] the day before I received yours. The sheriffs were prick'd to day,[190] I was in a great great fuss for I did not know it till near eleven forenoon, so I thought the best way was to go to Court & there by Winningtons help I came to the speech of My Lord Chancellor [Hardwicke] in an inner room where I could not have gone by my self, his Lordship readily promised his favor, and writ it down among his Memoranda. Smith was first on the List & had certainly been prick'd if I had not spoke.[191] I presume before this Mr. Philipps of Bosherston[192] has heard from his son, Haycock was at the Admiralty to day to enquire & was assured he was well at Portsmouth. I was very glad to hear it, he might now correspond with his father through my hand.

I am really glad there was no opposition at Carmarthen[193] for I think it might have look'd rather like opposeing the Kings Servant than Sir John Phillipps, and I am not one

---

[187] That is, the new administration was established, with Henry Pelham at its head.

[188] Elizabeth Pitt.

[189] Jeffreyston parish, south Pembrokeshire.

[190] Pricking the sheriffs – selecting those listed for each county by pricking or piercing the parchment next to their names.

[191] John Wogan of Wiston was chosen high sheriff for 1745.

[192] Rev. Jeremiah Philipps, vicar of Bosherston, Pembrokeshire 1728–66.

[193] Sir John Philipps of Picton Castle, Pembrokeshire, was re-elected on 3 Jan. after appointment to office as a lord of trade.

of those who are for runing down the Kings Service because they are not in it.[194] I don't know how far the arm'd Vessels were right in their demand, but I think the behaviour of the Privateer shewd that sawcy inclination to despise all Authority which by the righteous endeavors of Macbeth & Company has to long prevaled, has done so much Mischief and yet threatens more to this unhappy distracted Nation. It is now the third day of a hard frost Wee had cold raw weather with foggy mornings for some time before. My Dearest Mr. Rowe seems to think it will not be disireable for you to go to the University immediately from spending two or three Months here, which you know must necessarily be pretty idle. What do you think of comeing up the beginning of March, & returning with me to the Country for the summer and Comeing to the University in Autumn. I expect but a short session so hope to be early in the Country this year. My Love & Blessing to your Brothers and kind service to Mr. Rowe. I am ever . . .

I think the arm'd Vessels were greatly to blame in fireing so as to endanger innocent People & their Houses on Shoar.

I hear now Lord Baltimore has not resign'd[195] but will not attend the Board which is a sort of Conduct I don't well understand, though I incline to think he has reason to complane, & that Lord Vere might have been content to return to the same Chair[196] he left, with Anson & Grenville below him now, as Lord Glenorchy & Thompson were then. What I gave you some account of in my letter by Johnny Furlong,[197] most unhappily continues to such a degree that I really am much concern'd at it & fear the consequence. When I was at Court to day while the King was at Council pricking the sheriffs, the Duke of Newcastle seeing me came & took me by the hand & led me aside complaned of it, and gave me an instance but desired me not to speak of it. Then he said excuse me I am so full I can't help venting my self to you, and was pleased to add, you are a sensible and an honest Man pray come to me that I may talk a little with you about it, dont come on Wednesday (the public day) but early any other morning, which I promised to do. I need not tell you all this should be quite secret. But pray when you talk upon politic's, with any Whigs tell them it was impossible for Macduff & his friends to go on with Macheath unless they could have resolved to submit both their reason & Consciences to his Will, whose schemes they thought not agreable to the true Interest of their Country, or such as the old Corps would be willing to support that when Macheath was removed they found they could not depend on those who were attach'd to him & Macbeth, this obliged them, the True Trojans not being Strong enough to act alone, to treat with the Opposition, who were too sensible of the advantage they had from several unhappy circumstances, & therefore insisted on such terms as to be sure were not very agreable but were necessarily to be submitted to, that it is our busyness to make the best of it, that if the Whigs attend well and are hearty & resolute to support their own leaders, they have still an undoubted superiority in the Administration and may hope to see better days, but if they give way to resentment and fly off in disgust,

---

[194] A reference to Carteret.

[195] He resigned as a lord of the admiralty in Apr. 1745. J.C. Sainty, *Office-Holders in Modern Britain, IV: Admiralty Officials 1660–1870* (1975), 108.

[196] On the admiralty board, which he had left in 1742.

[197] The deliverer of the letter.

what now seems dangerous to the Whig cause, will soon become fatal, and they will bring themselves from a state of uncertain danger, to sure ruin. When you are with Tories or Jacobites as I take the family of Foes, who I believe are now with you, to be, it is better to hear their thoughts upon the State of Affairs, than to let them know much of yours.[198]

122.
John Campbell to Pryse Campbell, [16] January 1745
Your writeing to me two Posts together gives me great pleasure & satisfaction for what indeed can give me greater than to see that I am thought of with affection by the Person I love most in the World.

Your Mama told me of Watty's arrival & I believe I told her my real sentiments of the Matter that Watty deserves to lose his ears and the other Gent his money. Last night the Committee of Elections[199] met and Dick Lloyds Petition was appointed for the 27 of March the day named by me.[200] Sir John Philipps by Mr. Pryse's[201] direction moved for a day in February, he said little & was calm & civil but Sir Watkins Williams Wynn was in a perilous passion, sputter'd & swagger'd like [202]ny Turkey cock, but we beat them on two divisions I think 26 to 21.[203] That Committee has so little to do that I rather wonder there were so many, than so few, they talk of moveing the House for an Instruction but if they do, I hope they can't carry it. I was very much obliged to Winnington for attending & Speakeing, without him I could not have carried it, though H[enry] Fox, Legge, T[homas] Townshend[204] and several others attended very readily & kindly at my desire.

I hope my Dearest to hear by your next that the swelling is quite gone out of your foot, I must repete my entreaties that you will in every respect & on all occasions be most carefull of your health and Limbs. I pray God . . .

I fancy poor Mr. Hooke was mighty happy in meeting the four Miss Lloyds.

123.
John Campbell to Pryse Campbell, 17 January 1745
I was so late at the Marlow[205] Election that I can say but very little, it will last a day or two longer but Wee had a division tonight about a piece of Evidence and carried it 223

---

[198] Campbell is here referring to the Philippses of Pentyparc, Pembrokeshire, related by marriage to John Campbell.

[199] The committee of privileges and elections met at about 7 p.m. It was a committee of the whole House.

[200] *CJ*, xxiv, 707, 15 Jan. 1745. The House had divided 125 to 162 in the negative on a motion to hear the petition on 22 Feb. Campbell was one of the tellers for the noes.

[201] Thomas Pryse (?1675–1745), of Gogerddan, Cardiganshire; tory MP for Cardigan boroughs 1741–5. Related by marriage to Campbell.

[202] Part of the letter is missing.

[203] The vote of the committee of privileges and elections.

[204] Thomas Townshend (1701–80), of Frognal, Kent; MP for Winchilsea 1722–7 and Cambridge University 1727–74. Undersecretary of state to his father the 2nd Viscount Townshend 1724–30; teller of the exchequer 1727–80; secretary to the lord lieutenant of Ireland 1739–45. Brother of Charles William and Roger Townshend.

[205] Great Marlow, Buckinghamshire.

against 173[206] so I hope we shall carry the Election as well. Yesterday we had an unexpected division, Lord Strange moveing to put off the voteing the estimate for the Ordnance because there were some Articles for the Army in Flanders which is not yet voted, it was a mere cavill for the money is given on account so if the Army abroad was recall'd or disbanded, these things could be paid no longer than the Army continued to want them. Lord Strange was seconded by Sir John Philipps and George Grenville spoke in a sort of moderate way. The question was put for leaving the Chair, being in the Committee of Supply Ays 113 No's 238. Sir J[ohn] P[hilipps], Mr. Pitt & Sir J[ohn] Hind[e] Cotton, & Mr George & Mr. James Grenville in the minority.

I send you a letter I had tonight from P. Williams. My love to your Mama & Blessing to your Brothers & Sisters. I am . . .

Mr. Owen came to Town on Tuesday even.

124.
John Campbell to Pryse Campbell, 19 January 1745

I find that in my hurry on Thursday I put up another letter instead of Pry Williams's which I now send you. I am greatly provoked at the account I received both from you & R[oger] Evan[s] of Chathorses Stubborn & insolent behaviour, I really think he ought not to be suffer'd to come about the House upon any account, and that he should be turn'd out of his House. I think Wee had better run the hazard of his family comeing on the Parish than keep such an impudent incorrigible Theef, if you are of the same opinion you may give directions to R[oger] Evans accordingly. I am surprised they attempted to launch the Forereach[207] so soon they might I think as well have gone about it the next week after she was stranded, January is very often as bad a month as any in the Year.

I was exceeding glad to hear from your Mama last Post that the swelling was quite gone from your Ancle; I hope my Dearest will be very carefull for the future, both walking & rideing. I have got an Equipage which I expect you will hold in great contempt when you come. I went in it today to wait upon Molly I suppose I should make her Compliments, though I believe her thoughts were quite taken up with herself & her Christmas box which I gave her to day, I can't positively say she mention'd anything else. My Dearest, I pray God bless you . . .

I was a good while in private with the Duke of Newcastle on Thursday last, He told me that the day before he had better entertainment in a certaine Place,[208] than anytime before since Octavius [Carteret] retired, but our Conversation turn'd cheifly on what passed the day before in the House of Commons of which he had heard but a very imperfect account and indeed I could give him but an indifferent one for not expecting any debate I went late into the House & was obliged to sit at the bottom under the

---

[206] *CJ*, xxiv, 710. The hearings on this election, in which government candidate Henry Conyngham, the petitioner, was defeated by two votes, continued over three days, ending with the petition being withdrawn. Conyngham (c.1705–81), of Minster, Kent, and Slane, Co. Meath, became MP for Tiverton 1747–54 and Sandwich 1756–74. *CJ*, xxiv, 715; *HPC, 1715–54*, i, 199.

[207] The *Forereach*, of Tenby, Pembrokeshire, was re-launched and continued to ply its trade, mainly between Liverpool, Dublin, Tenby and London, well into the 1750s.

[208] At court – where George II was hostile and quarrelsome with the Pelhams who had been instrumental in having the king's favourite, Carteret, dismissed. R. Browning, *The Duke of Newcastle* (1975), 130.

Gallery where one cannot hear well, but I told him as much as I could. He said they must expostulate with the cheif men about it for there was no such thing as going on in that manner. Next Wednesday [23 January] they are to move, unless it should be defer'd, for the Army in Flanders,[209] Wee shall then see how these Gentlemen will behave. Mr. Pitt has not yet been well enough to attend the House, I met him to day airing in his Chariot wrapt up in a Cloak. Sir William Younge is also yet confined by the Gout, it was sometime a doubt whether the possessor or expectant of that Place would hold out longest with that distemper.

125.

John Campbell to Pryse Campbell, 24 January 1745

Yesterday in the Committee of Supply came the question for the Army in Flanders.[210] Sir William Yonge who has been laid up with the Gout for a month & Mr William Pitt who has been ill much longer both came to the House on this occasion, and though Sir William is yet weak he was in good spirits & open'd the Matter very well, Mr Pelham seconded and more fully explaned it. Then Mr. Vere Poulett brother to the Earl spoke & concluded with moveing the Army might be granted only for two months, as that Gentleman is no great Orator he did not engage any one to second his Motion. Then Sir Watkin Williams Wyn spoke for agreeing to the Motion,[211] and most earnestly entreated all his friends to join with him, he expressed great regard for & confidence in the new part of the Ministry, but if I understood him right he shew'd a true Tory inveteracy against the old Whig part, one expression was, that if some People could sink alone he would be the last man, I think he must mean to give them any assistance, but some Noise in the House at that made him leave the sentence unfinish'd; Sir R Newdigate[212] spoke next to agree with Sir Watkin and though he was not so rough & surly in his expressions seem'd to be entirely in the same way of thinking. Sir Watkin said if the Dutch did not heartily come in, he would move for an address to disband those Troops. Then Lord Strange spoke and he was against Voteing the Troops for any time, till wee should know what Answer the States [General] would give to Lord Chesterfield,[213] but no body seconded his Opinion. Then Mr William Pitt[214] rose & though he look'd thin & weak & doubtless is so, yet his Voice was Strong and he indeed spoke as finely in support of the Question as ever he did in opposition, he express'd his good opinion of & confidence in Mr. Pelham,[215] in as high and strong terms as was possible, and said if ever any Minister deserved well of his Country he certanely did in

[209] *CJ*, xxiv, 714: committee of supply.

[210] *CJ*, xxiv, 714–15; *PH*, xiii, 1050–6, for the debate.

[211] *PH*, xiii, 1054, citing Philip Yorke, states that Sir Watkin Williams-Wynn, 'to the surprise of the generality, spoke for the question, and as he said himself, agreed with the court for the first time in his life'.

[212] Sir Roger Newdigate (1719–1806), of Arbury, Warwickshire; tory MP for Middlesex 1742–7 and Oxford University 1751–80.

[213] Chesterfield was given the mission by Newcastle of persuading the Dutch to join the war against the French. *ODNB*.

[214] *PH*, xiii, 1054, citing Philip Yorke, states that Pitt opened by saying: 'if this was to be the last day of his life, he would spend it in the House of Commons, since he judged the condition of his country to be worse than that of his own health'.

[215] 'From 1743 [until c.1750], Pitt had attached his prospects to the Pelham whigs, increasingly disassociating himself from Cobham and the tories'. M. Peters, *The Elder Pitt* (1998), 38.

the highest degree, meaning for delivering it from Lord G[ranville][216] whome he lash'd in a masterly way with general applause of the House, and without the abusive language that used to be thrown out against Ministers contrary, to all decency & good manners. He exhorted strongly to unanimity in this question, & insinuated for one strong reason that it would effectually secure us against the return of Lord G[ranville]. He express'd a warm zeal for the King whom he allways mention'd in a becomeing manner, his speech was a very great and fine performance. Sir John Barnard spoke after not long but with great warmth, in favour of Lord G[ranville] whose Measures he entirely approved, & applauded, look'd upon him as a very great able & Honest man, and said he believed it would be the greatest pleasure to that noble Lord to have every one of his actions while he was in Power strickly examined in the House of Commons. He express'd a good Opinion of Mr. Pelham but said that the closer he follow'd the steps of Lord G[ranville] the more it would be for his honor & the good of his Country. Whatever I may think of Lord G[ranville] I must confess there was somewhat great & manly in Sir John Barnard's behavior, so freely & boldly to profess his regard for and good opinion of him & readiness to defend him in a House of Commons so very strongly set against him; though I admired Sir John Barnard's abilities you know he was never a favourite with me, but I must give due praise to what appear'd brave & honorable. Mr. Bowes spoke for the question & wish'd for the examination Sir J[ohn] B[arnard]'s said Lord G[ranville] would so much desired [*sic*], he seem'd an Enemy to Lord G[ranville] but how far his confidence extended, I can't tell, the Committee not being at all attentive, & that Gent not the clearest speaker; Mr. Cholmondeley of Cheshire[217] spoke but was so little attended to, I can't really tell whether he was for, or against the question. Lord Barrington spoke for the question & pretty long to prove he was not inconsistant with himself though he voted against these Troops last year, but now he said the views & measures of the Ministry were alter'd; his Lordship had great volubility, & is not a bad speaker, and used to be well heard, but very little attention was given to him at this time, the Committee perhaps not thinking it of great public importance whether his Lordship was consistent with what he did last year or no or perhaps haveing heard Mr. Pitt they thought it was needless to hear anything more for the question. Mr. Edward Finch was very busy takeing Notes & I believe intended to speak in defence of his Friend & Patron Lord G[ranville] but was prevented, I think by Mr. Pitt going away on account of his health, while Mr. Cholmondleley was speaking, and Mr Finch to before did not think it proper to answer what Mr. Pitt had said, behind his back; and I do not think it was any Misfortune to Mr. F[inch] that he was prevented engaging Mr. Pitt.

As to the Marlow Election, after having fought bravely three days, our Ships blew up. It is said one who was Agent for the Petitioner at the Election, has been gained by the Friends of the sitting member, and would have appear'd to day to prove bribery on the Petitioner to prevent which the Petition was withdrawn last night. Wee were up between five & sixe, when the great Question was put Lord Strange gave a loud, and for ought I know, a single No; his Lordship also took care to day that the House should

---

[216] John, Lord Carteret who became 2nd Earl Granville on the death of his mother.

[217] Charles Cholmondeley (1685–1756), of Vale Royal, Cheshire; tory MP for Cheshire 1710–15 and 1722–56. A member of the jacobite October Club.

not agree Nem[ine] Con[tradicente][218] to the resolution of the Committee. When I went into the House to day I was surprised to see Mr [George] Barlow of Slebech, who surprised me more by accosting me in a very Friendly & familiar manner; Mr Carew of Carew Castle[219] moved today for a Bill to regulate the Elections for Countys,[220] what he intends to make of it I can't tell, but he has several Wise men[221] join'd with him to bring it in, I think there is room to make alterations for the better, but much doubt their doing so. Lord Baltimore being fix'd to relign H[enry] Legge is to succede him and Mr. Philipson to have Legge's Place, I suppose it will be done in a weeks time. Admiral Vernon took occasion to day upon agreeing to the Vote of the Committee for 10000 Marines,[222] to make a rambling speech in which he over & over express'd his great surprise & concern at Sir Barnards approveing the measures of Lord G[ranville']s Administration (Sir J[ohn] B[arnard] was absent today) and he ended with compareing Lord Winchelsea at the head of the Admiralty to a Monkey in a China Shop that jumps about breaking & destroying every thing. I pray God . . .

126.
John Campbell to Pryse Campbell, [29] January 1745
I heartily thank you for your kind letter. I readily consent to your setting out the 20th of february if the weather be good at that time. As to your going to the university I don't care to make a positive promise so long before hand, but I assure you it is my real intention to leave you there before you have completed your 18th year, you may at any time let me know Your inclination and I believe you are satisfied, I shall be very unwilling to deny you. I thank God my Dearest you have never given me occasion to use Commands, and it is much more agreeable to me to advise and desire; I love you too much to find any pleasure in haveing Power over you. If you love and regard me as your best Friend, it is the greatest happiness I can wish for and it shall be my study to deserve it.

Today Mr Sydenham moved to bring in a Bill for annual Parliaments[223] seconded by Alderman Gybbon, who did not speak above ten words, two or three more spoke very short, so little was said for it that no body thought it worth while to say one word against it, when the question was put there was a faint Aye & a pretty loud no, but they divided the House Ay's 113 Noes 145.[224] Among the Ays were Sir J[ohn] H[ynde] Cotton, Sir J[ohn] Philipps and Mr. George Greenville, but you may ghess how much in earnest they & many others were by the Motion being made by such a Man & so very slightly supported. Yesterday Mr. [George] Barlow of Slebech came & sat by me

---

[218] Without objection.

[219] This is Thomas Carew of Crowcombe, Minehead.

[220] *CJ*, xxiv, 718.

[221] *CJ*, xxiv, 718, lists the committee to prepare this bill as: Sir Watkin Williams-Wynn; Robert Williams (?1695–1763), of Erbistock, Denbighshire; tory MP for Montgomeryshire 1740–1 and 1742–7. He was a member of the jacobite Cycle of the White Rose, the leader of which was Williams' elder brother Sir Watkin Williams-Wynn; Velters Cornewall; Nicholas Fazakerley; Humphrey Sydenham, who seconded the bill on its introduction on 29 Jan.; and Sir John Philipps.

[222] *CJ*, xxiv, 718.

[223] *CJ*, xxiv, 726. A motion to introduce a bill for annual parliaments was a stock opposition device; *PH*, xiii, 1056–107, for the debate.

[224] *CJ*, xxiv, 726.

was mighty complaisant, ask'd where I lived that he might wait upon me, and said that Sir J[ohn] Philipps and some others accepting Places had made him think very differently of Parties from what he did before, he thought it was plane they only opposed in order to get the Places they now had. I said I believed People might be apt to say so, I was very civil but a little cautious what I said. I thank Val for his journal I am sorry I did not keep one at the same time here, if he continues I will. Haycock returns many thanks for your being so kind to remember him he is mighty glad to hear you are to come soon to Town. My Love & blessing to Trub & Ally & kind service to Mr. Row[e] I pray God . . .

127.
John Campbell to Pryse Campbell, 2 February 1745
I am very thankfull for your writeing to me so often, the sight of your hand allways gives me great Joy. I spoke to Mr. Hill this morning about Mr. Hookes Tenant, but had not your letter about me, so I must give him (as Gil Blas says) a Memorial in writing. I don't know whether Mr. Hill can do it if he can I dare say he will.

I am very well pleased with Dick Marchants haveing Charles Morse's house. I have already answer'd your question about your journey by agreeing to the time you proposed, you may if you please bring up Val & J Brown. Yesterday Wee had a Motion in the Committee of Supply[225] for £170,000 & some odds for services not provided for last session, but expended before this session met by a Clause in an Act[226] last year the King was impower'd to issue any Sum out of Supplies, notwithstanding the appropriation, to make good such Treaties as His Majestie should think fit to make for the good of the Common Cause, in consequence of which this money has been paid in subsidy's to the Queen of Hungary & the Electors of Mentz[227] & Cologne.[228] Sir John Philipps made a Speech in which he mistook the meaning of the Clause above mention'd in a surpriseing manner that seem'd to shew great slowness of apprehension & seem'd to hurt him very much in the Opinion of the House. Mr. Vyner and Sydenham spoke a little finding fault but were not minded so in effect there was no opposition. Mr. Vyner insisted upon the Treatys being read at length, which have[229] the Members not haveing patience to hear run out the House. I think Sir John Phillipps never made so bad a figure as yesterday. Two or three Spoke to set him right & could scarce make him apprehend the thing. Tis too long to explane in a letter, but I hope soon to tell it you, and you will wonder how a Man who studies busyness[230] so much could mistake so grossly.

Did I tell you that Mr. Wallace the Chirurgeon call'd here in his Chariot last Sunday was Sevenight, I hear he has married a Fortune. I have not time to write to R[oger] Evan[s] to Night, haveing sat all afternoon with the Bishop of Llandaffe who has a little

---

[225] *CJ*, xxiv, 735; *PH*, xiii, 1124–5.
[226] 17 Geo. II, c.33: an act for granting His Majesty the sum of one million pounds out of the sinking fund.
[227] Johann Freiderich Karl von Ostein (1689–1763), elector of Mainz, Germany, 1743–63.
[228] Clemens Augustus I of Bavaria (1700–61), elector of Cologne 1723–61.
[229] Half.
[230] Philipps was not only a lord of trade at this time, but also had extensive coal mining operations in south Pembrokeshire.

of the Gout. Pray tell him the Trees the Gardener gave me account of must be sent for to Bristol. I will send some flower seeds soon. I am my Dearest . . .

128.
John Campbell to Pryse Campbell, 5 February 1745
I received yours in favour of Matty Morgan, I should be very glad to oblige Mr. Rowe in the thing, but was not willing to ask for the Place till it is really vacant; indeed, if I had desired it, I could not have seen Mr. Pelham to day for he was not at the House, and he staid till three this morning, with poor Lord Orford, who was thought to be dying. He was pretty well & easy all last week and till yesterday toward three o'clock, when a stone or piece of a stone, came into the passage, so large that Mr. Ranby[231] was obliged to assist with an Instrument to bring it away, & soon after another came away in a clot of blood, and then for some time he thought himself happily relieved, but in about two hours he began to be in pain & to bleed through the urinary passage, which continued till one this morning. Some time after the bleeding ceased, he was free from pain but chilly sick at his stomach, and inclined to doze which made them think a Mortification was form'd which would very soon put an end to his life. Dr. Jurin[232] indeed said it was possible to account otherwise for those things which seem'd to be the symptoms of a Mortification. Lord Orford I believe all last night believed himself dying, he sent for, and talk'd sometime privately with Lord Walpole, his understanding was never the least affected, and his voice continued pretty strong. I call'd there in my way from the House, and Haycock was there at six this evening, he brings me word that they thought him a good deal better since I call'd there, and that they had hopes of his Life, but I much fear a worse account to morrow morning. I hear he has taken a great deal of the Bark[233] which has been found the most powerful thing to prevent or stop a Mortification. I am really much concern'd for him, no man is without faults, but I truely believe he was an able and honest Minister to the Public, and a friendly humane, amiable Man in private Life. If he dies at this time he will be sincerely lamented by great Numbers more I believe than any other Man in the Kingdom, and I fear it might have a bad effect on the Public no one haveing so great an influence to keep the Whigs togather.

My Dearest I pray God . . .

Past nine o'clock Mr. Hill sends me word from Lord Malton's that a Servant is just come from Lord Orford who brings word that Mr. Ranby says my Lord is better but not well. I fear he means not in a good way.

129.
John Campbell to Pryse Campbell, 9 February 1745
Lord Orford grows better so that they have hopes of his recovery, though I talk'd yesterday about it with Thomas Grahame & he seem'd very fearfull. Yesterday and

---

[231] John Ranby (1703–73), surgeon to the royal household from 1727, surgeon to the person 1740–3 and sergeant surgeon from 1743. He treated Walpole during his final illness, and then published *A Narrative of the Last Illness of the Earl of Orford* (1745). J.C. Sainty, *Officials of the Royal Household 1660–1837* (2 vols, 1997), i, 47.

[232] James Jurin (c.1684–1750), physician, Newtonian and natural philosopher. He became embroiled in controversy after prescribing his own medicine, lixivium lithontripticum, to Walpole which did not prevent his death and for which Jurin was subsequently blamed. *ODNB.*

[233] Willow bark was used for pain relief and to stop inflammation.

thursday mornings my Lord had a periodical return of the bleeding about two o'clock, & somewhat of a feaver fit came on before the bleeding so they hoped the Bark might help him & I believe it has, for this morning they sent me word that the return of the complaint was much less this morning and that in the main he was better, and to night Haycock brings me word they think him a good deal better than in the morning. I have not seen Mr. Grahame to day.

The master told me a thing today that I believe will divert you, Lord Orford's illness being spoke of in a Company of Lawyers, I believe at Westminster Hall, and somebody observing how many people express'd a great concern for him, one Mr. Brown repeted a passage from Horace,

Virtutem incolumen odimus
Jublatam ex oculis quaerimus invidi[234]

Ay says Mr. Bootle,[235] I allways thought him an insignificant fellow. I am much pleased to find H[is] R[oyal] H[ighness]'s[236] good Ch[ancello]r's [Bootle] Learning, so exactly correspond with his judgement and good sense.

I am sorry to hear that your Boot made your ancle swell again, pray be very carefull not to hurt in [*sic*], and I wish you would continue to use the Verjuice. Haycock tells me you talk of setting out the 18. Pray my Dearest be very careful of yourself & remember this accident of your ancle in your journey. Don't expose yourself to bad weather, nor be too much in hast. I pray God . . . Give my Love to your Mama & tell her I sent a Box to the Camer this morning. I intend to send her an account of the contents next Post. My Blessing . . .

[George] Barlow of Slebech to Mr. Pelhams Levee Yesterday morning.

130.
John Campbell to Pryse Campbell, 12 February 1745
Yesterday a Bill being read a 2[n]d time and committed, for continuing the Duty on Salt for a longer term, Mr. Cholmondeley moved for an instruction to the Committee to receive a Clause to disable the Officers concern'd in collecting that Duty, from being returning officers, or voteing in Elections of Members of Parliament. After a very short Debate Wee divided Ays 54 No's 159[237] in the Minority were Sir J[ohn] H[ynde] C[otton] Sir John Philipps, Mr. Dodington & Mr. John Pitt. Today Sir J[ohn] P[hilipps] thought he had discovered £35,000 not accounted for, but it proved a Mistake too long to write at length however he insisted upon recommitting a resolution of the Committee of Supply & his Friends were so complaisant to divide

---

[234] Horace, *Odes*, iii, 24, lines 31–2: 'filled with envy, hate chaste virtue, and only seek it when it's hidden from our eyes'.

[235] Thomas Bootle (1685–1753), of Lathom Hall, Liverpool; opposition whig MP for Liverpool 1724–34 and Midhurst 1734–53. A highly paid lawyer who had several anti-administration clients including the duchess of Marlborough and Pulteney. In 1731 he and Nicholas Fazakerley defended the publishers of *The Craftsman*, Nicholas Amhurst and Richard Francklin, against a charge of seditious libel. Bootle was the prince of Wales' chancellor 1740–51.

[236] The prince of Wales.

[237] *CJ*, xxiv, 747.

with him to cover his mistake, I have forgot the Numbers at the Division[238] being put out of my head by what follow'd which was the second reading of the Bill[239] for takeing away the negative of the Aldermen upon the Common Council of London, there was a debate upon the motion for committing it. Sir J[ohn] B[arnard] Alderman Heathcote,[240] Alderman Lambert, & Alderman Calvert & Mr. Fazakerly spoke for it. Lord Coke, Colonel Bladen, Mr Pelham, Mr Winnington, Mr Vere against it. Wee divided Ay's 90 No's 117.[241] Among the No's were Sir J[ohn] H[ynde] C[otton], Sir J[ohn] P[hilipps], Mr. Dodington, Mr. J[ohn] Pitt. I should have told you that in the morning a good while before the Bill was read Colonel Bladen presented a Petition from 8 Aldermen against it, there were some other speakers such as Carew & Sydenham, the Latter made us all laugh for saying how dangerous it was to disoblige the City of London, the Capital, which had so great an influence on the whole kingdom, he said we were takeing the Bull by the Horns;[242] indeed Sir John Barnard threaten'd us with the resentment & hatred of the Citizens in a manner that was, to me, much more provokeing than persuasive. I wish I could send you any good accounts of poor Lord Orford, but Mr. Ranby and both the Mr. Grahames despare of his recovery, at the same time some of his friends have good hopes. I went into the House this Morning before ten o'clock to enquire, & Lord Walpole happening to come down, came & talk'd with me some time. He thought his Father much better & was in great spirits upon it, but I fear he flatters himself with appearances, my Lord Orford is pretty easy, and has generally good cheerfull spirits, beyond what anybody could expect in his condition. Lord Walpole told me that one morning (I believe this day s'ennight), his Father thought himself dying, would have him go home about 4 o'clock took his leave of him expecting to see him no more, but spoke with the ease as if Lord Walpole had been going for a short time to the Country. Mr. G[raham] tells me as the ground of his fears, that there is a great quantity of extravasated gramous blood in the Bladder the weight of which hinders the Spincter to close as it ought, so the water come's away in small quantities & involuntary, tinged by that blood, he apprehends fatal consequences from that gramous blood lying long there, and yet can't see how it should be brought away, unless the sphincter of the bladder could close so as to retane a quantity of water to dissolve, and then bring off, that clotted blood. This seems to me too good a reason to fear the Case desperate, I heartily wish it otherwise.[243]

Give my Love & Blessing to your Brothers and my kind service to Mr Rowe. Pray my Dearest be very carefull of yourself & particularly of your ancle in your journey. I pray God . . .

---

[238] *CJ*, xxiv, 749. The division was 88 to 174 in the negative.

[239] Bill for repealing so much of an act for regulating elections within the City of London of 11 Geo. I. See *PH*, xiii, 1125–72, for the debate.

[240] George Heathcote (1700–68), of Walcot, Somerset; MP for Hindon 1727–34, Southwark 1734–41 and London 1741–7. Initially a whig but spoke increasingly for the opposition and by 1745 had become a staunch jacobite. Sheriff of London 1739–40 and lord mayor 1742.

[241] *CJ*, xxiv, 749.

[242] Sydenham's speech is not recorded in *PH*.

[243] Walpole died on 18 Mar. 1745.

Haycock desires me to give his duty & let you know he intend'd to write to thank you for your letter but had not time to day and hopes another Post will be too late to find you at Stackpole. He is very happy in the expectation of seeing you soon. Pray don't make more hast than good speed, & don't travel in bad weather. Wee have pleasant frosty weather, I believe very hard out of Town.

131.
John Campbell to Pryse Campbell, 10 January 1747

It gives me great Pleasure that you take my advice so kindly, I believe you are satisfied it is allways kindly meant. I hope my Dearest you will now endeavor to make good use of your time to improve yourself in usefull & polite learning, which will be a fund of real pleasure & entertainment to you when you are too old to relish such a hurry of diversions as you found at Bath and I must entreat you both in the Spending of your time & your Money to be guided by reason & not by fashion and common example. You never grieved me so much as when you used to say you must do as other People did, it is that maxim that ruins the fortunes & the manners of a vast part of mankind. I beg you would not think I mention anything past to reproach you, or as retaneing the least unpleasing thought about you on that account, for I assure you my Dearest I do not. Nay if the money you spent this last year has bought you experience that will make you prudent & frugal for the future, I think it the best laid out of any money I ever paid in my Life and if the time you spent in nothing but unmeaning diversions has made you weary of idleness, brought you to see the worth of time, and the necessity of a young Mans applying himself to gain Knowledge to make him acceptable to men of worth or ever supportable to himself in his riper years, then even that time was not lost. I know very well there are many who are highly satisfied with themselves, and well received in a great deal of Company, who have been idle all their lives and live, & will die in gross ignorance; but you have by Gods blessing too much sense to enjoy their sort of happyness nor could you be pleased with the approbation of such Company as they are well received by. They appear in high joy while they can run about or have mirth brought home to them, but if alone or with serious Company they are miserable, they know not such a thing as, Vacui tranquilla voluptas,[244] and their old age is sure to be either melancholy or very ridiculous. But if you lay up a stock of knowledge in your youth it will be every day improveing, you will have entertainment within your self for all times, and be able to find entertainment in all objects, you will when old be easy to your self & acceptable to all others whose esteme is worth haveing. All here are well Trub is just come home from seeing Jane Shore[245] which is so well acted at Covent Garden as to have brought crowded audience for a week or more togather.

I had a visit this morning from Captain Dusign with a magnificent feather in his hat. I hear the little Baron is in Town & I saw Short Jones the Gamester very spruce at Court yesterday morning. I pray God . . .

---

[244] 'The calmed desire of the empty', supposedly from Lucretius, *De Rerum Natura*: 'vacuique animi tranquilla voluptas'.

[245] *The Tragedy of Jane Shore* by Nicolas Rowe (1674–1718).

132.

John Campbell to Pryse Campbell, 27 October 1747

I give you joy of Admiral Hawkes Success[246] which you will See in the Newspaper,[247] it is indeed a very happy event. You will observe the Admiral says he order'd Captain Fox[248] to attack the Tonnant[249] had he obey'd 'tis believed she must have been taken. He will probably be hanged for cowardice and disobeying Orders. When the Councill of War was call'd all the Captains declared they would not sit with Captain Fox, if he is hanged he may probably have company; Captain Cruikshanks[250] & another whose name I have forgot being comeing home to be try'd for their Cowardice in letting a Spanish Ship worth above a Million Sterling escape the [sic] succesively. Captain Cruikshanks who met her first was in a 40 Gun Ship with another (I think of 60 Guns) under his command, that Ship being near of equal force with the Spaniard engaged her some time but haveing no assistance from the Commadore, who stood off after the first Broadside, left her. She was afterwards met by the other Captain whose name I forgot, he had two 20 Gun ships besides his own, he gave one Broadside and then run away. I think these Captains meet with a favorable Court Martial they may possibly offer their Service to the Burrough of Carmarthen[251] for the next Parliament. I believe there were several young men of quality in the French Ships for Mr. Corbett told me a Nephew of Monsieur Maurepas[252] was kill'd in the Action, I was glad to hear that the French Officers in their letters to their Friends in France acknowledge that Admiral Hawke treats them with great politeness.

I waited on the Duke of Bedford to day to recommend Lieutenant Foley[253] to his Grace. The Duke speaking of this Action said that if Bergenopzoom[254] had been preserved, as it might have been, if well defended, he believe that disappointment join'd with this loss, would have induced the French to have agreed to such Terms of Peace as Wee might have accepted.

---

[246] Edward Hawke (1705–81), 1st Baron Hawke. Campbell refers to Hawke's victory over the French in the second battle of Finisterre, 25 Oct. 1747, one of the decisive battles of the War of the Austrian Succession. Hawke stated of the French after the battle that 'They took a great deal of drubbing'. Browning states succinctly that after this engagement 'France no longer had a navy'. Browning, *War of the Austrian Succession*, 323.

[247] For instance the *General Evening Post*, 24 Oct. 1747.

[248] Captain Thomas Fox, of the *Kent*. Fox was court-martialled, but was only found partly guilty – he had attacked the *Tonnant* but had then allowed the French ship to escape. He was relieved of the command of the *Kent*, and in 1749 was retired from the navy at the rank of rear admiral.

[249] The French flagship under Captain Duchaffault was one of the ships that escaped. The overall command of the French squadron was in the hands of the marquis de l'Étanduère.

[250] Refers to a separate incident.

[251] Since 1746 Carmarthen borough had been run by two rival corporations, one tory, controlled by Sir John Philipps of Picton Castle, the other whig, controlled by Griffith Philipps of Cwmgwili. This situation obtained until a new charter was issued in 1764.

[252] Jean-Fréderic Phélypeaux (1701–81), Comte de Maurpas, Louis XV's secretary of the royal household and secretary of the navy 1723-49.

[253] Probably Thomas Foley, of Ridgeway, Llawhaden, Pembrokeshire. He was a lieutenant in the navy in 1746. NLW, Foley of Ridgeway collection. Bedford was first lord of the admiralty at this date.

[254] The three-month siege of Bergen-op-Zoom, the Netherlands, ended in Sept. 1747 in a French victory. It caused a rift between the British and Dutch forces, the former realising they had overestimated the latter's fighting capacity. After the fall of Bergen-op-Zoom the British re-entered negotiations at Breda which resulted in the Treaty of Aix-la-Chapelle of 1748, between France, Austria, Holland and the British, bringing the War of the Austrian Succession to an end. Browning, *War of the Austrian Succession*, 320–1.

There is no doubt the Archbishop of York[255] will remove to Canterbury. Dr. Hutton of Bangor to York & Dr. Pearce[256] be made Bishop of Bangor, who is said to be Lord Bishop's man & made upon an old promise. I do not like it. I believe Hutton owes his rise to Lord Chancellor [Hardwicke] who Carries the Duke of Newcastle with him of course. Besides I believe His Grace likes to prefer Cambridge men now our Chancellor[257] is so old.

I pray God . . .

My Love to Ally

Pray tell Frank Evans I intend to send a Lock for the Court Gate From this, but desire he would let me know what size of Lock the rail of the Gate will admit.

133. [BL, Add. MS 32723, f. 262]

John Campbell, Grosvenor Square to the duke of Newcastle, 12 November 1750

I am very unwilling to trouble your Grace so soon after your return with any small concern of my own but as I apprehend your Grace will receive another application, I take this Liberty to repete the request I made to your Grace before you went abroad, that you will be so good to grant the Living of Narberth in Pembrokeshire to Mr Henry Rowe, who was my Sons Tutor, and behaved very much to my satisfaction in that capacity.

I hope your Grace will pardon me if I Make this request with more than ordinary earnestness, and concern, because I must confess I shall be extremely mortified, if a different disposal of this living, should give the Gentleman of the Country occasion to believe, as I know they would, that I am not honor'd with any share of your Grace's favour, and that you are not willing I should keep up an Interest for my Family in that Country, where I flatter my self I have, at present a pretty good one.

I will wait upon your Grace in a few day's to receive your commands, and beg leave to hope for the continuance of that favor which your Grace has hitherto shewn me, in a greater degree than I could pretend to deserve; having no other merit, but that of being, with the greatest respect . . .

134.

John Campbell to Pryse Campbell, undated but c.1751[258]

I find Matthews is worse than I thought and not likely to recover, I know not what to say about it. G[riffith] P[hilipps] did indeed seem very desireous to have you chose but

---

[255] Matthew Hutton (1693–1758). He was translated to Canterbury in 1757.

[256] Zachary Pearce (1690–1774), bishop of Bangor 1748–56.

[257] The chancellor of Cambridge was Charles Seymour (1662–1748), 6th duke of Somerset. The duke of Newcastle succeeded him as chancellor.

[258] Only the second part of the letter has survived. A pencilled note in a later hand states that it was 'John C's last letter to his son', though perhaps the writer should have said last extant letter. Another note in a different hand dates it 1751, the year Mathews died. At the time of his death – Oct. 1751 – he was MP for Carmarthen. The content of the letter seems to confirm the date. However, Thomas dates the letter not soon after Mathews had been elected to Carmarthen, in 1747, though he used NLW, MS 1352b, which does not contain the pencilled note on the back of the letter. Thomas, *Politics in Eighteenth-Century Wales*, 126.

the debt I had contracted by my contest[259] with Mr Symmons made me so fearfull of expense, that I often told him I could not think of it, and indeed I had long ago told Mr P[elham]; upon which he had advised Mr R[ice] of N[ewton][260] to offer, and that makes the difficulty now, supposing Mr P[hilip]p's Message to be relied on. But indeed it seems odd that the Old Reciever who has been many Years well acquainted with me, should be silent; and his son who I think never spoke to me, & I believe is not acquainted with you, should make this offer and make it by word of mouth to a third Person. If that interest should seperate Sir J[ohn] P[hilipp]s would have the advantage & regain the Town. I wish I had been in the Country when Matthews first fell ill, I could then, by makeing a private journey to Carmarthen, or meeting the Old Reciever at St. Clare's[261] or some such Place, have known what to do, I am now quite bewilder'd. If I see light or certanety any way I shall let you know. I have not seen G[riffith] P[hilipps] lately, I will endeavor to see him to morrow or the next day.

[259] In 1741.

[260] George Rice (?1724–79), of Newton House, Llandeilo, Carmarthenshire. Rice was the duke of Newcastle's south Wales election manager in 1761, and in the same year, and at the behest of Bute, he was made a lord of trade. He married Cecil Talbot, only child of Charles, Lord Talbot (1685–1737) of Hensol, Glamorganshire, lord chancellor 1733–7.

[261] St Clears, west Carmarthenshire.

Chapter 5. 1755–6

Unless otherwise stated, all the letters in this chapter are from CRO, Cawdor/Campbell box 128.

135. [BL, Add. MS 51406, ff. 1–2]
Henry Fox, Holland House to John Campbell, 27 September 1755
Your prophecy is accomplish'd. The Necessity has been seen, of putting the House of Commons in some measure under a new regulation. And H[is] M[ajesty] (who is in the utmost Dejection on finding the Measures, taken for preventing His Electoral Dominions from being attack'd talk'd of by so many in the manner He is told they are, has call'd upon me; & yesterday declar'd His Intention of making me Secretary of State, & giving me the Conduct of the House of Commons.[1] I don't know that I ought to tell you this with much pleasure. I am sure I can't yet say it with any satisfaction, if I could not at the same time inform you that Sir Thomas Robinson[2] is made much happier by going to his old employment the Wardrobe, with a Pension besides of £2,000 a year for 31 years. Barrington will be my successor.[3] I can't kiss His M[ajesty]'s hand till after the first Days Debate[4] which it is expected will be a warm one, & at which I dare hope you will assist. Your good Opinion will be the greatest Use to me in my first Outset.

I will endeavour to, let me say, preserve, not obtain it, For your good Wishes & kindness are such as have convinc'd me I am in some degree possess'd of it, & I never will by my fault forfeit it, for I know the value of it. I am with most affectionate regard . . .

136. [BL, Add. MS 51406, ff. 3–4]
John Campbell to Henry Fox, 2 October 1755
I received from you last Post, with great pleasure, the account of H[is] M[ajesty] having done a thing which I think very much for his service. How far I ought to congratulate you upon it, is indeed a question; for I am sensible it is painfully preeminence. But everyone knows you must fill any station with ability and if you discharge the duty of

[1] It became public knowledge that Fox had accepted the lead in the house of commons and the office of secretary of state for the southern department on 26 Sept. This conclusion had been reached over the summer with Newcastle rejecting Pitt's demands in favour of Fox's. The latter's acceptance of Newcastle's terms finally ended any doubts regarding the animosities between Fox and Pitt.

[2] Sir Thomas Robinson (1695–1770), of Newby, Yorkshire; MP for Thirsk 1727–34 and Christchurch 1748–61. A great friend of Newcastle's who made him leader of the Commons on Henry Pelham's death, though he was incompetent in that office, Pitt commenting that Newcastle 'may as well send his jackboot to govern us'. HPC, 1754–90, iii, 367, citing Horace Walpole. Pitt and Fox combined to make Robinson's position untenable and he resigned after one year, retreating to the office of master of the great wardrobe (1755–60), a post he had previously held (1749–54). He was also secretary – to Horatio Walpole – at the Paris embassy 1724–30; minister at Vienna 1730–48; joint plenipotentiary Aix-la-Chapelle 1748; lord of trade 1748–9; secretary of state for the southern department 1754–5. He was created 1st Baron Grantham in 1761.

[3] As secretary at war. Fox had been in that office since 1746.

[4] Parliament had been prorogued on 25 Apr. and would not meet again until 10 Nov. 1755.

this, as I suspect it you will, with integrity and fidelity, to your K[ing] & Country, that will give a satisfaction, which none can take away, and scarce anything can excede.

Before I had the favour of your kind letter I very little thought of attending the House of Commons before Christmas. I now intend to be there the first day. Your partiality to me, does me great honor; but must not make me forget that I am useless and insignificant. I most heartily wish you may have Mr Legge[5] with you, you know he is an able Man, and I believe you are satisfied, as I am, that he is an honest man; and you know he has been slighted in a manner which no degree of patience could enable a Man of sense & spirit to bear: I say it with concern for those who were so ill advised as not to treat him as he deserved but I hope things may not be gone too far for you to retrieve. I know well, that, upon Mr Pelham's death,[6] it was his desire you should have the Part you are now called to. It would give me great pain to see those I love, and honor on different sides; and, in truth, all I have that regard for in the House of Commons might sit in one bench without crowding. I sometime ago writ my thoughts very planely in a long and (as this will make you easily believe) an impertinent letter to our friend Mr West.[7] I could now wish you saw that Letter, but I hope he has burnt both, & forgot it, long before.

Let me conclude with desireing you will give me permission, and opportunity to speak to you, upon Parliamentary Busyness, as freely as I am used to do; though I don't expect you should throw away much of your time, or attention, upon one, who has no other merit with the Public, but wishing you well, and meaning honestly; or with you, but that of having long been with sincere esteem, and warm good wishes.

137. [BL, Add. MS 32859, ff. 419–20]
John Campbell, Stackpole Court to the duke of Newcastle, 7 October 1755
I have a just and gratefull sense of the unmerited distinction your Grace has been pleased to honor me with, in your letter which I received yesterday. I have indeed a warm zeal for the honor & Interest of my King and Country, and am a sincere and Wellwisher to your Grace, but have nothing else to boast of. I hope to wait upon your Grace before the first day of the Session. I am extremely glad of the good Agreement between your Grace and Mr Fox, and I heartily wish, and hope, such Measures may be taken, as all who act upon right, and public, principles may concur in.

My son [Pryse] has not been in Town, unless for a day, and I believe will stay in the Country till near the meeting of the Parliament; When he comes to Town I hope he will wait upon your Grace, and be most ready to receive any information your Grace will be so good to honor him with. I had the favour of a line from Mr Fox, but have not yet heard from Mr West. I am, with the greatest respect, . . .

138. [BL, Add. MS 32859. ff. 325–6]
The duke of Newcastle, at Newcastle House, London to John Campbell, 9 October 1755
I desired Mr West to acquaint you in answer to your letter to Him, with my earnest Request that you would be at the opening of the session; if ever there was a Time,

[5] Henry Bilson Legge.
[6] Henry Pelham had died on 6 Mar. 1754.
[7] James West.

when the Presence of Able, Honest, and Disinterested Men in Parliament was necessary, It is the present. I cannot explain to give you by letter, the state of our Publick Affairs, or the Reasons, & necessity of the Measures which have been, or are pursued. I will only assure you, that the utmost Care has been taken to promote the great National Views of defending our Rights and Possessions in North America, without engaging in unnecessary Expenses and Doubt not to be able to convince you, That we have strictly adhered to that Principle:

You will find a new scene at Home, not I believe disagreable to you, from many things, which you have formerly said to me & the advice which You gave me. When I have the Pleasure to see you, I shall acquaint you with the Rise & Cause of the intended arrangement[8] which I am persuaded you will approve. Without looking back upon what has past, I can now assure you, That Mr Fox & I are perfectly agreed,[9] and equally satisfied with each other, I am in no doubt, but this agreement will last, because it appears to me both the Interest & Inclination of both Parties. When I mention myself, I always include My Lord Chancellor [Hardwicke] for I take no step without him, & he is a party to all I do. I hope to have the pleasure of seeing your Son [Pryse] who I hear is in Town. If he has any difficulties about measures I wish he would mention them to me, & I will endeavour to remove them.

139. [BL, Add. MS 51406, ff. 5–6]
Henry Fox to John Campbell, 16 October 1755
I have the pleasure to acquaint you that your son [Alexander] is an Ensign in the 3rd Regiment of Guards, & what he will (as I guess from your eldest son's [Pryse] Account of his Military turn) feel the force of, the eldest of two this day made.

I have wrote to Legge & want to see Him. I believe Him to be a very honest amiable Man, but cannot help thinking that He is the Dupe of People[10] whom I know you don't love, on Account of Intrigues which of all others you would least approve, and to which He is *hardly* privy. When I have seen him you shall know more, but I think He must be against these subsidiary Treaty's, and, being so cannot help keep the place He is at present in.[11] After all We have seen of Hessians hir'd on Account of Ripperda's[12] Treaty with Vienna[13] in Sir Robert Walpole's time; Expensive Regard to the Continent in Lord Granville's Administration, more expensively confirmed after his Dismission; and above all the applauded subsidys, given to several Electors for the suppos'd Election of

---

[8] Newcastle's reconstruction of the ministry after the defeat of the Fox–Pitt alliance. See J.C.D. Clark, *The Dynamics of Change: The Crisis of the 1750s and the English Party Systems* (Cambridge, 1982), ch. 2.

[9] Fox had been reconciled with Newcastle, and had accepted the post of secretary of state for the southern department under Newcastle on 26 Sept. but despite the duke reassuring Campbell, there was a huge amount of distrust between the first lord and the secretary. Newcastle believed Fox wished to control the Commons. Clark, *Dynamics of Change*, 190–5.

[10] Pitt and his supporters.

[11] Legge was dismissed as chancellor of the exchequer in Nov. 1755 after opposing the subsidiary treaties with Hesse and Russia.

[12] Johan Willem (1684–1737), Baron and then Duke Ripperda.

[13] Treaty of Vienna, 1725, between Charles VI of Austria and Philip V of Spain, guaranteeing the Pragmatic Sanction of 1713.

a King of the Romans,[14] in time of profound Peace; can one Dear Sir, after all this, imagine that mere Conscience dictates violent, & they say national opposition to subsidiary Treatys enter'd into merely (& exclusively of all other German consideration) to prevent or resist any attack on H[is] M[ajesty]'s Electoral Dominions, if invaded certainly invaded in a British Quarrel only. I am infinity glad & let me say oblig'd to you for your coming to town before the Parliament meets, when both with regard to public & private Measures, I have a Detail to give to you that tho' long will not be tedious. Don't form an opinion until we meet. Whatever it shall after that be on Public measures I am sure You will clearly be convinced of the earnest Desire I have to be esteem'd by you & that Desire founded, on the very great Esteem with which I have long been & now am, Dear Sir, your most obedient . . .

140. [BL, Add. MS 51406, ff. 7–8]
John Campbell to Henry Fox, 21 October 1755
I am extremely thankful for your kind recommendation of my son [Alexander]; and beg you will be so good to make my most humble & respectful acknowledgements where they are due; in the best manner Both my son, & I have a just sense of the honor; and favour done to him, in giving him the seniority. As all my family are here,[15] and my comeing so soon to Town unexpected, it would somewhat embarras me to bring the young Captain up with me. I should be very glad if he might stay here till after Christmas; but if that cannot be, he will be ready to obey your commands if you please to signifie them to him by Mr Calcraft,[16] for the badness of the Season, and of our roads, will make my journey so tedious, that I propose to leave this Place before I could receive your Answer. It gives me a particular pleasure that my son has his Commission before you leave the Office,[17] so that all my thanks are due where I can pay them with the greatest satisfaction.

I can say little of public Affairs at this distance, but as I am too weak to make wise determinations, I am too old to make very rash ones, so shall form no decisive opinion till I have the pleasure of seeing you, when I shall be most desireous to hear, all you will be so kind to communicate to me. However as you are pleased to mention somewhat to me of the Subsidiary Treaty's, I will take the liberty to tell you some of my thoughts, in my present state of ignorance.

I never hoped that, in case of a War with France, Wee should be able to confine it to the sea and N[orth] America; and if Hanover is attack'd on our account, I think we are obliged in honor, and justice to assist; but there I should think others ought to assist also. If the Elector of Hanover was not the King of Great Britain what would the

---

[14] Francis 1 (1708–65), holy Roman emperor from 1745 and duke of Tuscany. He was married to Maria Theresa who de facto wielded the power of his offices.

[15] At Stackpole Court.

[16] John Calcraft (1726–72), of Rempstone, Dorset and Ingress, Kent; MP for Calne 1766–8 and Rochester 1768–72. He was a protégé of Henry Fox, who, until 1763, promoted him in every way he could, most lucratively appointing him as a communications agent between chiefs of the army and Fox himself. By 1762 Calcraft had 57 of these agencies – covering over half of the army. However, an irreconcilable difference emerged in Apr. 1763 over changes in the ministry and whether Fox should leave the pay office once made a peer. Horace Walpole commented of Calcraft: 'this tool, this mushroom overdunged, rose against him [Fox]'. Calcraft retired from the agency work at the end of 1764, after amassing a fortune, to become an MP.

[17] Of secretary at war.

Empress Queen[18] and all the Princes's of the Empire, not corrupted by France, think if they saw that Electorate invaded by a French army, would they not say, proximus ardet,[19] and exert their utmost abilities, to drive the French out of the Empire. They ought not therefore now, to throw the whole burthen upon us. Wee have assisted them often, and powerfully, when the quarrel did not immediately concern us, and I think they should now assist us, for though this Quarrel is purely British, yet if Wee are much hurt, the consequences must affect them; and if they lag more upon us than Wee are able to bear, they will kill the Hen, that has laid them many a golden egg.

I know nothing particular of these Treaty's nor do I in the least know the schemes of those who intend to oppose them; But I must have a very short memory, if I could believe that mere Conscience either prompted, or conducted some Peoples Opposition. I have often express'd my opinion of them, very freely, both to you and Mr Legge. I lament that he has been thrown in their Way, I fully believe he is not in their inmost Secrets. And I am pretty sure, it is not very long, since he was well disposed to Friendship with others. I may venture to assure you, that you will find in me, an honest disposition for the Service of my King, and Country; no prejudice against the Administration and sincere desire to shew that I am, with true esteem . . .

141.

John Campbell to Mary Campbell, 13 November 1755

I received yours of the 7th inst[ant] and left that you inclosed for you sister with her last night in my way to the Cockpit. I have been in a sort of political hurry since I came to Town. I have been getting information from the secretary elect,[20] who I would have gone to, but, as he said, he found it more convenient to come to me, which he did on Saturday & staid about three hours, and upon my signifieing, that I wanted a word more with him, before the meeting at his house on tuesday, he came here between Court & dinner on the Birthday,[21] I had also some conference with him last night at the Cockpit.[22] Our Friend L[egge] was neither at Mr P[itt]'s on tuesday nor at the Cockpit last night, I knew before I left the Country, that he would be against the subsidiary Treaties, but I now fear, he will have no political intercourse with any in the Administration, and be too much connected with P[itt] & C[umberland?][23] for which I am extremely sorry; That with the uncertane [sic] of what my Son[24] will do, and the fear that he may take a course quite contrary to my judgement & wishes, has kept my mind in continual agitation. I am uncertane whether or no Wee shall have a very long debate

---

[18] Maria Theresa.

[19] Horace, *Epistles*, i, xviii, line 71. The full quote is: 'Nam tua res agitur, paries cum proximus ardet. [It is your concern when your neighbour's wall is on fire]'.

[20] That is, Henry Fox.

[21] The king's birthday was celebrated on 7 Nov. *London Evening Post*, 8 Nov. 1755.

[22] Fox stated that 287 members were present at the cockpit meeting, to hear his defence of the subsidy treaties which were to be debated in the House. Earl of Ilchester, *Henry Fox, First Lord Holland* (2 vols, 1920), i, 281–2.

[23] Both being anti-subsidy treaty but pro-war.

[24] Pryse Campbell, although expected to follow his father as a whig, showed much less hostility towards the tories than John Campbell liked. In 1757 he voted with Campbell's hated Pitt on the Minorca inquiry, and in the same year Newcastle believed Pryse to be a supporter of Pitt. *HPC, 1754–90*, i, 190–1. See Introduction.

this day.[25] If I come home time enough I will send a word to the Lyon.[26] I send you inclosed the Motion which is to be made upon the King's speech by Lord Hillsborough Seconded by Mr Wyndham Obrian.[27] The words in the last page which I have drawn a line through were struck out since this Copy was given to me which was last Saturday, the [sic] answer'd some words in the Speech which were left out on a scruple of the Solicitors that the Commons ought not to give any directions, however right in themselves, relating to the raising of money. Lord Egmont Doddington & Sir G[eorge] L[yttelton] will be with the Administration, so will old H[orace][28] who is soon to be a Peer. I was at N[ewcastle] H[ouse][29] on tuesday very well received & a little while in private & spoke a little very freely I was desired to come sometimes at nine o Clock on the most leisure days, which I promised to do, and said that while I had that liberty, I would endeavor to say to H[is] G[race] what I thought might serve him, rather than what I thought might please him. If he continues to like such Freedom I trust I shall use it honestly though perhaps very weakly, when he is weary of it, I can stay at home. Sir G[eorge] L[yttelton] will I believe be violent in opposition.

My Love to dear Lyon & Bessy Ally is very well busy preparing Regimentals &c I am very sorry for poor Mr Hooke.

List of Speakers on Thursday	Mr William Beckford ag[ains]t
Lord Hillsborough moved	Attorney General [William Murray] for
Mr Wyndham O'Brian seconded	Sir G[eorge] Lee ag[ains]t
Mr Colbrook ag[ains]t	Sir Thomas Robinson for
Mr Martin ag[ains]t	Mr Legge ag[ains]t
Mr Stanhope for	Mr Potter ag[ains]t
Mr Hamilton for	Mr H[orace] Walpole Senior for
Mr Alston for	Dr Hayes ag[ains]t
Mr Northey ag[ains]t	Mr G[eorge] Townshend ag[ains]t
Mr Ellis for	Lord Egmont ¾ for
Sir Richard Lyttelton ag[ains]t	Mr William Pitt ag[ains]t
Mr Dodington ½ ag[ains]t	Mr Fox for
Lord Barrington for	Admirable Vernon ag[ains]t[30]

[25] On leaving out of the address a resolution to support the king's German lands. *CJ*, xxvii, 298; Clark, *Dynamics of Change*, 214; Pitt started speaking at just after 1 a.m. and spoke for over 90 minutes. *PH*, xv, 537.

[26] The Lyon was John (Jack) Campbell (younger brother of Pryse), of Bangeston, Pembrokeshire and later Chareton, Kent. He was Lord Lyon king of arms of Scotland, a junior officer of state in Scotland (1754–95). See Introduction.

[27] Percy Wyndham O'Brian (?1723–74), of Shortgrove, Essex; MP for Taunton 1745–7, Minehead 1747–54 and 1761–8, Cockermouth 1754–61 and Winchelsea 1768–74. Lord of the treasury 1755–6; treasurer of the household 1757–61. O'Brian was created earl of Thomond (Irish peerage) on 11 Dec. 1756.

[28] Horatio Walpole (1723–1809), MP for King's Lynn 1747–57. He succeeded his father, Horatio Walpole of Wolterton, as 2nd Baron Walpole of Wolterton in 1757. He was created 1st earl of Orford in 1806.

[29] In Lincoln's Inn Fields, London.

[30] George Colebrook (1729–1809), of Gatton, Surrey; MP for Arundel 1754–74; Samuel Martin (1714–88), of Abingdon Buildings, London; MP for Camelfors 1747–68 and Hastings 1768–74; Philip Stanhope (1732–68), MP for Liskeard 1754–61 and St Germans 1761–5. He was the illegitimate son of Philip Dormer Stanhope, 4th earl of Chesterfield. Stanhope froze as he spoke and never uttered another word in the Commons; William Gerard Hamilton (1729–96), of Hampton Court, Middlesex; MP for Petersfield 1754–61, Pontefract 1761–8, Old Sarum 1768–74, Wareham 1774–80, Wilton 1780–90 and Haslemere 1790–6. Lord

Mr G[eorge] Grenville ag[ains]t
Sir G[eorge] Lyttelton for
Sir Francis Dashwood ½ ag[ains]t
Mr Nugent for

First Division Ay's 105 No's 311[31]
Second Division Ay's 290 No's 89[32]

142.
John Campbell to Mary Campbell, 20 November 1755
I will begin my Politics with a little explanation of Subsidies; They are sums of money paid to Foreign Princes, either for their troops actually in our Service or kept in readiness to come into our service when we require them. The Subsidys now the subject of Conversation, & debate, are to be paid in consequence of two Treaties[33] concluded this summer and autumn with the Empress of Russia & the Landgrave of Hesse Cassel.[34] That with the Landgrave was sign'd at Hanover June 18. It is for four years The Landgrave to furnish 3000 Men of which 1900 to be Horse. The king to pay £47643 15s 00d levy money, for the foot, half upon the exchange of Ratifications, the other half when they shall march and £144375 levy money for the Horse, the one half to be paid when he requires the 3000 Men, the other half when the Horse shall actually march. The King is also to pay a subsidy of £36098 15s per annum from the day of signing the Treaty, till he requires the Troops to March; and from that time till the Troops are in the pay of Great Britain a subsidy at the rate of £72187 10s while the Troops are in the Kings pay the subsidy to be the same as before the Requisition. When the Troops are in actual service the King is to pay them; if in Germany on the same foot with his own German Troops,

---

[30] *(continued)* of trade 1756–61, an office obtained for him by Henry Fox. Hamilton resigned this office to become secretary to Lord Halifax as viceroy to Ireland; chancellor of the exchequer for Ireland 1763–84. This was his maiden speech, and was reputedly written for him by his close friend Samuel Johnson. He also sat in the Irish house of commons for Kellybegs, 1761–68. *ODNB*; *HPC, 1754–90*, ii, 272–4; Thomas Alston (c.1724–74), of Odell, Bedfordshire; MP for Bedfordshire 1747–61; William Northey (?1722–70), of Compton Bassett, Calne and (after 1761) Ivy House, Chippenham, Wiltshire; tory MP for Calne 1747–61, Maidstone 1761–8 and Great Bedwyn 1768–70. He persistently attacked Newcastle and Fox and was one of the tories who met at the Horn Tavern, London, to discuss the Minorca inquiry in 1757; Richard Lyttelton (1709–73), of Hagley Hall, Worcestershire; MP for Okehampton 1735–56. One of Cobham's cubs and violently opposed to Walpole and his administration. Son of Sir Thomas Lyttelton, 4th bt. Lieutenant colonel 1744; colonel 1747; master of the jewel office 1756–62; major general 1757; lieutenant general 1759; governor of Minorca 1/62–6 and Guernsey 1766–73; William Beckford (1709–70), of Fonthill, Wiltshire; MP for Shaftesbury 1747–54 and London 1754–70. Sheriff of London 1755–6; lord mayor of London 1762–3 and 1769–70. A great supporter of Pitt; Thomas Potter (?1718–59), of Ridgemount, Bedfordshire; MP for St Germans 1747–54, Aylesbury 1754–7 and Okehampton 1757–9; also a great friend of Pitt; Thomas Hay, Viscount Dupplin (1710–87), whig MP for Scarborough 1736 and Cambridge 1741–65; George Townshend (1724–1807), of Raynham, Norfolk; MP for Norfolk 1747–64. Succeeded his father as 4th Viscount Townshend in 1764 and was created Marquess Townshend in 1787. 'The first great English caricaturist'. *HPC, 1715–54*, ii, 473; *HPC, 1754–90*, i, 524.

[31] *CJ*, xxvii, 298.

[32] *CJ*, xxvii, 298.

[33] The treaty between Britain and the landgrave of Hesse-Kassel, signed 18 June 1755, granting a £300,000 subsidy. And the treaty between Britain and Russia, signed 30 Sept. 1755, granting a subsidy of £500,000, plus an annual payment of £100,000.

[34] William VIII (1682–1760) ruled Hesse-Kassel, first as regent 1730–51 and then as landgrave 1751–60.

if in the Low Countrys as the Dutch Troops, and if in Great Britain or Ireland as his British Troops The King to pay the expence of recruiting, and for any Artillery taken by the Enemy, and to transport them if they come here, at his own expence. If desired the Landgrave agrees to add 700 Horse & 3300 foot on the like conditions.

The Convention with Russia was sign'd Sept 30. It renews the defensive Alliance of 1742.[35] It is for four years, and the Empress is during that time to keep 55000 Men: viz 40000 foot & 15000 Horse, on the frontiers of Livonia,[36] and 40 or 50 Galleys on the Coast of that Province, ready to act, in case of an attack on the King or his Allies, on the requisition of the King. An attack of the Kings German Dominions *on account of the Interests of his Kingdoms* shall be consider'd as a Case within the Treaty of 1742. The Empress is to pay all the expences of the Troops & heavy Artillery. The King to pay the Empress a subsidy of £100000 per annum till the day the troops shall go out of the Russian Territories at the Kings requisition, from which time the subsidy shall be £50000 per annum. The King to send a Commissary every year to examine the numbers & conditions of the Troops. N.B. By the defensive Alliance of 1742 the Empress is to assist the King in Case of an attack with 10000 foot & 2000 Horse or 500000 Roubles per annum. In case the Empress is attack'd, the King is to furnish 12 Men of War of the line of Battle or 500000 Roubles per annum which is about £100000 sterling. N.B. The Hessian Treaty is for even sums in foreign money, reducing to british occasions the odd money. And now I believe you know more of the subsidiary Treatys, than two thirds of the House of Commons, for the Treaties are not yet laid before the House, and the accounts of them in the Newspapers have been erroneous, but I write from abstracts of them which Mr Fox sent me 3 days before the Parliament met. You will observe that the Troops are not to March till required and before the requisition what Wee are to pay is half the Levy money for the Hessian Foot, and the lesser subsides to the Landgrave & the Empress of Russia.

Half levy Money to Hesse	£23821	17s	06d
Subsidy to Hesse	£36093	15s	00d
Subsidy to Russia	£100000	00s	00d
	£159915	12s	06d

The great opposition to these Treatys is on supposition that they are to bring us into a general War on the Continent at an immense expence.

L[egge] P[itt] & G[eorge] Grenville are to be immediately removed[37] the vacancys are not to be so soon fill'd only L[egge]'s office cannot be left vacant, so it is to be fill'd by Sir G[eorge] L[yttelto]n.[38] He is to be L[egge]'s successor, but as unlike, as I to Hercules.[39]

---

[35] The treaty between Britain and Russia, signed 11 Dec. 1742.

[36] A historic region on the eastern Baltic with an inland border with Russia.

[37] Legge as chancellor of the exchequer, Pitt as paymaster to the forces and Grenville as a treasurer to the navy, were removed from office on 20 Nov. (the same date as this letter) for voting against the government on the subsidies for Russia and the landgrave of Hesse-Kassel.

[38] As chancellor of the exchequer 1755–6. He was widely regarded as being unsuited to the post. Pitt respected him as a poet but feared his incapacity as a chancellor. Ilchester, *Henry Fox*, i, 309.

[39] A reference to William Shenstone's *The Judgement of Hercules, a Poem inscribed to George Lyttelton* (1741). However the following lines do not occur in the poem.

Who will not laugh, when such a thing they see
Who will not weep the time, such things must be.

I fancy Wee may hear in the House of Commons some reflections on the Conversion & Apostleship of St Paul.[40] The P.Ds family[41] were in the minority the other night.[42] Who thought Wee should in this Reign see another Lower House Opposition[43] but so it seems to be, is it decent, is it gratefull, is it wise. Lady Dalkeith[44] on her marriage with Charles Townshend[45] has got a Sedan finely adorn'd with French Plate I cannot say it has a good effect. There have been repeted Riots at Drury Playhouse,[46] this nights evening post gives account of the last. It was Gentlemen (Fools) who supported the Dancers against the Noblesse in the Gallerys & Pit. I hear that when the beaten party went to break Mr Garrick's[47] windows they said, if we can't get the better of him here, wee will attack him in his Electoral Dominions. A great Mob Assembled in the Street so that the Gentlemen who were victorious in the House were afraid to come out, and it was not empty till past twelve at night. The best of the thing is, that the poor Divels who were driven off our stage for being French, were some months ago, hiss'd of [*sic*] the stage at Paris, for not being French. It seems they were mostly Germans. You may communicate all my news to the Lyon . . .[48]

Ally [Alexander] is today on Guard for the first time at the Tilt yard.

We have had rain in abundance, only this day was never without rain.

I told Mr Fox & some others your Bon Mot Honesty, Legge has enough for us all, and they were much pleased with it, I did not steal the credit of it, but gave it where due.

It grieves me very much to see L[egge] drove as I fear he is, into the Clan Cobham.

---

[40] A reference to George Lyttelton who wrote *Observations on the Conversion of St Paul* (1747).

[41] P.D. is most likely to be Princess Dowager (Augusta), and her family, the Leicester House opposition headed by Pitt and the Grenville brothers.

[42] 13 Nov. 1755.

[43] The previous opposition was that led by the prince of Wales until his death in 1751. Horace Walpole asked, 'Who are the new opposition? – Why, the old opposition, Pitt and the Grenvilles; indeed with Legge instead of Sir George Lytttelton. Judge how entertaining this was to me, to hear Lyttelton answer Grenville, and Pitt, Lyttelton'. Walpole to Richard Bentley, 16 Nov. 1755, cited in *PH*, xv, 538. See Clark, *Dynamics of Change*, 201–5.

[44] Caroline Campbell (1717–94), 1st Baroness Greenwich, daughter of the 2nd duke of Argyll. By her first marriage she took the title countess of Dalkeith (her husband being Francis Scott, earl of Dalkeith who died in 1750). She married Charles Townshend on 15 Aug. 1755.

[45] Charles Townshend (1725–67), of Adderbury, Oxfordshire; MP for Great Yarmouth 1747–56, Saltash 1756–61 and Harwich 1761–7. Lord of trade 1749–54, of the admiralty 1754–5; treasurer of the chamber 1756–61; secretary at war 1761–2; first lord of trade 1763; paymaster general 1765–6; chancellor of the exchequer 1766–7.

[46] The *Evening Post*, 18 Nov. 1755, reported that in the affray one gentleman had his leg broken while another 'run one of the spikes of the Orchestry in his foot in getting on the stage out of the Pit'. Since 8 Nov. 1755 David Garrick had put on *The Chinese Festival*, a ballet by the Swiss choreographer Jean Georges Novere (1727–1810). Most of the dancers were French, and anti-French feeling was higher than usual since Britain was about to be immersed in the Seven Years War. *ODNB*.

[47] David Garrick (1717–79), actor, playwright, theatre manager and producer. He became the manager of Drury Lane theatre in 1747 until 1776.

[48] Two lines obliterated.

143.

John Campbell to Mary Campbell, 22 November 1755

Yesterday morning Lord Holdernesse[49] writ letters to Mr Legge, Mr Pitt, & Mr George Grenville to dismiss them from the Kings Service; I was at Legges soon after, he expected Lord Holdernesse between 12 & 1, to receive from him the seal of the Exchequer which was the same day deliver'd to Sir G[eorge] Lyttelton. The House of Commons was full that day[50] in expectation of a Motion from Mr George Townshend for a call of the House, which he made merely to have an opportunity to mention some letters[51] writ by Mr Fox to several members, in which he said he was to have the conduct of the House of Commons Mr Fox I think made no great matter of it; the letters were writ by a Clerk & only sign'd by Mr Fox who said that in the Draught there were words which alter'd the meaning which were by a slip in hast left out by the Clerk. Mr Fox had not one of those letters himself, so another member who did not think fit to appear must have lent Mr Fox a letter or given him a Copy, not much so that members credit neither do I Mr Fox did himself much honor. Nobody else spoke about it to so the call was without opposition, or occasion, the House being so full allready, order'd for that day sevenight.[52] Then Mr Ellis moved for 40000 Seamen including the Marines, Sir Richard Littelton [Lyttleton] made a very long Speech, of dislike, which make little impression & kindled no heat, I was sorry there were no Ladies in the Gallery as Sir Richard display'd an embroider'd velvet Coat a handsome face and a bright red Ribband[53] in broad effulgence.[54] When I thought all was over & the question just going to be put Mr Pitt got up, began with wishing for 50000 Seamen besides the Marines, but desired unanimity & therefore would make no Motion; he soon left the question and when [sic] into a long declamation against the Ministers and the Administration for several years past,[55] with very strong things personal to Mr Fox on his Ambition, struggle for Power, and complying with anything ever so bad to get into the Office he now has,[56] Fox answer'd & being in a Committee there were several reply's between them two, at length, the Attorney General [WilliamMurray] got up upon Mr Pitt's Speaking the granting but 8000 Seamen in 1748, as a giving up of

<hr/>

[49] Robert Darcy (1718–78), 4th earl of Holdernesse. He was ambassador at Venice 1744–6 and The Hague 1749–51; secretary of state at the southern department 1751–4 and at the northern department 1754–61.

[50] 21 Nov. 1755.

[51] Circular letters were a form of whip summoning members to attend parliament to vote on specific issues. See L.B. Namier, 'The Circular Letters: An Eighteenth-Century Whip to Members of Parliament', *EHR*, xxxiv (1929). Circular letters were sent out under Fox's name calling his supporters to attend the House for the debate on the subsidy treaties in which had been written 'the conduct of the House' rather than the customary 'The conduct of His Majesty's affairs in the House'. Some of the members drew suspicious motives from the change. Ilchester, *Henry Fox*, i, 280–1.

[52] *CJ*, xxvii, 306, gives the call to be made a fortnight hence – 5 Dec. 1755.

[53] Denotes a knight companion of the order of the bath. Lyttelton had received this honour in 1753.

[54] See P.D.G. Thomas, *The House of Commons in the Eighteenth Century* (Oxford, 1971), 3–5, concerning the sartorial elegance, or otherwise, of members.

[55] Clark, *Dynamics of Change*, 217.

[56] Pitt was hoping for a secretaryship but Newcastle plumped for Fox as being more reliable. Pitt was also excluded from the regency council. His subsequent spleen was vented in verbal attacks in the Commons such as the one described by Campbell.

the Maritime, & consequently the interest & honor of this Country. The A[ttorney] G[eneral] took it as a reflection on the memory of Mr Pelham. P[itt] express [*sic*] great regard for that and denied any intention to blame him, but said it was a collusion between two parts of the Administration, meaning that whoever was at the head of the Admiralty at the time (either the Duke of Bedford or Lord Sandwich I believe the latter)[57] gave up the Fleet to the Army that is to the Duke of Cumberland indeed I think there was a great deal pointed at him, great complaint that in this time of danger our Land Forces were not sooner increased, nor proper care to raise the additional force when order'd, all this though it might seem immediately to strike at Fox yet most I think be intended to rest on the Duke. He also heavily blamed the Regency[58] for these things, and Wee know who was the first name in it, compare this with what I told you before. I do not think Pitt hurt Fox at all last night though it is true Pitt was fine, and entertaining. I suppose Pitt intend's to give Fox little rest. George Grenville sat grinning all the while Pitt was speaking but said nothing Legge to my comfort sat sometime in a back seat then stood behind the Chair sometime & went away before it was over. Wee sat till between six & seven. Wee have rain every day, or night a great shower of hail to day & heavy rain. My Love to . . .

144.
John Campbell to Mary Campbell, 29 November 1755
Letters from Sir B[enjamin] Keen[e] our ambassador at Madrid came on thursday night confirming the dismal news from Lisbon. The Earthquake happen'd the 1st inst: at a quarter before ten in the Morning but the confusion & consternation were so great that no letters were writ till the 4th. A great part of the City was thrown down, and the fires that were in the fallen houses set the ruins in flames which being communicated to the standing houses, abandon'd by the terrifie'd Inhabitants, the City was burning when the Express came away, I should say the remains of the City. The Popes Nuntio dated his letter to Madrid, From the place where Lisbon was. There were no letters from or any mention of Mr Castres[59] our Envoy or Mr Hay,[60] Lord Dupplins brother, our Consul; Lord Drumlanrig[61] was at Mr Hays house. Sir B[enjamin] Keen says Mr Castres was so well known & so much esteem'd that he thinks he would have been mention'd if lost but perhaps he rather express's his wishes than his belief: The Palace was destroy'd and had the King[62] and royal family been in it they must have perish'd, but they were a little

---

[57] The duke of Bedford was first lord of the admiralty 1744–8 and Lord Sandwich in the years 1748–51, 1763 and 1771–82.

[58] A regency council was established in 1755, as a precaution, when the 77-year-old George II visited Hanover at the end of April. The prince of Wales was just 17. The council consisted of 16 members including Fox, with the duke of Cumberland as its president.

[59] Abraham Castres (*d.* 1757), an intimate friend of Keene, who became envoy extraordinary at Lisbon in 1749. Sir Richard Lodge, *The Private Correspondence of Sir Benjamin Keene* (Cambridge, 1933), xxvi.

[60] Edward Hay, consul at Cadiz and then, in 1753, at Lisbon. Lodge, *Private Correspondence of Sir Benjamin Keene*, xxxi.

[61] Lord Charles Douglas, Lord Drumlanrig, was the son of Charles Douglas, 3rd duke of Queensberry (1698–1778).

[62] Joseph I (1714–77), king of Portugal 1750–77.

way out of Town. Mr Fox told me that the King had writ to his sister the Queen of Spain[63] that he was encamped almost without necessary's. The Custom House and most of the Merchants Warehouses[64] were near the Palace I have heard the english loss supposed to be two millions, a great treasure was very lately arrived, much of it belonging to english. The King of Spain[65] has sent several Couriers with as much money as they could carry, and order provisions to be sent from the bordering parts of Spain, and to let the Portuguese have every thing duty free; he immediately declared the son of his Ambassador who was lost at Lisbon a gentleman of his Bedchamber, though very young. No letters have mention'd any particular number of People supposed to have perish'd at Lisbon but it must be very great. Yesterday Secretary Fox brought a message[66] from the King (the like sent to the Lords) upon the occasion of this dreadful Calamity, desireing the House would enable him to send some succour to the distress'd when the Speaker had read the Message, Mr Fox made a short Speech in which he read the Copy of a letter from Sir B[enjamin] Keen[e] and moved an Address to the King promising to make good whatever H[is] M[ajesty] should lay out for relief of these poor unfortunate People. Mr William Pitt seconded him and said if the Forms of the House did (not) require he should think it needless to second a motion that must upon hearing be seconded by the feelings of every heart, the question was immediately put, & in a full house, pass'd nemine contradicente,[67] then Wee adjourn'd to Monday. Mr Fox said he did not think more could be laid out than £100,000. I think it will do honor to the King & Parliament both at home & abroad. Before Wee received the message Sir T[homas] Stepneys[68] Petition[69] was deliver'd & by agreement order'd to be heard the 10th of February.

Wheather continues very bad Rain thursday night yesterday only very cold but at night the wind rose, what time it began to rain I don't know but before I waked it was high wind and heavy rain, and has continued ever since rain or snow or both together. All our Friends in town are well . . .

145.
John Campbell to Mary Campbell, 16 December 1755
What you say of disappointments is very just and it ought to teach us an entire resignation to the dissolutions of infinite Wisdom. Yesterday the resolutions of the Committee of Supply for the Russian & Hessian subsidies, were agreed to by the House

---

[63] Mariana Victoria (1718–81), eldest daughter of Philip V, king of Spain 1700–46.

[64] Probably belonging to the British Factory which was a prominent organisation of British merchants in Lisbon, established in 1642. Lodge, *Private Correspondence of Sir Benjamin Keene*, xxvii.

[65] Ferdinand VI, 'the Learnt', king 1746–79.

[66] *PH*, xv, 543–4: on 8 Dec. the Commons resolved 'That £100,000 be granted to his majesty', towards assistance to the people of Lisbon.

[67] *CJ*, xxvii, 320.

[68] Sir Thomas Stepney (1724–72), 7th bt, of Llanelli, Carmarthenshire.

[69] *CJ*, xxvii, 320: Stepney's petition asserted that the other candidate in the election, Griffith Philipps, was related to the returning officers who encouraged those non-qualified to vote for Philipps whilst rejecting those qualified to vote who would have supported Stepney. This petition was followed by one from the burgesses of Carmarthen borough stating that Stepney was not a burgess of the borough and therefore unable to stand for election.

after a Debate which lasted till nine at night.[70] The two principal speakers were the Attorney General [William Murray] & Mr Pitt, to me the Attorneys carried most conviction Pitts was indeed the most entertaining I think he out did his usual outdoings. I spoke a few words that I might declare my assent more explicitly than by mere voting. When Wee divided first on the Russian question, Mr Pitt Mr Legge & George Townshend being at the upper end of the House, inadvertently sat till the door was shut, and then it was against order to open it for them, Sir George Lee was shut in too, but he having been in solemans Porch[71] where he could not see the door shut was let out, the other three were obliged to be counted with us, so the numbers for agreeing with the Committee were Ay's 263, No's 69.[72] Mr Pitt seem'd very angry at first but recover'd his temper, and they had soon an opportunity to set the matter right, for the question being put to agree for the Hessian subsidy they divided again Ay's 260. No's 72.[73] My son did not attempt to speak that day.[74] Lord Egmont spoke for the Treaty's. I expected to hear Sir J[ohn] P[hilipps] but he was absent. You will see Melancholy accounts from Lisbon in this night's Paper . . .[75] I am very sorry for poor Mr . . . sister . . . dined with us to day upon a very fine pheasant[76] given me by Colin Donaldson, She seem'd in good health and spirits. Master Edwards & she dined with us on Sunday the Master blith & good humor'd.

The inclosed Bill was brought here to day, You will let me know if it is right, and as soon as you return it I will pay it. By mistake I left all the Bills & receipts you gave me when you came down lock'd in a drawer at Stackpole. My love to . . .

A storm of wind & rain last night, the Wind till 8 this morning the day pretty good, wind & rain again at night, but I think the wind is fallen again.

The three Gentleman being shut in the first question occasion'd an uproar of mirth in the House.

146. [BL, Add. MS 51406, f. 9]
Henry Fox at Bath to John Campbell, 5 January 1756
I have been in London since I last wrote to you from hence. Could I have given a guess at what would be the Result of the very extraordinary appearances I saw in the House of Commons, I would have wrote to you whilst there. I hope to hear your prophetick opinion soon, and write this to say that if you are not yet set out I hope you will set out time enough at least to be at the Call[77] upon the 20th.

---

[70] *CJ*, xxvii, 339; *PH*, xv. 660–4.

[71] A door at the back of the chamber gave access to a passage, called Solomon's Porch, on the way to the Speaker's room. Thomas, *House of Commons in the Eighteenth Century*, 2.

[72] *CJ*, xxvii, 339.

[73] *CJ*, xxvii, 339, gives 259 to 72; see Clark, *Dynamics of Change*, 220, for analysis of Pitt's failure to win any division at this time.

[74] Pryse Campbell had been returned for Inverness-shire in 1754.

[75] One line obliterated.

[76] From 'I am' to 'by' crossed through, and two or three words illegible.

[77] The call of the House was repeatedly adjourned until 6 Apr. 1756 when it was postponed indefinitely. *CJ*, xxvii, 567.

I shall be in town Tuesday next, & the moment you let me know, at Richmond House in Priory Garden;[78] that you are in Grosvenor Square,[79] I'll come to you, for it is with the utmost confidence & sincerest affection that I am . . .

147. [BL, Add. MS 51406, ff. 11–12]
John Campbell to Henry Fox, 6 July 1756
I spoke to Colonel Watson the next day after I saw you last at Holland House, but he was then going out of Town; and I had no opportunity to see him again, so for fear he should have forgot it, I have by this post put him a mind to lay before the Duke of Marlborough his representation for removing some Guns that now lye entirely useless at Tenby in this County, to a place upon Milford haven, where I believe at a very moderate expense they may be of Service to defend this Harbour and Country; which now lye exposed to the insults of any little Privateer.[80] I must beg your Interest with his Grace for the removing & planting of the Guns, and I believe, with his Royal Highness, for men to serve and discharge them on occasion; for I am not one of those who think Guns will fire of themselves. But I hope the expense of what I desire will not appear too great a price for our Security; and it is indeed a matter of very serious concern to me, who have many Tenants, and some friends, Gentlemen of considerable Fortune, who are so situated that they might be plunder'd in half an hour; and if they had more warning, I am of opinion that even the Crew of a Privateer, might drive the Aniere Ban[81] of our County, before them like sheep, I should say Goats.

I have read Mr Byngs[82] letter,[83] with great surprise. I am so ignorant of all Military matters both by Sea and Land, that for what reason I know, the Admiral may have done the best he could, and was not able to give a better account of the French Fleet. But how he could have any pleasure in giving such an Account, I cannot possibly conceive, nor what he means by calling it an important event; surely it was not an event of any good importance.

Can I hear of nothing but Misfortunes abroad & absurdities at home. It would give me great pleasure indeed if I could hear that my Cousin[84] had so just a sense of his own,

---

[78] Priory Gardens, Richmond, Surrey.

[79] Campbell had leased a house in Grosvenor Square in 1728, the year after becoming MP for Pembrokeshire. CRO, Cawdor/Campbell box 5/99. A lease dated 28 Aug. 1728, from Sir Thomas Pope Blount of Twickenham to Campbell.

[80] The coast around the south of Pembrokeshire is full of small inlets, which were a haven for privateers and smugglers. In 1798, Pryse Campbell's grandson, 1st Baron Cawdor, broke up a smuggling gang near Stackpole, though not without being beaten with a bludgeon. CRO, Cawdor/Campbell box 2/285.

[81] Arriere Ban: in French customs a general proclamation whereby the king summons to war all his vassals and their vassals.

[82] John Byng (c.1704–57), of Wrotham Park, Middlesex; admiral. MP for Rochester 1751–7. Byng was executed after failing 'to do his utmost' during the battle of Minorca (20 May 1756), the opening sea battle of the Seven Years War. Voltaire satirised Byng's execution in *Candide*: 'in this country, it is wise to kill an admiral from time to time to encourage the others'.

[83] Byng's account of what happened at Minorca in May. Whereas the unpublished letter was partly 'a palpable impeachment of the ministry [which, of course, included Fox], under whose orders he was acting', the published version had 'had every expression tending in anyway to cast blame on the minsters' carefully expunged. *Newgate Calendar*. http://www.pascalbonenfant.com/18c/newgatecalendar. Fox admitted altering the content of Byng's account, though he said that nothing material to the admiral's court martial was removed. Ilchester, *Henry Fox*, i, 337–8.

[84] The duke of Newcastle.

& his Masters[85] Interest; as to do, without reserve or any starting back what he told the Duke of D[evonshire] he must do. And I think I give the best proof of my Friendship to him in saying so; because I am satisfied he would meet with most generous return, and the more power he properly communicated, the more he would keep. It really grieves me, to see him like a man who, for fear of trusting any one, carrys all his money jingling in his pocket, and is flatter'd out of it by one sort of Knaves; bully'd out of it by another, has it stolen from him by Pickpocketts; and it is very good luck if after all, he is not knock'd down & rifle'd by Robbers. I do, not intend to trouble you with my impertinence often; but when I do, I trust you will forgive me writing with the freedom of a friend, rather in the manner that is proper from a poor Scots Laird, or Welch Mountain Squire[86] to a Secretary of State. Give me leave then to assure you, that my best wishes always attend you both in your public, & private life, and that I am very sincerely . . .

148. [BL, Add. MS 51406, ff. 13–14]
Henry Fox to John Campbell, 15 July 1756[87]
I am not like Mr Bing [Byng], & it is with *no pleasure* that I send you the inclos'd account which came yesterday. The Place[88] was it seems impregnable, & would have prov'd so had Mr Bing put in Succours[89] which might have made the Garrison sufficient to defend so many parts at once assaulted. The smallness of the Garrison is suppos'd to have been the loss of the place & Thus Mr Bing's Retreat to Gibraltar has been an important Event. The French have landed likewise a great many Regular Troops at Quebec.

You hear indeed of nothing but Misfortune from abroad and I fear will not find any probability from our Councils at home, of your hearing better. Your Cousin seems still to hold Ministerial power as dear, & to be as jealous of it as ever. *Habitet secum*[90] as well the thing as the Temper that is so tenacious of it. If I knew how to do any good with it, I should desire & envy it. But tho' I see how fatally ill things are going, as I don't know how to mend them I am not unreasonable enough to wish for what I could not conduct. If there is in this Island a Man who could give me Hope of success in War, or Security in Peace, I wish Him Minister.

In this Temper of Mind, Dear Sir, You may be assur'd that I can do no good. I shall however give no Disturbance. I have spoke to the Duke of Marlbro', will facilitate & expedite whatever Mr Watson may propose to Him as to the Removal of the Guns, and appointing Men to serve them. And I shall endeavor to remove H[is] R[oyal] H[igh-ness]'s objections if He has any. Among other like News, I am afraid that Beleisles'[91]

---

[85] George II.

[86] Proverbially ignorant.

[87] Date pencilled in.

[88] St Philip's Fort, Port Mahon, Minorca, was besieged by the French fleet at the end of 1755.

[89] Military assistance. *OED*.

[90] Let him live with himself.

[91] Charles Louis Auguste Fouquet, duc de Belle-Isle (1684–1761), French general and statesman. He was made a marshal of France in 1741 and secretary at war in 1757. His grand scheme, which had seemed on the verge of realisation in 1741, was mastery of Europe for France. His retreat from Prague, saving most of the French army, was one of the great events of the War of the Austrian Succession. R. Browning, *The War of the Austrian Succession* (Stroud, 1994), 123–7. He was captured by the British at the end of 1744 and spent the next year in London.

Orders are *de profiter de la premiere negligence des Anglors;*[92] and that an Invasion is determin'd either in Great Britain or Ireland. I ought to ask pardon for this melancholy Letter, But I believe it rather confirms the Thoughts you already have had, than presents any new prospect to you. If you can find one thought that has cheerfulness or hope in it, pray impart it to Dear Sir your ever oblig'd . . .

149. [BL, Add. MS 51406, ff. 15–16]
John Campbell to Henry Fox, 24 October 1756
By yesterday's Post I received, with more concern than surprise, the News of your having resigned the Seals.[93] I dare say you did not do it rashly, and am truely sorry that you should have reason for it.

I need not tell you, that my regard dos' not depend upon a Mans being in or out of Place. But I must allways desire to see the chief Parts of Government fill'd with such men as I can esteem.

As I have had no Political correspondence for some time I am quite in the dark. I shall be greatly oblig'd if you will favour me with as much information as you think proper. I cannot imagine how Busyness will be carried on in the approaching Session: Is the Administration to be preserv'd, like the roman Capitol, by cackling of Geese. Or will my Noble Cousin,[94] to keep himself in full, and sole Power, take the assistance of the modest; humble; unambitious Nephewhood.[95] In the mean time, while some are so eager to govern, others must be allow'd to think, with great anxiety, what will become of the poor Country to be govern'd; so unsettled at home, and so beset with dangers from abroad, that it seems every way threaten'd with Ruin. Good wish's are all that my power can afford; and of those I shall not be spareing, for the Peace and Prosperity of my Country, and for long health and happiness to your self, and your family. I am sincerely . . .

150. [BL, Add. MS 51406, ff. 17–18]
Henry Fox to John Campbell, 30 October 1756
I waited in hopes of writing you word that your noble Cousin[96] & I were more than ever united. When instead of that, H[is] M[ajesty] was, by very dishonest means indeed, made to discountenance, not to say detest me, & I was inform'd by the Duke of Newcastle himself that He did so. He then show'd me my insignificance in the strongest Light, & show'd it to others as well as me. I learn't by chance only long after it was

---

[92] To take advantage of the first omission of the English.

[93] Fox informed George II on 15 Oct. that he was going to resign as secretary of state for the southern department, 'but could offer no convincing defence to the charge of deserting the king and his government in a time of the acutest crisis'. Fox's reasons for resigning were many, but include the continuing rancorous debate over the loss of Minorca, the war which was going badly, and the attitude of the duke of Newcastle who continued to use Fox as an underling. Also, Fox was, at this date, 'sick of politics and its burdens'. R. Browning, *The Duke of Newcastle* (1975), 242, and *ODNB*.

[94] The duke of Newcastle.

[95] The Grenville brothers: George Grenville and Richard Grenville-Temple (1711–79), Lord Temple, the latter being tory MP for Buckingham 1734–41 and 1747–52 and for Buckinghamshire 1741–7. One of Cobham's cubs. Styled Lord Cobham after his uncle 1749–52 when he succeeded his mother as 2nd Earl Temple. He was first lord of the admiralty 1756–7 and lord privy seal 1757–61 and resigned both posts when Pitt resigned his. Hence Horace Walpole's description of Temple as 'the absolute creature of Pitt'. *HPC, 1715–54*, ii, 85.

[96] The duke of Newcastle.

taken a measure of the utmost consequence which I was expected to support. I was put in mind of what I had said that Mr Pitt should have my place if he would come in to support the Administration; & told if it would not offend me that it should be offer'd Him next Day; I then thought I had a right, & that it was time for me to resign. Mr Pitt was then sent for; he would not act with the Duke of Newcastle on any terms. The Duke of Newcastle with the advice of his Melancholy friends resign'd on Monday last.[97] Mr Pitt was sent to join with me. No, He could not act with me as a Minister & made monstrous demands which are since moderated a good deal. I fancy it will end in Pitt being Secretary of State,[98] which you won't approve & in Legge's being Chancellor of the Exchequer[99] my having some other Employment out of the Cabinet, Paymaster perhaps; and for accepting this you'd may be blame me. But when you consider that the Difference between my being more or less ambitious is the Disquiet or Quiet of the King & the Publick in this critical Session, you'd find it honest, & then what signifys what else it is? I am sorry to add that there is no certainty even of this or any Settlement. When one shall be made you shall hear again from me, But I may possibly have your opinion, & should be glad of it, in the mean time.

The Parliament is prorogu'd till Dec 2[n]d.

151. [BL, Add. MS 51406, ff. 19–20]
John Campbell to Henry Fox, 5 November 1756
I am very thankfull for your letter by the last Post; though indeed the contents of it gave me much trouble and vexation. H[is] M[ajesty] must have been very wickedly, and cruelly imposed upon, to give him such an opinion of you. I cannot help speculating, that the Pride, resentment, and duplicity, of a Person[100] you offended about four years ago, had some share in it. You certanely could not avoid resigning when you did. The Duke of Newcastle's behaviour to you, was beyond anything I could have expected from the worst of his Councellors. But the telling you such an offer should be made to Mr Pitt without having any reason to expect he would accept it, was somewhat. I can find no name for. I did not indeed think he could in any Case have given Mr Pitt a second opportunity, to insult him with a contemptuous refusal; and what else could be expected.

I do not wonder at Mr Pitt's refuseing to act with you as a Minister, no doubt he has his reasons for it. When I first heard of your resignation I thought it would end as you now fancy it will: I have from a very little after Mr Pelham's death, to this time, except some months last Winter been in great fear that the Duke of Newcastle's causeless jealousy's and his denying in fact all confidence, though promised it, to those who were disposed to be his friends, and would have used him honourably; must throw the power into the hands of those, who would shew him no favour, and whose Power I dreaded. I have said this often, and to Several People.

You say truely, that I shall not approve Mr Pitt's being Secretary of State; but Mr Legge's being Chancellor of the Exchequer, if you had continued Secretary, I should

---

[97] Newcastle resigned as first lord of the treasury on 26 Oct.

[98] Pitt, after much debate, became secretary of state for the southern department and leader of the house of commons in Dec. 1756. See Clark, *The Dynamics of Change*, 289–95.

[99] Legge was made chancellor for the second time on 16 Nov. 1756. He was removed on 13 Apr. 1757.

[100] The lord chancellor Hardwicke. In the debates over Hardwicke's clandestine marriage bill, Fox had attacked him both politically and personally. Ilchester, *Henry Fox*, i, 185–97.

have approved very much. Though I give due honor to the upright intentions of those who insist upon excluding you from the Cabinet; yet I shall by no means blame you, for accepting an Employment out of it. The sacrifice of Ambition, to the quiet of the King and the public Peace, is greater in my eyes, than anything Ambition could obtane. And I cannot express the pleasure, and warm approbation, with which I read 'If it is honest what signifes what else it is?'

I should tire you heartily, if I writ half that on this occasion, has, without any order, crowded into my mind. I shall be impatient till I hear from you again, for surely some speedy Settlement is absolutely necessary in our present situation. I do not intend to be at the meeting of the Parliament.[101] I could do no good, and should, most probably, meet with many things to disgust me; besides, to say truth the present state of my Finances do not very well suit with a long attendance. I should scarce say so much, even to you, if you were a Minister; you may then be very sure I will not say it to my Lord Protector,[102] or any Authority under him. I am dear sir . . .

I should pronounce my Noble Cousin[103] Felo de se,[104] if I did not think a Jury might very honestly bring him off, by a verdict of Non Com.[105]

152. [BL, Add. MS 51406, f. 21]
Henry Fox to John Campbell, 11 November 1756
Things have ended as you forsaw. The Duke of Newcastle saw the King for the last time today. The Chancellor [George Lyttelton] resigns fryday se'ennight. Pitt & Legge come in and have ev'ry demand granted. They have each in different ways shew'd that they were as little inclin'd to act with me as with a Gentleman, as they were to Act with me as a Minister. I have therefore refus'd to take the Pay Office or any Employment. This too must be honest whatever else it is, and the uniform part I shall act, will be allow'd to be of my own unbiased choice. I'll send you a list of the new Placemen as soon as may be & a longer account of what has pass'd than I have now time for. I see no Reason, Dear Sir, to press your Attendance. And after this sessions [sic] wherein I have a part of Honour to Act, I believe no Man will be a worse attender than you ever obliged & affectionate & sincere friend . . .

153. [BL, Add. MS 51406, ff. 23–4]
John Campbell to Henry Fox, 12 November 1756
You may be assured I will not show your letter, or impart what you write to me, with so much Freedom, to anyone. Principle would oblige me to do that justice to any Man, who trusted me, but in this Case esteem and affection are added. Though the News you tell me is, in effect, no more than I expected; yet the certanety of it gives me fresh vexation.

---

[101] This is, the opening of the new session on 2 Dec. *CJ*, xxvii, 621.

[102] Pitt.

[103] The duke of Newcastle.

[104] One who 'deliberately puts an end to his own existence, or commits any unlawful malicious act, the consequence of which is his own death'. William Blackstone, *Commentaries on the Laws of England* (4 vols, 13th edn, 1800), iv, 189. Campbell's comment on Newcastle's resignation.

[105] Non compos mentis – not of sound mind.

I don't doubt the Duke of Devonshire comes to the Treasury[106] with good intentions, but it is a difficult, and dangerous Part he undertakes, I wish he may go through with it in such manner, as to preserve his Character in every respect. What you say of Mr Legge both surprises and grieves me; for I have long had an extraordinary good opinion of him, and a great friendship for him. Indeed his conduct the last Session gave me great dissatisfaction. I thought his resentment, against those who I believed had used him very ill, carried him much too far; But I still persuaded myself that he would be an honourable Enemy to them, and did not suspect he would be any sort of Enemy[107] to you, who had given him no offence, but allways shewn a favourable disposition towards him. The Part you propose to act is most honest & honorable, will gain you the Love of every honest Man, and force respect from all. It will give an uncommon Dignity to your Character, for very few men have been so much Masters of themselves. I am very sure your declining any employment must greatly displease; for judging of you, by themselves, it will keep them in constant fear of your Opposition. But I do not think they will venture to attack you. Is Mankind quite so profligate that they could do it, in this Parliament? If they should, and God spare my Life, & health; nothing shall prevent me attending you. I am not used to leaving my Friends in persecution. When I do so, may I be forced to beg my bread, from those I hate. At present I do not intend to exercise my Patience by seeing them take Possession. I wish indeed I was within distance of having an hour or two's conversation with you I should then ask many questions, I cannot so well put into writing. I heartily pity the King's distress. Good God! what has the Duke of Newcastle brought upon the King, the Public, himself, and those that he ought to have look'd upon as his Friends.

Pray when you favour me next, give me a little pleasure, if you can, by naming some that have shewn themselves Men of Honor, and integrity, upon this occasion.

My sons [Pryse] political Conduct for a year past has been one of the greatest troubles I ever met with.[108]

Mr L[egge]'s appearance in the manner he did, at the L[eicester] H[ouse] indeed shock'd me. There is somewhat very immoral, in encouraging, & spiriting up.

154. [BL, Add. MS 51406, ff. 25–6]
Henry Fox to John Campbell, 13 November 1756
I have this day resign'd the Seals.[109] The Duke of Newcastle has resign'd[110] in a much better way, He has got his Dukedom entail'd on Lord Lincoln,[111] & 4 Reversions of

---

[106] Devonshire became first lord of the treasury on 16 Nov. 1756, replacing Newcastle. However, he was more or less a titular head, with Pitt as secretary of state for the southern department being the real driving force in this short-lived ministry.

[107] Legge was instrumental in opposing Fox's candidate in the borough of Stockbridge, where the latter had a controlling influence.

[108] Pryse had become an MP in 1754, and showed little antagonism towards those his father regarded as enemies, such as Pitt. See Introduction.

[109] As secretary of state for the southern department.

[110] As first lord of the treasury.

[111] Henry Fiennes Clinton (1720–94), 9th earl of Lincoln. He was the nephew and heir of the childless 1st duke of Newcastle (upon-Tyne and under-Lyme) who asked the king for a remainder for Lincoln to become the 2nd duke of Newcastle-under-Lyme upon his uncle's death, which occurred in 1768.

great value granted to Shelly, Pelham, Jones & West[112] & has made Sir G[eorge] Lyttelton a Peer.[113] Lord Hillsborough has got a Peerage[114] in lieu of his Place, which is the only thing that has happen'd in the whole agreeable to your Humble servant as you see in the enclos'd List [not extant].

155. [BL, Add. MS 51406, f. 27]
John Campbell to Henry Fox, 28 November 1756
I need not repete my promise to come to you if you want me for I should do it if able, unask'd & unpromised. But I will tell you, that if Lord Anson is attack'd,[115] though I have scarce any acquaintance with his Lordship, I shall think that Honor, Justice & Humanity, oblige me to attend. And I think whoever can tell that two & two make four, must see, that both Honor, & Interest, oblige the Duke of Newcastle to make the Case of those who served him is own. Yet allow me to say, I cannot easily believe they intend what they threaten. To single you out, would be such apparent Malice, that I think scarce any Man could stand it, with an unembarrass'd Countenance; to attack Lord Anson, without Mr Legge's Consent, would be dividing in the first Instance from the only Man among them who ever had a Character. And I have very often heard Mr Legge Speak to Lord Anson in such a Manner as forbids me to believe he can join to run him down.

I am very glad for what you tell me of the Dukes of Devon and Bedford. I have often been angry with the latter for using his Parliamentary abilities in a way I thought much beneath his dignity; but to see an error reported and forsake it, is all that either God, or man require. I greatly honor Lord Hillsborough for his generous offer so generously refused. And I am so much a Highlander that it gives me great Pleasure to know that my Chief[116] spoke to you honourably. I allways look'd upon the Duke of Marlborough as a Man of dearest, & finest honor. I know nothing of Lord Powerscourt,[117] but I wish him good success, it is indeed no Compliment, for I might possibly do as much for Mr Sydenham, if he was the only Man that would oppose Dr Hay.[118]

I thank you for the Grub[119] which was indeed worth sending but I would have avoided profaneing the Title of King by calling His Grandeur[120] Lord Protector.

---

[112] Sir John Shelley (1730–83), of Mitchelgrove, Sussex; MP for East Retford 1751–68, Newark 1768–74 and Shoreham 1774–80. Shelley was endowed with various sinecures by his uncle, Newcastle, including keeper of the records 1755–83 and clerk of the pipe in the exchequer 1758–83. As part of Newcastle's resignation deal he received a reversion of the pipe office; Tom Pelham (1728–1805), of Stanmer, Sussex; MP for Rye 1749–54 and Sussex 1754–68. Lord of trade 1754–61 and of the admiralty 1761–2; comptroller of the household 1765–74. He received a reversion of the customs office; Hugh Valance Jones, Newcastle's private secretary, received a reversion of comptroller of the customs. James West received a reversion of the auditorship of the land revenues. Clark, *Dynamics of Change*, 529.

[113] Lyttelton was created Lord Lyttelton on 18 Nov. J.C. Sainty, *Peerage Creations* (2008), 43.

[114] He was made Baron Harwich on 17 Nov. but relinquished his office as treasurer of the chamber.

[115] Anson had been removed as first lord of the admiralty on Newcastle's resignation and replaced by Lord Temple, Pitt's brother-in-law. There followed recriminations against Anson for not doing enough to support Byng at Minorca. However, Anson was reinstated as first lord in July 1757.

[116] Archibald Campbell, 3rd duke of Argyll.

[117] Edward Wingfield (1729–64), 2nd Viscount Powercourt (Irish peerage). Brought in by Henry Fox to oppose Dr George Hay, 'a worthless friend of Legge's', at Stockbridge. Clark, *Dynamics of Change*, 300–1.

[118] Dr George Hay (1715–78), MP for Stockbridge 1754–6, Calne 1757–61, Sandwich 1761–8 and Newcastle-under-Lyme 1768–78.

[119] A political journal?

[120] Pitt.

I had an odd Paper, though it Compliments you highly, sent by another hand call'd the Test.[121] He is a Drawcansir[122] that kills all on both sides, and is so singular that I suspect he must be the Noble Author of Faction detected;[123] who speaks one word for you, and means two for himself.

You know my opinion of my Lord Protector,[124] and the G's[125] has been the same this long time. I hope Mr L[egge] will not force me to loose my opinion of him; if he should it will not be my fault. I will consider against another Post if I have any Question to ask by letter, though if I come up so soon there is less occasion. Whether you are attack'd, or no I wish all who know me, should know that I have the Honor to [sic] your Friend, and that I am . . .

156. [BL, Add. MS 51406, ff. 28–9]
John Campbell to Henry Fox, 30 November 1756
If the Proceedings of our New Ministers[126] will oblige me to come to Town so soon, there is less need to trouble you with Questions by letter. But I shall wish to know, by whom, and by what means, H[is] M[ajesty] was so far imposed upon, as to cause him to discountenance you so much before your resignation. How the Duke of Newcastle was so infatuated as to imagine he could exchange you for Mr Pitt, and keep his own station: I shall desire much to be inform'd of what passed during the Anarchy, between the old, and new Ministries. And I shall ask many Questions about Mr Legge. For though when a Man forfeits the Character for which I loved, and esteem'd him; I must necessary withdraw my friendship and respect. Yet you will allow that one should have very plane proof, before one gives up an old friend. I now say this to one, who I believe is as firm in his friendships as any Man. For my part, if I saw the most just reason to withdraw my affection from an old friend, and even to drop his acquaintance, and avoid his conversation; I yet should not choose to go so far against him, as you say the two Dukes[127] think Mr Legge will go against Lord Anson. After all whatever, for some ends, they may threaten I can hardly believe they will in earnest prosecute; I am sure that last year they had but few Friends in the House of Commons, they cannot depend upon the

---

[121] *Test*, a virulently anti-Pitt paper which was first published on 6 Nov. 1756. According to John Thomas Hope, *Catalogue of a Collection of Early Newspapers and Essayists . . . Presented to the Bodleian Library* (1895), 87, it was set up by Henry Fox. It survived until July 1757, by which time all the ex-ministers it supported had been incorporated into Pitt's ministry. *Test* was opposed by *Con-test*, whose main target was Fox. Thomas Wright, *A Caricature History of the Georges* (1868), 206–8. But see letter 157, below: Fox denies authorship. Ilchester, *Henry Fox*, ii, 33–4, states that it was difficult to believe Fox had a personal share in the 'indiscriminate violence' published in the *Test*, though he acknowledges that the journal attacked almost everyone except Fox.

[122] Name of a blustering, bragging, character in George Villiers's burlesque, *The Rehearsal*, who, in the last scene, is made to enter a battle and kill all the combatants on both sides. *OED*. Henry Fielding wrote under the pseudonym Sir Alexander Drawcansir, knight, censor of Great Britain, to produce the *Covent Garden Journal* (1752).

[123] Lord Perceval, later earl of Egmont, *Faction Detected by the Evidence of Facts: Containing an Impartial View of Parties at Home and Affairs Abroad* (1743): 'one of the best political pamphlets ever written'. *PH*, xii, 411, citing Coxe.

[124] William Pitt.

[125] The Grenville brothers.

[126] The Devonshire–Pitt ministry.

[127] Devonshire and Bedford.

Tories, or with them make a sufficient number to carry on busyness. Their dependence I should think must be, upon those who will join to support the King's Interest, and the public Busyness, though it is conducted by those they cannot like. In this Case will the Members venture so highly to provoke? I find there is some talk of dissolving the Parliament. But I cannot apprehend that my Lord Protector would have any advantage by that. Where has he more friends to bring in, and how would he bring them in? And if in this Ferment a greater number of Tories should get in, what would he be the better for that? They will never be real Friends to any Administration under this Establishment; And I can conceive His Grandeur is particularly odious to them. If they should help to lift him up for a short time, I am persuaded it would be with no other view, than to let him fall graviore Casa.[128]

Some I hear blame you for resigning, saying it was that occasion'd, and began all this Confusion. But I do not see how you could avoid it. As it appears to me, if the Duke of Newcastle would lop the Bough he stood on, you could not help it. Perhaps very few mans Patience would have held so long. What has happened must certanely be the natural & necessary consequence of H[is] G[race]'s way of acting; since it could be foreseen, two years past & more, by one so ignorant, so retired, and so unpracticed in ways of Courts, as I am, Pray what does our Friend the Speaker [Arthur Onslow] think, and say upon this occasion. You see, now you are out of Employment I scribble to you as a man of much leisure which I will hope you will excuse; yet I Trust you are not Idle, but are honestly employ'd; and that it may be to good effect is the hearty wish of your sincerely affectionate humble servant.

Among many disagreeable things, I have heard one story of a more ludicrous sort. Verily it is said among the People, that the messenger of Satan has buffeted St Paul even that a son of Belial hath defiled the Tabernacle of our Sister Comfort.[129]

157. [BL, Add. MS 51406, ff. 30–3]
Henry Fox to John Campbell, 14 December 1756
I was answering your letters which came to me at Bath, when I had so many letters to blame my going out of town, that I must have been obstinate if I had staid & so set out to be at the House of Commons yesterday.

The Paper you mention in yours of the 28th call'd the Test is as you may suppose said to be wrote under my direction, but upon my Word I do not so much as guess who is the Author of it. But surely it is too ludicrous, & not well enough wrote to have come from the Pen of the Author of Faction detected.

Now as to your first Question in yours of the 30th who influenced the King to discountenance (say to hell & detest) me? it is as bad a story as you ever heard. I, to the Duke of Newcastle alone, advis'd his putting Lord Bute about the Prince, which the Prince had sued for singly to the Duke of Newcastle. At His Grace's desire I gave the same Opinion to Lord Chancellor [Hardwicke]. Take notice I never gave this advise but to them two. They to please the King had talk'd indecently and immoderately against it and therefore when they determin'd to do it, thought it best to tell the king that I was in league with Lord Bute, Duke of Argyll & Legge, & would carry on his affairs in the

---

[128] A more severe fall. Horace, Odes, ii, 10.
[129] A reference to Pitt (Satan) and his falling out with Lyttelton (St Paul)?

House of Commons without He [*sic*] satisfy'd Lord Bute. H[is] M[ajesty] believing this had been reason enough to hate me, till after the Break. He saw me more than anybody the Hate of Leicester House, & then satisfy'd Himself with saying he had wrong'd me, but how could He help it? And He now believ'd I was a very honest Man – And would fain have made me undertake the Administration, & so it has been manag'd that my choice has only been *all* or *none*, I do not, of the two, repent my Choice of the latter. My Memory is good, & I will when We meet go through the whole detail with you. I am very clear that when I do you will be confirm'd in your opinion that I could not avoid resigning when I did. Your Friend Legge I hear is discontented, & says He is forced into the Service.[130] Very odd, that the *Child of the Whigs* as he has call'd Himself, should be forced to come into a Ministry whose junction with the Torys is apparent, nay avow'd, I know particulars from undoubted Intelligence. I have seen an *original* circular Letter to the Torys to attend & support the new Ministers, who *they were convinced will pursue constitutional measures* sign'd by Lord Litchfield,[131] Lord Talbot,[132] Lord Windsor[133] & another Lord or two, & by Sir John Phillips, Sir Cordel Fairbrace,[134] Mr Amcots,[135] Sir C[harles] Mordaunt, & 8 or so more Commoners. I observ'd Prase's[136] Name was not among them, Nathey's was. Now the first Condition it should seem was not to thank the King for haveing sent us his Electoral Troops when ask'd. The Lords did thank Him,[137] & Lord Temple as He had promis'd Lord Westmoreland came singly to oppose it. We in the House of Commons were not permitted to thank & I believe never did Men do themselves so much violence as in being quiet on this Head. Had there been a Division that day or yesterday, when the foreign troops were said by your Friend Legge, to be unpopular & that they were to go away immediately.[138] The Ministers & Torys won't have been on one side, & the whole House besides upon the other. It was as much mark'd yesterday as a Division could have mark'd it, when the whole House applauded me, & Lord G[eorge] Sackville, Mr Conway[139] when We conjured them not out of false notices of popularity to send away the foreign troops, till they knew how to supply so great a Deduction from our Defence, & the applause given, by the Torys, & the Torys only, to Legge & Grenville; Pitt was not yet rectiore, & besides has the Gout still in one foot. This cannot last, but what it will break into I don't know. Into nothing I am sure that shall make you ashamed of me & I am almost as sure,

[130] Legge, as chancellor of the exchequer, had been dismissed by Newcastle in Nov. 1755, but in 1756 returned to that office under Devonshire, only to resign again in Apr. 1757 after Pitt had been dismissed as secretary of state for the southern department by the king.

[131] George Henry Lee.

[132] William, Lord Talbot.

[133] Herbert Windsor (1707–58), MP for Cardiff boroughs 1734–8. Succeeded his father as 2nd Viscount Windsor (Irish peerage) and 2nd Baron Mountjoy in 1738.

[134] Sir Cordell Firebrace (1712–59), 3rd bt, of Long Melford, Suffolk; tory MP for Suffolk 1735–59.

[135] Charles Amcots (1729–77), of Harrington and Kettlethorpe, Lincolnshire; tory MP for Boston 1754–61 and 1766–77.

[136] Pryse, that is, Campbell's son.

[137] *LJ*, xxix, 7.

[138] In the debate on the quartering of foreign troops in Britain. The bill, introduced on 14 Dec., was engrossed the following day and sent to the Lords where it was given royal assent on 18 Dec. *PH*, xv, 782, gives the date of 14 Dec. for the passing of this bill.

[139] Henry Seymour Conway.

into nothing that will alter my Situation. They certainly will pursue the Enquiry as far as they can. I hope soon to tell you that I am going out of town, & at the same time the Day when I hope you & I shall meet in it again I shall be glad to know what Legge says when you shall have examined Him or the Interrogatories, I will furnish you with. And I heartily wish he may answer so as to preserve Your Friendship. Do you know that Sir George, now Lord Lyttleton, who has engag'd with the Duke of Bedford for one & one at Oakhampton nam'd Pitt to his Grace as His Man to be chose in his Room?[140]

What you so humorously tell me You had heard, is true. But I hope Sir George has forgot it as He did the seals when he came to Court to resign; & Patent, Robes, & Writt, when He came to be introduced into the House of Peers, & sending for them one after another made them stay an hour.

In the mean time, Dear Sir, I fear no publick Business has been done these 2 Months, not thought of till within this Week. We are a Reproach & laughing stock to all Europe, & I fear shall soon feel still more Effects from our follys & absurdities.

Adieu ever yours . . .

---

[140] George Lyttelton was raised to the peerage as Lord Lyttelton in Nov. 1756. In the following month he nominated William Pitt to take his place as MP for Okehampton, Devon.

Chapter 6. 1757–8

Unless otherwise stated, all the letters in this chapter are from CRO, Cawdor/Campbell box 128.

158.

John Campbell to Mary Campbell, 27 January 1757

I have been much taken up, doing of nothing (except when attending the Honorable House) ever since I came here. Yesterday about 11 I went to Newcastle House, where I found no alteration from what used to be on private days, except that People came later, after sitting a long time with many others in the library the Duke called me into the little room within it, saluted me very kindly told me he was never better in health, or better satisfied with himself, he then asked me if I would come the next morning about 9. I promised I would and came away. I went today about that time . . .[1] and was alone with him till turn'd of twelve, when I came out I found the Library full as usual. He talk'd very free to me, and let me do so to him, though I thought it now useless to say several things which I would have said four month ago, perhaps they might have been useless then, but they would not have been improper. He said several things about public affairs which I thought right, because they agreed with what I have often said, and one is wondrous apt to think they speak wisely who agree with ones own sentiments. To morrow I am to go with Mr Fox to the Duke of Devonshires Levee. The Duke of Newcastle was very decent in regard to Mr Fox. I think he said nothing to me that he might not have said to Lord Ilchester;[2] he ask'd no question that could put me under any difficulty. Lord Fortescue[3] who look'd in here this even (Nanney gone to the Play) told me that Mr Pitt had now only the Gout in his right hand so I suppose Wee shall see His Highness[4] next week. My Lord shew'd me a Copy of the Duke de Richelieu's[5] letter[6] to Voltaire justifying Admiral Byng's behavior, Voltaire inclos'd it, or a Copy, in a short letter to Mr Byng. But what can the Duke de Richelieu know of Mr B[yng]'s behavior but by hearsay, and you or I may know as much. Lord F[ortescue] is wonderfully for Mr Byng. My Love . . .

Lyon [John Hooke Campbell] very much at home the Captain [Alexander] upon Guard at St James's.

[1] The next two lines are obliterated.

[2] Stephen Fox (1704–76), Lord Ilchester, Henry Fox's brother. See Introduction.

[3] Matthew Fortescue (1719–85), 2nd Baron Fortescue. The barony devolved to him on the death of his half-brother, the earl of Clinton and 1st Baron Fortescue who died in 1751. The 2nd baron married Anne, Campbell's daughter, in July 1752. Burke's *Peerage*. See Introduction.

[4] That is, Pitt. Walpole commented upon Pitt's gout that 'no aspiring cardinal ever coughed for the tiara with more specious debility'. Cited in J. Black, *Pitt the Elder: The Great Commoner* (Cambridge, 1992), 129.

[5] Louis François Armand du Plessis, duc de Richelieu (1696–1788), a marshal of France.

[6] Letter of c.Dec. 1756. He stated: 'Nothing could be more unjust than the present campaign against Admiral Byng'. Voltaire Society of America online: http://www.whitman.edu/VSA/

159.

John Campbell to Mary Campbell, 17 February 1757

The Judges[7] have declared the Sentence against Mr Byng legal, yesterday the Lord of the Admiralty [Lord Temple] sign'd a Warrant for his Execution on Monday sevenight. The new Ministers would fain save him if they could lay the Burthen upon others or get the House of Commons to take the unpopularity on themselves, but the Ministers seem willing rather to let him die than hazard themselves by saving him. If they really think him innocent, Surely they cannot persist in so base a conduct; if they do they are the last of Men. Mr Pitt was sworn today[8] & present'd a Message from the King in consequence of which he is expected to move to morrow for £200000 to be given to the King towards maintaining an Army to defend his Dominions, and for the Hessians to be confirmed in our pay abroad for the same end and to assist the King of Prussia to keep out the French & their Allies.[9] If he can do this with an unembarrass'd Countenance,[10] nothing can be too hard for him. How will poor Legge act – what distinction can he find.

160.

John Campbell to Mary Campbell, 1 March 1757

Wee had a tiresome time in the House for allmost a week past,[11] no long days, but no short ones, the longest was Saturday,[12] after 9 at night, yesterday past Seven. Some of the Court Martial being very uneasy in their minds have desired to open them but being, they think, restrained by the Oath of Secrecy, unless required by Act of Parliament, desired such an Act might be pass'd. It was first mention'd in the House on fryday by Sir F[rancis] Dashwood at the desire of Commodore Keppel[13] who sat by him & said a little himself. Sir Richard Lyttelton made a long speech & read a letter from Admiral Smyth.[14] I that day apprehended the whole Court Marshall desired such a Bill, and that all the Members of it were very uneasy in their minds. Most of the House seem'd then of opinion that they might say all they had occasion to say, without breach of their Oath, and that an Act was unnecessary, and it was agreed they should take that night to consider of it. But Mr Keppel continuing to think himself bound by the Oath. On Saturday H[is] H[ighness][15] brought a message from the King

---

[7] The lords justice of appeal.

[8] As secretary of state for the southern department from which he resigned in April.

[9] This was voted *nemine contradicente* on 21 Feb. *CJ*, xxvii, 738.

[10] Pitt had previously opposed such measures.

[11] *PH*, xv, 803–27, for the debates over Byng.

[12] 26 Feb. *CJ*, xxvii, 724.

[13] Augustus Keppel (1725–86), of Elveden Hall, Suffolk; MP for Chichester 1755–61, New Windsor 1761–80 and Surrey 1780–2. Groom of the bedchamber 1761–6; lord of the admiralty 1765–6; first lord of the admiralty 1782–3: Keppel became rear admiral in 1762, vice admiral 1770 and admiral in 1778.

[14] Admiral Thomas Smith (c.1707–62), the illegitimate son of Sir Thomas Lyttelton (1688–1751), presided over the court at Admiral Byng's trial, and did his utmost to ensure that the court's recommendation of mercy was upheld.

[15] That is, Pitt. *CJ*, xxvii, 738.

in consequence of which a Bill was moved for and brought in, read twice committed & reported the same day in order to be read a third time on Monday.[16] H[is] Highness] is so little skill'd in drawing Messages, that this Message was a direct breach of privilege, the Crown having been advised to say in it that H[is] M[ajesty] had been inform'd a Member of the House of Commons did, in his Place, acquaint the House &c Mr Fox took a decent proper notice of it, which drew upon him gross abuse from H[is] H[ighness] but the Speaker strongly asserted the irregularity of the Message and is to make an entry in the Journals to prevent the bad effects of such a precedent.[17] I was surprised on Saturday to find that it could not be asserted more than five of the Court Martial desired this Bill, viz Keppel, Admiral Norris,[18] Commodore Holms,[19] Captain Moor,[20] & Captain Geary[21] Mr Keppel, acquainting the House that the last four had impower'd him to speak for them. I was much more surprised yesterday Morning to hear that all except Mr Keppel had gone back; but when Wee were going to read the Bill a third time the House was inform'd that Commodore Holmes, was very Easy[22] and did not desire the Bill, Mr Keppel had mistaken him this was said by his Brother[23] who is a member. Captain Geary Wee were told was willing to speak if all the rest were obliged to speak but not otherwise. Admiral Norris and Captain Moore had writ a short letter to Mr Keppel which he read to the House desireing him to Solicit the Bill; I think I have good reason to believe that those two had gone back, though they at last thought better of it, and stood to what they had first said. Keppel has behaved so well that one is ready to believe his joining in the absurdities of the Court, proceded from too much modesty in yeilding to worse judgements than his own. Mr Fox mention'd many difficulties in regard to the Bill, but did not oppose it, so I thought it would have pass'd without division, but when half the Members were gone, Velters Cornwall & Sir John Glynne[24] divided the House against the Bill but it was carried by 153 against 23. What the effect will be God knows Wee are told the City are still extreme violent against Mr Byng. I think the Old Ministers have behaved

[16] *PH*, xv, 804–7. The bill was read for the third time on 28 Feb. 1757.

[17] In theory the crown had no knowledge of what was said in the Commons, hence Fox's protest that this was creating a bad precedent. P.D.G. Thomas, *The House of Commons in the Eighteenth Century* (Oxford, 1971), 334.

[18] Son of Admiral Sir John Norris?

[19] Charles Holmes (1711–61), MP for Newport, Isle of Wight 1758–61. Rear admiral 1758; commander-in-chief of Jamaica 1760–1.

[20] Sir John Moor (1718–79), from 1776 1st bt of Moor. Rear admiral 1762; vice admiral 1770; admiral 1778.

[21] Sir Francis Geary (1709–96), created 1st bt of Oxenheath in 1782. Rear admiral of the blue 1758; vice admiral 1762; admiral 1775.

[22] Writ large.

[23] Either Henry or Thomas Holmes. Henry (1703–62), MP for Newton 1741–7, Yarmouth 1747–62, both Isle of Wight, and governor of the island 1754–62; or Thomas (1699–1764), of Yarmouth, Isle of Wight; MP for Newton 1727–9 and 1734–41 and Yarmouth 1747–64, both Isle of Wight. 1st Baron Holmes (Irish peerage) 1760–4.

[24] Sir John Glynne (1713–77), 6th bt of Hawarden, Flintshire; tory MP for Flintshire 1741–7 and Flint boroughs 1753–77. In 1745 he was arrested and sentenced to three months after drinking the Pretender's health on a village green, although he was then released due to lack of evidence.

with great candor towards him in return for the Malice shewn to them, and the abuse thrown on them by his friends in their great Wisdom. H[is] H[ighness] shews daily the most inveterate Hatred to Mr Fox who I believe vex's him to the heart by not opposing the Measures, and by keeping his temper. H[is] H[ighness] begins abuse in every debate, and I believe would be very glad if he could put Mr F[ox] in such a passion as to be off his guard, but hitherto all his endeavors have fail'd. And though Mr F[ox] does not pretend to be an equal Orator, I can venture to say he has shewn superior abilities. H[is] H[ighness] has several times since I came to Town flatly denied what I am sure I heard him say, and he one day charged Mr F[ox] with saying somewhat which I think it was impossible for any man in the House to think he had said. I am sure he said nothing in the least like it. Let the Tories rejoice in H[is] H[ighness] and H[is] H[ighness] in them.

The House of Commons were up to day between five and six, and nothing worth relating happen'd there. But the Lords were sitting upon the Court Martial Bill[25] and like to sit sometime when I came away, I was in there sometime, and heard part of a Speech of Lord Mansfields[26] I greatly regret that I did not go Soon enough to hear it all, for what I did hear was very fine, he was for some alteration, and in the first place for summoning the Members of the Court Martial in order to put some questions to them; and what I greatly approved he Spoke warmly and affectionately for taking care not to let a difficulty be put upon the King but that they should rather take it upon themselves, & if there was occasion put themselves between H[is] M[ajesty] and popular clamer. Lord Temple spoke immediately after him I and many more left his Lordship Speaking, I return'd to the House of Commons, when I came away from Westminster I heard that Lord Hardwicke was speaking I had great desire to hear him but thought the heat & fatigue would be too much. It has been said that Mr Byng ruin'd one Minority when he was in the Mediterranean, and is like to ruin another now he is come home. I cannot think it can be justly said that the old Ministers have shewn partiality either for or against him, but the partiality of the new Ministry in his favor is very visible. Though they would not venture to shew their favor to him in an open manly way to save his life. I think his Fate is as yet very doubt full.

161.

John Campbell to Mary Campbell, 7 April 1757[27]

Yesterday I was at a meeting at Lord Royston's[28] relative to the Enquiry[29] on Lord Anson heard Papers read & some Conversation, staid from between 10 & 11 till about one. I then thought their would be no more changes till after the Enquiry,

---

[25] *PH*, xv, 807–21: it was ordered to reject the bill.

[26] William Murray, who had been created Baron Murray on 8 Nov. 1756. J.C. Sainty, *Peerage Creations* (2008), 42.

[27] See Figure 6.1.

[28] Philip Yorke (1720–90), eldest son of the 1st earl of Hardwicke, who took the courtesy title Lord Royston in 1754.

[29] The meeting was to prepare for the inquiry into the loss of Minorca which began in the Commons on 19 Apr. *CJ*, xxvii, 846.

Figure 6.1: John Campbell to Mary Campbell, 7 April 1757.

though not sure but the Secretary might go that day. But sometime after I was in the House of Commons had authentic information that Mr Pitt was dismiss'd[30] and that Mr Fox was nominated for Paymaster but I believe it is his own desire not to accept

[30] Pitt was dismissed on 6 Apr.

so soon.[31] I think Lord Egremont will be Secretary.[32] No doubt all the New Men will give up now their Leader is gone.[33] Mr Elliot[34] declines staying in the Admiralty and I believe Counsellor Hamilton's son will come in his room. And I am told[35] Lord Digby's[36] Brother[37] succeds him at the Board of Trade. I could write all had been defer'd till after the Enquiry, but it is over, and Wee must look forward; I don't doubt the opposition will be furious, I don't think they who come in now are to be envied, but if they come to support the King & with an honest intention to their Country; the less desireable, the more honorable will their Places be. I intend to set out for Lodington to morrow morning . . .[38] I went this morning to Newcastle House and had a private audience of the Duke as his Grace and Mr Fox have both treated me with confidence, you may believe I know more of late transactions than I can write, or indeed than I am at liberty to speak of. Pray God things go well, the Prospect is not pleasing, But I have duty & affection for my King & Country hate faction, and those who make family dissentions. I have allways had an esteem for Mr Fox; & hope I shall not find reason to alter my opinion, and that my behavior in the House, may shew a true regard to My K[ing] & C[ountry] friendship to him, and honor towards the D[uke] of N[ewcastle]. I will endeavor to follow the dictates of my Conscience, without giving just Cause of Complaint to anyone. I hope this Session may not be long, but cannot tell what the appearance may be after the holydays.[39]

General Conway[40] is made Groom of the Bedchamber to the King in the room of General Herbert[41] who died lately. I heard of no other Writs moved to day all are well

[31] Fox asked the king to defer his taking the paymastership until the inquiry into the loss of Minorca was over. J.C.D. Clark, *The Dynamics of Change: The Crisis of the 1750s and the English Party Systems* (Cambridge, 1982), 358.

[32] Egremont did not become secretary of the southern department until 1761. After Pitt resigned, Robert Darcy, 4th earl of Holdernesse, became southern secretary, but only until June 1757 when Pitt returned, staying in that office until 1761. See Clark, *Dynamics of Change*, 357, who states that Fox believed as late as 5 Apr. that Egremont was going to accept the secretaryship. Campbell could have had his information from Fox.

[33] Henry Legge resigned the same day, James Grenville and Thomas Potter on the 7th and George Grenville on the 9th. Clark, *Dynamics of Change*, 357.

[34] Gilbert Elliot (1722–77), of Minto, Roxburgh; MP for Selkirkshire 1753–65 and Roxburghshire 1765–77. Lord of the admiralty 1756–7 and 1757–61; lord of the treasury 1761–2; treasurer of the chamber 1762–70; treasurer of the navy 1770–7. He was a leader of the Edinburgh Literary Society and an intimate of David Hume.

[35] Campbell had this from Fox's memorandum of 12 Mar. 1757. The same source lists Campbell to have the seat of George Grenville at the treasury. BL, Add. MS 51430, ff. 61, 67.

[36] Edward Digby (1730–57), 6th Baron Digby, of Coldshill, Warwickshire; MP for Malmesbury 1751–4 and Wells 1754–7. Digby was a particular favourite of Fox's and his early death had a profound effect upon him. Earl of Ilchester, *Henry Fox, First Lord Holland* (2 vols,1920), ii, 104.

[37] Henry Digby (1731–93), MP for Luggeshall 1755–61 and Wells 1761–5. Undersecretary of state 1755–6; lord of the admiralty 1763–5. Henry was created Baron Digby of Sherborne, Dorset, in 1765 (the barony had previously been in the Irish peerage) and 1st Earl Digby in 1790. Henry was the son of Charlotte Fox, sister to Henry Fox.

[38] One line obliterated.

[39] One line obliterated.

[40] Henry Seymour Conway.

[41] William Herbert (c.1696–1757), MP for Wilton 1734–57, who voted with the administration. Groom of the bedchamber 1740–57.

at next door My Son & his wife Lord Fortescue tells me got Safe to Bath & she was rather better for her journey. I am . . .

162.
John Campbell to Mary Campbell, 30 April 1757
You will excuse any omissions and forgetfulness, when I tell you that of the last five days past 8 was the earliest riseing of the House. Now we are adjourned till Monday when I expect another very long day. Wee are sometimes very cool & good humor'd, sometimes fire & taw then cool again. Sometimes the Enquirers want to drop their Enquiry[42] as easily as they can, & sometimes seem to intend Mischief. But all this is no wander as they are guided by a Man [Pitt] who has not the command of his own passions, or resolutions; whose Ambition is boundless and his Pride without measure, and is intoxicated with the adulation of his followers, and the applause of Corporations, Coffee Houses &c. Mr Fox has happily shewn that they cannot put him in a passion or off his guard, though G[eorge] T[ownshend] has try'd it by a mad rudeness which even he has after been ashamed of.

I dined at one this morning yet rose a little before nine without headach though I did not drink Tea before I went to bed. As to the future Administration[43] I know no more than I did when I wrote last about it.

My son set out for Bath this Morning Wee have the last two or three days very fine warm weather, pleasant I believe everywhere, but in the House of Commons, which it makes more disagreable.

I think the Inscription the Test of this day sevenight gives for Mr L[egge]'s Gold Box[44] should mortifie that poor Gentleman extremely. The Play of Douglas pleased me much particularly the Epilogue, and Lady Randolphs comparison of herself with the supposed Mother of Norval.[45] Wee shall all subscribe to Mrs Porters Play. Love to bessy . . .

The Duke of Grafton is alive & has eat many poach'd eggs, but his Friends have not the least hopes of his recovering.[46] Lord Dupplin has been extreme ill with the Gout in his Stomach, but is now relieved by a good fit in his foot.

---

[42] The inquiry into the loss of Minorca. This was raised and then postponed in the Commons throughout the last week of April. *CJ*, xxvii, 851, 853, 854, 857, 858. The House divided on 22 Apr. to agree to debate the subject, the votes being 122 to 89 in the affirmative. *CJ*, xxvii, 853. The smallness of the numbers seems to be an indication of a lack of enthusiasm for the inquiry; for Resolutions of the Commons relating to the loss of Minorca see *PH*, xv, 822–7. The inquiry 'lasted six days till past midnight' and developed into a dull and 'very fatiguing' farce. Ilchester, *Henry Fox*, ii, 31.

[43] In the wake of the dismissal of Pitt and Legge.

[44] When Pitt was dismissed as secretary of state for the southern department in Apr. 1757, Legge was also dismissed as chancellor of the exchequer. Popular support for both men outside the Commons manifested itself when they were given the freedom of several cities and towns and awarded gold boxes – in the case of London and Bath the boxes were worth 100 guineas each. *British Spy or Universal London Weekly Journal*, 23 Apr. 1757; *London Evening Post*, 28 Apr. 1757; M. Peters, *The Elder Pitt* (1998), 69.

[45] *The Tragedy of Douglas*, by the Scottish playwright Rev. John Hume (1722–1808), was first performed at the Theatre Royal, Covent Garden, on 14 Mar. 1757. Lady Randolph and Norval are two of the characters. The play was well praised in the press.

[46] Grafton died on 7 May 1757.

163. [BL, Add. MS 32870, f. 467]
John Campbell to the duke of Newcastle, fragment only: undated, c.April 1757[47]
Every honest Man, though in the most private station and of the most limited capacity, must as a time like this, feel some concern for the Public, and be desireous of seeing such a settlement at home, as he thinks would be most advantageous for the Nation, and most for the honor and ease of the King. I confess my wish is, that the Duke of Newcastle may return to the head of the Treasury Board, with such a Chancellor of the Exchequer as he can entirely confide in. Lord Dupplin I think is such a one, has a universal good Character, and has given offence to no Man. Mr Fox, in the Office of Paymaster[48] would support the Measures of Government, in the House of Commons without being a Minister, and I presume Mr Pitt might be again secretary,[49] if he would consent to come in upon reasonable and decent Terms. As to Mr Legge, after the unhappy steps he has taken, I should think the best thing for him would be to have the Title of his Ladies Family.[50]

Such a settlement I am persuaded Mr Fox thinks more desireable both for the Public and himself than for him to be in a Ministerial Office; not to avoid being responsible, but to avoid all appearance of what some are, and perhaps many more pretend to be, afraid of. As Mr Fox was of the Cabinet Councill[51] before he was secretary of state, it would probably be thought proper he should be so again if he is Paymaster; and then, according to Mr Pitts doctrine, he will be as responsible as if he was a Minister. I cannot, but think Mr Fox is sincere in desireing to see the Duke of Newcastle at the head of Affairs; and himself in no Ministerial Office, because it seems agreable to his Interest; and such a settlement would, I think, promise him more ease, and stability, with sufficient honor, and advantage than he could expect in a higher station. And I do believe he is truely inclined, and desireous to use his utmost endeavours to make it easy, and agreable to the Duke of Newcastle. I wish his Grace and Mr Fox might talk freely together, rather than by third Persons, all Mistakes would then be prevented, and the Duke would be guided by his own good sense, and upright Intentions; without any danger of being misinform'd, by the Passions, the Prejudices, the Interests, or wrong Judgements of other People.

If Mr Pitt will not accept being Secretary upon such terms as he ought, or if there should be any other difficulty, of a higher nature, in the way of his returning to that Office, a Secretary may be named who is a sure Friend to the Duke of Newcastle. Sir Thomas Robinson is so, and it may be presumed would be agreable to his Majesty. In such a Case I cannot but think that a hearty union of the Kings friends and Old servants,[52] might be able to carry on the public Busyness, and support themselves, even against Mr

---

[47] This letter was written at the beginning of the tortured negotiations which led, in June 1757, to the formation of the Newcastle–Pitt administration which survived until 1762.

[48] Fox remained as paymaster until 1765. Ilchester, *Henry Fox*, ii, 95, claims that since this was an inferior post it is a sign of Fox's waning political ambition, a theme that the letters to Campbell confirm. See Introduction.

[49] This became so, but Pitt's main concern was with the conduct of the British in the Seven Years War.

[50] That is, send him off to the house of lords, where he could do little harm. His wife was Mary Hill, Countess Hillsborough, until 1755 when she lost the title on the death of her father. She was created Baroness Stawell, of Somerton, Somersetshire in 1760. Contrary to Campbell's advice, Legge was made chancellor of the exchequer for the third time in the new administration, a place he kept until 1761.

[51] He had been a member of the cabinet council since 1754. Ilchester, *Henry Fox*, i, 237–9.

[52] The whigs.

Pitt and the Common Councill.[53] Nobody could think such a settlement the Ministry of the D[uke] of C[umberland] and none but Mr Pitt's new Friends the Tories, could think it reasonable, to exclude the ablest Parliament Man in the House of Commons, from the Public Service, and refuse his assistance in supporting the Government, merely because he is honor'd with H[is] R[oyal] H[ighness]'s[54] favour. I freely acknowledge my good opinion of Mr Fox, and Friendship for him. But I should be a very base, and bad Man, if I could be led by that, to offer an advice to the Duke of Newcastle, which I did not think the best for the Honor, Interest, and Satisfaction of his Grace.

In the present unhappy state of Affairs there is too much reason to apprehend such Events as may raise popular clamor, against the Wisest, and most blameless Administration. If such happen all the Kings servants must resolve to stand firm, and fearless, by their Master, and by each other; which will be the natural consequence of honest Mens acting in unreserved Confidence together.

164. [BL, Add. MS 51406, ff. 34–5]
Henry Fox to John Campbell, 9 July 1757
You heard before you left Town that I was to be persecuted to the last, & I doubt not imputed my not waiting on you to the Opposition which call'd me immediately to Windsor, where I underwent all the trouble, with all the Expence[55] that could be crowded into five Days, except that the Day of Election was, at last, quiet; I carry'd it by 137 agst 86. There was no encouragement from hence to my opposers, & the Duke of Newcastle wrote very warmly in my favour. But whether Example influenced, or it was my Fate, I know not; The Corporation, Whiggs a bucler[56] & who have complain'd that the D[uke] of M[arlborough]'s & my friends were not Whig enough, join'd with Mr Bowles[57] of Oxfordshire, & oppos'd me with all the Crys as well as blue streamers of the Oxfordshire Election, &, as they said, in Revenge for that. The Beauclerk Interest likewise strongly join'd them.

I am at last however quiet, & as much so in my Temper as in my situation. I have acted in everything the honest part, & the Knowledge that one, such Man as you are, thinks so, overbalances the railing Talk of all the Coffee Houses in Town. And a few such Testimony's as yours have made me quite easy. As easy, that is, here, as you can be in Pembrokeshire, for in neither place can either of us cast our eyes towards Lower Saxony,[58] Bohemia,[59] or America,[60] without the greatest apprehension of such Evils as

[53] Of London, who were great supporters of Pitt.

[54] Cumberland.

[55] Fox spent £4,000 on the election. See Ilchester, *Henry Fox*, ii, 62.

[56] Buckler: 'To act as a buckler to; to shield, defend, protect'. *OED*.

[57] Bowles was a large landowner in Oxfordshire. Richard Rigby wrote on 2 July 1757 to the duke of Bedford: 'Fox's election at Windsor is very doubtful. There is a Jacobite subscription of £5000 raised against him, with Sir James Dashwood's name at the head of it. The Beauclerk interest has joined it, and I am in the greatest fear for him; at all events it must cost him a vast deal of money'. *Correspondence of John, Fourth Duke of Bedford*, ed. Lord John Russell (1842), ii, 261.

[58] Frederick II, under the Convention of Westminster, Britain's new ally, had invaded Saxony in Sept. 1756.

[59] Bohemia was ruled by Maria Theresa, an ally of Britain, until the latter's alignment with Frederick II, when she aligned herself with France.

[60] Defeats in the war against France in America, in particular General Edward Braddock's fatal expedition to Duquesne in June 1755 and then at the battle of Oswego in Aug. 1756, making the colony's future look insecure for the British.

no Pitt, no God of our own making, can avert. May the grace of God do it, who alone can amend a state so desperate.

Adieu, My Dear Sir, You have conferr'd on me the greatest good one Honest Man can confer upon another, Your Friendship founded on your good opinion; I will never forfeit it, nor till I cease to be an honest Man, cease to be your most affectionate, your most faithfull & most oblig'd & humble servant.

165. [BL, Add. MS 51406, ff. 36–7]
John Campbell to Henry Fox, 15 July 1757
Many hearty thanks for your most kind letter. The regard you express for me, and the value you are pleased to set upon my friendship, founded upon a just esteme, give me more pleasure than I am able to express.

I know no Man that has more reason to be satisfied with his own conduct than your self, your friends must rejoice in it, and may justly boast of it. The temper with which you have bore so much base usage, is indeed a singular happiness. I have a hundred times had at my tongues end Thy steady temper Portias[61] &c.

Lord Digby told me of Windsor opposition the last day I was at the House; and I was really uneasy till I saw the account of your success[62] which overtook me on the road. Those who used to complane that your Friends were not Whig enough, joining a true blue Opposition, would some time past have made me wonder; but now no degree of impudence, or inconsistence can surprise. I am glad the Duke of Newcastle writ warmly for you; though I could not bring myself to wait upon him before I went into Town; not that I was unwilling to show him a decent respect, and civility; but I knew not how to look, or what to say. To speak my thoughts would have been rude, and to no purpose; and to speak contrary to what I thought, to what he knew I thought, was impossible. So I contented myself with desireing Mr West to present my most humble respects to his Grace, and very freely told the reason I did not go myself. Why should I disturb the endearments between H[is] G[race] and his good Friend Mr Legge.

I agree with you, that no Place can make an honest Man easy, when he thinks of the dangerous situation of our Country on every side, and in every respect. In this remote place every post puts me in a Fright, and to hear & read Fools & knaves prate of our being saved by the Councills of Pitt &c moves me to the last degree of indignation & contempt. Wee have no hope but where you look for it.

My neighbor and friend[63] who I told you had sent for my second Son [John (Jack)], the Lyon, died a week before I came into the country and had sometime before made a Will, about which I am in a good deal of anxiety; it being drawn, and writ by a Country Attorney, who is a very bad scribe, I wish he may be a sufficient lawyer. But if he has validly executed the intention of the Testator, my son will have a very pretty Fortune; He will go to London very soon upon this occasion, I will order him to wait upon you; and shall venture to promise him your friendship, because I think he deserves it, being satisfied that he is a sensible, good natured, perfectly honest young Man. He

[61] Joseph Addison, *Cato: A Tragedy* (1713), I, 1, line 13.

[62] Fox was seeking re-election after appointment to the office of paymaster. He won 137 to 86, his opponent being Charles Bowles.

[63] John Hooke (c.1699–1757), of Bangeston, Pembrokeshire.

Allways shews the greatest affection and duty to me; and it gave me great pleasure to find his was of thinking the same with mine, when he heard several of our great Debates last Session.

Dear Sir I do not in the least fear your altering your Conduct for the worse, and I do not desire you to do it for the better, therefore I have no doubt that I shall always continue with the sincerest esteme and affection your most faithfull and obliged humble servant.

I shall hope for a line now & then, at a leisure hour as anything occurs.

166. [BL, Add. MS 51406, ff. 38–9][64]
John Campbell to Henry Fox, 21 October 1757
Though you could not be particular, the general account you were so kind to give me, was enough to fill me with concern, & astonishment, and has raised in me a great curiosity, which, at the same time, I must confess is a very idle one; for I am very sensible that my knowing the whole, could not do the least good, to my Country, my friends, or even to my insignificant self. I am heartily sorry H[is] R[oyal] H[ighness][65] has found it necessary to resign. I see no one that can properly fill the Place, and this is a strange time to be without a General. You hear my Lord Protector behaved handsomely. I believe it, but cannot help saying, I believe also that it was only outward and insincere; though I would scorn to say so, if I had not seen so many public shameless influences of his prevarication, self contradiction, and disregard to truth.

I know not what to think of the expedition.[66] I truely thought the Commanders well choosen, I am sure I know not by whome, yet I confess the appearance seems against them. If they did wrong where shall we find Officers that will do their Duty. If they did their best, then I fear it is impossible for us to make any impression upon France; and I must ask, when or how is this ill fated War to end?

I do not understand, I suppose it is my dullness, the Declaration made to all the foreign Ministers, sign'd by Lord Holdernose.[67] Wee will vigorously support the K[ing] of P[russia][68] how can we do it, is there any way possible but by money, and if £200,000 was of so little effect (as you I think foretold) this year. Will it do more the next year. Or will they who so obstinately refused to give any more last year, be ready to give more, when there is so much less hope of doing any good by it. Perhaps, being quite in the dark, I write Nonsense. But there is one thing that I think you may tell me by the Post. Why are you glad that P[itt] is sole Minister.[69] I am not far from the same

---

[64] This letter was published privately in *Letters to Henry Fox, Lord Holland*, ed. earl of Ilchester (1915).

[65] The duke of Cumberland signed the treaty of Kloster-Zeven in Sept. 1757, after a disastrous military campaign against the French in Germany. On Cumberland's return to England he was accused by his father of ruining his country and his army, and resigned, his military career at an end. *ODNB*.

[66] The failed expedition to Rochefort. The raid was the first of a campaign of 'descents' on French coastal towns, a favourite project of Pitt's – who was attempting to lure the French away from their victorious Germany campaign. R. Middleton, *The Bells of Victory: The Pitt–Newcastle Ministry and the Conduct of the Seven Years' War, 1757–62* (Cambridge, 1985), 26–30.

[67] Robert Darcy, Lord Holdernesse (1718–78). 'Holdernose' could be Campbell's comment on his personal hygiene.

[68] Frederick II.

[69] Pitt had become leader of the Commons and secretary of state for the southern department in June 1757, with Newcastle as first lord of the treasury.

thought, I don't know whether for the same reasons; for, to tell the truth, I have no very high opinion of his abilities as a Minister. For your own ease it is lucky you were not made a Minister at the end of last Session; but I sincerely think, that if any good could have been done for this unhappy Country, you were much more likely to have done it, than those now in Power. I may at this time venture to say so, not only to yourself, but to any body, without being suspected of flattery; which you seem in no situation to receive. I have the honor to agree entirely with Lord Granville in his opinion of the Times.

I admire Lord Halifax's greatness of mind.[70] The entire submission of Lord H[ardwicke] & the Duke of Newcastle is what I expected, and what was foretold to them. I am very sincerely . . .

The Estate my son has the inheritance of is, I suppose, good £1,100 per annum. The Annuities out of it, for the respective lives of the Annuitants, about £500 per annum. He will have at least I think £1,000 ready money after paying Debt and legacies. A House not quite finished, but enough for use elegantly fitted up, & furnish't; with some necessary Plate and other odd things.

167. [BL, Add. MS 51406, ff. 40–1][71]
John Campbell to Henry Fox, 18 November 1757

Before I was favor'd with yours of the 10th [not extant] I had given my opinion very freely both in words and writing, upon the mean, unconstitutional Message.[72] If such submissions are unavoidably necessary, our Government is in effect dissolved; if they are not, how great is the Wisdom of those Ministers who take such ignomious steps.

I am not much Surprised at the Convention between France and the King of Prussia.[73] If France acted vigorously against him in conjunction with the Empress Queen I suppose he must very soon be destroy'd; but it seems to me more natural for the French to preserve him, that he may serve them, another time against the August House of Austria; and I said I believed the French would save the King of Prussia, for that reason, before I heard anything of this Convention. I don't doubt it will renew the cry against the Treaty of Stade[74] but the right, or wrong of that, must be determined by the necessity. If it was, as seem'd to me, necessary it must still be right, whatever the King of Prussia has done, or may do and he would doubtless have done the same if the Army of observation[75] had been cut in pieces, or made Prisoners of War. But if that Treaty was not necessary, it was wrong; though the King of Prussia should have made no Treaty

---

[70] Halifax had resigned his place as first lord of trade in June, but was reinstated in Oct. 1757.

[71] This letter was published privately in *Letters to Henry Fox*, ed. Ilchester.

[72] The king's address to parliament. Middleton comments that the address was of 'florid tone'. *Bells of Victory*, 8.

[73] The Convention of Kloster-zeven, signed 10 Sept. 1757, by France and Hanover in the wake of the defeat by the forces of the latter, under the command of the duke of Cumberland. The Convention left Hanover mainly in French hands.

[74] That is, the Convention of Kloster-zeven.

[75] The Army of Observation was established under Cumberland. It was initially proposed in the House by Pitt on 18 Feb. 1757 as an army of 50–60,000 to defend Hanover. Cumberland refused to accept command until Pitt had been dismissed, which he was on 6 Apr. F.A.J. Szabo, *The Seven Years War in Europe, 1756–63* (2008), 76.

with France. But how came they to think these Things of so much consequence to Us, who two years ago, thought Wee ought not to concern our selves in the least with the Continent; nor make the least attempt to prevent the French takeing possession of our Kings German Dominions. I think the Affairs of Germany will now, at worst, be only in the state they expected, and thought (I mean said) it was right for us to acquiesce in; with generous intention, I confess, to give the Hanoverians a Brief or so, to make them some recompense for their Losses, at the end of the War.

I am told our Pembrokeshire Address was drawn by Mr Whitakers lawyer, whose name is Ayres. But be that as it will, I believe you are so far right, that whoever drew it, it is adorn'd with some flowers that have fallen from C[harles] T[ownshend] himself. As to the Wisdom of our Great Welchman[76] I can say nothing, because I never saw anything of it. But I assure you they have Pride enough. You will please remember that great pride is most frequently accompanied with great Meanness; for example, compare the Message to the House of Commons last session, with the late Message to my Lord M[aste]r. I am Allways Dear Sir . . .

I begin to be apprehensive, I shall trouble you too much, with my opinion about Things of which I know little, and understand less.

168. [BL, Add. MS 51406, f. 42]
Henry Fox at the Pay Office to John Campbell, 17 December 1757
What you so kindly condole is indeed a Misfortune that I fear even Time will not efface in the Mind of my miserable Sister; & which we all lament & except the Mother no Body so much as the present Lord. For my Part it is the greatest affliction I ever met with; & as such makes it very difficult for me as yet to turn my thoughts to any other subject. If I could, you should hear more from me than what you I hope are already convinced of, that I am with the sincerest Regards, Esteem, & Gratitude Dear Sir . . .

169. [BL, Add. MS 51406, ff. 44–5]
Henry Fox at the Pay Office to John Campbell, 28 March 1758
I receiv'd yours of the 20th [not extant] yesterday, & set down to answer it tho' very unequal to the hard task it imposes. 'Give you a little' Notion of the Scene you are coming towards Nemo dat quod not habet.[77] And I doubt whether the same answer might not with truth be given you by ev'ry one of the chief Actors in the Scene, if you ask'd them a Notion of it. It seems to me that we take up and carry thro' with Violence what ever by chance is call'd or thought popular. And for future Measures I really think the London Evening Post more likely to suggest to you what they will be than I or perhaps any body.

In the mean time the Lord Protector,[78] as you call Him sees nobody, cultivates no Individuals but on the contrary last fryday[79] was se'ennight attack'd the Lord Chancellor

---

[76] Almost certainly a sarcastic reference to Sir John Philipps of Picton Castle.

[77] No one gives who possesses not.

[78] Pitt.

[79] *PH*, xv, 871–95: Proceedings in the Commons on the Bill to explain and amend the Habeas Corpus Act. Pitt's speech is not recorded.

J[ustice] Mansfield in particular & all Westminster Hall[80] in general most furiously. *I love the Law, but I hate the lawyer, I would never have any Lawyer whatever concern'd in Government*, were among his wise sentences. I have a good Memory & will, when I see you repeat all I have heard; out of which you must form what notion you can. I am still abus'd & in the Pamphlet you mention,[81] which is [Thomas] Potters, for an Opinion the contrary of which I have always maintain'd; for I think & ever shall think that however foolish the scheme was, they who had undertaken should have at all hazard gone further than they did in the Execution. You are so good as to avow (what I did not fail to brag in contradiction to Mr Potters obliging assertion) Your Friendship; And as it is the greatest Honor to me, so I am sure not to forfeit it, by any change in Conduct; nor do I see any Body likely or at all desirous to vie with me in those poor plain good qualitys for which I flatter my self you value me. As to foreign Affairs they wear something a [*sic*] better aspect, & We shall I hear feed good Fortune as we ought to do, this year. More Assurance was never shown than by the great Man [Pitt] in bringing out this Measure. I rate still, not surpriz'd, but really good to hear him for once so impudently in the right. Nobody mentions your Cozen of Newcastle[82] & yet He gives away every thing, & has just made Secker[83] (the only Bishop profligate enough to vote for the Bill to indemnify[84] & reward Evidence against Sir Robert Walpole) Archbishop.

When We meet you will see me better in Health than Business would let me be; & with more Ease, in as good Humour as notwithstanding Business you know I always would be.

Poor Lord Digbys Death[85] still hangs, at times heavy upon me. And I have griev'd for Sir Charles [Hanbury] Williams,[86] but he is quite well again. When I see you I trust we shall both be well & in a Disposition to enjoy without Alloy the pleasure of free & friendly conversation, only I am a little afraid that you will be angry when you hear

[80] That is, the lawyers. The courts of king's bench, chancery and exchequer were all situated in Westminster Hall.

[81] *The Expedition against Rocheforte Fully Stated and Considered in a Letter to the Right Honourable Author of Candid Reflections . . . by a Country Gentleman* (1758), was Potter's response to *Candid Reflections on the Report (as Published by the General-Officers, as Appointed by His Majesty's Warrant of the First of November Last to Enquire into the Causes of the Failure of the Late Expedition to the Coasts of France* (1758), attributed to Henry Fox.

[82] That is, the duke of Newcastle.

[83] Thomas Secker (1693–1768), rector of St James's, Westminster 1733; bishop of Bristol 1735; bishop of Oxford 1737; dean of St Paul's 1750; archbishop of Canterbury 1758–68.

[84] The Bill to Indemnify Evidence against Sir Robert Walpole. For a copy of the Bill see *PH*, xii, 638, and for the debate in the Lords, *PH*, xii, 640–733.

[85] Edward Digby died suddenly on 30 Nov. 1757 at the age of 27.

[86] Sir Charles Hanbury Williams (1708–59), of Coldbrook, Monmouthshire; MP for Monmouthshire 1735–47 and Leominster 1754–9. Envoy at Dresden 1747–9, at Berlin 1750–1 and ambassador at St Petersburg 1755–7. Whilst on diplomatic duty he became increasingly unstable mentally. On his way back to London in 1757 he 'showed signs of being deranged; by the time he reached London he was hallucinating, making extravagant claims, and acting violently, no doubt the result of tertiary syphilis'. Fox helped him and put him in the care of Sir William Battie, physician and writer of the *Treatise of Madness*, and then Dr John Munro, physician to Bethlehem hospital and writer of *Remarks on Dr Battie's Treatise on Madness*. However, in May 1759 Williams was declared a lunatic in May 1759, and died in November of the same year. Hanbury Williams was best known as the savage satirist whose poetry attacked without compromise opposition politicians. *ODNB*. Hanbury Williams, Thomas Winnington and Fox were especially close friends: Riker comments that 'The same love of revelry which characterised the less dissolute minds of Fox and Sir Hanbury Williams had knit them in a common bond with Winnington, and the three had long been boon companions'. T.W. Riker, *Henry Fox, First Lord Holland* (Oxford, 1913), 67.

altogether what has come to my knowledge by degrees only, & without in the least rattling me. I am Dear Sir . . .

170. [BL, Add. MS 51406, ff. 46–7]
Henry Fox to John Campbell, 19 August 1758
You will see in the inclos'd the good & truely important News from Cape Breton.[87] It is a great naval Victory as well as a place of the utmost consequence taken. Had not the French behav'd very ill, I hear We could not have landed without great Loss, if at all.

I fear it is too true that in another part of N[orth] America Lord How[88] is kill'd.

An Account is come to day from Cherbourgh[89] that We have done all the *petty* Mischief We propos'd, & are reimbark'd to some other Destination which is not griev'd at, by me at least. The Duke of Marlbro' has join'd Prince Ferdinand,[90] & it is hop'd Westphalia may be defended. If I go further into Germany the prospect will be very bad; so I shall return to good News, which is that the King, I am sure, looks & am told is as well as ever He was in his Life. We have lost no Officer at Cherbourgh but Captain Lindsey, a Man well spoken of. I should have told you our safety before, because I do not know but that you have a Son [Alexander] on the Coast of France. Adieu My Dear Sir, I mistook my time or maybe should have write more, perhaps this short account is better than a longer would have been.

171. [BL, Add. MS 51406, f. 48]
John Campbell to Henry Fox, fragment [n.d. but August 1758]
I have seen an Address, which I at first thought, dictated to the C[ommo]n[s] most indecently, & impertinently but when I recollected the Message to the Lord Mayor sent last year by Mr Blair,[91] I was forced to confess the C[it]y only exercised an acknowledged Privilege.

I have also seen a Letter, the stile of which did not seem to me suitable to the Dignity of the name, it is supposed to be sign'd with; and some expressions seen to carry a reflection, that could not come from – I take it for granted the inditing such letters is a work of Office, and therefore am at liberty to think it a Pittiful[92] performance.

---

[87] Cape Breton Island, Nova Scotia. More precisely Fox is referring to the capture of the fortress of Louisburg, on the island, in July 1758. It was a major British victory in the Seven Years War, ending the French colonial era in Atlantic Canada. The victory enabled the British to attack and defeat the French at Quebec in 1759, and by the following year to control all of North America.

[88] George Howe (c.1725–58), 3rd Viscount Howe. A brigadier general, Howe was killed whilst attempting to capture Fort Carillon, North America.

[89] Cherbourg was captured on 7 Aug. and the British set about destroying the harbour and fortifications which had been constructed at the end of the 17th century at a cost of over £1,000,000. The spoils were large: 35 ships and 22 brass cannon which were sent to London to be displayed in Hyde Park. The navy occupied the port until 16 Aug. Middleton, *Bells of Victory*, 78.

[90] Prince Ferdinand of Brunswick (1721–92), overall commander of the allied army in the Seven Years War. The duke of Marlborough was sent to join Ferdinand in mid-June, after a change of policy by Pitt from coastal raids to a theatre of war centred in Germany. Middleton, *Bells of Victory*, 72–4.

[91] William Blair, a clerk of the privy council, had sent a message to the lord mayor of London on 31 Oct. 1757, stating that the king had given instructions for an inquiry into the behaviour of the commanders-in-chief of the failed raid on Rochefort of Sept. 1757. The inquiry recommended that the army commander, Sir John Mordaunt, be court-martialled, but that court acquitted him.

[92] The implication being that Pitt was the author.

I have read a Pamphlet call'd Things as they Are[93] The unknown author is a drawcansir, kills all on both sides, and gives some suspicion of Jacobitism. Yet his account of the Character, Rise & Progress of my Lord Protector, appears to me just, and pleased me much.

When shall Wee give over, for this Year, going in quest of Adventurers on the Coast of France?[94]

172. [BL, Add. MS 51406, ff. 49–50]
John Campbell to Henry Fox, 10 September 1758
I heartily congratulate you, and Lord Illchester, upon the happy surprising recovery of Lord Stavordale.[95]

You may safely swear I never believed there was anything political in your journey to Chatsworth,[96] but as I heard that story from a Lady, my only doubt was whether it was idle chat among Women, or whether H[is] H[ighness] and his friends (if he has any) were really jealous; which I thought probable; because most Men judge others by themselves, and if you had been in his Place, and he in yours, I am very sure he would not have let the Summer pass without political Cabals. I remember with great regret the Congress of Suning Hill[97] both on public, & private account; for my son happen'd to be there that summer,[98] and from that time I date his takeing a different Part from me; which has been a great affliction to me, and much the greater because all togather unexpected; for I thought myself secure that all his prejudices were in my favor, and I could not fear that the strength of reason would carry him to the other side.

I am satisfied you are the happier for not being a Minister,[99] yet I believe I ought to wish you were; for a reason that is no great Compliment because the public would certanely gain by the change. I believe my cousin[100] has no right to any honor on account of Louisbourg,[101] but has H[is] H[ighness][102] to whom so much is given, a better

---

[93] *Things as They Are* (1758), has been attributed to John Perceval, earl of Egmont.

[94] Campbell is here displaying his ignorance of the administration's foreign policy, since he was no longer intimate with anyone in it, as Pitt had changed his policy regarding the coastal raids in June. Middleton, *Bells of Victory*, 73–4.

[95] Henry Fox-Strangways (1747–1802), known as Lord Stavordale 1756–76; MP for Midhurst 1768–74. Son of Stephen Fox-Strangways, 1st earl of Ilchester, elder brother of Henry Fox. Succeeded to the earldom on the death of his father in 1776.

[96] Chatsworth House, Derbyshire, home to the Cavendish family and the seat of dukes of Devonshire since 1549. This branch of the Cavendish family was one of the richest and most powerful aristocratic families in Britain. Fox was a political ally of William, the 4th duke, who was, however, reluctant to hold high office.

[97] Sunninghill Park, Berkshire was one of Pitt's favourite spas. This could refer to a meeting between the duke of Newcastle and Pitt to establish the Newcastle–Pitt administration, which was finalised in June 1757.

[98] Of 1757.

[99] Fox had written to Hanbury-Williams in July 1757: 'I am paymaster, which I like better than any post I could have had; and I am *indeed*, not in name only, no minister'. Cited in Ilchester, *Henry Fox*, ii, 95.

[100] The duke of Newcastle.

[101] The Siege of Louisbourg.

[102] Pitt.

Clame. I never doubted that he who can flatter as well & as grossly as he can abuse, might make himself well in the Closet, but probably he do's not desire to be very well there, for fear of giving jealousy in another Place.[103] When I see you next I hope to convince you that Stackpole is not so far out of the world but you might Spend a fortnight in the Summer, with the Hermit of that Place. St Paul[104] eat a mess of Leak [*sic*] Pottage with me last year, but you will say that the Apostle to the Gentiles is obliged to visit the remote & dark corners of the Earth. However the difficulty is not so great as you seem to imagine. For my part when I left London June was twelve months; I said This world was made for Cæsar. And I left behind me all appetite for parliamentary busyness; yet I must, if I live, keep my word next Winter about the Judges, and shall have a little honest satisfaction if I carry that matter through.

I rejoice greatly for the D[uke] of M[arlborough']s escape[105] and for the King of Prussia's Victory;[106] if he had lost that Battle he would, I suppose, have been absolutely ruined; I wish this may enable him to stand his Ground. The bad behaviour of the French Troops in Germany, at Louisbourg, and, as my Boy [Alexander] tells me, at Cherbourg is one of my greatest Comforts, and gives me some hopes that Wee may obtane a tolerable Peace, before Wee are quite undone. I am always . . .

My eldest Son [Pryse] & his wife came here fryday. His opinion of my Lord Protector is, I believe, a good deal sunk.

173. [BL, Add. MS 51406, ff. 51–2]
Henry Fox, Windsor Great Lodge, to John Campbell, 18 September 1758
I with my whole heart congratulate you on your Sons [Alexander] being come safe out of the great danger He must have been in. But what is to be said to those whom one is to condole on this occasion? I do not in this last affair[107] see even the shadow of an Object. I don't know what can be suppos'd to have been the Design, good or bad, of this last landing which has ended in a Tragedy which truly Mr Bligh[108] seems to treat very lightly. It is (forsooth) one of those things that must happen. I am sure then that such a Descent as this, is one of those things that never ought to happen.

---

[103] Leicester House.

[104] George Lyttelton.

[105] The escape referred to was from the attempted raid on St Malo in June 1758. Marlborough left in such haste that he 'left his silver spoons behind, which the French commander politely returned'. *ODNB*.

[106] At the battle of Zorndorf, 25 Aug. 1758. Frederick claimed the victory over the Russians, but both sides suffered heavy losses.

[107] The battle of St Cast, 11 Sept. 1758. The final 'descent' on the French coast which ended in disaster for the British forces.

[108] Lieutenant general Thomas Bligh (1685–1775), Irish parliament MP for Athboy, Co. Meath 1715–75. He was appointed commander of the 'descents' at the age of 73 and was blamed for the disaster at St Cast. On his return to England George II refused to receive him, a slight Bligh responded to by resigning, and retiring to his Irish estates. The British failure at St Cast began a pamphlet war attacking Pitt's war policy in which Bligh may have had a hand. The pamphlet *A Letter from the Hon. L-t G-l Bligh to the Rt Hon. W-m P-t Esq* (1758) was based on his correspondence with Pitt. Middleton, *Bells of Victory*, 83, and *ODNB*. Middleton refers to Bligh as William but other sources name him Thomas.

I give you many thanks for your letter of the 10th. You will see by the inclos'd that on receiving yours of the 7th I immediately apply'd to Lord Keeper [Sir Robert Henley].[109] He is not only engag'd, but by his not naming the Gentleman, I fear to a wrong man. I am very sorry for it.

I take the Letter you mention to be the Work of the Person who sign'd it, &, alass! Much the more likely to be so for those Reflections.

I beg my Compliments to your Son, & his Lady, & am to you & your whole Family a most sincere Welwisher, & to you in particular a most oblig'd & grateful humble servant . . .

At the time this Disgrace happen'd to us in France We had got a shew & Triumph of captive Canon in Hide Park,[110] & (what no thinking Man could see without blushing for his Country) the Union Flag flying on a high pole with the French Flag revers'd & under it, as an English Ship brings in a French one that she has taken. We had conquer'd france, no doubt, & by the concourse & behaviour of the Mob one may believe they thought so.

174. [BL, Add. MS 51406, ff. 53–4][111]
John Campbell to Henry Fox, 26 September 1758
I am truly thankfull for your most Frindly [*sic*] congratulations on my sons [Alexander] safety. I did not know the extent of the danger they were in, till yesterdays Post. If that account is true, the French were very near getting between them and the sea, with a superior Force. In that case they must all have been Prisoners, or been cut in Pieces. If People loose their Relations, or Friends in a rational service, they must lament, but they Cannot complane and they have a real Comfort to support them in their Affliction. They whose Friends have been sacrificed in this, as it appears to me, most absurd Expedition, have indeed occasion for more than human Patience. To land Troops with design to attempt a Town, which the same Troops had a little before found it impracticable to attack by Land, and where the Rocks had shewn them the Fleet could not assist. To let a small Army on Shoar in an Enemies Country, where they knew not what Force might come, in a Place the Fleet could not take them on board again, but was obliged to go Several days March distant from the landing. Surely this was madness, and such a Madness as I think no soldier, or sailor, could have been guilty of, unless obliged by Orders from an Office, from whence Wee have seen reason to expect every thing that can procede from Mad Ambition, mean Popularity, Pride, and most intemperate Passion. I cannot help believing that H[is] H[ighness][112] was the sole Author of the Project and left his brother M[iniste]rs (I beg his pardon for using such forms of equality) no other share than that of mean submission. Can you then blame me for

---

[109] Robert Henley (1708–72), MP for Bath 1747. Attorney-general 1757; lord keeper of the great seal 1757–61; lord chancellor 1761–6. Created Baron Henley 1760 and 1st earl of Northington in 1764. Henley was a member of the group known as the King's Friends and was responsible for procuring the dismissal of the marquess of Rockingham and the recall of Pitt to office in 1766.

[110] See L. Colley, *Britons: Forging the Nation, 1707–1837* (1992), for anti-French feelings in Britain in the 18th century.

[111] Published privately in *Letters to Henry Fox*, ed. Ilchester.

[112] Pitt.

wishing you a Minister. I do not say you could extricate your Country out of the present dangers, & difficulties, and procure a safe, and honorable Peace. But I am sure you would not precipitate us to Ruin, you would not expose our Troops in this Manner, nor add Disgrace to Misfortune, and make us, in the midst of our Calamity, the Objects rather of scorn & derision, than of Pity. I was much ashamed of our most Childish Cannon Triumph, before I heard of the smart rebuke our folly met at St Cas.[113] But how ridiculous & contemptible must it now appear to all the World. Surely even the unthinking Mob must see themselves abused.

I am as much obliged to you as if our request had been successful, but I a little wonder that the Living is allready engaged, because I never could find the seals willing to promise a Living before it was actually Void. However since it is so, though I am sorry my Friend[114] has lost all expectation & Preferment, I esteem my Lord Keeper [Sir Robert Henley] for observing his Promise, which I suspect was given to one who I am sure is not very scrupulous in that Point himself. My son desired me to make his compliments to you. I am always Dear Sir . . .

After all I have said, I do not wish that you should attempt to make yourself a Minister. I am sure you scorn the means others have made use of to rise by infamy, to Power. Indeed you could have no occasion for such Lyes as have been spread to blast your Character. For others have furnish'd Truths enough to satisfie any reasonable Men. But such indeed in factious Times have little Weight. Like a talkative Old Man I tire you often with prating about things you know much better than I.

I know no particulars of the late Disaster but from Newspapers.

175. [BL, Add. MS 51406, ff. 55–6]
Henry Fox, Bath to John Campbell, 15 November 1758
I thank you kindly for the friendly intentions of your Letter of the 5th [not extant], & the true Character you give of my lost Friend.[115] I came here in hope that the journey, & a little Bath Water might make me sleep better than since I heard of his Death, I have been able to do so. I have not succeeded yet. Methinks the Anni recedentes[116] have particular disadvantage on these sad occasions. When We are younger, We dissipate, We have new Views, new senses arising; & new Friendships may make us forget the former & have time to become old, confirm'd, & valuable. At my Age, Life of itself grows every day less palatable without such horrid Ingredients to embitter & make it almost insupportable.

To the sudden putting off of the meeting of Parliament,[117] I 'ave the opportunity of taking this journey; But what can the ministers say to Gentlemen at Your Distance from Town, for the Inconvenience, their uncertainty, & I believe too very unnecessary Fickleness, may put you to. I shall be at the House on 23[r]d that I meet you there?

---

[113] Battle of St Cast, 11 Sept. 1758.

[114] Legge.

[115] Was Fox still grieving over the death, on 30 Nov. 1757, of his nephew, Edward, Lord Digby?

[116] Receding years.

[117] Parliament was initially prorogued on 3 Aug. and after further prorogations the new session began on 23 Nov. 1758. *CJ*, xxviii, 316.

Chapter 7. 1760–4

Unless otherwise stated all letters in this chapter are from CRO, Cawdor/Campbell box 128.

176. [BL, Add. MS 51406, f. 57]
Henry Fox to John Campbell, 15 November 1760
The first paragraph of your Letter of the 9th [not extant], receiv'd yesterday, hurt me. It would hurt me more if I at all deserv'd it. You will see by the little I can say now that I had nothing to say at first, and I shall I believe when I see you convince you thoroughly that you was not out of my thoughts.

I, with the rest of the Privy Council[1] here or hereabouts, waited on the King[2] on Saturday, the Day of the late King's Death.[3] I am of opinion they were as much unprepar'd as if the late King had been only 25; & seem'd to have determin'd nothing but to be extremely civil to . . .[4] & this Civility is receiv'd & return'd, by King & Duke [of Cumberland] in a manner that pleases the Publick & do's them both Honor. It was soon found that there must be some Settlement; & Friend & foe agreed to press the Duke of Newcastle to remain. The Junto then is Mr Pitt, Lord Bute, Duke of Newcastle, Lord Hardwicke and already the favour has fluctuated & given uneasiness. But they go on, will go on sometime, & I am afraid not very long. Certainly at first the King was inclined to neither Pitt nor the Duke of Newcastle nor much perhaps to either now. The Plan for the present it should seem is to remove as few people as possible. There is . . .[5]

177.
John Campbell to Mary Campbell, 8 January 1761
I at first apprehended, as you did, that the new subscription was intended only for Ladies, and such as had no Land in the County, and I think they had been much wiser to make it so. If the Assessment[6] is too low they might have proposed the raising of it higher to 9d or 1s per pound. I think they are not very wise who spread such an impertinent story about the Country, relating to the D[uke] of

---

[1] Fox had been made a privy councillor on 23 July 1746.

[2] George William Frederick (1738–1820), King George III 1760–1820.

[3] George II had died, aged 78, on 25 Oct. 1760. Fox probably means the day of official mourning which began on 2 Nov.

[4] Part of the letter is missing.

[5] The rest of the letter is missing.

[6] The land tax assessment. Before the introduction of income tax, the main source for tax was land. It was introduced in 1692/3, 4 Wm & Mary c.1. It was not finally abolished until 1963.

R[ichmond][7] which you may boldly Contradict. Lord Fitzmaurice[8] being made Aide de Camp was the reason given by the D[uke] of R[ichmond] to the King and to every body else, all his Friends blame him, he himself is now sorry for it.[9] And H[is] R[oyal] H[ighness] the Duke of Cumberland gave him a gentile, and Friendly, but plane rebuke for it. You may be sure my information is good in this matter.[10]

Many People express without reserve their weariness, and dislike of the War in Germany[11] where, say they, Wee are at an immense expence, and yet unable to obtane the end either in regard to H[anover] or the K[ing] of Prussia. The difficulty of continuing to raise such sums of money is already a very serious thing, and the loss and want of Men is yet more so. Lord Granby[12] is expected over very soon, if he do's not contradict what is now so much talk'd. P[rince] F[erdinand] will I Believe grow very unpopular I do not mean with the lowest of the People, though it will soon catch among them. All his Complaints will not make amends for what our Men have suffer'd, with which every body from the very Highest, are much affected. You know I have not been satisfied with him for a long time, and in regard to Lord G[ranby]'s thought, from the first, that though His Lordship might possibly be in the wrong H[is] S[erene] H[ighness][13] could not possibly be quite right. Affairs are very bad in Ireland[14] & the Lords Justices are either intimidated or trying to be popular, I think they desire to resign and are like to be taken at their Word, but such a ferment there with such War abroad is very bad. Lord Kildare[15] behave's much better than I should have expected.

---

[7] Charles Lennox (1735–1806), 3rd duke of Richmond. Brother-in-law to Henry Fox, who as secretary at war assisted Lennox to establish his military career: by 1753 he was a lieutenant colonel in the 33rd regiment of foot, with which he served in Germany, and in 1758 he was made a colonel of the 72nd foot. He was an advocate of parliamentary reform, which led him to support John Wilkes (see p. 264, Note 137), a move that ensured a falling out with Fox.

[8] William Petty (1737–1805), Viscount Fitzmaurice, succeeded his father as the 2nd earl of Shelburne in 1761. He was created marquess of Lansdowne in 1784. MP for Chipping Wycombe 1760–1. First lord of trade 1763; secretary of state for the southern department 1766–8; home secretary 1782; first lord of the treasury 1782–3. A friend of Fox's, he was also much in favour with Lord Bute, a connection Fox used to his advantage. Earl of Ilchester, *Henry Fox, First Lord Holland* (2 vols, 1920), ii, 122.

[9] In Dec. 1760 Richmond resigned, after a stormy interview with the king, as lord of the bedchamber, after only one month in office, on hearing that Fitzmaurice had been promoted to colonel and the king's aide-de-camp, thus slighting (in Lennox's eyes) Lord George Lennox, his brother. Ilchester, *Henry Fox*, ii, 124.

[10] Probably from Fox.

[11] One of the major theatres of the Seven Years War.

[12] John Manners (1721–70), marquess of Granby, son of the 3rd duke of Rutland; MP for Grantham 1741 and Cambridgeshire 1754–70. His father made him colonel of the Leicester blues regiment in the 1745 rising, which was the start of a long military career. He led British forces to victory at the battles of Warburg (July 1760) and Villinghausen (July 1761). However, he was a very poor administrator and lacked the ability to discipline his men. He was also a gambler who died leaving £10,000 debts. *ODNB*. George II referred to Granby as 'a sot, a bully, that does nothing but drink and quarrel, a brute'. Cited in *HPC, 1715–54*, ii, 241.

[13] Pitt.

[14] In 1760 the Irish Patriot Party, led by Henry Flood (1731–91), of Farmley, Co. Kilkenny, Irish MP for Callan 1759–61, Longford borough 1768–9, Enniskillen 1777–83, Kilbeggan 1783–90 and British MP for Winchester 1783–4 and Seaford 1786–90, had appeared in the Irish house of commons, advocating reforms and stirring up popular support for an Irish nationalist party.

[15] James Fitzgerald (1722–73), 1st duke of Leinster and from 1744, 20th earl of Kildare. He married Emily Lennox (1731–1814), daughter of Charles Lennox, 2nd duke of Richmond, whose wife's brother-in-law was Henry Fox. Kildare was a leading member of the Irish Patriot Party. As such he and Fox had a stormy relationship which was never to come to an understanding since Fitzgerald had an 'inability to contemplate political compromise'. *ODNB*.

Sir J[ohn] Phillips is come to Town, presented an address yesterday and after came to the House, he seems now in good spirits. He was not so bad at Oxford as was said.

My little Grandson[16] son is very full of the Measles, but I hope in a very good way, he was bad yesterday, but relieve'd by bleeding, he had bled at the Nose in his sleep which went down his throat, and increased his uneasiness, but after he was blooded in the Arm, he brought up the blood that had gone down his throat. I had a letter from Nanny yesterday, they were to set out today. My love . . .

178. [BL, Add. MS 51406, BL, Add. MS 32919, f. 153]
John Campbell, Grosvenor Square, to the duke of Newcastle, Friday evening, 20 February [1761]
In obedience to your Grace, I send this to you if you have any commands, and at the same time take the liberty to inform your Grace that my son [Pryse] had, by accident, another Conversation with Mr George Ross[17] last night, in which that Gent renew'd his Proposal, and said if my son [Pryse] would undertake it, he was satisfied that with his Fathers[18] Interest he might get somewhat done for Col[one]l Fraser[19] that would satisfie the Col[one]ls Friends. My son repet'd the Answer he had made before, and, being press'd, let fall an unguarded expression that may increase the displeasure against him. Mr Ross talk'd of himself,[20] or a Brother in Law of his standing on the Fraser Interest in Invernesshire. I beg pardon for being so troublesome and am, with the greatest respect . . .

179. [BL, Add. MS 51406, f. 58][21]
Henry Fox, Pay Office to John Campbell, Grosvenor Square, 19 March 1761
Come in for Invernesshire[22] yourself to help Telemachus & Mentor.[23] And when it drags make the Vacancy for your 2[n]d son [John Hooke Campbell, Lord Lyon] who will then find no Difficulty. This is my humble advice, as well as hearty Wish.

This wise and kind advice I very foolishly refused to follow.[24]

---

[16] Either John, Alexander or George.

[17] George Ross (1700–86), of Cromarty; MP for Cromartyshire 1780–84 and Tain burghs 1786. Ross was taken under the wing of Argyll, and during the Seven Years War amassed a fortune with an army agency business. Ross intervened in the Inverness-shire election of 1761 on behalf of Simon Fraser against Pryse Campbell, who was the sitting member but had offended the duke of Argyll. Despite Pryse appealing to Bute, and his father's efforts with the duke of Newcastle, Fraser was returned for Inverness-shire in May 1761, a seat he held until 1782. *HPC, 1754–90*, iii, 378. See Introduction.

[18] Andrew Ross of Pitkerrie, Ross-shire.

[19] Colonel Simon Fraser (1726–82), of Lovat, Inverness; MP for Inverness-shire 1761–82. Lieutenant colonel of the 78th foot (Fraser's Highlanders) 1757; major general British army 1772; colonel of the 71st Regiment (which he raised) 1775; lieutenant general 1777.

[20] Ross was considering standing himself but decided otherwise.

[21] Fragment only.

[22] Pryse Campbell was the MP for Inverness until 1761, but had offended his constituents and Argyll by supporting the Irish cattle bill of 1759. See Introduction.

[23] Telemachus and Mentor, perhaps Argyll and Bute.

[24] Note in Campbell's hand.

180. [BL, Add. MS 51406, ff. 59–60]
Henry Fox, Holland House to John Campbell, 9 July 1761
I can hardly wish I had seen you, because I possibly should not then have had your Letter of June 25th [not extant] which I am infinitely oblig'd by, & proud of, & shall transmit as a real & valuable Honor to my Posterity. They will think it Flattery, & indeed, Dear Sir, so should I if I did not know you as well as myself. You may be sure of heering [*sic*] from me as often as I know any thing worth writing to you. I stay'd now for the Event of a most extraordinary Summons to Council[25] on the most urgent & important Business. (The A[rch] Bishop[26] I am told dictated the Word urgent). Messages were sent throughout England. We were more than 60 who met yesterday, when the King declar'd His intention to marry Charlotte Princess of Mecklenburg-Strelitz[27] & order'd his Coronation for the 22[n]d of September.

This Princess is 17, & they say handsome; but it were difficult to find one here who has seen her. We shall all see Her very soon, for she is to come immediately. I must not, I am afraid, hope that the fine sight will bring you to town, I wish it would. In the midst of this Joy; Peace seems to be slipping away; a Battle[28] is suppos'd to be by this time fought; & Pitt has so far carry'd his wicked point as to have delay'd at least our Recovery, if Recovery is a Word to be still us'd, or the thing hop'd for by any sensible Man for this perishing Country. But you had better read the Address of the Common Council[29] than such desponding thoughts as mine. So adieu, Dear Sir, & believe me with truth & with the greatest affection . . .

181. [BL, Add. MS 51406, f. 61]
Henry Fox to Dear Sir, 7 November 1761
The Historical Memorial,[30] which is a faithfull translation I believe of that printed at the Louvre, & which I send you, will probably answer your Question (in yours of Nov[ember] 1st receive'd yesterday) [not extant] better than I could. It confirms the Opinion I had form'd, that in March the Duke de Choiseuil[31] wanted Peace at any Rate.[32] Pitt dreaded it, & evaded it, & the Council then said it was impossible to prevent the Mischief which might be done by the Man [Pitt] who held the Pen. Only look into the first long, verbose Paragraph of Page 14 and you will see what use He [Pitt] made

---

[25] The privy council.

[26] Thomas Secker.

[27] Charlotte, princess of Mecklenburg-Strelitz (1744–1818). She arrived in London on 8 Sept. and George married her the same day at St James's Palace. *ODNB*. Horace Walpole, writing to his cousin Henry Seymour Conway the day after the wedding stated: 'The Queen is come: I have seen her, and have been presented to her, she looks very sensible, cheerful, and is remarkably genteel'. Cited in *PH*, xv, 1110. Fox was deeply involved with the king's choice of queen since for a time it looked likely that Lady Sarah Lennox, his sister-in-law, could have become George's wife. See Ilchester, *Henry Fox*, ii, 130–7.

[28] The battle of Vellinghausen was fought on 15 July 1761 and was a victory for Prince Ferdinand against the French. R. Middleton, *The Bells of Victory: The Pitt–Newcastle Ministry and the Conduct of the Seven Years' War, 1757–62* (Cambridge, 1985), 189.

[29] Of London.

[30] The *Memoire* from duc de Choiseul to Pitt was of French overtures for peace. Temple published *Remarks upon the Historical Memorial Published by the Court of France in a Letter to the Earl Temple* (1761).

[31] Etienne François, duc de Choiseul (1719–85). He was closely associated with the defeat of France in the Seven Years War.

[32] Referring to the Declaration of the French king of 26 Mar. 1761. TNA, SP78/251.

of that Pen. The Epoches[33] propos'd by France, the most advantageous to us that could be, were put of to give time for the nonsensical Expedition to Bellisle,[34] (into which He [Pitt] overul'd the council) & such other opportunity, as might occur to prevent Peace. France soon saw that He [Pitt], & therefore (prot Pudor!)[35] England, did not mean it. Nor were there probably the most lavish Offers wanting from the Empress Queen to get France to break off the Negotiations. You will be amaz'd to see how little ground there were, for the Advice, which He [Pitt] made a point of, & overul'd, went out upon.

Yesterday in the House of Lords,[36] Lord Temple enter'd into the whole matter, hidiously, insolently, & ill.[37] It would have done you good to hear with what readyness, spirit & good sense the Duke of Bedford answer'd Him. I shall wait to see how the next Week, passes in the House of Commons, & then I'll write to you again; & in my Letter put you *au fait*, of my situation which I hope You will like for me as well as I do for myself.

Do you take the London Chronicle, & the Daily Gazetteer, which us'd to be both reckon'd Pitt's Papers? If you do not, pray do; & send for, & at any rate get them from the time of Pitts Resignation. You will see some Letters admirable, & if Fools & Madmen, were to be reason'd with, conclusive & convincing. For the present Adieu My Dear Sir, you had not receiv'd the Pamphlet I sent last, or you would have thank'd me for it. They say it was wrote under Lord Bath's Direction.

182. [BL, Add. MS 51406, ff. 63–4]
Henry Fox to Dear Sir, 19 November 1761
I am honor'd with yours of the 13th [not extant] & it cannot but be the greatest satisfaction to me to correspond with a sensible & honest Man who so entirely agrees with me; Did we agree in thinking (instead of the contrary that) things were going on to a right and happy Conclusion, it were more satisfactory. But I fear with you that the opportunity is lost; My last points out Elliot as the Man who drew Lord Bute into acquiescing in these Councils the effect of which you so justly describe. The same Man has I fear influenc'd Him upon Pitt's going out,[38] into the weak notion of beating Pitt at his own Weapons, & out doing Him, by building on his Foundations; in consequence of which, instead of saying to France, Pitt is gone let us see if We can now agree. Besides warlike language sent to every Court in Europe, letters have been sent to Spain, to require a Communication of their Treaty[39] with France. In answer, Mr Wall[40] has

---

[33] The epochs were the time limits of the peace talks relating to the three areas of conflict: Europe, America and the East Indies. Middleton, *Bells of Victory*, 184–5.

[34] The island of Bellisle fell to the British at the beginning of June, defeating any attempts at peace talks.

[35] For shame!

[36] *PH*, xv, 1109. The king's speech on opening the session where he announced his marriage to Charlotte. The king also announced that peace negotiations with France had been broken off. Did this cause Temple's outburst since it foiled his and Pitt's plans for asking for a large supply? *PH*, xv, 1111–2.

[37] No reference to this in *PH*, xv, 1111–2. Probably concerning Shelburne's announcement that he favoured withdrawing British troops from Germany.

[38] Pitt had resigned as southern secretary in Oct. 1761.

[39] The 'Family Compact' treaty between France and Spain, signed 15 Aug. 1761.

[40] Richard Wall (1694–1777), commonly known as Ricardo Wall; Irish-born military man who became the Spanish minister of foreign affairs – in effect the Spanish prime minister (1754–63).

held the most angry & hostile language, & orders are I believe gone to Lord Bristol[41] to repeat His demand, &, refus'd, to leave Madrid in 48 Hours. The provoking part of it is, that no Minister or Men can say, that, in great part of the Dispute which Spain these six years past has wanted to settle amicably, We are not in the wrong, or have one word to say for ourselves. The Militia will be prolong'd this year I believe & then drop.[42] Nobody is seriously for it after the War shall be over but the Duke of Bedford & some few sanguine ones, who harshly engag'd in it. I believe Pitt, in his Inclination as much against it as anyone. The Pamphlet given to Lord Bath was not his, nor Murphy's[43] not Hor[ace] Walpole's. It has come from some unknown friend of Legge's but I don'd know whom. The Author of your Milford Workes[44] Charles Townshend; talks every Language every Day. But for the most part Pitt's.

You ask why We did not refute the reasonings of France about the Restitution of Captures. I am told that Mr De Choiseul told Stanley[45] that should not prevent Peace. So We had no need of Refuting. Elliot I fancy hopes to bring Lord Bute & Pitt together again. But let who will agree or quarrel; the scandalous yeilding to Pitts villainous Politicks this summer, & it is an honor that cannot or will not be retreiv'd; has My Dear sir, in my opinion ruin'd us. Why We did not agree to the Epoches at first; or to the mutual withdrawing our Troops in Germany in the progress; or broke off the Negotiations at last; are three Questions to which no sensible, satisfactory, or honest answer can be given.

For myself, Dear Sir, I shall do nothing to forfeit your good opinion or my art, & that in these times is fully sufficient for you most faithfull & most affectionate . . .

183. [BL, Add. MS 51406, f. 65]
Henry Fox to John Campbell, Grosvenor Square, 9 October 1762
I never was more glad in my life than to find I shall see you. It is what I want. I have a great deal to say to a sincere & sensible Friend, of Importance to the Publick, & of the greatest in the World to me.

I'll be with you by to morrow morning.

184.
John Campbell, Pandamonium[46] to Mary Campbell, 14 October 1762
I entirely agree with you that it is a shocking thing for British and French to be knocking one another on the head in Germany if Peace is so nigh as reported. How

---

[41] George William Hervey (1721–75), 2nd earl of Bristol, eldest son of John Hervey, 2nd Baron Hervey. Bristol was ambassador to Spain 1758–61. He was initially ordered to return to England by the 2nd earl of Egremont, on 2 Nov.

[42] The statutes relating to the militia were to expire in May 1762 and debate inside and outside parliament centred on whether a new act was needed. The militia act of 1762 was the result. J.R. Western, *The English Militia in the Eighteenth-Century: The Story of a Political Issue 1660–1802* (1965), 184–93.

[43] Arthur Murphy (1727–1805), playwright and actor. He gave up acting in 1756 to edit and write articles for the *Test*.

[44] Townshend had been chairman of the committee of privy councillors responsible for making Milford Haven a secure and fortified place according to an address published in the newspapers from the high sheriff of Pembrokeshire. *Lloyd's Evening Post and British Chronicle*, 24 Oct. 1757.

[45] Hans Stanley (1721–80), of Paultons, Romsey, Hampshire and Ventnor, Isle of Wight; MP for St Albans 1743–7 and Southampton 1754–80. A lord of the admiralty 1757–65; envoy to Paris 1761 and vice admiral of the Isle of Wight 1764–6. He committed suicide in 1780.

[46] London.

right it is I cannot say, but am satisfied Lord Bute[47] will make Peace very soon, if he is allow'd to do so, and is not hinder'd by the Malice of some, the Madness & folly of Many and the Cowardice, & selfish fears of others. When the Duke de Nivernois[48] heard of the retaking of New foundland[49] he said to Lord Halifax It is not the thing it self that so much vex's me, though I might wish it otherwise, but to see how like Poltrons our People act everywhere, and how well you are served. If Wee don't make a Peace now you will go on to take all our Colonys till you raise all Europe against you and then it will be our turn, or to that effect. Lord Halifax & Mr Grenville are to change Places the first to be Secretary, the other at the head of the Admiralty and Mr Fox to conduct busyness in the House of Commons this perhaps you may have heard from others, but maybe not from so good authority as I tell it.[50]

Pryse Campbell was very well when he went to Bath but had some bilious uneasiness a little before, and I thought it very right for him to take a month of Bath Waters before the Session which may prove a busy one.[51] Wee have fair cold weather with east wind, to day very cold. Yesterday after dinner I went & sat some hours with the late Speaker [Arthur Onslow] who converses very cheerfully, but is allways in Town & allmost allways within, he lives in an unfashionable Place great Russell Street, but has a gentile & comfortable Room for his study he enquired very kindly after you as an old acquaintance, and indeed seem'd very glad to see me. He seems Moderate as to Parties has not the least acquaintance with Lord B[ute] but is vastly fond of the King, who saw him in his Closet. Since my last Mr Fox has been here & sat two hours with me. The Sluices of Abuse will be again let out upon him stronger I suppose than ever. And he will be abused for leaving the Duke of Cumberland that is for not following him where it is amazing he should desire to lead. Who some years ago could have thought of a league between him & my Cousin of Newcastle. But People at my age should wonder at nothing . . .[52] lest the Evening Post should give a particular account of Newfoundland I send you the Morning Paper . . .[53] Lord B[ute] is I believe by no means insensible of the danger, as a Minister, he stands in, yes is not fearfull, and profess's to be easy from a consciousness of meaning to do right. I have heard that he said he would sign a good Peace though he knew Felton[54] stood behind him. For this I have no Authority though it do's not seem out of Character. Mr Fox keeps the same Place,[55] and is not to be, as yet at least, a Cabinet Counsellor. God knows how soon the H[ouse] of C[ommons] may turn all upside down; I wish the best and fear the worst.

---

[47] Bute had become the first lord of the treasury at the end of May 1762.

[48] Louis-Jules Mancini-Mazarini (1716–98), duc de Nivernais; French diplomat and writer. He arrived in London in Sept. 1762 to begin negotiations which led to the Treaty of Paris (10 Feb. 1763), thus ending the Seven Years War.

[49] A French attack on Newfoundland began in June and had completely failed by Sept. 1762.

[50] Almost certainly Fox.

[51] One line obliterated.

[52] Four lines obliterated.

[53] Four lines obliterated.

[54] John Felton (c.1595–1628) assassinated the despised George Villiers, 1st duke of Buckinghamshire in 1628.

[55] Paymaster of the forces.

185.

John Campbell to Mary Campbell, 2 December 1762

The inclosed [not extant] from Ally [Alexander] came here yesterday, Nanny had one from him at the same time. The other Paper will a little ease you of your fears and satisfie that the Majority of the Whigs will not be against Peace. I won't pretend to say that all the 213[56] will be in every Question for the Peace and the Administration, but I fancy there will be but few exceptions. The Division was unexpected, and made by the zeal of one Mr Coventry[57] a Lawyer, I believe against the inclination of his Friends of the Opposition. John Y[orke][58] younger son of Lord H[ardwicke] was in the majority, but I don't say he will continue on that side. Sir C[harles] M[orduant] as well as Sir A[lexander] W[edderburn][59] hearty with the Administration.[60]

Mr Ferrier[61] May be assured there was nothing else in Lord Egr[emon]ts Letter[62] to make the D[uke] of D[evonshire] resign.[63] My wonder is that H[is] G[race] did not intimate his resignation, at the same time that he refused to attend the Court Counsill for after he refusing [*sic*] to attend upon so particular a Summons he could not continue to hold a Place which allways is in the Privy & Court & Counsil. Sir William Temple[64] once told K[ing] C[harles] 2[n]d when he refused, I think, to hear his advice, that H[is] M[ajesty] might choose & change his Counsillors as he pleased, and might refuse to follow their Advice, but to have Counsillors, who should not give Counsil, he humbly though [*sic*] not possible. And surely it is at least as absurd to have a Counsillor who will not give Counsil; The D[uke][65] might decline attending, and H[is] M[ajesty] acquiesce for a time, in hopes the D[uke] would think better of it. But when the D[uke] had a particular summons by letter from a Secretary of State, to attend on a particular day upon Busyness of the highest importance, the matter was

---

[56] Those who voted in the majority to defeat the motion to defer the debates on the peace preliminaries until Pitt was able to attend the House. Pitt's supporters mustered 74 votes. *CJ*, xxix, 387.

[57] Thomas Coventry (c.1713–97), of North Cray Place, Bexley, Kent; MP for Bridport 1754–80.

[58] John Yorke (1728–1801), of Sonning, Berkshire; MP for Higham Ferrers 1753–68 and Reigate 1768–84. Lord of trade 1761–3, 1765; lord of the admiralty 1765–6.

[59] Alexander Wedderburn (1733–1805), MP for Ayr burghs 1761–8, Richmond 1768–9, Bishop's Castle 1770–4 and 1778–80, and Okehampton 1774–8. Solicitor-general 1771–8; chancellor to the queen 1771–80; attorney-general 1778–80; lord chief justice, common pleas 1780–93; first commissioner of the great seal 1783; lord chancellor 1793–1801. Wedderburn supported the Bute and then the Grenville administration.

[60] Concerning the preliminary Treaty of Peace between Great Britain, France and Spain. See *CJ*, xxix, 360–7, 29 Nov. 1762.

[61] One of the Ferrers family, originally from Westminster, who had owned the Bangeston estate, Angle, Pembrokeshire, until Elizabeth Ferrers died in 1736, when the estate passed to her fourth husband, John Hooke, who bequeathed the estate to John (Jack) Campbell in 1757. CRO, Cawdor/Campbell box 5/240.

[62] On 3 Oct. Egremont had written a letter to Devonshire summoning the latter to attend the cabinet council, which he had ceased doing when he had resigned as first lord of the treasury. Ilchester, *Henry Fox*, ii, 205.

[63] William Cavendish resigning as lord chamberlain.

[64] Sir William Temple (1628–99), 1st bt of Sheen; sometime adviser to Charles II. Temple published *Essay on the Origins and Nature of Government* (1672) and *Observations upon the United Provinces of the Netherlands* (1687).

[65] Devonshire.

brought to a point, and H[is] G[race] must either attend or not keep that Place, which by long & constant usage, made him a Counsillor, and this I may venture to say was the D[uke']s own declared opinion.

The very damp gloomy weather continues it do's not rain but the flags in the back yard are all day and every day as wet as if it was just after a shower and Ty Bach[66] as if it was just done over with a wet mop. But the weather rather warm and calm. I have seen Mr Mcquicke he was so good to call here twice, but is not so fix'd in a lodging yet, he looks extremely well. My Love . . .

Mrs Morris of Pembroke is a good old Woman. I hear she had taken down her sign, what shall Wee of the Opposition do for an Inne at Pembroke. My son & I are obliged to night to attend the Funeral of Lady Culloden[67] Wife to Lord President Forbes's[68] Son,[69] Wee shall also wear a Weeks mourning for her.

186.
John Campbell to Mary Campbell, 11 December 1762
To give you a short account of Thursday [9 December], which I could not do that night, I will begin with what, to be base, is most important, H[is] S[erene] E[xcellency][70] spoke, without intermission, three hours & an half;[71] he came into the House with his legs cover'd with a great deal of somewhat under large white woollen, or flannel stockings, & some black things that came up half his legs over that like half boots, and with a Crutch under one arm. On account of his Infirmity the House indulged him to speak, when he pleased, sitting,[72] so he was enabled to hold out the time I mention. Some short pieces of his speech were good & spirited, but the greatest part verbose, tedious, round about, & back again, over and over.[73] Indeed what Man in the most perfect health could speak to the purpose, & without useless, disagreable repetitiveness 3½ hours. I could not help thinking he wanted to damp the Debate that there might be no division. However Mr Dempster[74] a *Wild Scot* who they say is an

---

[66] Welsh for toilet: literally the small house.

[67] Jane, daughter of Sir Arthur Forbes (1709–73), 4th bt of Graigievar, Aberdeenshire.

[68] Duncan Forbes (1685–1747), Lord Culloden; MP for Ayr burghs 1721–2 and Inverness burghs 1722–37; lord advocate 1725–37; president of the court of session 1737–47.

[69] John Forbes.

[70] Pitt.

[71] *PH*, xv, 1259–71, for Pitt's speech in the debate on the preliminary treaty of peace between Britain, France and Spain.

[72] The rule was that members stood whilst speaking. The House granted Pitt the privilege of sitting on this occasion because of his infirmity. P.D.G. Thomas, *The House of Commons in the Eighteenth Century* (Oxford, 1971), 203.

[73] Horace Walpole simply stated that, for Pitt, 'It was not a day on which his genius thundered'. Cited in Ilchester, *Henry Fox*, ii, 213.

[74] George Dempster (1732–1818), of Dunnichen, Forfar; MP for Firth burghs 1761–8 and 1769–90. An independent whig, much influenced by Hume, Rousseau and Montesquieu. He was a member of the Select Society and he rated 'intrinsic merit' high above rank or wealth. As a 'true blue Scot' Dempster was dedicated to the encouragement of agriculture, industry and the arts, and to the establishment of a Scottish militia. *HPC, 1754–90*, ii, 313. In Nov. 1761 he made a speech pleading for the extension of the militia scheme to Scotland and Campbell's essay, 'The Substance of a Letter, to a Friend in Scotland upon the Militia Scheme', written in 1762 (see Appendix 5), may have been directed at Dempster. In May 1765 he supported Pryse Campbell's motion against any female regents marrying a Catholic. *HPC, 1754–90*, ii, 314.

honest Man with Parts but most truly what I have called him, did divide the House just at eleven o'clock ays 319 No's 65.[75] So if every Member had been in the House Wee were a majority by 83 of the whole. Several on both sides went away thinking there would be no division. I did not see but am assured Lord Royston was in the Majority,[76] his two Brothers[77] I believe went away.[78] The Motion was made by Mr Harris[79] of Salisbury a Man of sense & universal good Character, seconded by Lord Verney[80] Lord Strange not being very well. In the House of Lords the Motion[81] was made by Lord Wycombe (Shelburne) who spoke well, seconded by Lord Grosvenor,[82] who the opposition hoped for. It is now past twelve & so dark I must stop a little till it grows lighter. Though it continues a dark day, I am in a little time able again to write; I can give but an imperfect account of the Lords. The Duke of Newcastle, Lord Hardwicke, Lord Temple, Duke of Grafton,[83] spoke against some parts of the Preliminaries. Lord Halifax Lord Mansfield, Lord Chancellor [Robert Henley] & Lord Bute for them there might be others on both sides that I forgot. The last said he knew what hazard he ran, but he would have sign'd what he thought a good an honorable Peace at the hazard of what he valued more than life that when he died he desired no better Epitaph than Lord B[ute] who had a principal hand in making the Peace of 1762. The Duke of Grafton who, otherwise, I am told spoke well, abused Lord B[ute] in terms unbecoming his own rank & the dignity of the place he spoke in. Lord B[ute] very prudently forbore to answer till another had spoke, least as he said, he should have been too warm. He said he could lay his hand, upon his heart & say he did not deserve any of the Epithets the noble Lord had given him & in the con- sciousness of his innocence he could hear such language with the contempt it deserved. Lord Fortescue says Lord Bute spoke extremely well. The Dukes of

---

[75] *PH*, xv, 1272.

[76] Only the minority list is extant. See *PH*, xv, 1272–3.

[77] Charles Yorke (1722–70), MP for Reigate 1747–68 and Cambridge University 1768–70. Solicitor- general 1756–62 and was nominated lord chancellor in Jan. 1770 but committed suicide before taking up the office; John Yorke (1728–1801), see p. 253, Note 58.

[78] That is, neither voted.

[79] James Harris (1709–80), of Salisbury, Wiltshire; MP for Christchurch 1761–80. A lord of the admiralty 1762–3 and of the treasury 1763–5; comptroller to the queen 1774–80. A classical scholar of note, Dr Johnson referred to him as 'a sound sullen scholar'; Gibbon, more kindly, as 'learned and amiable'. He kept a journal of the Commons debates 1760 6 which has survived in full. *HPC, 1754–90*, ii, 588. The motion referred to was an address in favour of the peace preliminaries.

[80] Ralph Verney (1714–91), styled Viscount Fermanagh 1743–52, 2nd Earl Verney 1752–91 (Irish peerage); MP for Wendover 1753, Carmarthen 1761–8 and Buckinghamshire 1768–84 and 1790–1.

[81] *LJ*, xxx, 307; *PH*, xv, 1251–2, gives notes on Lord Hardwicke's speech but little else.

[82] Richard Grosvenor (1731–1802), Baron Grosvenor 1761 and Viscount Belgrave and 1st Earl Grosvenor 1784.

[83] Augustus Henry Fitzroy (1735–1811), of Euston, Suffolk, 3rd duke of Grafton. Styled earl of Euston 1747–57. MP for Boroughbridge 1756 and for Bury St Edmunds 1756–7. Lord of the bedchamber to the prince of Wales 1756–7; secretary of state of the northern department 1765–70; leader of the house of lords 1766–70; first lord of the treasury 1768–70; lord privy seal 1771–5 and 1782–3. He became duke in 1757 on the death of his grandfather the 2nd duke. As secretary of state he was nominally the head of the administration but real power resided in the gout- and depression-hit Pitt. Grafton, although incorruptible, was 'more interested in horse racing than governing', and he did his job 'in a desultory manner'. A.H. Cash, *John Wilkes: The Scandalous Father of Civil Liberty* (2006), 196.

C[umberland], N[ewcastle], G[rafton] & D[evonshire] went away on purpose to prevent a division, so for want of a Lord Dempster[84] there was none. I forgot to say Lord Pomfret[85] spoke, & handsomely for the Motion.

Yesterday I went to the House of Commons expecting the Address to be reported but no Debate, many of the Majority I believe thinking the same did not come down, my son went to Wandsworth, where I trust the little boy is recovering safely and though he came home at four o'Clock had no thought of coming to the House till I sent. It was resolved by the Opposition to have a debate, that many who could not have the opportunity to speak the first day, might declare themselves the second, and some young men had a mind for a division knowing the majority would by absence be less than the night before. This their elders did not want as knowing that whoever saw the number of the first day 319 printed by order,[86] would not believe that those who were absent next day, had changed their opinion in their Beds; Wee had many speech's chiefly I think from new Members and divided at or after 10 o'Clock ay's 227 No's 63.[87] The Attorney General, Charles Yorke spoke against some of the Articles coolly & decently, declared he did not desire a division and, if there was one, should not be in it, he accordingly went away his Brothers were absent. So you see the Peace is in no danger and though I believe the Opposition not unwise enough, and I hope not wicked enough, to desire to obstruct the Peace. Yet I think, if they could have great numbers upon any question, they could, & would have found an early opportunity to shew them, though upon some question of no real importance in its self. It has been very dark again for some time I can just write with my greatest magnifying spectacles. I thank God I am not the worse for these two days attendance.

Nanny got a Cold & neglected it, so she had a pain in the head and face which made her feaverish but a Blister made her easy. I was with her today & she was very cheerfull and I heard just now she was pure & well (8 at night) Lord Fortescue thinks Lord Bute was the next best speaker to Lord Mansfield. The first day H[ans] Stanley made a most excellent Speech for the Peace, and Charles Townshend spoke finely & warmly for it, his Conduct I cannot comprehend. I am . . .

187. [BL, Add. MS 51406, ff. 66–7]
Henry Fox to John Campbell, Grosvenor Square, 6 January 1763
I have this moment receiv'd Yours, & am much troubled how I must have misrepresented Lord Bute. So far from your son's [Pryse] being in a worse situation, He express'd for you & Him & your whole Family a great, I might say kinder, Regard, and in, I verily think, great sincerity. So that let us but find the thing, the Grant of it will come most easily. I can see how the mistake has happen'd, but had you heard Him say what

---

[84] Referring to George Dempster who had caused the division in the Commons.

[85] George Fermor (1722–85), 2nd Earl Pomfret.

[86] The House ordered that the resolution for the address and the votes for and against should be published in the *Votes*. *CJ*, xxix, 394.

[87] *CJ*, xxix, 395. *PH*, xv, 1273–4, lists 31 members absent from the previous day's vote.

has occasion'd it you would not have thought as you do from my Report of it. Pray let the suspicion vanish, or I shall not forgive myself for having so horridly given rise to it.[88]

188.
John Campbell to Mary Campbell, 8 March 1763
The House sat last night till past ten, yet Wee had no Division,[89] and most of the time very poor entertanement. But there was one very remarkable Incident. Mr G[eorge] G[renville][90] took as I thought the Chancellor of the Exchequers [Sir Francis Dashwood] Business out of his hands, and made a very long speech, which was answered or rather ridiculed by the good Brother in law H[is] S[erene] E[xcellency] who treated poor G[eorge] G[renville] with the greatest Insolence, and contempt for a long time, seeming in mighty good humor all the while to make it, the more provoking. G[eorge] G[renville] provoked rose to answer him, but had spoke but two or three sentence's when H[is] S[erene] E[xcellency] rose look'd at G[eorge] G[renville] with a smile of contempt & walk'd very leisurely out of the House.[91] It was to be sure the most rude impudent, thing that was ever done. The House seem'd to show little concern for G[eorge] G[renville] many laugh'd while H[is] S[erene] E[xcellency] was abusing, and when he walk'd out . . .[92]

The same day [7 March] Lord Ravensworth[93] ended, as I hear, a long unintelligible speech with a Motion[94] for the same Papers that are to be consider'd by our famous Committee,[95] Lord Hardwick answer'd him & it was soon thrown out. Lord Talbot said somewhat that Mr Fox's Friends thought meant as a sort of insinuation against him, as Paymaster, having great accounts to pass. Lord Hillsborough, who gave me account of it to day, took him up short & assur'd the House that no Man could be more desireous to have his Accounts examined than Mr Fox. Lord [William] T[albot] denied his intending any reflection, but I think it plane his meaning was not friendly; yet this Man has acknowledged the Service done by Mr Fox's undertaking Business, in the strongest & highest terms. The behavior of sub Ministers in the House of Commons to Mr Fox particularly G[eorge] G[renville] & G[ilbert] Elliot do's not please me by any means.

---

[88] The rest of the letter is missing.

[89] In the committee of ways and means regarding the tax on cider. *CJ*, xxix, 531; *PH*, xv, 1307–9, for the debate.

[90] Grenville and Pitt had fallen out after the former became leader of the House upon Pitt's resignation. Pitt attacked Grenville mercilessly on several occasions in the Commons.

[91] *PH*, xv, 1307–8, for the exchange between Grenville and Pitt, though no mention is made of Pitt walking out. Walpole, with glee, also describes the incident in H. Walpole, *Memoirs of the Reign of King George the Third* (4 vols, 1894), i, 198.

[92] Half a line obliterated.

[93] Henry Liddell (1708–84), MP for Morpeth 1734–47, created 1st Baron Ravensworth 1747.

[94] *LJ*, xxx, 346.

[95] *CJ*, xxix, 528: Sir John Philipps proposed the motion to establish a committee to consider the estimates and accounts since the commencement of the Seven Years War. This was a veiled attempt to investigate Fox's accounts at the pay office. However, the committee failed to produce any evidence or conclusions.

And I find it is seen in the same light by some other of Mr F[ox]'s Friends, and by his Enemies. It is marvellous to me. I had a good deal of talk about it to day with Lord Hillsborough who I found at the bottom of the House of Commons and sat by him, some time with nobody near us, so could speak Freely.

There was a great political dinner to day I think, at D[evonshire] House,[96] the Dukes of D[evonshire] & N[ewcastle] Lords Hardwick & Temple Mr Pitt & James Grenville, I suppose more but I know not who.

A parliamentary Commission of Accounts[97] is a certane number authorised by Act of Parliament to examine &c. they may be Members, or not as the House's Please; being by Act their Power do's not end with the Session like a Committee.

Four last morning foggy, sat[urda]y & sunday frosty yesterday & to day not, the fog this morning they tell me was very stinking, but I lay pretty late, the day was good & warm.

Nothing so foolish as a Pembrokeshire Christianing.

On the Debate of the Army[98] Wee had a very full House both of Members and strangers, and Two Ladies[99] in the Gallery. I am sure either young, or old should have been greatly out of Countenance to have been one of only two then in an Assembly of 400 Ladies, but these two Ladis [*sic*] had greatness of mind superior to such foolish bashfulness. They were People of fashion I heard their names but being nere the wiser forgot them.

I send the Chronicle,[100] lest you should want News; but not for Dr Brown's[101] fashion Cant, or the Postscript wicked Exhortation to all disbanded soldiers to turn robbers & Murderers. Love & compliments . . .

I wish you can read this hasty scrawl I did not come from the House till five to day.

189.
John Campbell to Mary Campbell, 10 March 1763
The title of Subminister I give to all Gentlemen in Office who take upon themselves to talk like Ministers, or Managers for Administration; but on this occasion I chiefly intended Mr G[eorge] Grenville & Mr G[ilbert] Elliot who spoke for a Committee,[102] these were no very remarkable Speech's. Mr Glover[103] was for a Commission, & freely offer'd himself to serve without any Salary. I doubt not Sir J[ohn] P[hilipps] would have done the same. But I think Mr Glover gains very little attention, he is very full of

---

[96] Piccadilly, London.

[97] This was proposed by Sir John Philipps on 22 Feb. 1763 (*CJ*, xxix, 489) and was a 'clumsy and antiquated procedure of a permanent body that had long since been replaced by Commons Committees of Inquiry'. Sir Francis Dashwood persuaded Philipps to accept the latter, which was proposed by Dashwood on 23 Feb. *CJ*, xxix, 491. P.D.G. Thomas, *Politics in Eighteenth-Century Wales* (Cardiff, 1998), 195–6.

[98] *CJ*, xxix, 530.

[99] Is Campbell jokingly referring to two of his relatives?

[100] The *London Chronicle (Semi-Annual)*, 5 Mar. 1763.

[101] Dr John Brown (1715–66), author and moralist, preached at St Paul's Cathedral about the effects of true christian liberty.

[102] That is, the committee to consider the estimates and accounts since the commencement of the Seven Years War (see letter 188 above).

[103] Richard Glover.

his own abilities and importance, but cannot I think convince the House of them. The Complaint to Nanny was made by Lord Lyttelton who was that day in the House of Commons and is you well know allways in extremes. Some have done me the honor to say I killed the Briton & Auditor[104] by smothering them in the Scavengers Cart, I don't know that but the N[orth] Briton[105] was not hurt but told me next day at the Coffee House, in great good humor that he was much pleased with the Idea. My Speech the Second day[106] was very short, and had been none at all, if Mr G[eorge] Grenville had not forced me to rise, by misrepresenting what I said the first time (ten days before)[107] and turning his fair Countenance allmost round to look at me two or three times, in his Speech! Mr G[ilbert] Elliot having spoke just before me, and insinuated, very planely that both K[ing] & M[inis[t]er were for an Examination of accounts; I added a few Words to let Him know that great Names would not fright me out of my opinion. I believe both G[eorge] G[renville] & G[ilbert] E[lliot] were angry & thought me impertinent; but whoever might think so I can't help it, I must have spoke when I was so called up, and if I do speak, I must say as I think.

Yesterday I presented Ally [Alexander] at Lord Bute's Levee, who told me that he was glad, as no doubt I was, that my son was come from Germany and very glad he was not likely soon to have occasion to return there, I said I hoped not while I lived, my Lord Said he hoped the same, meaning his own life. You will not quarrel him he for that.

Lord Maynard is come to town this afternoon, to kiss the King's hand, and be sworn Lord Lieutenant of Suffolk in the room of the Duke of Grafton,[108] he is very well disposed to Lord Bute, Lord Albemarle & Lord Cornwallis[109] & the Duke of Grafton were all at the Great dinner. Ally [Alexander] tells me Lord Fortescue is told they will do mighty things I fear his Lordship has some tast for a Riot.

Wee have had good days with great Fog every morning but today was not so clear as yesterday but warm enough & not unpleasant I had a little Walk in Hyde Park in my way to the House. My Love . . .

I think they can make no great Battle this session, I suppose they will set their Wits to work against the next. For my part I am more afraid of the impertinence & wrong

---

[104] The *Briton* was a pro-Bute newspaper established by the novelist Tobias Smollett at the end of May 1762. The *Auditor* was a journal of Arthur Murphy (1727–1805), the editor of the *Spectator*. This comment may be referring to Campbell's speech.

[105] The *North Briton*, a radical paper first published on 5 June 1762 and closely associated with John Wilkes, the radical MP. Wilkes was also known by the pseudonym North Briton. The paper attacked the Bute ministry and was backed openly by Lord Temple and secretly by the dukes of Devonshire, Newcastle and Portland. Cash, *John Wilkes*, 69. Issue 45 was published on 23 Apr. 1763 and caused a storm, since it attacked the king's speech. A large number of lawsuits, and a constitutional crisis over the issue of general warrants by parliament, ensued.

[106] On the unpaid accounts. This was raised in the Commons on 1, 9 and 10 Mar. 1763. *CJ*, xxix, 513, 537, 542. Campbell's speech is not recorded in *PH*.

[107] That is, the second of the three days the accounts were raised in the Commons – 1 Mar. 1763. *CJ*, xxix, 513.

[108] The duke of Grafton was one of the victims of Fox's 'purge of the Pelhamite innocents', in which he rid the administration of as many pro-Newcastle office holders as he could, in the wake of Newcastle's dismissal as first lord of the treasury in May 1762. See Introduction.

[109] Charles Cornwallis (1738–1805), Earl Cornwallis 1762–92, and 1st Marquis Cornwallis 1792–1805.

judgment of the subministers, and of the Tories our New Friends, than of the declared Opposition.

190.

John Campbell to Mary Campbell, 12 March 1763

I must begin with the Weather that being at present uppermost with me & I believe with everybody else. Thursday was a mild day, in the night after it rain'd and before light on Fryday the wind rose very high; it blew fresh all day & excessive cold, last night a very sharp frost, today the streets dry & hard & Ice wherever there was water, the wind has been strong easterly all day, the sun shone, but in the Wind & out of the sun, as cold as it was at Christmas, Ally [Alexander] went out ½ past 8 and he thought it the coldest day he had felt this year he went today to dine with the Marquiss of Granby at the Duke of Rutlands.[110]

I am sorry your things were wet, though I can't wonder when I consider the rains and floods. Pray don't reserve the Cheese Toaster for me, as I seldom eat toasted Cheese, though, as in duty bound, I reverence the name.

Wee sat till about 8 yesterday to lay a duty on Cider the Gentlemen of the Cider Countrys were unreasonable, they divided and opposition People divided with them for opposition sake.[111] Glover made a Puritan, ridiculous speech against Excise Laws in the manner of a wretched tragic stroller.[112] Velters Cornwall called him the tragic Roseius[113] of the age & ridicule'd him well in his particular manner. Our Chancellor of the Exchequer [Sir Francis Dashwood] do's not shew the Man of Busyness so much as might be wish'd.

Though the subministers behaved absurdly, there is not the least misunderstanding between Lord Bute & Mr Fox not for want of true pains taken to make them jealous and set each against the other. I think Mr Fox has sense enough to see if he was ill used by Lord Bute and at the same time is too honest a Man to be of a suspicious temper. It diverts me to see those who lately said Lord Bute would not be bad if he was not influenced to wrong things by Mr Fox now speaking kindly of Mr Fox & wondering he will bear the ill usage. You see, said one to me, how he is used by these People, who could not have stood at all without him; why will he not return to his old Friends, who would receive him with open arms. As it was in the House, I did not care just then to ask were those old Friends the Duke of Newcastle, H[is] S[erene] E[xcellence] and Mr L[egge] you know enough as to the two first, and I know it is but a little while since the last spoke of him with the greatest bitterness. Indeed the Duke of D[evonshire] is yet in terms of civility with him, but H[is] G[race] may be duped by the other, but cannot guide them.

---

[110] John Manners (1696–1779), MP for Rutland 1719–21; 3rd duke of Rutland 1721–79.

[111] CJ, xxix, 545, 11 Mar. 1763; PH, xv, 1307–9, for a short report on the debate, principally Pitt's attack on George Grenville.

[112] Glover said that Charles Jenkinson 'made the strangest enthusiastic speech against excises I ever heard . . . the House was in a laugh; he was the only person serious in it. Not a word however of what he said had any relation to cider'. Cited in HPC, 1754–90, ii, 505.

[113] Roscius – after Quintin Roscius Gallus (126–62 BC), Roman actor. The name Roscius became a paradigm for excellence in acting and referred to David Garrick. Cornewall is being facetious regarding Glover.

I fear my P[ryse] C[ampbell] is not well, he was not in the House yesterday Sir W[illia]m Owen has left a card at Mr Fox's belike he may not know of his public day, or may be too prudent to appear there as yet. My son is still in St James's street. I will pay the half price for Ally's [Alexander] Picture. I am ever yours . . .

I at present make no doubt the Parliament will rise some day in April.[114] Mr Fox told me he thought so this morning and the speaker[115] told me so last Sunday. Mr Fox still insist with me that I made Sir John Phillips a P[rivy] C[ouncillor][116] I am not very proud of it. And certes Sir John would never forgive either of us if he heard Mr Fox said so.

191. [BL, Add. MS 51406, ff. 68–9]
Henry Fox to John Campbell, 30 March 1763
Could I have foreseen what I now see I should not have come to court; consequently you (to whom *I* shall really never forget my obligation) would not have come into Parliament.

I believe the Message as it is call'd to the City has been much exaggerated & was innocent. I will go to the House of Lords when I hear it will be explain'd to day.[117]

I want to talk to you, but I want first to be at Liberty to tell what I know & which vexes me & will vex you. The moment I am I will send to you. In the mean time I take to converse with you by halfs. My own secrets I would tell, but other Peoples I can not, & without them, my Communication would be very lame & not worthy to come from me to you, whom I love & esteem above all Men, & much above some whom till lately I had a good Opinion of. Yours . . .

192.
John Campbell to Mary Campbell, 7 April 1763
I earnestly wish poor R[oger] Evans recovery but can scarce flatter myself with any expectation. I don't know that my Contemporary and old acquaintance Mr Rice Brown was any akin to me; there is scarce another I think of my age left in the Country. I mean among such as reckon themselves Gentlefolk.

I shall now tell you a secret, which I was told last night, and which may possibly be made public while I am writing it, but in these days I can answer for nothing. Lord Bute intends to resign tomorrow;[118] it will surprise you more to know it is by no means a suddain resolution, but has been his intention a good while, perhaps before the Session began; though known till lately, only to himself & his Master. G[eorge] G[renville][119] is to be first Lord of the Treasury and Chancellor of the Exchequer Charles Townshend

---

[114] Parliament was prorogued on 19 Apr. *CJ*, xxix, 666.

[115] Sir John Cust (1718–70), MP for Grantham 1743–70; Speaker of the house of commons 1761–70.

[116] Phillips had been sworn a privy councillor on 10 Jan. 1763. Thomas, *Politics in Eighteenth-Century Wales*, 194.

[117] *PH*, xv, 1309–10, citing *The History of the Minority*, refers to a petition from the city committee to the king which was prevented from reaching him by Lord Bute, regarding the repeal of the cider act.

[118] *PH*, xv, 1322–30, gives various accounts of Bute's resignation which, as Campbell rightly reported, was announced on 8 Apr. Adolphus stated that just as Bute was by enemies and friends considered 'permanently fixed in office . . . he astonished the public by so sudden a resignation'. Bute gave the principal cause of his resignation to be the want of support in the cabinet. Sir Francis Dashwood resigned as chancellor of the exchequer at the same time.

[119] He became first lord of the treasury and chancellor of the exchequer on 13 Apr.

first Lord of the Admiralty. Mr Fox will I believe go to the House of Lords[120] next week that I knew somewhat sooner. I think Lord Bute has not judged well of men, and has made many Mistakes, I cannot say he judges right in retiring at this time; but I must say that his intention & principle of acting seems great, and honest. To take the whole weight & odium upon himself, even at the hazard of his Life,[121] in order to make a Peace which he judged absolutely necessary for his King & Country, and when that has been completed ratified and approved, to retire without any Office. If this was truely the Case and I have no reason to think otherwise It may attone for a hundred Errors. How his will go on next Session I cannot say. Heaven defend us from Pitt, & Temple. There certanely is not the least inclination towards them at present. Mr Fox might be what G[eorge] G[renville] is to be,[122] if he could, and would, but he neither has the Will, nor is his health anyway equal to it. If it was I should heartily wish he had the Will . . .[123] I hope to get soon out of Town, though perhaps I can't make so much hast as if I intended to see the opening of next session, I find no inclination, at present, to see any Part of it, but it would seem vanity to answer for oneself at a time one can answer for no other Person or thing; nay can scarce form a ghess.

Lord Waldegrave[124] is very ill of the Smallpox, which I am sorry for, believing him a very worthy Man, and he might have been in some considerable Place. The two secretaries are to continue.[125] The Parliament is intended to rise the 16 inst[ant]:[126] The weather is good but a somewhat sharp air.

You will be sure I am in no pleasant disposition. My love and respects . . .

193. [BL, Add. MS 51406, ff. 70–1]
Henry Fox to John Campbell, 10 April 1763
I thank you kindly for your Letter, which inclines I think to the House of Lords; not to be put out of my way or, seem to mind, as indeed I do not, the Viscount's Coronet which they ought to Christ to have refus'd, & I should blush to be anxious about. Upon the whole, having heard that the K[ing] is displeased at my having left Him in Uncertainty whether I accept the Baronacy or no. I intend to morrow, to tell Lord Bute

---

[120] Fox had been made 1st Baron Holland on 16 Apr. J.C. Sainty, *Peerage Creations* (2008), 46. He had been hoping for a peerage since at least 1760, when he had asked the duke of Cumberland to intervene on his behalf with the new king. Cumberland had tarried in this and the deadline had passed. Ilchester, *Henry Fox*, ii, 119–20. Fox was very disappointed with a barony and was hoping for a viscountcy or earldom. *HPC, 1754–90*, ii, 465.

[121] Political rivals had fanned popular hatred, including assassination threats, for Bute after the Treaty of Paris, which was his great achievement, and his desire to establish a cider tax.

[122] That is, first lord of the treasury.

[123] Two lines obliterated.

[124] James Waldegrave (1715–63), 2nd Earl Waldegrave. Lord of the bedchamber 1743–52; governor of the prince of Wales and Prince Edward 1752–6; he attempted to form a ministry 8–12 June 1757, but fearing he would lose his friendship with George II, stepped down. Waldegrave married Maria Walpole, the illegitimate daughter of Edward Walpole, Sir Robert's younger son. He died of a smallpox attack on 13 Apr.

[125] Lord Egremont remained as secretary of the southern department until his death in Aug. 1763. He was replaced by the 2nd earl of Halifax, whose place as secretary for the northern department was given to the 4th earl of Sandwich.

[126] Parliament was not prorogued until 19 Apr. *CJ*, xxix, 666.

that perfectly sensible that by Lord Shelburne's[127] Practices the Disappointment of my not resigning[128] has entirely effaced the sense of my Merit in coming in; I shall ask no Favour, but that he would tell me honestly whether the K[ing] will be offended if I decline; If He bona fide will not I shall chuse to remain Mr H. [Henry] Fox. This I suppose will end in the House of Lords; My dear Sir, if you don't approve of this, pray extend your Friendship to giving yourself the trouble of another Letter so wight [*sic*] to me who loves & will love you as long as He lives. Adieu.

194. [BL, Add. MS 51406, f. 72]
Lord Holland to John Campbell [no date but before 19 April 1763]
H[is] M[ajesty] has sent Lord Mansfield to see what terms may be had on the scheme comprehending all H[is] M[ajesty] parted with me very kindly,[129] & I, with truth, assur'd Him; that if He should make the bitterest of my Enemies his Ministers, I would support his Measures. He bid me particularly give his *thanks* to you as one of the few honest Men He had met with. I'll tell you more when We meet. In the mean time you are only to say that Lord Mansfield was with the King but it was necessary He should not leave the seals till Monday. Adieu.

195. [BL, Add. MS 51406, f. 73(i)]
Lord Holland, Calais[130] to John Campbell, 11 May 1763
We arriv'd here at 4 o'clock this morning very well; which I am sure you will be glad to hear, & the certainty that you will be so, makes me have a Pleasure in telling you. I can with truth soe assure you that I make a Progress in forgetting,[131] beyond my most sanguine Expedition. I hope I shall soon remember no more than what is enough to make me love an honest Man better than ever. And you dear Sir; I can not love you better than I have long done with the greatest Reason.[132]

196. [BL, Add. MS 51406, ff. 75–6]
Lord Holland, Spa[133] to John Campbell, 19 July 1763
I have since your Letter of May 20th [not extant], receiv'd a fresh Instance of your kindness, by the alarm Lord Digby[134] tells me the Report of my Death[135] gave you.

---

[127] William Petty (1737–1805), Viscount Fitzmaurice of Bowood, Wiltshire; succeeded his father as 2nd earl of Shelburne and 2nd Baron Wycombe in 1761.

[128] As paymaster. Fox kept this office until May 1765.

[129] 'George III regarded him with obvious distaste, openly telling Grenville on 11 October [1762] "we must call in bad men to govern bad men" but their relationship improved as Grenville's abilities became increasingly obvious'. *ODNB*; P. Lawson, *George Grenville, a Political Life* (Oxford, 1984).

[130] For an account of Fox's travels in Belgium and France at this time see Ilchester, *Henry Fox*, ii, 262–5.

[131] His disappointment over not receiving a viscountcy and his subsequent falling out with Shelburne.

[132] Part of the letter is missing.

[133] In Belgium. Famed for its healing hot springs. The Hollands had left England for Calais on 11 May and travelled to Paris, to meet their son Stephen, before journeying to Spa. Ilchester, *Henry Fox*, ii, 262–3.

[134] Henry Digby (1731–93), 7th Lord Digby (Irish peerage) 1757, Baron Digby 1765–93, 1st Earl Digby 1790–3. Son of Charlotte Fox and the 5th Baron Digby, Henry owed many of his advances in the peerage to his uncle, Lord Holland.

[135] Several newspapers and Churchill's *Epistle to Hogarth* reported Fox's death whilst he was on the continent.

I was fatigu'd for two days after I came here which was the 13th, but except that, I have not had a quarter of an hour's uneasiness since I left London, & and am in such a state of Health & spirits as promise me as much happiness as the *anni recedextes*[136] will admit of.

What satisfaction the Inventors & Spreaders (for I hear it was diligently spread) of the Report of my Death, or what design they could have in it I can't imagine. I don't forget the publick, which I will never have any more to do with, but I do not fear for it much from Mr Wilks[137] & Lord Temple[138] &c perhaps because I was not as you was in London, But at this distance it seems to me like a Thunder storm,[139] such as at this instant there is here, which makes a Noise will hurt no body, & be over in half an hour. A Minister should think continually of the Interest of the People, & be totally regardless of its Voice. I do not see their Interest in the least concern'd in this commotion, or any point which the Opposition have now, right or wrong, to write in contending for, & therefore do not think it can be either permanent or of consequence. I could give other reasons for this opinion which however well the present Ministers may like the thing they would not thank me for. But I shall before the Parliament meets[140] come & be ready to give my Assistance in my new situation, & am glad to think I shall meet you in town, & if I do, spend much time with you.

Lady Holland[141] is pretty, well but as yet the Waters don't seem to do her Good. So it is well she do's not want them much. I don't want them at all, but drink two or three Glasses a day for pleasure. A brother of the King of Prussia's[142] & his Princess,[143] Prince Clement of Saxony,[144] the Hereditary Prince of Brunswick,[145] & (on a visit to him) Duke Ferdinand our general,[146] are now here. Will you envy me when I tell you Lady Holland & I din'd with them all (every one of them) at the Prince's Yesterday? Will you envy me when I tell you that in France, & among the Foreigners here; I am in as much

---

[136] The receding years.

[137] John Wilkes (1725–97), radical MP for Aylesbury 1757–64 and for Middlesex 1768–9 and 1774–90. He was sheriff of London 1770, and lord mayor of London 1774. From the late 1770s Wilkes was regarded as increasingly reactionary and in 1780, during the Gordon Riots, he ordered troops to open fire on the mob.

[138] Temple was Wilkes' main support, both financially and morally.

[139] Referring to the trial of Wilkes and the printers of *North Briton* No. 45 (under the issue of general warrants) which had taken place in the second week of July. Wilkes left for Paris on 26 July. Cash, *John Wilkes*, 136.

[140] Parliament was prorogued on 19 Apr. and then on 23 June, 6 Sept. and 11 Oct. It finally met on 15 Nov. 1763. *CJ*, xxix, 666–7.

[141] Lady Georgiana Caroline Lennox (1723–74), eldest child of Charles Lennox, 2nd duke of Richmond and Lennox. See Introduction.

[142] Either Frederick Henry Louis, Prince Henry (1726–1802) or Prince August Ferdinand of Prussia (1730–1813).

[143] Either Princess Wilhelmina of Hesse-Kassel (1722–87), married 1752, or Elisabeth Louise of Brandenburg-Schwelt (1738–1820), married 1755.

[144] Prince Clemens Wenceslaus of Saxony (1739–1812), archbishop of Trier 1768–1803.

[145] ?Charles William Ferdinand (1735–1806), duke of Brunswick-Wolfenbuettal, nephew of Duke Ferdinand.

[146] Prince Ferdinand of Brunswick, who was commander of the allied forces.

higher reputation than I deserve, than (you I am sure will give me leave to say) my Reputation is in lower & worse Esteem than I deserve in England? My Avidity for Praise is certainly over, for I am neither elevated with one nor depress'd when I think of the other. Charles[147] thinks what you say of Him a great Compliment & thanks for it. Lord Digby was born and will dy [*sic*] with as honest a Heart as any Man ever had.

I hope I am in the right in my conjectures, but don't let that hinder you, & such as you, nor shall it me from being at all the meetings of the next session. I look upon it now that We have an appointment. Yours ever . . .

197. [BL, Add. MS 51406, ff. 77–8]
Lord Holland, Paris[148] to John Campbell, Stackpole Court, 24 March 1764
Your letter of the 3[r]d [not extant] gives me, as all yours do, a great deal of pleasure. I love flattery from you whatever I do from others; & you shall find that I don't dislike to be told of my faults by you, nor will I disown them. I'll help you in making a List of them, & a numerous one, but I hope they have been all the faults of an honest Man. I heartily wish the sea side may have as good Influence on your Health, as it has hitherto allways had on mine. And since this Session of Parliament could not draw you from it, I approve highly of the use you intend to make of your seat, by resigning it for some Advantage to your younger son.[149] Is it not high time you should set about it? My son Charles really deserves all that can be said of his Parts, as I will convince you when I see you at Holland House; But he has what I value much more, good sense, good Nature, & as many good & amiable Qualitys as ever met in any body's Composition. His Friend Lord Carlisle,[150] is what His Performance speaks him. I have two sons here;[151] the eldest bids fair for being universally, & as much beliv'd as ever I was hated. The rest of my Family too, are ev'ry thing I could wish them. This happy in private Life, am I not in the right to leave the Publick? We leave this Place Monday the 16th or Monday the 23[r]d of April next; & you may allow 6 or 8 Days for coming from Paris to London. By that time the Parliament may be up, so if you intend to execute your scheme this session, you have no time to lose. Your Privy Councillor[152] is just what you describe him.

---

[147] Charles James (1749–1807), Lord Holland's second son. He became a prominent whig statesman, and arch-rival to William Pitt the younger, mirroring his father's relationship with the elder Pitt, *ODNB*. MP for Midhurst 1768–74, Westminster 1780–1 and 1801–6 and Tain burghs 1784–6. Foreign secretary 1782–3 and 1806; leader of the house of commons 1782–3 and 1806. Charles was Holland's favourite son, whom he greatly indulged.

[148] Holland had been in Paris since January.

[149] This came to nothing. Campbell was at this time MP for Corfe Castle and remained so until 1768. The younger son was John (Jack) Hooke Campbell.

[150] Frederick Howard (1748–1825), 5th earl of Carlisle. He became earl at the age of ten. He was the father of Caroline, who became the wife of John Campbell, 1st Baron Cawdor.

[151] The Foxes had four children: Stephen (1745–74), Henry, who died an infant, Charles James (1749–1807) and Henry Edward (1755–1811). The two sons with him in Paris were Stephen and Henry. Charles was at Eton.

[152] Pryse Campbell footnotes this: 'Sir J[ohn] Philipps of Picton Castle Lord Holland being ask'd to say that what my Father said in Confidence to him & Lord Bute was the Occasion of Sir J[ohn] P[hilipp]'s being made a P[rivy] C[ouncillor]'.

He do's no harm; so I shall be glad to think He do's not mean any; tho' that may not be, I'm afraid, a logical conclusion.

Yours ever . . .

198. [BL, Add. MS 51406, ff. 79–80]
Lord Holland, Piccadilly[153] to John Campbell, 16 May 1764
It is a Grief to me that I don't find you here but that you shall not come & return without my seeing you, for I will come from Kingsgate[154] on purpose. I shall go next Week, to make my poor Brother[155] a Visit, return to appear at the King's Birth Day,[156] & about the 6th of June set out for Kingsgate. Now tell me your Intentions, & be afraid of seeing me for a Day at least, when I know it will be convenient. When I will tell you very particularly what I know. I will now only say that in general things are as you & I can't wish. Your scheme for your son may be difficult, but is very reasonable. Set about it soon, I think it the best & wisest thing that you can do.

I am, My dear Sir . . .

199. [BL, Add. MS 51406, ff. 81–2]
Lord Holland, Holland House to John Campbell, 7 November 1764
Six weeks ago I had a letter from Mr Edwards, to help a Man in the east India Service which might be of great service to Sir R[ichard] Phillips.[157] I thought I could not be in the wrong to be against Sir W[illiam] Owen. So I wrote to the Deputy Chairman[158] of the E[ast] In[dia] Company[159] and sent Mr Edwards his Answer. If I remember right Mr Edwards wanted to be Custos Rotulorum of Haverford West[160] Himself, and I advised Him to write to Lord Sandwich Himself. This is all I know & should have never thought of Pembrokeshire since, but for your letter. I have done no harm. Can I do any good? I think not. I am enter'd into my 60th as you into your 70th year & deserve more than you do, & submit as much, to be call'd Lumber. I am ready to do all the harm I can to the Owens & all the good I can to your Friends. But I don't know how to go about it. If you can suggest, I'll obey. But I am nobody, & except on this or any other occasion to serve you, not only content but desirous to continue so.

---

[153] Holland had purchased part of The Albany, Piccadilly, in 1763.

[154] Kingsgate was Fox's home at Broadstairs, Kent, which was built in the 1760s.

[155] Lord Ilchester (1706–76).

[156] 4 June.

[157] Sir Richard Philipps (?1742–1823), 7th bt, of Picton Castle, Pembrokeshire; MP for Pembrokeshire 1765–70 and 1786–1812, Plympton Erle 1774–9 and Haverfordwest 1784–6. He was created Baron Milford (Irish peerage) in 1776. He defeated the Pittite Kensington in the Haverfordwest election of 1784. In 1797, as lord lieutenant of Pembrokeshire, he handed over the responsibility (either because of age and gout or apathy) of defeating the French invasion of Pembrokeshire to John Campbell's grandson John Campbell, 1st Baron Cawdor.

[158] John Dorrien. L.S. Sutherland, *The East India Company in Eighteenth-Century Politics* (Oxford, 1952), 95.

[159] East India Company: a joint-stock trading company 1660–1874.

[160] In Haverfordwest, Pembrokeshire, the office of custos rotulorum and lord lieutenant was a separate creation to that of the county, for the years 1761–1974. Sir John Philipps held the office 1761–4, but after that date, until 1770, the office remained vacant.

Lord Sandwich looks on Mr Edwards as his Friend, Sir J[ohn] Phillips was well with Mr Grenville, and Lord Chancellor [earl of Northington] had a much better opinion of you than of Sir W[illiam] Owen. These are all the Hints I have to give you. Sir Richard Phillips being so bad a Canvasser seems an incurable sore. As the Parliament meets the 10th January I think there must be a new sheriff before the Election. The appointment is in the Chancellor not the President,[161] and if you will name one & answer for his honest impartiality I am sure the Chancellor [George Grenville] should & I hope would appoint Him.

You never read one word true of me in the News Papers. I have built a Ruin of Flint & behind the Well of it a Stable, & some other whims but nothing in stone or near Ramsgate. Sea Air had its usual good Effects on me. And I am very well, except that Gout or Rheumatism makes me weak & walk miserably, but I have no swelling or Pain whatever. Till I have Pain I shall be content. When I have, I believe not at all so.

I have been vastly concern'd for the Duke of Devon. He acted neither from Faction or Malice in any Degree. He was misled into whatever he did that was wrong, by weak, good, nature. He had two fleshy substances growing in his Brain. Surely Death had ways enough of killing, I never heard of this before.[162]

Here I shall stay till the 6th of January without stirring unless you command me. I observe with concern that you say nothing about your coming. In your next I hope you will, for nobody has a higher Esteem or a sincere Affection for you than ever yours.

200. [BL, Add. MS 51406, ff. 83–4]
Lord Holland, Holland House to John Campbell, 24 November 1764
You can not overrate my high Esteem and great Affection for you, but I must with the same sincerity assure you that you much over value my Abilitys, or the opinion others have of them. To be nobody is indeed my Choice; And I believe not less that of other People.

I don't remember Lord Chancellor's[163] answer when you ask'd by me a Living. I have a lucky Knack of forgetting the disagreeable things I have met with, resolv'd at the same time to incur no more. However, Sir R[ichar]d Phillips was here, & could not get at Lord Chancellor, I thought of your & not of his Father,[164] expected no answer, but prepar'd for a queer one if any, & wrote to his Lordship, to desire an impartial Sherriff & to propose Mr Meyrick[165] as such. I have had no answer. It is not the more unlikely to succeed, but I don't know, nor shall but by the event whether it will or no, I wish it may.

---

[161] Lord president of the council, John Russell, 4th duke of Bedford (1710–71) was in the office 1763–5.
[162] William Cavendish, 4th duke of Devonshire, had died on 2 Oct. 1764.
[163] Robert Henley.
[164] Campbell's father was Sir Alexander Campbell and Sir Richard Philipps' father was Sir John Philipps, 6th bt.
[165] John Francis Meyrick of Bush, Pembrokeshire.

I walk a little better very little, but am in all other Respects perfectly well. How can you advise me to ride Dear Sir? I eat, I sleep well, & whilst I continue to do so surely setting [*sic*] still is preferable to riding. So much so, that I can't find in my conscience to press you to come to town, tho' I should be happy to see you here. I was in hopes to have wrote that Chancellor York[166] was again Attorney General;[167] but that Treaty hangly [*sic*] if it is not quite off. I wish'd it as it would have been a *Coup de Grace* to the expiring Opposition. Adieu! Dear Sir.

---

[166] Referring to Charles Yorke.

[167] The attorney-general was Sir Fletcher Norton (1716–89), of Grantley, Yorkshire; MP for Appleby 1756–61, Wigan 1761–8 and Guildford 1768–82. Attorney-general to the duchy of Lancaster 1758–63; solicitor-general 1762–3; attorney-general 1763–5; Speaker of the house of commons 1770–80.

Chapter 8. 1765–6

201. [BL, Add. MS 51406, ff. 85–6]
Lord Holland, Piccadilly, to John Campbell, 3 January 1765
I am just come from Goodwood,[1] & find your letter of the 25th [not extant] I fear I may
have done wrong. When Sir Richard [Philipps] was with me He was in great Distress
how to apply to Lord Chancellor. I therefore wrote to His Lordship, & on the 30th of
November spoke to Him at Court; He was very gracious. And I nam'd Mr Meyrick as
a very worthy Man, & in doing so am sure did what was agreed to Sir Richard, & what
I thought would be so for you. Lord Chancellor told me the three nam'd were very
improper & the Judge must name new ones. Sir W[illia]m Owen was with me since; I
told him I had nothing to do in Pembrokeshire, less there & ev'ry where else, was, &
should be at your Command. If I have mistaken, the Mistake proceeded from the Love
I shall ever bear you whilst Holland.
    I know no circumstance but what I have wrote here.

202. [BL, Add. MS 51406, ff. 87–8]
Lord Holland to John Campbell, 2 February 1765
Meyrick is Sherriff, & I have had a great hand in making him so. It is owing to you &
I hope I have not gone too far. What dependence could there be on what was said, on
either side, when the most interested were the solicitors? I stepp'd in with your known
Character in my hand, who would not say an untruth to carry ten Elections. And told
them you said Mr Meyrick was a Man of Probity & would act impartially. I trust
He will.
    I have time to say no more than that I am very glad, & very much favour yours . . .

203. [BL, Add. MS 51406, ff. 89–90]
Lord Holland, London to John Campbell, Stackpole Court, 26 February 1765
The News has kill'd me, upon no other foundation than the worst fit of asthma I ever
had & a Cough with a little fever, which is now gone.
    I am very sorry for your Complaint, & will comfort myself for you, as I do myself
& try to be contented whilst there is no pain. I congratulate you on your Triumph over
Sir W[illia]m Owen, really owing to the superiority of your Character to his.
    I am Dear Sir . . .

204. [BL, Add. MS 51406, f. 91]
Lord Holland to John Campbell, 28 February 1765
My attendance on your kinsmans cause was not of the least use, I had the pleasure to
see you there, as you are everywhere in the Right.

---

[1] Goodwood, Sussex, was the family seat of the Lennox family, dukes of Richmond, Holland's in-laws.

I should not write, but to tell you, how Glad I am, that your Journey had no ill effect, and that I am perfectly well again.

I am, Dear Sir . . .

205. [BL, Add. MS 51406, ff. 92–3]
Lord Holland, Kingsgate [Kent] to John Campbell, 29 May 1765
You know I'm sure as much by this time of the Regency[2] as I do; I'll now send you the most rational Account I have receiv'd from any of my Correspondents of the Motions of what has happen'd since. You'll not pay so bad a compliment to my understanding as to think I had any share in the Contrivance of a Matter so conducted. Upon my Honour I had no knowledge of it & came away Sunday the 19th without any but what was publick in the streets. On Thursday the 23[r]d I was turn'd out[3] without the least Civility; as a Party to what I really knew nothing of. But perhaps, Mr Campbell, My Behaviour to Lord B[ute] was an unpardonable Reproach to Bedford House[4] who have had ten times the obligations to Him that I have. They I understand have been the chief Actors, & ungratefull themselves are angry that I am not so too. But Good God! this is nothing. The Ministers who were to be turn'd out, were (wisely!) the first who were told it. Temple & Pitt joined [with][5] them & the Newcastles standing member they had the King in their Power & used him cruelly, notwithstanding the strongest efforts made by the Duke of Cumberland (who had been solely employed by the King) to save him.

They made him[6] turn out Mackenzie[7] protesting all the while that it was making him break his Royal Word, & that He never would forget it. They said they did not make it a Petition but a Condition & He was forc'd to give it to Sir Frederick Campbell.[8]

Thank God the Times don't admitt of it, or else Faction is ready for as many Murders now as it used to perpetrate 4 or 500 years ago. What more you may hear to vex you I don't know. Now for something that you will be so good as to be pleased with. This

---

[2] The king had fallen ill at the beginning of the year and some, including Holland, believed he was not going to survive. J. Brooke, *King George the Third* (1974), 188. *PH*, xvi, 52–8 gives the king's speech recommending the consideration of a regency bill and the responses of the Houses. The upper House excluded the dowager princess of Wales from the bill, which was seen as a slur on the royal family, and an insidious attack on Lord Bute, which determined the king to remove Grenville and Bedford from the administration. The Commons reinstated the dowager in the bill which received royal assent on 15 May as the Minority of Heir to the Crown Act (5 Geo. III, c.27), 1765, or regency act.

[3] From the office of paymaster.

[4] Bedford House, originally Southampton House, was in Bloomsbury Square. It was the home of the duke of Bedford. Holland is referring to the faction which was led by Bedford, an erstwhile political ally of Holland. On 17 May 1765 London weavers had surrounded the house after Bedford had spoken harshly of them in the Lords, when opposing a bill to tax foreign silks. Troops were used to disperse the rioting crowd; however they returned three days later. *ODNB*.

[5] This word is smudged.

[6] The king.

[7] James Stuart Mackenzie. The Grenville ministry made it a condition of continuing that Mackenzie should be removed from his office of lord privy seal (Scotland). He was removed on 23 May 1765, though was returned to the office in 1766 on the fall of that ministry.

[8] Lord Frederick Campbell (1729–1816), of Ardencaple, Dunbarton, and Coombe Bank, Kent; MP for Glasgow burghs 1761–80 and Argyllshire 1780–99. Lord privy seal (Scotland) 1765; chief secretary (Ireland) 1767–8; lord clerk register (Scotland) 1768–1816; lord of trade 1786–1801; vice-treasurer (Ireland) 1787–3; member board of control, India 1790–3.

place, as usual, gives me such Health as is miraculous, & whilst it continues nothing can put me out of humour. Had this employment been taken from me civilly (for it must I know go to the House of Commons) I should have had another Feather maybe in my Cap. But what then! That's all I loose, and as for Pride, anger, & all such Passions I think the Sea Air wafts them all away. They don't at all molest me. But the humbled K[ing]! the mortify'd & oppress'd Lord Bute! My Heart bleeds for them. I have, Dear Sir, the happy consciousness, of having had a great Hand in bringing about a Regency. Not in the mode it appears, I only was anxious for a Bill, no matter what. And would you believe it? Lord Temple (Pitt if he had been there) & several others were against any Bill Lord Shelburne said the Parliament were the natural Guardians,[9] & you should let things take their Course, let things break. That is let there be War & confusion & see what will come of it.

Well there is a Bill & I am heartily glad of it. If you, Dear Sir, come this summer I shall never let you go back without seeing you. You'll tell me your Motions when they are fix'd. May every thing happy attend you & yours. Adieu. Most Faithfully and affectionately yours.

206. [BL, Add. MS 51406, ff. 94–7]
Lord Holland, Kingsgate to John Campbell, Stackpole Court, 26 August 1765
The Extract of a Letter [not extant] I sent to you, gave as good a general Account of the Motions & beginning of these things[10] as could be. And I could not answer your Questions, and it was so impossible to forsee what would happen, that I did not write. I have now yours of the 15th inst[ant] & am sorry I did not answer yours of June 7th [not extant] only to tell you that I could not tell who were, or would be together; or who was not ungrateful to Lord Bute; nor or had Esteem or Friendship for me. Who I comprehended then under the words Bedford House I can tell. There was a meeting at Bedford House of George Grenville D[uke] & D[uche]ss[11] Bedford & the 2 Secretaries[12] & Lord Gower[13] & others from whence G[eorge] Gr[enville] went late at night to the K[ing]'s & insisted on my being turn'd out.[14] I meant these by Bedford House. Now to your Letter of the 15th inst[ant] [not extant]. You say you differ from me, inasmuch as to your Eye no Light can give a pleasing aspect to late Transactions. I don't at all recollect what I said, But you, Dear Sir, will consider what ever I said, it was before most of what We now see had happen'd, or could be forseen. Pratt made a

---

[9] Of the prince of Wales, who had been born in Aug. 1762.

[10] The nascent Rockingham ministry.

[11] The duchess of Bedford was Lady Gertrude Leverson-Gower (1715–94), daughter of John, 1st earl of Gower (1694–1754).

[12] Northern secretary, appointed on 11 July, was Augustus Henry FitzRoy, 3rd duke of Grafton. Southern secretary, appointed on 10 July, was Henry Seymour Conway.

[13] Granville Leverson-Gower (1721–1803), Viscount Trentham; MP for Bishop's Castle 1744–7, Westminster 1747–54 and Lichfield 1754. Lord of the admiralty 1749–51; lord privy seal 1755–7 and 1784–94; master of the horse 1757–60; master of the wardrobe 1760–3; lord chamberlain 1763–5; lord president of the council 1767–79. He was created 2nd Earl Gower in 1754 on the death of his father. In 1737 his sister Gertrude married John, 4th duke of Bedford, which led to a political group being formed: the 'Bloomsbury gang' or the Bedford Party. The 2nd Earl Gower was ranked second in this group, and after Bedford died in 1771, he led it until the 1790s when it fell apart. *HPC, 1754–90*, iii, 38.

[14] As paymaster of the forces. According to *ODNB*, he was ousted in May 1765.

Peer,[15] Norton disgraced,[16] are such Blows to Government, as a wise & shady Administration could not recover in twenty years. And what you justly complain of besides, the supporters of Government given up to the Rage & Ridicule of Faction, had not happen'd when I wrote. Lord Bute, who talks to ev'ry body in my Praise did not ask, but indeed avoided asking my Advice. The late Ministers[17] were the first who knew their Disgrace was determin'd. I should not have advis'd that. Then all was thrown into the Duke of Cumberland's Hands.[18] I should not have forseen what has happen'd from it. But I should have advis'd asking what He would do with it before all Power was given him, but He was not even sounded. When Pitt would have nothing to do with Him & made him come to Hayes[19] on purpose to be told so. H[is] R[oyal] H[ighness] was oblig'd to advise his taking his old Ministers again.

Then insolently & foolishly as you observe, they drove away Mackenzie. And when after that Lord Temple's Influence had made Pitt go from what He had agreed & H[is] M[ajesty] was very near being forc'd to come back to them again. Then, *I know*, that in that Event *Bedford House* had prepar'd many of the most offensive things that they could think of to force the King to.

You know Grenville's Council, perhaps you don't know the Extent of his Insolence.[20] The Duchess of Bedford's Pride Resentment & Ingratitude[21] cooperated, & it was indeed impossible they could continue, & the Government remain on the Footing it ought to do.

I thought therefore, tho' I never said so, that the King must dismiss them, & was glad he did so. But what follow'd My Dear Sir, I am strangely mistaken if I spoke of with applause. When they were first dismiss'd I thought new Ministers on one side, & the Crown on the other tir'd of Changes would have moderation & forbearance. The K[ing] alone seems hardly to have been consulted which I hop'd He would have been. He can't approve of a great deal that He[22] has done; but He resists nothing, & seems

---

[15] Charles Pratt (1714–94), of Camden Place, Kent; MP for Downton 1757–62. He was knighted in 1761, created 1st Baron Camden in 1765, on Pitt's insistence, and Earl Camden 1786. Attorney-general to the prince of Wales 1756–7. Pratt was made attorney-general in 1757, again on Pitt's insistence and instead of Lord Hardwicke's son Charles Yorke; lord chief justice, common pleas 1762–6; lord chancellor 1766–70; lord president 1782–3 and 1784–94. Pratt's most distinguished achievements were his decisions in 1763 as lord chief justice, when he freed John Wilkes, declaring him, as an MP, immune from seditious libel.

[16] Sir Fletcher Norton was regarded by the Rockingham ministry as a follower of Grenville and Bute and was dismissed as attorney-general in July 1765.

[17] The Grenville ministry which was dismissed on 13 July 1765.

[18] The king had requested that Cumberland have talks – which failed – with Pitt regarding the formation of a ministry.

[19] Pitt's residence in Kent.

[20] In 1763 Fox referred to Grenville as a 'hindrance not a help, and sometimes a very great inconvenience to those he is joined with', and someone who was deficient in good nature, good sense and honesty. Fox to Lord Bute, 11 Mar. 1763, cited in earl of Ilchester, *Henry Fox, First Lord Holland* (2 vols, 1920), ii, 227.

[21] Holland also thought the duchess of Bedford, who 'could twist her lord and master this way and that', 'vain, foolish, wicked, with a very defective understanding'. Ilchester, *Henry Fox*, ii, 290.

[22] The duke of Cumberland, who had recommended to the king that Rockingham should form a ministry. However, Cumberland was, in the first months of the new ministry, 'the head and soul of all'. R. Browning, *The Duke of Newcastle* (1975), 310. For the relationship between Lord Holland and Cumberland, see Introduction.

satisfy'd with his Deliverance, from Gr[enville] &c. He speaks of & to His new Ministers as his Deliverer but I fear do's not think of what you mention, the many, who have stood by Government, for its own sake & not for G[renvil]l[e]'s or Bedford's &c. I hope too that Lord Bute satisfy's himself with Revenge on *his Calcraft's*,[23] & thinks no further. But the contest now is. Which shall shew most Aversion to Him. And which shall pay most Court to Pitt & Temple. Many think that the two last (or rather the last) intend to force G[eorge] Gr[enville] in again & take the whole Government, & that they will succeed. So many strange things happen, that I don't think about Events no Experience or good sense can help to form a judgement of. For my Part in all the good Health that threescore will in a constitution like mine admit of, in good Weather, a pretty place, & with a happy Family & retir'd with good Humour, I am going down the Vale of Life with Ease & Chearfullness, & the more that I don't look upon the Publick, in that serious Light which perhaps, & to dream your Praises certainly I ought to do.

Lord Winchilsea's[24] Friendship got a Promise to Lord Digby[25] perform'd now which I'm afraid without it would have been shuttled off.[26] If you have the least inclination after reading this Letter to ask Questions, of one so little in the Secret as I am; Pray do, It will be a Pleasure Dear Mr Campbell to me to write to you, & as I ought to do without Reason. Yours ever . . .

Allways, Dear Sir, mention your Health; which I fear, like mine, gives little pleasure but I hope, like mine too, gives no pain.

207. [BL, Add. MS 51406, ff. 98–101]
Lord Holland, Kingsgate to John Campbell, 22 September 1765
I had often heard of the circular Letter & particularly of that sent to Sir J[ohn] Phillips, which you send me, but never seen it. Perhaps one or two Observations upon it may tend greatly to the Eclaircissement[27] you Want. Mr G[renville] says *upon Lord Eg[remont]'s Death*,[28] *H[is] M[ajesty] was advis'd . . . to send for Mr Pitt*[29] *& after him &c &c.* But He do's not say by whom; It was by the Duke of Bedford, I had this from the King himself, & Lord Bute tells me *upon his honour* that He never advis'd or thought of it. But the Help He wish'd & wanted for the Administration, which all Mankind I am told then said could not stand as it was, was the accession of the Duke of Bedford; instead of that His Grace advis'd Pitt as above on Wednesday & His Grace had only employ'd Caleraff.[30] Then, says Lord Bute & not till then, I thought it best to inform my self, and

---

[23] This may be referring to George III. Bute was tutor and then favourite to the prince of Wales, later George III, until 1765 when they became estranged, as the king increasingly fell into the lap of Pitt. Similarly, Fox nurtured John Calcraft but the latter later turned against his mentor.

[24] The 8th earl of Winchilsea.

[25] Henry Digby. In 1757 he was created Baron Digby in the Irish peerage, and Baron Digby in the English peerage in 1765.

[26] Digby had been promised a peerage in 1763 by Fox.

[27] An explanation. *OED*.

[28] Egremont died on 21 Aug. 1763.

[29] To replace Egremont as secretary of state for the southern department. For this to have materialised Pitt would have would have had to make a reconciliation with his brother-in-law George Grenville.

[30] John Calcraft.

met Mr Pitt at Beckford's[31] *thursday*. Pitt was sent to, to come to the K[ing] Saturday, & then, on *Fryday* the K[ing] Spoke for Mr Grenville. *Saturday* & afterwards *Monday* Pitt saw the King, & it went off. Sandwich went to Wobourne,[32] & that *gratefull* Family[33] made it so themselves, & to their Colleagues a condition[34] to banish Lord Bute. *In this situation* G[eorge] G[renville], said *that Lord Bute had declar'd* &c. And this He would not you think untrue to say if it were not true. The venture was not great for Lord Bute says He never heard or dream'd of such a thing's being reported till February when some expressions in a Letter of Sir John Phillips, gave him a hint, & the next day He came to town. He assures me that He never was ask'd to make such a Condition or Promise nor ever had done so. You'll observe that G[eorge] G[renville] says the Declaration was made to the K[ing], not to Him; and you are very good if you think Ministers always make true Reports of what passes with the K[ing] alone. They have a most respectfull Maxim that: what passes in the Closet must never be repeated. The use they make of it is that as there can be no feuding & proving they may report what they please. The late King said that His Ministers told Him Lyes all day long. The Duke of Cum[berland] very kindly & very respectfully said that He had never observ'd that bad quality in me, No says the King, I'll do him Justice I don't believe He ever did tell me a Lye, but if He did not, He's the only Man that ever came into my Closet that did not. I suppose however, He lump'd me with the rest always in his mind & did not seem to like me the better for it. You'd observe too, Mr Campbell, that Mr Gr[enville] avoids saying that the K[ing] told him so. So there's the Lye *convey'd* & not told.

You ask me instances of Ingratitude to Lord Bute – if you read the Pamphlets,[35] known to be wrote by their Orders,[36] you will not be at a Loss. Had you convers'd with them, you would have met with it in ev'ry conversation with ev'ry one of them; And I know a Fr[ien]d of Lord Halifax's who after a publick dinner, went to him & desir'd him to consider the Prudence, as well as the decency, of holding such Langage [*sic*] of Lord Bute before 12 Guest & all his servants; as would justify, nay make a Quarrel necessary, between the two calmest Gentlemen in the World. Yet I have never been able & I have taken pains to find one Fact, offensive to them laid to His charge. It is hardly credible how sure they made themselves that they could not be remov'd, &, Mr Gr[enville] to make amends for the great offence of his tiresome Conversation, grew to think that the K[ing] was not entitl'd to the least Complaisance; perhaps, that absolute & rough Government was the surest. The Kings only Passion is Gardening & Building, He had made some Contracts, for buying little Bargains &c to enlarge & embellish Richmond. Gr[enville] refus'd them to him (out of his own Civil List too), and tho' the whole did not amount to £6,000 tho' the Contracts were made, oblig'd him to cancel them very unwillingly I am told. I don't know that Lord Bute could have perswaded the

---

[31] William Beckford.

[32] Woburn Abbey, Bedfordshire, the seat of the duke of Bedford.

[33] The Bedfords.

[34] To come into the ministry.

[35] *A Letter to the Earl of B – Relative to the Late Changes that have Happened in the Administration; The Political Apology; or Candid Reasons for not Taking Part in the Present System*, and *An Honest Man's Reasons for Declining to Take any Part in the New Administration* (all 1765), being three such pamphlets.

[36] The Grenvilles and Bedford.

K[ing] to keep them in. He might have found a better way of changing them, & for not doing so I blame him. They were acquainted with the K[ing]'s Intention to remove them before He had thought of successors to them. A strange Fault sure! To find them was left to the Duke of Cumberland, without I believe sounding his Intentions. A great Absurdity, but I by no means call this as you do giving up every thing to his own Anger. I believe the K[ing] was full as angry on his own account, as Lord Bute could be on his. And could Lord Bute forsee what the D[uke] would do? You say Yes. I am sure my knowledge of him, as well as what I have heard from his Family since, would have made me sure, that however far He might go in rewarding the Opposition; Lord Campden [Camden], Wilkes, & all concern'd in that affair had not more determin'd Enemys than He would be. I should not have thought He would send for, as He did immediately, to Lord Temple. No Treachery therefore or ill meaning can I accuse Lord Bute of, but great & inexcusable Indiscretion. Tir'd to Death, & unsuccessful He would let another Hand try, without a previous trial of that Hand. It might certainly have been done otherwise, & should have been. The four late Ministers besides – have been surely the greatest Fools that live. The bad consequences of Lord Butes Indiscretion, seem, many, to have happen'd by chance for I cannot find who made Pratt who dismiss'd Norton yet. The shadow of Mr Pitt I think. The shadow – for Mr Pitt & every body else denies it. In many things that have been done; the K[ing]'s Behaviour has been to blame I think. You ask who has stood by me, I make no Party & belong to none so that is not the Question I have no Reason to complain of any Body, but the D[uke] & D[uche]ss of Bedford Lord Gower Mr Rigby[37] Mr Calcraft Lord Shelbourne. Charles Townshend came here fryday to receive my thanks *very due to him*,[38] & I delay'd that I might be the better able to write to you. But I am not, nor shall I, should I ever be Friends again with the Duke of Cumberland, (the only thing I wish & shall endeavour ardently) for I think We should not talk politicks. [Welbore] Ellis, Lord Hillsborough Selwin,[39] Sir E[dward?] Winnington,[40] Lord Baltimore & many others are faultless to me, or if you will to my memory, I am politically dead. Lord Bute has been faulty to Himself, but of my conscience not intentionally to the King. The King talks of & to his uncle[41] of the New Ministry, as his deliverers. And do's not think enough of those who suffer innocently or how a little Firmness might have sav'd many whom He wish'd to save. But what you seem to wish, is found *raro in illa conditione*;[42] & I never expect it. What is still to happen I have no guess at.

---

[37] Richard Rigby (1722–88), of Mistley Hall, Essex; MP for Castle Rising 1745 7, Sudbury 1747–74 and Tavistock 1754–88. Lord of trade 1755–60; secretary to lord lieutenant (Ireland) – the duke of Bedford – 1757 61, vice-treasurer (Ireland) 1762–5 and 1768; paymaster general 1768–82. Attached to the duke of Bedford, and for some time a supporter of Fox, to whom he owed much of his political advancement. He broke from Fox when the latter refused to resign the office of paymaster on his being raised to the peerage. Rigby may have coveted the office for himself, since he seems to have sought lucrative offices wherever he could.

[38] A reference to Townshend succeeding Fox as paymaster of the forces – without, it seems, any rancour on either side. This occurred in May 1765, hence the comment. Ilchester, *Henry Fox*, ii, 302–3.

[39] George Selwyn (1719–91), of Matson, Gloucestershire; MP for Ludgershall 1747–54 and 1780–91, and for Gloucester 1754–80. He was made paymaster of the board of works 1755–82, an office he owed to Holland's patronage.

[40] Sir Edward Winnington (1727–91), 1st bt, of Stanford Court, Worcestershire; MP for Bewdley 1761–74.

[41] Cumberland.

[42] Rarely in that condition.

Kingsgate, a thing much more worth thinking of, is a small Bay in the Isle of Thanet directly opposite to Flushing,[43] an open very pretty Corn Country, my House just 30 yards from the Sea, very small, & round about it many odd & useful Buildings design'd by Mr Wynne[44] (my good friend Sir John's son) who is very ingenious; & executed without great Expence by me, & so my no small Amusement, & still [*sic*] go on, while the Sea Air Night & Day, gives me good Nights, & appetite enough, & all together as equal & contented a Mind as you wish me. I make no Excuse for this long Letter, & am ready to write again with Great Pleasure whenever you desire. But allways before you open my Letter consider that I left London the 19 May, have not seen or heard from Lord B[ute] since 22[n]d of April, & am not in a situation, to know, or desiring to know any thing. Adieu My Dear Sir & believe me, as indeed you may, with the greatest sincerity, Affection, and Esteem . . .

208. [BL, Add. MS 51406, BL, Add. MS 32970, f. 103]
John Campbell, Stackpole Court to the duke of Newcastle, 29 September 1765
[45]The occasion of my giving your Grace's trouble is a letter I receiv'd from my son, informing me of an infamous falshood which has been told your Grace relating to the last Election[46] for this Country. viz That our Militia[47] Colonel Mr Owen[48] was opposed[49] merely because he was a friend of your Grace. I have experienced so much falshood, and baseness from that Family, as prevents my being surprised at any mean Action they do, or any Lye, they tell. And I am fully satisfied there was not one Person that gave his Interest against the Colonel: who saw him in that light, or would not laugh at his pretending to that Character. If I thought it worth while to recriminate upon those I so much and so justly despise, I could easily, and with truth, say enough to convince your Grace that neither the Colonel: or his worthy Father,[50] deserve to be called Friends to your Person, though I don't question their allways paying adulation to your Power. As for my self who had a principal share in what this Gentleman calls Opposition to him, I defy any Malice to say, with a shadow of truth that I ever shew'd or express'd disrespect, much less Emnity to your Grace. If your Grace could trouble yourself with remembering my sentiments, or words, you would know, my Opinion, of the late War,[51] in the Manner, and in the extent, to which it was carried, and of the

---

[43] That is, Flushing in the Netherlands.

[44] Thomas Wynne, 'unknown architect', was a long-time friend of Lord Holland. See J. Newman, *The Buildings of England: North East and East Kent* (1969), 352.

[45] The beginning of the letter is not extant.

[46] At the end of 1764 occasioned by the death of Sir John Philipps. Hugh Owen petitioned on his defeat at the election and wrote to Newcastle that 'Some of the late ministry [Fox?] exerted the hand of power most violently against me in regard to my election . . . and no reason could be alleged but that I had expressed a strong attachment to your Grace'. Cited in *HPC, 1754–90*, ii, 241.

[47] The Pembrokeshire militia was formed in 1759. B. Owen, *History of the Welsh Militia and Volunteer Corps, 1757–1908* (Wrexham, 1995), 69.

[48] Lieutenant Colonel Hugh Owen (1731–86), of Orielton, who was the commanding officer 1759–78. He was MP for Pembrokeshire 1770–86. Owen, *History of the Welsh Militia*, 69.

[49] Owen was opposed by Sir John Philipps of Picton Castle, thereby commencing an electoral rivalry which outlasted the century. P.D.G. Thomas, *Politics in Eighteenth-Century Wales* (Cardiff, 1998), 203.

[50] Sir William Owen.

[51] The Seven Years War, 1756–63.

hand[52] that was said to *Guide* those Measures, was such, that I must be glad to take any opportunity to assist in putting an end to what I thought so destructive. I will not pretend to say I was a competent Judge of the particulars which were objected to in the Peace. If any of them were wrong, I heartily wish they had been better; yet must still be Free to say that I should have rejoiced for the conclusion of the Treaty[53] if it had been worse. In this I had the Misfortune to differ from your Grace. But I could not think that a reason why I should loose my respect for your Person, or forget my relation to your Blood, which I must allways look upon as a great and valuable Honor. Some of your Graces Friends can, if they please, witness for me, that I regretted my not paying my respects to your Grace when I was last in Town, and told them the reason. I never was unwilling to wait upon your Grace, or afraid to justifie my self to you, in your Closet; but I was not unwilling to expose my self to what, I apprehended, I might hear in your Antichamber. The only time that I spoke in this Parliament was in opposing a Motion[54] made by the late Sir John Phillipps I then very much displeased a Gentleman who was lately at the head of the Treasury [George Grenville]; and gave, as they were pleased to tell me, some satisfaction to your Graces Friends.

My Lord I have sat many years[55] in Parliament, during all which time, it has been my Opinion, that though an honest Man, may often comply with Things not quite agreable to him, rather than give any advantage against an administration which he approves, yet there are some Things in which he must follow his own Judgement, such as he has, without regard to Persons.

In consequence of this Opinion I did, in some Instance's Vote contrary to the inclinations of Sir Robert Walpole, when he was Minister, of your Grace, and of your beloved Brother [Henry Pelham], at the same time that I was firmly, and warmly attach'd to those Administrations.

If I was now able to attend the House of Commons, your Grace should find me acting upon the same Principle; heartily, and cheerfully supporting the King's Government conducted by your Grace, and your Friends, yet voting with those for whom I have far less esteem, if Questions were moved in which I have already declared my Opinion, and not been convinced that I was mistaken.

I ask your Grace's pardon for this tedious letter, presuming that your Equity, and natural Goodness will permit me to say, that if you ever lend an Ear to such sycophants, as by their shameless falshoods have occasion'd this trouble, you must also give a patient hearing to honest Men in their refuting of senseless and infamous calumnies. I have the honor to be, with great respect . . .

209. [BL, Add. MS 51406, ff. 102–3]
John Campbell to Lord Holland, [n.d.] received 18 October 1765
For your last kind letter I return a thousand thanks which might probably have been paid sooner, if I had not fear'd my Idleness might be too tiresome to you; though I

---

[52] Pitt's.

[53] Treaty of Paris, signed 10 Feb. 1763.

[54] Philipps' motion for a commission on public accounts. Campbell was the sole MP to oppose the measure.

[55] Campbell had been an MP since 1727 and only retired from politics in 1768 at the age of 73.

know you will allow much to one who I believe you are satisfied sincerely loves, and esteme's you, and is an honest Man; the only Merit I pretend to you.

You have set me right in what I had mistaken, shewn things in a new light, and given me a good comment on G[eorge] G[renville]s letter, the Narrative from which you should have had as soon as I had it, if I had thought you had not seen it. When I sent it I only thought to refresh your Memory with a thing I imagined you must have seen, but might have forgot. I believe I now differ with you about nothing; except one Person[56] who I think has acted an inexcusable Part, and does not deserve the happiness of being restored to y[ou]r Friendship & Conversation. When Men plunge so deep in Faction as he did, they will endeavour to preserve some outward decency's as long as conveniently they can, which made him seem an Enemy to Wilkes, Prate [Pratt] &c, but when they come to Action all must give way to their ruling Passions, and Desires. You must give me leave to say that it is not in one Instance only that you [*sic*] discernment, and clear, sound judgement have been over power'd, by the amicable weakness, of a warm hearted, and too credulous Freindship. Otherwise you would not have so long continued to load Rigby & Calcraft with favors and zealously to serve Bedford, Sandwich, Sh[elbur]n[e][57] &c. I dare say a Man of less Friendly warm, [*sic*] with less than half your Understanding would have found them out, before they came to the Tryal that unavoidable [*sic*] discover'd them. I have read but few Pamphlets and was not so well informed as to know which were writ by direction of the late Ministers.

I find Kingsgate is much nearer the Sea than this Place[58] though Wee are within what I used to think an easy walk, and should yet, with a little resting by the way, if it were not for the bloody water. But I fancy Wee have greater variety of Rocks, Cliffs, & Caverns, which used to give me great delight, when, in a fine day, I could walk to them sit among them and

> Silent pass amid the deafening roar
> Of tumbling Billows on the lonely shoar[59]

Wee have also I dare say a good deal more barren Ground, which though it adds a little to my Profit, helps to give a pleasing wildness to some scenes, which I think I could improve and heighten, if I had money; but they satisfie me as it is. If I live to another summer, I shall wish Harry Walpole would send me an enchanted Chariot from Otranto,[60] I would fly in it to Kingsgate, take you up, and shew you various romantic wild scenes and among others the seat of an Ancient Hermit, who now as a Saint, performs wondrous Cures with the Water, of a shallow well, which he drank in his mortal state, I would carry you in an instant, I could lately have gone in ¼ hour, from the likeness, of a very tolerable part of the improved inclosed Country of England, to

---

[56] The duke of Cumberland.

[57] All five men named had benefited from Fox's influence or friendship and all had deserted him to pursue either more lucrative posts or influence.

[58] Stackpole Court was about two miles from the sea.

[59] Lines slightly misquoted from Homer's *The Iliad*, as translated by Thomas Tickell (1685–1740):
   Silent he pass'd, amid the deafening roar,
   Of tumbling billows, on the lonely shore.

[60] *The Castle of Otranto* by Horace Walpole was published in 1764 and is regarded as the first gothic novel.

a pattern of the Deserts of Arabia. When I had done all this I would restore you safe to good Lady Caroline who I think deserves you because I believe she knows how to value your worth and that your Ease and happiness are the great objects of her wishes, and her Cares. I hope she would pardon me making free with her.

I think my complaint is, in the main, much as it was sometimes a very little walking purges my Water, and sometimes a good deal more has no effect. But thank God never any pain, or sickness, as yet, and very good rest appetite, and spirits. May you long enjoy good health, and give happiness to all about you, receiving it yourself from their sincere love, and from mens conscia recti.[61] I am always sincerely and affectionately Yours . . .

I hope your House is a good deal raised above the Sea otherwise I should advise you to Keep a good well deck'd Boat, that in this weather, you may have a good Chance to make safe & well at Flushing.

Your gratitude to C[harles] T[ownshend] is just, but you may carry your good Opinion too far. Though I think he can force one to think well of him, in spite of one's teeth, if he will.

210. [BL, Add. MS 51406, ff. 104–7]
Lord Holland, Holland House to John Campbell, 22 October 1765
I received on the 18th your letter not dated, I am now come here (to stay 'till after Christmas) in good Health, if some other Word should not be found out, for what is call'd health at our Age, so very unlike what we remember to have understood by that term formerly; If you can love hearing from me, I do assure you, I spend no part of my great leisure more pleasantly than in writing to you, I don't think I should have set down to do it to day, but for the enclos'd, which I cut out of yesterdays Public Advertiser,[62] it is so exactly the state of the case, I should have drawn up, & so exactly espress'd in the terms I should have used that I can't help sending it you, I shall not wonder if it is imparted to me, and I think it necessary to give you my word of Honour, that I have not the least guess, who is the author of it.

Since I came to Town, I hear, from Undoubted authority, that Lord Bute hearing of the letter to Sir John Phillips, wrote one to him to the purport I mention'd, Sir John should have made that as publick as he had done Mr Grenvile. It seems my Lord Chancellor [Northington] wrote Mr Grenvile the other day his letter of dismission,[63] Mr Grenvill[e] answer'd it, supposing He said that it was grounded on a Misapprehension of the Kings that he Grenvill had intended to resign; assuring him, that was not his intention, and not without some insinuations, that he would continue to serve on whatever Conditions H[is] [Majesty] might impose. In this mean, & silly, endeavour to stay in, did he persist so far, as when he carried the seals, to keep The King an hour and a half, And when they parted H[is] M[ajesty] looked tired to Death, & Grenvill miserable beyond description; certain it is they had all of them, brought themselves to an Opinion, that the K[ing] could not turn them out; And now I here, [*sic*] they

---

[61] A mind conscious of its own rectitude. Virgil, *Aeneid*, i, 604.

[62] The *Public Advertiser*, 21 Oct. 1765, carried an article by a Pomponius Atticus, defending Lord Bute.

[63] He resigned in July 1766.

lay the fault, of their common folly, upon one another; *Delirant regis, plectunter achivi*[64] has been unhappily verified upon this occasion, I believe you may be Assur'd, that Mr Pitt tho' he would not come in without Lord Temple is by no means pleas'd at having been prevented & in mere outward show reconciled to Mr Grenvill has no conversation with him nor better opinion than he has always express'd of him, Mr Grenvill I hear grows very unpopular, & you won't wonder at it, when you hear, that he actually, (compell'd to it by no law treaty or even application from the Spaniards) obtain'd orders to the Captains of Men of War, Persuaded them swear to prevent all smuggling as he call'd it of English goods for Spanish dollars; I could not easily believe this; but it is true, that he has been such a fool; & too true that the effects of it, are very . . .[65] I send you enclos'd in another letter;[66] I wont defend the part, the first person [Cumberland] you mention'd acted; but at last there were great difficultys in his way; and withall the Blame that can be cast upon it, my heart & my Judgement, avow the friendship & wish to be restor'd to it, I will go thro' with all the others you have mention'd; Rigby; as to him I very ingenuously own, I was deceiv'd, I took him to be a very honest Man I lov'd him, excessively, others wiser than me, knew him better, I have nothing to say for this mistake; which has given me more pain than any. As to Calcraft – his bad Nature could not bear to be so much oblig'd; I am told & I believe that I owe his ingratitude to nothing else; Tacitus[67] I think says, that it is in human nature, that a Man may be oblig'd into being a bitter enemy; But could I, Mr Campbell, suspect such a Nature? A Man who cou'd have such suspicion must be miserably wise indeed, Suspicion carry'd so far as that, Siculi non invenere tyranny Tormentum majus[68] . . .[69] Sandwich, I had no reason to expect much from, nor have I any thing to complain of in his Regard; Lord Shelborn [Shelburne], Here I can quite acquit myself I could not help trusting him, Lord Bute trusted him for me, I own I did not see him, so bad as he prov'd to be, but I think I am sure, I should never have trusted him, and put it so far in his Power, to betray me, Lord B[ute] trusted him, not I; and indeed without that necessity He would never have been so intimate; I did not like him well enough.

The shore at Kingsgate is a very Bold one & there is a Chalk Cliff of fifty foot perpendicular, thirty yards distance from my door; I am interrupted here; & here is certainly full enough for one time, so much, that I shan't begin again I believe 'till you call upon me. Adieu . . .

I can't defend the part the 1st person [Cumberland] you mentioned acted.

[BL, Add. MS 51406, f. 108 is a draft of BL, Add. MS 51406, f. 107 from: 'I can't defend', though the following is in the draft but missing from the final version:]

---

[64] Horace, *Epistles*, i, 2, line 14: 'quidquid delirant reges plectuntur achivi': 'Whatever wrongs the Grecian kings are guilty of their subjects must suffer for'; as a general proverb: whatever errors the great commit the people must atone for.

[65] Part of the letter is missing.

[66] 'The Duke' is written superscript here in pencil.

[67] Publicus (or Gaius) Cornelius Tacitus (56–117 AD), Roman senator and historian.

[68] Horace, *Epistles*, i, 2, line 57: 'Siclui non invenere tyranny Majus tormentum': 'no greater punishment than envy was devised by Sicilian tyrants'.

[69] Part of the letter is missing.

Bedford I was not mistaken in, he is governed by one[70] in whom I was not mistaken neither, Vain foolish Wicked with a very defective understanding & so I always thought him.

211. [BL, Add. MS 51406, ff. 110–11][71]
John Campbell, Stackpole Court to Lord Holland, 3 November 1765
October 22 you could not expect I should be long silent. I must begin with what is most interesting to me, your health. You do not speak of it quite in the manner most pleasing to me. I must in regard to that say in the stile of St Paul (not the Lyttel St Paul)[72] I wish that you were not allmost but all together such as I am, save only bloody Water. For I eat well, digest well, sleep well, when nothing of a private concern vex's me (which sometimes happens) have as good spirits as ever; and, if the said complaint did not hinder, could walk to the sea with pleasure. If my Memory, and small share of Understanding decays, I shall be the last to find it out.

I give many thanks for the slip from the Daily Advertiser I make no doubt it will be laid to you. I do believe it was some Friend of yours, who carefully concel'd it from you lest you should prevent his publishing it. The account is given in so plane, distinct, coherent, & dispassionate a manner, and looks so like truth, that all impartial Men, and one may hope there are some few such, will believe it. If any Nobleman think that depressing the just power of the Crown, will raise that of the Peers, & I believe they will be greatly disappointed. If the Crown sinks the Peerage will sink with it. I have no fear of Aristocracy. I rather apprehend, a Confusion of Democracy, Oligarchy, Ochlocracy[73] and Anarchy, to end naturally, and by swift progress, in Despotism. Not in our Time, but I fear our Children may see it. The last time it happen'd,[74] there was a suddain Restoration of regular Government, can that be expected again? I shall now change the title of *Protector*[75] for that of *Montebank*;[76] it being more reasonable to call a Man what he is, than what he would be. I hear the said Montebanks Brother in Law[77] talks as if he repented standing out. If those two are stowe'd into the Administration, I shall think Things are at the worst, and then by the old Proverb, I may hope they will mend.[78] As to the Great Person who wish [*sic*] to be Friends with, I will not say a word more, because I fear I could say nothing agreable to you upon the subject. If what a Newspaper said of your dining in company with the P[rince]ss A[mel]ia[79] at Lord

---

[70] The duchess of Bedford.
[71] Published privately in *Letters to Henry Fox, Lord Holland*, ed. earl of Ilchester (1915).
[72] George, Lord Lyttelton, wrote a treatise entitled *Observations on the Conversion of St Paul* (1747).
[73] Mob rule.
[74] The protectorates of Oliver and Richard Cromwell, 1653–9.
[75] One of Campbell's names for Pitt.
[76] Mountebank: a quack or charlatan. *OED*.
[77] Lord Temple.
[78] 'When things are at their worse they begin to mend' (late 16th century).
[79] Princess Amelia (Amelia Sophia Eleanor) (1711–86), second daughter of George II. In his 'Memoir', Holland refers to her as 'a lively, meddling, mischief-making & mischief-meaning woman [who] has parts without any understanding; and has employed them all her life in doing all the harm she can'. He also states that she was the complete opposite to her brother the duke of Cumberland, who was, until 1763, Holland's patron. 'Memoir', 11–12.

Holdernesse's be true, you may probably have your wish. I believe there are few wishes of yours to which I would not cheerfully saw [*sic*] Amen.

I confess he must be a bad Man himself, who could make a general application of what Tacitus says, and believe that no man can be, in the highest degree, obliged, and yet continue honest, and gratefull. God Forbid. All I mean is, that I think Men so very bad as Calcraft &c. must have had Plague spots upon, them, which a Man of much less discernment would have been, if his Eyes were not dazzle'd by the worth of an affectionate and Friendly heart, too hasty in believing too ready to trust strong Profession. Yet I confess it is better to be so deceived, than never to believe, love, or trust. The Print entertaned me, though not quite to my mind, for I must confess I have never yet been convinced by any thing but *Authority* the *strongest* indeed of all Arguments that General Warrants,[80] in the Case of reasonable, and seditious Libels, are either illegal, or inexpedient. I indeed now planely see that all the Writers are satisfied that they may say, whatever they please, of any Person, or of any Thing, with impunity.

I heartily wish Lord Bute had sought good Advice where he might have been sure to find it. How much Mischief what Confusion might have been prevented.

I will not yeild the superiority to Kent. Your Cliffs are Chalk ours are Marble (commonly called Limestone), I have, within a walk, stupendious Rocks, lofty & spacious Caves, two sandy Bays, and a beach of Pebble's. If I could but get the Inchanted Chariot I would shew you fine Things. Wee never wanted more than three viz. Wood, Water I mean fresh, and verdure. I have now three or four green Fields just by my House, Trees of my own planting, allmost as big as my self, and somewhat taller. And a Serpentine River few Men can piss over, or throw a stone the leng [*sic*] of. The Post hear [*sic*] now relieves you, and I can only add the warmest wishes for your good health and happiness . . .

I am told that G[eorge] G[renville] denies he had any hand in preventing Trade with Spanish America, & lays all the blame on the Admiralty.

212. [BL, Add. MS 51406, f. 112]
John Campbell to Lord Holland, 8 November 1765
I most heartily condole with you for the Death of the Duke of Cumberland.[81] I know the sensibility of your Friendly heart will feel it deeply. I am now sorry for my last. A Man should say nothing to his Friends, unless necessary for his service that may be disagreable to him. I clame the Title of your Friend as having a sincere esteem and Affection for you, from my knowledge of your great, and amiable qualities and my full persuasion of the Integrity of your heart. I must beg of you to divert your mind, that you may not hurt a health you know is so valuable to your Family, and Friends. May you long continue to make them happy. I am sincerely and affectionately yours . . .

---

[80] General warrants were issued by the secretary of state for the arrest, for instance, of authors of seditious libel. 'No persons were named in such a warrant, and such a warrant left it to the person entrusted with the warrant to decide who it was that should be arrested.' E. Jowitt, *Dictionary of English Law* (2nd edn, 1977), 862.

[81] Cumberland died on 31 Oct. 1765. For the relationship between Cumberland and Holland, see Introduction.

213. [BL, Add. MS 51406, ff. 114–16]
Lord Holland, at Holland House to John Campbell, 11 November 1765
In the first Place, I'll tell you, a letter directed to me here, always comes a day later, than it wou'd do, directed to me in Piccadilly London.

I am not quite so hearty, as you describe yourself to be, and yet, I am pretty well to [*sic*]; May you long continue as you are; And now to the reason of my writing again so very soon. Things appear to me in a New light, & will to you, if you can believe, as I do, what I did not at all imagine. But I have not the least doubt of, Now my Lord Bute has told it me, upon his word; The King consulted the Duke of Cumberland before he turn'd out his late Ministers,[82] And not Lord Bute he has consulted upon everything, ever since, The Duke of Cumberland; & not Lord Bute. Lord Bute do's not see & for many Months has not seen the King in Private.[83] You will hate the Duke more than ever, But I will have something to say, to that by & by. How far Lord Bute, could have prevented, H[is] M[ajesty']s putting Himself, under such an adviser, how soon he foresaw it, or guess'd at it's consequences, I don't know, But so it was, And you will no longer wonder that those who had been contending with the King, this last two year and were quite beat out of the Field, gain'd an entire conquest in their view of the Case, I cou'd only Blame Lord Bute, in facilitating the K[ing]'s consent to Mr Mckensizes[84] dismission, as he owns he did. A false punctillio, but what with you or me Mr Campbell wou'd have had a very different effect. The Earl of Straffords letter to King Charles ye first,[85] did not make H[is] M[ajesty']s Passing the Bill of Attainder more excusable. The Late King[86] when he nam'd his promise of the Garter to Lord Granvill[e],[87] was told by the Duke of Newcastle, that H[is] M[ajesty']s. knew, My Lord Granvill[e] had given up that promise, the King answer'd (as the Duke of Newcastle told me) and *dos he deserve it less for that?* McKenzie was turn'd out by the last Ministry, the Duke is only Blameable in that Case for his advising, H[is] M[ajesty']s to submit; The late Ministry[88] likewise had made themselves odious & intolerable to the King, and brought on that Resolution the execution of which he gave the Conduct of to his Uncle, as long ago as the beginning of April last.

And hear [*sic*] I will tell you a Notion of my Own, which every minutes recollection, confirms me in, which will soften a little, your anger to the Duke, and solve many of the Phænomana, which have appear'd this last summer. My Notion is, That the King, put himself, into the Hands of a Man [Cumberland], whose Understanding, was

[82] George Grenville's ministry which was turned out in July. The king had been using Cumberland as a go-between/adviser since March.

[83] In May 1765 George Grenville had been promised by George III that he would no longer consult Lord Bute. However, there was a widespread belief, which continued into 1766, that Bute was still the king's adviser. In July 1766 the king wrote his last letter to Bute, letting him know that Chatham had formed a ministry.

[84] James Stuart Mackenzie.

[85] Thomas Wentworth (1593–1641), 1st earl of Strafford, was Charles I's chief adviser, but was hated by parliament who demanded his execution. Strafford's letter, dated 23 Apr. 1641, stated his willingness to die if it meant reconciliation between monarch and subject and he absolved the king from his promise to save him. Charles signed a bill of attainder for his execution and Strafford was executed on 12 May 1641. *ODNB*.

[86] George II.

[87] John, Lord Carteret, had been made a noble member of the garter in 1749.

[88] The Grenville ministry.

weaken'd, and impair'd by Palsy, & yet, gave him Credit, for the same strength of Mind, that he had once, (& only had) been Master of he could not govern his own People, and yet went on, 'till he made them govern. H[is] R[oyal] H[ighnes]s [Cumberland] show'd all along great tenderness for the King, which I suppose had great Weight, and was certainly very sincere; he frequently fell into fits of crying, and they were almost always followed, by submissive Councils; The yielding even if it had been without terms, and but for half an hour, to the Old Ministry; The not being able to govern, and yet going on with his Friends, whom he could not govern; Being able to hear, of Pitt, after the Treatment he had met from him; His temper so little sanguine, that he could think him or Lord Temple or courting the People (For H[is] R[oyal] H[ighnes]s made Lord Campden [Camden]) necessary; The having any fears any diffidence of the Power of the Crown, whom there was spirit to exert it; these *Traits* have none of them the least resemblance of the Duke of Cumberland I knew.

I find too from his Family that his Head, has at times, fail'd this last twelvemonths, do's not this soften you. But a letter this morning receiv'd from you, of Nov[ember] the 8th shows me, that his Death alone, had already obtain'd his Pardon. People say Mr Pitt has been again sent to, and has again declin'd because of health, 'tis certain; that Lord Temple's preventing him from coming in, has exceedingly disgusted, & disjoin'd him from Lord Temple; he has the same opinion of G[eorge] Grenvill[e] as formerly, and, the reconciliation betwixt them two, has gone no further, than being able to bring themselves to dine at the same Table, in a good deal of Company at Stowe.[89] When Mr Pitt declar'd that they were now disjoin'd, and parted with Lord Temple, he quoted out of the 4th Book of Virgil

> Extinxti, me, teque, Soror, populumque patres que
> Sidonis, urbemque tuam[90]

Great, & magnificent! I heartily wish, the Division, between these two Brothers[91] may hold, for I think the Peer, a much worse Man, than the Commoner; I don't my Dear Mr Campbell know what *Ochlocracy* is, but I with you think there is nothing to be fear'd but Confusion, to which I think, News Papers may a great deal Contribute.

Whenever I am mention'd in them, be assur'd it is not true; I did not dine at Lord Hollderness's, nor have been in the way of any Royalte, do News Papers do any Good? would it not serve not hurt the cause of Liberty, if they were not to be Publish'd, but by a Licence, think of that Mr Campbell, and give me your opinion. George Grenvill[e] obtained those orders from the Admiralty, which made the Captains, of the King's Ships, Customs House Officers, they were unwilling to take the Oath, and may be, because not used to it, observ'd it; But they have behav'd honourably, making no advantage to themselves; But that the Orders came, from George Grenvilles wise Head, & not from the Admiralty Originally, the thing speaks it self.

---

[89] Stowe House, Buckinghamshire, seat of the Temple-Grenville family. At this date it was occupied by Richard Grenville (1711–79), the 2nd Earl Temple.

[90] 'Extinxti me teque, soror, populumque patresque Sidonis, urbemque tuam': 'You have, oh sister, brought to ruin me and you, and the people and fathers of Sidon [modern-day Saida in Lebanon] and your city'. Virgil, *Aeneid*, iv, 682–3.

[91] Grenville and Lord Temple.

I dare say you have a very pretty Place, this place is pretty enough, But I want, Sea sands to drive upon, Sea Air to breath, Sleeping or waking, & am sorry to say, that I already feel the want, of it. Here is a very long letter but I think, it will be some measure entertain you, and if it dos, in ever so small degree, the intent is perfectly answer'd, Of My Dear Sir, you ever affectionate and faithfull humble servant . . .

This letter was begun the 11th and finish'd the 14th.

214. [BL, Add. MS 51406, ff. 117–18]
John Campbell to Lord Holland, 25 November 1765
Your letters give so great and pleasing entertanement to me, that I must allways think the longer they are, and the oftener they come the better. The only danger is, that they may give me too much encouragement to be troublesome. Your last has set things in a new light. If the D[uke] of C[umberland] was now alive, all my Anger would be turn'd to pity. And I see I have blamed the much injured Lord Bute for things of which he was quite innocent. His false delicacy should indeed have a very different effect upon his Friend,[92] who I fear will find that he has bought present ease, by lasting servitude. I am of opinion that proper spirit, upon occasions that called for, and would justifie the exertion of it would have had very good effects both for himself, & the Public. I think Lord Bute made the greatest political mistake when he resign'd his Office.[93] I wish he had been more advised by a Friend of mine,[94] and never admitted such Creatures as the late Sir H[enry] Erskine[95] Sir Alexander Grant[96] of Billiter Lane, Leonidas Glover[97] &c., to any political familiarity with him. I am sorry he do's not, & has not for so long time, seen the King in private. If Lord Bute had admitted me I should have talk'd to him honestly, & Freely, I do not pretend to say Wisely; but to believe it was scarce possible to have talk'd mere foolishly, than some he did admit; possibly I might add, or less honestly.

The Montebanks[98] quotation from Virgil shew'd more vanity, and arrogance, than I ever heard of being express'd in so few Words. If the Brother in Law[99] is a worse Man, surely he has great Luck in Wickedness. Be that as it may, I heartily wish the Division between them may continue, and increase.

I should not have used such a crabbed word as Ochlocracy, but that I thought I had seen it in some of the political Papers, for I am, in truth, a very very poor Grecian; it signify's Mob Government. (Οχλος, Turba, Multitudo) I have long, & often thought that great Mischief was done by Newspapers; and have many times said that I wish'd

---

[92] George III.

[93] As first lord of the treasury, 1763.

[94] That is, Holland.

[95] Sir Henry Erskine (?1710–65), 5th bt of Alva, Clackmannan; MP for Ayr burghs 1749–54 and Ansthruther Easter burghs 1754–65. Erskine was utterly partisan in all matters relating to Bute and referred to himself as *sous ministre* to his master.

[96] Sir Alexander Grant (d. 1772), 5th bt, of Dalvey, Elgin; MP for Inverness burghs 1761–8. In the early 1740s Grant had become a leading merchant of Billiter Lane, London, making his money in the West Indies.

[97] Richard Glover.

[98] Pitt.

[99] Temple.

there were none but the Gazette.[100] I am much pleased to find you have the same thoughts; for though I sometimes think differently from you, I allways, sincerely, believe it a strong confirmation of my own judgement, when I find it agree with yours.

I have lately had a little correspondence[101] with the Duke of Newcastle which has pleased me. It was occasion'd by my being certanely inform'd that our Militia Hero[102] Colonel Owen had, in a letter, affirm'd to H[is] G[race] that the said Hero was opposed in this County merely because he was a Friend of the Duke's. I had such a share in the Election, that this must affect me, or nobody, so I writ to the Duke upon it; treated the Hero & his Father[103] with just contempt, in truth they could not easily deserve more than I express'd. I defy'd their Malice to say that I ever shew'd, or express'd, personal disrespect, much less Enmity to his Grace. But said my Opinion of the late German War,[104] & the Hand[105] said to Guide those Measures, was such, that I could not avoid being glad of any opportunity to join in putting an end to them, that I was no competent judge of particular parts; if any were wrong I heartily wish'd they had been better, but was still free to say, that I would have rejoic'd at the conclusion of the Treaty,[106] if it had been worse. That if I could attend Parliament I would cheerfully join in supporting the King's Government in the hands of H[is] G[race] & his Friends though I might sometimes Vote with those for whom I had less esteme, if Questions were moved, in which I had allready declared my Opinion, and seen no reason to alter it. The Duke gave me thanks for, what he was pleased to call, a very kind, and very honest letter; acknowledged that he very well remember'd all I now said, to have pass'd between him, and me; and though Wee sometimes differ'd in opinion, he never did, or could blame me for acting according to my own. He earnestly wished for my attendance in Parliament with very strong expressions of regard for me, and his knowledge of the integrity of my heart.

At present it is impossible for me to think of any journey. I have thoughts of taking a Medicine by the Advice of a Physician (not a Welch one) who has taken it himself. He thinks it may cure me of the bleeding so as to enable me to use exercise. But the recovering from a Chronical Distemper, at 70, seems to me a vane expectation. I believe I may be well content, and should be very thankfull while I continue, otherwise, so well, and easy.

If I was to attend Parliament I believe I should please very few. And if I did please *some* few I should be satisfied. I should probably fancy myself obliged to talk oftener than ordinary in order to explane the Principles of my Conduct. So perhaps it is not unlucky that I am confined here.

Pray use what exercise you can. I most earnestly wish the continuance of your health being ever affectionately & Faithfully yours . . .

---

[100] The *London Gazette*, first published in Nov. 1665 as the *Oxford Gazette* before changing its name in February the following year. An official court journal.

[101] See letter 208 above.

[102] Meant facetiously: Owen was Campbell's political foe.

[103] Sir William Owen.

[104] The German theatre of the Seven Years War.

[105] Pitt as driving force behind the Seven Years War.

[106] The Treaty of Paris.

215. [BL, Add. MS 51406, f. 119][107]
John Campbell to Lord Holland, 27 November 1765
Have you read the inclosed [not extant] writ by a Friend, as seems, of Lord Bute's, & observed the paragraphs I have mark'd. He should appear to be well inform'd, by telling so expressly the Contents of Lord Bute letter to the King. But he either express's himself ill, in that particular, or greatly mistakes the time of Earl Granville's death.[108]

Has Capel Hanbury,[109] in his possession any number of letters between You, Mr [Thomas] Pelham, Mr [Sir Edward] Winnington and Sir Charles Hanbury Williams? If he has how came he by them? He is a worthless fellow.

216. [BL, Add. MS 51406, ff. 120–1]
Lord Holland, Holland House to John Campbell, 21 December[110] 1765
I waited till after the Parliament met,[111] that I might have more to write to you; I thought Lord Bute would speak the first day, & that I should be there to hear Him. There was not it seems a glance at Him, not a word which could possibly give him, the opportunity he longed for of speaking, nor was I well enough to go there. The Question was, upon an Amendment, moved by Lord Suffolk,[112] of no Consequence; the Majority was, 80,[113] I enclose you a list of the Minority.[114] Lord Temple made many Compliments to Mr Pitt, But Lord Shelbourn [Shelburne] being of the Majority, and Beckford, not only with the Ministry, But at their previous meeting, are undoubted proofs, That my Lord Temple & Mr Pitt are disjoined;[115] I wish as you do, that the Session may be lasting; That Mr Pitt intends to lend his Countenance to this Ministry and show it, as soon as he is well enough to come to Town I believe is true.

What more is to follow I know not; In the House of Commons, The Ministry,[116] had as many, & Mr Grenvill[e], as few, as the Ministry could wish. I always knew it would be so; And Mr Grenvill[e] who never was thought to speak well, 'till he was

---

[107] Fragment only.

[108] The *Public Advertiser*, 4 Nov. 1765, in an article signed by 'J.J.' referred to Lord Granville dying in the summer of 1763, when in fact, he died in January of that year.

[109] Capel Hanbury (1707–65), of Pontypool, Monmouthshire; MP for Leominster 1741–7 and Monmouthshire 1747–65. An 'old whig' who supported Fox until he fell out with him in c.1761. Hanbury's brother was Charles Hanbury Williams.

[110] Parliament adjourned on 20 Dec. until 14 Jan. 1766. *PH*, vxi, 90.

[111] 17 Dec 1765. *LJ*, xxi, 225.

[112] Henry Howard (1739–79), 12th earl of Suffolk, and 5th earl of Berkshire. Lord privy seal 1771 and northern secretary 1771–9.

[113] *LJ*, xxxi, 227. The vote was regarding amendments to the motion for an address to the king's speech regarding the 'tumults and insurrections' in America. The amendment was rejected: contents 24 not contents 80; *PH*, xvi, 83–7, for the address and proposed amendment.

[114] See letter 217 below.

[115] Lord Temple fell out with his brother-in-law Pitt over America, the former believing the colony was heading for independence, a view Pitt could not support. The split with Pitt was further advanced when the Chatham ministry rejected George Grenville. However, the three men were reconciled after the fall of that ministry, and united over the controversy surrounding the Middlesex election of John Wilkes in 1768. *ODNB*. Holland wrote to his brother, Lord Ilchester: 'Pitt alone is surely infinitely better than Pitt and Temple'. Cited in Ilchester, *Henry Fox*, ii, 311.

[116] The first Rockingham ministry, 1765–6.

Chancellor of the Exchequer, Is now again the most wretched speaker in the House; I hear Charles Townshend trounced Him, dos not he deserve it? for giving him my Place?[117] and did not he give it luckily? for had he not moved the Writ, the Last day of the last sessions,[118] Charles could not have been, the only Cabinett Councellour[119] in the House, The first day of this.

I approve very much, of your Correspondence, with The Duke of Newcastle; The News Paper you enclose, was much remark'd, & has had very great effect here; every Body wonder'd, that a writer so well inform'd, could place Lord Grevills Death Eight Months later than it happened, I can't imagine who could; or who did write the Paper, taken altogether.

I have heard since his Death, that my Friend Sir Charles Williams;[120] never kept a receipt, or burnt a Letter, His Brothers as Executors, I suppose, have I know a great many of mine, a great many which Capel show'd to many People; I have not the least guess, where they are now, I wish you could see them; they were writ with all the freedom, inaccuracy, & unreserv'd intimacy, that I write with to you, and on all occurrancies; I don't doubt, they might make me many Enemies, they would not make you less my Friend, than you are. I suspect, much that some expressions in them (I can't in the least guess what) made Capel my Enemy, who profess'd to be much other ways, 'till about two years agoe, and then without giving any Reason, would have no Commerce or Correspondence with me. I suspect this & in Consequence of it, that He show'd them, to whoever would be Offended by them, it is three or four years ago, that George,[121] show'd one of these letters among others, at the Hot Wells at Bristol; in which amongst other things, was this expression. *That Ungovernable and ungover'd Man, The Duke of Bedford.* Mr Campbell[122] an Irish Gentleman, a very grand & very honest Man, ask'd G[eorge] Hanbury, how he came by these letters, and then very gravely represented to him, that he thought he should not show them, without he had my leave. I did not know this 'till long afterwards, when Mr Upton,[123] Mr Campbells Brother in Law, a very worthy & great friend of mine told me.

But Prot Facinus![124] Would you believe it? some of these letters were given to Wilkes & Churchill,[125] I suppose they could find nothing in them, to their Purpose, and they was

---

[117] Townshend replaced Holland as paymaster of the forces in May 1765.

[118] *CJ*, xxx, 433, 24 Mar. 1765: Writ to re-elect Townshend as MP for Harwich as he had been appointed to the paymaster's office.

[119] That is, the ministry.

[120] Sir Charles Hanbury Williams.

[121] George Hanbury, brother to Sir Charles Hanbury Williams.

[122] Dr Thomas Campbell (1733–95), 'Irish Dr Campbell', writer and church of Ireland clergyman. Author of *A Philosophical Survey of the South of Ireland in a Series of Letters to John Watkinson* (1778), a response to Campbell's dismay at the lack of knowledge of Ireland among the English.

[123] Clotworthy Upton (1721–85), created Baron Templeton (Irish peerage) in 1776.

[124] Declare the crime!

[125] Charles Churchill (1732–64), poet and satirist, described by Wilkes' biographer as a parson who hated preaching, parish life and family life but instead chose a 'libertine life'. A.H. Cash, *John Wilkes: The Scandalous Father of Civil Liberty* (2006), 66. Churchill edited and wrote articles for the *North Briton* with John Wilkes. His satirical poem *The Duellist* (1763) attacked Wilkes' enemies in the house of lords.

offer'd to me to purchase, from Mr Churchills Brother & Executor. On Consideration, I refus'd to treat for them; & if you have any doubt, about my reason for declining it, I will tell you in my next.

For the present Adieu Dear Sir and let the Consideration of what a world we live in, have no other effect upon us, then to lessen our concern, when we think, we are so soon to leave it.[126] Yours ever . . .

217. [BL, Add. MS 51406, ff. 122–3]
Lord Holland, London to John Campbell, 2 January 1765 [1766][127]
My Secretary, is very positive, that the List of the Minority, was in your letter, & must have been lost in opening it. But it shall signifie nothing you will certainly find a list in this. Tom Earl[128] us'd to say, that, *de mortuis nil nisi bonum*[129] was the silliest of all maxims; I own, I don't find much, to say for it; Sir Earlby Wilmot[130] whom I don't know told Lord Mansfield, that Capel Hanbury had shown my Letters to Him, and by his account, I had no reason to be concern'd; But my Reason, for not buying the letters, was this; Lord Bute who did not know, But that the Publication of Lady Mary Worthye letters,[131] Might be disagreeable to Lady Bute,[132] enter'd into a treaty, gave Three hundred Guineas, & had all the Original letters given to him. The day . . .[133] three weeks afterwards, they were printed in Holland.[134] there is no more talk, nor as I believe thought . . .[135] now of attacking Lord Bute, in the house of Lords, then the most Private Character there. What seriously now employs, I believe, the thoughts of serious Men, is the sad situation with regard to the colonies.

Mr Pitt, leaves it uncertain whether He comes to Town or not, or what part he shall take if He dos come; This furnishes many idle reports and gives Lord Temple room to say whatever He pleases, a Liberty which he freely takes, without the least regard to Truth. I would not trouble you, with Reports, that are just as likely, to be absolute inventions, as to have any foundation; And therefore go to the true reason of my *Empressement*[136] to write to you to day, which is to know your reason as soon as Possible, for wishing me not to buy the Pembrokeshire Annuity; I have begun to treat for it, But not engag'd, tho' inclin'd to purchase it; I can't imagine, what objection, there may be to it;[137]

---

[126] Holland died 1 July 1774, and Campbell in Sept. 1777.

[127] Holland has written 1765, but from internal evidence he must mean 1766.

[128] Rev, Thomas Earle (*d.* 1749), vicar of Malmesbury 1705–14 and West Port St Mary 1721-49, both Wiltshire; father of William Earle (1728–74), one of Fox's chief supporters.

[129] Speak no ill of the dead.

[130] Sir John Eardley Wilmot (1709–92), judge; lord chief justice of common pleas 1766–71.

[131] Lady Mary Wortley Montagu (1689–1762), aristocrat and writer. Her letters were first published in 1763 and a year later a pirated edition appeared which included unauthentic material.

[132] Mary Stuart (1718–94), daughter of Lady Mary Wortley Montagu.

[133] Part of the letter is missing.

[134] Part of the letter is missing.

[135] Part of the letter is missing.

[136] Animated display of cordiality. *OED.*

[137] Ends with a semi-colon.

I have had a feaverish Cold, attended, with Asthmatick Symptoms, very unpleasant, But still more unpromising. Yours ever . . .

Tuesday December 17th List of the Minority in the House of Lords, 1765[138]
  Wentworth
  Bedford
  Trevor
  Gower
  Vere   5
  Marlbro'
  Hide
  Littleton [Lyttelton]
  Bridgewater
  Suffolk   10
  Sandwich
  Scarsdale
  Essex
  Abercorn
  Coventry   15
  Halifax
  Waldegrave
  Buckinghamshire
  Powis
  Temple   20
  Weymouth
  Bolingbroke
  Bishop Carlisle
  Bishop of Bangor[139]   24

---

[138] See *British Parliamentary Lists 1660–1800*, ed. G.M. Ditchfield, D. Hayton and C. Jones (1995), 59, 248, for other sources of this list.

[139] Edward Noel (1715–74), de jure 13th Baron Despencer, 1st Viscount Wentworth; Robert Hampden Trevor (1706–83), 1st Viscount Trevor; secretary to the embassy at The Hague 1734–46; postmaster general 1759–65. Succeeded his brother as 4th Baron Trevor in 1764. Initially he was a supporter of Robert Walpole and corresponded regularly with Horace Walpole, though by the accession of George III he had become a follower of George Grenville. *ODNB*; George Spencer (1739–1817), 4th duke of Marlborough; lord chamberlain 1762–3; lord privy seal 1763–5. Although his father was a supporter of Henry Fox, the 4th duke was firmly in the duke of Bedford's camp, especially after he married the duke's daughter Lady Caroline Russell in 1762; Thomas Villiers (1709–86), of The Grove, Watford, Hertfordshire; whig MP for Tamworth 1747–56. Envoy to Poland 1744–6 and Prussia 1746; joint paymaster general 1763–5 and 1786; chancellor of the duchy of Lancaster 1771–82 and 1783–6; lord of the admiralty 1748–56. Raised to the peerage as Baron Hyde in 1756 and created 1st earl of Clarendon 1782; Francis Egerton (1736–1803), 3rd duke of Bridgewater, known as Lord Francis Egerton until 1748; famous as the commissioner of canals; Nathaniel Curzon (1726–1804), of Kedleston, Derbyshire; tory MP for Clitheroe 1748–54 and Derbyshire 1754–61. Created Baron Scarsdale in 1761; William Anne Capell (1732–99), 4th earl of Essex; James Hamilton (1712–89), 8th earl of Abercorn (Scottish peerage); styled Lord Paisley 1734–44 and created Viscount Hamilton 1786–9; George William Coventry (1722–1809), 6th earl of Coventry, of Croome Court, Worcestershire; known as Viscount Deerhurst 1744–51. MP for Bridport 1744–7 and Worcestershire 1747–51 when he succeeded his father as earl; lord of the bedchamber 1752–70; John Waldegrave (1718–84), 3rd Earl Waldegrave; MP for Orford 1747–54 and Newcastle-under-Lyme 1754–63; groom of the bedchamber 1760–3; master of the horse to Queen Charlotte 1770–84. Waldegrave was a military careerist, becoming a colonel in 1743, major general

218. [BL, Add. MS 51406, ff. 124–5]
Lord Holland, Piccadilly to John Campbell, 23 January 1766
Before I receiv'd yours of the 17th [not extant] I had order'd the Annuity to be bid for, resolving if I bought it, to offer it at the price I gave, to Mr. Wogan;[140] But I have now, forbid the bidding for it, and shall have nothing to do with it. I never wanted to buy in Pembrokeshire, my motive was to make it, part of a Jointure, that a Mother & son, might have less matter of Account between them. I can satisfie this view without meddling, with this annuity, which You wish to Mr Wogan, I hope your wishes will succeed.

I was wrong in my Conjectures, Mr Pitt they say, has been too extravagant to be comply'd with, even by Mr Conway;[141] The Ministry remains as it was.[142] When I hear more you shall in the mean time, I am excessively sorry to see, by a word in your letter, that you have, vexation, of a private nature, to employ your mind. Much more so, than at my own ill health, which has been a little worse then usual, this last Week.

Adieu Dear Sir . . .

219. [BL, Add. MS 51406, ff. 126–7][143]
John Campbell to Lord Holland, 28 January 1766
I am grieved to hear of your ill health and that it has been lately worse, I regret my being so long, at so great a distance from you, and the uncertanety of being able to come nearer. Your health is most valuable to your Family, & Friends. And, if it had been as good as I wish it, would I believe have been of the greatest service to the Public. But Wee do not deserve an able, honest disinterested Minister, whose Counsils would neither be rash, or timid. You will know that by disinterested I do not mean that Affectation which may make a Man refuse the just dues, or fair profits of an Office,[144] for the sake of the Dear Country which, at the same time, he would sacrifice to his Ambition, or even to his Vanity. I am glad Pitt has been too extravagant even for those who were grovelling in the dirt of his feet; glad I am of any King that may keep him from Power.

[139] (continued) in 1757, lieutenant general in 1759 and general in 1772; Thomas Thynne (1734–96), 1st marquess of Bath; master of the horse to Queen Charlotte 1763–5; lord lieutenant of Ireland 1765; secretary of state for the northern department 1768 and 1779; secretary of state for the southern department 1768 -70 and 1775–9; groom of the stole 1782–96; Viscount Weymouth 1751 -96 and created marquess in 1786; Frederick St John (1732–87), 2nd Viscount Bolingbroke and 3rd Viscount St John; known as 'Bully' by his contemporaries, he was renowned for his extravagant lifestyle of gambling and drinking. He married Lady Diana Spencer (1734–1808), daughter of the 3rd duke of Marlborough, and artist, whom he abused and later divorced; John Egerton (1721–87), bishop of Bangor 1756–68, bishop of Lichfield 1768–71 and bishop of Durham 1771–87.
[140] Probably John Wogan (1735–79) of Wiston, Pembrokeshire.
[141] Henry Seymour Conway.
[142] That is, there were no changes in the Rockingham ministry during the Christmas recess. This ministry remained in power until July 1766 when it was dismissed in favour of the Chatham ministry.
[143] Published privately in Letters to Henry Fox, ed. Ilchester.
[144] A comment upon Pitt's refusal to accept profits from the office of paymaster. Fox, on the other hand, took everything that was due to him, thereby amassing a fortune. See Ilchester, Henry Fox, ii, 333–6. See Introduction.

I was many years ago delighted with an expression in Swifts Baucis & Philemon.[145] *Two Hermits Saints by Trade.*[146] The two sorts of Men[147] I think most Mischievous, and for whom I have the greatest aversion are, *Saints by Trade* and *Patriots by Trade.* You may, with good reason, add *Friend by Trade.*

My private Trouble is on account of my poor Daughter Fortescue.[148] To whom, if you knew her, I am sure you would wish well, on her own account, as well as mine; for I think I may, without a Parents partiality, say she is a Woman of an innocent, and amiable disposition. She is now with us here, deserves all the kindness I can shew her, and wants all the Comfort that can give her.

The Professions of your Friendship to me give me the greatest Pleasure, as I have long been satisfied that no Man can be more incapable of falsehood; and I promise my self you never doubt my sincerity when I send you my best Wishes, with assurance that you are loved, estem'd and honor'd by Yours always . . .

You are very good with regard to the Annuity. I had fancied you wanted something here to exchange with Mr Edwards, which made me mention the Land. I don't know what Sir T[homas] Stepney will do, he has been busy lately about geting rid of his Lady, who I believe used him very ill.[149]

I hope the exceedingly fine, mild, dry weather for a week past, may have a good effect on your health.

220. [BL, Add. MS 51406, ff. 128–9]
Lord Holland, London to John Campbell, 31 January 1766
I am by no means able to go down to the House of Lords, but upon my word neither on a Public or a Private account, ought that to give you the least concern I did not guess right; Monday last[150] was in the House of Commons such a day, as you wou'd have rejoic'd to seen;[151] the Colonies, sent each of them, a representative to New York and those illegal delegates,[152] a remonstrance[153] to the House of Commons here; Mr Cook[154] of Middlesex carried it on Monday, and Mr Pitt, with all his insolence about him, went down to order it to be received; But never was Man so disappointed; He set out with the utmost extravagance declaring in attempting to tax the Colonies, we had broke the

---

[145] Jonathan Swift (1667–1745), writer, satirist and priest. *Baucis and Philemon* was published 1706–9.

[146] Line 7.

[147] Campbell has Temple and Pitt in mind, who both nurtured the merchants of the City as political allies.

[148] Anne, Lady Fortescue. See Introduction.

[149] Stepney's wife was Elizabeth Eleanor Lloyd, daughter of Thomas Lloyd of Derwydd and Danyrallt, Carmarthenshire. They had a very stormy relationship, though they never divorced. Personal communication with Dr David Davies, currently undertaking research into the Stepney estate and family.

[150] 27 Jan. 1766.

[151] *CJ*, xxx, 499–500.

[152] A reference to the Stamp Act Congress, a body that was established to organise opposition to the Stamp Act by several American colonies. In England it was widely believed to be an illegal assembly, though Pitt stated in the debate that it was no more illegal than political clubs in Britain. P.D.G. Thomas, *British Politics and the Stamp Act Crisis: The First Phase of the American Revolution 1763–1767* (Oxford, 1975), 189.

[153] *CJ*, xxx, 499–500: the Massachusetts Bay petition.

[154] George Cooke (c.1705–68), of Harefield, Middlesex; MP for Tregony 1742–7 and Middlesex 1750–68. Horace Walpole called him 'a pompous Jacobite'. Cited in *HPC, 1754–90*, ii, 249. A follower of Pitt, he unexpectedly presented the petition sent from the Stamp Act Congress, 'in evident collusion with Pitt'. Thomas, *British Politics and the Stamp Act Crisis*, 189.

Original Covenant, & they were freed from all Allegiance; Sir Fletcher Norton[155] told him, that he set the Prerogative above all Law, when he suppos'd, that the Crown cou'd by it's Charters emancipate & set free from the Legislature of G[reat] Britain, any Part of its subjects; that such Doctrine was extremely Dangerous, and that if he thought the House wou'd approve of it, He would not scruple, moving, to send the Gentleman, to another Place.[156] You'll easily believe, Sir F[letcher] Norton's superiority in point of Argument was great. But I am told the Roughness with which he treated him, (which you will say cou'd not be too great) was full great enough. The House was as much against Pitt on Monday, as it had been with Him the Tuesday[157] before; Conway, & Dowdeswell,[158] declar'd against receiving the remonstrance, and, it was rejected without a Division.[159] It is Prodigious to what a degree Mr Pitts Popularity in the City, they say is fallen off; It should seem, as if they really expected He could do them good, & wou'd do them no harm, & expected Him to conquer every thing, but don't understand His giving up Anything. George Onslow,[160] stuck to him, and spoke for him and was for bringing up the remonstrance, which is look'd upon as a Mark of the Duke of Newcastle being still afraid, holding up a finger against Him. Nor indeed have I heard, that he has spoke with any resentment, But only with concern, that Mr Pitt shou'd treat him so. At first every Body thought, as your Correspondent did, that the Influence he meant was Lord Butes. But he took care both in Publick & in private, to make that very

---

[155] Norton accused Pitt of 'sounding the trumpet to Rebellion' in the debate. H. Walpole, *Memoirs of the Reign of King George the Third* (4 vols, 1894), ii, 193.

[156] To the bar of the House – members who violated the rules or privileges of parliament were ordered there by the Speaker.

[157] *CJ*, xxx, 478–9, 21 Jan. 1766, when petitions from various colonies were received asking for repeal of the Stamp Act.

[158] William Dowdeswell (1721–75), of Pull Court, Worcestershire; MP for Tewkesbury 1747–54 and Worcestershire 1761–75. Chancellor of the exchequer in the first Rockingham ministry, he was replaced by Chatham with Charles Townshend. Horace Walpole stated that Dowdeswell was 'so suited to the drudgery of office, as far as it depends on arithmetic, that he was fit for nothing else'. Cited in *HPC*, *1754–90*, ii, 333. He was a strong opponent of the cider tax. Walpole also stated that in the debate on the cider tax Dowdeswell 'sunk much in the estimation of mankind, and seemed but a duller edition of Mr Grenville without his malignity'. Walpole, *Memoirs of George III*, ii, 219.

[159] Walpole states that only five MPs were for hearing the petition: Richard Hussey (1715–70), of Truro, Cornwall; MP for Mitchell 1755–61, St Mawes 1761–8 and East Looe 1768–70; Isaac Barré (1726–1802), of Manchester Buildings, Westminster; MP for Chipping Wycombe 1761–74 and Calne 1774–80. Joint vice-treasurer (Ireland) 1766–8; treasurer of the navy 1782; paymaster general 1782–3; clerk of the pells 1784–1802. In his maiden speech in the Commons Barré attacked Pitt at the instigation of Fox. However, in 1765 he seconded Beckford's motion against the stamp tax, and sided with Pitt regarding the American colonies. *HPC, 1754–90*, ii, 50–1; Edward Thurlow (1731–1806), MP for Tamworth 1765–78. Created Baron Thurlow of Ashfield 1778, and Baron Thurlow of Thurlow 1792. Solicitor-general 1770–1; attorney-general 1771–8; lord chancellor 1778–83 and 1783–92; teller of the exchequer 1780–1806. In the Commons he was one of the Bedford group, and voted against the repeal of the Stamp Act; and two ministers: Richard Howe, 4th Viscount Howe (I), MP for Dartmouth 1757–82; Colonel George Onslow (1731–92), of Ockham, Surrey; MP for Guildford 1760–84. Nicknamed 'cocking George' because of his love of cockfighting. He became lieutenant colonel of the 1st foot guards in 1759.

[160] George Onslow (1731–1814), of Imber Court, Surrey; MP for Rye 1754–61 and Surrey 1761–74. Lord of the treasury 1765–77; comptroller of the household 1777–9 and treasurer 1779–80; lord of the bedchamber 1780–1814. Created Baron Cranley 1776; Onslow succeeded a cousin as 4th Baron Onslow (1776) and was created earl of Onslow 1801. During the debates on the repeal of the Stamp Act and on the declaratory bill he spoke frequently, and also corresponded with Pitt and was 'anxious to please him and win his esteem'. *HPC, 1754–90*, ii, 229.

clear. On Monday[161] Mr Pitt mounts the stage again, and the same day in the House of Lords, Lord Cambden [Camden] & Lord Shelbourn [Shelburne], it is suppos'd will hold Pitts Language; it is said Lord Bute, with many of his Friends, are against the repeal of the Stamp Act, which the Ministry is suppos'd to intend Repealing; I think they shou'd not repeal, but Suspend it; what the result of all this will be, I can't guess. I am told, Lord Temple is as Violent in his Conversation, against Pitt, as ever he was for him; You shall hear from me again, next Week. Perhaps I may know no more to Conclude upon, than I now do. But whilst Pitts popularity, is going as they assure me it is, I thought I wou'd give you the Pleasure of telling it you, & sending you a Printed Paper, which came out on Thursday, & is much sought after. I fancy youll excuse the indelicacy of it, in favour, of it's intention.

Ireland, which is very Natural, is laying in the same claim of Independency,[162] & I don't know that this bad affair, is at all the worse for it.

221. [BL, Add. MS 51406, ff. 130–1]
Lord Holland, Piccadilly to John Campbell, 7 February 1766
I give you many thanks for your letter of the 28th January. I am within this four days a great deal better, but I have given over all thoughts of making any figure good or bad in the strange World of Politics. Here I shall stay at Home Nursing myself till it is warm enough to go to Kingsgate, and when it is too Cold to stay there any longer, I will go to the South of France or to Naples; I wish I could leave England, in a better situation with regard our Colonies, then I fear she will ever be again;

I never heard one word of Lady Fortescue but what was in her favour, I never pry'd or . . .[163] pity her, & you, as I do most heartily.

I thought this extraordinary Week, wou'd have produc'd some News to send to you, But no: I can tell you what had pass'd, what the Consequences will be, you must Guess, & may tell me.

On Monday [3 February][164] last Mr Pitt spoke in a much more moderate way, & very ill; on Wednesday,[165] with the same moderation, but better; The Subject on Wednesday trifling, only about wording some resolutions; On Monday whether we cou'd tax America. Mr Pitt held the same Doctrine, and most ignorantly argu'd, from the exemption of the Clergy, that those could not be tax'd who were not represented; no Division either day. But yesterday,[166] encourg'd by the strange things that had happen'd in the House of Lords, Mr Grenville, mov'd an address to the King, to assist, to support the Stamp Act; Mr Pitt went down to oppose it, a previous question was mov'd, & the Division for the previous Question, was 274 against

---

[161] 3 Feb. 1766. *CJ*, xxx, 513. For the debate, regarding five resolutions to do with the petitions laid before the House by various merchants and the American colonists, see Walpole, *Memoirs of George III*, 197–201. See also Thomas, *British Politics and the Stamp Act Crisis*, 195–9.

[162] The Irish Patriot Party, led by Henry Flood, was becoming vociferous in its demands for more independence for Ireland at this time.

[163] Four lines crossed out.

[164] *CJ*, xxx, 513.

[165] *CJ*, xxx, 517.

[166] Actually 7 Feb. – the same day the letter is dated.

134[167] altho' Lord Mountstuart,[168] Mr Mackenzie Mr Elliot Mr Oswald Mr Wedderbourn [Wedderburn], & almost all Lord Butes Friends, were with Mr Grenvills, among the 134.

Now for the House of Lords. On Monday [3 February] the Question was, on our right to tax America, a 125 to 5. The 5 were Lord Paulett, Lord Shelbourn [Shelburne], Lord Cornwallis, Lord Torrington,[169] & Lord Camden. Lord Shelbourn [Shelburne], & Lord Camden spoke Mr Pitts Language which is decry'd and held in Contempt everywhere. Lord Camden lost his Credit entirely, Lord Littelton [Lyttelton] made a fine Speech on the other side, & Lord Mansfield, they say absolutely the Best that was ever spoke. On Tuesday [4 February] a Resolution was mov'd, to address the King, to direct His Goverours [sic],[170] to recommend to the several Assemblys,[171] to make Compensation, to those, who had suffer'd, by the late Outrages;[172] The Late Ministry mov'd to make it require instead of Recommend, and they carried there [sic] Question 63 against 60. Amongst the 63 were Lord Bute & his friends, & 8 Lords of the Bed Chamber. Not only Rumours, but appearances too, were very strong, that Lord Bute, & His Friends, who certainly had gather'd together, their Force in both Houses, had join'd Mr Grenvill[e] Duke of Bedford &c.[173]

On Wednesday Morning [5 February], The Ministers went to the King, who desir'd them to stay in, and declar'd for the repeal of The Stamp Act, which is with the Ministers a Condition *sine qua non*[174] and which Lord Bute has declar'd against Repealing.

On Thursday [6 February], there was another division, upon words mov'd by Lord Sandwich, in which Lord Talbott Lord Harcourt,[175] Lord Litchfield, who had voted against the Court on Tuesday, Voted with them. However the Court lost it 59 to 55 & Lord Sandwich's words were receiv'd. Lord Bute spoke, he said he had no wish to differ with The Ministry, but in National Points, even the wish of the King, for whom he had the greatest Duty & Affection, should not weigh. He & several Lords of the Bed

---

[167] *CJ*, xxx, 521–2, does not record the division. For the debate, see Walpole, *Memoirs of George III*, ii, 202–4. See also Thomas, *British Politics and the Stamp Act Crisis*, 205–10.

[168] John Stuart (1744–1814), MP for Bossiney 1766–8. 1st marquis of Bute, styled Lord Mountstuart until 1792.

[169] George Byng (1740–1802), 4th Viscount Torrington.

[170] That is, the governors of the various colonies.

[171] The several assemblies of the American colonies.

[172] In the American colonies reaction to the stamp duties was often in the form of riot. See R. Middlekauff, *The Glorious Cause: The American Revolution, 1763–89* (rev. edn, Oxford, 2004), ch. 5.

[173] Walpole comments: 'The astonishment and mortification of Grenville and the Bedfords were unequalled. They had quarrelled with and defied the Favourite [Bute] when they were in power; and were now seeking and courting his support, when he seemed to have lost his power almost as much as they had'. Walpole, *Memoirs of George III*, ii, 204.

[174] Essential condition.

[175] Simon Harcourt (1714–77), 1st Earl Harcourt, of Stanton Harcourt, Oxfordshire. A supporter of Bute and Grenville, though mostly a court supporter, Walpole stated that Harcourt was 'an empty man, devoted to the Court but diffident and complaisant'. Cited in *ODNB*. In 1761 he was created ambassador to Mecklenburg, charged with requesting the hand of Princess Charlotte on behalf of George III. Harcourt was made master of horse to Queen Charlotte 1761–3 and then lord chamberlain to the queen 1763–8. He became British ambassador to France in 1768–72, but was never committed to the post. In 1772–8 he was viceroy to Ireland where he carried out several beneficial reforms. *ODNB*.

Chamber, voted for Lord Sandwich's words; And Lord Temple, The Duke of Bedford &c were not asham'd, to praise him, all round the House, extravagantly.

Surely Mr Grenville, had better have staid to let the ferment at Court, work a little before he came to the Division of Yesterday, of which I have . . .[176]

222. [BL, Add. MS 51406, ff. 132–3][177]
Lord Holland, London to John Campbell, 25 February 1766
An accident last Week, brought me very near Death indeed. Physick exceeding too strong for me, brought me into a situation, which I never felt before, & am convinc'd I shall never feel again, 'till the two or three Hours that may precede my Death; I hope not then; I am very weak, but in other respects, well again, as far as relate, to the horrible accident.

Now for Politicks. Mr Pitt contrary to His Custom, Condescended to Submit to the judgement of the House and to suppose tho' not convinc'd, that He must have been in the wrong. G[eorge] Grenville flush'd, with the overrated accession of Lord Bute &c brought on a Question Last Friday was se'nnight[178] very injudicious, & indeed unfair: as it forejudg'd the question of repeal on which they were then hearing Evidence. Pitt got again on the right side & with all His Merchants,[179] triumph'd in a Great Majority 270 to 134.[180] What made this more extraordinary, is that all Lord Bute's Friends, almost every Scotch man, and many Country Gentlemen, were in the Minority.[181]

On Friday last, [21 February] The Question of repeal came on, every Man, adhering to his former opinion; which could not but give, great doubt of the real inclination of the Court. For the Repeal 275 against 166.[182]

On Wednesday [19 February] last, was se'nnight, The Duke of Bedford, Lord Bute, G[eorge] Grenville, met together, at Lord Eglingtons;[183] Lord Temple, was to have been there but from some Villainous trick, of which I don't know the design, fail'd. Lord Eglington, ask'd Lord Bute, whether if they express'd their Penitence, he could forget

---

[176] The rest of the letter is missing.

[177] This letter repeats information included in letter 221.

[178] This is 14 Feb. but the debate referred to took place on 7 Feb.

[179] A great number of merchants' petitions opposing the Stamp Act were read and debated in the Commons, often until after midnight, during the period 7 Jan.–21 Feb. 1766. The Commons also examined several persons on the same subject, including Benjamin Franklin. *PH*, xvi, 133–59.

[180] Walpole, *Memoirs of George III*, ii, 202–4; see Thomas, *British Politics and the Stamp Act Crisis*, 205–8, for an account of the debate.

[181] Walpole comments: 'though Lord Rockingham with childish arrogance and indiscretion vaunted in the palace itself that he had carried the repeal against the King, Queen, Princess-dowager, duke of York, Lord Bute, the tories, the Scotch, and the opposition (and it was true he had), yet in reality it was the clamour of trade, of the merchants, and of the manufacturing towns, that had bourne down all opposition'. Walpole, *Memoirs of George III*, ii, 212.

[182] *PH*, xvi, 161, gives ayes 275 noes 167 in the negative to amend the bill to replace 'repeal' and insert 'explain and amend'. Walpole gives the same numbers and states that this 'majority, though the question was but a prelude to the repeal, decided the fate of that great political contest'. Walpole, *Memoirs of George III*, ii, 211.

[183] Alexander Montgomery (1723–69), 10th earl of Eglinton; gentleman of the king's bedchamber 1760 and Scottish representative peer 1761. A 'worthless and silly wretch' according to 'Memoir', 17. In Oct. 1769 he was shot, and died from his wounds in a dispute with an excise officer over the right to hunt on Eglinton's lands.

& forgive; He said Yes; they met, But when it stop'd here, you may believe, they were discontented. Lord Bute declar'd he knew nothing, nor would know any thing, of the intentions of The Court, But only adhere strictly, to those Essential National points, upon which He had already declar'd his opinion.

Here let me ask, whether you are of my Opinion; I think, & have let Lord Bute know it, that in going thus far, He has gone a great deal too far; He could not with . . .[184]

Yesterday on the report of the Committee. Mr Pitt was not there, the Majority still very Great, 240 to 133.[185] If there was any such thing as stability in these times, this would give it, to the Ministry.

But when Lord Bute with 8 Lords of the Bedchamber, Nine Bishop's Votes against The Court, (The words of the Question were not of the least significance) when Oswald, Elliot, Jenkinson,[186] Mr Mackenzie, Lord Mountstuart, Sir James Lowther,[187] &c are Active & eager, on Mr Grenvill[e]s side, People will doubt whether H[is] M[ajesty] is sincerely for the repeal. And I fear . . .[188] with great parade, was ushered into the House of Commons amidst Loud Huzzah's. Lord Temple, held up his hands, as if astonish'd, & scandaliz'd at such behaviour. However you must dislike the thing, do join with me, in being pleas'd with this Circumstance attending it.

I am very sorry to unsay what I began my last letter with, I have by no means got over, the effects of that horrid Physick; were I ever so well, I cou'd not however, give you any Probable insight to what is likely to happen. Another fortnight, will I suppose produce another letter, such as it may be, which however, I shall have a pleasure in writing . . .[189]

223. [BL, Add. MS 51406, ff. 134–7]
Lord Holland, London to John Campbell, 11 March 1766
I thank you for your letters of the 2[n]d 3[n]d & 4th [none extant] my declining, or rather ruin'd health, is not enough better or worse, to make it worth mentioning; I think the same, of American affairs. The conceited insolvence, of The Late Ministry,[190] who not only disregarded, But secreted the Accounts they had from America, has brought to light, the rebellious spirit there, which is not new, & I believe remedyless.

---

[184] Part of the letter is missing.

[185] *CJ*, xxx, 602, on the report of the committee of the whole House to the American papers. This was seen as a last attempt by Grenville's friends to divert the repeal of the Stamp Act. In the debate Grenville said that both America and England were governed by the mob. Walpole, *Memoirs of George III*, ii, 213.

[186] Charles Jenkinson (1729–1808), of Addiscombe, Surrey; MP for Cockermouth 1761–6, Appleby 1767–72, Harwich 1772–4, Hastings 1774–80 and Saltash 1780–6. Undersecretary of state 1761–2; private secretary to Bute as first lord of the treasury, and treasurer of the ordnance 1762–3; joint secretary to the treasury 1763–5; lord of the admiralty 1766–7 and the treasury 1767–3; joint vice-treasurer, Ireland 1773–5; secretary at war 1778–82; president of the board of trade 1786–1804; chancellor of the duchy of Lancaster 1786–1803. Jenkinson was attached to the crown 'as the one stable element in the political scene; a born bureaucrat, of restricted sympathies, his passion was for the detail of office'. *HPC, 1754–90*, ii, 675.

[187] Sir James Lowther (1736–1802), 5th bt, of Lowther, Penrith, Westmorland; MP for Cumberland 1757–61, 1762–8 and 1774–84, for Westmorland 1761–2 and Cockermouth 1769–74. He married Lady Mary Stuart, daughter of the 3rd earl of Bute.

[188] Part of the letter is missing.

[189] The end of the letter is missing.

[190] George Grenville's ministry, 1763–5.

The declarotary Bill [Declaratory bill][191] for securing the Independency of America, and the Bill for the repeal of the Stamp Act, went hand in hand thro' the House of Commons.[192] Mr Pitt upon the first, like a fool return'd to his old Doctrine, & spoke very ill; But the latter end of the day, an Accident happen'd, of which he took advantage; spoke better, & was heard, I am told, with more applause, than Man ever was;[193] I think it was on Wednesday last [5 March]. Bamber Gascoigne,[194] read a letter no Body knows why, from Sir William Meredith[195] to the Mayor of Liverpool,[196] which mention'd an Agreement, between Lord Bute & the late Ministry. But hoped, & believ'd that Mr Pitt wou'd soon be at The Head of Affairs; Mr Pitt was surpriz'd, that so private a Man as he was, who had but five people of his mind in the House of Lords, and perhaps not four in the House of Commons, should be so spoke of, But the Birds of the Air, sang unaccountable Storys, one had lately reach'd his Ears, of a meeting[197] at Lord Eglingtons, and The Bird sang likewise of what pass'd there, so agreable to the usual Honour & good intentions of Lord Bute, that it was very creditable. He forgave, & was ready to bury in oblivion, many affronts he had receiv'd. But when they had a mind, to go further, & began with their factious Proposals, he declar'd off. And wou'd have nothing to do with them. That Noble Lords Name, had been so banded about, so infamously us'd, That to be sure, he would never think, of coming into any share, of The Government of this Country. He disculpated[198] himself, from having had any share in the Vile Calumny, that had been so spread, & the distinctions, that had been invidiously made, and then again he flatter'd Lord Bute, the Scotch, & his old Friends the Torys. But when he came to that Part, of The Late Ministrye, Persecuting Mr Mackenzie, because he was Lord Butes Brother, & turning out others from Synacure Places, merely because they were his Friends, & *eo nomina*,[199] that was *errant* Faction. And whether the Monument, shou'd be illuminated, or hung in Mourning, (in which it is supposed, he alluded to an expression of Lord Temples) he would stand at the foot of that Monument, and declare his abhorrence, of such as he would call them again, Factious Measures. With a great deal of Wit, as well as reason, they say, He describ'd the meeting, at Lord Eglingtons. And when Mr Grenville talk'd of meetings at Hayes, silenc'd him, by making no secret of them, and appealing, to him, as well as every Body that knew any thing of the matter, whether they had been of his seeking; much less

---

[191] The bill was given royal assent on 18 Mar. 1766.

[192] Both the declaratory bill and the repeal bill were introduced on 26 Feb. and encountered very little opposition until their third readings.

[193] The debate was reported in the *Gentleman's Magazine*, Apr. 1766.

[194] Bamber Gascoyne (1725–91), of Bifrons, Barking, Essex; MP for Maldon 1761–3, Midhurst 1765–8, Weobley 1770–4, Truro 1774–84 and Bossiney 1784–6. Lord of trade 1763–5 and 1772–9; lord of the admiralty 1779–82; receiver-general of customs 1786–91. He was encouraged by Holland but remained as independent as possible. When he failed to be returned for Maldon in 1763, he systematically pursued the corporation via lawsuits until it was destroyed. *ODNB*.

[195] Sir William Meredith (?1725–90), 3rd bt, of Henbury, Cheshire and Pierrepoint, Surrey; MP for Wigan 1754–61 and Liverpool 1761–80. Lord of the admiralty 1765–6; comptroller of the household 1774–7.

[196] A John Crosbie was mayor 1765–6.

[197] Also referred to in letter 222 above.

[198] To clear from blame or accusation. *OED*.

[199] By that name.

suing for:[200] I still think, Lord Bute in the wrong to meet them, But nothing can have turn'd out more, for this Honour, & to their shame.

The repeal pass'd 250 to 122.[201] They are at this time about it in the House of Lords. Mr Pitt seconded the repeal of the Excise part of the Cyder Bill,[202] and I hear, that most Unjustifiable measure is to go without opposition.[203] I hear Lord Temple is like a Madman, & talk'd an hour yesterday of his Contempt of Popularity; What a strange degree of Vanity, & folly, must there be, in his Composition who could think, that Because after abusing His Brother [George Grenville] for years together, one day in June last they were reconciled; Court, Nation, Parliament, should immediately, be at his Beck.

Lord Cambden [Camden] Yesterday on the Bill, to secure the Independency of America, again talk'd, against our right to Tax.[204] His arguments were absurd, But his flattery of Mr Pitt, much more so; what to day will produce, you shall know by Thursdays Post.

Thursday 13 March 1766[205]

The House of Lords, sat 'till Eleven, last Tuesday;[206] and I hear, there was a great deal of good speaking; for committing the Bill to repeal, were 73, Proxys 32, 105 against committing 61 Proxys 10. 71.[207]

Lord Bute with 8 Lords of the Bed Chamber Lord Northumberland, Lord Harcourt, Lord Townshend, Lord Litchfield, & others, to the Number of twenty, were among the 61 & the Duke of York;[208] so that the countenance of the Court, is not yet clear; There was a report, yesterday, that Mr Pitt, had sent his Proposals[209] in writing, to the King. But this is mere Report. Lord Temple went out of his way yesterday, to quote words, of Mr Pitts & to ridicule them. It should seem then, that they two, are thoroughly at variance, & this pleases me & is the only thing that does.

The Duke of Grafton, I hear, spoke excessive well, He said if you did not repeal the Stamp Act, you wou'd run into, inconveniences, immediate & certain, to avoid such as were visionary & remote. This I own, is my whole argument, for in these matters, whatever is remote, I think is visionary.

[200] The previous four words are written superscript and it is indicated that they should be included after the semi-colon.

[201] *CJ*, xxx, 627. The debate on the Declaratory Bill of Right and the Repeal of the Stamp Act took place on 4 Mar. 1766. *PH*, vxi, 206, gives 275 to 161. Walpole, *Memoirs of George III*, 218, agrees with Holland's figures.

[202] *CJ*, xxx. 627. The cider tax was seen by petitioners wanting its repeal as an attack on personal liberty, 'both with respect to the tax itself, and to the mode of collecting it under the powers of the excise laws', the latter allowing a person's house to be searched. *PH*, xvi, 206.

[203] The bill to repeal the tax on cider, which had caused great discontent in 'cider counties', was given royal assent on 11 Apr. *PH*, xvi, 207.

[204] *PH*, xvi, 177–80, for Camden's speech.

[205] This letter is additional to the one of 11 Mar. rather than a separate item.

[206] 11 Mar. 1766. Thomas states that this Lords debate was 'one of the most important . . . of the century'. *British Politics and the Stamp Act Crisis*, 244.

[207] *PH*, xvi, 181. *British Parliamentary Lists*, ed. Ditchfield, Hayton and Jones, 62, for lists of the minority.

[208] Prince Edward Augustus (1739–67), duke of York 1760–7.

[209] That is, his proposals for forming a ministry.

Lord Chancellor [Northington] spoke well for the Repeal, Lord Mansfield against it, I think they say ill. Lord Cambden [Camden] is by some much commended; But I have observ'd this whole Winter, that Men & very sensible Men too, hear the same words, with ears so very different, that I had no notion, to have been possible;

Adieu. Dear Sir, nor can I name a time because I don't know when, I shall have any thing to write again. I don't know whether it effects your part of the World, enough, to make it worth while to tell you, That the Duke of Beaufords Marriage,[210] with a Daughter of the Late Admirall Bosscowen who has ten thousand Pound, is fix'd, made by his choice, but much to the vexation, of his Mother & his Family. Adieu.

224. [BL, Add. MS 51406, ff. 138–140]
John Campbell to Lord Holland, 6 April 1766

You began your last with what is most interesting to me, your health, which I am very glad to hear so much mended; and hope as the season advances it will daily grow better. The weather is very mild, indeed Wee had not here the great snow I see so much of in the Papers or any thing like it.

I heartily wish you may have as much satisfaction and Comfort from your sons Marriage[211] as so tender a Father deserves. May He and all your sons pay you the duty and affection which they owe you, I am sure none can owe more.

If the Duke of Bedford could after so many years of Friendship be persuaded to use you ill,[212] there can be no security he would not do the same again, if you were now reconcil'd, and where you can have no confidence all intercourse must be disagreable. It is insolent to expect you should forget it, because he is willing to do so; it is taking upon himself the Part of the injur'd, and he should be made to know that do's not belong to him; and to see that you have a just sense, and feeling of his unworthy behavior: You may very justly think your self his superior. Every honest Man has the most valuable superiority over one that is not so. The Duke by his unjust, and base treatment of you made himself inferior to you. And to preserve the Dignity of your Character is what you owe to yourself. Yet your sons near connection with him will bring you into some difficulty; but you will know how to conduct yourself in it. I can't help thinking you were too partial to Rigby, otherwise I believe a Man of less discernment would not have been so long imposed upon by him.

The repeal of the Cyder Tax, and their submission to Pitt gives me no high Idea of the present Ministry. If they acted Like men, they would have let Mr Dowdeswell know that a Chancellor of the Exchequer is not to be the head of a little Party or the

---

[210] Henry Somerset (1744–1803), 5th duke of Beaufort, married Elizabeth Boscawen, daughter of Admiral Boscawen (1711–61) in 1766. Somerset was master of the horse to Queen Charlotte 1767–72. Holland's comment refers to Somerset being lord lieutenant for Monmouthshire 1771–99 and Breconshire 1787–1803.

[211] Stephen Fox (1745–74), Lord Holland's eldest son, who briefly, upon his father's death became the 2nd Baron Holland, married Lady Mary FitzPatrick (c.1751–78), daughter of the 1st earl of Upper Ossory on 20 Apr. 1766. Lady Mary's mother was the duchess of Bedford's sister.

[212] Bedford, under the influence of the duchess and Rigby, fell out with Bute and his supporters in 1765. Holland rejected overtures of a reconciliation in Mar. 1766, declining to receive either the duke or his duchess. Ilchester, *Henry Fox*, ii, 290, 312.

Champion of a County; he might keep Word with the Cyder Men as Mr Dowdeswell, but should not think to carry the weight of a Minister in that Affair.[213]

I have seen some letters (in the printed Papers)[214] from the submissive secretary [Conway] to Governor Barnard[215] & another,[216] which seem to me quite inconsistent with the repeal of the Stamp Act: surely both cannot be right; and I am very apt to believe that if the repeal was necessary, it was in great Measure, made so by the behavior of the present Ministers, as a Faction while they were out; and as some what between a Faction and a Ministry since they came in.

Though I am much inclined to the Opinion of the protesting Lords,[217] yet I can never approve protesting with Reasons; A Libell upon the Determination of the House, to be enter'd, unanswer'd as it must be upon their own Journal has allways appear'd to me very absurd. It is however a matter above me, & out of my sphere. I was apprehensive that the Act,[218] and the Resolutions of both House's asserting the dependence of the Colonies, might, be resented by them allmost as much as the Stamp Act. I now suppose they will be satisfied Britain is as submissive as the Secretary, that those Things mean no more than Conways letters, so they may light their Pipes with them, and take no farther Notice of them.

I think Pitt, and Prate [Pratt], for their behavior in the American Affair, deserve to be look'd upon as Traytors. I begin to consider myself as one that has left the World, so far as to form, & speak my opinion of Political Affairs in the present Time; as of those in Times past, Matters in which I have no personal concern. One must indeed have some thought of those Wee are to leave behind us, but Wee must commit them to the Care of Providence, satisfied that no Wreck can finally destroy a Good Man. If things look'd ever so promising, now, they might suddainly alter to very bad when Wee are gone; and ill as they now appear it is *possible* they may soon mend.

When I write to you I can't help being tiresome desiring to express my thoughts to one I so much love, honor, and confide in. I am with every Good wish affectionately yours . . .

Our little spiteful Fool[219] has withdrawn his Petition. I am satisfied he never intended to try it for in all this Time he had prepared no List of objections to the Members Voters. It is the Principle of His Family to give as much trouble & vexation as they can, and they pride themselves in doing so.

---

[213] Dowdeswell had led the opposition on the cider tax in 1763 and 1764 and became committed to its repeal on behalf of the 'Cyder men'. P. Langford, *The First Rockingham Administration, 1765–66* (Oxford, 1973), 214–15.

[214] Some of Conway's letters were published in the *Gentleman's Magazine*, Apr. 1766, and most were published in 1813 in *PH*, xvi, 112–20.

[215] Sir Francis Bernard (1712–79), 1st bt, of Nettleham; British-born governor of New Jersey 1758–60 and Massachusetts Bay Colony 1760–9. See Middlekauff, *The Glorious Cause*, 143–7, for Bernard's role during the Stamp Act crisis.

[216] Letter from Conway addressed to 'the Governor of a neighbouring colony'. *Gentleman's Magazine*, Apr. 1766.

[217] Those lords voting against the repeal of the Stamp Act: Camden, Cornwallis, Poulett, Shelburne and Torrington. *LJ*, xxxi, 262–3.

[218] The Declaratory Act or American Colonies Act 1766. 6 Geo. III, c.12.

[219] Sir William Owen of Orielton, Pembrokeshire.

225. [BL, Add. MS 51406, ff. 140–1][220]
John Campbell to Lord Holland, 29 April 1766
You are very happy in your Sons having made a Choice so agreable to you. I rejoice in your happiness, as all must who know, and think of you as I do. May you long enjoy it, and the Young Couple much longer.

I think Lord Shelburne has done great justice both to himself, and to Mr Calcraft who is most undoubtedly Tali dignus Amico.[221] If I am not mistaken, the one owes his most valuable Title, to the same Person [Holland] to whom the other owes his Riches. So they may well admire each others Honor, Honesty, truth, and Gratitude. Far be it from every honest Man to break in upon their sacred Friendship; but if His sublime Protectoral Highness[222] should, in imitation of an ancient benevolent Potentate, desire to make it a triple League; I wish he may be admitted. As to Mr R[igby] I confess honest Men are not apt to be suspicious; and being sometimes deceived, and ill treated, by supposed Friends, is not so grievous, as that constant suspicion which haunts those who, conscious of their own baseness, judge all of Mankind by themselves. Since that brave Gentleman openly shew'd himself I have often recollected an Incident the last Session you were in the House of Commons.[223] One day that I thought you had been ill treated by some of the, at that time, sub Ministers in that House; meeting Mr R[igby] in the Lobby, I express'd my resentment to him, who I made no doubt had, as your Friend, the same feeling; He made me no answer, but slipt from me. It struck me at first; but knowing the confidence you had in him, I persuaded my self that he was in a hurry, and his thoughts engaged before I spoke; or at worst, that his neglect was rather of the Man who spoke to him, than of you. However I now think I ought to have told you of it, and confess that, when I mention'd him to you last, I blamed you, when I was myself in fault; for I now planely see it was his guilty Conscience made him silent, and slip away.

If I had on tuesday morning 22[n]d instant seen a Motion, then intended to be made, I should have said that it was impertinent, nugatory, and ridiculous. The Resolution[224] pass'd that night, or rather the next morning does great honor to the Wisdom of the present Administration. I do not wish a change because I think frequent changes encrease the weakness, and confusion of this Government & Country; and in Truth I know not who to wish in their Places. The appearance is very bad, but I resolve to make myself easy like the Man, who when he was told the ship he was in was near sinking said what is that to me I am but a Passenger. I have wish'd myself in the House every time they have been overhauling what was done in former sessions, but I think that work is now pretty well finish'd. They have only to reverse Wilkes outlawry[225]

---

[220] Published privately in *Letters to Henry Fox*, ed. Ilchester.

[221] Juvenal, *Satires*, v, line 173: 'Such a worthy Friend'.

[222] Yet another term for Pitt.

[223] Fox was made Baron Holland of Foxley on 16 Apr. 1763. *LJ*, xxx, 404.

[224] *PH*, xvi, 207–9, regarding the illegality of general warrants to arrest persons accused of a libel (and if that person was an MP that it was also a breach of privilege). The motion passed in the affirmative 173 to 71. This was drawn into a bill, which was passed in the Commons, but was rejected in the Lords on 14 May 1766. *CJ*, xxx, 753–4.

[225] On 1 Nov. 1764 Wilkes was declared an outlaw for failing to appear at court for sentencing with regard to the publication of *North Briton*, No. 45, which had been declared a seditious libel. He was freed from outlawry on 8 June 1768.

bring him again into the House, and Address i.e. command the [King] to give him some lucrative employment for honor to be sure he does not want. I really think he has as much, or more, than P[itt] T[empl]e R[igby] C[alcra]ft Sh[elbu]rne and some others. I don't doubt Mr Secretary [Conway] would be very proud to be one of his Introducers.

I think it is best to laugh at what Wee cannot care or help. I am allways truly and affectionately yours . . .

226. [BL, Add. MS 51406, ff. 142–3]
John Campbell to Lord Holland, 11 July 1766
I was heartily glad to hear that you bore your journey to Kingsgate so well. I hope the sea air will have its usual effect and make you strong for your Expedition to Naples from which I do not doubt your receiving great Benefit. It is a grief to me that I could not see you. If I had no infirmity but Age I should at this time be confined here, for I am told, the Road between this & Carmarthen the first *great* Town[226] in our way to London, are in some parts allmost impassable for any Carriage, and probably this letter may swim several times before it reaches London. I hope you have better weather in the East than Wee have on this West Coast, for I think I scarce ever saw so much heavy rain in any summer. I fear it will do much hurt both to our Hay & Corn. Though this Place is naturally very dry.[227] Our two harvests are of much more consequence to us than who is in or out of the Cabinet; and as I can no more make fair weather there than here, I will not trouble my head about it. But look upon the Duke of Newcastle sheding classic tears over the statue of the late King, and the Americans worshiping those they erect to Mr Pitt of Burton Pynsent,[228] with as little concern as I would on any other Farce.

The more I see and hear of the other states Men the more I must honor one [Holland] whose access to Power gave me much joy, and whose retreat I so much lamented and shall continue to lament, though I could not blame, because I saw his Body had not strength to hold the Rudder, his Mind was so able to direct with Wisdom, Fortitude, and Integrity. But 'tis past and to regret is all in vane. I do not know Mr Upton, but I honor & wish well to any Man who is a sincere Friend of you.

My best wishes attend you & all your fellow Travellers being allways affectionately & faithfully . . .

I can not promise to let you go without receiving more trouble of this sort from me.

227. [BL, Add. MS 51406, ff. 144–5]
John Campbell to Lord Holland, 22 August 1766
Though I had pretty given up any concern about Politics, I cannot help asking your Opinion of the late jumble, and the present state of the Ministry, for in these Times I

---

[226] Carmarthen had a population of about 2,500–3,000 and was one of the largest towns in Wales at this time.

[227] Lack of groundwater (despite the wetness of the climate) in this part of Pembrokeshire caused problems for farmers well into the second half of the 19th century.

[228] In Somersetshire. The house was built by William Pitt after he had inherited the estate from Sir William Pynsent in the mid 1750s.

cannot think of using the word Settlement. You will be sensible that my curiosity is in great measure owing to my Sons being in Office.[229] An Event quite unexpected to me and I believe to him. He was at Bath intending to make some stay there, when he receiv'd, by a Messenger a letter from the Duke of Grafton to come and kiss the kings hand the next day. The Duke was extremely gentile and obliging, and I have no objection to his Grace.

There have been Times when such a Thing would have given me great joy. But I know not what to say, or think of it now, as I see no stability in Government and can look with no pleasure on a Cabinet where Chatham,[230] Camden, Shelburne sit.[231] Nor can I look with any esteme upon a Man who was so desireous to serve under Pitt. Lord Hillsborough[232] would be a credit I believe to any Administration. The violent Quarrel between the Par Nobile[233] gives me pleasure. The new E[arl of Chatham] has out witted his Brother in Law,[234] and fairly got rid of him; who has vented the rage of his disappointment in a curious Pamphlet Methinks you are very black quoth the Devil to the Collier. Pitt has sold his Popularity for a very good Price, he has no longer any use for that, or for Lord Temple. I heard that Lord Bute solemnly denies his having any hand in this Town, and I hope it is true. Have I lived to see R[ober]t H[arle]y make a Revolution in Administration, and W[illia]m Pitt dispose of all the great Offices as a Sovereign? Government is surely sunk very low. But I do not suppose the House will fall upon our Heads. And things may happen as contrary to the present appearance's, as they are to former expectations.

I must enquire after your health, which will be allways a serious concern to me, at this distance, for the very bad account I hear of every body of our Roads, and the continuance of my disorder leave no present, if any, hope of taking my wish'd for journey.

I shall rejoice to hear you have found benefit from the sea air, and hope sometimes to hear that you kindly remember your affectionate servant. My best wishes always . . .

228. [BL, Add. MS 51406, ff. 146–7]
Lord Holland, Lyon to John Campbell, 13 October 1766
I receiv'd your kind letter, of the 12th of September [not extant] just before I left England.[235] I thought you would like it better, that I should stay to acknowledge it,

---

[229] In Aug. 1766 Pryse Campbell was appointed one of the lords of the treasury, in the Chatham administration, which must have rankled.

[230] Pitt was created 1st earl of Chatham on 4 Aug. 1766.

[231] Chatham was lord privy seal and prime minister, Camden lord chancellor and Shelburne secretary of state for the southern department. Edmund Burke, in a speech of 1774, described the Chatham administration as one of 'patriots and courtiers', king's friends and republicans, Whigs and Tories . . . indeed a very curious show, but utterly unsafe to touch and unsure to stand on'. Cited in J. Brooke, *The Chatham Administration, 1766–68* (1956), 237. Campbell seems to have had similar feelings.

[232] Hillsborough was made first lord of trade by Chatham.

[233] *Par nobile fratrum*: A noble pair of brothers.

[234] 2nd Earl Temple, whose reconciliation with his brother George Grenville in May 1765 marked the beginning of the end for the close political friendship that existed between him and Pitt.

[235] The Hollands, with their youngest son, Henry, left England for France and then Italy on 23 Sept. 1766 and did not return until the summer of 1767.

till I was advanc'd in my journey. I am I think, I may now say much advanced in my recovery too. I am much better than when I left England. Insomuch that I have as little doubt, as I had, two months ago, hope, of comeing back again. I leave all thoughts of a Court & politicks, (incomprehensible if not absurd) and of all business, behind me; and find great benefit by doing so, my illness being; I am persuaded, chiefly upon my nerves. Lady Holland, whose kindness is proof against this long journey which she hates, is here and well. Ste[phen] & His Charming wife [Mary] and Charles [James Fox] and Harry[236] are so too, you are in Wales what have I to think of in England? We are setting out in a few days, some by sea some by land, for Naples. Fannen,[237] at my House in London will allways be able to tell you where I am. And how I am, or, if you chanse To enquire by a line, to send that line to Dear Sir, your most faithful, most oblig'd & most Affectionate Friend . . .

---

[236] Henry Edward (1755–1811).
[237] Mr Fannen was the Hollands' factotum. Ilchester, *Henry Fox*, ii, 285.

Chapter 9. 1767–71

229. [BL, Add. MS 51406, ff. 148–9]
John Campbell, London to Lord Holland, 20 August 1767
I luckily forgot to take an impression of your seal of Arms which, gives me a pretense to draw from you, I hope, a good account of your arrival and health at Kingsgate.

I had last monday an opportunity to enquire about Lord Ch[atha]m[1] I was inform'd he had been thought a little better, but was now worse, see's nobody, has at times, but not constantly, a very great tremor; but constantly. Spleen that to Misery swells each anxious thought. This I apprehend is to the highest degree; though I am told his understanding is not impair'd. But I believe the poor Man is in a most unhappy state. Thank God I can sincerely pity him though my Opinion is not Alter'd. Lucas[2] will have the Excise. It is believed to be a promise of Lord Ch[atha]ms brought forth & witness'd by Lord Granby.[3] Lowndes[4] is by some means, I don't know how, quite satisfied.

If Mankind could take warning, what a damp[5] would P's[6] present state of Body & Mind cast upon criminal Ambition. Mens Conscia Recti[7] can never be deprived of all Comfort. When I read as I have often done, the Lines of which I have now quoted one; I cannot help feeling some regret & envy for the great, the undeserved honor done to R[igby]. But when I think that he could not only cast off such a Friendship, but receive and ever shew those lines, without feeling the most bitter remorse, and expressing the deepest sense of shame, sorrow and repentance, I regularly despise, and detest him.

My best wishes ever attened your Lady Holland and all your Family. And nothing can hinder me being proud to avow to all the World that I am Lord Holland's Friend.

230. [BL, Add. MS 51406, f. 150]
Lord Holland, Nice to John Campbell, 6 March 1768
I was so happy as not to hear from Fannen of your severe illness till I heard of your recovery. I am glad to see your hand again, which is as good, and I hope you are as well, as ever. Your letter did not come to me so soon, as, by it's date it should have done,

---

[1] Chatham's health had deteriorated badly in 1767. His mental health was of particular concern. Lady Chatham was given power of attorney for his affairs in August. M. Peters, *The Elder Pitt* (1998), 182.

[2] Anthony Lucas was made a commissioner for the revenue of excise. *London Evening Post*, 29 Aug. 1767.

[3] General John Manners (1721–70), marquess of Granby; MP for Grantham 1741–54 and Cambridgeshire 1754–70. He was appointed commander-in-chief of the army by Chatham in 1766.

[4] Richard Lowndes (?1707–75), of Winslow, Buckinghamshire; MP for Buckinghamshire 1741–74.

[5] A discouragement or check. *OED.*

[6] Pitt.

[7] Virgil, *Aeneid*, i, line 604: A mind conscious of integrity.

which I mention for fear, Tho' I think you would hardly imagine I should not thank you, as I do, by the first Post.

You are too wise to let any Election thoughts disturb you, except about your son's. That by what I read in the papers, is I suppose as I hope, secure.[8] I shall let mine know how you command his advertisement,[9] which will please him prodigiously. Your namesake Doctor Campbell,[10] commands it too. For my part upon looking it over, I think it is well enough, But at first the length of it only struck me I must confess. He will be mighty pleas'd with your approbation, and they write me word His election is sure. I know little from England, and nothing is to be learnt here; two days ago our winter begun, which I am told will not last above two days more. It dos not affect me, nor is it worse than such weather as we have very often in England in the midst of Summer. I continue as I have been these three months, and that they tell me, is very well; and I can't deny that I am so. But then . . .[11]

231. [BL, Add. MS 51406, ff. 151–2]
Lord Holland, Lyon to My Best Friend, 20 April 1768
Mr Fannen gives me your letter of March the 3rd the Cardigan Election was over, long before I received it, and I am very glad to see it ended, as we wish'd.

Fannen came here, to fetch Harry, But we can't find in our Hearts, to part with him, so he will set out with us, on Monday, and by a round about way, on purpose, to lengthen our Journey; I fancy we shall be at Calais, the 18th or 19th of May.

Let me beg you to write to your Son [Pryse] and speak early, to Sir Richard Phillips, & other Friends, in my son Ste[phen]'s favour.[12] I think verily a Deputy Recorder, can have one vote, & that is the only Question in his Case. Surely Dear Sir, what you foretold, as soon to happen, is begun & has made great progress already; at least I see, in a very serious light, Mr Wilkes's Triumph[13] over Religion, Law, Majesty, & Liberty; & Liberty destroy'd, under the name and pretence of Liberty. I think it Portends, the approach of some great Mischief. I should not know what to advise But I thank God, I am not to advise. And whatever may be deem'd proper, I don't see, where there is Spirit, or resolution enough, to go through with it.

Irresolution, has been a General fault, & is surely, a most fatal Weakness. I think *Pitt* almost the only Man, that I have seen in Power, who had not that *fault*, tho' he had

---

[8] Pryse Campbell was elected for Cardigan boroughs, 24 Mar. 1768.

[9] Charles' election address to the voters of Midhurst, Sussex.

[10] Dr John Campbell (1708–75), historian, who wrote, inter alia, *The Present state of Europe* (1750) and *Political Survey of Britain* (1774).

[11] Letter ends.

[12] Referring to efforts to obtain a Commons seat for Stephen Fox? He failed to win the election of Mar. 1768 for Salisbury, losing to the standing member Edward Bouverie. *Lloyd's Evening Post*, 18 Mar. 1768. Earl of Ilchester, *Henry Fox, First Lord Holland* (2 vols, 1920), ii, 326, states that Stephen had to 'face a strenuous six months' work, in order to woo the electors of New Sarum [Salisbury]', before he became an MP in Nov. 1768.

[13] Wilkes, despite still being an outlaw, had won the Middlesex election at the end of March. He gave himself up to the king's bench on 20 Apr., the first day of the parliamentary session. Lord Chief Justice Mansfield stated that he did not recognise anyone in the court who was an outlaw, and Wilkes was free to go. He presented himself a week later and this time was arrested and taken to the king's bench prison to await trial. A.H. Cash, *John Wilkes: The Scandalous Father of Civil Liberty* (2006), 210–14.

many *others*; for which Reason, I wish he was again well; & for the first time in my Life, should be glad to see Him, at the head of every thing;[14] Undertaking to stem that Torrent, which he so long, & so much Contributed to severally. I hope, I shall be too wise, to let my Comfort, if any still remains for me, be embitter'd, by failing as I do, in my last request. But my Dear Mr Campbell don't impute *Calcrafts* exorbitant riches[15] to me; I gave him, & was continually giving him, the means. But the use he made of those means, was not inspired, nor was he assisted in it, by me. As to his Ingratitude, you must allow me to say, that it was impossible to suspect. One so oblig'd, & who had no Interest in it, no conviction whatever & could get nothing by his Ingratitude. I had read that *you may oblige a Man, 'till you make him your Enemy*; (which must have been Calcrafts Case) but I look'd upon it, as the Ingenuity, rather than the opinion of the Writer. I had, and indeed, have even now, no notion of it. I would be justify'd to you Dear Sir in every thing. I hope I shall be able, to bear the abuse, which I see pursues me still, and which a less partial Eye than yours, must easily see I don't deserve.

Adieu! My Dear Sir, my mind gives me, to believe what I sincerely wish, that some how, when I come to England, I shall see you again. I hope at Holland House, which is now Lady Hollands, who will be very glad to see you, because indeed she thinks of you, as you deserved [*sic*], I hope you will of me, that I shall ever be most faithfully, & affectionately, yours . . .

232. [BL, Add. MS 51406, ff. 153–4]
Lord Holland, Kingsgate to John Campbell, 26 August 1768
I am afraid (and Lady Holland says I do) that I write too seriously about my low spirits. Your kind letter of Aug[ust] 19th [not extant] shews so much regard for me, that I would not upon any account let you remain in such an error about me; as I thank God you are If you think I am absolutely void of chearfullness. Indeed I talk a good deal of chearfull nonsense in a day & in every day. The truth is, that I divert myself, but yet cannot help thinking very often, that it were better it were all over and these thoughts I call low spirits; But are indeed the affects of old age. I am as much out in the air as you can wish me, and in my one Horse chair or post chaise every day, eat and drink only what experience has taught me agrees with me, and, taught by experience too, have nothing to do with Physick or Physicians.

My Tower in honor of Mr Harley[16] is built I believe more for my private amusement than from Publick spirit. But he is really allmost the only man that has not been a Coward. This gave me the thought, But I own the desire of makeing Kingsgate still

---

[14] Chatham was nominally still head of the administration – until mid Oct. 1768 – but continued ill health kept him away from parliament.

[15] See Chapter 5, Note 16.

[16] Thomas Harley (1730–1804), of Berrington, Herefordshire; MP for London 1761–8 and Herefordshire 1776–1802. Alderman of London 1761–1804; sheriff of London 1763–4; lord mayor of London 1767–8. As mayor he was responsible for putting down a riot at St George's Field – the site of the king's bench prison where Wilkes was being held – on 10 May 1768 (the opening day of parliament), in support of Wilkes. Several people lost their lives in what was to become known as the St George's Field massacre. Harley was praised by parliament for the part he played, and asked the king to award him with a mark of distinction. He was made a privy councillor. There is a good account of the riot and the turmoil in London at this time in support of Wilkes in Cash, *John Wilkes*, 222–5.

prettier than it is, put it in execution. I have not the least acquaintance with Mr Harley, which made me like doing it all the better. I will find some means soon, of sending you a sketch of it, and some other things here. I would have this letter go to day, so must not say a word more than yours ever . . .

The weather whatever it is dos not affect me at all.

233. [BL, Add. MS 51406, ff. 155–6]
Lord Holland, Kingsgate to John Campbell, 21 September 1768
I read in yours of Sept[ember] the 9th [not extant] the letter of an amiable, sensible, and good natur'd Man. I honor you for it, without being at all surprised. Who ever had Children, that do not when they are young men, do, what their Fathers had rather they would not do? I have found it, Dear Mr Campbel, in a very essential instance and, Memor illum puerum isse, me fuisse,[17] I acted as you do, and I dare say you will applaud yourself for the success of your good natured behaviour. I do not repent mine. Ste[phen]'s marriage indeed, was with my consent, and His, the happyest, choice, man ever made. But he could not have made it, not have been ever happy, had I acted, as I have seen many Fathers act, upon less provocation. You & I Mr Campbel, have from dispositions, thank God, better, and greater, happyness than Popularity can give; But still old age annihilates all happyness, and I cannot imagine the reason why mine should be worse to me than yours. That yours is better than mine I am very glad.

Your catalogue of the objects of Popular applause, and your reason why Lord Ch[atha]m is no longer Popular (which I veryly believe is the true one) are delightfull. Inclosed you have Harley Tower and the inscriptions upon it. It is entirely finished except the Vases upon the basement and I don't yet know whether I shall not put some Eagles upon that, instead of four Vases.

I shall soon send you something else.

I find I can send one by this post upon the Hill, two or three hundred yards from the House, there are two Tumuli, or Hillocks, time out of mind called Hackendume banks,[18] under which (for they have been opened) are sculls and bones; and there, I last year, Built what I send you. My Friend Mr Wynn[19] gives me the designs, and I think them very Pretty. There are more done and doing, which I will send you, if they amuse you; and which will give me more opportunity of telling you, how sincerely I am . . .

234. [BL, Add. MS 51406, ff. 157–8]
Lord Holland, Kingsgate to John Campbell, 16 October 1768
I am very sorry to find in you letter of October the 4th [not extant], that your Eldest son [Pryse], has so painful an Illness, which However, often goes off, without being apt to return, & I heartily wish that may be his case.

---

[17] Remembering that he is a boy, and I was one.

[18] Hackemdown Tower was built on this site by Holland, who assumed he had discovered the site of a Saxon–Danish battle.

[19] Thomas Wynne, architect.

I hear from London, that the Queen's Pardon, only waits for Miss Meadows's, and that Mrs Campbell,[20] will have the first bed Chamber, Womans, place that falls. Your son too, cannot want hands ready to help him, & upon the whole, it will be a very happy Match, I dare say. I am a great Friend to Matches of Inclination.

I think Eagles, will be better than Vases, & have order'd them, there are no Stairs. Harley Tower, is to be look'd at, not from; and I agree with you, in thinking, that the lower opening is too long one Bushel of Flints, in two hours time, may cure that, next year. I shan't send you any more draughts, because all the things I have done here, that are thought, in the least worth it, are going to be engrav'd, and as fast as they are done, you shall have them. We shall never agree, (& for your sake, I am glad of it) about Old Age.

On Thursday I go to Holland House, Lady Holland is there already, & Ste[phen] and Lady Mary, in Wiltshire. Adieu!

235. [BL, Add. MS 51406, ff. 159–60]
Lord Holland, Piccadilly to John Campbell, 22 December 1768
Why can't I answer your letter of Dec[ember] the 9th [not extant] as I wish'd to do? I have this week been unable to answer it as I must; with expressions of the deepest concern for you and Mrs Campbell; which I can say nothing to alleviate.

Oh wearisome condition of mortality! My only reason for writeing, is, least you should think me the very worst of those bad creatures men, as I should be if I forgot you. When I hear that it would not be Impertinent to try to entertain you with any of their follies, I will write again; in the mean time, I remain with grief of heart your most faithfull . . .[21]

236. [BL, Add. MS 51406, ff. 161–2]
Lord Holland to John Campbell, 18 April 1769
I don't know what to say about the mistake, Charles made; as to the Frank, But that I am glad, that you found it out.

I cannot help believing, as I sincerely wish, that Lady F[ortescue's] situation may henceforth be a very happy one; Her joy on the occasion, I hope promises, I am sure it deserves it.

You lament the Times, I wish you may not have, every day, more reason, it is easy to point out, the Men, & their Weakness, or Wickedness, which have brought things to this pass, But I am afraid it is already, difficult to cure the mischief that has been done. I wish most sincerely, you was now in the House to try, and you would have this satisfaction, that not one Man in the House, whom you have any opinion of, would not be ready to join with you. Both my sons, would attend you, & I can with pleasure tell

---

[20] Frances Meadows, only daughter of Sir Phillip Meadows, married Captain Alexander Campbell, of the 3rd regiment of guards, on 3 Sept. 1768. Frances had been made a maid of honour to Queen Charlotte in 1761, which she had to give up on her marriage and seek pardon from the queen, before she could again hold office in the queen's household. However she never became a woman of the bedchamber. IHR, http://www.history.ac.uk/resources/office/queencharlotte; CRO, FJ/13, Cawdor pedigree.

[21] This letter is Holland's response to the news that Pryse Campbell had died on 14 Dec. 1768.

you, they neither want Courage, nor ability. Ste[phen] has spoke[22] once or twice upon this occasion, & very well. But I am told, that few in Parliament, ever spoke better, than Charles did on Friday.[23] Off hand with rapidity, with spirit, & such knowledge of what he was talking of, as surprize'd every body, in so young a Man.[24] If you think this Vanity, I am sure you will forgive it.

And Now, to my Narrative. On Thursday [12 April], Mr Wilkes stood at Brentford Nominated by Mr Sawbridges[25] & seconded by Lord Shelbourn [Shelburne']s Young Townshend,[26] in a speech that I believe, you would think Treasonable; they had both been in the House, when, without a Division, Mr Wilkes was declar'd, incapable of being elected.[27] Yet they propos'd Him. I think they should have been expell'd, But as I don't know, the motive for not doing it, I am not a Judge.[28] Mr Luttrel[29] was named by Mr Dodd,[30] seconded by my Son, Ste[phen]. Mr Luttrel was not supported, as he had reason to expect, Great pains indeed were taken, to intimidate, and with too much effect. When it came to the House, Mr Dowdeswell &c Oppos'd, sending for the Return, or proceeding, 'till a Petition should be prevented, then my son Charles spoke. The Division was 207 against 115[31] & on Saturday, the Motion was, that Mr Luttrel ought to have been return'd. The Division was 197 to 143[32] and the Return was amended. It was a very long, & fine debate. The Attorney General,[33] spoke excessive well, & with great spirit, so did Thurlow, Jenkinson,[34] Dyson,[35] Sir F[letcher] Norton, most convincingly, to the Question, but no

---

[22] Stephen Fox made 'crisp and concise contributions' to debates in the Commons but had 'acquired an unhappy knack of making himself appear ridiculous; and this, combined with a surprising rotundity of figure for one so young, prevented his contemporaries from taking him seriously'. Ilchester, *Henry Fox*, ii, 350–1.

[23] *CJ*, xxxii, 385, 14 Apr. 1769. In the debate on the Middlesex election, in which Fox spoke in support of Luttrell. Fox's speech is not reported in *PH*, xvi.

[24] Fox was 21 at this time and had been an MP since he was 19, which was technically illegal.

[25] John Sawbridge (1732–95), of Olantigh, Kent; MP for Hythe 1768–74 and London 1774–95. Sawbridge was also alderman of London 1769; sheriff of London 1769–70; lord mayor of London 1775.

[26] James Townsend (1737–87), of Bruce Castle, Tottenham, Middlesex; MP for West Looe 1767–74 and Calne 1772–87. Alderman of London 1769; sheriff of London 1769–70; lord mayor of London 1772–3. Shelburne was a close friend of Townsend's and supported his political ambitions.

[27] 17 Feb. 1769. However, there had been a division, the vote being 235 to 89 in favour of expulsion. *CJ*, xxxii, 228–9.

[28] The ministry did discuss ways of expelling Sawbridge and Townsend, but finally decided not to do so. Cash, *John Wilkes*, 251.

[29] Sir Henry Lawes Luttrell (?1737–1821), of Painshill, Surrey; MP for Bossiney 1768–9 and 1774–84, Middlesex 1769–74 and Ludgershall 1817–21.

[30] John Dodd (1717–82), of Swallowfield, Berkshire; MP for Reading 1741 and 1755–82.

[31] *CJ*, xxxii, 385; *PH*, xvi, 585.

[32] *CJ*, xxxii, 387; *PH*, xvi, 588.

[33] William de Grey (1719–81), MP for Newport 1716–70 and Cambridge University 1770–1. Solicitor-general to the queen 1761–3; solicitor-general 1763–6; attorney-general 1766–71; lord chief justice, common pleas 1771–80. De Grey entered politics mainly to further his legal career. *HPC, 1754–90*, ii, 308.

[34] Charles Jenkinson (1729–1808), of Addiscombe, Surrey; MP for Cockermouth 1761–6, Appleby 1767–72, Harwich 1772–4, Hastings 1774–80 and Saltash 1780–6.

[35] Jeremiah Dyson (?1722–76), of Stoke, Guildford, Surrey; MP for Yarmouth, Isle of Wight 1762–8, Weymouth and Melcombe Regis 1768–74 and Horsham 1774–6. He was clerk to the house of commons 1748–62; secretary to the treasury 1762–4; lord of the treasury 1768–74; cofferer to the household 1774–6. An expert in parliamentary procedure, Dyson was called upon to write a paper regarding the 'most efficacious as well as the most proper mode of effecting the expulsion' of Wilkes. *HPC, 1754–90*, ii, 373, citing Lord Grafton.

farther. Mr Grenville who was in the Minority spoke better than he ever did before, in the opinion of every Body, but[36] my son Charles.

I believe, from what I have heard, out of his speech, you would have been of Charles's opinion, and would not have been less willingly of the Majority, because Ste[phen] with *the Calcrafts*, were on the other side, under the Auspices, and Eye of Lord Temple, who sat there, 'till two o'clock in the morning. Indeed, indeed, Mr Campbell, he is a worse Man, than ever Lord Chatham was. A Mr Payne[37] M[ember] of P[arliament] for Shaftsbury, spoke most excessively well,[38] I am told for the Question, & the great Mr Burke,[39] very ill, against it. What is to be done now, I don't know, But whatever the Populace can do, they are very ready for. It is most certain that the Mob, that went to St James's, was hired, & yet the Attorney General [William de Grey], cannot yet get legal evidence of it, nor has a reward of six hundred Pounds yet discover'd the Man who broke Mr Rose's Coach & almost kill'd him.[40] I am sometimes in hopes, that this being without dispute, a Contest,[41] not with any particular Man, but with the House of Commons, is a lucky Circumstance I don't well see, how they can Assasinate or depose a House of Commons, as I dare say they would very readily do, a Minister, or a King. But if this Circumstance is Comfort, it is not such a one, as I would wish to send Mr Campbell, I hope he will send one better. Adieu! Adieu!

237. [BL, Add. MS 51406, ff. 163–5]
Lord Holland to John Campbell, 11 May 1769
I delayed thanking you, for your kind letter of April the 27th [not extant] 'till the Parliament should be up, which it was, on Thursday.[42] After a Debate of Monday[43] 'till two o'clock on Tuesday Morning, in which I am told, (& willingly believe it), Charles Fox spoke extremely well it was all off Hand,[44] all argumentative; in reply, to Mr Burke, & Mr Wedderbourn; & excessively well indeed; I hear it spoke of by every Body as a

---

[36] Meaning 'except'.

[37] Ralph Payne (1739–1807), MP for Shaftesbury 1768–71, Camelford 1776–80, Plympton Erle 1780–4 and New Woodstock 1795–9. He was created Baron Lavington (Irish peerage) in 1795. He was governor of the Leeward Isles 1771–5 and 1799–1807 and clerk of the green cloth 1777–82.

[38] Walpole said his language was 'wonderfully verbose' and that a defence of the administration he and Dr Johnson were preparing was using words so long 'that the reply must be printed in a pamphlet so large as an atlas, but in Elzevir type, or the first sentence would fill twenty pages octavo'. *The Yale Edition of Horace Walpole's Correspondence*, ed. W.S. Lewis et al. (48 vols, New Haven, CT, 1937–83), xxxiii: Walpole to Lady Upper Ossory, 14 Nov. 1779.

[39] Edmund Burke (1727–97), of Beaconsfield, Buckinghamshire; MP for Wendover 1765–74, Bristol 1774–80 and Malton 1780–94. Private secretary to the first lord of the treasury 1765–6; paymaster general 1782–3. Burke most famously wrote *Reflections on the Revolution in France* (1790).

[40] Hugh Ross, septuagenarian, merchant of the City of London, was attacked by the mob on 22 Mar. 1769. One of the mob hit Ross several times with a hammer. The king offered a reward of £500 and Ross offered £100. *Gazeteer and New Daily Advertiser*, 10 Apr. 1769.

[41] The parliamentary and constitutional battle over the unseating of Wilkes in favour of Luttrell. The Commons had voted the latter duly elected on 15 Apr., though he came last in the poll. Only in the winter of 1770 did the 'uproar about the Middlesex election die down in the House of Commons'. *HPC, 1754–90*, i, 331–5, and iii, 65; Cash, *John Wilkes*.

[42] Parliament was prorogued on Tuesday, 9 May (*CJ*, xxxii, 453), not Thursday which was the day Holland wrote the letter.

[43] 8 May 1769. *CJ*, xxxii, 451.

[44] That is, extemporaneous.

most extraordinary thing, and am, You see, not a little pleas'd with it. My son Ste[phen], spoke too; (as they say, he always dos) very short, & to the purpose, they neither of them aim at Oratory, make apologye, or speak of themselves, but go directly to the purpose, so I do not doubt, they will continue speakers. But I am told Charles can never make a better speech, than he did on Monday.

I send you a List of the Speakers, & the Numbers. I hear Nortons Speech, was the best that ever was made and convincing to the Last degree. Lord Temple, Lord Shelbourne, G[eorge] Grenville, Lord Rockingham, & Lord Lyttelton, Notwithstanding, all their disagreements, are now thoroughly united, to carry on, the Wick'd work they have been always engaged in, when they have not been in place, and dined together with the Minority on Tuesday at the Thatch'd House;[45] Invited by Mr Dowdswell [Dowdeswell], when they were all together in the Lobby.

The King was extremely insulted, when He went to The House,[46] which I should hope, might make Him, less unconcern'd, than He seems to be, He carry's himself so, it is really hard to know, whether He is concern'd or not. A Lord who is near Him, told me, that after the Great Riot[47] at St James's or rather in the midst of it, when he came out to the Levee! You could not find out either in his Countenance or His Conversation, that every thing, was not quiet, as usual. My notion of the Mob is, that it is hired by French Money; that D'Eon,[48] is a distributor of it; & that Lord Temple, & Lord Shelbourne, encourage it. You are mistaken in thinking, I cou'd be of service, If I was consulted, for I really cannot foresee the Consequences, nor the design, of what they are about, and should therefore not know how to advise.

Mr Wilkes has quarrel'd with His Friends,[49] because He says, they divert the attention of the Publick from him. They do so, & I believe He is near, meeting with His reward, a just Contempt, as well as abhorrence; But the Spirit of disorder, Licentiousness, & faction, still continues; & whether 'twill be better or worse, for not flowing from Mr Wilkes's direction, I can't tell.

You must Observe I don't mention Lord Chatham, no body dos now, and that is a Step as far as it goes to your more favourable opinion of Him, I believe.

Lord Temple has been telling Lies these three Months and no longer ago than Sunday last, assured several People That Lord Chatham, had prevailed to have the Prorogation of the Parliament put off for three or four days, & would come down on Monday & speak; whereas the poor Man, has all the time, been confirm'd to His Room, if not to

---

[45] The Thatched House Tavern, St James's Street, Westminster.

[46] The house of lords on 9 May 1769. *LJ*, xxii, 382.

[47] The St George's Field riots of 10 May 1769.

[48] Chevalier d'Éon (1728–1810), French diplomat, spy, soldier and cross-dresser. In 1763 he became plenipotentiary minister in London, but was superseded by a new French ambassador, which led to his falling out with the French king and his exile in London where he remained until 1774.

[49] In Feb. 1769 the Society of Supporters of the Bill of Rights formed as a defence against what it thought were the king's increasing powers. It believed that Wilkes was the only man capable of standing up to this encroachment, so agreed to pay off his debts which they accepted had been accrued in the fight for liberty. However, by Apr. 1769, the Society, now called the Bill of Rights Society, divided, with several members resigning (encouraged by Lord Shelburne) over the continued payment of Wilkes' debts. Although they appeared to be standing against Wilkes, the splinter group still agreed with him on all other aspects of the defence of liberty. Cash, *John Wilkes*, 249, 289–91; *ODNB*.

his Bed. If I know nothing else of Lord Temple, but this profligate & scandalous lying disposition, I should hate him, as I do.

Except two or three days, that I shall go to Kingsgate I shall be, to be found here, and never so happy as when found by you. You may then tell my Sons, what they have desir'd me to ask of you. Whether you cared about the Pembrokeshire Petition,[50] & what part you wou'd have them take in it. Did they get any instructions from Pembrokeshire at Last? Which I see is Asserted in the Newspapers, If they did not, I think the Sheriff,[51] should advertize the falsity of it.

Ever dear sir . . .

The Question was that Mr Luttrel is duly Elected.
Ayes 221   Noes 152[52]   Majority 69
Tellers for the Ayes:
Sir Alexander Gilmore   p[53]
Mr Bradshaw[54]   p

For the Noes
Frederick Montagu   c[55]
Mr Harboard[56]   c

Speakers
Dowdswell [Dowdeswell]   contra
Stanley   Pro
Sir G[eorge] Osborne   p
Lord J[ohn] Cavendish   c
Blackiston   p
Glynn   c
Ellis   p
Grenville   c
Norton   p
Sir G[eorge] Saville   c
Half an hour after one[57]
Wedderbourn [Wedderburn]   c
Thurlow   p

[50] Regarding the 1768 election. *CJ*, xxxii, 755–6.

[51] Thomas Skyrme, of Vaynor, Pembrokeshire.

[52] *CJ*, xxxii, 451.

[53] 'Pro', that is, for Luttrell being placed as MP for Middlesex.

[54] Sir Alexander Gilmour (c.1737–92), 3rd bt, of Craigmillar, Edinburgh; MP for Edinburghshire 1761–74; Thomas Bradshaw (1733–74), of Hampton Court; MP for Harwich 1767–8 and Saltash 1768–74. Clerk in the war office 1757–9 and first clerk 1760–1; chief clerk at the treasury 1761–3; commissioner of taxes 1763–7; secretary to the treasury 1767–70; lord of the admiralty 1772–4.

[55] 'Contra', that is, opposed to Luttrell being elected MP for Middlesex.

[56] Frederick Montagu (1733–1800), of Papplewick, Nottinghamshire; MP for Nottingham 1759–68 and Higham Ferrrers 1768–90. Lord of the treasury 1782–3; Harbord Harbord (1734–1810), of Gunton Hall and Suffield, Norfolk; MP for Norwich 1756–86. Created Baron Suffield in 1786.

[57] In the morning. The time at that point in the debate.

Cornwall   c
A[nne] Powlett   p
Morton   p
Burke   c
C[harles] Fox   p
Seymour   c
Whitworth   c
Seymour   c
Blackiston   p
Cavendish   c
Beckford   c
S[tephen] Fox   p
Barre   c
Col. Onslow   p
Grenville[58]   c

238. [BL, Add. MS 51406, ff. 168–9]
Lord Holland, Nice to John Campbell, 4 March 1770
I have your kind letter of the 9th of Feb[ruary] [not extant]. Lady Holland desires me to tell you, that she is very much oblig'd to you, and that the fine weather, and the very fine accounts of Charles that we have here, have done her great good. They have given me, as much pleasure as I am capable of, But they cannot make me set much value upon my life; or even prevent my being sorry, every day, that I cannot foresee, as I us'd to

[58] Sir George Osbourn (1742–1818), 4th bt, of Chicksands Priory, Bedfordshire; MP for Northampton 1768–9, Bossiney 1769–74, Penryn 1774–80 and Horsham 1780–4. Groom of the bedchamber 1770–1812; Lord John Cavendish (1732–96), MP for Weymouth and Melcombe Regis 1754–61, Knaresborough 1761–8, York 1768–84 and Derbyshire 1794–6. Lord of the treasury 1765–6; chancellor of the exchequer 1782–3. Lord John said in this debate that he was sorry the Commons 'have got into so unbecoming a contest with so unworthy an antagonist [Wilkes]'. According to Walpole, who opposed Lord John, the latter inflamed the party towards Pitt by resigning his treasury office. H. Walpole, *Memoirs of the Reign of King George the Third* (4 vols, 1894), ii, 250; William Blackstone (1723–80), of Wallingford, Berkshire; MP for Hindon 1761–8 and Westbury 1768–70. Solicitor-general to the queen 1763–70; Blackstone was attacked after the debate in which George Grenville pointed out that the lawyer's speech confuted his own *Commentaries on the English Law* (1765–9) with regard to the expulsion of Wilkes, since Blackstone mostly followed the government in speaking against the radical MP. *ODNB*; John Glynn (1722–79), of Cardinham, Cornwall; MP for Middlesex 1768–9. Sergeant at law 1763; recorder of London 1772–9. Glynn was Wilkes's lawyer. At the Middlesex election Glynn's opponent, Sir William Proctor, hired a mob led by the then notorious Edward Macquirk. This mob killed a lawyer by the name of George Clarke and the poll was closed until the end of the year, when Glynn won. Cash, *John Wilkes*, 235–6; probably George Grenville, rather than his brothers Henry (1717–84) or James (1715–83), the former never having a speech recorded, and the latter opposed to all George would have stood for, especially his opposition to the expulsion of Wilkes; Sir George Saville (1726–84), 8th bt, of Thornhill, Yorkshire and Rufford, Nottinghamshire; MP for Yorkshire 1759–83. One of the most respected men in the Commons, he believed the voting of Luttrell as MP for Middlesex after Wilkes had clearly won the poll to be an 'attack on the right of electors freely to choose their representatives'. *HPC, 1754–90*, iii, 407; Charles Wolfran Cornwall (1735–89), of Barton Priors; MP for Grampound 1768–74, Winchelsea 1774–80 and Rye 1780–9. Lord of the treasury 1774–80 and speaker of the house of Commons 1780–9. Anne Poulett (1711–85), MP for Bridgwater 1769–85; John Morton (?1714–80), of Tackley, Oxon; MP for Abingdon 1747–70, New Romney 1770–4 and Wigan 1775–80. Attorney-general to the queen 1770–80, deputy high steward, Oxford University 1770–80; Henry Seymour (1727–1807), of Sherborne, Dorset; MP for Totnes 1763–8, Huntingdon 1768–74 and Evesham 1774–80. Groom of the bedchamber 1763–5. Active follower of George Grenville; Richard Whitworth (?1734–1811), of Batchacre, Staffordshire; MP for Stafford 1768–80.

think I could, that it would soon end. 'Tho my sons have, and indeed I believe they have, as much honesty, and good nature as comes to any bodys share. I think I am myself an example, of how little use that may happen to be to them. You know the news you heard of Charles & Ellis,[59] was true, and I believe you hear, as I do, a very good account of Lord North[60] of whom, without knowing him, I have a very high opinion; but whether good omens will be follow'd by good events or no, you will not wonder that I don't guess; you may be glad, if you will, that I don't try. You are very kind in wishing to see my name in my own hand writeing. I can add to it, with the greatest truth, that I am with the greatest esteem, Dear Sir . . .

I just now heard that Sir Richard Philips has at lost his Election,[61] which for your sake, I am very sorry for. But both my sons I find attended for him to the last. I could not easily have forgiven them if they had not.

239. [BL, Add. MS 51406, f. 170]
Lord Holland, Holland House to John Campbell, 18 June 1770
I would not write to you whilst I was in such Pain as I have been for these three weeks, from a very large Tumour on my Thigh, which broke during the journey. I was in very great pain till Saturday, I am now free from it. This is a great deal to say, and all that I shall ever be able to say that will please you, for I am very ill, and in extreme low spirits. I thank you kindly for your letter, which I found at Calais, and was glad to hear, since I came home, that the best speech Charles has made, was on the Pembrokeshire Election. I am Dear Sir . . .

240. [BL, Add. MS 51406, ff. 171–2]
Lord Holland, Holland House to Dear Sir,[62] 21 June 1770
I have just receiv'd your letter of June the 14th [not extant]. I have allready told you how falsely the Newspapers, represented my health, (as they allways do, every thing that relates to me) Such as my haveing been at the Kings Levee, Haveing conference with Ministers &c. I have not talk'd nor am I able to talk of any business. I have not seen any body, But my own Family and a few private acquaintance, Nor been once out of the

---

[59] Charles being made a lord of the admiralty in Feb. and Welbore Ellis being made joint vice-treasurer (Ireland), though not officially until Apr. 1770.

[60] Frederick North (1732–92), Lord North (a courtesy title allowing him to sit in the Commons – he was heir to the earl of Guildford); MP for Banbury 1754–90. Lord of the treasury 1759–65; joint paymaster general 1766–7; chancellor of the exchequer 1767–82; first lord of the treasury 1770–82; home secretary 1783; leader of the house of commons 1783; president of the Foundling Hospital 1771–92. North considered that Wilkes' expulsion from the Commons was the correct decision, believing his behaviour to be 'unconstitutional and a threat to law and order'. The parliamentary battles over Wilkes, during the first five months of 1769, 'laid the foundation for North's long ministry', his worth as a parliamentarian rising greatly in the eyes of his colleagues in the House. *ODNB*. He formed the short-lived North–Fox coalition administration in 1783, with Charles James Fox.

[61] The Pembrokeshire election of 1768 was declared void in the House when it was decided there had been an irregular poll and it was thus impossible to decide upon a winning candidate. At the ensuing by-election Philipps put up John Symmons of Llanstinsant, who refused the poll because the sheriff decided to hold the election at Pembroke, an Owen stronghold, rather than the county town, Haverfordwest. Hence the tory Hugh Owen was returned, keeping the seat until his death in 1786, when Philipps once again became the county MP. *HPC, 1754–90*, i, 467; P.D.G. Thomas, *Politics in Eighteenth-Century Wales* (Cardiff, 1998), 206–7.

[62] Written by Holland's amanuensis, hence addressed to 'Dear Sir'.

chair I sit in, since I came. I told you in my last, that I was free from Pain. I can with pleasure say, that I continue so. This is all I shall ever have to bragg of, and I hope to God it will continue for it is a great deal I am very glad to tell you (though I much doubt whether it will do much good) That Beckford is dead.[63] I am glad of it, Because he was the most ill natur'd being, I believe, that ever existed. I never pretended to guess at Lord Chatham's intentions; I never comprehended him; But I did not expect that I shou'd be at the same loss about his words, yet I am assur'd (by several Ear witnesses of veracity) That in one speech in the House of Lords,[64] He said, 'That the Livery of London, was a most respectable part of the Constitution; older than King Lords & Commons, and that *Androgeus* was Lord Mayor of London, when Julias Ceasar came here.' Where did he find this? and what could he mean by a Lord Mayor & Livery, where every body went stark naked?

In another speech,[65] he said 'Your Lordships have all of you read Robertson's life of Charles the 5th.[66] It is a very proper Book to read *under the shade of a tall oak tree*'. For God's sake what could this mean? And yet you may be assur'd that he said both these things. I find he appears to be as well in health, as ever he was, and that his speaking, of which I was always a great admirer, meets with great applause. Well I have some hopes, that he will not immediately find a person to succeed Beckford. And so I bid you adieu? [*sic*] giving you very many thanks, on Lady Holland & Charles's account, as well as on my own.

241. [BL, Add. MS 51406, ff. 173–4]
Lord Holland's amanuensis at Holland House to John Campbell, 8 September 1770
Lord Holland haveing found a friend of his alarm'd at seeing the news Paper, that he was dangerously ill at Kingsgate, thinks it right to let Mr Campbell (whom he is proud to think his friend) know that he has not been at Kingsgate But is at Holland House, better than when he wrote last to Mr Campbell; whom he assures that he dos not remember that he ever saw his name, in the news paper, But with a lye about him. He sincerely hopes Mr Campbell is well.

242. [BL, Add. MS 51406, f. 175]
Lord Holland, Holland House to John Campbell, 11 February 1771
I am very glad to find, that the weather had no bad effect upon you, though it had upon your letter, which I did not receive so soon as I should have done. Indeed to hear of you, & of your welfare, is the greatest pleasure I am capable of, and a very great one.

As to the squabbles you mention, they neither divert nor vex me. *Omnia hæc Subjeci fidelibus.*[67] I don't get off my chair nor have since I came to England. The News Papers

[63] William Beckford died on 21 June, the same date as this letter.

[64] *PH*, xvi, 968, 4 May 1770. Chatham is reported as saying: 'The livery of London . . . were respectable in the time of Cæsar's invasion'.

[65] *PH*, xvi, 651, 9 Jan. 1770. Chatham is reported as saying he 'begged leave to refer their Lordships to a most important passage in history, described by a man of great abilities, Mr Robertson. This writer, in his life of Charles the Fifth . . .'.

[66] William Robertson (1721–93), Scottish historian, published his *History of the Reign of Charles V* in 1769.

[67] All those faithful subjects.

never mention me without a lye which I sometimes cant guess the reason of. My Lady Holland desires to be remembered to you, & joyns with me in compliments to Mrs Campbell.

Yours ever most oblig'd & most affectionate Holland[68]

243. [BL, Add. MS 51406, ff. 177–8]
Lord Holland, Holland House to John Campbell, 2 April 1771
I am some days, a great deal worse than others, But I don't find the weather affects me, which is lucky this winter. I waited however in hopes, if I could give you no better news of myself, that I might say something of the Publick that would please you, But I cannot say, I yet see a prospect, I can make anything of. The leaders of the opposition[69] quarrel, which is a good thing, But dos not seem likely, to have all the good consequences, one might expect from it. You know the point in dispute[70] now, and if anything could surprize where party is concerned, it would be amazing that any body should be against the House of Commons, But such as were very near demolishing My Lord North, and did destroy my Sons [Charles] Chariot[71] last week, I would not have them afraid, But I would have them more cautious of a Mob than they are, But calling them a Mob is an offence, and some Gentlemen in the House of Commons of great property, were very angry, that the people of England, (the dirtyest blackguards, I am told, and the lowest rabble you ever look'd at) should be so term'd; and Dukes & Marquises, have been in procession to compliment the Protectors of them. When I have any thing pleasanter to write, I will write again. I thank you very kindly, for the advice you give me, and Lady Holland, if she was at home would certainly joyn in it, if she was not convinced by four years[72] experience, that I am too old to mend. Your good wishes my Dear Mr Campbel, do me more good than any advice can do. If my best wishes, could do you, or your family any good, you have them most sincerely, for no body can be more than I am, your oblig'd & faithfull & affectionate servant . . .

[68] Only this line is written by Holland himself and it is in a very shaky hand.

[69] In the house of lords the opposition leaders were Chatham, Rockingham, the dukes of Richmond, Portland and the 5th duke of Devonshire and Lords Shelburne and Temple, whilst in the lower House the opposition leaders were Burke, Barré, George Grenville and Dowdeswell. Thomas Wright, *A Caricature History of the Georges* (1868), 317.

[70] The dispute over the right of the press to report debates in the Commons, which had sprung up at the beginning of 1771, when George Onslow had raised the question of parliamentary privilege in the Commons after taking umbrage when he was referred to in the *Middlesex Journal* (19 Mar. 1771) as 'little cocking George . . . the Jack-pudding of the House. He always attempts to excite a laugh; he is often successful: but it is generally at his own expense'. Several Commons debates ensued, and Charles Fox was one of the most outspoken MPs. The mob surrounded the Commons for several days. Wright, *Caricature History*, 325.

[71] On 27 Mar. According to some reports Fox, together with his accomplice George Selwyn, was earlier in Alice's coffee house in Palace Yard, Westminster, 'shaking his fist at the people, provoking them by all the reproachful words and menacing gestures that he could invent'. *London Evening Post*, 28 Mar. 1771. However, a letter signed 'C.D.' in the *Public Advertiser*, 30 Mar. 1771, stated that Fox and Selwyn were merely jesting with the mob rather than inciting them to riot. The *General Evening Post*, 28 Mar. 1771, stated that Fox's new chariot was attacked on at least two separate occasions.

[72] The period Holland had been suffering ill health?

Appendix 1: Account of the Pembrokeshire Election (1727)[1]

In the Evening Post[2] of Sept[ember] the 16th an account was given of the election for the County of Pembroke in which it is said that upon closeing the Books to Poll stood thus for Sir Arthur Owen 374 for John Campbell 229 notwithstanding which Majority the High Sheriff[3] thought fit to return the latter affirming that his Undersheriff had taken another Poll in a Garrett four foot wide over the Hall. This being a gross & injurious misrepresentation it is thought proper to give the true state of the Case as follows.

The High Sheriff had several times before the day of Election told Sir Arthur Owen & several of Sir Arthur's Friends that he intended to have two places of polling for the ease & dispatch of the Country; and for that reason, on tuesday the fifth of September as soon as a Poll was demanded he ordered two Clerks to be sworn. The High Sheriff being indisposed stayed but a short time in Court that day, and the Gentleman who acted as his Deputy in absence did not appoint a second place of Polling. But the next morning when the High Sheriff came into Court he declared publickly (the Hall being then full) that he would have the Poll taken at two places, Sir Arthur Owen & some of his Friends objected against it, but the objection not appearing to the High Sheriff to be founded upon any Law or Reason he persisted in his Resolution, thinking it was his Duty not to detain the Freeholders longer than necessary, and that he was not obliged in that instance, to consult the pleasure of either Candidate. He therefore order'd the Undersheriff to go with one of the sworn Clerks to take the Poll in a place which had formerly been made use of without objection upon the like occasion; and he called aloud to the Freeholders, desireing that some of them would go & poll at the place where the Undersheriff Sate; upon which, some Gentlemen were pleased to stand up and desire that none of Sir Arthur Owens Friends would Poll in that place, and accordingly none of them did.

There is no Garrett over any part of the Hall; the place where the Under Sheriff Sate is a Loft within the Hall, fifteen foot long six foot & a half broad, and about eight foot above the floor of the Hall, with stairs going up from the floor, it is at the lower end of the Hall opposite to the Bench where the Highsheriff & Candidates Sate who could see the Persons & hear the voices of those in the Loft.

A gentleman who had been appointed an Inspector by Sir Arthur Owen acted as such, and several Gentlemen acted as Managers for him in that place, and all who voted there took the Freeholders Oath.

---

[1] CRO, Cawdor/Campbell box 2/285.
[2] The London Evening Post was the leading opposition newspaper.
[3] Sir Richard Walter of Rhosmarket, Pembrokeshire.

© The Parliamentary History Yearbook Trust 2014

It will therefore appear that they who voted before the Under Sheriff in the Loft, were as legally & regularly polled, as they who voted with the High Sheriff at the Bench.

Upon casting up the two Sheriffs Books the Poll stood thus for Sir Arthur Owen 374 for John Campbell 541.

The High Sheriff must then have acted contrary to all Reason and Justice if he had not returned the latter.

This Account will at anytime be attested by many Gentleman of undoubted credit.

Appendix 2: Copy of a Letter to a Nonjuring Gentleman in Scotland[1] Writ in the year 1727

Dear Sir,

I very readily comply with your desire to acquaint you with my reasons for thinking that our present Establishment is such as a Man of Honor, and Integrity may submit to serve, and support. To do this, I must briefly consider the Nature of Government in general, and our own constitution in particular.

Government is called the Ordinance of God, and all Parties agree that its Original, and Authority are divine.[2] Yet it does not appear that ever God by Revelation instituted Government in general or any particular form of it, unless Wee except the Theocracy of the Jews, which concerns no other Nation and is a Precedent they cannot follow. The old Testament whenever it mentions Government, among the Gentiles, speaks of it as a Thing known and established; and let me, by the way, observe that if you believe the Book of Genesis, you must acknowledge that Liberty, Property and limited Monarchy are not the Inventions of Modern Heretics, & Rebells for if the People of Egypt had not been possessed both of Liberty & Property, they could not have sold, first their Estates, and then themselves, and their Familys to Pharaoh for Corn; and Joseph needed not to have used that Expedient to enlarge the royal Prerogative, and make all the Country Crown Land. If our High Clergy boast that Joseph is not blamed for that Action, they may please to remember that Moses was not writing the History of Egypt, and that many Facts are related in the Bible, without being censured by the Penmen, which are yet undoubtedly sinful; it is not indeed necessary that whenever an account is given of a Robbery or Murther, it should be gravely observed that Robbery & Murther are sins. But I will venture to say that I would give my Vote for impeaching any Minister that should attempt to follow this Example. And I must confess it is much to be lamented, that mistaken notions of Loyalty, & Gratitude should prevale upon so good and humane a Man as Joseph to become the Instrument to inslave a Nation.

---

[1] The 'penal laws instituted against the Church and its adherents for supporting the Jacobite cause divided it into those clergy and congregations willing to swear loyalty to the Hanoverian monarchs and those unwilling: respectively the Juring or "English" chapels and the non-juring or "Scottish" chapels. The latter were technically illegal ... but ... they were meeting freely by the 1770s in the strongly episcopalian areas of the north-east "by tacit connivance"'. C.G. Brown, *Religion and Society in Scotland since 1707* (Edinburgh, 1997). Campbell's ancestral home was, of course, in the north-east of Scotland. The letter copied into a notebook by Campbell defends the Lockean, and whig, theory of the social contract, opposing the divine right of kings theory which was espoused by supporters of the Stuart clan and many tories.

[2] See John Locke's *Second Treatise on Government*, published in 1689. Campbell's essay is infused with Lockean theory.

Since then neither the Institutions of Government, or the Rights of Governors are to be found in the earliest Revelation, how is their Original derived from Heaven? I Answer, that god has made us rational and sociable Creatures; Wee can scarce subsist without Society and yet our Nature is so imperfect, & corrupt, that Wee cannot live in society without Government; Therefore our Reason tells us that Government is necessary. Every determination of right Reason must be true and Truth must be agreable to the Will of God; so Wee may justly say, it is the Will of God Wee should have Government. If this be the Original of Government, it is plane that the End and Design of it, must be the Good of the Governed, and Wee must allways keep that in view when Wee are discussing, or settling the Rights and Powers of Governors. Let the Constitution of any Kingdom, or State, place ever so great and arbitrary a power in the Prince it must allways be understood that he is obliged to be the Guardian, not the Destroyer of his People. And if he planely shews himself an Enemy to them, and the whole tenor of his Actions, is in opposition to their Wellfare; the same Reason which instituted Government in general, will put an end to his Reign; for it would be the highest absurdity to say that the People are obliged to submit to a Governor whose Actions and avow'd Intentions, are directly contrary to the Design and Nature of Government. Some Divines have however assented that Christianity has enjoin'd absolute passive Obedience to Princes as necessary to Salvation, and our high Clergy have presumed to call it the Doctrine of the Cross; to prove which, they would not only oblige us to take the Text in the strict literal sense, but that not coming up to their purpose, they have strained it beyond what the Letter can bear. By which zealous endevors they have shewn their good Will to Mankind, and as far as in them lay, have discredited the Religion they pretend to defend; yet should you take his Gunn from one of these passive Gentlemen, I believe the letter of the Text could not persuade him to give you his Cassock also, or should you strike one of these humble Non resisters on the one cheek, I would not have you expect him to turn the other. I think too that St Origen[3] is the only instance of a Divine who cut off his offending Members; The Church, Wee know, says he fell into many gross Errors, and that Action is allways allowed to be one of them. So, it seems, Wee must understand or rather force, some Texts in a sense that would make all mankind Wretched slaves, at the same time that Wee may use a reasonable liberty in giving an easy turn to others, in order to save a Coat, revenge a small affront, or the like. But our Comfort is, Wee are not obliged to be led by these blind Guides. God is perfectly Wise and Good therefore nothing inconsistent with those Attributes, can be the genuine sense of his Commands.

The New Testament cannot be thought to institute Government which had subsisted so many Ages before the birth of Christ; it can only declare that Institution to be agreable to the Will of God who Wee may be sure, would not declare his approbation of the rational Institution of Government, and, at the same time give such Rules for Obedience, as would be destructive of the Wise, and good Ends for which it was instituted. How can a reasonable Man believe that the Supreme Being would delegate his Power to Kings, in so absolute a manner, as our high Clergy pretend, without

---

[3] Origen (c.185–254) was one of the most distinguished early fathers of the Church. He died as a result of torture.

giving them a proportionable share of his other Perfections? How dreadfull would the Idea of infinite Power be, if not join'd with infinite Goodness? However general then, or strong the terms of Scripture which enjoin obedience to Governors may be, they must still be understood in such a sense as is agreable to the Nature of God, and consistent with his other commands; to which I think this Doctrine a direct contradiction. Some Men I know, have gone so far as to assert, that absolute Nonresistance is for the Good of Mankind; for say they, when did ever any Tyrant commit so many Rapes, and Murthers or burn, and plunder so many Houses, and Towns, as the Armies in a civil war allways have, and ever will.

I need not dispute the Fact with these Gentlemen I would only tell them, that this Argument will carry them much farther than they are willing to go. For suppose a foreign Nation was coming to invade us with a great, and well appointed Army, with design to make an entire Conquest of the Kingdom; it is certane, if Wee defend our selves by Arms, much blood will be spilt, and probably Many Virgins and Church's defiled and many Houses, and Towns burnt, and plundered whatever may be the event of the War. Wheras if Wee submit without resistance, it is not likely that the Invader will butcher his New peaceable subjects only for diversion, or make Bonfires of our Towns when Wee have made them so freely, his own. Yet, should you put the Question to our passive Divines, I dare say they would all desire you to fight, and promise to assist you with their Prayers. They would exhort you, rather to die bravely, in the defence of your Country, than live slaves to an unjust Invader, who will, it may be, spare your lives, and allow you to preserve a shamefull Being; but your Liberty, your Estates, and even your Lives will be precarious, and subject to the caprice of your New Master. It is better, they would tell you, to die honorably, than to wear out a miserable Life in perpetual dread of Poverty, Chains, & Death. Now the same are my sentiments in regard to a domestic Tyrant; his Invasion of our Liberties, & Property is as unjust as the other, nay it is a great aggravation that, in this Case, a People are ruin'd by the Person whom they appointed to protect them. But when true Notions of Government are taught, and encouraged it will not be a matter of so great hazard to pull down a Tyrant, whom none then will defend but the Partners of his Crimes, the base Instruments of his tyranny, and they will not dare to shew their Faces to a brave, injured People. The false enthusiastic Notions of pretended Christian obedience with which the high Clergy filled the heads of their hearers & Pupils have indeed made many good, well meaning Men unreasonably struggle against the Laws of Nature, and their Country, on the side of Lawless, cruel Power, and imaginary Right. This is in truth an afflicting thought. However, to do the High Clergy justice, though they are allways ready to be the Fools they never mean to be the Objects of arbitrary Power. Of this Wee have a remarkable Instance in the Case of King James the Second[4] who having luckily, dealt some of his first, and heaviest blows upon the Church, the high Clergy, though they had been thundering out Damnation to all Resisters ever since the Restoration, yet when they found their own Interest struck [*sic*] at revolted to Reason, and Commonsense, appear'd for once on the side of Justice and Mercy, joined with, and animated, the People in the Glorious Cause; and so the Nation was saved from a near prospect of all the Evils any People can suffer, or fear; in the space of a few

---

[4] James II (1633–1701), king 1685–8; the last catholic king of England.

Weeks, without more Blood than has been shed in a common Riot, and with less disorder than the Tories raised to insult the Legislature acting regularly at Dr Sacheverels Tryal.[5]

It is often said that the original Contracts between Nations, and their Princes, are no where to be found nor can be proved, by history, ever to have been. If the Objectors can prove any other Original of Government, they need be at no trouble to disprove such a Contract; but if that cannot be done, this Argument will serve rather to prove the power of Princes unlawfull, than unlimited. But indeed it proves nothing; for every one knows there is such a thing as tacit consent and a People may give their Assent by Actions as well as by Words. When wee see many thousands obey one Man no stronger than each of them, where is the absurdity in saying, they give that Power to him, which they Freely permit him to exercise, though Wee see no writing, nor hear any Words, by which they formally confer the Title, and Office of King upon him. Or where can there be a greater absurdity than to suppose they give him that Power for their own destruction. The Patriarchal Scheme has been setup as an Original of Government, in opposition to that I and all the Friends of Liberty espouse, Mr Lock has examined and confuted it admirably well, but to a Man of your good sense, and Candor, I need only recommend the reading of Sir Robert Filmers Book[6] writ in defence of it, and I am satisfied you will want no help to see the Inconsistence, and vane empty Nonsense of that Doctrine.

As to our own Constitution, it is certane that the power of our Kings is very much limitted, not only by the Law of Nature, or an original Contract, either express, or tacit; but also by many Laws made from time to time even with the consent of the Kings themselves. The subjects have many Rights, and great Privileges, which our Kings have often most solemnly acknowledged, and confirm'd. And every King at his Inauguration swears to observe the Laws, maintain & preserve the Rights, Liberties, and Properties of his People. I think the Coronation is a plane express Contract between the People, and their King, in which Allegiance, and Protection are reciprocally promised; He is to govern, and they are to obey accordingly to the Rule of Law, and the Constitution. I know it is answer'd, that he is as much King before, as after the Coronation, which is a proper decent and pompous Ceremony, but not necessary to confirm the King in the Government of his Kingdom. But surely it is not reasonable to look upon a solemn Engagement by Oath, as a mere Ceremony and I must think that the King being allowed to exercise the royal Authority before his Coronation, is in confidence, that he will on that occasion agree to the Conditions of Government that will then be proposed to him, and give the People the Satisfaction and Security, at that time to be required. And by this mean Wee avoid the Inconveniencies of an Interregnum. To explane this a little, you may consider, that all Officers, civil, and Military, are obliged by Law to take the Oaths to the Government to qualifie them for their Places, yet they are allow'd

---

[5] Rev. Henry Sacheverell (1674–1715) was tried in early 1710 for sermons he published regarding the danger to the Church from the whigs. He was suspended from duties for three years and his sermons ordered to be burned, a sentence that caused widespread riots.

[6] Sir Robert Filmer (1588–1653), his most famous book being *Patriarcha* published in 1680. It espoused the theory of the divine right of kings, and as such was attacked by John Locke in the first part of his *Two Treatises of Government*, published in 1689. Locke's social contract theories had great influence on Enlightenment thinkers.

to exercise their Offices, with full Power, for several Months before they take those Oaths; but if they refuse or neglect it to take them, within the time limitted, their Places are void, and if they presume to act after that time is lapsed they are highly criminal. If the subjects have no right to defend their Libertys, and Property's, what are they but empty Names? If the King is accountable only to Heaven why should our Laws direct his Government, and set bounds to his Power? The Law of Nature would, in that Case, be sufficient, and Heaven Wee may trust would punish him for acting contrary to it. But why should Wee mock our selves by making Laws, for the breach of which, Wee could have no remedy on Earth.

It is a known Maxim of our Law, that the King can do no Wrong, this has I believe been frequently misunderstood, and misapplied; but the true meaning of it is; that if the King commands anything contrary to Law, it is not a royal Act, and is no way to be regarded, or obey'd, and if those in Office under the King execute such Commands, they are Answerable, and ought to be punish'd for so doing, the royal Authority not going along with any illegal order. If our Kings understand this right, allow the Laws to have their Free course, and their Ministers to be called to account, either in the Common Courts of Justice, or Parliament, as the Case may require, the Crown will be sure and their sacred Persons need fear no sacrilegious Violence. But if they stop the Course of Justice, and force their Will into the Place of the Law, they renounce the benefit of those wise, and excellent Provisions it has made for their safety, and with their hands, throw down the strong Fence our Constitution had set about them. Examples of both sorts may be found in our History. To come to the Particular Case of King James the Second, I think all the accounts of his Reign, and the best attested Facts in them, planely shew that he not only broke, but defy'd our Laws; he openly asserted a Power to dispense with, which was, in effect, to annul them His whole endeavor was to overturn our Constitution both in Church, and State; he look'd upon our Religion as Heresy, and every restraint of his Will as Treason. And as he did all this not only contrary to his Coronation Oath, but to his own voluntary Promise at his Accession; what reason could the Nation have to depend upon any assurance he might give him of amendment for the future. All hopes of legal Remedy were taken away, by his dissolving the Parliament because they would not acknowledge his dispensing Power; and filling the Bench's in Westminster Hall, with such shameless mercenary Wretches, as would avow, and support it. To what then could the People have recourse but the Ultima Ratio?[7] Some of the high Tories have gone so far as to acknowledge that in Cases of extreme necessity Resistance may be lawfull; but they think King James had not gone that length, and the People should have stay'd yet longer, to see if the King's designs were really so bad, as represented by his Enemies, and, they might add, as boasted of by his Friends.

This had been to wait till his Army was modall'd to his Mind; and then when they were naked in his hands, and his sword at their throats, the sad Consequence of Resistance had been to double their Chains, by provoking an Oppressor, whose yoke they were unable to shake off; Or at best, they must have purchased their Liberty, by a Long, and bloody Contest; Whereas it was gain'd allmost without a blow.

---

[7] The last resort.

It is however asserted that the Crown of England &c were hereditary, and that the son[8] of King James was an innocent Infant, who could not have offended himself, and in Reason & Justice ought not to suffer for his Fathers faults; and if his Birth was suspected, it ought to have been examined into, in a public and regular way Great Clamor has been made, that there never was such an Examination, though earnestly desired by King James, and both the Parliament & King William[9] solemnly called upon to do it, as promised by the Prince of Orange's Declaration,[10] in which that was set forth as one Motive of his Expedition. When the Opposers of the Revolution have said this, they triumph greatly, and imagine no Answer can be given them.

That the infant son of King James was innocent is most certane, and I am very Free to declare my Opinion that it is not just to punish a Child for his Fathers faults. But I deny the consequence that he ought therefore to possess the Crown his Father once wore and to examine into his Birth, unless his succession to the Crown was the necessary consequence of his legitimacy was wholly needless, let King James, and his Friends, call ever so solemnly upon Parliament to do it. That Assembly had no reason to enter into an Affair of no consequence to the Nation, and therefore not proper for their Consideration. As to the Prince of Orange's Declaration, the Parliament was not bound to fullfill the Prince's Promises; nor indeed is the Prince himself to be blamed in this Matter. At the time he emitted that Declaration, the Child was undoubtedly, if legitimate, Heir apparent to the Crown, and, then the truth of his royal Birth, was of great importance to the Nation in general, and to the Prince, and Princess of Orange[11] in particular; it might then be worth while for the Prince, if he suspected an imposture, to come over on purpose to detect it. The Prince of Orange had no Right to dethrone King James, or disinherit his son, he could not certanely know, before he came, what would be the Event of his Expedition, how King James would behave, whether he would quit the Kingdom, or what Measures the Estates of the Realm would take upon that Occasion. But when King James, with his Queen, and son, were fled, When the Representatives, and Constitutional Trustees of the People, had declared the Throne vacant, and after that placed the Prince & Princess of Orange on it, and settle'd the Crown upon them, the Princess Anne of Denmark [Queen Anne of Great Britain], and their respective Issue in such order as was judged most expedient for the public good, and agreable to Equity, and the spirit of the Laws; It would have been as improper for King William to enter into an Examination of the Pretenders Birth, as it would have been for the Prince of Orange to have omitted that Article in his Declaration.

You will call me back, I know, to prove that the Childs Right of Succession was not a necessary consequence of his Legitimacy. The high Clergy have, I confess, often and most confidently asserted that Hereditary Right is divine and indefeasable, but without any Evidence of the one, or reason for the other. Let them produce, if they can, any divine Command for it; I dare affirm they can never do so; and surely there is no natural reason why a son should, necessarily succede his Father in a Kingdom, more than in a

---

[8] James Francis Edward Stuart (1688–1766), the 'Old Pretender'.

[9] William III (1650–1702), formerly prince of Orange, from 1688 joint monarch of England, with Mary Stuart (1662–94).

[10] The Declaration of Reasons for Invading England, dated 16 Dec. 1688.

[11] That is, Mary Stuart, Queen Mary.

Bishoprick or any other Office. The Hereditary Right of our Princes must then be founded upon the Laws of the Land, and consequently must be regulated by them, and subject to the Legislature. Were the Power of our Kings so unlimited as the assertors of indefeasible Hereditary Right would have it, nothing could be more wrong than to make the Crown Hereditary. What dreadfull Work might a Weak, or Wicked son make? In how little time might he undo, all the Good which a Wise, and Virtuous Father had been doing, in the Course of a long and happy Reign? Though he was surrounded by honest, and able Councillors, he might reject their Advice, and the extravagant Wickedness or folly of one Man might lay wast a flourishing Kingdom, and make Millions Miserable. Our Constitution takes away this Objection, the Law being a Rule by which the King both may, and must, direct his Government; and if he refuses to be guided by it, he renounce's his Kingly Office, which is to execute the Laws, not to govern by his own Will, and Passions.

The Case being so, the Hereditary descent of our Crown will appear a just and Wise Provision, to prevent the dangerous Intrigues that might be carried on when a Demise was in View, and the violent Contests when it came to an Election. It may also be consider'd as the Reward, given by a gratefull People, for the pious Cares of a good Prince. This last reason cannot argue for the son of a Tyrant; and Wee shall easily see whether the others will take Place in this Instance; that is, whether it was more for the safety and quiet of the Nation[12] to admit than to set aside the Son of King James, for such I all along suppose him to be, not thinking it of any moment to our Cause, or worth my time, to question his birth.

The Child was then in the hands of his Father, and Mother, who had carried him into a foreign Country; it cannot be imagined they would upon any account have sent him back, to be educated by such as they called perjured Rebells, and in Religion which they look'd upon as a damnable Heresy. And surely no one could ever seriously propose or think of, so ridiculous a Project, as to allow his Parents to breed him up till he was of age, and then accept him for our King, to argue against such a scheme would be an affront to the meanest understanding. Suppose then that the Child had been left in the Kingdom when the King, and Queen withdrew, and had been by the Convention, after an Inquiry into his Birth, declared King. What a dangerous, and distracted Condition must the Nation have been in during his long Minority, in such a posture of Affairs. I need not enlarge upon it; reason will presently suggest a thousand inconveniencies, and even an impossibility of any calm Settlement, or safety, upon such a Foot; And you will planely see, that according to the Rule of Government first laid down, the People had a Right as well to reject the Son, as to depose the Father. And their Trustees, the Members of the Convention, were bound in duty to do it. It being then necessary for the Convention to disinherit the infant Son of King James, they shew'd all the regard the suprema Lex salas Populi[13] would permit to the order of succession in the royal Family by giving the Crown to his eldest Daughter, by whose consent, and desire, her Husband, the Kings Nephew, was join'd with her in the Title, and the Administration put solely in his hands.

---

[12] In an endnote Campbell writes: 'I think I should rather have said Consistent with the safety of the Nation for a supposed, or expected Utility will not be sufficient to Justifie great alteration contrary, to the ordinary course of the Laws'.

[13] ' Let the good of the people be the supreme law'. Cicero, *De Legibus*, III, pt iii, sub. viii.

The Crown was afterwards by the whole legislature, regularly, settle'd, failing the Issue of the Princess Anne, & King William, upon the Family of Hanover who were the first Protestants of the Royal Blood to which still all the respect was shewn which could possibly consist with the preservation of our religious, and Civil Rights.

The asserters of indefeasable Hereditary Right very frequently ask those they dispute with, whether they would be willing to have their Fathers Estate taken from them. Wee might answer directly, that if our Fathers were guilty of Treason, the Laws would cut off our succession to their Estates and if Noblemen, to their Honors; but I rather chose to tell these acute Disputants that they bring together two Cases widely different.

My Estate is that part of the good Things of this World which Providence, and the Laws of my country have allotted, and secured to me, for my private enjoyment, and the maintenance of me, and my Family. The regal Office is a Trust reposed in the Person who wears the Crown, for the good of the Community. Where then is the Parallel? or what Argument can be drawn from the one Case, to the other? A Man may squander away, or Mismanage his own Estate, and be answerable to no one for it; But I believe Trustees are accountable by the Laws of all Nations, by the Law of Reason they undoubtedly are. Can Wee then think that Kings may without controle abuse their Trust, which is of the highest Nature, and concerns a whole Nation, in every thing that can be dear to them on Earth. Surely they must be accountable, either in their own Persons, or which is most for the security and advantage both of Prince, and People, in those who administer the Government under them. I am sure you cannot think, and will not say the contrary. And I dare promise, that if you will take the pains to examine all the other pretence's, and arguments, of the Advocates for absolute Power indefeasible Hereditary Right, and Passive Obedience, you will find them all equally empty, and inconclusive.

I have now Sir told you freely and briefly, my thoughts upon this subject. And the Reasons upon which I judge the present Government to be just & legal, and the Revolution Settlement[14] such as ought, not only to be submitted to but earnestly contended for by every Man of Reason, and Virtue who is on the side of Truth, a Friend to Mankind, and a Lover of his Country.

If you think me too bold in undertaking to determine in a Letter, a Question upon which so many Volumes have been writ; I desire you to consider, that Error is an intricate, and endless Maze; but Moral Truth is simple, and plane: and I believe not difficult to be found by those who sincerely, & impartially seek for it. May their Number still increase. If any of the Tory Party can shew that what I have said is contrary to Reason, and that their scheme is consonant to it. They need not endeavour to strengthen their Cause, by the Authority of Fathers Councils &c. But if Reason fails them, to what purpose serve pompous Catalogues of those who have maintained their Doctrines but to shew how many then have been mistaken, a discovery, to me, neither strange, or pleasing.

In consequence of the Revolution Settlement Wee are now happy under a King truly great and good; who scorns the mean Ambition, of setting his Will above the Laws, but makes the exact observation, and due execution of them his Pleasure, and his Glory. In whose Reign the worst complaints of the disaffected are, not that themselves

---

[14] That is, the Glorious Revolution and the Act of Settlement.

are Deprived of Liberty, but that their Neighbors enjoy it. For so exquisitely cruel are the high Clergy to the souls of Men, that they would force numbers of their innocent fellow subjects, either not to worship God at all, in public, or to do it in a way that they believe is not acceptable to Him. When did any Unbeliever shew such a scandal upon Christianity as do these Men, who would be thought its most zealous Advocates. For what impartial Reasoner could believe that Religion to come from God, if it really taught two such monstrous Doctrines as Persecution, and absolute passive Obedience. To what Misery would Mankind be reduced, if thus exposed defenceless, to the Rage of the Tyrant, and the Priest. You will think perhaps that I have stept out of my way to mention Persecution; but I would not seperate two Doctrines which the high Clergy have made inseperable: And indeed they are the result of the same temper of mind, equally repugnant to Reason, and Humanity, and destructive of Society. Whoever maintains them do's, in effect, though it may be he neither intends, or knows it, declare himself Humani Genens Hostis.[15]

Dear sir I beg of you to consider this matter seriously and coolly, lay aside all prejudices, and let your Reason give impartial Judgement: And then I am sure the Cause of Liberty cannot fail; though I fear in this letter it may suffer by the weakness of its Advocate.

If you have any Objections to what I have writ pray let me know them, and I will answer in the best manner I am able; but then I must entreat you to keep close to the Argument, and not amuse yourself with Words, which is the usual practice of your Party; but why do I call it yours. Before you can Answer this letter, I trust it will be no longer so for though what I have said is very imperfect, and ill express'd; yet I hope it may prove a usefull hint, and that you will have converted yourself before you come to the end of the Letter.

I need not tell you, that if you came over you must expect to be called a Knave and Fool, by the Party you leave, in all the various Phrases they can learn, or invent. But I am satisfied you have strength of Mind, to despise the Abuse, and goodness of heart, to pity those who give it. Never to be mistaken, is more than any Man can hope for; the next thing is, to see, acknowledge, and forsake an Error which Education and long habit had render'd even dear to us. To hear that you have done so will be a very great satisfaction and Pleasure to Dear Sir.

Yours &c JC

---

[15] Enemy of mankind.

Appendix 3: Essay on the Act of Settlement c.1758

Mr Walpole[1] returns Mr Campbell a thousand thanks for the perusal of this Ms which has given him great pleasure, both from the clearness of the proof & the short & judicious manner in which it is stated. Mr W[alpole] fears it is a bad return, but having no better, begs Mr Campbell to do him the honour of accepting the inclosed Volume.[2]

The above mention'd volume was entitled Fugitive Pieces's.[3]

The Clauses of Provision in the Act of Settlement 12 W[illiam] 3[r]d[4] having been made great use of, much insisted upon, and spoke of in the highest terms, by several Gentlemen in a Debate the last session of Parliament, upon a Bill to enable the King to grant Military Commissions to some foreign Protestants, to act in America only. And the same having been since mention'd in a most invidious manner, in a Malicious Libel printed in the Newspapers, which I saw in the Country in Autumn 1756. I was led to reconsider that mater, and to put my thoughts upon it, in Writing.

By an Act 1. W[illiam] & M[ary]. Sess[ion] 2.[5] The Crown of England was settled, upon the Issue of Q[ueen] Marie,[6] in default of such, upon the Princess Anne of Denmark,[7] and her Issue, in default of such, upon the Issue of King William.[8] And by the same Act it is provided, That no Papist, or Person who shall marry a Papist, shall be capable to inherit, or possess the Crown, And in every such Case the People are absolved from their Allegiance, and the Crown is to descend to such Person, being Protestant, as would have inherited the same, if the said Person being a Papist, or married to a Papist, were naturally dead.

No further provision was made for the Succession dureing the life of the Duke of Glo[u]cester,[9] son to the Princess Anne of Denmark; but upon the death of that young Prince, the Friends of Liberty, and the Protestant Religion Judged it necessary that a more particular Settlement should be made. For if King William, and the then Princess

---

[1] Horace Walpole (1717–97).

[2] This note from Walpole is pasted on to the inside of the front cover of the notebook containing this essay.

[3] This line is in Campbell's hand and refers to *Fugitive Pieces in Verse and Prose* by Horace Walpole, printed at Strawberry Hill in 1758 in a limited edition of 200.

[4] The Act of Settlement (12 &13 Wm III, c.2) of 1701 which secured the British monarchy in the protestant line.

[5] An Act declaring the Rights and Liberties of the Subject and Settling the Succession of the Crown (the Bill of Rights), 1689.

[6] Mary II of England (1662–94), joint sovereign with William (1650–1702).

[7] Anne (1665–1714), fourth daughter of James, duke of York and his first wife Lady Anne Hyde. In 1683 she married George, prince of Denmark, who was subsequently created an English subject, knight of the garter and duke of Cumberland. Anne became queen of England in 1702.

[8] William III (1650–1702) of England, who reigned 1689–1702 with Mary II (1662–94) until her death in 1702 and then as sole monarch.

[9] Prince William (1689–1700), duke of Gloucester, the only son of Queen Anne to survive infancy.

of Denmark, had died without Issue, any of the popish branches of the royal Family or even the Pretender himself, as the descent of the Crown is said to purge all Attainders, might by a pretended conversion to the Protestant Religion, have clame'd the Crown, without any impediment from the foremention'd Act. King William therefore, being desirous complete our deliverance from Popery and slavery and to secure, as far as possible, to the latest Posterity; those religious, and civil Rights, which he had rescued from the most imminent danger. His Majesty did his speech at the opening of a new Parliament[10] Feb[ruar]y 11, 1700/1 tell them That the loss of the Duke of Glo[u]cester had made it absolutely necessary that there should be a farther Provision for the succession to the Crown in the Protestant Line. And he earnestly recommended it, to their early and effectual Consideration.

All who have converted with those who lived, and had any concern in public Busyness, or sat in Parliament, at that time, know. That the majority of the then House of Commons, were no Friends to King William, and had no great inclination to the Thing he so warmly recommended to them.[11] Indeed any one may be satisfied of this, by looking into the Journals of the House of Commons, where they will find how this most important and necessary Busyness, was delay'd, and put off, from time to time, so that the Bill was not pass'd by that House,[12] till the 14th of May. Their time was a good deal taken up, by Enquiry's and Impeachments, which came to nothing,[13] of the Lords Sommers, Portland, and Halifax.[14]

As the body of the People too well remember'd the Reign of King James the Second, to bear the thoughts of falling back into those dangers from which they were saved by the Revolution;[15] The House of Commons dared not refuse to settle the Crown in the Protestant Line. But under pretence of care, and zeal for the Liberties of the People, they endeavor'd to dog the settlement with such Provisions, as might either occasion the loss of the Bill by raising Debates, and causing Amendments to be made, in the House of Lords, where the Majority were zealous Friends to the Revolution, or if the Bill should pass both Houses, might render the Government impracticable, when the Settlement should take place. Several of the Provisions could not but be very disagreable to the greatest part of the Lords, and some were disposed to make Amendments; But the most knowing, and experienced in that House, advised and prevailed, to pass the Bill as it was sent up by the Commons, Wisely judging that if the settlement was once

---

[10] *LJ*, xvi, 594–5.

[11] That is, the majority of the house of commons upon William's accession supported the catholic James II.

[12] *CJ*, xiii, 540.

[13] They were impeached by the Commons for the part they took in negotiations relating to the partition treaty of 1698. However the decision was overturned by the Lords.

[14] *CJ*, xiii, 497. John Somers (1651–1716), 1st Baron Somers; whig lawyer. Lord keeper 1693–7; lord chancellor 1697–1700; Hans William (1649–1709), Baron Bentinck, 1st earl of Portland; Charles Montagu (1661–1715), Baron Halifax 1700–15; 1st earl of Halifax 1714–15; MP for Maldon 1689–95 and Westminster 1695–1701; chancellor of the exchequer 1694–9; first lord of the treasury 1697–9 and 1714–15. Edward Russell (1653–1727), earl of Orford; MP for Launceston 1689–90, for Portsmouth 1690–5 and for Cambridgeshire 1695–7; admiral of the fleet 1690–7; treasurer of the navy 1689–99; first lord of the admiralty 1694–9, 1709–10, 1714–17, was also impeached.

[15] The Glorious Revolution of 1688 which removed the catholic James II from the throne and replaced him with the protestants William and Mary.

made, it would be very easy, at a convenient time, to make the proper amendments. Whereas the insisting upon any amendment then, would be falling into the snare the Commons had set for them, and if the Bill was then lost, the opportunity might never be retrieved, as the Kings life was very precarious, and it was by no means sure, that the Princess Anne would be so well disposed to the desired settlement. I am pretty confident that my opinion may be justified by a fair, and impartial consideration of the Act of Settlement which was framed by that House of Commons. It is entitled An Act for the further limitation of the Crown, and better securing the Rights, and Liberties of the subject.[16] And it consists of two very different Parts. The first and essential Part, which was the great desire of all true Friends to the Constitution as restored and improved at the Revolution, declares the Princess Sophia Electress Dowager[17] of Hanover the next in succession to the Crown, after King William, the then Princess Anne of Denmark, and their respective Issue; settles the succession upon the Heirs of the body of the said Princess Sophia, being Protestants, and repetes the Provisions made against Papists, and Persons marrying Papists, made in the first of William and Marie [Mary].

The Second Part of the Act, which is introduced by a new Preamble, consists of those Provisions for the Security of the Rights, and Liberties of the subject, made by that zealous, patriot, Tory House of Commons.[18] But I will venture to say, that if the Love of Liberty was really the actuating Principle, there was very little skill shewn in framing the Provisions, which those Wise Men were so long about. For some of them were absurd in themselves, and some absurdly worded, for the pretended intention of security to the subject, though extremely well adapted to the end of reflecting upon, and insulting King William. They are as follows,

1) That whosoever shall hereafter come to the possession of this Crown, shall join in Communion with the Church of England as by Law establish'd.
2) That in case the Crown, and imperial Dignity of this Realm shall hereafter come to any Person not being a Native of this Kingdom of England, this Nation be not obliged to engage in any War for the defence of any Dominions, or Territory's which do not belong to the Crown of England, without Consent of Parliament.
3) That no person who shall hereafter come to the Possession of this Crown, shall go out of the Dominions of England, Scotland, or Ireland, without consent of Parliament.
4) That from and after the time that the farther limitation by this Act shall take effect, all Matters and Things relating to the well governing of this Kingdom which are properly cognizable in the Privy Councill by the Laws and Customs of this Realm, shall be transacted there; and all Resolutions taken thereupon, shall be sign'd by such of the Privy Council as shall advise, and consent to the same.
5) That after the said Limitations shall take effect as aforesaid, no Person born out of the Kingdoms of England, Scotland, or Ireland or the Dominions thereunto belonging,

---

[16] Ch. 12 & 13 William III c.2.

[17] Sophia of the Palatinate (commonly known as Sophia of Hanover) (1630–1714), heiress to the crowns of England and Ireland and then of Great Britain. She was declared heir presumptive by the Act of Settlement, 1701. She married Ernest Augustus (1629–88), elector of Brunswick-Lüneberg, and was the mother of George I (1660–1727).

[18] The house of commons was dominated by the tories until 1714.

although he be naturalized, or made a Denizen (except such as are born of English Parents) shall be capable to be of the Privy Councill, or a member of either House of Parliament, or to enjoy any office, or Place of Trust, either civil, or military, or to have any Grant of Lands, Tenements, or Hereditaments from the Crown, to himself, or to any other, or others, in trust for him.

6) That no Person who has an Office, or Place of Profit under the King, or receives a Pension from the Crown, shall be capable of serving as a member of the House of Commons.

7) That after the said Limitation shall take effect, as aforesaid, Judges Commissons be made, Quam diu se bene gesserint,[19] and their salarys ascertaned, and establish'd: but upon the Address of both Houses of Parliament, it may be lawfull to remove them.

8) That no Pardon under the Great Seal of England, be pleadable to an impeachment by the Commons in Parliament.

Of these eight Provisions the fourth, and sixth were repele'd before the succession in the Family of Hanover took Place, the third was repele'd, and the fifth amended in the first session of King George the 1st's first Parliament.[20] So there were but four of these famous Provisions that had not been repele'd, or alter'd, before the accession[21] of King George the Second.[22] But I will consider each of the Provisions distinctly, to see how far they deserve, that high regard, and veneration, with which some Gentlemen have thought fit to treat them. The first, I will say no more of than to express my doubt, whether the Good Churchmen who composed it, were aware that it left the King at Liberty to be an Occasional Conformist.

The Second is very improperly expressed, if it was really intended to guard against the partiality which the Family of Hanover might retane for their German Dominions. In that Case, it ought to have provided, that whenever the Crown should be possessed by a Prince who had other Dominions not subject to the Crown of England, the English Nation should not be engaged in War for the defence of any such Dominions, without consent of Parliament. But this Provision is only for a Prince not born in England, and would of course expire upon His Majesties demise and is as much against a War for the defence of Holland, or Austria, as of Hanover. It should be observed that King William, though born in Holland, was not a sovereign of that Country, not in possession of any Dominion, except Scotland,[23] which I suppose was forgot, not subject to the crown of England.

The Third was I believe thought an indecent restraint upon the royal Person, and therefore repeled in the first year of King George the first: It looks too like an unkind reflection upon King William, who had so often gone abroad[24] to hazard his Life, in the Common Cause of England, and the rest of Europe.

---

[19] As long as he shall behave himself well. This was established by the Act of Union, 1701.

[20] *LJ*, xx, 21–2, 17 Mar. 1715.

[21] In 1727.

[22] George II (1683–1760).

[23] William III was also William II (King Billy) of Scotland.

[24] William II as Stadtholder William III of Orange played a major role in the European war of the Grand Alliance 1688–97, which meant he spent large parts of those years on the continent.

The Fourth Provision is so worded that I cannot take upon me to say how far it was intended to extend. It seems, I think, to bring all matters of state to be debated in the Privy Council, and if the meaning was, that the Crown should be determined by the Resolutions of the Majority, it would have given the Privy Council, a Power like that of the Senate in Sweden,[25] and made an entire alteration of the Constitution. But however it was understood, it would probably have occasion'd great Inconvenience, and Confusion, and made a seat in the Privy Council not very desireable. It was repeled the fourth of Anne, Chap. 8. The fifth is so drawn, as to exclude all Foreigners that were naturalized before this Act, yet every subsequent Act of Naturalization might, and of course would, have been a repele of this Provision, as to the Person naturalized by such Act. This surely was very absurd; unless it was in truth design'd to affect those Foreigners only who came over with King William, and had been naturalized and prefer'd by him. It was explained, and made sense of, by an Act in the first year of King George the first.

The sixth, was repeled in the fourth of Queen Anne, and a more rational Provision enacted in the room of it. I believe indeed such an execution of all Persons employ'd in the executive part of the Government, from the Legislature, had never been thought of before; nor could have enter'd into the heads of any Men who had just Idea's of a Free state. Even Faction it self has since been ashamed of it, and never pretended to attempt the reviving of it, in the full extent.

The Seventh is indeed a Wise and just Provision, but imperfect, as the Judges Commissions determine, it seems, with the Life of the King who gave them, so that upon a demise of the Crown, an able, and upright Judge, may be arbitrarily turn'd out, notwithstanding the Quam diu se bene gesserit!

The Eighth Provision, if it only means, as I think the words naturally imply, That no Pardon, should prevent any Person being try'd upon an impeachment by the Commons; Is also in my opinion just, and wise. But if it should be understood to take away the power of the Crown to pardon, after sentence, upon such Impeachment I think it would then be an improper, and cruel restraint of the royal Prerogative.

I hope I have allready said enough to shew, that these Provisions, do not deserve to be spoken of with such respect, and solemnity, as those who have not examined them, may think due. But I will venture to go farther, and shall not fear to affirm, That the Right of His Majesty King George to the Crown of Great Britain, do's not rest upon this Act of Settlement, which was made to regulate the succession to the Crown of England, by an english Parliament, that neither had, nor pretended to have, any Power to settle the Succession to the Crown of Scotland. Wherefore when the Commissioners of the two, then Separate, and Independent Kingdoms, were met to Settle the Terms upon which they were to be united into one Kingdom. The Great Men of each Nation who managed that Treaty,[26] knowing that this english Act could not direct or limit the Succession to the Crown of Great Britain, and being at the same time justly sensible, that the preservation of the Liberties, the Civil, and Religious Rights of the People of

---

[25] The senate or high council of Sweden consisted of the king's personal advisers.

[26] Treaty of Union between Scotland and England, agreed 22 July 1706. It led to the Acts of Union between the two countries of 1706 and 1707, uniting the two kingdoms. Prior to these acts the two countries had been separate states with a shared monarchy.

the United Kingdom, must entirely depend upon the Succession to the Crown in the Protestant Line. They resolved to fix it, upon a firm, and humanly speaking, immovable foundation; and to that end, made it the Second Article, indeed the first condition of the Union. That the Crown of Great Britain, in default of the Issue of her Majesty Queen Anne, should defend to the Princess Sophia Electress & Duchess dowager of Hanover, and the Heirs of her body being Protestants and that all Papists, and Persons marrying Papists, should be excluded from, and forever incapable to inherit, possess, or enjoy the Imperial Crown of Great Britain. The Protestant succession in the present royal Family, and the Execution of all Papists, and Persons marrying Papists, being thus made an Article of the Union, absolute and without any reference to the future consideration of the British Parliament. I may presume to say, that it cannot be repeled, or alter'd by the Parliament of Great Britain; which owes its Being, and its Authority over the united Kingdom, to that Treaty of Union. And may it prove in the Event, that this Settlement of the Crown of Great Britain on the present royal Family. Imperium sine fine dedit.[27] I will secondly venture to affirm that seven of the before recited eight provisions, being not mention'd in the Articles, are repele'd by the Act of Union. The english Act of Settlement is indeed refer'd to in the second Article of the Union, but merely as descriptive of the Person on whom the Crown is settle'd. And so great care was taken in drawing up this Article to avoid giving any pretence to say, that the english Act of Settlement was adopted into, or made part of the Article; that at the end of the Provision, in the Article, against Papists, and Persons marrying Papists, the reference is not made to the Act of Settlement the 12th of W[illiam]3[r]d. but to the Act of the first of William and Marie [Mary]. The 25 Article of the Union says, All Laws and Statutes inconsistent with the Terms of these Articles to be void. But in truth, without any such Article, every Law in either Kingdom inconsistent with the Union must upon the Commencement of it, necessarily become Void. The Parliament of England had no Power over Scotland and seven of the so often mention'd Provisions, could not have a partial effect in England only, but if they had any force, must affect the whole united Kingdom, were therefore inconsistent with the Union, and consequently repele'd by it. And what ever Force any of them now have, they received from Acts of the British Parliament. The Seventh Provision only, must be allow'd to have always continued in force as to the english Judges.

These things were I believe well understood at the time of the Union, but I confess they seem to have been forgot since; and I fear the english Lawyers &c. have been too apt to look upon the poor Kingdom of Scotland, as being annex'd to, rather than united with, the rich, and powerfull Kingdom of England. But I would desire them to consider, whether if these Provisions had been in an Act of the Scots Parliament, made to regulate the Government of Scotland, it would ever have been thought, that they were binding upon the Crown, and Kingdom of Great Britain. Yet as before the Union each Crown was equally Imperial, and Independent; the Argument would be the same on one side, as on the other. The different strength and Riches of the two Countrys will make no difference in point of Right. The King of France has no more Right to regulate the Government of Geneva, than that Republic has, to regulate the Government of France.

---

[27] Virgil, *Aeneid*, i, 279: 'I have given him rule without end'.

It may perhaps be said that this Argument would not at this time, readily have occurred to any but a Scotsman. Be it so, if the Argument is just, what is that to the purpose? Truth is the same on whatever side it appears, and has in it self the same invincible Force, whoever it helps, or hurts.

The first Parliament of Great Britain[28] were [*sic*] so sensible that the Acts of the English Parliament could have no force upon the whole united Kingdom, that they pass'd an Act entitle'd, an Act for the Security of Her Majesties Person and Government, and of the Succession to the Crown of Great Britain in the Protestant Line. The greatest part of which Act is in the very same words with an Act of the English Parliament passed in the fourth of Queen Anne entitled, An Act for the better Security of her Majesties Person & Government and of the Succession to the Crown of England in the Protestant Line. And in this British Act they declared, and enacted, the Act made in England, in the sixth of William & Marie [Mary] for the frequent meeting and calling of Parliaments to extend to the Parliament of Great Britain; as fully, and effectually, to all intents constructions, and purposes, as if the same were therein and thereby particularly recited and enacted. A strong proof that they were sensible the Act commonly called the Triennial Act,[29] was virtually repeled by the Union.

The Second Article of the Union.[30]

That the Succession to the Monarchy of the United Kingdom of Great Britain, and of the Dominions thereto belonging, after Her most sacred Majesty and in default of Issue, of Her majesty, Be, remane, and continue, to the most excellent Princess Sophia Electress and Duchess dowager of Hanover, and the Heirs of her body being Protestants, upon whom the Crown of England is settled by an Act of Parliament made in England in the Twelfth year of the Reign of his late Majesty King William the Third intitled An Act for farther the Limitation of the Crown, and better securing the Rights and Liberties of the Subject. And that all Papists and Persons marrying Papists shall be excluded from, and forever incapable to Inherit, possess, or enjoy, the Imperial Crown of Great Britain and the Dominions thereunto belonging, or any Part thereof, and in every such Case the Crown and the Government shall from time to time, descend to, and be enjoy'd by such Person, being a Protestant as should have inherited, and enjoy'd the same, in Case such Papist or Person marrying a Papist was naturally dead. According to the provision for the descent of the Crown of England, made by another Act of Parliament in England in the first year of the Reign of their late Majesties King William & Queen Marie [Mary] Intitled an Act declaring the Rights and Liberties of the Subject, and settling the Succession of the Crown.

N.B. In page 10. I would by no means be understood to say. That any Law do's or can, supersede that inherent Right, which the People have, to preserve their Liberties, and to defend the continuation by which those Liberties are secured.

---

[28] That is, those from 1707, after the Acts of Union (of 1706 and 1707) between England and Scotland, and the Treaty of Union of 1706.

[29] Triennial Act (1694), also known as the Meeting of Parliament Act (1694) (6 & 7 Wm & Mary, c.2) established yearly parliaments and general elections every third year. It was superseded by the Septennial Act of 1716 which allowed for general elections every seven years and established a period of political stability.

[30] Campbell has copied the second article word for word.

Enclosed:[31]

From the Glo[u]cester Journal

Let us look round one moment and observe how our Fine serving Patriots change, as the Objects of their Interest or Ambition vary. It is but a little while ago that Mr Pitt hated General Conway, put a negative on Lord Melbourne, and was abused to his face by Coll Barré. Lord Temple hated Lord Lyttelton, abused Lord Gr and his Friends threaten'd to impeach the Duke of Bedford, and a thousand times, called his Brother G[eorge] G[renville] odious, and contemptible.

Padet hæc Opprobria

Et diu potuisse, et non potuisse refelli[32]

Uter est insanior horum[33]

---

[31] There is an indication that this has been torn from the bottom of one of Campbell's letters.

[32] 'I am not ashamed that these reproaches can be cast upon us, and that they can not be repelled.' Ovid, *Metamorphoses*, i, lines 758–9.

[33] 'Which of these is more mad?' Horace, *Satires*, 2.3, line 102.

Appendix 4: Comments on the Preface to Spelman's Sixth Book of Polybius, and upon P. Francis' *Orations of Demosthenes* (c.1759)[1]

Page 1. By the spoils of conquer'd Nations Cæsar[2] enabled to bribe &c.

Cæsar did not only bribe, but flatter the roman People to their Ruin. Which all must do, who would raise themselves to exorbitant Power in a Free state. For great Alterations though projected by, and for the advantage of, a single Person, or a Few, must be executed by the Many, who are therefore to be made believe they shall be great Gainers by the Change. To which end they must be flatter'd in their inclination to Licentiousness, their desire of Power, and their Envy of all above them. The Laws must often be represented as injurious restraints of their Liberty, and the legal Majestrates as public Enemys, Oppressors, and Plunderers. And those who have cancell'd, interested, Designs, must boast themselves to be the honest uncorrupted friends of the People, who labor incessantly, and run all hazards to preserve, or retrieve, the public Liberty, and do Right to an injured Nation.

Page 2 & 3. The excellence of our Constitution is the Ballance of the three constituent Parts, Regal, Aristocratical, and Democratical. But I fear what the People are so much in Love with, and so jealous of loosing, is not the Ballance, but their own share, of Power, which they are apt to think can never be too great. And I have seen pretended Patriots use all their Arts to persuade the People that their share of the Government was in danger, at the same time that it was daily encreasing; And to raise a jealousy of the royal Power, though visibly declining. Perhaps indeed the depressing of the legal Kingly Power, may be the Occasion of our falling at length under a Despotic Monarchy. If it happens, Wee shall owe our Misery to false pretended Patriotism. Hec savior ulla Pestis, et Ira Deum, stygus sese extulit undis.[3]

Page 4. It is said. The Party quarrels with things and the Leaders with Persons consequently a change of Measures may appease the first, but nothing less than a change of Ministers can satisfie the last. He should rather have said. That the Leaders quarrel with Persons, because they envy and covet their Power, and Office's, and they gain followers by persuading, and confidently assuring them, that the measures of the administration are either Weak, or Wicked; consequently the Leaders will not be

---

[1] Edward Spelman (*d.* 1767) republished his Preface to Polybius in 1758 as an appendix to his four-volume translation of *The Roman Antiquities of Dionysius Halicarnassensis*, as a defence against Nathaniel Hooke's (*d.* 1763) repudiation of the earlier work. Spelman's Preface included a demand to repeal the Septennial Act, while the volume as a whole included an attempt to parallel the tripartite government of Rome with that of mid 18th-century Britain. All four volumes are available at www.archives.org.

[2] Gaius Julius Cæsar (100–44 BC), Roman general and consul.

[3] 'Hec savior ulla Pestis, et Ira Deum, stygus sese extulit undis. Recte: Nec saevior ulla pestis et ira Deum Stygiis sese extulit undis.' 'No crueller plague ever rose from the waters of Styx at the anger of the Gods.' Virgil, *Aeneid*, iii, 214. (This is from Virgil's description of the Harpies.)

satisfied without a change of Ministers, and, though the desire, and expectation of gaining by the change, extends much further than this Writer Seems to think, yet perhaps the Bulk of the Party may believe they should be satisfied with a change of Measures. But in that Case their Leaders would easily find, new Grievance's to complane of, or means to persuade them, that the alteration of measures was made at a wrong time, or only through fear, and that the Ministers had still the same Designs, or were incapable of carrying the right Measures in a proper Manner. Nay when the Leaders of Faction have got full possession of the public credulity, they sometimes will not be ashamed to inveigh against Measures they have a little before warmly recommended, or to declare for such as they lately declamed against. And a Party may follow their old Leaders in the persute of the very same Measures, they zealously opposed, under a former Administration. These Things will appear strange and surprising to Library Politicians, but are made familiar to such as have sat long in public Assemblys.

When the Resentment of the People against the Administration arises, naturally from Evils or Oppressions, which they sensibly feel; the Case is very different. I do not call that Faction or Party. Though even then, Ambitious, interested, & designing Men, will find opportunities enough, to do mischief, and to prevent Good. I agree however with this Writer, that Parties, and Opposition ever were, and ever will be, in all free states. Some degrees of them may be necessary, will be usefull. But the excess of them must be destruction of the best Government. Therefore the reasoning will allways be fallacious, when they are spoken of in general, without distinguishing the degrees. When Opposition, or Parties run high, an honest Man will join himself to that which he thinks the right side; but he should guard himself, as much as possibly he can, that he may not be carried too far by Prejudices, or Passions on the one hand; and be carefull not to let speculation, make him too delicate on the other. The best Administration will sometimes do wrong, and the most just, and necessary Opposition, will not be constantly in the Right. A prudent Man will not desire, lightly, to make frequent Changes in the Administration, lest he should, prejudice the Public, which he intends to serve, and become the Fool of other Men's Ambition, who possibly may not be found more able, or more honest, than those they labor to displace.

Page 5. It is true what is there said, that in these Contests both Parties appeal to the Public. But do they desire equal judgement, will not one side, at least be conscious, that their proceedings will not bear an impartial full & fair examination, and will not they endeavor, by all the arts they are Masters of, to prejudice, and by false Evidence mislead, those judges they affect so much to revere. And have not the People, by such means, been often prevaled upon to give the most mistaken, and unjust judgements, and to gratifie the worst of Men, by destroying the best Citizens, who had most faithfully served the Public. Good Men will act uniformly, and resolutely, for the true Interest of the People, will inform them truely, and endeavor to bring them to a right way of thinking. But the Designing, and irregularly Ambitious, will always flatter them, and say what they think will captivate, and please, without any regard to the Truth. They who oppose Government have generally the Advantage; for the Multitude are easily prejudiced against their Governors, and readily hearken to any thing that is said to the disadvantage of the Rich, and Great. I most heartily agree with this Writer, as to the End of every Institution of Government, and what is the Duty, and the True honor of every one of the Orders, our Government is composed of. And I think that the present

Constitution of the British Government is the best I have heard, or read of. But everything Human, the Political, as well as the natural Body carries in it the Seeds of Corruption, which will, in time, destroy it. Both Body's may by proper care, and the judicious application of wholesome Remedies, be kept alive and preserved in health, for a considerable time. Yet their very food breeds distempers and Commerce, which polish's, inrich's and strengthens; will in time, corrupt, infeeble, and by those means destroy, the very state it has raised to envied Greatness.

Page 6. Mr Spelman roundly declares his belief, that there is not a Man in Great Britain, who is not convinced, nor a Man not actually in the Administration, or expecting one day to be in it, who will not own, that annual Parliaments are an effectual Case for all the Evils that are felt, fear'd or complane'd of. If this Gentleman's fondness for his own Fancies would have given him leave to consider the nature of Man, and of all human Affairs; he must have seen, that such an effectual Care for all political Evils; was like the Philosophers stone, only to be found in Imagination and he could not have thought, that a Maxim must necessarily appear self evident to all Men, because it seem'd so to him. There is no Man in Britain who expects less to be in the Administration than myself. Yet I am by no means convinced of the expediency of annual Parliaments. Indeed there appears to be a fallacy in very Terms, as used by this Writer. One would naturally suppose that by annual Parliaments, he meant Parliaments chosen annually, and sitting regularly every year. But was that the Case for some hundred years? Can Mr Spelman shew in History a long tract of Time during which the People enjoy'd annual Parliaments, in this, the only proper, sense of the Words? If he cannot, all that he has built, upon a mistaken fact, must fall to the Ground. He is pleased to say that the Treaties of Bretigny,[4] and Troyes[5] were concluded, and the Victories of Crecy,[6] and Agincourt[7] gained, under the Auspices, as he pompously expresses it, of annual Parliaments. Should that be granted, would it prove such Parliaments to be an effectual Case for all Political Evils? Was not the Ambition of Edward the 3d[8] and Henry the 5[9] to conquer France, a very great Evil? which their Parliaments were sometimes sensible of, could not Cure, but submitted to maintain.

Statutes have indeed been made for Parliaments to be held annually; but it does not appear that they were observe'd Parliaments were called, Pro re nata,[10] and dissolved when the Busyness they were called for was dispatch'd. Sometimes there were several Parliaments in a short space, and sometimes a considerable interval without a Parliament. It is but since the accession of William the 3d[11] that the Parliament has regularly, and constantly sat every Year. In truth it appears to me, that the Statutes of the 4th and 36th[12] of Edward the 3d were not made to provide against long Parliaments; but to

---

[4] Treaty of Brétigny (1360), between England and France, ending the first phase of the Hundred Years War.

[5] Treaty of Troyes (1420), between England and France, after Agincourt.

[6] Battle of Crecy (1346), between England and France.

[7] Battle of Agincourt (1415), between England and France.

[8] Edward III (1312–77), king of England.

[9] Henry V (1386–1422), king of England.

[10] In the circumstances.

[11] William III (1650–1702), king of England.

[12] 4 Edw. iii, c.13 and 36 Edw. iii, st. i, c.10.

secure the sitting of a Parliament every Year. Long Parliaments were not I believe thought of in those days. The Kings, Wee may suppose, did not desire, by keeping a Parliament allways in being, to make it a constant fix'd, necessary Part of the Government. And the Power of the House of Commons was not then risen so high, as to make the Members desire to serve for several years togather.

This Writer allows that the Democratic Part of our Government cannot conveniently be exercised by the collective Body of the People; But thinks that a Representative, under proper regulations, answers all the Purposes of the People's voting in a Collective Body, and is subject to none of the inconveniences of it. If so, I think I may venture to say, that whatever raises, or sinks the Power of the House of Commons, must, till they cease to be Representatives of the People, raise or sink the Democratic part of the Government. And this might have help'd Mr Spelman to answer his own Question viz: How comes it to pass, that so many successive Oppositions have never, in the warmest season of their Contest, taken one step to restore annual Parliaments. Not to dispute about the use of the word restore, it may be said; that if the Leaders of those Oppositions had the least remanes of good Intention in their hearts, or of sincerity in their Professions, they did not attempt to make Parliaments annual, because they knew it would sink the Power of the House of Commons, and be productive of many Inconveniences; some of which this Writer has mention'd. But in his Answer to the objections he states against annual Parliaments, and in his commendation of the Times, when he imagines they were so, he forgot to take any notice of one thing relating to those Times, though a most notorious Truth, I mean that in the days he thinks so happy, and glorious, the People of England, were, beyond comparison, less free, than they have been since the Revolution in 1688; which yet did not establish annual Parliaments. It may be true that at some times, for a short space, they possessed themselves, not only of their due, but of an exorbitant share of Power. Yet their regular, legal, Settled liberty never bore any proportion to what Wee now enjoy. And I suspect that sometimes when they appear to be asserting their Liberties, and assuming a high degree of Power, they were in reality only acting as the Dupes, and Fools, of the great lords. There is not allways the greatest enjoyment of Liberty; where the name is most used. There is no Country in Europe where Liberty is more talk'd of; or in higher terms, than in Poland; yet where is there greater slavery, or fewer Free Men? This Gentleman confess's that endeavors have been used to restore triennial Parliaments, but that, he says, would have been only a palliative remedy, not a Cure; which he proves by reminding us, that several essential Clauses in the Act of Settlement[13] were repele'd, the Peace of Utrecht[14] confirm'd, he means approved, and Schism Act[15] passed by triennial Parliaments. As to the Clauses, he is pleased to call essential, in the Act of Settlement, I think that whatever Parliament repele'd them, did very right. And if the Parliaments had been annual in the latter part of Queen Anne's Reign,[16] I am so far from believing they would have refused, to pass the Schism Act, or approve the Treaty

---

[13] 12 &13 Wm III, c.2. The Act of Settlement was passed in 1700 to ensure a protestant monarchy.

[14] The Treaty of Utrecht (1713) established the Peace of Utrecht and ended the war of the Spanish Succession.

[15] 13 Anne, c.17 (1714). A tory act which was aimed at repressing dissenters and dissenting schools. It was repealed by the Religious Worship Act of 1718. 5 Geo. I, c.4.

[16] Anne (1665–1715), queen of England.

of Utrecht, that I am persuaded they would have enable'd the Enemies of Liberty, then in Power, to make larger, and more hasty steps towards the ruin of our Constitution. And as Mr Spelman has not favor'd us with his reasons for believing they would have done better, I am as Free, as he, to assert my own opinion.

For my own Part I do not determine against septennial Parliaments. Human Nature is such, that there must be some degree of self Interest mix'd, to make men be assiduous in the discharge of their public Duty. All men naturally love Power, but few would think such a Power, to be held only one Year, in effect no more than six months, was worth taking any trouble to obtane, or giving much attention to, when it was conferr'd upon them. Nor would the Members of any Parliament be very earnest to engage in, or persue Measures, which might be all undone, by another set of Men, before the Year came round.[17] A term of seven Years is not long enough to make the Representatives forget their Constituents, but so short a Term as one Year, would make them too subject to popular Humor, and Clamor, and too fearfull, even of doing right if it was contrary to the present Bent of the People, perhaps imposed upon and inflamed, by designing, wicked Men. If there is a strong objection against septennial Parliaments it is rather, as I think, that they raise the Power of the Commons too high, and too much depress, that of the Crown, and the Lords.

When I have said this, I will freely acknowledge that, in my opinion, the Part of the Septennial Act[18] which continued the then sitting Parliament four Years beyond the time for which they were chosen, was an irregular, and illegal stretch of Power; which could only be justified by the Necessity. I am indeed satisfied the necessity was real, and in such a Case, Salus Populi Suprema Lex.[19] But though this Writer said, at first, that Annual Parliaments were an effectual Cure for all our Political Evils, he tells us page 12. The People have a right to have a Place Bill go hand, in hand, with the Bill for Annual Parliaments, in support of which Right, he quotes from Whitlock a Clause formerly incerted in the Writs of Summons viz: Nolumus autem quod aliquis de retinentia domini Regis aliqualiter sit electus.[20] Whether the Word retinentia[21] will include Officers of state, and all persons in public Employments under the Crown, whether it was a Clause of exclusion, or of favourable exemption, and whether a long disused Clause, in the old Writs, proves a Right, are Questions I will not take upon me to answer. But I believe an exclusion of all Persons employ'd in the executive part of the Government from the Legislature, was never known in any Free state. I think it very absurd, and of dangerous consequence. There are many strong Arguments against a Place Bill, but I will so far agree with Mr Spelman as to allow, that it is very fit to go hand, in hand, with a Bill for annual Parliaments. This gentleman has upon second thoughts in Page 13 added to his annual Parliament, another necessary viz That the People be equally represented. In what manner he would regulate the Representation, he has not been pleased to say, nor can I Ghess; therefore I shall only observe, that it

---

[17] One line has been erased here.

[18] 1 Geo. I, st. ii, c.38 (1715).

[19] 'The welfare of the people is the supreme law'. Cicero, *De Legibus*, 3.

[20] 'We do not however desire that anyone of the lord king's retinue be in any way elected', from a parliamentary writ *de eligendo*.

[21] Retinue.

is very dangerous to make, or attempt, great innovations in the Constitution, how plausible soever they may appear, without they are absolutely, & evidently necessary.

It is easy to make fine schemes when the Government, and the People to be govern'd, are equally the Creatures of the Imagination. But to govern the World, such as Wee find it, is a very different Task.

Liberty is the greatest temporal Blessing, and the natural Right of Mankind. Many are too apt to call Licentiousness by that sacred Name; though nothing is more contrary to or can be more destructive of it. Liberty cannot subsist without Law, which it is the busyness of Licentiousness to weaken, and render ineffectual. Therefore all those, who really aim at undue Power, and to free themselves into the highest stations, but affect to be Patriots, use their utmost endeavors to bring the Laws, the Magistrates, and regular Administration of Government, into Contempt; magnifying on all occasions the Power of the People, and flattering them by calling their Envy, public Spirit, their Malice Justice, and their Rage virtuous Bravery. In hopes to be raised, by the rash Folly, and blind Credulity of the Populace, to those Heights that are the objects of their Ambition.

N.B. the first Page of this Preface is the 371 page of the Volume I should suppose that an english translation of a Greek Author was design'd for the use of such Englishmen as have some tast for Learning, but have little knowledge of the Greek language. I am therefore surprised to find that Mr Spelman has writ english Notes many of which cannot be well understood by anyone that has not a pretty good knowledge of the Greek. I think, with a little more trouble, he might have made his notes of greater use to an english Reader. And I confess I do not see any great entertainment to an Englishman, in his very frequent corrections of the two French Translations.

Translation of Diononisus Halicarnass:[22] Volume 1 Page 93 End of the Note I approve limitted Monarchy as much as Mr Spelman. But his assertion in this Place goes too far. One cannot promise so much for any Human Government. Besides the Roman Empire was too large to be govern'd by limitted Monarchy; unless he means that Italy, or some part of it, should have been a limitted Monarchy, and all the rest dependent Province's govern'd by Vice Roys, much in the same manner as they were by the Proconsils.[23] In that case it is probable some Vice Roy would have acted the part of Cæsar, or the Provinces would have rebelled, and if Rome had not, as most likely she would, lost her Liberty, she would at least have lost her dominion.

Page 209. last note. There is indeed no flattery in saying that the Romans had lived like Greeks from the time they were assembled in the same City, and did not at the time he wrote attempt anything more illustrious in the persute of Virtue, than they had done formerly. But I must confess I cannot see that oblique Reflection on their lost Virtue which Mr Spelman observe's reachs even to the throne of Augustus.[24] I suspect that he imputes his own Thoughts to Dionysius.

Page 299. Curtius[25] seems to have done what is said to be impossible. I know not how he threw himself into the Water, which was surrounded with so much Mud, nor

---

[22] Dionysius Halicarnassus (c.60 BC–c.7 BC), Greek historian.

[23] Proconsul – the governor of a province in the Roman republic, appointed for one year by the senate.

[24] Founder of the Roman empire and its first emperor from 27 BC until his death in 14 BC.

[25] Mettius Curtius was a Sabine warrior who fought under Titus Tatius during the time of Romulus.

how, or where he got out did he full armed wade through the Mud, and swim through the Water, or did he come out again and *Advance retireing* through the Enemy that were parted on all sides.

Vol 2. Page 324. I think the behaviour of the first Brutus[26] in regard to his sons, a disgrace to Human Nature, and to the Names of Virtue and Liberty. I did not, in my judgement, procede from a Strength of Mind superior to the tender passions, but from a hardness of heart a Disposition, incapable of feeling those Passions, or rather from a savage Pride, that had rooted them out of his Nature, and rendered him capable of committing any Barbarity to indulge that ruling Passion. Had he, as a Judge, condemned his sons to that punishment which was due to the Crime they were convicted of, and had he even suffer'd them to be executed, shewing at the same time that he felt all that inexpressible Anguish which Humanity would naturally fall upon such a dreadfull Occasion, there might have been room to believe that he was guided by a Principle of Virtue, in which Case he would have been an Object of the greatest compassion. But his whole demeanor, during that most shocking scene, was such as must raise the Honor and detestation in every humane breast. How much more respectable was the tenderness of Collatinus.[27] Unfit indeed to be the Colleague of such a Master, or to preside in an Assembly inflamed and inraged by him. One rejoices to find that the Good Man lived to old age in peacefull retirement. And surely he must have felt himself happy in being removed from among his ungratefull, cruel Countrymen, and from the hateful sight of Brutus.

Page 392. Note. I am not Grecian enough to understand the necessity of changing $Eυθυς$[28] for $αυτης$.[29] I should have thought that the first word might be used to express the sudain Alarm. But Hudson has left it out, without substituting any other in its room.

Page 412. In this third Dispute about the Abolition of Debts, both Extremes seem to be wrong. It was very fitting to give some relief to the Poor, who by Misfortunes, were become Insolvent. And, on the other hand, Appius Claudius[30] gives unanswerable Arguments against a general abolition of all Debts. It is probable that the Demands of the Plebians[31] were unreasonable, and extravagant; and I doubt not that, at the same time, many of the Patricians were so avaritious and tyrannical as to oppose all reasonable Concessions. Alike wrong were the Extremes, of placing all Power in the Senate[32] without Check or controle, or of giving up all, even executive, Power to the People. Absolute Oligarchy's, or Aristocracy's, are very bad, and tyrannical Forms of Government, but the arbitrary Power of the Collective Body, which will be exercised by what Wee call the Mob, is of all Tyranny's the worst.

---

[26] Lucius Junius Brutus, founder of the Roman republic and one of the first consuls in 509 BC.

[27] Lucius Tarquinius Collatinus (c.6th century BC), one of the leaders who overthrew the Roman monarchy.

[28] Immediately.

[29] This.

[30] Appius Claudius Crassus, decemvir of Rome, c.451 BC.

[31] The plebs was the body of free landowning Roman citizens. A member of the plebs was known as a plebeian.

[32] A deliberative assembly of elders (senate means 'old men'), the Roman senate was one of the longest surviving governmental institutions in the ancient world, traditionally founded in 753 BC, surviving until 603 AD.

Page 429. In the note, it is said, that the best thing that can be said of the Magistracy of the Dictators[33] is, that after the death of Julius Cæsar it was absolutely abolish'd. But what benefit had the People from that abolition, was not the Imperial a worse, and more absolute Magistracy, without any appeal. The successors of Julius could have no occasion, or desire to revive the Office of Dictator, when greater Dignity, and more uncontrollable Power, were annex'd to their Title of Imperator.

Vol 3 Note page 18. Surely Mr Spelman mistakes in thinking that the Popes call their Ambassadors Legates imagining that name can procure them the same consideration as the Ambassadors of old Rome for doubtless they expected, and not vainly, that the Ambassadors of the Vicar of Jesus Christ[34] should have not the same, but much greater consideration, than those of old Rome.

Page 47. Both the Consuls[35] seem to blame, both Insolent & obstinate and both appear to be actuated by Ambition & to aim at Power though be different ways, but Claudius[36] seems to have had a cruel disposition which he shew'd both to his Enemy and his fellow Citizens. Servilius was not mercifull to the enemy, but that was the common fault of the People of Rome, and of the Times he lived in.

Page 90. Nothing can be more true than what Appius Claudius says that flattering the People is the common & direct road to Tyranny. But his Proposal Page 95 in regard to the Familys of the seceder's is cruel and unjust.

258. I cannot think the Collective Body of the People could ever make a proper Court of Judicature. It may be true that this Power was executed well or ill accordingly as the Tribunes[37] were good or bad Men but as I know no way to secure the Election of good Men *only* to that office. They who acted uprightly in the Administration, had but a very precarious security. No human Institution can be perfect, but I should think a Court of Justice might have been so constituted as for the most part to secure the public Liberty against the Attempts, & designs of Ambitious Great men; and at the same time preserve worthy Magistrates from being destroy'd, or ruined by Factious, or maliciously wicked Tribunes.[38]

Page 416. I think there can be no doubt that the Roman Custom was right, and the Grecian very iniquitous, the only reason given to justifie it being false in Fact viz: That it is contrary to the Course of Nature for Virtuous sons to be the offspring of Wicked Fathers, or wicked sons of Virtuous Fathers. Whereas it is a notorious Truth that Good men have often Wicked Children, and the Children of very bad men are sometimes eminently Virtuous.

Vol 4. Page 87. It appears to me to have been a great happiness that the Romans did not wear arms in the City. If they had, it is likely this contest instead of ending in blows would have had a very bloody End.

---

[33] In the Roman republic the dictator was an extraordinary magistrate with extensive powers.

[34] The pope.

[35] The consul was the highest elective office in the Roman republic, and an appointive office under the Roman empire.

[36] Tiberius Claudius Cæsar Augustus Germanicus (10 BC–54 AD), Roman emperor.

[37] Tribune was the title shared by elected officials in the Roman republic.

[38] Is Campbell thinking here of the downfall of Walpole?

Page 132. The Consuls & Senate could not make a more impudent or wicked avowal of Tyranny, than by refusing to make the Law the Rule of their Government, for the being Govern'd by known laws is the very essence of Liberty, at least it is a condition without which Liberty cannot exist.

Page 133. There is not the least resemblance between the raining of flesh here mention'd and the Quails that are recorded to have fallen in the Camp of the Israelites, which are refer'd to in the 88 Psalm. Mr Spelman may believe as he pleases, but he should not misrepresent in order to explode or ridicule.

138. No thing could be more villainous than the conspiracy of the Tribunes to destroy Caso[39] by false Evidence. And it is not at all to be wonder'd at that the Animosity of the Young Noblemen was not extinguish'd, but inflamed by it, and that they opposed a Law, good in it self, when it was proposed by such profligate Men; But indeed there might be reason to fear that the Decemirin[40] to be chosen, in consequence of their proposal, would not prove very upright, equal Legislators.

300. The Judgement given by the Roman People, in this instance, was very shamefull, and what one would expect from a Mob.[41] The behavior of the consuls was becoming their Dignity.

Francis' Demosthenes, Essay on the Political State of Greece[42]
Page 44. Poverty & Probity. I could wish the Author had spared these sentence's. For though public Virtue & Love of Country have indeed Allways been the language of what Wee call the Opposition, yet that language will by no means prove a rectitude of intention. The Love, & fear of God have ever been the language of the Worst Hypocrites, and those words are more frequent in the mouths of such, than of truly honest, & religious Men. I could never see reason to believe, that Love of Country and Probity, were the spring, & rule of Action to the Opposition in my time. I can scarce believe that public Virtue, & Love of Country were ever, as such, avowedly laughed at and treated as proper objects for ridicule in any Nation, or by any Party. It is true that when faction, Ambition, & private resentment, have put on the Mask of Patriotism, and assumed the Names of Virtue, and public spirit, they have been, most deservedly, ridiculed, and treated with contempt. Nay I make no doubt that real Virtue, and true Love of country have been often ridiculed; but then the Men by whom they were so treated, did, at least, pretend to believe them false, and counterfeit; Otherwise such ridicule could have done no hurt, could never have met with any encouragement, and would have served only to raise a general indignation against those who openly declared themselves lost, to all sense of Virtue, Honor, or Shame.

---

[39] Cæso Quinctius who was the son of Lucius Quinctius Cinncinnatus (520–430 BC), dictator, was falsely accused of murder.

[40] Decemviri (ten men), commissions established between 451 and 49 BC to write up the code of law defining the Roman administration. The magistracy was suspended while the commissions sat, though the latter soon became notorious for corruption and were abolished after two years.

[41] This refers to the attempt by Appius Claudius Crassus, decimvir in 451 BC, to abduct the beautiful young girl Verginia. When she rejected him he had Marcus Claudius declare that she was his slave. Rather than let her lose her freedom, her father stabbed her.

[42] *Orations of Demosthenes*, i (1757) and the *Orations of Demosthenes and Æchines*, ii (1758), translated by the Rev. Phillip Francis (1708–73), with a dedication to Henry Fox. These translations were deemed inferior to others. John Campbell was one of the subscribers to these volumes. See Introduction.

Page 46. The Observation that in their Address to the People Æschines[43] allways says O Athenians, & Demosthenes[44] O Men of Athens; is not strictly true, for Æschines, in the very first sentence of his Oration against Timarchus,[45] says O Men of Athens, and repetes the same Words twice again in a very short space.[46]

Orations Page 11. First line. The words military operations are here, undoubtedly, put by mistake, for military Preparations.

Page 138: The close of the Notes seems to hint at the Case of the late Admiral Byng, but the Author concluded a little too harshly.[47] He afterward saw that the Protection afforded to that unhappy Gentleman, by some Orators, who were indeed at the same time Ministers, was weak, & unavaileing. In our Country the popular Orators were not allways Ministers and I Doubt if they were allways so at Athens. In truth they have been too often able, to destroy the best Ministers, and raise to Power Men of very different Characters.[48]

Page 140. Note. I am not well acquainted with the state, and course of corruption at Athens. But in our own Country I know, it is not, so much advantage taken of the People's Poverty to corrupt their Honesty, as the licentiousness of the People taking advantage of the Ambition of the Gentry, & Rich, to extort extravagant Price's for their Votes.[49]

Page 160. There cannot be a more just Observation than, That flatterers are never the most Faithfull, or most usefull servants, in public, or private life, to the Prince, the People or Particulars.

Page 180. The man who sells his vote is allways infamous and corrupt, whether he gives a wrong Vote for hire, or insists upon being paid for giving a right one. But there is the widest difference between him that hires a Man to do a bad Action, and him that pays a Man for doing right, who would not do his duty without reward.

Page 191. Though I have scarce any knowledge of the Greek language, I cannot think the word Φιλανθρωπος,[50] in this place, is rightly express'd in English. When the Orators insisted upon the Acts of Hostility committed by Philipp,[51] and his perpetual Violations of the Peace, their Orations might well appear full of public spirit, and the

---

[43] Aeschines (389–14 BC), Greek statesman and orator.

[44] Demonsthenes (384–22 BC), Greek statesman and orator.

[45] Timarchus was a usurper in the Hellenistic empire of Seleucid, in the years 163–60 BC.

[46] The oration of Timarchus contains a large bulk of Athenian law.

[47] Admiral John Byng (1704–57), executed for failing to do his utmost to prevent the French from taking Minorca. See Chapter 6, letters 158–60. Francis' note reads: 'how near to Ruin must be that maritime state, whose Admiral dares to be a Coward or a Traytor, yet is protected from the vengeance of his Country, by the Administration, and the Ministers: for such were the Orators of Athens'.

[48] Campbell's comment here is referring to Pitt and his part in the downfall of Walpole.

[49] Francis comments of the people how 'Advantage was taken of their poverty, to corrupt their Honesty in giving their Votes for Places and Employments. They were intimidated by Menaces, or deceived by promises, or seduced by Adulation . . . In the last Excess of Corruption they were debauched in their sobriety and Temperance by drunken Riots and Luxurious Entertainments. From hence . . . proceeded the Destruction of Greece and Rome. And from the same Principle will invariably and forever proceed the Destruction of all future States'. Campbell's view seems strange to modern readers – that the poor corrupt the rulers.

[50] Philanthrops – Francis comments on page 191, footnote, that it has been translated as 'humane'.

[51] Philip V (238–179 BC), king of Macedon 221–179 BC.

love of their fellow Citizens, but it seems to me rather ludicrous to say they appear'd, to the People, to be filled with sentiments of exceeding moderation.

Page 225. Nothing can be more just, Wise, & honorable than the Advice here given by Demosthenes to the Men of Athens.[52]

Page 232. Nothing can be more noble than the sentiments express'd in this Page.[53]

Page 240. How beautifull is this description of a Wise and Honest speaker in a public Assembly, but such it seems were not allways the best heard, or most admired, at Athens, more than in other Places.[54]

---

[52] See Introduction.

[53] Demosthenes comments on the indolence of the Greeks in the face of a common enemy – Philip V, king of the Macedonians. Campbell could have in mind Britain's precarious position in the Seven Years War at this time.

[54] Demosthenes writes that 'who never speaks for popular Favour, but always for the public Good . . . this is the Citizen of Real courage, and Useful Abilities. Far different from those, who with daily Adulation have destroyed the Power and Grandeur of the Commonwealth'. Campbell's dislike of 'popular favour' is very evident from his letters, and Pitt's pursuit of such popular politics in particular raised the ire of the dour Campbell.

Appendix 5: The Substance of a Letter, to a Friend in Scotland upon the Militia Scheme, August 1762[1]

Decipimur Specie Recti.[2]

I think the principal Arguments made use of in favor of the Militia Scheme, are. The danger to our Liberties from a standing Army. The great Expence of keeping up, in time of Peace an Army sufficient to secure us against sudain attempts from abroad. The great advantage of being defended by Men who, in Case of an Invasion, will fight, not merely for pay, but for their own Properties, their Wives, their Children, their Liberty, and Religion. With all that is dear, and valuable to them, allmost in their sight. And the Justice of puting Arms into the hands of a Free People, to defend their Country, against foreign Enemies, or their Rights, and Liberty, if illegally invaded by their Governors at Home.

I confess my apprehensions of danger, from the Army to the public Liberty, are not very great while I see it commanded, for the most part, by Men of Rank, and Property, or the younger sons of considerable Familys. And I am strongly inclined to believe it will allways be so commanded: And then I trust such Officers will not give up the most valuable Rights, Privileges, and Propertys belonging to themselves, or their Family's, for the sake of precarious Commissions. An Officer, if he is but the younger son of a Noble, or Opulent Family, will not only have an attachment to, and a regard, and affection for his Family, and near Relations, but he will also consider his own Right of eventual succession to their Homes, and Fortunes.

The expence of our Army is indeed great; but that of the Militia when drawn out, is I believe as great; besides the Provision for their Wives and Children in their Absence; an Advantage not given to the Army. And when, upon a Peace, the Militia are return'd to their respective Homes, and only to be brought togather, and exercised, by Regiments or Battallions, twenty eight days in a Year, I am affraid it will be very unsafe to rely upon them for our defence, so far as to reduce our regular Forces to a small Number.

The Name of Mercenaries has been frequently given by the favorers of this scheme, as a term of reproach and contempt, to our regular Forces. Yet the Militia, when drawn out, are as much Mercenaries as they. And indeed all soldiers, if they have not means of their own, sufficient to maintain them at a distance from home, must when drawn away, either be paid, live upon free Quarter, or starve. Much has been said, and writ, to shew the danger from Mercenary's, and with great truth when apply'd to foreign hired Troops; for if such are sufficiently numerous, employing them for defence at

---

[1] A bill for the continuance of the English militia was debated in Mar. 1762. Scottish members considered bringing in a separate bill for Scotland, but nothing came of it. J.R. Western, *The English Militia: The Story of a Political Issue 1660–1802* (1965), 174. See Introduction.

[2] 'We are deceived by the appearance of what is right.' Horace, *Ars Poetica*, line 25.

home, must put the Liberty of the Country, where they are so entertan'd, to the utmost hazard. Nor can it be denied, that Nations may, and have been enslaved, and ruined by Armys of their own Natives. There are dangers which no human Prudence can foresee, or Caution prevent. I would ask whether, in King Charles the first time,[3] the Liberties of England might not have been endanger'd by a militia constituted exactly like the present. It is certane they were overturn'd, by a [*sic*] Army of English Volunteers raised for their defence. I did not wonder, in the last two Reigns,[4] to hear the Name of Mercenaries, given, in Odium to our regular Forces, by a Faction violent in opposition to every Measure of Government, when there was, perhaps, too much reason to suspect that many were angry with the Army for supporting a settlement, and Constitution, with which they were dissatisfied. But now that Wee boast of being all united, Jacobitism, and Faction extinct, I cannot help wondering that any warm Friends of the present Establishment should affect to treat with contempt and aversion, those regular Force's who have fought for the Interest, and Honor of their Country, with as much bravery, and fidelity as ever were shewn by them.

The private soldiers in our regular Forces, list voluntarily, I believe a great Part of them allur'd by the levy Money.[5] The Volunteers, and substitutes in the Militia, will be the same sort of Men, and in list for the like reasons; and therefore cannot justly be prefer'd to the Regulars. To expect that Men of substance, who are balloted for the Militia will serve themselves, is surely a vane imagination; and if some, who would not if they could help it; should be obliged to serve; because they cannot afford to pay substitutes; how constraint, and the loss of a comfortable Livelyhood, which many such may have, will encourage them to fight with alacrity, and resolution, for Liberty, and Property, I leave to the Consideration of the Patrons of this scheme.

When Men are press'd into the regular Army I believe they are generally, in a short time, pretty well reconciled to their Condition, as they do not, probably find it changed for the worse, and, if they were dismissed, could not easily alter it for the better. But the Case of a Man forced by Ballot into the Militia, will be very different. He will have a sensible, and lasting feeling of his Misfortune, unless he looses it, by drinking, and Debauchery.

The last Argument I have stated for the Militia scheme, may to some sound very fine, and, the speculation may be pleasing. But I fear, in fact, it will rather qualifie them for Mischief, than for any Honest, and Good Purpose.

The Militia are allmost as much under the power of the Crown as the Regulars. The Crown appoints the Lieutenants in every County, and the Lieutenants appoint the Deputy Lieutenants, and the Officers, who must indeed have such Estates as are specified in the Act,[6] to qualifie them, but however they are qualified, they cannot be commission'd unless they are approved of by the Crown.

If then the Crown should ever be misadvised and imposed upon by evil Ministers, designing to subvert the Constitution, and destroy the Liberties of their Fellow subjects, could such Ministers find in each County, a sufficient number of qualified Officers, who

---

[3] Charles I (1600–49), king from 1625 until his execution by parliament.

[4] George I (1660–1727), king from 1714, and George II (1683–1760), king from 1727.

[5] Levy money was that granted by the house of commons to pay for recruits to the militia.

[6] Probably the Militia Act of 1758. 32 Geo. II, c.20.

would concur in an attempt so wicked, and unnatural, the Nation might be in a great danger, from the Militia, as the most suspicious Friends of Liberty can apprehend from the regular Forces. It will no doubt be said that so profligate a set of Militia Officers could never be found. I do believe so; and may I not, with equal justice, and as good reason affirm that there is not the least probability such a Number of the Nobility, and Gentry as are in the command of the Army, should ever be made the Fools of evil Ministers to enslave themselves and their Country. But it may possibly be allege'd that the appointment of Officers for the regular Forces being originally, and absolutely, in the Crown, without any qualification, the whole set may be changed, every Man of Honor, or Property may be dismissed, and their Places fill'd by Men of no Principles, and desperate Fortunes. To this I answer, that such a Design could not be put in execution at once, so wild and barefaced an attempt could never succede, the Army would not submit to it, the whole Nation would rise against it. And if the same was endeavor'd to be effected by Degree's, the Design would appear before any considerable Progress could be made; it would be remonstrated against, and withstood; and would surely end in the Destruction of such abandon'd Men as should dare to undertake it. Whatever may have been in Times past there is a great and happy Alteration since the Revolution in 1688. The Power of the Crown, the Privileges, and Rights of the Parliament, and People, are more known, ascertained, fix'd, and secured. Liberty is better, and more generally understood, in consequence, more valued, and seems now universally allowed to be the natural Right of Mankind, as well as the legal Right of the People of Britain. And if it was really in danger, I see no cause to doubt, that much the greater Part of the Nation would be ready to assert, and maintane it, with spirit and Resolution. The Nobility, and Gentry who are in the Army I am satisfied would appear, among the first, in a Cause so just, and so honourable. The Annual meeting of the Parliament is become so necessary, and so much expected by the People of all Ranks, and Degrees, that it would scarce be possible for the Crown to avoid assembling those Guardians of our Liberty's before whom no Traytor to our Free Constitution would dare to shew his Face.

I am indeed glad that the Militia are so much under the Power of the Crown. Had they been made more independent, no Man can say, and it would be terrible to think what disorders, and convulsions such an Institution might have occasion'd, in the Kingdom, at some future, perhaps not very distant, Time.

In Case of a foreign Invasion I can see no reason to fear that even the private Men in the Army would be indifferent to their Country, or fight worse for it at home, than they have done abroad; Wee need not desire them to do better. And surely I may presume their Officers would do their Duty as well as those of the Militia; to suspect the contrary after what Wee know of their behavior, in every Quarter of the World abroad, would be most unjust, and ungratefull.

The People of Britain have been taught, by too many, to desire things that seem to me, allmost incompatible. I mean to be a mercantile, and at the same time a Military People. And Both these desires have been carried to extravagance. There are some who will not be satisfied unless Wee engross, the whole Trade of the World; and the Projectors of this scheme would, by Rotation, have made every Man in the Kingdom a soldier. I readily allow that Men in a trading Nation may be as good soldiers as any in the Worlds But if the original profess'd intention of this Militia scheme was to be carried into Execution, I fear Wee should find, by dear bought Experience, that a Military life very much indisposes most Men, for the common busyness of civil Life, either in Agriculture, Manufactures or Commerce: In truth the Notion of making every Man in a Nation like this a Soldier, was too chimerical to be, at anytime, put in Practice; the Patrons therefore of this Plan found themselves obliged, even in the first Act,[7] to consent that every Man might have a substitute, who could afford to procure one. I do not know whether they gave themselves time to observe, that by this Concession, their favorite boasted scheme, of making us a Military People, and all the imaginary fine Consequences drawn from it, fell to the Ground. And, instead of it, there came out the most inconvenient, and oppressive method of raising a Militia, that could easily be invented – laying a heavy Tax,[8] by Lot, which must necessarily fall upon very many who are unequal to the Burthen. A Gentleman of several thousands per annum, and a Man who maintains a Wife and Children upon a Farm of ten pounds per annum, which he holds at rack Rent may both be ballotted for the Militia Men; for the first to serve would be ridiculous, to the other it would be ruinous; yet it may cost as much to redeme the poor Man, as the Rich. How unequal, is how hard is this? It would be very tedious to recount the numerous, and various Cases, in which a balloted Man would be ruined, or at least greatly and grievously distress'd if he served, who yet could very ill afford to pay the Hire of a Substitute. And such I believe will very often be found the most sober, and usefull set of Men in the Kingdom. But as many of them as go into the Militia are in great danger of being debauch'd, corrupted in their Morals, and render'd both Idle, and dissolute; not likely, if they return home, at the end of three years, to be as usefull Members of Society as they were before, but rather troublesome, and burthensome to the Neighbourhood, slothfull, vicious, and insolent. And when in the course of several rotations, the Number, of sober, and industrious Men is considerably lessen'd, some of the springs of our wealth will I fear run very low.

There is another Mischief attending the present state of our Militia, which seems not to be thought of; yet to me, appears a Matter of consequence, deserving very serious consideration. Healthy and vigorous Young Men from the Country, being quarter'd in great Towns, will run much hazard of getting there, and if they return home, carrying with them, a cruel, and often fatal, distemper; to Places, and among a Set of People where it was scarce known. It might be said there is the like danger from the regulars; but they are not changed, and sent home at the end of three years, and besides will not probably carry it to the same sort of People among whom it may even in matrimony, be unknowingly propagated by the better sort of Militia Men. And by the rotation far greater Numbers may, in no long course of years, be debauched, and infected in the Militia, than in the Army.

The Militia Act orders the Men to be chosen by Lot, but gives no directions how, or by whom the Ballot shall be managed; that is left, as I shall say, to the Honor, and Discretion; some perhaps may call it the Will, and Pleasure, of a respectable Triumvirate of Deputy Lieutenants, and Justices of the Peace.

---

[7] Of 1758. 32 Geo. II, c.20.

[8] Under the terms of the Militia Pay Act (32 Geo. II, c.21), which allowed for the raising of £100,000 to pay for the militia.

The Inconveniencys of the Ballot, though fairly managed, are so great so many, and so manifest, that Wee now see the Parliament has been made sensible of them, and given such means for Procuring Volunteers, and Substitutes, as may often prevent the Ballot or save the balloted Man from the Ruin it would bring upon him if he served. Which seems to imply an acknowledgement of the absurdity, and impracticability of the Original scheme, and it may I think be conjectured that the Ballot would have been quite taken away, but to avoid giving Offence to the Projectors of it, who might be unwilling to see, and yet more unwilling so explicitly to confess, their Mistake.

What is done by the last Act[9] palliate's but does not cure the evil; for a Man who is ballotted may yet be obliged to pay half the price of a substitute, which the Act supposes may amount to five pounds; and it cannot be doubted that the Idle Fellows in every part of England, and Wales, will know how to take the advantage, and make their Market, of the Sober and Industrious many of whom can but ill afford to pay five pounds. But if it is taken for granted that by the help of this Provision, every Man to whom it would be ruinous or greatly inconvenient, will avoid the Militia Service; then as I before observed, instead of making all the good People of England soldiers, Wee have with much Care, and repeted Pains, form'd a most troublesome, severe, and unequal scheme, for raising a Militia of little use for our safety against Dangers from abroad, and of no security to our Constitution at home; form'd, as to the private Men, of much the same sort, as are in our regular Army; and as to the Officers in the Militia it must I think be expected that many of them who possess, or are Heirs to small Estates will be in great danger of being made more Idle, debauched, and expensive than as yet they are, though Luxury has made, allready, an unhappy progress even in the most remote Countys. This scheme will I doubt not hasten its destructive March. There are, I am satisfied many good, and gallant Officers in the Militia; but I cannot help fearing that no small number of them will be spoil'd for Country Gentlemen, without being much improved as Officers.

It has not come much in my way to observe the Militia; but I think one would not naturally expect they should be kept under as good Discipline as the Regulars. In the Army the Officers, and private Men, know each other only in their military Relation. In the Militia the Officers and their Men are known to each other in their civil state; and a Man will probably think it very hard to be punish'd, or severely reprimanded, by a Gentleman whom he, his Father, or some of his Friends may have served at home, or have obliged on some occasion in civil Life; and the Mans Friends may remember, and resent it. An Officer may be unwilling to provoke such, or any who themselves, or Whose Friends have follow'd, or may follow him, or those he is attach'd to, at an Election. On the other hand the Officers may be tempted to gratifie private resentments, and bear hard upon such who themselves, or whose Friends are in an opposite Interest, or have any way disobliged them in private Life. I wish, rather than expect, they may all be superior to such temptations. Wee seem at present to have two Armys in the Kingdom upon very different Establishments. A Policy I am not able to understand; and what makes it the worse one (the Militia) has in several instances; particularly the provision for their Wives and Children, had partial favour shewn to it. Is there not room to apprehend that the different Constitutions of these Army's may sometime, or other,

---

[9] The 1762 Militia Act. 2 Geo. III, c.20.

breed ill blood between them? Possibly it might have so happen'd before now, but for the Notion the Regulars entertane, fortunately at least I think, of their Superiority to the Militia. It has been said, that if the Militia had not been raised and drawn out, Wee could not have sent so great numbers of our regular Forces abroad. This I believe is true in fact, But how far it has been an advantage to the Kingdom, let those tell who have found it so; I am not of that Number.

To most that I have said, it would probably be answer'd. That in time of public danger, and in Cases of public necessity, all Particulars must submit to many Inconveniency's for the safety of the Whole. A Proposition which no Man in his senses can deny. But to say that the Mischiefs I complane of, are necessary is beging the Question. And no unnecessary much less useless Hardships, or Burthens, should be laid upon a Free People.

I wish the happy day of Peace was near in view, though many seem as little to desire, as I see ground to hope, Wee may soon enjoy that Blessing. Whenever it does come, I am sensible the bad Consequences of this Militia Scheme will not be so severely felt. The Militia Men will not then be in so great danger of being made absolutely good for nothing. They will only I suppose, be made worse servants, worse Laborers, worse Neighbors &c. without being made good soldiers, such Young Fellows as take a likeing to the Busyness, will probably learn by it, where any care is taken to teach them; and then, it may be expected, they will take the first opportunity to list into the regular Forces; where I think they will be best disposed of. The rest, I believe will learn little, and forget that little very soon.

The last Act directs that in time of Peace the Militia shall be train'd, and exercised, by Regiment, or Battalion, twice in a year for fourteen days, at each time, or once a year for twenty eight days togather. It will be necessary for them, on those occasions, to be quarter'd in Towns of pretty good reception. And whether or no the appointed times will be sufficient for them to learn the Military Art; I fear they will be very sufficient for many of them to learn Idleness and Debauchery which will not be so readily forgot as the Military Exercise.

It would be tiresome, and unnecessary to point out the many opportunities given, in this Plan, for Gentlemen to shew Partiality as Justices of the Peace, or Deputy Lieutenants; and I have no desire to reflect upon any who bear those honourable Commissions. But Wee must all be sensible, the frailty of human Nature is such, that every Power, though plac'd in the most proper hands, that can be chose, is very liable to be abused. What cannot be avoided, or help'd, should therefore be bore with patience. Yet surely the Legislature of a Free People will never knowingly grant unnecessary Powers, or such as are not usefull to some good end. And will always take the best care and precaution, they possibly can, to guard against the abuse of necessary Powers, or of such as may be of public utility when rightly exercised. If in this Case, the best care was taken that the Nature of the Scheme could admit, as in duty Wee ought to believe, I think I may conclude that the original Draught was too wrong, for any care to set it right.

I do not pretend fully to discuss this matter or to enumerate all the Misfortunes that will, or may arise from this scheme; but it seems to me that enough is obvious, to make us wish to get rid of it as soon as Wee can. And if some who fancy they can have a warmer zeal for Liberty than their Neighbors, still insist upon the danger to the

Constitution from our regular Forces; I am confident I may affirm that the danger from the Army is distant, and uncertane whereas the Mischiefs occasion'd by this scheme are great, certane, and immediate. And I dare defy any Man to say, with truth, that they who disliked the Militia Scheme have not shewn, as just notions of Liberty, and as true an Affection for it, as the greatest Patrons, and Promoters of this Plan.

Young, warm and Speculative Politicians, are too apt to make hasty conclusions upon a partial view of the subject they take into consideration, and to be charmed with Ideal Plans not fit for practice. Some Gentlemen may have seen, read, or heard of, a Militia in Switzerland, or some other foreign Country, the Plan of which pleased them; and it may be, they immediately thought, it would be very practicable, and beneficial, to have somewhat like it in England; without duely attending to the difference of Countrys, and People. Whereas all Circumstances should have been thought of, well weigh'd, and maturely consider'd; before any step had been taken towards putting such a Project in execution.

England is an extensive Country, has much Agriculture, and may have a good deal more; the English are a trading, manufacturing, rich, luxurious, and I am sorry I must add, licentious People. I know of no Country where Liberty is so fully enjoy'd; but, by *the Many* it seems not to be so well understood.

The Contrivers and Promoters of this scheme would do well to inform us, what Nation circumstanced like England, has now, or ever had, an usefull well disciplined Militia upon a similar Plan, and not productive of any Evils that overballanced the Advantages received from it. Untill that is done, I may take leave to suspect; that no such Thing ever was, or will ever be.

It is well known, that when this scheme was first proposed, the greatest Men in the Kingdom declared strongly against it, and one House of Parliament[10] rejected it, by a great majority.[11] It had indeed passed the House of Commons; but there, the number of those who declared for it was small,[12] it was never fully debated, seem'd neglected by the Majority, and only suffer'd to pass, be cause every one expected it would be thrown out, upon a debate in the other House. How the cheif Persons who then opposed it so warmly, and let me say bravely, and worthily, were towards the close of another, very memorable session, converted to it, or perhaps brought to acquiesce, without being convinced; if known, might not be proper to be told. Those who know, and remember, what was doing at that time, want no Information.

Some Persons express'd a very earnest desire to have this Plan extended to Scotland;[13] and a great deal of Oratory was made use of, to persuade the Scots that they were unkindly, and unjustly treated in being denied their share in this Patriotic scheme, which, most probably, would never have been imposed upon England, if it had not happen'd to be opiniatre'd [*sic*] by some when the Great Men were, at that time, for particular reasons, very desirous, to humor and oblige. The People of England had been artfully persuade to desire it, before they knew what it was. But I believe, the much

---

[10] It was rejected in the Lords on 24 May 1756. *LJ*, xxviii, 612. See Western, *English Militia*, 132–40, on this rejection in the lords and the bill's success in 1757.

[11] The Lords rejected it 59 to 23.

[12] It was passed in the Commons without a vote on 10 May. *CJ*, xxvii, 600.

[13] See J. Robertson, *The Scottish Enlightenment and the Militia Issue* (Edinburgh, 1985), especially ch. 4.

greater Part of them, disliked, as soon as they understood it. And it occasion'd Disorders in some Countrys, which were not quieted without capital Punishments.

The People of Scotland live remote from the seat of Government, and Legislature. This scheme, for a considerable time, was not well known, or explaned among them, and being recommended by general florid Declamation, a great part of them were induced to desire it, and complane of its being deny'd them, as an injury, and disgrace. But the Scots are now better inform'd, and many of them have declared against it, with much good sense, and great spirit. Which I presume prevaled upon some Scots Members to alter a Resolution they had come to, pretty early in the last session, to move for a Bill to extend this noble Plan, as a great Benefit, to their Native Country.[14]

It is an unquestionable Truth that Scotland has an equal Right with England to all proper means, that the Wisdom of the British Legislature can provide, for securing the Liberty, and Property of the People at home, and for their defence against all Dangers from Abroad. Therefore if I had thought, before it passed, or had since been convinced, that this Law was salutary for England, I should have been, and would now be, as zealous as any Man in the Kingdom, for extending it to Scotland. But while I continue to see it in the light in which it has allways appear'd to me, I must rejoice that the Country of my Fathers, to which I have so strong, and natural a tye, has hitherto escaped a Burthen I hope it will never feel; and that I think fits heavy upon their Neighbors. A great Part of what I have said in regard to England, may be apply'd to Scotland; though it must be confess'd that Scotland is not, by many degrees so rich as England, and therefore it may be hoped that as the People cannot be so luxurious, they are not, as yet, so licentious. That the common People are not so riotous, my own eyes have convinced me. And probably the great Draughts of brave, and able Men that have been made from that Country, for the regular Forces, have occasion'd a greater want of Hands in many parts of it, than is in England. If so, the Militia Plan would be more immediately prejudicial to Scotland.

I am humbly of opinion, that if Wee co[u]ld moderate our Ardor for Conquests, and eagerness for engrossing of all Trade; Wee should not have occasion for so great a Force to defend us. Wee should then have fewer Enemy's, and might perhaps have some Friends. But if Wee resolve to go on, conquering America in Germany, and France and Spain in America. And, in the conceit that all our Enemys are at our feet, haughtily reject all reasonable Terms of Peace, expecting to take, and hold, every Place by which Wee imagine Wee may increase our Commerce, and accommodate Wealth; I fear no Riches Wee can acquire, will be sufficient to preserve a Nation, exhausted of Men, and overloaded with Taxes and Debt. But Wee may be ruin'd in the midst of our Conquests, in the height of our Pride, and the full Blaze of our vane Glory.

---

[14] See Robertson, *Scottish Enlightenment*, 115–21.

Appendix 6: Statement upon the Removal of Army Officers from the House of Commons, 1765

Both in the late, and present, Reign a Clamor has been raised upon the Crowns dismissing a very small number of Military Officers who were members of the House of Commons and had engaged in a form'd Opposition there. It was invidiously, and malitiously, called Garbleing[1] the Army. Such will allways be the Practice's, and the Arts of Faction; which real Patriots will despise, well knowing that nothing could be more dangerous to our Constitution, than to make the Army independent of the Crown, the legal Head of the Civil Government.

---

[1] To sift or weed (an army, corporation etc.) so as to exclude unfit or uncompliant members. *OED.*

Appendix 7: Observations (c.1770)

On a Bill[1] to regulate the trail of controverted Elections, as it came from the Committee in April 1770 I should not have thought it adviseable for the House of Commons to call in the aid of the whole Legislature unless absolutely necessary, to regulate their Judicature, in Matters relating to the Elections of their Members; which seems to me a necessary and essential Privilege of that House. And I think every desireable purpose might have been answer'd by such regulations as could have been made by the Power of the House it self; the effects of which would have appear'd to the House, and might have been confirm'd or alter'd, and amended, as should be found proper. I confess the House of Commons alone could not have imposed new Oaths; but having long thought, the frequency, and multiplicity of the Oaths, a great Misfortune to this Kingdom; as the solemnity with which they ought to be administer'd, is thereby necessarily lessen'd, and consequently the awfull impression they should make upon their Mens Minds. By which means the great security every Man has for his Life, Liberty, and Property is much weaken'd. I should rather have wish'd to see many Oath's abolish'd, and many others alter'd, and abridged; than such an Amazing increase of swearing. It may be said; that all other Rights are try'd by evidence upon Oath, and therefore it is proper to put the Right of an Election to Parliament, upon the same footing. But it should be consider'd, that in the Trial of a controverted Election, every Witness is, in effect, a Party, heated and imitated by the preceding Contest. The House had a power to punish a Witness, when they discover'd falshood, or prevarication in his Evidence; and supporting some inconvenience to arise from the trust of those sanctions, and solemnities, establish'd by law in other Trials; I must still think that this great increase of Oath's is for the greater Evil.

This new Judicature is call'd a Committee. Names, it is true, are in themselves of no importance, but giving wrong names, often leads to great Mistakes in regard to Things. And surely this Judicature can with no propriety be call'd a Committee; as the Persons to compose it are not to be chosen by the House, or in any respect, subject to it: though they must, indeed, be Members of it.

The first Clause directs, that when any Petition is presented complaning of an undue Election, or Return, The House *shall* appoint a day, and hear, for taking the same into *Consideration*. Yet, when that day, and hour come, it does not appear to me, that any power is left in the House, to consider upon it; but they *must*, if the presented number of Members are present, after some ceremonies performed, be witness's to the Clerks drawing Lots for those who are to compose this new Judicature, named by the Bill a Committee. And when, between Chance, and the Contending Parties, the said Committee is settled, without any interposition of the House, save only to accept

---

[1] This became the Parliamentary Elections Act of 1770. 10 Geo. III, c.15, known as Grenville's Act, since George Grenville was its main protagonist. It transferred the power of trying controverted elections from the house of commons to a committee of 13 selected by ballot from the judiciary. The Act was repealed in 1828.

excuse's from serving, to be verified upon *Oath*. The power of this new Judicature is then absolute, and independent of the House. There was in the first Draught of the Bill a Clause, requiring this new species of a Committee, to report to the House, for their opinion, any Resolution they should come to, previous to the final Determination. The House to confirm, or disagree with, such Resolution, and make such Orders thereon, as to them shall seem proper. But that this New Committee, may have no sort of resemblance to any other Committee, that no Trust may be left in the House, but this Sovereign Councill may be made absolute; The Committee of the whole House have to my unceasing astonishment, between the word (shall) and the word (Report) inserted those, to the House, most humiliating, words (If they think proper). This is, for anything I know, the first instance of any Judicature having it left to their own option, whether their Resolutions shall be submitted to the Revision of a Superior Court. If indeed I may yet call the House a Court superior to this Councill of fifteen, which is (I had almost said in Mockery) called a Committee. I cannot help thinking that, any Delay or Inconvenience to be apprehended from that Clause, as first drawn, might have been fully obviated by inserting the word (General) between the word (any) and the word (Resolution) And that the Clause, as it now stands, gives to this New Judicature, an extent of Power very dangerous to be lodged in the hands of so small a Number, mostly chosen by Lot.

If this Clause, as it now stands, had been Law in the first session of the present Parliament, I apprehend that Chance might have thrown it into the power of eight or even of seven, Men, to have resolved, that Mr Wilks,[2] was after his Expulsion, eligible, and consequently duely elected, for the County of Middlesex; And such a Resolution, the House having no power to reverse it might, at one blow, have destroy'd the Dignity, Authority, and necessary Power of the House of Commons leaving both Prince, and People, law, and Liberty, to the discretion of an enraged, desperate Faction. It may now be disputed whether these nominal Committees are bound by preceding Resolutions of the House. And as every Election is to be try'd by a New Committee, whether one Committee is obliged to take notice of, & conform to, the general Resolutions of a preceding Committee. If not, Wee may have many inconsistent Determinations, in the same Session. For different sets of Men, though all acting bona fide, upon Oath, may form very different opinions, upon similar Cases, and there is no appeal to the House left by this Bill.

It will probably be allow'd that these Committees are obliged to judge according to the Law and usage of Parliament, as part of the Law of the Land, yet, there Wee see, they will find room for different Opinions; a Party in the House of Commons having on Several occasions declared against the Decisions of the House in terms that would not sometime ago have been thought proper, or decent and upon questions that some years past, would I am fully satisfied, not have been thought disputable. It is therefore very possible, and perhaps not improbable, that a Majority of some Committee, that is seven, or eight Members, may come to generall Resolutions very contrary to the Opinion of the House. Yet, strange as that must appear, I can see no Remedy, as long as this Act continues in force, and unamended; This bill not leaving these *new* sorts of Committee's accountable to the House, for any thing they may do in the exercise of

---

[2] John Wilkes (1725–97).

their Judicial Power. They have an unlimitted power to send for Persons, Papers, and Records and examine upon Oath; which they may use as they think fit, the House having no Right left to interfere; nor do I see that a Peer of the Realm can refuse to obey their summons, or to be examined upon Oath by them. And if they do any thing grievous, or oppressive, there is, I think, no help, as they act by the Authority of the whole Legislature, and where their power is not limitted by the Bill, there is no Authority, less than the Legislature, that can controle, or stop their Proceedings.

By the Act Geo: 2nd, commonly called the Bribery Act,[3] such votes are to be deem'd legal, which have been so declared by the last Determination of the House of Commons. But there are, I believe, several Boroughs in which the Right of voting has never been fully ascertane'd, by the House. In such Places the Resolution of one of these Committee's, cannot surely be called a Resolution of the House; so the Disputes in those Boroughs may be left for ever without any final Determination except by an Act of Parliament and perhaps some such Questions may arise even in Counties; which different Committees may judge different ways.

They who think this Bill will prevent, for the future, all complaints of partiality, and injustice, in the Determinations of contraverted Elections, and all reflections upon the House of Commons, on that account; may be so far right, that, as no power is left to the House, in those Cases, the whole House cannot be blamed for any particular Decision, however disliked. But Gentleman may be pleased to consider, that Juries are upon Oath, and all the Evidence, before them, is also upon oath; And then let them remember, how the Jury has been treated which, most justly acquitted Mr Guillam;[4] and how that has been applauded; which found the two chairmen Guilty of murdering Clark;[5] all though, supposing he had died of the Blow, there was not the least proof of any connection between them, and the unknown Person, by whom Clark was struck down. He might, for any thing that appear'd in Evidence be of the same Party with Clark, or Clark might have assaulted him first. Nothing was proved, but that Clark was struck down by a tall man. If then the Majority of a new instituted Committee, should decide contrary to the popular Humor, the Gentleman who make such Decision, may be exposed to greater Odium, and Reproach, than can now fall upon any particulars. For neither Integrity, or Wisdom can prevent the Censure of Malice, or silence the Rage, and abuse of Faction. In such a Case where will our Modern Patriots seek for redress. An Act of the whole Legislature, proposed by themselves has made the judgement of such a Committee final. Will, even they, address the Throne to dissolve a Parliament, because they dislike the Determination of a Committee of fifteen? They must, I suppose, have recourse to that executive power which assaulted the Merchants, going with an Address to St James's, and the Officers of the Kings Household, within the gates of his Palace.

---

[3] Corrupt Practices at Parliamentary Elections Act. 2 Geo. II, c.24.

[4] Samuel Guillam, the justice of the peace who read the riot act during the Spitalfields riots in Sept. 1769.

[5] At a court/tory-instigated riot during the Middlesex by-election of 14 Dec. 1768, George Clarke, a lawyer, was clubbed to death by Edward MacQuirk, a leader of the mob, and one other person. The perpetrators were sentenced to transportation but both received a royal pardon. The house of commons, furious at the royal intervention, reopened the poll which had been closed by the sheriff. John Glynn (1722–79), the radical Wilkite candidate, beat the tory Sir William Beauchamp Procter (1722–73), 1,548 votes to 1,272.

Some would have us believe, that this Bill will put an end to Bribery in Elections. If that was true, this Bill would, probably, in a short time, become one of the most unpopular that was ever brought into Parliament. But when it is consider'd, how many in this Nation, of otherwise very private Characters, are possess'd of great wealth, which naturally inspires men with Ambition, not, in this Country, to be in any degree satisfied, without a seat in Parliament. And when it is also remember'd how great a Number of indigent Man have Votes in Elections; who are very little interested in public Affairs, who are unqualified to judge, of such matters, or of the merits of the Candidates often quite Strangers to them; I leave it to those who have greater knowledge of human Nature, and superior abilities to form a judgement upon that knowledge, to determine whether any Laws can prevent Bribery, in a Nation so circumstance'd. It may indeed be kept somewhat out of Countenance, and out of Sight; And I am of Opinion that a great deal of the Riot, Intemperance, and consequent Idleness, occasion'd by treating, might be prevented, by proper Laws. But I believe no Man will pretend, to affirm that the Bribery Act has put any great stop to Corruption at Elections. I doubt if it has at all lessen'd it. Sure I am, it has brought a Flood of Perjury upon the Kingdom; which I fear this Bill may increase, with very melancholy effects.

The Bill is intended, among other good Effects, as the Preamble sets forth, to prevent the obstruction to public Busyness, and to lessen the expence, trouble, and delay, to the Parties, which were occasion'd by the former Mode of trying Elections. It may probably do so, in some Cases; but in others I fear, it may rather increase those inconveniency's. I think also it may subject Members to much trouble, to many things very disagreable, and to great indignities. Many other Persons it may expose to vexatious Prosecutions. If, in Times like the present, any Gentleman, even a member, should give Evidence, upon a Trial, of a controverted Election, according to his Conscience, but not agreable to the Prejudice's infused into the Populace; I apprehend he might be in a very dangerous situation, if try'd, for Perjury, by a Middlesex Jury, upon the Evidence of Remonstrants. It is my Opinion that former Acts have submitted Cases relating to Elections, too much to the Courts of Common Law. But this Bill has gone beyond all Example, or Expectation, and, in effect, given a final stroke to the Authority of the House of Commons in Matters relating to the Elections of Members. A Thing, perhaps, of much greater Consquence than it seems now to be thought. It has been well observed by Gentleman of good knowledge, and judgement, that these Committees, being to consist of Members present at the drawing of the Lots, it is much to be fear'd that few Gentlemen, not some way interested, will be very ready or willing, to attend on those days. Which may well deserve very serious Consideration.

I am persuaded that many honest Gentlemen who, with upright intentions, voted for this Bill, may live to repent it; and to see, in the instance, how much the Constitution may be hurt; by too hasty attempts to amend it.

It appears to me there will be more politeness, than propriety, in offering a Petition to the House, for Redress, which they cannot give; or for *what is called a Committee* which they cannot refuse. And I think it will be matter of some difficulty to draw a proper, & yet decent Petition; which must, in effect, be a Requisition.

Appendix 8: Some Account of the Great Demagogue, 1765[1]

He[2] was a younger Brother of a good family, with very small Fortune, but a sufficient stock of Pride, Vanity, and Ambition. It has been said he began very early to study popular Oratory, expecting, probably, that it wou'd some time help him to gratifie his ruling Passions. And it has, in truth, well answer'd such expectations. A Cornetcy was purchased for him, by his Brother,[3] and while he had that Commission, he was brought into Parliament to assist in the Opposition against Sir R[obert] W[alpole]. His first remarkable Speech was a labor'd Panegyric upon the late P[rince] of W[ales] but so contrived that every one might see it was, at least, equally intended, for a severe Satyr upon the late K[ing]. For this speech he was, most deservedly, broke, which no doubt made him heartily angry. He on all Occasions attack'd Sir R[obert]W[alpole] with the greatest appearance of rancour and malice; but in that he was not singular. When that truely great Man retired, This Gentleman continued to oppose the New mix'd Administration, and particularly Lord C[artere]t, afterward E[arl] of G[ranvi]lle who was made Secretary upon that Change, and soon look'd upon as Prime Minister. That Lord was not of a temper to be dictated to by this Gentleman, who seems not disposed to agree long with any Minister to whom he cannot dictate. He was most violent against those Continental German Measures, by which it was believ'd Lord C[artere]t had gained so much Favor and Credit, in the r[oya]l C[lose]t. He spoke most abusively of the Hanover Troops; And, with a sort of Parliamentary guard upon his words, not very civilly, or decently of the r[oya]l P[ri]n[ce]. Lord C[artere]t not meeting with so great compliances, as have been since made to this Gentleman, found himself obliged to retire about Christmas 1744. And the D[uke] of N[ewcastle] became Prime Minister, but without the share of Favor and confidence necessary to make him easy, or enable him to Act Freely, in that situation; though his Brother, Mr P[e]l[ha]m[4] was at the head of the Treasury. Therefore in February 1756 H[is] G[race] resign'd the Seals and His friends followed his example in resigning their Places as fast as they could. Lord C[artere]t was again made Secretary, and intended Prime Minister. But his lordship finding in a few days, that he cou'd not have a proper support in Parliament, he once more resign'd the Seals, and seem'd from that day to give up Ambition, of which he had shewn as large a share as most Men. A rare Instance. The Duke of Newcastle was not only restored to his Place, and the appearance of Prime Minister, but gained the real Power, And very soon after, This Gentleman acceded to the Administration, and condescended to accept

---

[1] This essay is not in the hand of John Campbell, Pryse Campbell or Henry Fox. It is to be found among the correspondence of Campbell senior at CRO, Cawdor/Campbell box 252.

[2] William Pitt, the elder. He is also referred to throughout the essay as this Gentleman.

[3] Thomas Pitt (c.1705–61), of Boconnoc, Cornwall.

[4] Henry Pelham.

© *The Parliamentary History Yearbook Trust 2014*

the Office of a V[ice] T[reasurer] of Ireland,[5] a Place very lucrative, but quite a Sine Cure. It was then said, that he wish'd to have been Secretary at War, but that the Ministers cou'd not prevale upon the K[ing] to give him any Office that wou'd bring him into the r[oya]l Cl[ose]t, and did not choose, or wou'd not then venture, to insist upon it. The next Session This Gentleman it seems, thought he had so far run riot against the Hanover Troops, that he cou'd not vote for their being continued in british Pay. A pleasant expedient was therefore found out, to get over that difficulty. The Queen of Hungary was desired to take them into her pay and an additional subsidy was granted to H[er] A[ugust] M[ajesty] equal to the expense of those Troops; which it was not thought proper to spare from the Army of the Allies, though this Gentleman had, not long before, represented them as rather a Burthen, than a help to it. Risum teneatis.[6] This Gentleman began soon after to court the Relations, and Friends of the deceased Sir R[obert] W[alpole] E[arl] of Or[for]d; blamed himself for his violent Opposition to him, And, even in the H[ouse] of C[ommons] excused it by his youth, Inexperience, and Misinformation. To a Friend of Sir R[obert] W[alpole] he lamented, in private, that the Opposition to that Great Man had gone near to ruin the Kingdom, the true Interest of which, he said Sir R[obert] understood better than any of them, and persued it, as long as he had power to do so. Yet this Gentleman did, after that affirm in the House of Commons that he still thought he was right at the Time he opposed him.

Upon the death of Mr Winnington[7] this Gentleman was made Paymaster. And in that Office he made an Ostentatious Refusal of a Sum of Money offered him by order of the King of Sardinia,[8] as usual, upon the ready payment of the subsidy granted to that Prince; by which heroic Action H[is] S[erene] M[ajesty] saved £3000 but what Profit, or Advantage this Nation got, or will ever get by it, We are yet to learn. For some time this Gentleman seem'd to go on very cordially with the Administration, spoke of the D[uke] of N[ewcastle] in the House of Commons as the greatest, and the best Minister, to whom this Country was more oblig'd than to any one, regretted his not having known him, and been with him sooner; And laying his hand on his breast, said he now hoped he shou'd be with him allways. He was once thought of by some in the H[ouse] to insinuate a comparison between H[is] G[race] and his Brother Mr Pelham, in which he gave the preference pretty strongly to the D[uke].

Toward the latter part of Mr Pelhams time, This Gentleman was visibly dissatisfied. It may be supposed, he wanted a more directing share in Business; and was impatient to have access to the r[oya]l Cl[ose]t, where he did not doubt, he cou'd make himself agreeable. This Gentleman happening one day to sit next to old Mr H[orace]W[alpole] in the House of Commons. Mr W[alpole] was overheard to express his concern for the coldness he observ'd between Mr Pelham and This Gentleman, which he thought began with the latter. This Gentleman at first affected, and it was plane only affected, not to understand Mr W[alpole] but that Gentleman insisting upon it, He denied it, in the manner People usual [sic] do, when they are unwilling directly to acknowledge a thing,

---

[5] In Feb. 1746.

[6] 'Can you keep yourself from laughing?' Horace, *Ars Poetica*, line 5.

[7] In 1746.

[8] Charles Emmanuel III (1701–73), king of Sardinia 1730–73.

and yet do not desire to have their denial believed. And neither of the Gentlemen seemed solicitous not to be overheard by those who sat next to them.

When Mr P[e]lh[am] died[9] this Gentleman was at Bath, He very soon appeared much displeased, and complaned, that he was not consulted, or much taken Notice of on that occasion; though the Duke of Newcastle sent to desire he wou'd come up, to be present, and give his assistance, in the Settlement then made. It is therefore reasonable to believe, that the true Cause of this Displeasure was his not being immediately invited to a Ministerial Office. The Duke of Newcastle then came to the head of the Treasury, Mr L[egge][10] was made Chancellor of the Exchequer, and Mr F[ox][11] named for Secretary, but before he had accepted the seals, he imagined he saw reason to think he should be so soon much restrained in his Department, that he declined, And Mr L[egge] had not been a week in his office, before he became uneasy, for a like reason. Sir T[homas] R[obinson] now Lord G[rantham][12] was made Secretary. A worthy Man, but having lived long abroad, where he was an able Minister, and coming later into the House of Commons he cou'd not be well qualified to lead Business there, nor did he think he was, or in the least desire to do it. And Mr L[egge] and Mr F[ox] being both dissatisfied; at the same time that this Gentleman was watching Opportunities, and trying all means, to form, and to declare an Opposition; that session was the oddest public scene that could be shewn. The majority of the House of Commons were like sheep without a Shepherd. The necessary Motions for Business, were made by those in office, and neither warmly opposed, or warmly supported, but past for the most, part, pretty quietly. In other Matters the P[riv]y C[ouncillo]rs had no concert, often opposed one another without design; and in things unexpected, were all quite at a loss. This in, another Session, might have produced very bad Consequences, and Things cou'd not possibly continue long in such a state. For speculative Men may think, and designing Men may say, what they please; but whoever knows a little of the World, will be sensible that in Great Assembly's there must be some Leaders, though they should not be Drivers. Every body seem'd convinced of this Truth, at that time. And, in consequence, it was resolved to put Things upon some footing, and in some Order before the next Session. It was accordingly settl'd that Mr F[ox] should be Secretary, and lead the public Business in the H[ouse] of C[ommons]. The D[uke] of N[ewcastle] and that Gentleman were said to be firmly united, and perhaps for some time they both thought so. In the mean time this Gentleman had gained Mr L[egge] whom he praised beyond measure, telling everybody, at least such as wou'd tell him again, that Mr L[egge] was the greatest Man in public, and the most amiable in private Life. They hoped for some time to set the D[uke] of C[umberland] at the head of what they, most ridiculously, called a Whig Opposition, complaining most grievously that the D[uke] of N[ewcastle] consulted with Tories, and encouraged them so much, as made it necessary for the Whigs to unite in opposing him. If they cou'd have had the D[uke] of C[umberland] to head them, they depended upon Mr F[ox]s assistance in the H[ouse] of C[ommons] and thought that, in such Case, nothing cou'd stand before them. But finding their first

---

[9] In Mar. 1754.

[10] Henry Bilson Legge.

[11] Henry Fox.

[12] Robinson was made Baron Grantham in 1761. J.C. Sainty, *Peerage Creations* (2008), 44.

Project disappointed, by the refusal of the D[uke] of C[umberland] and Mr F[ox], they applied themselves elsewhere resolved to head the Opposition in the H[ouse] of C[ommons] themselves, and conceived an irreconcileable aversion to Mr F[ox] who it is probable they believed had occasioned their disappointment. And poor Mr L[egge] to his great, and lasting Misfortune, became the Dupe of this Gentleman. They took occasion to begin their opposition, the first day of the next Session, on account of the Subsidiary Treaties that had been concluded with the late Zarina, and Langrave of Hesse Cassel; they sat together most part of that Session Mr L[egge] commonly seconding this Gentleman whom he called, and probably then thought, his honourable Friend; though it has been believ'd, on very good Authority, That this Gentleman had, before that time, spoke as disrespectfully, and contemptuously of Mr L[egge] as he did some time after. Their Opposition occasioned their both being dismissed from the K[ing]s service about Christmas, and brought them a shower of fulsome Compliments, and Gold Boxes, from the City of London, and other Corporations. But the equality with which they were treated on those occasions, it has been thought, was rather provoking, than pleasing to this Gentleman.

S[i]r G[eorge] now L[or]d L[yttelto]n was made Chancellor of the Exchequer and notwithstanding the Opposition of This Gentleman, Mr L[egge] &c the Administration carried their Questions in Parliament by great Majorities. Mr F[ox]s conduct in the H[ouse] of C[ommons] gave general satisfaction to the Friends of Government, and this Gentleman seem'd to be greatly distressed because he cou'd not put the Secretary in a passion, or, by any provocation, put him off his guard; though in endeavouring to do it, he himself went beyond all bounds of decency, or discretion; of which he had shown himself sensible, by solemnly denying words, he had been distinctly heard to speak, in the same Debate. It should not be omitted that This Gentleman, forgetting, how much he had praised the D[uke] of N[ewcastle] a very few years before, now treated H[is] G[race] as an unable, and Criminal Minister. But this fair prospect on the side of Government, was soon change'd. The D[uke] of N[ewcastle] and Mr F[ox], became greatly dissatisfied with each other, before the end of the session, and their Discontents continued increasing after the Prorogation. The D[uke] of N[ewcastle] was very desirous to get rid of Mr F[ox], and he very weary of his situation. The D[uke] imagined that This Gentleman wou'd gladly accept of the Secretarys Place, and that then all wou'd go well, and smoothly on. Mr F[ox] was given to understand as much, and he resign'd in Oct[ober] 1756. But to the surprise, no doubt, of the D[uke] of N[ewcastle] This Gentleman refused the offer of the Secretarys Place, and *at that time* absolutely rejected any proposal to join with H[is] G[race] upon which the D[uke] himself resign'd. For some time every thing was in confusion, and Government at a stand. After a short interval, a ministry was formed. The late D[uke] of D[evonshire][13] first Lord of the Treasury, Mr L[egge] Chancellor of the Exchequer Lord Temple at the head of the Admiralty, the Great Seal in Commission, Lord H[ardwicke] having resign'd with the D[uke] of N[ewcastle], and This Gentleman Secretary. He, or his followers at least, talk'd at first very high of an Inquiry into the Conduct of the late Ministers; and severe threatenings were given out. But being soon sensible they had no bottom to stand on, without the support of the D[uke] of Newcastle] Friends in Parliament, the note was

[13] He died on 2 Oct. 1764.

immediately chang'd, and care was taken to make it publicly known that they wou'd give no trouble to H[is] G[race] he might be perfectly easy. However not to disappoint openly, and immediately, the expectations they had raised; an Inquiry was moved for, and not opposed, but agree'd to be carried on in a Committee of the whole House, and was said to be chiefly pointed at Lord Anson. The new Ministers, that is to say This Gentleman and his followers, having declared they wou'd not disturb the D[uke] of N[ewcastle], and Mr F[ox] having been so short a time in Ministerial Office, and so little in confidence, that they cou'd not make him the Object of their Inquiry, though he certanely was very much the object of their Resentment. It was easy to see before the Inquiry was finished, that it must end in nothing. The D[uke] of N[ewcastle], however disgusted with Mr F[ox], having declared, like Man of honor, that he wou'd look upon the Cause, of all who were in the cabinet with him, as his own.

In the mean time both the D[uke] of N[ewcastle], and Mr F[ox] joining with the Ministers in public Business, there was no obstruction, and This Gentleman and his followers were not much disturbed, till a little before Easter 1757 when the late K[ing] who had rec'd This Gentleman L[or]d T[emple] and Mr L[egge] into his Cabinet with great reluctance, took occasion from some offence given him by L[or]d T[emple] in the affair of Admiral Byng, to dismiss both his Lordship, and This Gentleman; upon which Mr L[egge] resign'd the seal of the Exchequer, which was put into the hands of the L[or]d C[hief] Justice] and L[or]d W[in]ch[ilsea] was put at the head of the Admiralty but the Secretarys place left Vacant. At the same time H[is[M[ajesty] sent to Mr F[ox] to take the Place of Paymaster, but it being in the middle of the Inquiry, he thought it proper to defer receiving it till that shou'd be ended. From this time to near the close of the session, private Negotiations were carried on, in which all Partys, and Persons, from the King inclusive, made court to the D[uke] of N[ewcastle] H[is] M[ajesty] shew'd and expressed the utmost aversion to This Gentleman and his adherents, and for a long time continued in hopes of the D[uke] of N[ewcastle] wou'd comply with H[is] Majesty']s desires. The Duke kept in generals, and avoided, as long as he cou'd, making any positive, explicit declaration to either Party: But against the time that it became necessary to declare, H[is] G[race] had concluded a Treaty with This Gentleman, the terms of which being laid before the K[ing] for his approbation, were absolutely refused by H[is] M[ajesty] who earnestly pressed the D[uke] of N[ewcastle] to take the first place in Administration, and form a Ministry with Mr F[ox] and without This Gentleman, which H[is] Grace] thinking fit to decline, the K[ing] try'd to form an Administration, without either of them. But means were found to disappoint H[is] M[ajesty']s endeavours so far, that they into whose hands he wish'd to put the public Business, found it proper to advise, and desire that H[is] M[ajesty] would yeild [sic] to the cruel Necessity; which the K[ing] did with great Grief, and Resentment. This Gentleman being then prevaled on to make some concessions, A ministry was soon settled. The D[uke] of N[ewcastle] return'd to the Treasury, with Mr L[egge] Chan[cellor] of the Ex[che]q-[uer] This Gentleman resumed the seals as Secretary, and L[or]d Anson who had so lately been the great Object of their Inquiry, was with the full consent of the Party, and, as was then said, at the desire of This Gentleman, brought again to the head of the Admiralty. If their accusation of Lord Anson had been just, he ought not to have been restored, and as it was false and malicious; if they had been capable of shame, or remorse, they must have felt them strongly, for their abuse of him, and the popular

Odium they had raised against him. But they had very cogent private reasons for this scandalous Inconsistency. At the same time Mr L[egge] who appear'd so closely united with this Gentleman, and been so much flatter'd by him, was from the day of their return to their Officies [*sic*], treated with incivility, and contempt, which was carried by This Gentleman in the H[ouse] of C[ommons] to a surprising length, very seldom seen from one Minister to another on the same Bench. And Mr L[egge] was thereby brought to a necessity, either to retire or attach himself to the D[uke] of N[ewcastle]. He chose the latter. This Gentleman being got again to the r[oya]l Cl[ose]t made it his business to attone for past Offences, by going such lengths in German Measures, as were never attempted, or imagined, by any former Ministers. Yet he still acted the part of Demagogue so well, as to make even those Measures popular.

On the accession of the present K[ing] all the prudent and honest Men entertaned a reasonable hope, that H[is] M[ajesty] who gloried in the name of Briton, wou'd put a stop to this Useless, and destructive profusion of Blood, and Treasure. And there can be no doubt that the K[ing] from the first sincerely desired it. But the dangerous state into which This Gentleman had brought the Kingdom, in pursuing his own Views, cou'd not move him to comply with the desires of his S[overei]gn, and the Opinion of every wise, and honest Counsellor, in accepting reasonable Conditions of Peace. He abruptly broke off the first Negotiation and soon after proposed a Measure, that was disapproved by the whole Cabinet except L[or]d Temple] making a wild declaration that he was for crushing the whole House of Bourbon. And when he saw that he cou'd be no longer implicitly obey'd, in anger he resign'd. H[is] M[ajesty] being, unhappily advised to give him, immediately a Pension of £3000 per annum for three Lives and a peerage for his Lady, it was said, that the surprise of such Favors, perhaps as unexpected as they were undeserv'd, had so great a temporary effect upon him, that he burst into tears with the warmest expressions of Duty, and Gratitude. But he soon got the better of that weakness, and return'd to himself. For on the Lord Mayors day in 1762 he triumph'd over his beneficent P[rince] and insulted him openly, in a manner that shocked every one who had a just sense of Duty, Decency, or good manners. He has, since that time, appeared in Opposition, when he did appear, but has affected to act by himself, in no concert with the most of the Opposers. He was applied to on the late Turn; but after long deliberation, or hesitation, and, as is said, frequent change of his mind, or, at least, of his seeming Intentions, he refused to come into Administration. What he now mediates is not known; but that he may persist in his Refusal is devoutly to be wished. His Eloquence is chiefly of the invective, and inflammatory kind, sometimes rising to allmost unintelligible Bombast, sometimes strong, and fine; often very unequal in the same speech. He must in justice be acknowledg'd, that after his first coming into Court Measures when his Brother and he were on different sides, This gentleman always treated his brother with the greatest respect, and carefully avoided giving him the least offence; though his Brother seem'd to take a pleasure in making illnatured reflections on what he said; yet he was never provoked to make a like reply, or give his brother one angry, or disrespectfull word.

His written Compositions are not extraordinary. Not long after he was first made Secretary, he drew a Message from the C[row]n to the House of Commons which was so manifest a breach of Privilege, that he had the Mortification to see by order of the H[ouse] an Entry made in the Journals to note it, least it shou'd be made a Precedent, though the House was satisfied there was no ill Intention. This threw him into the most intemperate Passion. The mistake as doubtless made without Design, had been very excusable, if he had not been too haughty to take advice, and to amend it. But neither his fellow Counsellors, or the Speakers, to whom, of Course, it was shewn, before it was delivered to the House, could prevale with him to alter it.

It must be allowed he has admirable Talents for execution and knows how to make his orders Speedily, and punctually obey'd. His abilities to do real service to his King and Country in the Cabinet are not so well known.

The Expeditions to the Coast of France in the late War, which may be look'd upon as most peculiarly his own, do him no great Honor. As it seems that in those Adventures, the public Treasure was thrown away, a considerable part of the K[ing']s Army fatigued, and exposed to great hazard, and some loss, merely to gratifie This Gentlemans Passions, keep up his Popularity, and procure the Huzzars of a giddy and ignorant Mob. Such is the Man so long celebrated in Newspapers, and admired in Alehouses, obscure Coffee Houses &c As the Favorite of the People, and the only Person capable to support the Honor, and Interest of the Nation.

Virs sapiens non quid verissimum sit, sed quid velit Vulgus exquiet? Ille vero nostras Ambitiones, levitatesque, contemnet, honoresque Populi, etiam ulto delatos, repudiabit.[14]

Nihil est tam molle, tam tenerum, tam aut fragile, aut flexible, quam voluntas erga nos, sensusque Civium: qui non Modo improbitati irascuntur, sed etiam in recte factio sape fastidiunt.[15]

Populus non delictu alique, aut sapientia ducitur, sed impetus non nunquam, et quædam etiam semeritate. Non est enim Consilium in vulgo, non ratio, non discrimen, non diligentia.[16]

October 1765

---

[14] 'Should the wise man seek not what is most true, but what the mass desires? He, truly, will condemn our ambitions and vanities and will reject the honours of the people, even when freely offered.' Cicero, *Tusculanae Disputationes*, v, 36.

[15] 'For there is nothing so soft, so tender, so frail, so flexible, as the inclinations and feelings of our fellow citizens towards us; for they are not only angry at any impropriety, but they often even take offence at virtuous actions.' Cicero, *Pro Milone*, 42.

[16] 'The people are not led by any careful choice or by wisdom, but not infrequently by impulse and also by a certain rashness. For there is no wisdom in the common people, nor reason, nor discrimination, nor diligence.' Cicero, *Pro Plancio*, 9.

Index

John Campbell, Pryse Campbell and Lord Holland/Henry Fox have only been indexed where they are mentioned within the text but not as writers or recipients of letters. A letter 'n' after a page number denotes where biographical information of the person noted is to be found. Names in brackets denote spellings used by the letter writers. [S] denotes Scottish peerage and [I] denotes Irish peerage.

Abercorn, James Hamilton, 8th earl of [S] 290
Aberllefenni estate, Merioneth 8
acts and bills of parliament
  Act for the Further Limitation of the Crown, 1
    Wm & Mary, c.2 (1701) 332, 336
  Act of Settlement, 12 &13 Wm III, c.2 (1701)
    17, 328, 330–2, 334–5, 341
  Bill of Rights, 1 Wm & Mary, c.2 (1689) 17
  Cider Act, 6 Geo. III, c.14 (1766) 298, 300
  Cider Bill/Act, 4 Geo. III, c.7 (1764) 257, 260–2
  Corrupt Practices at Parliamentary Elections Act,
    2 Geo. II, c.24 (1728) 360
  Declaratory Act, 6 Geo. III, c.12 (1766) 293,
    297–8, 301
  Indemnity Act, 7 Geo III, c.7 (1766) 40
  Militia Bill, 33 Geo II, c.2 (1759) 19, 350–6
  Parliamentary Elections, Grenville's Act, 10 Geo
    III, c.16 (1770) 22, 358
  Peerage Bill (1734) 14
  Place Bill (1742) 107, 109, 342
  Schism Act, 13 Anne, c.17 (1714) 341
  Septennial Act, 1 Geo I, c.38 (1715) 17–18,
    91–2, 112, 338, 342
  Stamp Act, 5 Geo III, c.12 (1765) 39, 40, 292–301
  Triennial Act, 6 & 7 Wm & Mary, c.2 (1694)
    336
Adam, 'friend of Pryse Campbell' 48, 53, 55, 58, 61
Adams, Joseph 26
Addison, Joseph 236
address of thanks 15, 29, 45–6, 48–9, 50, 52, 54, 57,
    63, 70, 91–2, 96–8, 102, 161, 163–5, 168, 169,
    170–2, 180, 192
Aeschines 347
Ailesbury, Thomas Brudenell-Bruce, 1st earl of 186
Albemarle, George Keppel, 3rd earl of 175, 257
Allen, John 183
Alston, Thomas 208, 209
Ambrose, Captain John 47
Amcots, Charles 225
Amelia Sophia Eleanor, Princess Amelia 281
America 52, 74, 205–6, 236, 241, 243, 256, 287,
    294, 296–7, 299, 330
  Georgia 69
  Massachusetts Bay Colony 300
  New York 292
American colonies 289, 292–5, 300–1
American independence 299

Anderson, James 5
Androsgeus 317
Anna Leopoldovna, regent of Russia 74
Anne, queen of Great Britain 54, 68, 158, 326,
    330–2, 341
Anson, Admiral George 184–6, 189, 222, 224
Appius Claudius Crassus 244, 346
Archer, Harry 49
Argyll, Archibald Campbell, 2nd earl of [d. c.1513] 1
Argyll, Archibald Campbell, 7th earl of [d. 1638] 2
Argyll, Archibald Campbell, 3rd duke of [d. 1761]
    43n, 87, 108, 140, 160, 222, 225, 248
Argyll, Colin Campbell, 1st earl of [d. c.1493] 1
Argyll, John Campbell, 2nd duke of [d. 1743] 8, 46n,
    62, 71, 83–4, 101, 108, 115, 172, 176, 181
Arundell, Richard 141, 184–5
Ashe, John Wyndham 126
Astley, Sir John 126
Aswarby, Lincolnshire 32
Athenian law 347
Atholl, 2nd duke of [S] see Strange, James Murray,
    4th baron
The Auditor 259
August Ferdinand, prince 264
August II the Strong, king of Poland 170
Augusta, princess dowager 211
Augusta of Saxe-Gotha, princess of Wales 99
Austen, Jane 41
Austria, house of 238
Ayres (a lawyer) 239

Bacon, Sir Edmund 27, 67n
Bacon, Sarah 27
Bailey 70, 77, 91
balance of powers 338
Baldwin, archbishop of Canterbury 6
Baltimore, lord 51, 67, 92–3, 114, 135, 143, 162,
    184–6, 189, 194, 275
Bankes [Banks], John 66
Banks, Henry 142
Barlow, George 97, 130, 137, 147, 194–5, 197
Barlow, Hugh 127, 132, 147, 188
Barlow, John 8
Barnard, Sir John 13, 66n, 85, 97, 106, 114, 128,
    166–7, 193–4, 198
Barré, Colonel Issac 293, 315, 318

Barrington, William Wildman Shute, 2nd viscount
    109–10, 134, 142, 164–5, 172, 193, 203, 208
Barrymore, James, 4th earl of Barrymore [I] 119
Bassett, Eustacia 25–6
Bassett, John Francis 25
Bath 25, 27–8, 52, 121, 127, 199, 233, 245, 252,
    303, 364
Bath, Thomas Thynne, 1st marquess of 290–1
Bath, William Pulteney, 1st earl of 9, 24, 28, 39,
    49n, 53, 63, 65, 78–9, 87, 91–2, 101–2, 105, 112,
    119, 122–5, 129, 132, 134, 145, 159, 171, 176,
    181, 186, 250–1
Bathurst, Allen, lord and 1st Earl Bathurst 147
battles
    Agincourt (1415) 340
    Crecy (1346) 340
    Dettingen (1743) 132, 138, 140, 144, 173, 177
    St Cast (1758) 243, 245
    Villinghausen (1761) 247, 249
    Warburg (1760) 247
    Zorndorf (1758) 243
Beauclerk family interest 33, 235
Beaufort, Charles Noel Somerset, 4th duke of 62
Beaufort, Henry Scudamore, 3rd duke of 157, 169,
    172, 299
Beckford, William 208–9, 274, 287, 315, 317
Bedford, Gertrude, duchess of 271–2, 275, 280, 300,
    304
Bedford, John Russell, 4th duke of 93n, 130, 182,
    184–6, 200, 213, 222, 224, 226, 235, 250–1, 267,
    271, 273–5, 278, 280, 288, 290, 295–6, 300
Bedford House, as political entity 270–2
Belle-Isle, Charles Louis Auguste Fouquet, duc de
    217
Bentinck, Hans William, *see* Portland, 1st earl of
Bentinck, William *see* Portland, 2nd duke of
Bergenopzoom 200
Berkeley, Norborne 116
Berkley, Elizabeth 62
Bernard, Sir Francis 300
Birmingham 160, 163
Bishop, Mr 165
Black, Jeremy 41
Blackerby, Nathaniel 76
Blackstone, William 220, 314–15
Bladen, Martin 107, 114, 198
Blair, William 241
Bligh, Thomas 243
Boethius [Anicius Manius Severinus Boethius] 60
Bohemia 236
Bolingbroke, Frederick St John, 2nd viscount 290–1
Bolton, Charles Powlett, 3rd duke of 139
Book of Genesis 321
Bootle, Thomas 197
Boroughbridge, Yorkshire 100
Boscawen, admiral 300
Boscawen, Elizabeth 299
Bourbon, house of 367
Bowen, Rev. Hugh 103
Bowen, John 48, 91, 156
Bowen, Matthew 9

Bowen of Camrose, Pembrokeshire 103
Bowes, John 65–6, 192
Bowles, Charles 236
Bowles, Mr 235–6
Braddock, General Edward 236
Bradshaigh, Sir Roger 137, 139
Bradshaw, Thomas 314
Bramston, Mrs 159
Brandenburg-Schwelt, Elizabeth Louise, princess of
    264
Breadalbane and Holland, 3rd earl of [S], John
    Campbell, styled Lord Glenorchy 186, 189
Brentford 311
Brereton, Thomas 16, 100
Brett (gardener at Stackpole Court) 113, 116
Bridgewater, Francis Egerton, 3rd duke of 290
Brighton 26
Bristol 63, 100, 195, 288
Bristol, George William Hervey, 2nd earl of 251
British constitution 338, 340, 342–3
The Briton 259
broadbottom, opposition 100, 101, 105, 109
    administration of Henry Pelham 96
Broderick, Captain Thomas 157–8
Brodie, Alexander, of Brodie 10
Brodie, Alexander, of Lethen 10n, 43, 105–6, 108,
    151
Brodie, David 2
Brodie, Elizabeth 2
Brown, Dr John 258
Brown, John 67, 195, 197
Brown, Rice 261
Browning, Reed 35
Bruce, Robert the 1
Brudenell, James 73
Brudenell-Bruce, Thomas *see* Ailesbury, 1st earl of
Brunswick-Wolfenbutal, duc de 264
Buckingham, George Villiers, 1st duke of 252
Buckingham, George Villiers, 2nd duke of 223
Bunbury, Lady Sarah 25
Burke, Edmund 312, 314, 318
Burnet, Bishop Gilbert 162–3
Burton, William 117, 187
Burton Pynsent House, Somersetshire 303
Bussy, François de 125
Bute, John Stuart, 3rd earl of 18, 23, 30, 34, 36–8,
    104, 108n, 202, 224–5, 246–8, 250–3, 255–6,
    259–62, 266, 270–6, 280–3, 285–9, 293–9, 304
Bute, John Stuart, 1st marquess of, styled Lord
    Mountstuart 294, 297
Bute, Mary, lady 289
Byng, George *see* Torrington, 4th viscount
Byng, Admiral John 19, 36, 216n–17, 222, 227–8,
    230, 347, 366

cabinet council 50, 137, 160, 186, 234, 288, 303
Calcraft, John 36, 206n, 273, 275, 278, 280–1,
    301–2, 308, 312
Calthorp, Henry 143
Calvert, William 162, 167, 198

Cambridge, Clare Hall 4, 26
Camden, lord, Charles Pratt 272, 275, 278, 284, 293, 299, 301, 303–4
Campbell, Alexander [*d.* 1697] 3, 176
Campbell, Alexander [*d.* 1785] 26–7
Campbell, Alexander [John Campbell's 3rd son] 26, 47, 63, 70, 75, 84, 86, 88, 89–90, 92–3, 99, 101–2, 123, 126, 129–30, 176, 195, 201, 205–6, 211, 227, 241, 243–4, 253, 259–60, 310
Campbell, Anne 3
Campbell, Anne [Nanny] 25, 113, 227, 248, 253, 256, 259, 292, 294, 310
Campbell, Archibald *see* Argyll, 2nd earl of
Campbell, Archibald *see* Argyll, 7th earl of
Campbell, Archibald *see* Argyll, 3rd duke of
Campbell, Archibald of Lochell 3
Campbell, Charles 26
Campbell, Colin [*d.* 1647] 3
Campbell, Colin of Ardersier 2
Campbell, Colin *see* Argyll, 1st earl of
Campbell, Colin 'lord of Argyll' 1
Campbell, Daniel 5
Campbell, Elizabeth 'Bessy' 26, 47
Campbell, Frederick, lord 270
Campbell, Admiral George 26
Campbell, Gilbert 3
Campbell, Gill-Easbuig 1
Campbell, Henrietta 26
Campbell, Sir Hugh 2, 176
Campbell, Sir James, 5th bt of Auchinbrek 3
Campbell, John [*d.* 1592] 2
Campbell, John *see* Argyll, 2nd duke of
Campbell, John *see* Cawdor, 1st baron
Campbell, Brigadier general John 143
Campbell, Dr John 307
Campbell, Sir John [*d.* 1546] 2
Campbell, Sir John [12th thane of Cawdor] 2
Campbell, John 'the fiar' 3
Campbell, John Duncan Vaughan, *see* Cawdor, 5th earl
Campbell, Mary (daughter of John and Mary) 26
Campbell, Mary (John Campbell's wife) 310, 318
Campbell, Mary (daughter of Pryse Campbell) 26
Campbell, 'Molly' 70, 90, 113, 140, 151, 191
Campbell, Pryse 9–13, 15, 19, 24, 26–30, 37–9, 41, 204–5, 208, 215–16, 221, 225, 248, 252, 254, 256, 266, 303, 307, 309–10
Campbell, Susanna 3
Campbell, Dr Thomas 288
Candid Reflections 240
Canterbury 201
Capel, William 115, 120, 123
Capell, William Anne Holles, *see* Essex, 4th earl of
Cardiganshire 5
 Gogerddan [house] 5
Carew, Thomas 97, 106–7, 124, 128, 186–7, 194, 198
Carey, Thomas chirargion [surgeon] 100
Cargill, Mr 44
Carlisle, Frederick Howard, 5th earl of 265

Carmarthenshire 6, 95
 Carmarthen 8–9, 75, 115, 124, 127, 129, 133, 142, 188, 200, 202, 303
 Llandovery 95
 New Inn 95
 Newton [house] 202
 St Clears [St Clares] 202
 Ystradffin estate 6, 176
Caroline of Brandenburg-Ansbach, queen 142
Carte, Rev. Thomas 172
Carteret, John *see* Granville, 2nd earl
Cartwright, Thomas 66
Castle of Ontranto (H. Walpole) 278
Cato the younger 89, 92–3
Cavendish, John, lord 314–15
Cavendish, William *see* Devonshire, 4th duke of
Cavendish, William *see* Devonshire, 5th duke of
Cawdor, John Campbell, 1st baron 26–8
Cawdor, John Duncan Vaughan Campbell, 5th earl 28
Cawdor, Muriel, 9th thane of Cawdor 2
Cecil, William 172
chancellor of the exchequer 64, 82, 87, 93, 97–8, 105, 107, 111, 114, 117, 123–6, 134, 138, 142, 149, 210, 219, 234, 257, 260–1, 267, 288, 293, 300, 364–6
Chandler, Samuel 21
Charles I, king of England 31, 283, 350
Charles II, king of England 174, 253
Charlotte, princess of Mecklenburg-Strelitz, queen 249, 310
Chatham, William Pitt, 1st earl of 12, 16, 18–20, 22–4, 28–9, 30–1, 33, 35–7, 39, 57n, 68, 77, 79, 85, 91, 96–7, 106, 108, 111, 114–15, 126, 128, 134–5, 142–4, 148, 156, 159, 160, 162, 167, 169, 171–2, 179–80, 183–4, 188, 191–3, 203, 205, 207–15, 218–29, 230–44, 246–7, 249–51, 254–5, 257–8, 260, 262–3, 265, 270–6, 280–1, 284–7, 289, 291–304, 306, 307, 308, 309, 312–13, 315, 317–18, 347, 362
Chatsworth House, Derbyshire 242
Chesterfield, Philip Stanhope, 4th earl of 51, 57, 70–1, 82–3, 86, 110, 164, 181, 185, 192
Chetwynd, William Richard 184–5, 187
Choiseul, duc de 249, 251
Cholmondeley, Charles 193, 197
Cholmondeley, George, 3rd earl of 71, 146–7, 181, 184–5
Cholmondeley, Colonel James 107
church of England 322
Churchill, Charles 18, 288–9
Cibber, Colley 123
cider, duty on 260–2
circular letters 212, 273
Clarendon, Edward Hyde, 1st earl of 31, 64, 66, 114, 162, 290
Clark, J.C.D. 41
Clarke, Charles 134
Clarke, George 360
Clayton, William *see* Sandon [Sundon], 1st baron [I]
Clemens Augustus I of Bavaria, elector of Cologne 195

Clemens Wenceslaus of Saxony, archbishop of Trier 264

Clutterbuck, Thomas 11, 69n, 94, 99–100, 141

Cobham, Richard Temple, 1st viscount 57, 65, 77, 86, 109, 115, 182–3, 186, 192, 218, 223

Cobhamites, 'clan' Cobham 185, 211

cockade gentlemen 138

Cockburn, John 185

Cockpit 96–7, 157, 207

Coke, Edward 169, 198

Colby, Lawrence 186

Colebrook, George 208

commission of accounts 258

common council of London 198, 249, 258

commons, house of 5, 8–11, 13–14, 15–17, 19–22, 24, 29, 32–7, 39, 40–1, 63, 69, 74–5, 87, 93, 109, 110, 112, 129, 132, 137, 146, 164, 166, 168, 182, 191–3, 203–4, 210–12, 215, 219, 224–5, 228–36, 239, 242, 245, 250, 252–3, 256–9, 260–1, 331–4, 341, 350, 355, 357–61, 363–5, 367
  call of the House 44, 126, 135, 168, 212, 215
  committees
    elections (1741) 72, 75, 77, 129, 190
    secrecy 78, 101
    supply 93, 98, 111, 114, 115, 117–18, 158, 171, 179, 180, 191–2, 195, 197, 214
    ways and means 165–6
    whole house 46, 153, 190, 359
  Journals of the House of Commons 331
  petitions to
    from dean and chapter of Westminster Abbey 116
    from Massachusetts Bay 292–3
    master colliers 134
    merchants 61, 79–81, 84, 88, 91, 296
    public urination by women in the public gallery 25, 129

Compton, Sir George 87, 185, 187

Compton, James *see* Northampton, 5th earl of

Compton, Spencer *see* Wilmington, 1st earl of

congress of Sunninghill 242

Con-Test 223

Convention of Westminster 236

Conway, 2nd baron *see* 1st earl of Hertford

Cooke, George 292

Cope, Sir John 164

Corbett, Thomas 139, 154, 182, 200

Corfe Castle 10–11

Cornbury, lord *see* Clarendon, 1st earl of

Cornewall, Captain James 177

Cornwall 83

Cornwall, Charles Wolfran 314–15

Cornwall, Velters 9, 109n, 124, 162, 229, 260

Cornwallis, Charles, 1st marquess 259, 294, 301

coronation, of George III 249

Cotes, Charles 66

Cotton, Sir John Hynde 49n, 82, 96–7, 105, 111, 114, 126, 128, 135, 153, 163, 197–8, 169, 185, 191, 194

court martial (Byng's) 228–30

Courtney [Courteney], William 67

Coventry, George, 6th earl of 290

Coventry, Thomas 253

Crewe, John 172, 187

Cromwell, Oliver 282

Cromwell, Richard 282

Crosbie, John 298

Crosse [Cross] 77

crown of England 330, 333–4, 336

crown of Great Britain 334

crown of Scotland 334

Crowther, Dr 136

Cruikshanks, Captain 200

Culloden, Duncan Forbes, lord 254

Culloden, Jane Forbes, lady 254

Cumberland, Prince William Augustus, duke of 34–5, 132n, 172, 207, 213, 235, 237–9, 247, 252, 255, 261, 270, 272, 275, 278, 280–5, 364–5

Cuningham, Dr Thomas 48, 55, 61, 76, 94, 120, 125, 166

Curzon, Nathaniel *see* Scarsdale, 1st baron

Curzon, Sir Nathaniel 67

Curzon, William 67

Dalkeith, Lady Caroline 211

Dalton, Richard 129

Dalrymple, John *see* Stair, 2nd earl of [S]

Danby, earl of *see* Leeds, 1st duke of

Darcy, Robert *see* Holdernesse, 4th earl of

d'Arenberg, Leopold Phillipe, 4th duke 179

Darnley, Henry, lord 2

Dashwood, Sir Francis 142, 162, 209, 228, 257–8, 260–1

Dashwood, Sir James 67, 235

Dawkins, Dick 130

de Chaillou, Jean-Jacques Amelot 169–70

de Grey, William 311

de la Warr, John West, 1st earl 147

Declaration of Reasons for Invading England (1688) 326

Demonsthenes 338, 346–8

Dempster, George 254, 256

d'Eon, Chevalier 313

Devon
  Heaton court 25
  Okehampton 209, 226

Devonshire, William Cavendish, 4th duke of 161–2, 217, 221–5, 227, 242, 253, 255, 258–60, 267

Devonshire, William Cavendish, 5th duke of 318

Devonshire–Pitt administration 36

Digby, Edward 67, 162

Digby, Edward, lord 32, 232n, 236, 240, 245

Digby, Henry, lord 232, 363, 265, 273

Digby, William, 5th baron 32

Dionysius Halicarnassus 343

Dodd, John 311

Dodington, George Bubb 25, 64n, 79, 83, 96, 101, 106–8, 110–11, 129, 134, 142, 144, 153, 165, 180–1, 183, 184–5, 197–8, 208

Dodsley, Robert 44

Donaldson, Colin 215

Dorrien, John 266
Dorset, Lionel Sackville, 1st duke of 140, 185
Douglas, James *see* Morton [Moreton], 14th earl of [S]
Douglas, James *see* Queensberry, 2nd duke of
Dowdeswell, William 293, 300, 311, 313–14, 318
Downing, Sir Jacob 33
Dunbartonshire 1
Duncomb, Anthony 150
Dungeness 175
Dunwich, Suffolk 33
Dupplin, viscount *see* Kinnoull, 9th earl of
Dusign, Captain 199
Dyson, Jeremiah 311

Earle, Giles 72–3
Earle, Rev. Thomas 289
East India Company 266
Edward, prince, duke of York 299
Edward III, king of England 340
Edwardes, William 94
Edwards, Mr 137, 141–2, 292, 266
Edwin, Charles 117
Egerton, Francis *see* Bridgewater, 3rd duke of
Egerton, John, bishop of Bangor 290–1
Eglington, Alexander Montgomerie, 10th earl of [S] 296, 298
Egmont, John Perceval, 2nd earl of 14–15, 39, 84, 106n, 114, 116–17, 131, 153, 208, 215, 223
Egremont, Charles Wyndham, 2nd earl of 161, 186, 232, 251, 253, 262
election petitions
    Carmarthen (1741) 8, 75, 124, 130, 132–3
    Carmarthen (1755) 214
    Chippenham (1741) 81
    Denbigh (1741) 104, 125, 132, 166, 168
    Haverfordwest (1741–2) 79, 124–5, 132
    Pembrokeshire (1727) 8
    Pembrokeshire (1741–2) 9, 75, 97–8, 100–4, 124–5, 132
    Pembrokeshire (1768) 4, 31
    Wiston (1741–2) 94–5, 100
elections 358–60
    Cardigan boroughs (1768) 307
    Chippenham (1741) 81
    controverted 358
    Denbigh (1741) 160, 166, 168
    Great Marlow (1745) 190, 193
    Middlesex (1768) 360
    Pembrokeshire (1727) 319–20
    Pembrokeshire (1768) 316
    Westminster (1741) 73–4, 117
    Windsor (1757) 235–6
    Worcester (1743) 151
    Yorkshire (1742) 78
Elidyr de Stackpool 6
Elliot, Sir George 19
Elliot, Gilbert 232, 250–1, 257–9, 294
Ellis, Welbore 143, 208, 212, 275, 314, 316

Elizabeth Farnese, queen of Spain 177
Elizabeth Petrovna, empress of Russia 74, 209–10
Emmanuel III, king of Sardinia 121, 128, 139, 156, 158, 363
England 332, 333, 335, 350, 353, 355–6
English Channel 157, 161, 163, 167–8, 175
    the Downs 163
Egypt 321
Ernest Augustus, elector of Brunswick-Lüneberg 332
Erskine, Sir Henry 285
Essex, William Anne Holles Capell, 4th earl of 290
Eton, rebellion at 26, 32
Evans, Frank 46–8, 55, 69, 201
Evans, Roger 48, 55, 58, 69, 113, 118, 122, 145, 155, 157, 177, 191, 195, 261
Evelyn, John 67
The Expedition against Rochefort (Potter) 240
Eyles, Sir John 174

'Family Compact' 250
Fane, Sir Francis 96, 105, 167, 180
Fane, John *see* Westmorland, 7th earl of
Fane, John *see* Westmorland, 9th earl of
Fannen, Mr 40, 305–7
Fazakerley, Nicholas 101, 111, 153, 194, 197–8
Felton, John 252
Fennick, Robert 67
Ferdinand of Brunswick, prince 241, 247, 264
Fermor, George *see* Pomfret, 2nd earl of
Fermor, Lady Sophia 180
Ferrers, Elizabeth 253
Ferrers [Ferriers], Mr 253
Fielding, Henry 155
Filmer, Sir Robert 17, 324
Finch, Daniel *see* Nottingham, 2nd earl of
Finch, Daniel *see* Winchilsea, 8th earl of and Nottingham, 3rd earl of
Finch, Edward 143–4, 192
Finch, Henry 150
Firebrace [Fairbrass], Sir Cordell 106, 225
Fitzpatrick, Lady Mary 300, 310
Fitzroy, Augustus Henry *see* Grafton, 3rd duke of
Fitzroy, Charles *see* Grafton, 2nd duke of
Flanders 60, 96, 110, 132–3, 150
Fleury, Andre-Hercule de 158
Flood, Henry 247
Forbes, Duncan *see* Culloden, lord
Forbes, Jane *see* Culloden, lady
Forster, Brooke 142
Forster, James 187
Fort Carillion, North America 241
Fortescue, Matthew, 2nd baron 25, 227n, 233, 255–6, 259
Fox, Charles James 18, 23, 37, 40, 265n, 304, 311, 312, 315, 318
Fox, Charlotte 32
Fox, Christian 32
Fox, Henry Edward 265, 304, 307
Fox, Stephen 300, 304, 307, 309–12, 315

Fox, Sir Stephen (1627–1716) 31–2
Fox, Captain Thomas 200
Fox-Strangways, Henry *see* Ilchester, 2nd earl of
Fox-Strangways, Stephen *see* Ilchester, 1st earl of
France 11, 20, 126, 128, 158, 161, 164–5, 170–2,
    174, 200, 206–7, 236–9, 241–2, 244, 335, 340,
    356, 368
  Calais 170, 175, 177, 307, 316
  Cherbourg 241
  Dunkirk 160, 162–3, 172
  Paris 177
  Rochefort 237, 241
  St Malo 243
  Toulon 166, 168, 170, 173
  Ushant 157
Francis, king of the Romans 206
Francis, Rev. Philip 18–19, 338, 346–8
franking 70, 84, 106, 118
Frankland, Sir Thomas 72
Fraser, Simon *see* Lovat, 11th lord [S]
Frederick I, king of Prussia 59
Frederick I, king of Sweden 135
Frederick II, king of Prussia 175, 228, 238–9, 243,
    247
Frederick Louis, prince of Wales 86, 132, 158, 168,
    172, 181, 197, 362
Fugitive Pieces in Verse and Prose (H. Walpole) 330

Gage, Thomas, 1st viscount 67, 174
Gage, William, 2nd viscount 82
Gaius Julius Caesar 338, 343, 345
Garrick, David 211
Gascoigne, Bamber 297
Geary, Sir Francis 229
general warrants 282, 302
Geneva, government of 335
George I, king of Great Britain 9, 332–4, 350
George II, king of Great Britain 48, 57–8, 62–4, 71,
    86, 91, 99, 114, 122–3, 138, 143, 146, 158,
    161–2, 168, 169–71, 173, 189, 193, 195, 196, 203,
    206, 214, 218–19, 223, 225, 229–30, 247, 262–3,
    281, 283, 333, 350
  official birthday of 138, 207
George III, king of Great Britain 246, 253, 263,
    271–2, 274–5, 279, 283, 312, 313, 317
Germany 74, 209, 246–7, 250–1, 259, 356
  Berlin 135
  Hanover 15, 64, 70, 96–7, 110, 112, 114–15,
    206, 209, 213, 362–3
  Lower Saxony 236
  Philipsburgh 173
  Prussia 74, 102, 104
Gibraltar 47
Gilbert, John, bishop of Llandaff 120, 131, 138, 147,
    183, 195
Gilmour, Sir Alexander 314
Gilmour, Sir Charles 150, 168, 176, 186
Glamorganshire 183
  Llandaff 147
Glorious Revolution 3, 70, 328, 341

Gloucestershire
  Cheltenham, Frogmill Inn, Andersford 136
  Gloucester 136, 180
  Huntley 136
Glover, Richard 'Leonidas' 39, 80n–1, 88, 182, 258,
    260, 285
Glynn, John 314–15, 360
Glynne, Sir John 229
Godschall, Sir Robert 75
gold boxes 233, 365
Goodwood, Sussex 269
Gordon, George *see* Huntley, 6th earl of and 1st
    marquess
Gordon, Sir William 78, 86
Gore, Charles 66
Gore, Thomas 66
government
  nature of 321–5, 327–8
  rights and powers of 322
Gower, Granville Leveson-Gower, 2nd earl 271,
    275, 290
Gower, John Leveson-Gower, 1st earl 132, 146,
    271
Grafton, Augustus Henry Fitzroy, 3rd duke of 255,
    259, 271, 299, 303
Grafton, Charles Fitzroy, 2nd duke of 140, 147, 233
Graham, Thomas 168, 173, 178, 196–8
Granby, John Manners, marquess of 247, 260
Grant, Sir Alexander 10, 285n
Granville, John Carteret, 2nd earl 72, 82–3, 97, 112,
    114, 121, 129, 139–40, 151, 156–7, 159, 178,
    180–1, 186, 189, 191, 193, 194, 238, 283, 287,
    362
  as Macheath [cant name] 180–2, 184–6, 189
Great Britain 206, 209, 218, 292–3, 301
Great Marlow, Buckinghamshire 190
great seal of England 333, 365
[Great] Yarmouth 152
Grenville, George 22, 40, 142n, 148, 153, 179, 180,
    185–6, 191, 194, 209–10, 212–13, 218, 223,
    252–3, 257, 259, 260–3, 267, 270–4, 277, 279,
    283–4, 287, 293–6, 298–9, 304, 311, 313–15, 318
Grenville, James 104, 106, 159, 258
Grenville ministry 270, 272, 283, 297
Grenville, Richard 142–3, 179
Grenville-Temple, Richard *see* Temple, 2nd earl
Griffin, Sir John 154
The Groans of Germany 70, 72
Grosvenor, Richard, 1st earl 255
Groves, friend of Pryse Campbell 156
Guernsey, lord 67, 93, 116, 180
Guillam, Samuel 360
Guthrie, William 22, 41,100
Gwynn, Dorothea 174
Gwynn, Priscilla 174
Gybbon, Phillips 64, 87, 126, 167, 184–5, 194

habeas corpus, suspended 169
Haceby, Lincolnshire 32
Haddock, Admiral Nicolas 46

Halifax, George Montagu, 1st earl of 331
Halifax, George Montagu-Dunk, 2nd earl of 49,
  145–6, 185, 209, 238, 252, 255, 262, 274, 290
Hamilton, Sir Archibald 67, 185
Hamilton, Charles 150
Hamilton, James *see* Abercorn, 8th earl of [S]
Hamilton, William Gerard 208, 209
Hammond 170
Hampden, Robert Hampden Trevor, 1st marquess
  see Trevor, 4th baron
Hanbury, Capel 287, 289
Hanbury, George 288
Hanbury-Williams, Charles 107, 181, 240, 287–8
Hanover
  electoral dominions 203, 206, 211
  electorate of 71, 97, 143, 207, 225
  troops 96, 97, 110, 112, 115, 128, 131, 132, 142,
    146, 147, 153, 157, 158, 159, 175
Harbord, Harbord 314
Harcourt, Simon, 1st earl 295, 299
Hardwicke, Philip Yorke, 1st earl of 12, 14, 35, 38,
  71n, 157, 171, 188, 201, 205, 219, 225, 230, 238,
  246, 255, 256, 365
Hardy, Sir Charles 141, 150
Harley, Edward 4, 65, 67
Harley, Robert *see* Oxford, 1st earl of
Harley, Thomas 308–9
Harrington, William Stanhope, 1st earl of 71, 148,
  185
Harris, James 255
Harwich 141
Haversham, Maurice Thompson, 2nd baron 146
Hawke, Admiral Edward 200
Hay, Charles, lord 101–3, 119
Hay, Edward 213
Hay George 222
Hay, John *see* Tweeddale, 4th marquess of
Hay, Thomas, viscount Dupplin *see* Kinnoull, 9th
  earl of [S]
Haycock, James 70, 86, 93, 95, 119, 126, 130, 133,
  135–6, 149, 152, 154–5, 157, 159, 163, 174, 180,
  183, 187–8, 195–6, 197, 199
Haylor, James 152
Heathcote, George 198
Heathcote, William 66
Henley, 'Orator' John 125, 154
Henley, Robert *see* Northington, 1st earl of
Henry, prince, Frederick Henry Louis 264
Henry V, king of England 340
Herbert, Henry Arthur *see* Powis, 1st earl of
Herbert, General William 232
Hereford 136
Hereford, dowager viscountess 116
Hertford, Francis Seymour-Conway, 1st earl of
  116
Hervey, George William *see* Bristol, 2nd earl of
Hervey, John, lord 11, 22, 32–3, 52n, 58, 83–4, 105,
  112, 118, 122, 125, 132
Hervey, Mr 83
Hervey, Thomas 73
Hessian troops 205, 210, 214–15, 228

Heydon, Norfolk 186
high clergy 321–3, 326, 329
Hill, John 50, 195
Hillsborough, Mary Hill, countess of 234
Hillsborough, Wills Hill, earl of 104, 106, 142, 180,
  208, 222, 257–8, 275, 304
'Historical Memorial' 249
Hobart, Sir John 185, 290
Hobbinol (Somerville) 54
Holcombe, Essex 61
Holdernesse, Robert Darcy, 4th earl of 212, 232,
  237, 281, 284
Holland, Caroline, lady 37, 264n, 278, 304, 306,
  308, 310, 315, 317, 318
Holland, Henry Fox, 1st baron of Foxley 10–14, 16,
  18–19, 22–3, 28, 30–3, 36–41, 65n, 85, 94, 96,
  98, 107, 109, 114, 132, 134, 138, 141, 143, 146,
  150, 154, 162, 179–80, 190, 203–14, 216, 219,
  221, 223, 227, 229–36, 246–7, 252, 257,
  259–63, 265–6, 269–70, 272, 275, 281, 285,
  287–9, 297–303, 306, 309, 346, 362, 364–6
  as paymaster of the forces 231–2, 234, 236, 242,
    270–1, 275, 288, 291
Holles, John *see* Newcastle, 1st duke of
  (1662–1711)
Holles, Lady Susannah 4
Holmes, Charles 229
Holmes, Henry 229
Holmes, Thomas 229
Homer 278
Hooke, John 13, 25–6, 116n, 154, 173, 187, 190,
  194, 208, 236
Hooke, Nathaniel 338
Hooke-Campbell, John 208, 211, 236, 248, 265
  as Lord Lyon, king at arms 10, 13, 25, 211,
    236–7, 248
Hooper, Edward 106, 285
Hope, Rev. Charles 32
Hope, Christian 32
Horace [Quintus Horatius Flaccus] 54, 60, 63, 84,
  197, 207, 224, 279, 280, 337, 349, 363
Horner, Susanna 33
Howard, Charles 15
Howard, Frederick *see* Carlisle, 5th earl of
Howard, George 77
Howard, Henry *see* Suffolk, 12th earl of
Howe, George, 3rd viscount [I] 241
Howe, George, 4th viscount [I] and 1st earl 203
Howe, John 66
Howell, D.W. 42
Hume, David 233
Hume-Campbell, Alexander 106, 167, 179–80
Hume-Campbell, Alexander *see* Marchmont, 2nd
  earl of [S]
Hume-Campbell, Hugh *see* Marchmont, 3rd earl of
  [S]
Huntley, George Gordon, 6th earl of 2
Hussey, Richard 293
Hutton, Matthew, archbishop of Canterbury 201
Hyde, Edward *see* Clarendon, 1st earl of
Hylton [Hilton], John 67

Ilchester, Henry Fox-Strangways, 2nd earl of 242
Ilchester, Stephen Fox-Strangways, 1st earl of 30, 32–3, 227, 266
impeachment 331, 333–4
independent electors of Westminster 155
instructions
    London 99
    Merionethshire 129
    Westminster 100
    Worcester 99
Irby, Sir William 67
Ireland 247, 288, 294, 332
Irish Patriot Party 247
Isham, Sir Edmund 187
Italy 174, 178
    Rome 338, 343–5, 347

jacobites 64, 67, 72, 86, 87, 107, 116, 119, 123–4, 132, 137–8, 146, 167, 172–3, 190, 193–4, 235, 242
Jamaica 122, 125
James II, king of England and Scotland 3, 162, 323, 325–7, 331
James IV, king of Scotland 1
Jeffreys, John 102
Jenison, Ralph 185
Jenkins, Mr, exciseman, Carmarthen 142
Jenkinson, Charles 311
Jews 321
Johnes, Thomas 27
Johnson, Samuel 41, 312
Jones 'the Gamester' 199
Jones, Hugh Vance 222
Jones, Thomas 138
Joseph [son of Jacob] 321
Julius Caesar 317
Jurin, James 196
Juvenal [Decimus Iunis Iuvenalis] 302

Keene, Sir Benjamin 85, 213–14
Keith, James Francis Edward, marshall 74
Keith, Mary 2
Kent 163, 172, 282
    Hayes [house] 272, 298
    Kingsgate House 266, 276, 278, 280, 294, 302, 306, 308, 314, 317
        Hakemdown Tower (folly at Kingsgate) 309
        Harley Tower (folly at Kingsgate) 309–10
Keppel, Augustus 228–9
Keppel, George see Albemarle, 3rd earl of
Ker, John see Roxburghe, 1st duke of
Ker, Robert see Roxburghe, 2nd duke of
Kildare, lord 247
king's speech 15, 70, 140
Kinnoull, Thomas Hay, Viscount Dupplin, 9th earl of [S] 13, 208–9n, 213, 222, 233, 234

la touche, James Digges 155
Lambert, Daniel 162, 198

Lane, Sir Richard 151
Laughton, Richard 5
Leach, Mr 47
Lechmere, Edmund 67
Lediard, Thomas 77
Lee, Dr George 72, 107–8, 208, 215
Lee, George Henry, viscount Quarenden see Litchfield, 3rd earl of
Lee, Nathaniel 158
Lee, Sir William 72
Leeds, Thomas Osborne, earl of Danby, 1st duke of 31
Legge, Edward 175
Legge, Henry Bilson 13, 85n, 102, 106, 141, 160, 175–6, 184, 190, 194, 204–5, 207–8, 210–13, 215, 219–26, 228, 232–4, 236, 245, 252, 260, 364–7
Leicester House 211, 221, 225
Lennox, Charles see Richmond, 2nd duke of
Lennox, Charles see Richmond, 3rd duke of
Lennox, Emily 247
Lennox, George, lord 247
Lennox, Georgina Caroline, lady 264
Lennox, Sarah, lady 249
Lever, John 77
Leverson-Gower, Evelyn, lady 304
Leveson-Gower, Granville see Gower, 2nd earl
Leveson-Gower, John, see Gower, 1st earl
levy money 350
liberty 338, 341–6
Liddell, Henry see Ravensworth, 1st baron
Limerick, James Hamilton, 1st viscount [I] 63, 66, 84, 106, 114, 165, 167
limited monarchy 343
Lincoln, lord 221, 227
Lisbon 213, 215
Litchfield, George Henry Lee, Viscount Quarenden, 3rd earl of 114, 187, 225, 295, 299
Livonia 210
Lloyd, David of Derwydd 292
Lloyd, Elizabeth Eleanor 292
Lloyd, Herbert of Peterwell 30
Lloyd, misses 181, 190
Lloyd, Richard 56, 59, 104, 190
Lobkowitz, prince of, Johann Georg Christian 178
Locke, John 5, 17, 321
Lodington, Leicestershire 77
London 3–4, 11, 23, 28, 99, 105, 123, 126, 136, 152, 163, 166, 173, 191, 198, 233, 235, 237, 241, 243, 249, 251–2, 264–5, 270, 276, 282, 287, 303, 305, 310, 313, 317
    The Albany, Piccadilly 258, 282
    Bedlam 170
    Charing Cross 141
    Chelsea 75, 93, 155
    City of London 198, 284, 293, 312, 365
    coffee houses 233, 235
        British Coffee House 166
    Drury Lane theatre 211
    Fountain Tavern, The Strand 84
    Great Russell Street 252
    Green Hatch, Holborn 153

London (cont.)
  Grosvenor Square 11, 126
  Hanover Square 177
  Holland House 216, 265, 308, 310, 317
  Hyde Park 241, 244
  Kensington 57
  Leicester Fields 99
  Leicester House 99
  Lincoln's Inn 4
  Newcastle House 208, 227, 232
  River Thames 116–17, 163
  St James's barracks 227
  St James's Palace 52
  St James's Park 173, 312–13
  St James's Square 102
  St James's Street 260
  Spring Garden, The Mall 173
  Wandsworth 256
  Wimbledon 52, 57, 137
Lonsdale, Henry Lowther, 3rd viscount 132, 146, 164
lord chancellor 71–2, 146, 153, 157, 171–2, 188,
  201–2, 205, 219, 225, 269, 272, 279, 299, 304,
  331
Lord Granville's administration 205
lord privy seal 132, 184–5
lords, house of 13, 20, 32, 35–6, 44–5, 49–51, 70,
  72, 100, 109–10, 117, 131–2, 134, 146, 157–9,
  161–2, 164, 171–3, 214, 225, 230, 234, 240, 250,
  255, 261–3, 331, 355
  protest against rejecting Lord Stanhope's motion
    134
Lort, Elizabeth 4
Lort, George 4
Lort, Gilbert 4
Lort, Sir John 3, 4
Lort, Susanna, lady 4
Louis XV, king of France 131–2, 170
Louisbourg, siege of 243
Lovat, Simon Fraser, 11th lord [S] 29, 248
Lowndes, Richard 306
Lowther, Henry see Lonsdale, 3rd viscount
Lucas, Anthony 306
Lucium Tarquinius Collatinus 344
Lucius Quinctius Cinncinnatus, dictator 346
Luff, Peter 37
Lumley, Richard see Scarbrough, 2nd earl of
Lumley-Saunderson, Thomas see Scarbrough, 3rd
  earl of
Luttrel, Sir Henry Lawes 311–12, 314–15
Lyttelton, George, lord 65, 97, 101, 106, 111, 126,
  173, 179–80, 184–6, 208–12, 220, 222, 224, 243,
  281, 290, 294, 313, 365
Lyttelton, Sir Richard 208, 212, 218
Lyttelton, Sir Thomas 228

Macdonald clan 2
Macduff see Pelham, Henry
Macheath see John, Lord Carteret
Mackenzie, James Stuart 101, 108, 270, 272, 283,
  294, 297–8

Mackworth, Herbert 66
Macquick, Edward 360
McQuicke, Mr 254
Manners (Paul Whitehead) 44, 100
Manners, John see Granby, marquess of
Manners, John see Rutland, 3rd duke of
Manners, William 141, 187
Mansel, Rawleigh 94, 100, 132
Mansell, Bussy 66
Mansfield, William Murray, 1st earl 100, 102,
  105–6, 111, 128, 135, 142–3, 153, 159, 166,
  169, 208, 213, 215, 255–6, 263, 289, 295, 299
Marchant, Dick 195
Marchmont, Alexander Hume-Campbell, 2nd earl of
  56
Marchmont, Hugh Hume-Campbell, 3rd earl of 54,
  56
Marcus Junius Brutus 344
Maria Theresa of Austria, queen of Hungary 74, 93,
  97, 113, 118, 121, 128, 133, 140, 148, 165, 175,
  195, 207, 236, 238, 363
maritime powers 74
Marlborough, Charles Spencer, 3rd duke of 140,
  147, 158, 164, 216–17, 222, 235, 241, 243,
  291
Marlborough, George Spencer, 4th duke of 290
Marlborough, 'Turianum Maxima', Sarah, duchess of
  68, 158, 197
Marshall, Henry 66, 162
Martial, Marcus Valerius 107
Martin, Samuel 208
Mary, princess 59
Mary II, queen of England 326, 330
Mathews, Admiral Thomas 166, 168, 173–4, 177,
  183, 201–2
Maurpas, comte de 200
Maynard, Charles, 1st viscount 132, 182–3, 259
Mead, Dr Richard 121
Meadows, Frances 26, 310
Meadows, Sir Philip 26, 310
Meare, Mr F. 93, 123
Mediterranean 73, 163, 168–9, 230
'Mentor' 248
Meredith, Sir William 298
methodists 113, 160
Mettus Curtius 343
Meyrick, John 4, 7
Meyrick, John Francis 137, 269, 270
Middlesex 287, 292, 359
Middlesex jury 3, 361
Middleton, Dr 130
militia 349
Minorca 19, 29, 36
  inquiry into the loss of 230, 232–3
  St Philip's Fort, Port Mahon 217
Miscellaneous Thoughts (Lord Hervey) 105, 112,
  140
mob 76–8, 92, 100, 244–5, 285, 296, 281, 312–13,
  315, 318, 344, 346, 368
  Westminster mob 100
Montagu, Charles 187

Montagu, Frederick 314
Montagu, George, *see* Halifax, 1st earl of
Montagu, John *see* Sandwich, 4th earl of
Montagu, Lady Mary Wortley 289
Montagu-Dunk, George *see* Halifax, 2nd earl of
Montague, Wortley 64
Montgomerie, Alexander *see* Eglington, 10th earl of [S]
Moor, Sir John 229
Moore, William 66
Moray, James Stuart, 8th earl of [S] 168
Moray and Argyll, Agnes Keith, countess of 2
Mordaunt, Sir Charles 67, 225, 253
Mordaunt, Sir John 49, 241
Morgan, Matty 196
Morgan, Thomas 183
Morrice, Bezaleel 173
Morris, Edmund 'uncle Morris' 55n, 61–2, 77, 86, 151
Morris, Johnny [Jack?] 117, 121, 139, 154
Morris, Lewis, governor of New Jersey 119, 149
Morris, Mr 164
Morris, Mrs 254
Morse, Charles 195
Morton [Moreton], James Douglas, 14th earl of [S] 147
Morton, John 314–15
Moses 322
Mountstuart, lord *see* Bute, 1st marquess of
Murphy, Arthur 251, 259
Murray, James *see* Strange, 7th baron
Murray, John, lord, colonel 181
Murray, William *see* Mansfield, 1st earl of

Naples, kingdom of 178, 302, 305
National Archives Scotland 38
the Netherlands (Dutch Republic, Holland, Low Country) 119, 121, 162, 200, 209
    Brill 119, 12
    Dort 119, 121
    Flushing 276
    The Hague 177
    States General 119, 148, 177, 192
New Windsor, Bedfordshire 33
Newcastle, John Holles, 1st duke of (1662–1711) 4
Newcastle, Thomas Pelham-Holles, 1st duke of (1693–1768) 8, 10, 12–14, 29–30, 34–6, 38–9, 57n, 65, 71, 82, 85, 87, 100, 109, 115, 131, 140, 147, 150, 169–71, 181–4, 189–92, 201, 203–4, 207, 209, 212, 216, 218–19, 220–5, 227, 234–8, 240, 242, 246, 248, 252, 255, 259–60, 270, 272, 276, 283, 285, 288, 293, 303, 362–7
Newdigate, Sir Roger 192
Newton, Sir Isaac 39
Nivernais, duc de 252
Noel, Edward, *see* Wentworth, 1st viscount
Noel, James 66
Noel, Thomas 66, 142
Noel, William 67, 142
non-jurors 17, 321

Noorthouck, John 21
Norris, Admiral 229
Norris, Admiral Sir John 64, 89, 157, 160, 162–3, 167, 172–5, 177, 182
North, Frederick 316, 318
North–Fox coalition 316
Northampton, James Compton, 5th earl of 87
Northcote, Harry [Henry] 67
Northey, William 208–9
Northington, Robert Henley, 1st earl of 244–5, 255, 267
Northumberland, Hugh Percy, 1st duke of 67, 299
Norton, Sir Fletcher 268, 272, 275, 293, 311, 313, 314
Nottingham, Daniel Finch, 2nd earl of 162–3
Nova Scotia
    Cape Breton 240
    Newfoundland 252
Nugent, Viner 13, 106n, 142, 209

oaths 69, 77, 324, 325, 358–60
    coronation 325
    of secrecy, Byng's trial 228, 229
O'Brien, Percy Wyndham 208
*Observations on Miscellaneous Thoughts*122
Ogle, Sir Charles 125
Oglethorpe, James Edward 143
'Old Coachman' 181–2, 185
Onslow, Arthur 15, 69n, 79, 128, 160, 162, 224, 252
Onslow, Denzil 150
Onslow, George 293, 315, 318
oration of Timarchus 347
Ord, Robert 146
Orford, Edward Russell, 1st earl of (1653–1727) 331
Orford, Sir Robert Walpole, 1st earl of (1676–1745) 1, 7, 8–12, 14–15, 19–20, 23–4, 32, 35, 38–9, 41, 43, 45n, 48, 57, 63–5, 72, 73, 75, 79, 81–6, 93, 97, 100, 102, 105–8, 110, 112, 126, 132, 134, 159, 161, 164, 168, 171, 173, 181, 184, 196–8, 205, 212, 240, 345, 347, 362–3
Origen 322
Osbourn, Sir George 314–15
Ostein, Johann Frederick Karl von, elector of Mainz 195
Osterman, Count Andrey Invaovich 74
Oswald, James 153, 186, 294
Owen, Arthur 7, 8, 115n, 319, 320
Owen family of Orielton, Pembrokshire 4, 7, 8
Owen, Hugh 276, 285–6, 316
Owen, Hugh (transcriber) 38, 276, 285–6
Owen, John 9
Owen, John (historian) 39
Owen, Thomas 4
Owen, 'uncle' 94, 112, 125
Owen, William 8, 9, 94n, 266, 276
Oxenden, Sir George 187
Oxford, Robert Harley, 1st earl of 67, 304

Oxfordshire 235
   Christ Church, Oxford 32
   Henley 113
   Nettlebed 112
   Oxford 113
   Woodstock 99

Packer, Wichcombe Howard 66
Pakington, Sir Henry 66
papists 330, 332, 335–6
Parker, Sir Thomas 102
parliament
   annual 194, 340–2
   of England 335
   of Great Britain 335–6
   Scottish 3
   septennial 342
   triennial 341
patriots 15, 49, 56, 78–9, 82, 89, 92, 106, 112, 159,
   162, 166, 184, 188, 338, 343, 346
*The Patriots are Come or, a New Doctrine for a Crazy
   Constitution* 106, 112
Payne, Ralph 312
Paynter, David 134
Pearce 139
Pearce, Zachary 201
Pelham, Catherine, lady 85
Pelham, Charles 67
Pelham, Henry 12, 14–15, 23, 31, 33, 35, 65n–6, 69,
   97, 103, 106–7, 111, 121–2, 124–5, 127–8, 134–5,
   137, 140–1, 145–7, 149, 160–1, 165–7, 169–71,
   179–80, 182, 184, 186, 188, 192–3, 196–8, 203–4,
   213, 219, 277, 362–3
   as Macduff [cant name] 180, 183–4, 186, 189
Pelham, Tom 222, 287
Pelham-Holles, Thomas *see* Newcastle, 1st duke of
   (1693–1768)
Pelhamite innocents 34, 36
Pembroke Society 113
Pembrokeshire 3–4, 6–10, 12–13, 16, 21, 24, 26–7,
   38, 79, 81, 86, 104, 154, 158, 201, 235, 239, 266,
   269, 276, 289, 291, 303, 319
   Bangeston 153, 253
   Burton 165
   Carew 4
   Gresholm [Grassholm] 133
   Haverfordwest 8–9, 79, 124, 133, 137, 139, 147,
      149, 266, 316
   Hubberston 43
   Kilgetty House 24
   Milford Haven 43, 216, 251
   Narberth 201
   Orielton [house] 7, 9, 38, 115, 122
   Pembroke boroughs 8–9, 100, 124, 254
   Pentyparc [house] 125, 151, 187
   Picton Castle [house] 4, 7, 95
   Rosemarket 319
   St David's 147
   Stackpole Court [house] 3–7, 21, 24, 26–8,
      38–41 47, 51, 53, 58, 122, 125, 137, 141, 151,

   206, 215–16
   Stepaside 60
   Tenby 216
   Wenn 4
   Wiston 94, 100
Perceval, John *see* Egmont, 2nd earl of
Percy, Henry, lord 31
Percy, Hugh *see* Northumberland, 1st duke of
Perry, M. 66
Petty, William *see* Shelburne, 2nd earl of
Philip V, king of Macedon 348
Philip V, king of Spain 97
Philipps family of Picton Castle, Pembrokeshire 4, 7
Philipps, Griffith 132, 201, 214
Philipps, James, 'uncle Philipps' 59, 93, 122, 142,
   145, 152, 156
Philipps, Jane 59
Philipps, Rev. Jeremiah 188
Philipps, Sir John (1666–1737) 7, 8
Philipps, Sir John (1700–64) 7, 9, 24, 75n, 82, 94,
   97–8, 104, 111, 114–16, 124, 129–30, 131–3, 141,
   147, 162, 169, 171–2, 184–5, 188, 190–1, 194–5,
   197, 200, 215, 239, 248, 258, 261, 267, 273–4,
   279, 276–7
Philipps, Sir Richard 266–7, 269, 307, 316
Phillipps, Sir Erasmus 7, 21, 95n, 98, 124, 129, 132
Phillips, Rev. George, 'monocle' 103
Phillipson, John 141, 150, 185–6, 194
Pitt, Elizabeth 187
Pitt, George [Jack] 117
Pitt, John 185, 188, 197–8
Pitt, Thomas 144, 362
Pitt, William, the elder, *see* Chatham, 1st earl of
Pitt, William, the younger 27, 37, 265
The Play of Douglas (Hume) 233
plebeians 344
Political Club (Pembrokeshire) 113
Polwarth, lord *see* Marchmont, 3rd earl of
Polybius 18
Pomfret, George Fermor, 2nd earl of 256
Porter, Mary 122, 233
Portland, Hans William Bentinck, 1st earl of 331
Portland, William Bentinck, 2nd duke of 140, 259,
   318
Porto Bello, Panama 55–8
Portsmouth 50, 157–8
Potter, John, archbishop of Canterbury 138
Potter, Thomas 208–9, 240
Poulett, Anne 314–15
Poulett, John, 1st earl 149
Poulett, John, 2nd earl 148
Poulett, Vere, 3rd earl 148, 192, 198, 294, 301
Powell, Thomas 124
Powis, Henry Arthur Herbert, 1st earl of 72, 290
Powlett, Charles *see* Bolton, 3rd duke of
Powney, Peniston 106
Praed [Prade], William Mackworth 66
Pratt, Charles *see* Camden, lord
Price, Mr 95
privy council 50, 64, 241, 246, 249, 332–4
Proctor, Sir William Beauchamp 360

protestant/s 330–2, 336
    protestant line to the crown 330–1, 335–6
Prowse, Thomas 67, 173
Prust, John 147
Pryse, John Hugh 30
Pryse, Lewis 5, 124
Pryse, Mary 5
Pryse, Thomas 190
Pulteney, William, *see* Bath, 1st earl of
'Punch' 154–5

Quarenden, viscount *see* Litchfield, 3rd earl of
Quebec, North America 217
Queensberry, James Douglas, 2nd duke of 87
Quinctius Caeso 346
Quintin Roscius Gallus 260

Ranby, John 196, 198
Ravensworth, Henry Liddell, 1st baron 257
Raymond, Robert, 2nd baron 147
Redlynch [house], Dorset 32
regency
    1755 212–13
    1765 270–1
Rice, George 202
Rich, Sir Robert 78
Richelieu, duc de 227
Richmond, Charles Lennox, 2nd duke of 82, 140,
    147, 247, 264
Richmond, Charles Lennox, 3rd duke of 246, 247,
    315
Richmond House, Priory Gardens, Richmond 216,
    275
Rickson, Captain William 122
Rickson, Mr 93
Ridley 169–70
Rigby, Richard 36, 235, 275n, 278, 280, 300, 302,
    306
Ripperda, duc de 205
Robertson, William 317
Robinson, Sir Thomas 203, 208, 234, 364
Rockingham ministry 271–2, 287, 291, 293, 296
Rockingham, Thomas Watson-Wentworth, 1st earl
    of 70, 196, 313, 318
Rolle, Henry 44, 66
Roman
    consul 345
    decemviri 346
    empire 343, 345
    magistracy of dictators 345
    proconsul 343
    republic 343–5
    senate 343–4, 346
Romulus 343
Rose, Hugh 10
Ross, Andrew 248
Ross, Captain Charles 142, 144, 147
Ross, George 248
Ross, Hugh 312

Rowe, Rev. Henry 47–8, 51–5, 57–8, 60, 62, 63,
    89–90, 93, 95, 98, 102, 105–6, 112, 115–16, 123,
    129, 130, 133, 134, 136, 137, 140, 145, 151, 156,
    165, 186, 189, 195–6, 198, 201
Roxburghe, John Ker, 1st duke of 87
Roxburghe, Robert Ker, 2nd duke of 77
Royston, Philip Yorke, lord 230, 255
Rushout, Sir John 87, 98, 134, 141, 146, 150, 184
Russell, Edward *see* Orford, 1st earl of (1653–1727)
Russell, John *see* Bedford, 4th duke of
Russia 74–5, 104
Rutherford, John 66
Rutland, John Manners, 3rd duke of 260
Ryder, Sir Dudley 65, 106, 169

St Aubyn [Auben], Sir John 114
St George's Field riots 313
St Helena [St Helen's] 160, 176
St John, Frederick *see* Bolingbroke, 2nd viscount
St Paul, the Apostle 281
Sacheverell, Dr Henry 324
    trial of 324
Sackville, George, lord 96, 225
Sackville, John Philip, lord 96
Sackville, Lionel *see* Dorset, 1st duke of
Salust 89
Sandon [Sundon], William Clayton, 1st baron [I] 76
Sandwich, John Montagu, 4th earl of 131, 146,
    157–8, 182, 184–6, 213, 262, 266–7, 274, 278,
    280, 290, 295
Sandys, Samuel 50, 63–4, 73, 79, 82–3, 87, 93, 97–8,
    107, 109–11, 114, 117, 123–6, 134, 138, 141–2,
    146, 148, 150, 181, 185
Saville, Sir George 314–15
Sawbridge, John 311
Saxe, comte de 170, 173, 177
Sayer, Rev. Dr George 138
Scald Miserable Procession 100
Scarbrough, Richard Lumley, 2nd earl of 49, 50–1
Scarbrough, Thomas Lumley-Saunderson, 3rd earl of
    133
Scarsdale, Nathaniel Curzon, 1st baron 290
Scotland 1–4, 6, 10, 13, 17, 19–20, 25, 160, 164,
    321–3, 349, 335–6, 356
    Argyllshire 131
    Edinburgh 99
    Glasgow University 2
    Inverness burghs 3, 10, 29
    Inverness-shire 1, 3, 9–10, 13, 27, 29, 30, 248
    Islay and Jura 2, 5
    Nairn 1, 4, 5, 10, 28
Scudamore, Henry *see* Beaufort, 3rd duke of
seceders 51
Secker, Thomas, archbishop of Canterbury 240, 249
Secker, William 39, 86
Seleucid empire 347
Selwyn, George 275, 318
Seymour, Catherine 186
Seymour, Charles, chancellor of Cambridge
    University 201

Seymour, Henry 315
Seymour, Henry Conway 21–2, 116n, 225, 232, 271, 291, 293, 300–2, 315
Shelburne, William Petty, 2nd earl of 36, 247n, 250, 255, 263, 271, 278, 287, 293–4, 301–4, 311
Shelley, Sir John 222
Shippen, William 67–8, 82, 96, 110, 114
Shrewsbury 154
Shuttleworth, Richard 172, 187
Sicilies, kingdom of the two 157, 179
sinking fund 64
Smith, Mr, of Jeffreyston, Pembrokeshire 188
Smith, Admiral Thomas 228
Smollett, Tobias 259
Society of Supporters of the Bill of Rights 313
solicitor-general 102, 106, 111, 128, 135, 143, 148
Somers, John, 1st baron 332
Somerset, Algernon, 7th duke of 186
Somerset, Charles Noel, lord *see* Beaufort, 4th duke of
Sophia, princess, electress of Hanover 112, 332, 335–6
Southwall, Edward 65–6, 100
Spain 49–50, 52, 57, 64, 71, 99–100, 170, 174, 177, 250–1, 253–4, 356
    Alicante 174
    Madrid 251
Spanish America 282
Speke, George 126
Spelman, Edward 18, 338, 340–6
Spencer, Charles *see* Marlborough, 3rd duke of
Spencer, Lady Diana 291
Spencer, George *see* Marlborough, 4th duke of
Stair, John Dalrymple, 2nd earl of 138, 143–4, 164, 169
Stamp Act congress 292
Stanhope, Charles 67
Stanhope, Philip 208
Stanhope, Philip, 2nd earl 131–4
Stanhope, Philip Dormer, *see* Chesterfield, 4th earl of
Stanhope, William, *see* Harrington, 1st earl of
Stanley, Hans 251, 256, 314
Stavordale, lord, *see* Ilchester, Henry Fox-Strangways, 2nd earl of
Stepney, Sir Thomas 214, 292
Stowe House, Buckinghamshire 284
Strafford, Thomas Wentworth, 1st earl of 283
Strange, James Murray, 7th baron and 2nd duke of Athol [S] 25, 95, 126, 134–5
Strange, James Stanley, lord 158–9, 160, 162, 165, 168–9, 171, 191–3, 255
Strangways, Thomas 33
Strangways-Horner, Susanna 33
Strickland, Captain William 142, 144, 146–7
Stuart, Charles Edward Louis Philip Casimar, 'Bonnie Prince Charlie', the Young Pretender 161–2, 168–9, 170, 172
Stuart, Henrietta, lady 3
Stuart, James *see* Moray, 8th earl of [S]
Stuart, James Francis Edward, the Old Pretender 161–2, 168, 170, 326
Stuart, John *see* Bute, 3rd earl of

Stuart, John *see* Bute, 1st marquess of, styled Lord Mountstuart
Suffolk 259
Suffolk, Henry Howard, 12th earl of 287, 290
Sunninghill Park, Berkshire 242
Sussex 172
Sweden, senate of 334
Swift, Jonathan 292
Sydenham, Humphrey 126, 171, 194–5, 198
Symmons, John 9, 75, 95, 98n, 104, 124, 132–3, 202, 316

Tacitus, Cornelius 280–1
Talbot, William, 1st Earl Talbot of Hensol, Glamorgan 51, 225, 257
Taylor, Joseph 67
Taylor, William 67
'Telemachus' 248
Temple, Richard *see* Cobham, 1st viscount
Temple, Richard Grenville-Temple, 2nd earl 218, 222–3, 225, 228, 230, 250, 255, 259, 264, 270–3, 275, 280–1, 284–5, 287, 289–90, 292–3, 295–9, 302, 304, 312–13, 318, 365–7
Temple, Sir William 253
Tencin, Cardinal Pierre Guerin de 158
The Test 223–4
Things as They Are 242
Thomas, Sir Edward 81, 106, 114
Thomas, P.D.G. 40, 42
Thomas, Wil 58, 119, 122
Thompson, Rev. Anthony 169, 170, 174, 189
Thompson, Maurice *see* Haversham, 2nd baron
Thurlow, Edward 293, 311, 314
Thynne, Thomas *see* Bath, 1st marquess of
Tiberius Claudius Caesar Augustus Germanicus 345
Tickell, Thomas 278
Timarchus 347
Titus Tatius (king of Sabines) 343
Torbay 160, 173
Torrington, George Byng, 4th viscount 294, 301
Townsend, James 311
Townshend, Charles 211, 239, 251, 256, 261, 275, 279, 288, 293, 299
Townshend, George, 4th viscount, 1st marquess 208–9, 212, 215, 233
Townshend, Thomas 190
treasury 11–13, 29, 31, 33, 35, 37, 83, 87, 92, 108, 121, 125–8, 138, 141, 146, 149–50, 182, 184–6, 221, 232, 303, 362
    first lord of 37, 57, 45, 82, 90, 166, 219, 221, 234, 252–3, 259, 261, 262, 277, 362, 364–5
treaties
    Alliance (1742) 104
    Bretigny (1360) 340
    Great Britain and Hesse-Kassel (1755) 209
    Great Britain and Russia (1755) 209
    Hanover (1725) 64, 70
    Kloster-Zeven (1757) 237–9
    Neutrality (1725) 70
    Paris (1763) 10, 36, 108, 252, 262, 277, 286

treaties (cont.)
    Subsidy (1755) 205–7, 210, 365
    Troyes (1420) 340
    Union (1706) 334, 335–6
    Utrecht (1715) 158, 341–2
    Vienna (1725) 205
    Worms (1743) 138, 156–8
Trevor, John 72
Trevor, Robert Hampden Trevor, 4th baron 290
triumvirate 106
Trojans 176, 183, 186, 189
Trubshaw 47–8, 50–1, 53, 55–63, 69–70, 75, 86,
    88–90, 92–3, 100, 102, 108, 130, 137, 139, 146,
    195, 200
Tucker, Josiah 147
Turnor, Sir Edward 106
Tweeddale, John Hay, 4th marquess of 87, 129, 139,
    176

Upton, Clotworthy 288, 303

Val, Pryse Campbell's valet 48, 53, 58, 84, 90,113,
    119, 130, 133, 149, 177, 178, 195
Vane, Henry 184
Vaughan, Erasmus 62
Vaughan, Sir John 8
Vaughan, William 129
Veil, Sir Thomas de 177
Vere, Lady Diana de 78
Vere, lord 184–6, 189
Verginia 346
Verney, Ralph 255
Vernon, Admiral Edward 55–6, 64, 78, 123, 125,
    134, 136, 142, 162, 170–2, 194, 208
Vernon family of Hadden Hall, Derbyshire 3
Vernon, George 67
Vernon, George (d. 1565) 4
Ville, Jean Ignace de la 177
Villiers, George see Buckingham, 1st duke of
Villiers, George, see Buckingham, 2nd duke of,
    playwright
Virgil [Publius Vergilius Maro] 56, 60, 89, 90–1,
    127, 156, 177, 278, 284–5, 335
Voltaire, François-Marie Arouet 227
von Münnich, count 74
Vyner [Viner], Robert 66, 135, 195

Wade, George 150n, 159, 164, 169
Wade, Kathleen 26
Wade, William 25–6
Wager, Admiral Sir Charles 11, 59n, 73, 78, 86,
    88–9, 100, 117
Waldegrave, James, 2nd earl 262
Waldegrave, John, 3rd earl 290
Wales 1, 3–9, 14, 20, 27, 31, 38, 83, 85, 115, 303,
    305
Wall, Richard [Ricardo Wal] 250
Wallace, surgeon 195

Waller, Edmund 12, 104n, 106, 111, 114–15, 134–5,
    142, 156, 161, 165, 171, 180, 183, 185
Waller, Henry 187
Walpole, Edward 106–7, 145, 262
Walpole, Horatio [Horace] (1717–97) 13, 15–16, 21,
    23, 91n, 159, 208, 251, 278, 330
Walpole, Horatio, 'Lord Sheffield' (1678–1757) 45,
    114, 121, 143, 145, 363
Walpole, Mary [Marie] 262
Walpole, Sir Robert see Orford, 1st earl of
Walpole, Robert, lord, eldest son of Sir Robert 65,
    196, 198
Walter, Peter 96
Walter, Sir Richard 8, 319
Watson, colonel 216–17
Watson-Wentworth, Thomas see Rockingham, 1st
    earl of
Wedderburn, Sir Alexander 253, 294, 312, 314
Wemyss, James, 5th earl of 172
Wentworth, Edward Noel, 1st viscount 290
Wentworth, Thomas see Strafford, 1st earl of
Wentworth, General Thomas 123, 125, 134,
    164
West, James 149, 150, 204, 222
West, John see de la Warr, 1st earl
Westminster
    Abbey 120
    Alice's Coffee house, Palace Yard 318
    palace of
        court of requests 124, 166
        Solomon's porch 215
        Westminster Hall 240
    Thatched House Tavern, St James's 313
Westmorland, John Fane, 7th earl of 77, 159
Westmorland, John Fane, 9th earl of 159, 225
Weymouth 110
Whichcot, Thomas 66
Whitaker, Mr 239
Whitefield, George 69
Whitehead, Paul 44, 100
Wilhelmina, princess of Hesse-Kassel 264
Wilkes, John 18, 29, 39, 40–1, 246, 259, 264n, 272,
    275, 278, 287, 288, 302, 307–8, 311–13, 315–16,
    359
Willes, Edward, bishop of St David's 120
Willes, John (1685–1761) 151
Willes, John (1721–84) 151, 154
William, prince, duke of Gloucester 330–1
William III, king of England 326, 328, 330–4, 336,
    340
William VIII, landgrave of Hesse-Kassel 209–10,
    365
Williams, 'Pry' 191
Williams, Robert 194
Williams-Wynn, Sir Watkin 52, 79, 86, 88, 92, 104,
    109–10, 114, 125, 129, 133, 163, 169, 190
Willoughby, Thomas 113
Wilmington administration 12
Wilmington, Spencer Compton, 1st earl of 82,
    121–2, 126–7
Wilmot, Sir Earlby 289

Winchilsea, Daniel Finch, 8th earl of and 3rd earl of
    Nottingham 129, 139, 141, 154, 162, 165, 194,
    273, 366
Windsor, Herbert 225
Winnington, Sir Edward 275, 287
Winnington, Thomas 11, 73n, 97–8, 105, 111, 114,
    125, 133, 134, 141–2, 146, 150–1, 153, 162, 176,
    179–80, 184–5, 188, 190, 198, 363
Woburn Abbey [house] 274
Wodehouse, Thomas 26
Wogan, John 291
Wogan, John (1713–15) 183
Wogan, John of Wiston 188
Worcester 151, 154
Wiltshire 310
    Hindon 33
    Old Sarum 33
Windsor 235

Wright, John 187
Wright, John 'Gil Blas' 45, 69, 84, 86, 88, 90, 106,
    131, 139, 195
Wurtemburg, Karl Eugen, duke of 118
Wyndham, Charles *see* Egremont, 2nd earl of
Wyndham, Sir William 53
Wynn [Wynne], Sir John 104, 146, 176, 276
Wynn [Wynne], Sir Thomas 111
Wynne, Thomas, architect 276, 309

Yonge, Sir William 109, 111, 153, 179–80, 188,
    192
Yorke, Charles 255–6, 268
Yorke, John 253, 255
Yorke, Philip, *see* Hardwicke, 1st earl of
Yorke, Philip *see* Royston, lord
Yorkshire 113, 163